The
International Critical Commentary

on the Holy Scriptures of the Old and
New Testaments.

UNDER THE EDITORSHIP OF

The Rev. SAMUEL ROLLES DRIVER, D.D.,

Regius Professor of Hebrew, Oxford;

The Rev. ALFRED PLUMMER, M.A., D.D.,

Master of University College, Durham;

AND

The Rev. CHARLES AUGUSTUS BRIGGS, D.D.,

Edward Robinson Professor of Biblical Theology,
Union Theological Seminary, New York.

PROVERBS

Professor C. H. TOY

THE INTERNATIONAL CRITICAL COMMENTARY

A

CRITICAL AND EXEGETICAL COMMENTARY

ON

THE BOOK OF PROVERBS

BY

CRAWFORD H. TOY

PROFESSOR OF HEBREW IN HARVARD UNIVERSITY

EDINBURGH

T. & T. CLARK, 59 GEORGE STREET

PRINTED IN SCOTLAND BY
MORRISON AND GIBB LIMITED
EDINBURGH AND LONDON
FOR
T. & T. CLARK LTD., EDINBURGH

0 567 05013 0

LATEST IMPRESSION . . 1988

INTRODUCTION.

§ 1. NAMES.

1. The Masoretic title is *Proverbs of Solomon* (משלי שלמה, *Mishlē Shelōmō*, by the later Jews usually abridged to *Mishlē*). That this is old appears to be shown by the Grk. (𝕲ᴮ) title παροιμίαι (the subscription is simply π. in Cod. B, π. Σαλομωντος in א, π. Σολ. in A and C). The name might naturally have been suggested by 1 K. 4³² (5¹²), but would originally have been given to the collection 10¹–22¹⁶, whence it would have been extended to the whole book as additions were made to it from time to time. That this was the common Talmudic title is shown by Bertheau.* On the meaning of *mashal* and its synonyms see notes on 1¹·⁶ within.

2. By early Christian writers the book was commonly called *Wisdom* or *All-virtuous Wisdom*,† ἡ πανάρετος σοφία, names which were also given to *Ben-Sira* (*Ecclesiasticus*) and *Wisdom of Solomon*.‡ Other designations were ἡ σοφὴ βίβλος (Dionys. of Alex.) and ἡ παιδαγωγικὴ σοφία (Greg. Naz. *Orat*. 11). Whether this σοφία represents an ancient Heb. title חכמה is uncertain. Fritzsche (*Die Weisheit Jesus-Sirach's*, *Einl*. p. xx) holds that the name σοφία given to *Ben-Sira* bears witness to a similar name for our *Proverbs*; but this is not certain. It is possible that the title *Wisdom* was common in Jewish circles, and thence passed to the Christians; so Hegesippus (quoted by Euseb. *ubi sup*.) refers the

---

* *Einleitung* to his Comm'y on *Sprüche*.

† Clem. Rom. *Cor*. 1⁵⁷, Euseb. *Hist. Eccl*. 4, 22.

‡ Cf. Fritzsche, *Weish. Jes.-Sirach*; Nowack, *Sprüche Salomo's*., The expressions σοφια and ἡ παν. σοφ. sometimes, however, designate Wisdom simply (as the speaker), and are not titles of books. Cf. Frankenberg, *Die Sprüche*, *Einl*., § 1.

designation to "unwritten Jewish tradition." But in that case it would be rather a descriptive term than the official title, and in the former sense we may naturally take the Talmudic name *Book of Wisdom*.* In the same way we may explain the somewhat curious fact that the Midrash on *Proverbs* begins by citing Job 28¹² : "and wisdom, where can it be found?" the author has merely in mind the fact that *Proverbs* deals with wisdom, which term was obviously used to define the contents of all the philosophical books.†

§ 2. DIVISIONS.

The divisions of the Book indicated in the text itself are as follows :

I. A group of discourses on wisdom and wise conduct (1–9) : 1. General title (1¹), purpose of the Book (1²⁻⁶), central or fundamental principle (1⁷) ; 2. Warning against consorting with sinners (1⁸⁻¹⁹) ; 3. Wisdom's appeal (1²⁰⁻³³) ; 4. Wisdom as guardian against bad men and women (2) ; 5. Advantages attending obedience to the sage's instruction, the fear of Yahweh, and devotion to wisdom (3) ; 6. Exhortation to obey the sage (4) ; 7. Warning against unchaste women (5) ; 8. Three paragraphs, against suretyship, indolence, slander, here misplaced (6¹⁻¹⁹) ; 9. Warning against unchaste women (6²⁰⁻³⁵) ; 10. A similar warning (7) ; 11. Function of Wisdom as controller of life, and as attendant of Yahweh in the creation of the world (8) ; 12. Wisdom and Folly contrasted as hosts (9¹⁻⁶, ¹³⁻¹⁸), and an interjected, misplaced paragraph of apophthegms on wisdom (9⁷⁻¹²).

II. A collection of aphorisms in couplet form (10¹–22¹⁶).

III. Two collections of aphoristic quatrains (22¹⁷–24²², and 24²³⁻³⁴).

IV. A collection of aphoristic couplets (25–29).

V. A collection of discourses of various characters (30. 31) : the "words of Agur" (30¹⁻⁴) ; the certainty of God's word (30⁵, ⁶) ;

---

* ספר חכמה, the name given to *Proverbs* in *Tosephot Baba Bathra*, 14 *b*.

† See Hermann Deutsch, *Die Sprüche Salomo's nach der auffassung im Talmud und Midrasch*, 1885. Deutsch also cites a synagogal prayer of the 12th century, in which *Proverbs* is styled ספר החכמה ; but this hardly proves anything for the earliest times.

prayer for moderate circumstances (30^{7-9}) ; against slandering servants (30^{10}) ; a collection of aphorisms citing certain things arranged in groups of fours (30^{11-33}) ; instruction to a king (31^{1-9}) ; description of a model housewife (31^{10-31}).

The purpose of all these sections is the inculcation of certain cardinal social virtues, such as industry, thrift, discretion, truthfulness, honesty, chastity, kindness, forgiveness, warning against the corresponding vices, and praise of wisdom as the guiding principle of life.   If we compare *Proverbs* in this regard with *Ben-Sira*, we find that the latter, while it deals in general with the same moral qualities, goes more into detail in the treatment of social relations, and has more to say of manners as distinguished from morals.

§ 3. STRUCTURE OF THE MATERIAL.

The divisions indicated above suggest, by their differences of tone and content, that the Book has been formed by the combination of collections of various dates and origins.   It is not probable that one man was the author of the philosophical discourses of chs. 1–9, the pithy aphorisms of 10^1–22^{16}, the quatrains of 22^{17}–24, the couplets of 25–29, and the mixed material of 30. 31.

A similar conclusion is indicated by the repetitions which occur in the Book.   Thus, as between II. and III. we find *variant couplets :* cf. 11^{15} and $22^{26.\ 27}$; 18^5 and 24^{24} ; *identical lines :* 11^{14} and 24^6 ; 13^9 and 24^{20} ; 14^1 and 24^3 ; 20^{22} and 24^{29}.   As between II. and IV.: *identical couplets :* cf. 18^8 and 26^{22} ; 19^1 and 28^6 ; 19^{24} and 26^{15} ; 20^{16} and 27^{13} ; 21^9 and 25^{24} ; 22^3 and 27^{12} ; *variant couplets :* 12^{11} and 28^{19} ; 13^{24} and 29^{15} ; 15^{23} and 25^{11} ; 16^{12} and 25^5 ; 16^{28} and 26^{20} ; 22^2 and 29^{13} ; 22^{13} and 26^{13} ; *identical lines :* 10^1 and 29^3 ; 15^{18} and 29^{22} ; 17^3 and 27^{21} ; 19^{13} and 27^{15}.   As between III. and IV., an *identical line :* cf. 24^{23} and 28^{21}.   Cf. also $6^{10.\ 11}$ with $24^{33.\ 34}$.

From these repetitions we infer that the collectors of II., III., IV., were mutually independent — no one of them was acquainted with the work of the others.   In I. and V. we find no matter that can be called repetition ; the peculiar tone of each of these divisions kept it apart from the others ; 6^{1-19} and 9^{7-12} are misplaced.

Subdivisions or smaller collections also appear to be indicated by repetitions within each of the three middle sections. Within II.: *identical* or *equivalent couplets:* 10^1 and 15^{20}; 10^2 and 11^4; 11^{15} and 17^{18} and 20^{16}; 13^{14} and 14^{27}; 14^{12} and 16^{25} (and cf. 21^{2a}); 14^{20} and 19^4; 16^2 and 21^2; 19^5 and 19^9; 20^{10} and 20^{23}; 21^9 and 21^{19}; *identical* or *equivalent lines:* 10^6 and 10^{11}; 10^8 and 10^{10} (perhaps scribal error); 10^{15} and 18^{11}; 10^{27} and 19^{23}; 11^{13} and 20^{19}; 11^{14} and 15^{22}; 11^{21} and 16^5, 12^{14} and 13^2; 14^{31} and 17^5; 15^{33} and 18^{12}; 16^{18} and 18^{12}; 19^{12} and 20^2. Within III.: *couplets* or *lines:* 22^{23} and 23^{11}; 22^{28} and 23^{10} (the couplets which in $23^{10.\ 11}$ form one quatrain are in $22^{23.\ 28}$ divided between two quatrains); 23^{17a} and 24^{1a}; 23^{18} and 24^{14} (a similar division of couplets); on $23^{3.\ 6}$ see notes. Within IV.: 28^{12} and 29^2.

In some cases these latter repetitions may be scribal errors. Ewald, Delitzsch, and others, endeavor to determine the limits of the smaller subdivisions, which are held to be indicated sometimes by similarity of material, sometimes by catch-words; see the notes. The paragraphal divisions are obvious in I. and V., and in parts of III. and IV.; in II. the absence of logical arrangement makes it very difficult, if not impossible, to recognize any such paragraphs, and the divisions which have been suggested are commonly arbitrary and useless, as is pointed out within.

The misplacement of certain passages, as 4^{18}, $6^{1-5.\ 6-11.\ 12-19}$, 9^{7-12}, and of a number of lines in II. is discussed in the notes.

§ 4. Rhythm and Parallelism.

1. Hebrew poetry, as is now generally agreed, has neither metre in the Greek and Latin sense, nor systematic rhyme; there are occasional sequences of syllables, which may be called iambic, trochaic, anapaestic, etc., and occasional assonances or rhymes; but these are of irregular occurrence, and obviously do not belong to the essence of the form of the verse.*

---

* On the rhythmical form of Hebrew poetry see J. Ley, *Grundzüge des rhythmus* etc., 1875, and *Leitfaden der Metrik*, 1887; G. Bickell, *Carmina Vet. Test. metrice*, 1882, his additions in *Zeitschr. f. Kath. Theol.*, 1885-1886, and the introductory remarks to his *Kritische Bearbeitung d. Proverbien* in the *Wiener Zeitschr. f. d. Kunde d. Morgenlandes*, 1891; C. A. Briggs, *Biblical Study*[8], 1891, *Hebraica*, 1887, 1888, *General Introduction to the Study of Holy Scripture*, 1899, chs. xiv-xvii;

The rhythmical form of the poetic line or verse is marked not by the number of words or syllables, but by the number of accents or beats. The accent of each word or group of words is fixed by the laws of Hebrew accentuation ; accepting the Masoretic system as correct (and we have nothing else to guide us), we can with reasonable probability determine the number of beats in any line. The chief source of uncertainty lies in the presence of possibly un-accented words, which are to be combined into rhythmical unity with following words ; such are short prepositions, conjunctions, negatives, and nouns defined by following nouns (*status construc-tus*). These may or may not have an accent ; in determining this point we may sometimes be aided by the Masoretic punctu-ation (the Maqqef or hyphen), which gives the pronunciation of the seventh century of our era; but this is not always decisive, and we must, in the last instance, be guided by the general nature of the rhythm.

In order to avoid the possibly misleading suggestions of the terms "dimeter, trimeter, tetrameter, pentameter, hexameter," etc., the lines are here called *binary* ("having two beats"), *ter-nary*, or *quaternary*. For the guidance of the English reader (the translation rarely giving the rhythmical form of the Hebrew) the rhythmical definition of every couplet is marked in the com-mentary ; thus, *ternary* means that both lines of the couplet are ternary, *ternary-binary* that the first line is ternary and the second line binary, etc.

In *Proverbs* the lines are arranged almost without exception in couplets (distichal). A certain number of triplets occur (tris-tichal), and these must be dealt with every one for itself. The presence of triplets, even in a passage predominantly distichal, must be admitted to be possible. In some cases the third line appears to be a corruption of some other line, or the remains of a separate couplet, or an erroneous scribal insertion ; where there is no reasonable ground of suspicion, beyond the irregularity, the triplet form must be accepted.

2. Strophes (quatrains and other forms) occur in all parts of the Book except II. It is not to be assumed that a discourse

---

Grimme, in *ZDMG.*, 1896. On Babylonian rhythm see Delitzsch, *Bab. Weltschöpf-ungsepos ;* H. Zimmern, in *ZATW.*, 1898.

must be strophic in form; in every case the question must be decided by the logical connection of the material.*

The principle of arrangement by couplets and strophes may properly be used for the criticism of the text, always, of course, with due caution; it may easily be pressed too far.

3. The form of the parallelism varies in the different Sections. In I. it may be said to be, in accordance with the tone of the discourses, wholly synonymous; the apparent exceptions are $3^{27-31.\ 32-35}$, 9^8, all occurring in misplaced or doubtful paragraphs. II. divides itself into two parts: in chs. 10–15 the form is antithetic, in $16-22^{16}$ the couplets are mostly comparisons and single sentences, with a few antitheses. III. is made up of synonymous lines, except 24^{16}. IV. shows a division into two parts: in chs. 25–27 we find comparisons and single sentences, except in 25^2, $27^{6.\ 7.\ 12}$, which contains antitheses, while in chs. 28. 29 the two forms are nearly equal in number (33 antithetic couplets, 22 comparisons and single sentences). In V. the parallelism is, with a few exceptions (see $30^{12.\ 24-28}\ 31^{30}$), synonymous.

So far, then, as the rhythmical form may be regarded as an indication of origin we must put in one group chs. 10–15 and part of chs. 28. 29, and in another group chs. $16-22^{16}$, 25–27 and part of chs. 28. 29. I. and V. stand by themselves, and III. stands midway between II., IV., and I.

If we compare the rhythmical forms of *Proverbs* and the *Psalter*, we find that most of the Psalms, being connected discourses, resemble I.; the aphoristic ψ 37 shows the same variations as II., III., IV. *Lamentations* is rhythmically unique, but belongs in the same general category as I., as does also *Canticles*.

§ 5. Thought.

Proverbs may be described as a manual of conduct, or, as Bruch calls it, an "anthology of gnomes." Its observations relate to a number of forms of life, to affairs domestic, agricultural, urban (the temptations of city life), commercial, political, and military.

---

* On strophic structure in the Old Testament see, besides the works mentioned above, D. H. Müller, *Die Propheten*, 1895, and *Strophenbau und Responsion*, 1898.

Many of the sayings are simply maxims of commonsense prudence, enjoining industry and caution ($6^{1-5.\ 6-11}$ $10^{4.\ 19}$ 11^{15} 12^9 14^{20} 16^{26} 20^3 $23^{1.\ 2}$ 25^6 28^8 30^{10}, etc.), sometimes with what seems to be a humorous or sarcastic turn (6^{3-5} 19^{24} 23^{33-35} 30^{2-4}). The most are ethical, inculcating lessons of truth and general goodness. A religious tone is found in different degrees in different sections : in I., if we omit the cosmogonic hymn in ch. 8, the references to God occur almost exclusively in chs. 1–3, and there partly in passages (such as 2^{5-8} 3^{27-35}) which appear to be editorial insertions; the divine name is mentioned most frequently in II. (21 times in chs. 10–15, 13 times in chs. 16. 17, 21 times in 18–22^{16}) ; in III. there are 6 occurrences, and 8 in IV. (2 in chs. 25–27, and 6 in chs. 28. 29) ; in V. a reference to God is found only in 30^{2-9} (3 times). It appears then that II. is relatively more religious, the rest of the Book more definitely ethical.

None of the aphorisms, however, — not even such as " go to the ant, thou sluggard," or " answer a fool according to his folly," or the tetrads in ch. 30, — are popular proverbs or folk-sayings. They are all reflective and academic in tone, and must be regarded as the productions of schools of moralists in a period of high moral culture. The ideas of the Book may be considered under their ethical, religious, and philosophical aspects.*

A. *Ethical.*

1. The high ethical standard of the Book is universally recognized. Its maxims all look to the establishment of a safe, peaceful, happy social life, in the family and the community ; the supposed exceptions, cases of alleged selfish prudence (as, for example, the caution against going security), are only apparent, since proper regard for self is an element of justice.

Honesty and truthfulness in public and private life, especially in business-transactions and courts of justice, are throughout insisted on, and respect for human property and life is enjoined ; the moralist has particularly in mind the urban crimes of perjury, theft,

---

* Cf. A. F. Dähne, *Geschichtl. Darstellung d. jüd.-alex. Relig.-philosophie*, 1834; T. K. Cheyne, *Job and Solomon*, 1887 ; C. G. Montefiore, *Relig. Value of the Book of Prov.*, in JQR., 1890; R. Pfeiffer, *Relig.-sittliche Weltanschauung d. B. d. Sprüche*, 1897; Cheyne, *Jewish Relig. Life after the Exile*, 1898.

robbery, and murder. A fine conception of political equity is given in the picture of the king (not a Messiah, but an ideal sovereign in general), who is represented as the embodiment of justice in his dealings with his people ; the references to royal authority occur almost exclusively in chs. 16–29 (the other instances are 8^{15} $14^{28.\,35}$ 30^{31} 31^{2-9}). The idea of justice is prominent in all parts of *Proverbs* (as also throughout OT., and in Egyptian and Greek ethical systems) ; and, as the fundamental virtue in human intercourse, it is identified with general probity or righteousness, the same terms being used to express both conceptions (see notes on 1^3 *al.*). Warnings against unchastity constitute a special feature of I. (they are found elsewhere in 22^{14} 23^{27} 30^{20}) ; one of the terms used for harlot, " strange woman " (2^{16} *al.*), designates the vice in question as an offence against the well-being of the family. Kindness to man (3^3 *al.*) and beast (12^{10}) is enjoined frequently in II., and once in I. and V. each ; the fact that the term (as elsewhere in OT.) is several times associated with " truth " (3^3 14^{22} 16^6 20^{28}) may indicate that the element of justice entered into the conception of kindness. Love is extolled (10^{12}) as ministering to peace. There is a sharp polemic against slander and malicious gossip ($6^{12-15.\,19}$ 16^{28} *al.*). Special regard is shown for the interests of the poor (22^{22} *al.*). Irascibility is condemned (14^{29}), and pride (13^{10}) ; and modesty or lowliness is approved (11^2). Frank acknowledgment of wrong is enjoined (28^{13}). Revenge is forbidden (24^{17}), and kindness to enemies is insisted on. Industry is praised, sloth is ridiculed, temperance in eating and drinking is urged. The ideal of family-life is high (especially in I., III., and ch. 31) : monogamy is assumed ; parents are the responsible guides of their children, and entitled to their obedience and respect (love to parents is not mentioned, but is doubtless involved), the mother having equal honor with the father. Woman is spoken of only in the relations of wife, mother, and housewife : she is a power in the house, capable of making home miserable (19^{13} *al.*) or happy (18^{22} 31^{28}) ; she has not only housekeeping-capacity, but also broad wisdom (1^8 31^{2-9}) ; her position is as high as any accorded her in ancient life (Egypt, Greece, Rome). *Proverbs* speaks (1^8 *al.*) of the training of children at home ; but of the method and extent of the education of children in Hebrew postexilian communities we know little (cf. note on 22^6). The frequency with which terms for "instruction" occur in the Book makes it probable that a definite apparatus of training existed.

Among the virtues not mentioned in *Proverbs* are courage (see note on 28^1), fortitude (see 3^{11}), moderation in thought, self-sacrifice, intellectual truthfulness. The silence of the sages (and of OT. generally) respecting these traits is doubtless to be interpreted as indicating not that they did not exist among the Israelites, but chiefly that the moralists attached more importance to other qualities as effective forces in the struggle of life ; the last-mentioned virtue, further, belongs to a mode of thought which was foreign to the Jewish mind. The obligation to seek truth is recognized in I. (1^2 3^3 *al.*), but the "truth" is that law of conduct obedience to which secures prosperity and happiness. Of beauty as an element of life nothing is said ; the failure to mention it is due not to the religious character of the Book (for much of the material of *Proverbs* is non-religious), but to the fact that the Jewish sages had not been trained to distinct recognition of the value of the beautiful in the conduct of life. So also the silence of *Proverbs* in regard to international ethics must be referred to the times ; the Jews were not then a nation, and could not have political relations with the surrounding peoples, and moreover, a science of international ethics did not then exist in the world.

2. Life is contemplated on its external and visible side, as a mass of acts. The freedom of the will is assumed, but there is no inquiry into its nature and its relation to the absolute will of God or to conditions of temperament and education. There is no reference to such inward experiences as swaying between opposed lines of conduct, struggle with temptation, and the mistakes of conscientious ignorance. Men are judged, without allowance, according to their actual conformity to law, and are sharply divided into good and bad ; in 1^{22} "simpleton," "scoffer," and "fool" are equivalent terms, and these classes are set over against the obedient in $1^{32.\ 33}$. In II.–V. characters are regarded as fixed ; in I. the exhortations assume the possibility of change, but it is said (1^{28}) that when the hour of punishment comes it will be too late to turn. There is no reference to sorrow for sin or in general to processes of conversion from bad to good, or from good to bad

(so in Ez. 18). The advantages and disadvantages, for practical morality, of this strictly external conception of life are obvious.

The absence of all inquiry into the psychological basis of the moral life (which *Proverbs* has in common with the rest of OT.) is due to the Jewish practical, unspeculative habit of thought. There are no terms for "conscience" and "duty" in Hebrew, and no Hebrew prophet or sage troubles himself to examine into the origin of the sense of obligation. The OT. ethical thought is wholly occupied with the question how to make the best of life.

3. The same practical point of view controls the determination of the grounds of moral judgments, and the motives for the good life.

For the standard of rightdoing the appeal in *Proverbs* is to commonsense or to the command of God. There is no reference to the good of society as a whole, no recognition of society as an ethical cosmos,* no attempt to define the relation between society and the individual or to harmonize egoism and altruism in the unity of the cosmos.

The motive urged for good living is individualistic utilitarian or eudaemonistic — not the glory of God, or the welfare of men in general, but the well-being of the actor. Nor is there specific reference to man's obligation to seek moral perfection for its own sake. The only point directly insisted on is that happiness follows obedience to the law of right. It is unnecessary to call attention to the fundamental value of this principle in practical life, and to its ethical limitations. On the other hand, it cannot be assumed that the broader and more ideal points of view were unknown to the Jewish moralists; we can infer only that such points of view did not seem to them to have practical importance.

The scheme of life in *Proverbs* cannot strictly be called either optimistic or pessimistic. The existence of moral and physical evil is recognized, without attempt to explain its origin or to reconcile it with the moral perfection of God. But there is also recognition of the possibility of escaping or rising superior to all evil; universal happiness is contemplated as the ideal ultimate lot of humanity.†

---

* That is, no recognition by the individual as guide of his own life. The philosophical conception of the cosmos is found in ch. 8; see p. xvi.

† On a supposed pessimistic sentiment in 14[18] see note on that verse.

B. *Religious*.

1. Monotheism is taken for granted, God is regarded as supreme and absolute in power, wisdom, and goodness, and the only trace of anthropomorphism in the theistic conception is the unsympathetic (hostile and mocking) attitude of God toward the sinner (1^{26} 11^{20} *al.*). This conception is in the main that of OT. generally, and is a part of the practical point of view of the moralists.

2. Of other supernatural beings (angels and demons) there is no mention (see note on 30^{15}). The existence of such beings no doubt formed part of the popular belief of the time (Job 1^6 33^{23} ψ 91^{11} 1 C. 21^1) ; but the sages, dealing with the everyday moral life, saw no occasion to refer to these administrative agencies, and confined themselves to the visible facts. Idolatry is not mentioned — the audience addressed in *Proverbs* is Jewish.

3. Sin is the violation of law in the most general sense, and salvation, which is deliverance from earthly evil, is secured by obedience to law, human and divine. There is no reference or allusion to a Messiah, or to any national deliverance (see notes on the passages relating to kings).

4. The only national element in the Book is the mention of sacrifice, which occurs five times ; of the occurrences only three (15^8 $21^{3.27}$) have an ethical tone, the others (7^{14} 17^1) being merely allusions to feasting in connection with sacrifices. There is no mention of temple or priests. As to a supposed reference to tithes in 3^9 see note on that verse. Obviously the temple-cult is recognized, but is not supposed to have a close connection with moral life.

5. The sage speaks in his own name, without reference to divine inspiration or to any book as authority. The " law " of which he speaks is the law of his own conscience and reason ; he does not name Moses or the prophets. In some cases (as in 6^{32-35}) he appears to depart from the Pentateuchal legislation. He does not mention a collection of sacred books ; but this silence is due partly to the literary custom of the time, partly to the nature of his material ; even the author of the *Wisdom of Solomon*, though in chs. 10–19 he follows closely the narrative of the Hexateuch, does not name that book. In *Proverbs* ($30^{5.6}$) there are two quo-

tations, one from ψ 18³¹, the other from Dt. 4² 13¹, and neither of these books is mentioned. The sages were doubtless acquainted with the greater part of our Old Testament, but they use its material freely as literature, and do not cite it as a Canon of Scripture. *
Proverbs does not mention a class of scribes or extol learning as *Ben-Sira* does (38²⁴–39¹¹), but it makes mention of sages, and assumes the existence of systematic instruction, in which the study of the literature no doubt played an important part.

6. The eschatology is of the simple and primitive sort that is found in the greater part of OT. : Sheol, the abode of all the dead, has no moral significance ; there is no judgment after death, and the position of men in Sheol has no relation to their moral character ; see notes on 2¹⁸. ¹⁹ 5⁵ *al.* The divine judgment is manifested in the last moment of life (אחרת, 5⁴ *al.*). The idea of ethical immortality was either unknown to the sages or was regarded by them as unimportant for practical life.

7. The thought of the greater part of the Book is definitely religious, standing in sympathetic and reverent contact with the conception of a just and wise divine government of the world. The sages are independent thinkers, but refer their wisdom ultimately to God.

C. *Philosophical.* †

1. In agreement with other Wisdom books, and in contrast with the rest of OT., *Proverbs*, in all its parts and especially in I., identifies virtue with knowledge. Its position is thus sharply distinguished from that of the Prophets, the Law, and the Psalmists, in which Yahweh, as national God, is always ready to favor his people if he alone be recognized and obeyed. The central idea of the Book is " wisdom," which performs all the functions elsewhere in OT. ascribed to Yahweh (1²⁰⁻³¹ 2¹⁰⁻²² 3¹³⁻¹⁸ 9¹⁻⁶ 22¹⁷ *al.*). This wisdom is, in parts of the Book, also identified with religion (1⁷ *al.*) — a point of view proper and necessary for a Jew. But the sage's chief interest, particularly in I., is in the intellectual grasp of practical truth ; in certain places, as in 2⁵⁻⁸, an editor has thought it

---

* Cf. the manner in which Jeremiah is referred to in Dan. 9², and the way in which the translator of *Ben-Sira* puts his grandfather in the same category with the prophets and other Israelitish writers.

† Cf. H. Bois, *Origines d. l. philosophie judéo-alexandrine*, 1890.

desirable to introduce a specifically religious statement into the sage's picture of the all-sufficiency of wisdom. The religious coloring in I. and elsewhere is, however, not to be referred to a desire on the part of the philosophers to placate the orthodox party (Oort), but must be regarded as a natural expression of the view of the authors of the Book.

The conception of the world as a physical and moral cosmos or orderly arrangement is found, at least in germinal form, in such OT. passages as Gen. 1, ψ 104. But the conception is far distincter in Pr. 8, in which wisdom is said to control all human society and to have been present at the creation of the world.*

Wisdom in *Proverbs* is a human quality, generally (in II.–V.) regulating the ordinary affairs of men, but sometimes (in I.) appearing in the larger character of sovereign of life. It is then only a step to the still broader conception of her in (8^{22-31}) as a divine attribute, as in fact the chief attribute of God. How this scheme of different conceptions is to be unified is not explained by the sages, and we cannot be sure that they had worked out a self-consistent philosophical system. But the idea of "wisdom" appears to be parallel to the OT. idea of "spirit"—a life common to God and man, breathed into man by God—treated ordinarily in its human relations and activities merely, but, in the highest flights of the philosophical imagination (as in ch. 8), regarded as universal and all-controlling. The conception is not "pantheistic" in the modern sense of that term, but is an ethical and philosophical expansion and purification of the old tribal and national idea of the unity of the deity with his people. Cf. WS. 7. The question whether the representation of Wisdom in ch. 8 is a personification or a hypostatization is discussed in the notes.

2. An expression of philosophical skepticism appears to occur in 30^{2-4} (Agur) on which see notes; the doubt expressed relates to man's capacity to understand God. The parallels are all in the Wisdom books (Job 3, 9^{32} 19^6 *al.*, Eccl. 3^{11}). Elsewhere in OT. (as in ψ 139) the greatness of God is treated as a ground of awe and reverence; here it is regarded as a reason for refraining from attempts to define him.

---

* See footnote on p. xiv.

D. *Comparison with Other Books.*

1. In its ethical code *Proverbs* agrees in the main with the more advanced Jewish canonical and uncanonical books (the *Pirke Aboth* is especially important) and with the New Testament; in the later period of Jewish history there had come to be a generally recognized moral code.* In some cases (as in 6$^{32-35}$) *Proverbs* modifies the old law for the better, and its prohibition of revenge (24$^{17.29}$ 25^{21}) not only stands in striking contrast with such sentiments as that of ψ 109, but appears to be unique in OT. (it is not exactly paralleled in Lev. 19^{18} ψ 120^{7}).

2. Its religious point of view is in general (in respect to God, sin, salvation, Messianic expectation, the future life) the same as that of the other Wisdom books except *Wisdom of Solomon;* but it is less national than *Ben-Sira* (see, for example, BS. 24), and differs from our book of *Job* in that it makes no mention of subordinate supernatural beings (cf. Job 1^{6} 3^{8} 5^{1} 26$^{12.13}$ 33^{23}); WS. is much later than *Proverbs*, and represents a different order of ideas.

3. In its picture of social life it most resembles *Ben-Sira* †; the two books deal, in fact, with the same sort of society, chiefly city life, with its commerce, its feasts, its gossip, its temptations to licentiousness, its relaxation of family-ties, its worship of money, and its close relations with royalty; cf., among other passages, Pr. 3^{29} and BS. 7^{12} (slander), Pr. 5. 7 and BS. 9$^{2-9}$ 23$^{18-26}$ (the harlot), Pr. 6$^{1-5}$ 17^{18} and BS. 29$^{1.7.10.18}$ (suretyship), Pr. 13^{24} and BS. 30$^{1.12}$ (chastisement of children), Pr. 11^{4} 22^{16} and BS. 5^{8} (riches), Pr. 14^{31} 22^{16} and BS. 4$^{1-6}$ (the poor), Pr. 14^{35} 28^{15} and BS. 10^{3} (kings), Pr. 15^{20} 30$^{11.17}$ and BS. 3$^{1-16}$ (conduct toward parents), Pr. 18^{24} and BS. 6$^{7-16}$ (friends), Pr. 20^{1} 23$^{29-35}$ and BS. 19^{1} 31$^{27-30}$ (wine), Pr. 20^{14} and BS. 27^{2} (buying and selling), Pr. 23$^{1-8}$ and BS. 32$^{1-11}$ (conduct at feasts). *Ben-Sira* goes more into detail than *Proverbs* in the description of social relations, but the social

---

* *Ben-Sira* sometimes falls below the general level; on this point and on the ethics of *Prov.* and *BS.* see C. G. Montefiore in *Jewish Quart. Rev.* II. (1889–1890), pp. 430 ff.

† And we may add the Syriac *Menander*, given in Land's *Anecdota Syriaca*, Vol. I.; see Frankenberg's article in *ZATW.*, 1895.

organization contemplated appears to be the same in the two books.

4. More generally, as regards the moral and religious point of view and aim of the books of the Wisdom group: *Job* is a passionate discussion of the question whether the divine government of the world is just; *Proverbs* and *Ben-Sira* ignore this question, and confine themselves to cheery practical suggestions for the conduct of everyday-life; *Ecclesiastes* treats life as a logically and ethically insoluble riddle, and advises a moderate and wise enjoyment of its good things; *Wisdom of Solomon* dwells on eternal wisdom, the architect and inspirer of the world, as the guide of life, and on the hope of happy immortality as the consolation amid earthly trials. *Proverbs* and *Ben-Sira* thus form a separate subgroup, devoting themselves to practical morals in contrast with the speculative element in the other books.

§ 6. ORIGIN AND DATE.

1. Various authors are named in the titles: to Solomon are ascribed chs. 10^1–22^{16}, 25–29, and apparently chs. 1–9 (though the title in 1^1 may be intended to refer to the whole book), to "the sages" 22^{17}–24^{22} and 24^{23-34}, to Agur 30^{2-4} (and possibly but not probably other parts of ch. 30), to the Mother of King Lemuel 31^{2-9}; 31^{10-31} and probably 30^{5-33} are anonymous.

No OT. titles are in themselves authoritative in the sense that they can be accepted without reference to the material involved. The name "Moses" stands for legislators of all periods; no psalm or other production ascribed by the tradition to David can be assigned him without examination of its contents; large parts of the books of Amos, Isaiah, Micah, Zephaniah, Jeremiah, and Zechariah were certainly not written by the prophets whose names they bear, and Jonah and Daniel had nothing to do with the composition of the books called after them. The name "Solomon" in titles is of equally doubtful import. The fact that he is said to be the author of *Proverbs, Canticles, Ecclesiastes*, and ψ 72. 127 * shows that the Jewish tradition came to regard him as the ideal of

---

* To which somewhat later were added *Wisdom of Solomon* and *Psalms of Solomon.*

wisdom and a writer of idealizing non-liturgical poetry,* and ascribed to him indiscriminately everything of this sort. If the titles in *Canticles* and *Ecclesiastes* cannot be accepted as authoritative, neither can those in *Proverbs* be so regarded. And if little or no weight is to be attached to 1^1 (as is now generally held), the same thing must hold of 10^1 and 25^1. As to the latter title it is sometimes said that so definite a statement (namely, that proverbs of Solomon were edited by scholars of Hezekiah's time) must have an historical basis. But still more definite statements are prefixed to certain obviously late psalms ascribed to David (see, for example, ψ 51–60), and the history of the Prophetic and historical writings makes it improbable that the collection and editing of literary material began so early as the reign of Hezekiah.

Agur and Lemuel's Mother are shadowy figures of whom little of a helpful nature can be said; see notes on 30^1 31^1. With "the sages" the case is somewhat different; the term specifies not an individual, but a class, and, since it is apparently derived from the nature of the material, so far carries with it its own justification; but from it in itself we get no more chronological aid than we should get in the criticism of the *Psalter* from the statement that the book was composed by "psalmists." Whether the ascription to "sages" is probable must be determined by an examination of the contents of tne sections in question.

In the body of the book of *Proverbs* there is no mention of any historical person or event from which a date can be drawn. *Ithiel* and *Ucal* (30^1) appear to be corrupt forms, the attempt of Geiger to find a King Alcimus in 30^{31} is unsuccessful, and the absence of historical allusions elsewhere in the Book is intelligible from the nature of the material.

For the determination of origin and date we must, therefore, ʌave recourse to internal data.

2. The following facts appear to point to the postexilian period as the time of origination of the Book.†

The tacit assumption of monotheism can hardly belong to an

---

* ψ 72 appears to have been referred to him because it gives the picture of a splendid monarch, and ψ 127 because of his fame as builder of the Tempie.

† Cf. Stade and Holtzmann, *GVI.*, II., pp. 292 ff.

earlier time. Ezekiel (Ez. 6. 8. 23 *al.*) declares that idolatry was rampant in Israel down to the destruction of Jerusalem by the Chaldeans, and its existence more than a century later is probably vouched for by Zech. 13².* It may be said that the sages, as moralists, might ignore purely religious errors, even though they were as common as in the preëxilian period; but astral worship is referred to in Job 31²⁶. ²⁷, and it is hardly likely that in a book of so wide a range as that of *Proverbs* there should be no hint of a usage that would have been the destruction of the "fear of Yahweh."

The absence of characteristic national traits points in the same direction. The terms "Israel, Israel's covenant with Yahweh, temple, priest, prophet" (see note on 29¹⁸), all common in the Prophetic writings, do not occur in *Proverbs*. These expressions are found in postexilian writings, and their absence in *Proverbs* is, therefore, not merely a matter of date; but it is difficult to understand how an Israelitish ethical and religious writer of the preëxilian time, whatever the literary form of his work, could refrain from mentioning them. The same remark holds of other religious ideas referred to above (§ 5, B). The fact that the term "law," which (whether priestly or Prophetic) in preëxilian writings always means the command of Yahweh, here denotes the instruction of sages is significant. As for the national name "Yahweh," frequent in *Proverbs*, it occurs in *Ben-Sira*, and we must assume that it was in common use among the Jews down to the second century B.C.† In a word, if for the name Yahweh we substitute "God," there is not a paragraph or a sentence in *Proverbs* which would not be as suitable for any other people as for Israel. This nonnational form of thought belongs to a sort of culture which did not exist among the Jews till they were scattered throughout the world and came under Persian and Greek influence.

The social life depicted in *Proverbs* does not bear the marks of

---

* Zech. 1–8 and Malachi bring no accusation of polytheism against their contemporaries; perhaps idolatry, held under in the period of reconstruction, showed itself at the later time represented by Zech. 13². It could not, however, have been very prominent or dangerous after the exile.

† When the Jews began to give up the utterance of the name Yahweh, and to substitute for it Adonay and other terms, is uncertain.

Old Israel. While polygamy is recognized as legal or is assumed in an exilian code (Lev. 18[18]), here monogamy is taken for granted. Agricultural pursuits are mentioned (3[9] *al.*), but the chief attention is given to city life with its special occupations and temptations (see § 5). There are numerous and emphatic warnings against malicious gossip, going security, greed of money, nocturnal robbery, murder, and unchastity — vices and faults which, though possible in any tolerably organized community, were specially prominent in the postexilian cities; on the last-named vice, to which so much space is given in chs. 1–9, see notes on 2[16] 5[3] *al.* The system of education assumed as existing is of a much more advanced sort than that indicated in Dt. 6. The frequent mention of kings as a class in the world, and as persons whom the private citizen might meet socially (see 23[1.2], and other references in § 5), belongs to an order of things foreign to the older life (cf. Dt. 17[14-20] Isa. 11[1-5] *al.*) ; the best commentary on it is found in the pictures of royal life given in Josephus and similar histories.

The philosophical conceptions referred to above (§ 5, C) are out of place in any preëxilian century or during the exile. They manifestly belong to the time when the Jews came into close intellectual contact with the non-Semitic world. It has been supposed that they were derived from Persia, but this is hardly probable if we may judge from the extant Persian sacred books : wisdom plays no such prominent part in the Avesta as it plays in *Proverbs;* in the Gathas, it is true, various qualities are personified, but among these it is wisdom to which least importance is attached, and the Avesta is in general more ecclesiastical than philosophical. In the West * it is only in Greece that we find that identification of knowledge and virtue which is characteristic of the Jewish Wisdom literature — a trait which in *Proverbs* is especially prominent in chs. 1–9, but appears also throughout the Book. The Jews seem not to have become acquainted with Greek philosophy before the conquest of Alexander.

3. The same date (postexilian) is indicated by the use of the terms "wisdom" and "wise" in OT. More than half of the oc-

---

* The Indian systems may be left out of consideration; there is no good historical ground for supposing a Hindoo influence on Western Asia as early as the third century B.C.

currences of these terms are found in the Wisdom books, and in the other books (except in half a dozen passages in late reflective psalms) no philosophical sense attaches to them. In the historical and Prophetical writings they refer to mechanical or artistic skill (Ex. 35^{10} Isa. 40^{20} 1 Chr. 22^{15}), cleverness in ordinary affairs (2 Sam. 13^3 14^2), political sagacity (Gen. 41^{33} Dt. 1^{13} Isa. 3^3 19^{11} Jer. 8^9 Ez. 27^8 28^4 Esth. 1^{13}), magical or prophetic knowledge (Ex. 7^{11} Dan. 5^{11}), or general intelligence (Hos. $14^{9(10)}$ Isa. 11^2). In *Proverbs* and the other Wisdom books they relate to a definite class of sages whose function is the pursuit of universal moral and religious wisdom — men who, unlike the prophets, lay no claim to supernatural inspiration, but make their appeal simply to human reason. In at least one passage of the later preëxilian time (Jer. $9^{23(22)}$) there is the suggestion that the ethical prophets looked with suspicion on the contemporary "wise men," whose wisdom appears to be contrasted with the true ethical knowledge of Yahweh; but in *Proverbs* the sages present themselves as legitimate and competent teachers of this knowledge. There occurred, obviously, a noteworthy change in the character and position of the wise men, and the change could have taken place only after the exile.

Confirmation of this view may be obtained from the consideration of the unity of the group of Wisdom books (*Job, Proverbs, Ben-Sira, Ecclesiastes, Wisdom of Solomon*). All these books, though there are differences among them, are substantially identical each with the others in their philosophical points of view and in their ethical codes. They have the same conception of wisdom, and, if we omit *Job*, they portray the same general condition of society. The similarity between *Proverbs* and *Ben-Sira* is especially striking.* It is not impossible that the similarity is due in part to borrowing (though it may be equally well accounted for by supposing that the two books drew material from the same sources, and BS. has not the tone of an imitator); but in that case the fact that Ben-Sira imitated *Proverbs* rather than the

---

* The most notable difference between the two books is the nationalistic conception of wisdom in one passage of the latter (ch. 24); but this does not impair the general similarity between them. *BS.* 24^{28} (which in its present form appears to identify wisdom with the Tora) is possibly a gloss.

Prophetical books suggests that his affinities, intellectual, moral, and religious, were with the sages, and that he belonged to their period. When we consider the uniqueness of the Wisdom group and the substantial mutual identity of the books composing it, it is difficult to avoid the conclusion that they all sprang from one intellectual and religious tendency, and that they belong to the same cultural period. Three of them (*BS.*, *Eccl.*, *WS.*) are certainly of the second and first centuries B.C., and the other two cannot be very far removed in time.

4. It may be possible to obtain a more definite date for *Proverbs* by comparing the Wisdom books one with another. A two-fold division of these books may be made, according to the point of comparison. In regard to speculative thought they fall into two sub-groups : *Job*, *Eccl.*, *WS.*, discuss the question of the justice of the divine government of the world ; *Prov.* and *BS.* ignore this question. In regard to literary form and general religious tone there are the sub-groups : *Job*, *Prov.*, *BS.*, which agree in rhythmical form, in the conception of the righteous and the wicked, and in the view of the future life ; and *Eccl.*, *WS.*, which depart from the old literary form, and attack and defend the new doctrine of immortality.

Though arguments from diction have to be used with great caution, the following statement of the occurrences of 24 ethical terms in *Job*, *Prov.*, and *Eccl.* may be of value, it being borne in mind that in extent the three books are to one another about as 35 : 32 : 13.* Of the terms involving the idea of *wisdom* the stem חכם is most frequent in *Eccl.*, somewhat less so in *Prov.*, much less in *Job;* the adj. נבן is found 9 times in *Prov.*, once in *Eccl.*, not at all in *Job;* of substantives מזמה (= *wisdom*) is peculiar to *Prov.* (chs. 1–9) ; בנה is frequent in *Prov.* (mostly in I.), much less frequent in *Job*, wanting in *Eccl.;* דעת is common in *Prov.*, much less common in *Eccl.*, still less in *Job;* תבנה is not infrequent in *Prov.*, rare in *Job*, not found in *Eccl.;* עצה and תשיה (more general terms) are equally common in *Job* and

---

* It would be desirable to include *Ben-Sira* in the comparison ; but this will not be possible till we have more of its Hebrew text. Cf. the list of Heb. words given in Cowley and Neubauer's *Ecclesiasticus* (*BS.* 39¹⁵–49¹¹) ; the list, however, needs revision. *Ben-Sira* appears to contain more late words than *Proverbs*.

Prov., and are lacking in *Eccl.* Of words expressing *folly* כסל is frequent in *Prov.* and *Eccl.*, and wanting in *Job;* אול is common in *Prov.*, very rare in *Job*, lacking in *Eccl.;* פתי is peculiar to *Prov.* The verb חטא *sin* occurs 8 times in the poem of *Job*, once in *Eccl.*, not at all in *Prov.*, the participle is not infrequent in *Eccl.*, less frequent in *Prov.*, lacking in *Job*, the substantive is about equally common in *Job* and *Prov.*, and is wanting in *Eccl.* Of terms for *instruction* the noun תכחת is found only in *Prov.*, the verb of this stem is about equally common in *Job* and *Prov.*, and is lacking in *Eccl.;* the stem יסר is rare in *Job*, frequent in *Prov.*, not found in *Eccl.* Of words signifying *way* in the sense of *conduct* מעגל occurs only in *Prov.*, דרך is common in *Job* and *Prov.* and rare in *Eccl.*, while ארח and נתבה, about equally common in *Job* and *Prov.*, are lacking in *Eccl.* The terms חסד and חן, *kindness* and *favor*, are not uncommon in *Prov.*, but the first is rare in *Job* and wanting in *Eccl.*, while the second is rare in *Eccl.* and wanting in *Job*. מצוה *command* is found 10 times in *Prov.*, twice in *Eccl.*, once in *Job*, but *tora* 11 times in *Prov.*, once in *Job*, and not at all in *Eccl.* Words = *ethically crooked* do not occur in *Eccl.;* עקש is common and נפתל rare in *Prov.*, and both terms are very rare in *Job* (on the other hand עות, found several times in *Job*, does not occur in *Prov.* and *Eccl.*). It will be observed that, so far as this list goes, *Eccl.* is nearer than *Job* to *Prov.* in certain terms of the more strictly scientific vocabulary (חכם, חכמה, נבן, דעת, כסל, חטא), in general avoiding terms that have a religious, ecclesiastical, or hortatory coloring ; *Job*, on the other hand, is nearer *Prov.* in the diction which the latter shares with the *Psalter*. We may thence probably infer that the philosophical conception of wisdom is less developed in *Job* than in *Proverbs*, and that the former book is earlier than the latter. The same conclusion seems to be suggested by a comparison of the representation of wisdom in Job 28 (in which wisdom is said to be undiscoverable by man, but is identified, as is also often done in *Prov.*, with obedience to God) with that in Pr. 8 (in which wisdom is almost identified with God himself).*

---

* For the opposite view see Budde's *Hiob, Einleitung*. Some critics regard v.[28] of Job 28 as an editorial addition ; the excision of this verse will not materially

The general inference from these considerations is that most of *Proverbs* stands in time between *Job* and *Ben-Sira*. The date of the latter book is about B.C. 190. For *Job* the similarity between its historical *milieu* and that of Isa. 53 Mal. 3[14.15] suggests a time not earlier than c. B.C. 400, and the non-national and speculative tone of the book points to a date fifty or a hundred years still later.* We thus have c. B.C. 300 as the upper limit for *Proverbs;* for the lower limit see the following paragraph. In this statement of the relation between *Job* and *Proverbs* there is one point that may seem to make a difficulty. It is held by some critics that the sceptical tone of the former must belong to a later period than the calm unspeculative attitude of the latter, which accords with the position of Job's Friends. But this point, very interesting in its suggestions, seems not to be decisive for the chronological relation of the two books. It is obvious, on the one hand, from *Malachi* that the sceptical movement began as early as B.C. 400,† and, on the other hand, from *Ben-Sira* it is no less obvious that the unsceptical attitude was retained as late as B.C. 200. What we have to conclude, therefore, is that the two points of view continued to be held side by side for a considerable period, and it is perhaps an accident that we have only hints of scepticism (as, for example, in Agur) between *Job* and *Ecclesiastes*. And that there was a continuous development of sceptical thought is made probable by a comparison of the tones of *Job* and *Ecclesiastes* — the one passionate and profoundly religious, the other indifferent and feebly religious ; these different phases appear to indicate widely different periods of culture. The difference between *Job* and *Proverbs* is one not merely of time, but of point of view as well. We must assume that the Jewish sages of the four centuries preceding the beginning of our era were of two general classes, the one content to consider the questions of practical everyday life, the other not satisfied with anything less than a solution of the great ethical and religious question

---

affect the view above expressed. Job 28 is, however, now out of place and interruptive, and may well belong in the same period with Pr. 1–9.

  * On the date of *Job* cf. the commentaries of Davidson and Budde, and the articles in Hastings' *Dictionary of the Bible*, Cheyne's *Cyclopaedia Biblica*, and Herzog[8].   † And cf. Jer. 12[1] 20[7].

of the world — the question of the justice of the divine government of men. The first line is continued in *Proverbs*, certain psalms, and *Ben-Sira*, the second in *Job*, certain psalms, *Eccles.*, and *Wisd. of Solomon*. In these parallel lines the chronological relations of the various writings may be measurably determined by such considerations as are presented above.

5. It remains to ask whether the internal indications enable us to fix the chronological order of the various parts of the Book. There is an obvious division into three parts, I., II.–IV., and V., and of these the central part appears to form the kernel of the Book.

a. Taking first this central part, we may begin by separating III. (22^{17}–24), which clearly differs from its context. It consists of quatrains, with synonymous parallelism, which form short hortatory discourses. It assumes a system of instruction by sages, and is marked by ethical inwardness and depth. It indicates, therefore, an advanced stage of reflection and teaching. In its rhythmical and strophic form it resembles *Ben-Sira*. Its two parts, 22^{17}–24^{22} and 24^{23-34}, though separate collections, are so nearly akin in form and thought that they must be considered to be products of the same period and the same circle of sages.

b. The remainder of the central part is composed of two sorts of aphorisms. 1. In chs. 10–15 and half of chs. 28. 29 we find antitheses, restrained and lapidary in style, expressing general moral sentiments, with frequent mention of the divine name and of the terms "righteous" and "wicked." 2. In chs. 16–22^{16} 25–27 and half of chs. 28. 29 there is a predominant employment of comparisons and other single sentences, the style is more flowing than in the first group (10–15, etc.), the material is more varied, and there is much less frequent use of the terms above-mentioned.

The question of chronological priority between these two sorts of aphorism is not easy to decide. The compressed and vigorous antithesis may seem to different persons to be earlier or later than the more flowing form. It is probable that the two do not stand far apart in time, but the more human and pointed tone of the second group accords more closely with the style of *Ben-Sira*.*

---

* It is this fresh picturesqueness that has given us a number of household words from chs. 25–29 (Davidson), but this characteristic does not in itself indicate great antiquity.

This analysis indicates that there once existed various small bodies of aphorisms (in oral or written form), and that these were variously combined into small books. They were all the products of cultivated ethical reflection, though part of their material was doubtless old. Thus the sub-section chs. 10–15 appears to have been a separate book of antitheses, and a similar work was used by the compiler of chs. 28. 29, and, more sparingly, by other editors. We have another aphoristic book in 16–22^{16}, and still another in chs. 25–27 and parts of chs. 28. 29. From portions of these works an editor compiled our section 10^{1}–22^{16}, and from other portions the section chs. 25–29 was independently put together. All this material was regarded by the tradition as Solomonic, and, when the sections were combined, the editor, aware of a difference, referred the formation of the second to the scholars of Hezekiah's time (see note on 25^{1}). This statement of the editor proves not the chronological priority of 10^{1}–22^{16}, but only that this latter collection was made before the other. Smaller collections, such as the Book of Fools (in 26$^{1-12}$) are referred to in the notes, and are further indicated in the lists of repetitions given in § 3. Throughout the central part (chs. 10–29) the marks of editorial hands are visible.

c. The first main division of the Book (chs. 1–9, except 6$^{1-9}$ 9$^{7-12}$) appears to be later than the central part. Such later date is suggested by its precise pedagogic form, its philosophic conceptions (ch. 8), and the prominence it gives to certain sins (robbery and unchastity). The question might be raised whether the section is a unit — whether it does not divide itself naturally into two parts, one (ch. 8 and parts of chs. 3. 4) philosophical and speculative, the other hortatory and practical. There is, no doubt, such a difference in the contents, but it is hardly of a sort to indicate duality of authorship: the general conception of wisdom is the same throughout, and the practical hortatory tone is not confined to the distinctively pedagogic paragraphs. The relation between the section and the Book of *Job* has already been referred to. The two have the same rhythmic form (synonymous parallelism, and frequency of quatrain arrangement) ; but a similar agreement exists between *Proverbs*, many psalms, and *Wisdom of Solomon*, and is of no use for the determination of relative priority in time between these books. The fact that the pessimism of *Job* is not found in *Proverbs* is referred to above (in paragraph 4 of § 6). It is held by some critics that in Job 15[7] there is a direct allusion to Prov. 8[22-31], that Eliphaz asks Job whether he is the personified Wisdom there described.* But this view rests on an improbable interpretation of the couplet. In the first line Eliphaz asks whether Job was the first man created, assuming, apparently, that the first man stood very near the counsels of God and was endowed with special wisdom (cf. v.[8]) The parallelism (synonymous throughout the chapter) suggests that the second line is identical in meaning with the first, and that the expression "before the hills" is a rhetorical synonym of "in hoar antiquity." Or, if the two lines be not mutually equivalent, the second must be regarded as a heightening of the first, with more cutting sarcasm: "were you created first of men? or, forsooth, before the world?" There is no obvious allusion to a primeval Wisdom, or to any cosmogonic history (and v.[8] relates not to the past, but to the speaker's present). Finally, even if the second line be supposed to refer to the same fact that is mentioned in Prov. 8[25], it does not appear why *Job*, rather than *Proverbs*, should be considered the borrower; the conception in the latter book is certainly the more highly developed. And, in general, the conception of wisdom seems to be more developed in Prov. 1-9 than in *Job;* in the latter book (omitting ch. 28, which, on exegetical grounds, is probably to be regarded as an interpolation) wisdom is the reflection of sages, handed down orally, on one great question — a question which has its roots in the Prophetic writings ; in Prov. 1-9 wisdom is the guide of life, with organized instruction, and in one passage (ch. 8) there is a philosophical personification which approaches nearer to WS. 7 than to Job 28.† Cf. notes on 30[4].

The paragraphs 6[1-5] 6[6-11] 9[7-12] belong partly in the same category with III., partly with V.

---

* So Ewald, Davidson, Budde, *al.* The couplet in *Job* reads:

Wert thou the first man born?
Wert brought forth before the hills?

† Cf. Seyring, *Die Abhängigkeit d. Spr. Sal. Cap.* I.-IX., etc., 1889; Strack, in *Stud. u. Krit.*, 1896; Wildeboer, *Litt. d. AT.*

d. Chs. 30. 31, a collection of unconnected fragments, have the appearance of an appendix. The cool agnosticism of Agur reminds us of *Koheleth* rather than of *Job*. The artificial tetradic form is probably late; see note on 30^{11} ff. The terms *wise* and *wisdom* either relate to common-sense sagacity (30^{24} 31^{26}), or when they denote philosophical depth, are treated with contempt (30^3). On the strange titles in 30^1 31^1 see notes on these verses.

The history of the formation of the Book appears to be somewhat as follows : Out of certain current collections of aphorisms were first put together our subsections chs. 10–15, 16–22^{16}, 25–27, and 28. 29, and from these by different editors the sections 10–22^{16} and 25–29 were made, the editor of the latter being aware of the existence of the former.* The two may have received substantially their present form between B.C. 350 and B.C. 300, the second a little later than the first. During the next half-century the section III. (22^{17}–24) was produced, and a book of aphorisms was formed by combining II. and IV. and inserting III. between them ; it is not apparent how this position came to be assigned III., but, as 25^1 ("these also are proverbs of Solomon") seems to presuppose 10^1 ("proverbs of Solomon"), and III. is referred not to Solomon but to the "sages," it is likely that it was added after II. and IV. had been combined ; it is possible, however, that it was first attached to II., the collection IV., with its title unchanged, being then added. The opening section (omitting 6^{1-19} 9^{7-12}) may have been composed about the middle of the third century B.C., and was combined by its author (or by some contemporary editor) with II.–IV. ; the introduction (1^{2-7}) is couched in the technical terms of the schools, and is probably the work of the author of the section ; he seems also to have prefixed the general title (1^1). The additions to the section (6^{1-19} 9^{7-12}), which resemble III., V., and II., may be due to the final redactor, or to a very late scribe. Finally the work was completed by the addition of the fragments contained in chs. 30, 31, the completion falling in the second century B.C. Succeeding copyists introduced into the text a number of errors, not only in words and phrases, but also in arrangement of lines and couplets.

---

* It is possible, however, that the title in 25^1 was inserted by the final redactor.

6. The linguistic phenomena of the Book are in accord with these dates : while the style, especially in the earlier parts, does not differ substantially from that of the " classic " period (which may be taken to include centuries 8–5 B.C.), there are passages, chiefly in the later parts, which show a nearer approach to the later usage. It is to be borne in mind, of course, that the vocabulary and syntax are probably to some extent affected by the nature of the material : in such a work there would naturally be a large number of philosophical terms, and the more popular aphorisms would use words which, though not new, might not be found elsewhere.* Such expressions may characterize the individual style of the Book, but do not determine its date. It is to be noted also that a certain number of peculiarities are to be set down as scribal errors. These deductions being made, there still remains a small number of expressions which appear to belong to the later usage. Some of these (as בר in 31²) are Aramaisms, others are late-Hebrew ; reference is made to these in the critical notes. *Ben-Sira*, so far as we can judge from the part of its Hebrew text which we have (chs. 39¹⁵–49¹¹), contains a greater number of late expressions than *Proverbs* — a fact which we might expect from its later date and its fuller and freer treatment of matters of everyday life. It is doubtful whether any Arabisms occur in *Proverbs ;* the words which have been so explained may all be otherwise satisfactorily accounted for. There are no Persian or Greek words.

§ 7. Text and Versions.

1. The text is not in good condition ; errors are more frequent in II.–V. than in I., the simple style of the latter having saved it to some extent from scribal misunderstandings and misrepresentations. The mistakes are to be set down partly to the ignorance of copyists, partly to the freedom which they allowed themselves in dealing with this book as with other OT. books ; we find much the same state of things in *Samuel, Isaiah, Ezekiel,* and *Psalms.* It does not appear that changes were made in *Proverbs* in the interests of theological opinion or from a sense of propriety or de-

---

* This is the case with most of the words mentioned as rare in Driver's *Introd. to Lit. of OT.*

cency (*causa honoris, c. reverentiae,* etc.).* Such changes were
made in other OT. books; the immunity of *Proverbs* is due in
part to its untheological character, in part to the fact that it was
looked on as less sacred and authoritative than the Pentateuch
and the Prophetic writings.

2. The extant Ancient Versions of *Proverbs* are the Septuagint
(from which were made the Coptic and the Hexaplar Syriac), the
Peshitta Syriac, the Targum, fragments of the later Greek translations (Aquila, Symmachus, Theodotion, etc.), and the Latin of
Jerome.

Of these the oldest and, for the criticism of the text, the most
valuable is the Septuagint. It represents in general an older text
than that of the received Hebrew tradition; † but its value as a
presentation of the old Jewish aphoristic thought and as a critical
instrument is impaired by the corruptions it has suffered and by
certain peculiarities in the mode of translation. In a number of
cases it offers good suggestions for the restoration of the original
Hebrew. In not a few instances the translator does not understand the Hebrew. ‡ He sometimes departs from the literal
rendering in order to give the translation a smoother and more
idiomatic Greek form, § sometimes also in order to obtain a better
antithesis or a more appropriate thought. Possibly he is sometimes influenced by the desire to reproduce the later Pharisaic
orthodoxy, ‖ but this is not clear; there is no trace of distinctively
Christian ideas. The Greek book is somewhat longer than the
Hebrew: some Hebrew couplets and lines it omits, but it includes
much that the Hebrew text has not. The omissions usually indicate a Hebrew scribal plus. The additions are sometimes in the

---

* Geiger, *Urschrift*, pp. 378, 400, 403, finds an example of such change in 7^{18},
and Hitzig in 30^{31}, on which see critical notes.

† The translation may have been made as early as 100 B.C.

‡ Such ignorance is found abundantly elsewhere in the Septuagint, but is here
especially obvious — a fact which may be due in part (as Frankenberg suggests) to
the absence of a good exegetical tradition; *Proverbs* was not so much read and
commented on as some other books. It is not certain that one man translated the
whole of *Proverbs*.

§ Cf. Jäger, *Observations in Prov. Sal. vers. alex.*, 1788. This, however, hardly
warrants us in supposing (Frankenberg) that the translation was made for a non-
Jewish public.

‖ This hypothesis is carried to excess by Heidenheim.

form of doublets, but oftener contain entirely new matter, which the Greek translator has either himself composed, or, as is more probable, has inserted from current collections of proverbs. They appear sometimes to be based on a Hebrew original, sometimes to have been written originally in Greek. There is rarely ground for supposing of any one of them that it formed part of the original *Book of Proverbs;* but they show that our Hebrew Book is only a selection out of a great mass of material then current, and they thus corroborate the view of date given above. An unsettled condition of the early Hebrew MSS. of *Proverbs* is possibly indicated by the Septuagint order of sub-sections in III., IV., V., which (if we designate the chapters as in the Hebrew) are arranged thus: 22^{17}–24^{22}; 30^{1-14}; 24^{23-34}; 30^{15-33}; 31^{1-9}; 25–29; 31^{10-31}.* From the point of view of similarity of material this arrangement is manifestly inferior to that of our Hebrew text — it breaks up III. and ch. 31 by the interposition of alien matter, and places IV. far from its natural connection. But it does not follow that the mal-arrangement is due to the caprice of a Greek translator.† The subsections composing III.–V. must once have circulated as separate treatises, and may have been combined in different ways by Jewish scribes or editors. What we know of the procedure of Greek translators elsewhere in OT. (for example, in *Jeremiah*) does not favor the supposition that they acted capriciously in this regard.

The Coptic Version is useful for the control of the Greek. It sometimes offers material not found in our Greek MSS.; all such cases must be judged by the critical rules applied to the Greek Version. ‡

The present Peshitta Syriac text of *Proverbs* has a perplexing mixture of readings, agreeing sometimes with 𝕳 against 𝕲, sometimes with 𝕲 against 𝕳; the more important readings are given in the Critical Notes. As it follows 𝕳 in general in material and

---

* Cf. the Greek arrangement of *Jeremiah*, and numbering of the Psalms, and the modern attempts at rearranging *Ecclesiastes*.

† So Strack and Frankenberg. The latter observes that the Greek arrangement divides the latter part of the Book into two Solomonic collections, with only two titles (10^1 25^1). This may have been the principle of arrangement, but the translator may have found it in his Hebrew manuscript.

‡ Cf. Bickell, who makes much use of the Coptic.

arrangement, it is probable that it is based on the Hebrew; at the same time we know too little of the history of Syriac translations to be able to say whether or how far the present text has been corrected from the Hebrew. On the other hand, the nature of the agreements between 𝔖 and 𝔊 favors the view that the former has in certain passages followed the latter; whether, in that case, this rendering from the Greek was the work of the original Syriac translator or of a later reviser is a difficult question, though the former supposition seems the more probable. If we add to all this that the Syriac translation is often free, it is obvious that it must be used with caution in the criticism of the Hebrew or the Greek.*

The Targum, as is now generally held, is based on the Syriac, though in a number of cases it follows the Hebrew.

Jerome for the most part follows the Masoretic text closely, and gives little material for getting back of it. Where he follows the rendering of 𝔊 or inserts from it couplets which are not in 𝔥, he probably retains the older Latin text, which was made from the Greek. He represents the Jewish exegesis of his time, but is rarely helpful in those cases in which the Hebrew is peculiarly difficult or obscure.

§ 8. CANONICITY.

According to Rabbinical authorities † the reception of the Book into the Canon was for a time opposed on the ground of its contradictory statements ($26^{4.5}$) and its too highly colored descriptions (7^{7-20}). The latter class of objections seems to have arisen early, if any chronological conclusion can be drawn from the statement of the tradition that they were set aside by the "men of the Great Synagogue." The solution of the question appears to have been found in the allegorical interpretation of the passage in ch. 7. The Talmud says nothing of any difficulty in connection with Agur. The doubts concerning *Proverbs* soon passed away, and its value was universally recognized. It is quoted or used in NT. frequently (over twenty times) and in the Talmud (especially in

---

* On details of 𝔖 and 𝔗 see J. A. Dathe, 1764, in Rosenmüller's *Opuscula*, 1814, Th. Nöldeke, in *Archiv f. wiss. erforschung d. AT.*, ii., and Pinkuss' articles in *ZATW.*, 1894.

† *Shab.* 30 b, *Aboth Nathan*, Cap. i.

Pirke Aboth), is cited abundantly by the early Christian writers, has always been highly esteemed for its practical wisdom, and a number of its aphorisms have become household words.

§ 9. BIBLIOGRAPHY.

On Text and Versions.

PROCOPIUS, 'Ερμενεία.

G. J. L. VOGEL, 1768 (in Schultens).

J. G. JÄGER, *Observv. in Prov. Sal. vers. alexandrinam*, 1788.

J. F. SCHLEUSNER, *Opuscula*, 1812, and *Lexicon*[2], 1829.

P. DE LAGARDE, *Anmerkungen z. griech. uebersetzung d. Proverbien*, 1863.

M. HEIDENHEIM, *Zur textkritik d. Proverbien* (in his *Vierteljahrschrift*), 1865, 1866.

DYSERINCK, *Kritische Scholien* (in *Theol. Tijdschrift*), 1883.

H. OORT, *Spreuken* I.-IX. (in *Th. Tijdschr.*), 1885.

A. J. BAUMGARTNER, *Étude critique sur l'état d. texte d. livre d. Proverbes*, 1890.

G. BICKELL, *Krit. bearbeitung d. Proverbien* (in *Wiener Zeitschr. f. d. Kunde d. Morgenlandes*), 1891.

H. PINKUSS, *Die syrische uebersetzung d. Proverbien* (in *ZATW.*), 1894.

H. GRÄTZ, *Exeget. studien* (in his *Monatsschrift*), 1884, and *Emendationes*, 1892-1894.

E. NESTLE, art. *Bibelübersetzungen*, in Herzog's *Real-Encykl.*[3] (and published separately).

Remarks on text in commentaries of Hitzig, Ewald, Delitzsch, Zöckler, Nowack, Wildeboer, Frankenberg.

Translations and Commentaries.

Midrash Mishle, ed. S. Buber, 1893.

SAADIA'S version, ed. J. Derenbourg, 1894 (cf. B. Heller, in *REJ.*, 1898).

RASHI, Lat. transl. by Breithaupt, 1714.

ABEN EZRA,* ed. C. M. Horowitz, 1884.

The commentaries of Rashi, Aben Ezra, and Levi ben Gersom are given also in A. Giggeius' *In Prov. Sal. Comment. trium Rabbinorum*, 1620, and are cited in L. Cahen's *La Bible*, 1847. In this last work Leopold Dukes, in his Introduction to Proverbs, gives a list of 38 Jewish commentators on the book, beginning with Saadia (d. 942) and ending with J. Löwenstein (1837).

H. DEUTSCH, *Die Sprüche Sal.'s nach d. auffassung im Talmud u. Midrasch dargestellt u. kritisch untersucht*, 1885.

J. MERCERUS, *Comm. in Sal. Prov.*, etc., 1573, 1651.

M. GEIER, *Prov. regum sapientissimi Sal.*, etc., 1653, 1699, 1725.

C. B. MICHAELIS (in J. H. Michaelis, *Uberiores annotationes in Hagiogr.*, etc.), 1720.

A. SCHULTENS, *Prov. Sal.*, etc., 1748, and abridged ed. by G. J. L. Vogel, 1769.

B. HODGSON, *The Prov. of Sol. transl.*, etc., 1788.

---

* It is not certain that this work is by Aben Ezra; it may be by Moses Qamhi (Kimchi). It was edited also, from another MS., by S. R. Driver (Oxford, 1880).

H. EWALD, in his *Poet. Bücher* [*Dich-ter*] *d. Alt. Bundes*, 1837, 1867.

G. R. NOYES, *New Translation of the Prov.*, etc., 1846.

M. STUART, *Comm. on the Book of Prov.*, etc., 1852.

F. HITZIG, *Die Sprüche Sal.'s über-setzt*, etc., 1858.

O. ZÖCKLER, *Comm. zu d. Spr. Sal.* (in Lange's *Bibelwerk*), 1866 (Eng. transl., 1870).

H. F. MÜHLAU, *De prov. quae di-cuntur Aguri et Lemuelis origine atque indole*, 1869.

FRANZ DELITZSCH, *Das Sal. Spruch-buch*, 1873 (Eng. transl. 1875).

E. REUSS, in his annotated transl. of the Bible, French ed. (*La Bible*), 1878, Germ. ed. (*Das Alt. Test.*), 1894.

W. NOWACK (in *Kurzgef. exeget. Handbuch z. AT.*), 1883 (revision of E. Bertheau, 1847).

H. L. STRACK (in Strack u. Zöckler's *Kurzgef. Comm. z. AT.*), 1888.

R. F. HORTON (in *Expositor's Bible*), 1891.

G. WILDEBOER (in Marti's *Kurzer Hand-Comm. z. AT.*), 1897.

W. FRANKENBERG (in Nowack's *Hand-komm. z. AT.*), 1898.

General Works.

L. DUKES, Introduction to Proverbs in Cahen, *La Bible*, 1847.

J. F. BRUCH, *Weisheitslehre d. He-bräer*, 1851.

H. BOIS, *La poésie gnomique chez l. Hébreux et chez l. Grecs — Solomon et Théognis*, 1886.

T. K. CHEYNE, in *Job and Solomon*, 1887.

C. G. MONTEFIORE, *Notes upon the date and religious value of the Book of Prov.* (in *Jew. Quart. Rev.*), 1889–1890.

R. SMEND, *Alttestamentliche religions-geschichte*, 1893.

R. PFEIFFER, *Die relig.-sittliche Welt-anschauung d. Buches d. Sprüche*, 1897.

Proverbs of Other Ancient Peoples.

Chinese: F. H. Jenings, *Proverbial Philosophy of Confucius*, 1895; W. Scarborough, *Chinese Proverbs*, 1875.

Egyptian: T. L. Griffith, art. *Egyptian Literature*, in *Library of the World's Best Literature*.

Assyrian: M. Jäger, *Assyr. Räthsel u. Sprichwörter*, in *Beiträge z. Assyri-ologie*, 1892.

Indian: Böhtlingk, *Ind. Sprüche;* Muir, *Sanskrit Texts;* M. Williams, *Indian Wisdom;* P. More, *Indian Epigrams*, 1898 ; C. R. Lanman, *Indic Epigrams*, 1899 ; see also the

Hitopadeça, the *Panchatantra*, and the *Jatakas*.

Greek: For the aphorisms which go under the name of Menander see the collections of Meineke and Koch.

Syrian: The so-called Syriac Menan-der is given in Land, *Anecdota Syr.*, I.; cf. *ZATW.*, 1895.

As a Semitic parallel we may add *Arabic:* Freytag, Meidani; Fleischer, *Ali's Sprüche.*

See also L. Dukes, *Blumenlese*, and his Introduction to Proverbs in Cahen, *La Bible.*

A COMMENTARY ON THE BOOK OF PROVERBS.

A COMMENTARY ON THE BOOK OF PROVERBS.

I. CHAPTERS I.–IX.

A series of discourses on the excellence of wisdom, with illustrations of its principles taken from everyday life. These are preceded by a general introduction, before which stands a general title. On the date and origin see the Introduction.

I. contains the title (v.¹), an introduction (v.²⁻⁷), and two discourses (v.⁸⁻¹⁹· ²⁰⁻²³).

1. Title. — *The proverbs of Solomon, son of David, king of Israel.* The title *king of Israel* belongs to *Solomon.* On the ascription to Solomon, and on the term *proverbs* (Heb. *mishlē*) as name of the book, see the Introduction. The title was probably prefixed by the collector of I., or by the editor of I.–IV., or, possibly, by the last compiler. The Heb. word *mashal* (*proverb*) probably signifies *similarity, parallelism* (nearly = *comparison*), and seems to have been used at an early time of all poetry, hardly with reference to the form (parallelism of clauses, clause-rhythm, being the distinctive formal characteristic of old-Semitic poetry), but, probably, with reference to the thought (short distiches made by the juxtaposition of related ideas, originally comparisons with familiar objects) ; * the men called *mashalists* (Nu. 21²⁷) appear, like the Greek rhapsodists and the Arabian *rawis*, to have been reciters (doubtless also sometimes composers) of narrative and descriptive poems. There is no one English equivalent for *ma-*

---

* There is no OT. word for *poetry*, though there are terms for various species of poetical composition, *song*, etc. On the late Hebrew terms for liturgical poetry and poets, *piyut, paitan* (ποιητής), see Delitzsch, *Zur Gesch. d. jüdisch. Poësie*, pp. 49 ff.

3

shal—it seems to cover the whole ground of Hebrew poetry. It may signify a simple folksaying or aphorism (1 Sam. 10¹² 24¹⁴⁽¹³⁾ Ez. 12²² 18²), an allegory (Ez. 17²), an enigmatical saying (Ez. 21⁵), a byword (Jer. 24⁹ Dt. 28³⁷), a taunting speech (Isa. 14⁴ Hab. 2⁶), a lament (Mic. 2⁴), a visional or apocalyptic discourse (Nu. 23⁷ 24¹⁵), a didactic discourse (ψ 49. 78), an argument or plea (Job 29¹).* In the Book of Proverbs it is either an aphorism (10–22) or a discourse (1–9, 23²⁹⁻³⁵ 27²³⁻²⁷).

2–7. Preface or introduction, stating the object of the book, namely, that men may be induced to accept the teaching of wisdom. — The structure is distichal, with synonymous parallelism (except v.⁷). The thought is similar to that of 22¹⁷⁻²¹, and the preface, like the title, was probably prefixed by a late, perhaps the latest, editor; the paragraph is syntactically a continuation of v.¹.

2. That men may acquire wisdom and training,
   May understand rational discourse,
3. May receive training in wise conduct —
   In justice and probity and rectitude,
4. That discretion may be given to the inexperienced,
   To the youth knowledge and insight.

5. Let the wise man hear and add to his learning,
   And the man of intelligence gain education,
6. That he may understand proverb and parable,
   The words of sages and their aphorisms.

7. The fear of Yahweh is the beginning of knowledge —
   Wisdom and discipline fools despise.

As the Hebrew text stands the introduction appears to consist of two parts, the statement of object (²⁻⁶), and the definition of knowledge (⁷) ; and the former divides itself into a general reference to men (².³), with special regard to the immature (⁴), and a particular reference to the wise (⁵·⁶) — that is, the work is said to be addressed to all classes of intelligence. The definition (⁷) stands by itself, being of the nature of a general reflection, an appendix to the statement of object. V.⁵ appears to be a parenthesis or an editorial insertion — the syntactical construction

---

* Cf. Delitzsch, *op. cit.*, pp. 196 ff.

here changes (to be resumed in v.[6]), and there is a certain incongruity in bidding a sage learn to understand the words of sages. If these two couplets be omitted, we have a symmetrical paragraph of two quatrains: [2.3], "that men may acquire wisdom," and [4.6], "that the immature may be educated into understanding the discourses of the sages."

2–4. The general object of the book. — The syntactical connection with v.[1] is close: *the proverbs of Solomon* . . . [whose object is] *that men may acquire*, etc. — **2**. Synonymous, ternary. Lit.: *to acquire* (or, *know*), etc., the subject of the Infinitive being "men" or "the pupil." The parallel expressions are practically equivalent in meaning. *Wisdom* is the general expression for knowledge of all good things; it is practical sagacity (Ju. 5^{29} 2 Sam. 13^3 14^2 20^{16}), the skill of the artisan (Ex. 31^3), wide acquaintance with facts (1 K. 4^{29-34} [5^{9-14}]), learning (Jer. 8^9), skill in expounding secret things (Ez. 28^3), statesmanship (Jer. 18^{18}), and finally, knowledge of right living in the highest sense. This last is its sense here — moral and religious intelligence. It excludes not only the morally bad, but also (in contrast with Greek wisdom) the philosophically speculative, though, in parts of Proverbs, Ecclesiastes, and Wisdom of Solomon, it is tinged with Greek philosophical thought. In it the religious element is practically identical with the moral: no stress is laid in Proverbs on the ritualistic side of life (sacrifices, vows), the devotional (prayer, praise, reading sacred books), or the dogmatic (monotheism, sin, salvation); the writers of chs. 1–9 and of the whole Book are concerned with practical affairs; the law of God is for them simply the moral law. — The second term, *training, discipline*, (or, *instruction*), signifies properly the fact of teaching, education (sometimes chastisement), but must here be taken to mean the result of right teaching, that is, wisdom; the teacher may be God, or a man who imparts the law of God. *Rational discourse* is lit. *words of understanding;* this last term = "discernment, comprehension," is in like manner identical with *wisdom.* — Man's relation to wisdom is expressed by the word *acquire* (lit. *know* or *learn*). So far as stress is thus laid on intellectual recognition of right as the basis of a good life the thought of our section (and of the whole Book) is allied to the Socratic-Stoic conception of morality. The OT. term, however, like the Greek, expresses more than bare intellectual recognition — it involves intellectual assimilation and practical acceptance of truth as the rule of life; see Am. 3^{10} Hos. 6^3 13^5 Isa. 1^3 Jer. 14^{20} Job 20^{20} ψ $51^{3(5)}$. Still, knowledge is here set forth as the foundation of conduct, that is, it is assumed that men will do right when its nature and consequences are clearly understood by them. The conception of a change of heart is not found in Proverbs. In the second clause the verb *understand = discern, distinguish, apprehend*, is a synonym of *know.* — **3.** Ternary; line 2 is the definition of the last word of line 1. The element of assimilation is expressed in the term *receive* = " apprehend, accept, and apply as a rule of life." — The term *training* (or, *instruction*) is usually defined by its source (v.[8], father, 3^{11} Yahweh), but here by its object or aim, as in Isa. 53^5 *the chastisement of* [= *which should procure*] *our peace.* The aim is here expressed by four terms (so RV.), *wise conduct, justice, probity, rectitude,* the three last of which are better taken as setting forth the content of the first. From the signification of these words they cannot be understood as objects of the verb *receive* (Nowack, Frankenberg), or as expressing the content of the term *instruction* (Delitzsch). Kamphausen * renders : *that men may accept instruction that makes wise (klug), righteousness and* [*sense of*] *the right and rectitude,* taking *instruction* as = " the fact of teaching," and leaving it uncertain whether the terms in the second clause are the object of *receive* or are in apposition with *instruction.* Delitzsch and Frankenberg, not so well : *to attain intelligent instruction.* — *Wise conduct* is action which springs from insight and sagacity, in ordinary affairs (1 Sam. 18^{30} Gen. 48^{14} 3^6 Prov. 10^5 14^{35} *al.*), and especially in the moral and religious life (Jer. 3^{15} ψ 119^{99}). Such action, in its best sense, is controlled by moral principle, and is accordingly here defined by several synonymous terms. *Justice* (RV. *righteousness*) is a forensic term, expressing the quality of the character and action of that one of the two parties to a lawsuit who has the right on his side, and thus comes to signify right conduct in gen-

---

* In Kautzsch's *Heilige Schrift.*

eral. *Probity* is the procedure of a judge, especially legal decision (Ju. 4[5] 2 Sam. 15[2]) or custom (1 Sam. 2[13] 10[25]), law (Dt. 4[5]),
God's acts of moral government in the world (Isa. 26[9] ψ 105[7]),
then general conduct in accordance with legal decision (assumed
to be morally right) whether made by man or by God. *Rectitude*
is levelness, straightness, straightforwardness of conduct, as opposed to the crooked ways of those who abandon the guidance of
moral truth. These three words are variant expressions of *rectitude*, and thus define the content of the general term *wise conduct*.
V.[2] declares that knowledge of right principle is the basis of true
life; v.[3] assumes that this knowledge necessarily leads to action
controlled by moral principle. — **4.** Synonymous, ternary. From
the point of view of the teacher; lit.: *to give discretion*, etc. The
inexperienced (RV. *simple*) are the uninstructed, the immature;
the word is here used in a negative, indifferent sense, to indicate
need of instruction (used in v.[22] with bad connotation). The Heb.
term appears to signify those whose minds are open to influence,
who can be easily led. The parallel *youth* likewise emphasizes the
idea of immaturity (so that there is no need to substitute a term
= *stupid*); the word may mean *babe* (Ex. 2[6]), *child* (2 K. 4[29]),
young man (Ju. 17[7]), or, without respect to age, *servant* (2 Sam. 9[9]).
The Book of Proverbs addresses itself to men only, not to women;
the silence respecting the latter is doubtless due to their domestic
isolation and comparative security from grosser temptations; more
attention is paid them in Ben-Sira (7[24. 25] 9[1] 22[4. 5] 23[22-26] 25[16-26] 26
36[21-26] 42[9-11]). — *Discretion* is cleverness in general (Gen. 3[1]), either
for good (so throughout Pr.) or for evil (Ex. 21[14]). The synonym
insight, or *discretion*, is the power of forming plans or perceiving
the best line of procedure for gaining an end, then the plan itself,
good or bad; in Pr. sometimes employed in a bad sense (12[2] 14[17]
24[8]), oftener, as here, in a good sense.

5. Synonymous, quaternary-ternary (possibly ternary). The
telic sense *that the wise man may hear* (RV. Orelli) is not a
correct rendering of the Heb.; the hortative sense *let . . . hear*
(De., Frank.) though not in accordance with the construction of
the rest of the paragraph, is that which best suits the expression
of object which characterizes the introduction. The declarative

rendering is adopted by the Vrss., Schult., Kamph.; the sentence
then breaks the connection, and must be taken to be parenthetical.   It seems, indeed, not to belong here, but in some such
connection as that in which the similar aphorism 9⁹ now stands.
It is perhaps an old gloss (found in all the Vrss.) the design of
which is to point out that the teaching of wisdom is appropriate
not only for the immature (v.⁴), but also for the wise.   *Learning*
is that which is received, the content or material of instruction.
The parallel expression in the second clause appears to be a nauti-
cal term (so the Grk. and Lat. Vrss.) derived from the word for
rope, and meaning *steering, guidance;* used in Job 37¹² of God's
guidance of the clouds; in Pr. 11¹⁴ 12⁵ 20¹⁸ 24⁶ = *counsel*, and
here *power of guidance, of sound direction* of life, = *education*.
— **6.** Synonymous, ternary.   The scholarly aim.   The verse connects itself immediately with v.²⁻⁴; these refer to the subject-
matter of teaching, v.⁶ to its form.   The allusion here seems to be
to organized schools, and to the habit of Oriental teachers of
couching their instruction in figures, parables, and allegories (see
especially ch. 30).   The reference is not to esoteric teaching
intended to conceal the highest wisdom from the mass of men —
there is no evidence that such esoterism existed anywhere in the
ancient world * — though the teacher would naturally speak more
freely to the inner circle of his pupils (cf. Mt. 13³⁴). — The three
terms here employed to describe the form of the sage's instruction
have no exact representatives in English.   On *proverb* see note
on v.¹.   The meaning of the stem of the second term (מליצה)
appears to be *turn, bend;* Gen. 42²³ an *interpreter* is one who
translates discourse from one language into another, and so the
Babylonian *ambassadors* or *interpreters* of 2 C. 32³¹; Isa. 43²⁷ the
mediators or *interpreters* are the representative men, prophets, and
priests (the Grk. not so well, *rulers*), who made God's words intelligible to the people, and the *mediating angel* of Job 33²³ interprets
man's case to God.   Our word thus appears to mean a turned or
figurative saying, one that looks toward another sense, a *parable;*
in the only other place in which it occurs, Hab. 2⁶, it has the

---

* This statement can, I believe, be substantiated. The Greek Mysteries, and
such passages as Dan. 12⁹, do not form exceptions.

connotation of *taunt, sarcasm;* cf. the similar use of *proverb.*
Here it signifies a didactic utterance (rhythmical in form), in
which the figurative need not be the predominant feature. — The
third expression (חידת) comes in like manner from a stem meaning
turn aside, and signifies some sort of deflected discourse. Its
earliest use seems to be that of *riddle,* as in Ju. 14, 1 K. 10[1]
(= 2 C. 9[1]) ; in Ez. 17[2] it = *parable,* and in Nu. 12[8] the parabolic
or visional form of the ordinary divine communication with priest
or prophet, in contrast with the direct speech which Yahweh
employed with Moses; in Dan. 8[23] Antiochus Epiphanes is described as understanding *ḥidoth,* which must mean tortuous (morally tricky) words or procedures ; a shading of scorn and ridicule
appears in Hab. 2[6], while in ψ 49[4(5)] 78[2], as in Pr., the sense is
simply didactic. Here it obviously = *aphorisms.* — The three
terms are here synonyms. Their etymology indicates that the
earliest teaching was figurative in form (riddle, proverb, parable,
allegory) ; but, as prophecy naturally advanced from ecstatic
utterance to straightforward discourse, so the Israelitish sages
gradually abandoned the figurative form in the interests of clearness, though it continued to be employed by popular teachers.
V.[6] assumes that it is a part of good education to understand
the aphorisms of the sages, and these, as Pr. and Ben-Sira show,
were simple and direct expositions and enforcements of duty. —
That a definite class of teachers with some sort of school-organi-
zation existed as early as the third century B.C. appears probable
from the way in which the sages are spoken of in Pr. (especially
22[17-21]), and Eccl. 12[11], and from the account given in *Pirke
Aboth* of the heads of schools and their sayings from the middle
of the second century on. The aphorisms, and particularly the
discourses, in Pr. and Ben-Sira are for the most part not popular
in form, but bear the impress of cultivated thought. Later the
title *sages* was given to the teachers of the law.*

If v.[5] be omitted, v.[2-4. 6] form a symmetrical strophe or paragraph :

To know wisdom and instruction, to discern words of understanding,

To receive instruction in wise conduct, in justice and probity and rectitude,

To give discretion to the inexperienced, to the youth knowledge and insight,

To understand proverb and parable, the words of sages and their aphorisms.

* See Schürer, *Jewish People,* Eng. tr., II. i. 324.

7. The motto. — Antithetic, quaternary. This general definition of wisdom may be regarded as the motto of the whole book, and is probably to be ascribed to the final editor ; see ψ 111[10]. The *beginning* of knowledge, its choicest feature, its foremost and essential element, is said to be the *fear of Yahweh*. The term *fear* goes back historically to the dread which was felt in the presence of the powerful and stern tribal or national deity ; Semitic deities were in the historical period generally conceived of as lords or kings, exercising constant control over their peoples, and inflicting punishment on them for disobedience. This is the prevailing attitude of the pious man toward God throughout the OT. ; only the sentiment gradually advances from the form of mere dread of the divine anger to that of reverence for the divine law. It never entirely loses, however, the coloring implied in the word *fear*. The OT. ethical conception of life is not love of a moral ideal as the supreme good, but regard for it as an ordination of the supreme authority ; the world is looked on not as a household in which God and man are co-workers, but as a realm in which God is king and man is subject. This conception, the result of the moral strenuousness of the Jewish people and of their Oriental governmental scheme of life, helped to develop moral strictness. It is a fundamental principle of moral life, though not the only principle. The idea of the Hebrew sage is that he who lives with reverent acknowledgment of God as lawgiver will have within his soul a permanent and efficient moral guide ; other conditions of ethical experience, such as native character, knowledge, temptation, surroundings, are left unmentioned, not deliberately excluded, but omitted because they are not prominent in the writer's thought ; his purpose is to emphasize the one principle of reverence as paramount, and he identifies the man's own moral ideal with the divine moral law. — The use of the name *Yahweh* instead of the more general *Elohim* is not significant as to date or as to ethical feeling. Yahweh, though in name nothing but the national deity of the Jews, is here regarded as the supreme and only God. The personal name was gradually replaced by *the Lord* (as in the ancient Versions, except the Targum), or *the Holy One* (as in the Talmud), or *God* (as in Ezra, Neh., Eccles., and some Psalms), but, as appears from some late Psalms, continued to

be freely used, in certain circles, down to the second century B.C.
It is possible, however, that both in Egypt and in Palestine it was,
in this later time, though written, not pronounced, but replaced in
reading by *Adonay* (*the Lord*). — The second clause states, not
formally but in substance, the antithesis to the first, the sense
being: "absence of the fear of Yahweh (in fools) is negation (contempt) of wisdom." The *fool* is primarily a person lacking in good
sense in general, uninstructed (Isa. 35^8), unskilled (Pr. 11^{29}), or
offensively ignorant (10^8 20^3 29^9), then, as here, one who is lacking
in the highest wisdom, and therefore devoid of piety toward God
(so the Grk. here). Such an one *despises* wisdom, is ignorant of
and does not value its high function, nor accept it as guide. —
Instead of the couplet of the Heb. the Grk. has a quatrain:

> The beginning of wisdom is the fear of God,
> And a good understanding have all they that practise it;
> Piety toward God is the beginning of knowledge,
> But wisdom and instruction the impious will set at naught.

The second line of this quatrain now stands in ψ 111^{10}, and the
third line appears to be a doublet of the first (except that the
terms *wisdom* and *knowledge* exchange places), but may be an
original parallelism. Whether the longer form of the Greek is an
expansion of Heb. or Grk. scribes, or belongs to the original
reading, it is difficult to say. As this verse is an isolated aphorism, its length does not affect the rhythmical structure of the
succeeding discourse. Cf. BS. 1$^{11-27}$.

I. 1. The primitive sense of the stem משל is doubtful. In all Semitic
languages it means to be *like* or *equal*, in Canaanitish (Heb., Phoen.) also
to *rule*, and in Arab. to *stand erect*, be *eminent, superior*. The original
force is perhaps to be *alongside of, above* (cf. על = *on*, superposition, and *at*,
juxtaposition), whence the notions of similarity and superiority. See Schultens, *Prov.*, Fleischer (in De.), Ges. *Thes.*, BDB. — 𝔐 מלך ישראל; 𝔊 ὅς
ἐβασίλευσεν ἐν Ἰσραήλ, possibly a variant reading (cf. Eccl. 1^1), but hardly
an indication (Jäger) that the Grk. translator considered the paragraph v.$^{1-6}$
to be non-Solomonic. — 2. The primary sense of the stem חכם seems (from
the Arab.) to be *firm, fixed*, whence the verb *control, restrain*, and the
noun *fixedness of opinion, knowledge*. — 3. השכל is taken as = *intelligence,
wisdom*, by Oort, *Theol. Tijdsch.*, xix. 380 (𝔏 *doctrinae*), as in Dan. 1^{17};
the Inf. occurs elsewhere in Pr. twice, in 21^{11} = *make wise, teach*, in 21^{16}
= *wise conduct:* the latter sense is preferable here. מישרים is collective

plu., *a mass of equitable actions = equity;* syn. מֵישׁוּר, Mal. 2⁶ Isa. 11⁴ ψ 45⁶⁽⁷⁾.
A different sense occurs in Dan. 11⁶. — 𝔊 divides the v. into three stiches:
δέξασθαί τε στροφὰς λόγων, νοῆσαί τε δικαιοσύνην ἀληθῆ, καὶ κρίμα κατευθύνειν.
On στρ. λογ. see Schleusner, *Lex.* What Heb. it represents is doubtful; Lag.
מוסבות *turnings* (cf. Ez. 41⁷·²⁴), which, however, is not used of speech; Heidenheim (in *Vierteljahrsschr. f. theol. Forsch.*, ii. 401) לקחי מוסר, *the teachings of*
discipline, which hardly explains 𝔊; νοῆσαι = להשכל, ἀληθῆ is scribal insertion
(Lag., on the contrary, rejects δικ. as usual rendering), κατ. = some form of
ישר, perh. מישר taken as Inf., less probably Hif. הושר. 𝔏 = 𝔥. 𝔖 *to receive*
instruction and fear, where דחלתא seems to be scribal error. 𝔗 = 𝔥, except
that it prefixes ו to צרק. — Graetz inserts הוכחת before מוסר (as in 6²³), and
writes להשכיל and מישרים, ומשפט, making a tristich (so 𝔊). — 4. פתאים, written
v.²²·³² פתים; the א is vowel-letter, and should be omitted. St. פתה = *open*,
wide (Gen. 9²⁷), then *to be persuaded, enticed, seduced;* פתי *open-minded, per-*
suadable, simple-minded, inexperienced; Ar. *fatā = broad-minded, generous,*
and *young man, fatwā = legal decision* (opening, expounding of a legal question), *mufti = judge.* — 𝔥 לתח; 𝔊 ἵνα δῷ, free rendering. 𝔥 לנער; 𝔊 παιδὶ
δὲ νέῳ, in which νέῳ is perh. dittogram (Jäg.), but may be orig. (Lag.); according to Heid. it is miswriting of νέος, the two words π. and ν. being designed to
form a parallel to plu. פ. For נער Graetz unnecessarily writes בער *stupid.*
Rashi נער = מנוער *cast out from* or *destitute of learning.* — 5. A telic force for
ישמע is hardly supported by such a construction as that of ישמיר Isa. 13⁹ in
which the two clauses are closely combined. — החבלות is denominative noun
of action; 𝔊 κυβέρνησιν, 𝔏 *gubernacula,* ΑΣΘ *gubernationes;* on 𝔖ᴴ see
notes of Lag. and Field; Fleischer (in De.) compares Ar. *tadbīr,* Syr. *dubōro.*
— V.⁵ is regarded as interpolation by Ziegler, and as parenthetical by Wildeboer. — 6. 𝔥 מליצה; 𝔊 σκοτεινὸν λόγον; ΑΘ ἑρμενείαν, and so 𝔏 Rashi, AV.,
against the parallelism, *the interpretation,* marg. *an eloquent speech;* RV. *figure.*
— 7. On the etymology of אויל as = *thick, dull, stupid,* see Fleisch., De., SS.,
BDB.; Malbim, Heid. (in De.) *sceptic,* from אולי *perhaps.* — Bickell (*Wiener*
ZKM. v. 86) adopts the reading of 𝔊 on the ground that *beginning of wisdom*
as well as *beginning of knowledge* is here absolutely necessary; he holds that the
Psalmist took the passage from Pr. and that the translator of the ψ followed the
translation of Pr., the clause falling out of 𝔥 by homoeoteleuton. It is, however, equally possible that Pr. followed the ψ. Further, it is not clear what Heb.
would be represented by 𝔊 εὐσέβεια εἰς θεὸν, which Bickell renders by יראת יהוה;
but εὐσ. nowhere else represents יר, and the expression looks like original Greek
rather than like a translation. It is found in Cl. Al., *Strom.,* 161. The Heb.
author may have written דעת in first clause because he had חכמה in second.

8–19. Discourse against organized robbery: exhortation to listen to instruction (v.⁸·⁹); the temptation to robbery and murder (v.¹⁰⁻¹⁴); warning against it, fate of the robber (v.¹⁵⁻¹⁹).

— The arrangement is in couplets, with varying number of beats.

Bickell further arranges it in quatrains : v.[8. 9, 10. 11. 12, 13. 14, 15. 17, 18. 19].
The text is not quite clear ; some good emendations are suggested
by the Greek.

8. Hear, my son, thy father's instruction,
    And forsake not the admonition of thy mother;
9. For a chaplet of beauty they will be to thy head,
    And chains about thy neck.

10. My son, if sinners entice thee, consent thou not,* —
11. If they say : "Come with us,
    Let us lay wait for the ‹ perfect,›
    Let us lurk for the innocent [],
12. Let us, like Sheol, swallow them alive,
    Sound as they who go down to the Pit;

13. All precious wealth we shall find,
    We shall fill our houses with spoil;
14. Cast thou thy lot among us,
    One purse we all will have," —

15. [] Walk not in company with them,
    Keep thy feet from their paths; †
17. For in vain the net is spread
    In the sight of any bird, —

18. And they for their own blood lay wait,
    They lurk for their own lives.
19. Such is the ‹ fate › of all who by violence seek gain :
    It destroys the lives of its possessors.

8, 9. Exhortation.   V.[8] is synonymous, ternary ; v.[9] synonymous, ternary-binary.   On *instruction* see note on v.[2]. *Admonition* (Heb. *tora*, sometimes = *law*) is here synonym of *instruction*.
Forsake, more exactly *reject, repel*. *Chains* = *necklace*.   The
address *my son* = *my pupil*, is characteristic of chs. 1–9, and
also, though less markedly, of 22^{17}–24^{22} ; it occurs once (27^{11})
in the section chs. 25–29, and once (19^{27}) in the central division

---

* Perhaps better :
  10. My son, if sinners entice thee,
  11. If they say : Let us lay wait for the ‹ perfect,›
  12. Let us, like Sheol, swallow them alive,
      Sound as they who go down to the Pit;

† 16. For their feet run to evil,
      And haste to shed blood.

of the Book, 10¹–22¹⁶. It indicates an organized system of instruction, probably in schools ; see note on v.⁶ above. The instruction here mentioned, however, is that not of sages but of parents. It is assumed that the teaching of father and mother will be wise, and this moral training of home would naturally form the basis of the fuller instruction of the schools. The reference is to the moral law in general, not specifically to the Tora (Law of Moses), though this would naturally be the foundation of Jewish home teaching. The Talmud (Ber. 35 *a*, Pes. 50 *b*, Sanh. 102 *a*) explains *father* here as = " God," and *mother* as = " Israel " (Ez. 19²) ; according to Rashi the *instruction of the father* is what God gave to Moses in writing and orally, while the *law of the mother* means the words of the Scribes or Rabbis whereby they made a hedge to the Law.* Ornaments of head and neck were anciently worn by men as well as by women.†

10–19. Alliance with bands of robbers and murderers can be attended only with disaster. The organized robbery here referred to suggests city life of the later time, the periods when, under Persian and Greek rule, Jerusalem and Alexandria sheltered a miscellaneous population, and a distinct criminal class became more prominent. The references in the preëxilian prophets are to a less organized sort of crime ; they speak rather of legalized oppression of the poor by the rich ; see Am. 8⁵·⁶ Hos. 4² 6⁸·⁹ 7¹ Isa. 1²³ 5²³ 10¹ Mic. 2² 3³ 6¹² 7²·³ Zeph. 3³ Jer. 5²³ 7⁶·¹¹ Ez. 18¹⁰⁻¹³ 22³⁻⁹ ; the passages in Hos. are the only ones that seem to relate to bands of robbers, and they represent a state of anarchy under the last kings of Samaria. The description here might be understood (so Frank.) as referring not to literal robbery and murder, but to spoliation under legal forms ; but the language of the paragraph (v.¹¹·¹⁸) and the manner of I. (portrayal of open vice chs. 5. 6. 7) favor the former view. Frank. compares BS. 31²⁵ᶠ.

10. The rhythm is irregular : the first clause is ternary, the second has only one beat ; the latter might be attached to v.¹¹, or

---

* On the education of Jewish children see J. Wiesen, *Gesch. u. Meth. d. Schulwesen im talmud. Alterthume ;* for the Greek customs, Becker, *Charicles,* Eng. tr. pp. 217 ff.; for the Roman, *Gallus,* pp. 182 ff.

† See Ju. 8²⁶; Maspéro, *Anc. Egypt and Assyria ;* Becker, *Char.,* 198, n. 6, *Gal.* 429 ff.

omitted as gloss, and [10. 11a] will then form the couplet. — *Sinners* is the general term for wrongdoers, persons of bad moral character, etymologically "those who miss the mark"; they are men who fail in the performance of duty, and thus miss the aim of life. The noun occurs most frequently in Ps. and Pr. (13^{21} 23^{17}), the verb is common in all parts of OT. Instead of the conditional construction the Grk. has the hortative: *let not impious men lead thee astray*, but the conditional protasis is a natural if not necessary preliminary to the hortative apodosis of v.[15]. — **11.** A triplet in the Heb., ternary-binary-binary; the verse division is doubtful (see note on v.[10]). The Heb. text instead of *perfect* has *blood*, and at the end of the verse adds *without cause;* the first emendation (requiring the change of one Heb. letter) is called for by the parallelism, and the addition *without cause* is superfluous, since the victims are described as innocent. If the reading *blood* be retained, it must be understood elliptically, as = *to shed blood;* it cannot be taken (Fleisch. in De.) to mean *a youth, a young blood.* The adv. *without cause* must qualify the verb *lurk;* the translation *innocent in vain* (that is, their innocence does not save them), while grammatically possible, does not accord with the connection. — Bloodshed is assumed to be a natural accompaniment of robbery, and it is accomplished by lying in wait in the dark places of the city. Ancient cities were badly lighted at night, and not usually well policed. Cf. ψ 10^8. — **12.** Synonymous, ternary. The word rendered *sound* is generally used of moral completeness = *perfect* (Gen. 6^9 Pr. 2^{21}), and is here so taken by some (as Kamph.); but the parallelism favors the physical sense *in full bodily health and strength*, equivalent to the parallel *alive* (as in Ez. 15^5, cf. the ritual use, Ex. 12^5 *al.*). The sense of the passage is: we will swallow them (Grk. him) alive and sound so that they shall be as completely destroyed from the earth as those that go down by course of nature into the pit of Sheol (that is, those who die). *Sheol* (and so its equivalent *the Pit*) is the Underworld, the abode of the dead, good and bad, a cheerless place whose denizens have no occupation (Eccl. 9^{10}) and no relations with Yahweh * (Isa. 38^{18}); descent to it is a misfortune, since it

---

* It is probable that in the oldest form of the Heb. religion (as in the Babylonian) Sheol was under the control of a separate deity, independent of Yahweh:

deprives man of activity and happiness, but not a punishment except when it is premature (ψ 55²³⁽²⁴⁾). — The second clause reads in the Grk.: *and let us take away the remembrance of him from the earth* (cf. ψ 34¹⁶⁽¹⁷⁾ 109¹⁵), which represents a different Heb. text from ours, the general sense being unchanged; in the Heb. the parallelism to the first clause is presented in the adj. *sound*, in the Grk. in the verb *take away*. The course of thought favors the Heb.; the Grk. is probably an imitation of the psalm-passage. — **13.** Synonymous, ternary. The object of the assault is treasure; the house is to be broken into (Mt. 6¹⁹). The robbers have their own houses, are residents of the city. The Vrss. give slightly different readings; 𝔊: *let us seize his costly possessions;* 𝔖: *all his wealth and glory;* 𝔗: *all wealth and glory* (or *property*). 𝔥 gives a good sense = "all sorts of wealth." — **14.** Synonymous, ternary. The word *lot* is primarily the thing (a die or something of the sort) used to procure the answer of the deity (as by Urim and Thummim) to a question (Lev. 16⁸), then the thing assigned to the questioner by the divine decision (Jud. 1³), then in general one's part in life (Jer. 13²⁵ ψ 16⁵ Dan. 12¹³); *cast thy lot among us = share our fortunes, identify thyself with us.* The disposition of the booty indicates a regular organization in the robber-band. There is to be *one purse*, a common fund of spoil to be equitably distributed among the members of the gang. This is held out as an inducement to the neophyte, who would thus get more than he could hope to gain by his own separate efforts. Murder is lightly passed over by the robbers as a natural and easy feature of their occupation; the young man is supposed to be accessible to the temptation of easily acquired wealth. The picture of manners here given is historically valuable. For another interpretation see note above (on v.¹⁰⁻¹⁹). — **15–19.** The reason for avoiding such companions: their path, though it may be temporarily successful, leads finally to destruction. — **15.** Synonymous, ternary. The received Hebrew text begins the verse with *my son*, as in v.¹⁰, and a justification for this expression may be found

---

but in OT. there is no trace of any divine government in the Underworld (which is an isolated and anomalous place) till late postexilic times when the one God became universal (Job 14¹⁸ 26⁶) and the idea of resurrection arose (Dan. 12², cf. the doubtful Isa. 26¹⁹).

in the length of the preliminary description, v.[10-14], which might make the resumptive *my son* natural (Baumg.) ; but, on the other hand, as it is not found in 𝔊, is unnecessary at the beginning of the apodosis, and is rhythmically undesirable, it is better to omit it.—16. Synonymous, ternary. On both internal and external grounds this verse is probably to be regarded as a scribal insertion. It breaks the connection between v.[15] and v.[17], the latter of which gives the ground (namely, the peril of the robbers' course) for the exhortation of the former ; and the section v.[15-19] is devoted to a description not of the character of the robbers (which is given in v.[10-14]) but of their fate. Verse [16], further, is identical with Isa. 59[7a], and is not found in the best Grk. MSS. It appears to be the gloss of a scribe who thought a reference to the bloodthirstiness of the robber-band here appropriate, or wrote, as a remark, on the margin this parallel expression, which was then inserted in the text by a subsequent scribe.—In the second clause we may take *feet* as subject of *make haste*, or we may insert the subject *they* (the robbers).—17. Single sentence, ternary. This statement is introductory to that of v.[18], and its meaning is fixed by the relation between the two : v.[18] declares that the robber murderer's course is destructive to him, and v.[17] must therefore set forth the destruction and the blindness not of the victim but of the murderer himself ; the comparison refers not to the futility of laying snares in the sight of birds (who thus see the trap and avoid it), but to the blindness and folly of birds who, though the snare is laid in their sight, nevertheless fall into it. In like manner the criminal, blinded by desire for gain, fails to see the snare which God (working through society and law) spreads for him, and falls irredeemably into it. The connection is not : go not with them, the net which they spread for thee is clearly visible, thou wilt surely not be blinder than a bird (Ziegl., De.), but : go not with them, for, like silly birds, they fall into the net, and thou wilt be entrapped with them (Ew., Nowack, Strack., *al.*, and cf. Schultens). Frank. renders : *for without success is the net spread*, etc., that is, the efforts of the snarers [the sinners] are without result for themselves — they catch no birds ; a possible sense and good in itself, but the couplet appears to state a fact always true of bird-snaring. Moreover, the sage probably intends

not to deny that sinners get booty, but to affirm that, though they
get it, it does not profit them in the end. — A different text is
offered by ⑮, which reads : *for not in vain are nets spread for
birds* (inserting *not*, and neglecting *in the sight of*), that is, not in
vain are there pitfalls for criminals in the shape of human laws and
dispensations of God — they (v.[18]) are laying up punishment for
themselves. This gives a natural connection of thought, but looks
like an interpretation of a text not understood. — The Heb. expression *possessor of wings,* = *bird*, is found only here and Eccl.
10[20]. — **18.** Synonymous, ternary-binary. Their criminal procedure, begun for their profit, turns out to be a plot against themselves ; they overreach themselves and become the executors of
their own doom. It is not said how this result is brought about,
but the allusion doubtless is to human law and divine judgments.
This is the old-Israelitish view that wrongdoing will be punished
in this life — perhaps also the belief that criminals cannot in the
long run escape the vigilance of the law. — ⑮ *for they who have
to do with blood lay up evils for themselves, and the overthrow of
lawless men is grievous*, in which the first clause is incorrect rendering of the whole Heb. verse, and the second clause is a parallel,
probably a scribal addition ; the contrast given in *own blood* is
ignored, in accordance with the Grk. reading of v.[17]. — **19.** Single
sentence, ternary. Lit. : *such are the ways*, the manner and outcome of life (or, the sense *latter end, fate*, may be got by a slight
change in the Heb. word). Grk., second cl. : *for by impiety they
destroy their lives*, an appropriate idea, but here probably not original. See 15[27] 28[16] Job 8[13] Hos. 4[11]. The term *gain* has here the
connotation of *violence, injustice*, as in Ez. 22[13] ; the simple sense
profit is found in Gen. 37[26] Mal. 3[14] Job 22[3]. — The argument of the
section v.[10-19] is an appeal not directly to the sense of right, but to
rational self-regard : robbery and murder bring destruction on the
perpetrator, and must therefore be avoided. The connection,
however, indicates that this law of prudence is regarded as the
law of God.

9. לויה, only here and 4[9], lit. *twisted*, any adornment for the head. ענק
apparently a denom. from ענק *neck*, a word which occurs in Jew. Aram. and
Arab., but not in Heb. Graetz, with little probability, emends to כלילת *perfect*.
𝕊 omits. — 𝔐 מוסר ; ⑮[B] παιδείαν, ⑮[NAC] νόμους (and so 𝕊) ; the latter is prob.

scribal variation (cf. 6²⁰), hardly (Lag.) rendering of נמוסי for מוסר; Heid. holds that it comes from a Pharisaic hand. — 狂 רֶד; 𝔊ᴮ δέξῃ, 𝔊ᴬ ἕξῃ, perh. free rendering (Heid.: allusion to phylacteries), perh. representing a variant reading, though the original in that case is not apparent. — **10, 11.** 𝔊 divides v.¹⁰·¹¹ as follows: *My son, let not impious men seduce thee, Nor consent thou if they urge thee, saying, Come with us, go shares in blood, And let us hide the just man unjustly in the earth.* Bickell, omitting ¹⁰ᵃ for rhythmical reasons, writes: *Consent not if they say, come with us, Let us lay wait for blood, let us lurk for the innocent.* The Heb. rhythm is not satisfactory, but it is hardly improved by these variations. Bickell's omission of ¹⁰ᵃ is unwarranted, and the resulting form is not good, either rhythmically or rhetorically. 𝔊 is rhythmically better, but its rendering of 狂 is partly incorrect, partly free. 狂 may be retained if we suppose ¹⁰ᵇ to be purposely short, and take ¹¹ as couplet: *If they say, come with us, Let us lay wait for the perfect, let us lurk for the innocent,* or, if we throw out ¹⁰ᵇ·¹¹ᶜ, and part of ¹¹ᵃ, and take the rest as couplet. It is hardly possible to recover the original form. — **10.** 狂 אם; 𝔊 μή = אַל. — 狂 הֹבֵא (from אבה), in which the א and ב have changed places (full form תאבה), or the א is the writing of an Aram. scribe for ה, the initial א of the stem being omitted because it was unpronounced. The regular form האבה is found in a number of MSS. (see De' Rossi), and either it should here be written, or we should, with Bi., write הֹאב; in several MSS. the verb is understood as בוא (תבא, תבוא), which is improbable. — **11.** After יאמרו 𝔊𝔖 have לָךְ, perh. repetition from following לְכָה. 𝔊 παρακαλέσωσι may = יא׳. — 狂 נארבה; 𝔊 κοινώνησον, from ערב or חבר (Lag.). — 狂 לְדָם; Dyserinck, *Theol. Tijd.* 17, 578, reads לְתָם, which suits the next clause; Oort, *ib.,* 19, 381, holds that the reading of v.¹⁸ (which ver. is clearly parallel to v.¹¹) sustains דם here. — 狂 נצפנה seems to be intrans. (as apparently in ψ 10⁸ 56⁷); elsewhere the Qal is trans., and so it is here taken by Frank. who renders: *we will set (a trap).* — 狂 לְנָקִי; 𝔊 ἄνδρα δίκαιον, either not having the ל, or (Lag.) taking it, according to the Aram. const., as sign of Acc. — 狂 חנם, found in the Vrss. (𝔖 בֵּעֵתָא *maliciously*), but superfluous, and probably a gloss (Bi.). The whole clause may be omitted without detriment to the sense, and with advantage to the rhythm. — **12.** 狂 נבלעם; Graetz Pi., as in 19²⁸ 21²⁰. — As 2d clause 𝔊 has καὶ ἄρωμεν αὐτοῦ τὴν μνήμην ἐκ γῆς, representing the Heb. of ψ 34¹⁷ 109¹⁵, perh. editorial variation; Lag. suggests that, the Heb. text of 𝔊 being effaced, it took the appropriate passage from the Ps.; for 狂 ותמימים may have stood ונחמם; Heid. supposes that 𝔊 may have had ותחמם ידיעותם מארמה, improb. late Heb. — **13.** 狂 הון; 𝔊 τὴν κτῆσιν αὐτοῦ; Bi. הונָם, not so good a reading as that of 狂. — **14.** 狂 תַּפִּיל; 𝔊𝔏𝔖𝔗 have Impv., which is better, though not absolutely necessary, since the assertory form of statement is possible; Bi. omits ת׳ as marring the parallelism, but *thy lot is with us* is hard. — 𝔊ᵇ has a doublet, a free and a literal rendering; the former is probably the original (Jäg., Lag., Baumgartner), the latter a correcting gloss. — **15.** 狂 בני; 𝔊ᵃˑ ᶜˑ ᵃ vlé, H-P 23 (= V), 252, 254, 295, 297, vlé μου, lacking in 𝔊ᴺᴬᴮᶜ, and should probably be

omitted. — 獨 נתיבה sing.; plu. in 𝔊𝕷𝕾𝕿 and several Heb. MSS., the diff. not
appearing in *script. defect.* — 獨 בְּרֹרָך, lacking in 𝕷 De'R 249. — **16.** Wanting
in the uncials of 𝔊 (exc. אׄc. ᵃ A) and in Copt. (Sahidic and Memphitic);
Cod. 23 (of H-P) adds to it from Rom. 3¹⁶·¹⁷, and the cursives which contain
it place it some before and some after v.¹⁷. It appears not to belong to the
original text. — After רם 𝕾 has זכיא (= נקי, as in Isa. 59⁷). — **17.** 𝔊 prefixes
οὐ; 𝕾 has ו instead of כי, and for 獨 מורה plu. act. Part. פרשׁין. — 獨 מֹזְרֶה in
sense of *spread* is difficult, the word elsewhere meaning *scatter, winnow;*
Schult. here *ventilatum;* Rashi, *in vain is* (*grain*) *scattered* (*on*) *the net.*
We should perhaps read מפרשׂה רשׁת (𝔊 δίκτυα) or חנם פרשׂו ר', which is
phonetically not too hard. In Hos. 5¹ 𝔊 renders 'פ by ἐκτείνειν, which is its
expression here. — 獨 בעל; plu. in 𝔊𝕷𝕬r. and 4 Heb. MSS. — **18.** 獨 יארבו;
𝔊 μετέχοντες; see v.¹¹. 獨 דְּמָם; 𝔊ᴮ ᵃˡ· φόνου (H-P 23 αἱμάτων) = דמים, not
so well. 𝔊, rendering יצפנו by θησαυρίζουσιν, adds κακά as necessary complement. 𝕾 appears to make v.¹⁸ a continuation of v.¹⁶ (Pink.) — **19.** 獨 ארחות;
𝔊 אחרית, probably to be adopted; see 5⁴ Nu. 23¹⁰ ψ 37³⁷·³⁸ 73¹⁷; אר' is not
elsewhere used as = *fate,* the sense here required by the connection. —
獨 בעליו; 𝔊 τῇ ἀσεβείᾳ = בעולה (Jäg.).

20–33. The appeal of Wisdom. — Wisdom, standing in a public
place, exhorts the ignorant and the scornful to listen to her words,
threatening them with destruction if they refuse. The section is
independent, having no immediate connection with the preceding
or the succeeding context. It resembles the first half of ch. 8,
but is minatory while that is persuasive in tone. As the text
stands, it is arranged in couplets (except v.²²·²³·²⁷, which are triplets), which may be naturally combined into quatrains. After the
introduction (v.²⁰·²¹) comes the address, which consists of a denunciation (v.²²·²³), the charge of disregard of her teaching (v.²⁴·²⁵), a
description of the fate of the despisers (v.²⁶⁻³¹), and a contrast
between the doom of fools and the happiness of the obedient
(v.³²·³³). Wisdom is personified, as in chs. 8. 9.

> 20. Wisdom cries aloud in the streets,
> In the broad places utters her voice,
> 21. Calls out at the head of the ‹ high places,›
> In the gates of the gateways [] * she says:
>
> 22. How long, ye dullards, will ye love ignorance [] †,
> And fools hate knowledge?

---

* The Heb. adds: *in the city.*

† The Heb. adds: *and scoffers delight in scoffing.*

23. [ ] * I will utter my mind to you,
    Will tell you my decision:

24. Because I have called, and ye refused,
    I have stretched out my hand, and none regarded,

25. Ye have ignored all my counsel,
    My admonition ye have rejected, —

26. I, in my turn, will laugh in [the day of] your calamity
    I will mock when your disaster comes,

27. When your disaster comes like a storm,
    And your calamity like a whirlwind. [ ] †

28. Then will they call on me, but I will not answer,
    They will seek me, but will not find me,

29. For that they hated knowledge,
    And chose not the fear of Yahweh.

30. They would none of my counsel,
    All my admonition they despised;

31. Therefore they shall eat of the fruit of their own conduct.
    And be sated with their own counsels.

32. For the indifference of the insensate will slay them,
    The careless ease of fools will destroy them.

33. But whoso hearkens to me will dwell secure,
    Will be free from fear of harm.

The interpretation of the paragraph depends in part on the view taken of the relation between v.²².²³ and the following verses. If the former are held to contain an exhortation to repentance (v.²³ᵃ), they can hardly be closely connected with the latter, since these presume that the call of Wisdom has been rejected, and the discourse should state, after v.²³, the repellant answer of the persons addressed; as the text stands, v.²⁴⁻³¹ constitute a separate discourse which states the result of disobedience. Unity of thought may be gained by omitting v.²³ᵃ, and taking the whole piece as minatory, the connection being: you have turned a deaf ear to me long enough (v.²²), I have lost patience and will tell you my decision (v.²³): because you have refused, etc. (v.²⁴⁻³¹).

20, 21. Introduction: the publicity of Wisdom's appeal. — Synonymous, ternary. After *gateways* the Heb. has *in the city her*

---

* V.²³ᵃ in the Heb.: *turn ye to my admonition.*
† Heb. v.²⁷ᶜ: *when distress and anguish befall you.*

words she says; the expressions *in the city* and *her words*, which mar the rhythm in the original, appear to be glosses, the former intended as an explanation of *gateways* (stating definitely that the reference is to city gates), the latter noting that the following verses give the words then uttered by Wisdom. The Grk. has a somewhat different reading : *Wisdom sings in the streets* (lit. *exits*), *in the broad places boldly speaks, proclaims on the summits of the walls, sits at the gates of princes, at the gates of the city boldly says ;* this seems to be partly misreading, partly expansion, of our Heb. text. — *Broad places* are the wide open spaces in front of city gates ; instead of *high places* the Heb. has a word which is commonly rendered noisy places, understood to mean crowded *thoroughfares* (including bazaars and market-places) ; but this sense is doubtful, and a better term is given in 8^2 (*high places*), or by Sept. (*walls*) ; *walls* may be included in the *high places;* these, together with *streets* and *gateways*, were gathering-places for the people. The *gateway* was a long structure entered at the extremities through *gates.* The verb *cries aloud* expresses an excited emotional utterance, usually of joy (Lev. 9^{24} Isa. 12^6 Job 38^7), sometimes of sorrow (Lam. 21^{19}), or general excitement ($\psi\ 78^{65}$), here of intensity of feeling. — Wisdom does not content herself with being wise at home, but seeks men out in their everyday life — she is a preacher. The custom of speaking in places of concourse was an old one, familiar to the prophets ; see Jer. 7^2, and cf. Mic. 1^8 Isa. 20^2 Jer. 5^1 ; so also Socrates (Xen., *Mem.* I. 1, 10). The later Jewish custom resembles both that of the prophets and that of the Greek philosopher, the former in its hortatory tone, the latter in its reflective, ethical subject-matter. The choice of the term *wisdom* to denote the religious teacher points to a phase of life which came after the great prophetic period (in the prophets wisdom is not religious), and probably indicates the influence of the Greek atmosphere in which the Jews lived from the close of the fourth century B.C. on * (see Introduction, § 6).

---

* Cf. the similar use of *wisdom* in Ben-Sira, Eccl., Wisd. of Sol. The title *Koheleth*, given in Eccl. to Wisdom (speaking in the person of Solomon), if, as is possible, it means a *caller* (or *member*) *of a public assembly*, supposes acquaintance with Grk. forms of life ; see the commentaries of Tyler, Plumptre, Reuss, Siegfried, Wildeboer, and Cheyne's *Job and Solomon.*

The exhortation in Prov. is not: put away all other gods and serve Yahweh alone, or: bring offerings to the temple according to the Law, but: listen to reason and conscience, which are the voice of God in the soul.

22–33. The discourse of wisdom in the received Heb. text falls naturally into two parts, an invitation, v.$^{22.\ 23}$, and a denunciation, v.$^{24-33}$. The connection between the divisions is not clear (see note above on v.$^{20-33}$). The denunciation is introduced abruptly, as if the invitation had been refused, though nothing is said of a refusal. On this point the Versions offer nothing different from the Heb., and there is not good ground for extensive alterations of the text (see below). A closer connection between the parts might be secured by giving v.$^{24.\ 25}$ the conditional form, the apodosis following in v.^{26}, but against this is the form of the verbs in v.$^{24.\ 25}$. Failing this we shall have to consider the divisions as separate discourses, or suppose that an explanatory transitional statement has fallen out after v.^{23}, or, what seems most satisfactory, omit v.^{23a}; v.$^{22.\ 23}$ will then contain not an invitation, but a denunciation. Cf. the connectedness and smoothness of the similar discourse 8^{1-11}.

22, 23. The Heb. has two triplets: v.^{22} is quaternary-quaternary-ternary, v.^{23} binary-ternary-ternary; on the text see below. The three classes of persons are practically the same, though the words have different shades of meaning. *Dullards* (or *simpletons*, RV. *simple*) are the *inexperienced* (v.^{4}), here those who positively love ignorance, and deliberately refuse to listen to instruction in right living. — The terms *scoffing* (or *scorn*) and *scoffer* (or *scorner*) belong almost exclusively to the later religious vocabulary of Pss., Pr.; they occur elsewhere only Hos. 7^5 Isa. $28^{14.\ 20}$ 29^{20} Job 16^{20}, in which passages they express contempt in general; in Pr. *scoffer = bad man*, one who turns his back on what is good (so ψ 1^1), the special element of contempt not being significant; the simple sense occurs in 20^1. In ψ 119^{51} the reference is to apostate Jews or foreign enemies; in Pr. there is no reference to the nation Israel. — *Fool* (Heb. *kesīl*) is also a term of the reflective moral literature, occurring, in the intellectual or ethical sense, only in Pss., Pr., Eccl. (the verb is found once, Jer. 10⁸) ; it seems to mean a stolid, dull person, in Pr. one who is insensible to moral truth and acts without regard to it. By these three terms the sages express the contrast to that wisdom which consists in acceptance of and obedience to the divine law of conduct written in man's heart. — As only two of these classes (*dullards* and *fools*) are mentioned in v.³² (which is a résumé of the preceding statement), there is ground for supposing v.²²ᵇ to be a scribal addition ; Wisdom is here dealing with the unwise. — In v.²³ᵃ of the Heb. these persons are urged to listen to instruction, to *turn* (that is, give heed) *to* (not *at*) the admonition of Wisdom ; she promises to impart her knowledge to them. *Admonition* (or, *reproof*) (used chiefly in Pss., Pr.) is exhortation tinged with imputation of blameworthiness. For the reason given above this line should probably be omitted ; the remaining couplet (v.²³) will then be Wisdom's declaration that she now utters her final word. The word rendered *utter* (RV. *pour out*) is a poetical synonym of *speak ;* so 15².²⁸ ψ 19²⁽³⁾ 78² 94⁴ 191¹⁷¹ 145⁷ ; and *mind* (*spirit*) = *thought*, here = *purpose* or *determination*. The Heb. word commonly rendered *spirit* means first *wind* and so *breath*, and then the inward life or being ; in Pr. it generally has this last sense, as 11¹³ 16².³² 25²⁸ 29¹¹ (so Isa. 40¹³ *the mind, judgment of Yahweh*). Here the meaning is given by the parallelism : *I will tell* (or *make known*) *my words* = *I will utter my thought.** The *words* (here = *decision*) and the *mind* are stated in the following address (v.²⁴⁻²⁷). *My spirit* may also = *myself.* — The Heb. introduces the second line of v.²³ with *behold.* — 𝔊 construes the two verses differently : *So long as the guileless hold fast to righteousness they shall not be ashamed, but the foolish, being lovers of insolence, have become impious, have hated knowledge, and have become liable to reproof; behold I will pour forth to you the utterance of my breath, and teach you my word.* The declarative form (instead of the interrogation of the Heb.) is improbable, and the contrast in v.²² is against the connection. — Bickell reads : *How long will ye love ignorance, and scorners delight them in scorning, and fools hate knowledge and incur my reproof ?* He thus gains a rhythmically symmetrical

---

* So Salomon ben Melek, cited by Heid.

quatrain, and (by obliterating the invitation of v.[23]) gets rid of the break between v.[22. 23] and the rest of the discourse.   But the substitution of *incur* for *turn* is arbitrary, v.[23b. c] (which he omits) is a natural introduction to the denunciatory discourse, and the omission of the subject (*dullards*) in v.[22a] is, from the parallelism, improbable.   𝔖 makes v.[23a] conditional : *if ye turn . . . I will*, etc. ; but this construction only introduces confusion, since v.[24ff.] assume that they have not turned.

24–33. The denunciation, consisting of a direct address (v.[24–27]), a description, in 3 pers., of the fate of the recusant (v.[28–31]), and a statement of the contrasted positions of the ignorant and the wise (v.[32. 33]).

24–27. Wisdom will mock at the calamity of those who reject her invitation. — The lines may be read as ternary, but the law or rule governing the beats is not clear. — V.[24. 25. 26] are couplets, v.[27] is a triplet in the Heb. ; the Grk. converts v.[27] into a quatrain (or two couplets) by adding at the end *when destruction comes upon you.* Bickell, by omissions, substitutions, and transpositions, makes out of v.[26. 27] a quatrain : *I also will laugh in (the day of) your calamity, when distress and anguish come upon you, I will mock when your fear comes as a storm and your desolation comes as a whirlwind.* V.[27] in the Heb. is expansion of the predicates of v.[26], a recognized poetical form.   It is not necessary to insist on absolutely symmetrical couplets at all hazards ; but, as the rest of the paragraph is arranged in couplets and quatrains, and as the two predicate-terms of v.[26], *calamity* and *disaster*, are given in v.[27a. b], and v.[27c] appears to be an afterthought (a scribal insertion), it is better to omit this last. — The verbs in v.[24. 25] refer to Wisdom's invitations in the past, that is, all the good influences of life ; warning has not been lacking, and on the despised warning follows this minatory discourse. The first verb in v.[25] is primarily *go freely about* and *let go free*, then *neglect, avoid, ignore;* the sense of "allowing full play or license" is found in Ex. 5^4 32^{35} Pr. 29^{18}, that of "neglecting, avoiding," in 4^{15} 8^{33} 13^{18} 15^{32}. — *Laugh at* (instead of *laugh in*, etc.), v.[26], is possible (Gen. 39^{14}), but does not agree so well with the designation of time in the following clause.   *Mock* is stronger than *laugh*, expressing bitterness or exulting derision.   The *I in my* *turn* (RV. *I also*) brings out the contrast of persons : " You have had your turn, and I shall have mine." *Disaster* is lit. *fear* (parallel to *calamity*) = ground or cause of fear. Instead of *storm* we may render by *desolation* (RV. marg.), but the former sense is favored by the parallelism. *Distress* and *anguish* are synonyms (cf. Isa. 8^{22} 30^{6}), both signifying distressful limitation, straitness, opposed to largeness, freedom of movement (ψ $31^{8(9)}$ 118^{5}). *Befall* is lit. *come upon*. V.^{27c} is probably not original ; see note above. — The address is minatory. The offence (v.$^{24. 25}$) is disregard of the exhortation of Wisdom — she has implored, they have turned a deaf ear. Their posture of mind is that of deliberate disregard — they have had sufficient warning. Whether their neglect came from lack of previous training, or from superficiality and frivolity of nature, or from conscious choice of evil in preference to good, is not said. The picture is presented objectively : these persons, for whatever reason, are outside the domain of Wisdom. This objective view is characteristic of the old-Israelitish thought, which does not seek nice psychological distinctions ; the prophets judge individuals and nations by their relation to the law of Yahweh or to the nation Israel, without examination of mental experiences ; compare also the distinction, in the Fourth Gospel, between the domains of light and darkness. Solidity of ethical judgment is thereby gained, though at the cost of sympathetic discrimination. — The result (v.$^{26. 27}$) is that when the punishment comes the disobedient will be without the support of Wisdom. The calamity (as everywhere in Pr.) occurs in this life — it is not said to be inflicted by Wisdom, but comes in the natural course of things ; it is inevitable, a necessary result of the divine government of the world, which includes both natural law and special divine intervention. On the one hand, the sage intimates, those who neglect Wisdom will naturally find themselves defenceless in the evil day which Wisdom alone can avert ; on the other hand, God as governor will punish the evildoer. Wisdom is here first ordinary human sagacity, which saves man from misfortune, and then that higher sagacity which is the comprehension and assimilation of the good as divine, of that highest truth and right which God has embodied in his law. There is an approach here to the conception of communion with truth, or with the divine source of truth, as the strongest support of the ethical life. The personified Wisdom, who speaks as the final arbiter of men's destinies, is the insight that rules the world, and is identical with God's moral law. —The discordant note in the announcement of retribution is Wisdom's mockery of the wretched sufferer. This is not in accord with her character as pure, divine intelligence, friendly to man (as she appears, for example, in 8^{31})*; the unhappy fate of the evildoer, it would seem, should call forth sorrow and not exultation. Such, however, is the tone of the old Hebrew thought; the prophets exult in like manner over the downfall of the enemies of Israel. The Hebrew, whether prophet, psalmist, or sage, was a thoroughgoing partisan, identifying himself with his circle, and identifying his interests with the eternal order. Further, his governmental conception of the world was purely external: the bad, from whatever point of view they were adjudged bad, were regarded as enemies of the realm, and their destruction was hailed with joy. Such seems to be the point of view of the writer of this passage. He does not feel that, though sin is to be denounced and its consequences set forth, the sinner has a claim on the sympathy of his fellowmen; he does not take into account temptations and struggles of soul. He contents himself with dividing men into two classes — those who heed and those who reject wisdom.

28-33. Resumptive description of the fate of the unwise (who are spoken of in third person), consisting of a detailed explanation of their punishment (v.$^{28-31}$), and a statement of the general rule of compensation in life (v.$^{32. 33}$).

28-31. Resumptive description of punishment. — Well formed couplets, synonymous, ternary, except that v.^{31b} is binary, the penult being a very long word. The correspondence with the preceding paragraph is close, with inversion of the order of thought: v.^{28} answers to v.$^{26. 27}$, and v.$^{29. 30}$ to v.$^{24. 25}$; the conclusion is repeated in v.^{31}. The rendering *seek early* (AV.) or *seek diligently* (RV.) rests on the derivation of the verb from a noun meaning *morning*, as if it signified to rise betimes in order to do one's work dili-

---

* According to the Masoretic Hebrew text; see note on that verse below.

gently; * but this derivation is improbable in the face of 7^{15} 11^{27}, Job 7^{21} — the verb means simply *seek*, here parallel to *call*. The terms *hated, chose not, would none, despised* (v.$^{29.\,30}$) are synonyms, expressing indifference or hostility to the instructions of Wisdom. In v.$^{30.\,31}$ the *counsel* (or *counsels*) and *admonition* (or *admonitions*) of Wisdom are contrasted with the man's own *way* (= manner or scheme of life, *conduct*) and *counsels* (or *devices*). In v.^{29} Bickell would read *the knowledge of God* as the appropriate parallel to *the fear of Yahweh* (so in 2^5), which is also, perhaps, rhythmically an improvement of the text; yet, as the former expression occurs only once in Pr. (and elsewhere in OT. only twice, Hos. 4^1 6^6, *knowledge of the Most High* once, Nu. 24^{16}), it is perhaps better to retain the general term *knowledge*, which in v.^{7} is identified with *the fear of Yahweh*. — The thought is the same with that of the preceding paragraph, only with an added touch of irremediableness in v.^{28}. The offenders who have deliberately rejected the counsels and appeals of Wisdom will find, when the day of punitive distress comes, that they need her aid, but they will ask it in vain; she will be deaf to their cries, as they were deaf to her appeals. This is only a more vivid statement of the principle affirmed in v.^{31}, that every one must eat of the fruit of his own doings — a universally recognized law of life. If it be asked, what room is here left for repentance? the answer of the sage is that the offenders have had ample opportunity to amend their ways, and have refused to change (v.^{30}). As to the term of repentance and the limit of Wisdom's patience, it is assumed that at a given moment God intervenes to punish, when sin has grown too great to bear, when the iniquity is full (Gen. 15^{16} $18^{20.\,21}$), but this moment is known to God alone. The point of view is external : at a certain moment retribution inevitably comes (whether in the course of natural or civil law, or by supernatural intervention), and then, in the nature of things, it is too late for the sinner to retrace his steps; there is no reference here to a state of punitive blindness and moral deadness in which the man desires to repent and cannot, or is conscious that he is morally

---

* It need hardly be added that the word *early* in this rendering of AV. has nothing to do with the time of life.

lost; * the cry of the sinner in v.[28] is for deliverance from physical evil.

32, 33. The general rule. — Both couplets are synonymous, ternary. — **32.** *Indifference* (משובת) = *averseness, apostasy, recusance, refusal,* is the "turning away" from instruction and consequently from right living. *Careless ease* (שלות) is primarily *quiet, freedom from care and anxiety* (as in 17[1]), here, in bad sense, repose gained by ignoring or neglecting the serious responsibilities of life (nearly = *negligence*). The two terms are, in their primary senses, mutually complementary : rejection of knowledge produces false security and deceptive peace, and the latter presupposes the former; they are here substantially synonymous : *refusal* is *indifference, negligence. Insensate* (= *dullards*) and *fools* as in v.[22]. — **33.** *Secure* may mean, objectively, *free from danger* (as in 3[23] Jer. 23[6]), or subjectively, *free from sense of danger* (as in 3[29] Ju. 8[11]). The contrast with the *slay* of v.[32] favors the former meaning, but the second line (*fear* = apprehension) makes the latter probable. The *sense of security* is thus put over against the *careless ease* of fools (v.[32]). — Wisdom sums up by stating the general principle that ethical folly is self-destructive (so 5[22. 23]) ; as to the means by which this destruction is effected see note on preceding verse. — In contrast with the false peace of the ignorant is put the true peace which comes from wisdom — a security which is assured by obedience to the laws of man and God. The reference is to freedom from outward misfortune ; the whole tone of the Book makes it improbable that the writer has in mind the inward peace which is independent of external experiences ; elsewhere *harm* (RV. *evil*) is visible "misfortune" or "mischief" (3[29. 30] 6[14. 18] 13[21] 16[4] 17[3] 22[3] *al.*). Inward peace, resting on consciousness of right and trust in God, was no doubt recognized and valued, but it is assumed in Pr. to be coincident with freedom from outward calamity, and is not treated as an independent fact.

20. The form חכמות, found elsewhere only 9[1] 24[7] (and by emend. 14[1]) ψ 49[3(4)], is prob. not abstr. sing. for חכמות (Ols., Ew., De.), but plu. of exten-

---

* This is the doctrine of J. A. Alexander's hymn, beginning: "There is a time, we know not when" (*New York Church Praise-Book*, 1881), or : "There is a line, by us unseen" (*Congregational Hymn-Book*, 1858), but it is not found here or elsewhere in the Bible.

sion and intensity (Bött., Now., Siegf., Strack in *Comm.*, Barth); its predicates are sing. exc. in 24⁷.*— תָּרֹנָּה, 3 sing. fem. Qal energic (or possibly Q. plu. of רנן); it is unnecessary to point הָרֶנָּה (as in Job 39²⁸); Heid.'s emendation בחוצֹת רנה, adopted by Oort, is simple, and secures parallelism in the nouns, but loses it in the verbs. ⅏ ὑμνεῖται (Lag. = הֵרֵנָּה) is perh. Mid., prob. error for ὑμνεῖ; a Pass. is inappropriate and improbable. — **21.** 𝔐 הֹמִיּוֹת; ⅏ τειχέων = חוֹמוֹת; so 𝕿 בירהא *the tower* (or *castle* or *palace*). The Partcp. ה' never occurs alone, but always as predicate (7¹¹ 9¹⁸ 20¹ Isa. 22² Jer. 4¹⁹ Ez. 7¹⁶), and it is doubtful whether it can here be taken as subst.; the reading מֵרֹמִים (8²) is graphically not too hard, or, after ⅏, we may read חֹמַת. — 𝔐 שְׁעָרִים; ⅏ δυναστῶν = שָׂרִים (here inappropriate) to which παρεδρεύει is added, apparently to fill out the clause. Jäg. thinks ἐπὶ ... παρεδρεύει add. from 8⁸. — Bickell omits שְׁעָרִים and אָמָר (both of which, however, are called for by the connection), and for בָּעִיר writes עָרִים. We should rather omit בָּעִיר and אמריה as glosses. The Vrss. (exc. ⅏) follow 𝔐 with unimportant variations, and the glosses must have been early. — **22.** עַד מָתַי (⅏ ὅσον ἂν χρόνον) is always interrog. in OT. — On פְּתָיִם see note on v.⁴ above; the final letter of the stem is omitted because not pronounced = חֲאֵהֲבוּ; Qal = הָאֵרְבוּ, ⅏ ἕχωνται, perh. free rendering, perh. (Lag.) scribal error for ἐρῶνται. — Instead of Perf. חמרו we expect Impf. — ⅏ ἀσεβεῖς γενόμενοι, perh. (Lag.) = להיתם כסילים (read בהיותם) instead of 𝔐 להם וכ'. — **23.** תִּשׁוּבוּ; ⅏ καὶ ὑπεύθυνοι ἐγένοντο possibly = יחובו (Lag., Heid., cf. *Aboth*, 1, 11) or (Bi.) = ויאשמו. But as חוב is prob. a loan-word from the Aram., found only Dan. 1¹⁰ (Ez. 18⁷ the noun is corruption, probably of שוב), its occurrence here is doubtful. If the line (v.²³ᵃ) be retained, the Impf. (which cannot have Impv. force) must be changed to Impv. שׁוּבוּ (the ח perh. repeated from preceding דעת); so also Dyserinck. — נבע *gush*, 18⁴; elsewhere only Hif. = *speak*, exc. in Eccl. 10¹, where the text is doubtful. — 𝔐 רוחי; ⅏ ἐμῆς πνοῆς ῥῆσιν, paraphrastic, perh. (Lag.) to avoid the expression πνοὴν πρόϊεσθαι = *die;* the verb has the sense of *utter*. — The change of pers. in the verbs in v.²²·²³ is a common rhetorical usage in OT. — **24.** 𝔐 יַעַן, omitted by Bi., apparently for the sake of the rhythm, is desirable, if not necessary, as introduction to v.²⁶. — 𝔐 וַתְּמָאֲנוּ; ⅏ καὶ οὐχ ὑπηκούσατε, free rendering of 𝔐, or from some form of ענה or שמע (hardly from הקשיב, as in 2²); 𝕾𝕿 לא האמינו, from לא תאמינו. 𝔊𝕾𝕿 render מַקְשִׁיב by a verb 2 plu., assimilation of the translator. — **25.** וַתּוֹכַחְתִּי, noun as obj. of אבה only here, elsewhere (as v.³⁰) with pref. ל, and so perh. to be written here (Oort). The two nouns in this v. are plu. in 𝔊𝕾, the second in 𝕷, variations coming from *script. defect.* — **26.** ⅏ prefixes τοιγαροῦν as natural connective. — 𝔐 אֵיד; ⅏ ἀπωλείᾳ, as Job 21⁸ 30¹²; Heid., = אֵבֶר.— 𝔐 פַּחַד; ⅏ ὄλεθρος, perh. = עִיר (Gr.), which, however, is nowhere else so rendered (24²² Job 30²⁴ 31²⁹). — **27.** K. שַׁאֲוָה, Q. שֹׁאָה, both from שאה; ⅏ freely ἄφνω, and so 𝕾, Rashi, and apparently 𝕿. — 𝔐 פַּחַד and אֵיד; ⅏ θόρυβος and καταστροφή, rhetorical varia-

---

** On הֵילִילִית, Eccl. 1¹⁷ 2¹² *al.,* cf. Barth, *NB.,* § 259 c, Comms. of Tyler and Palm, and Strack in *Stud. u. Krit.,* 1896, IV.*

tions from the renderings in v.[26]. — 𝔖 attaches v.[27a] to v.[26], and 𝔊 adds a fourth
line (Jäg., Lag.) in v.[27]; these changes show that the old translators found
difficulties in the rhythm. — Bi. takes v.[26. 27] in the following order: [26a. 27b.]
[26b. 27a], tranferring כִּשׁוּאָה to v.[26], throwing out בֹּא פַחְדְכֶם in v.[27] as scribal
repetition, and writing שֹׁרֶכֶם instead of אֵידְכֶם. The rhythm thus gained is
hardly better than that of 𝔐, except in that it gets rid of the triplet. It would
be simpler, if the triplet is judged insupportable, to regard v.[27c] as a gloss, the
addition of a familiar expression (see note on this line above); cf. the similar
expression in the triplet of ψ 116[8], in contrast with the couplets of ψ 18[5. 6]. —
28. 𝔊 wrongly puts v.[28a] as direct address. — The verb שׁחר occurs, outside of
Job, Pss., Pr., only in Hos. 5[15] Isa. 26[9]; 𝔏 here *mane consurgent* (and similarly
elsewhere in Pr., exc. 7[15]). Denominatives of the caus. stem (rarely of the
simple stem) are frequent in Arab. and Heb. (so הִשְׁכֵּם) to express the doing
of a thing at a certain time of the day, but they do not then contain a substan-
tively additional idea like *seek;* the primitive sense of the stem is doubtful. On
the old ending ן of the verb in יְשַׁחֲרֻנְנִי see Böttcher, *Lehrb.,* II. § 930, 1047 f.,
and Toy, in *Trans. Amer. Phil. Assoc.,* Vol. XI. 1880. — After יְשֵׁ 𝔊 adds
κακοί as subject, unnecessary general interpretative gloss, not (Lag.) addition
of a Christian scribe to avoid contradiction of Mt. 7[7. 8]. — **29.** 𝔐 רַעַת; 𝔊[B] σοφίαν, for which we should expect αἴσθησιν, yet σ. is not necessarily Christian
(Lag.) or Alexandrian (Heid.); 𝔊[A] παιδίαν, 𝔏 *disciplinam* (= מוּסַר v.[2]). —
𝔐 יִרְאַת; 𝔊[B] λόγον, perh. interpretation of an Alex. scribe. — **30.** 𝔊 has the
two nouns in plu. (*script. defect.*). — **31.** 𝔐 מֹעֵצָת; 𝔊 freely ἀσεβείας; מ is
used in OT. in bad sense, exc. Pr. 22[20]. — **32.** מְשׁוּבָה, always in bad sense in
OT. — 𝔊 ἀνθ' ὧν γὰρ ἠδίκουν νηπίους, taking מ as trans. = *turn aside, oppress,*
hardly = *retribution* (Jäg. *because of retribution for* [*their treatment of*]
children they shall be slain), or from מְשׁוּפָה (Schleusn.) *assailing,* or (Lag.)
מְבַצַּעַת *injustice.* — 𝔐 שַׁלְוַת; 𝔊 ἐξετασμὸς = שְׁאֵלָת or שֶׁלֶת (so 𝔖[H]) 𝔖𝔗 טוּפֵי
error, free rendering of 𝔐. — 𝔐 מִפַּחַד רָעָה; 𝔊 [33], ἀφόβως ἀπὸ παντὸς κακοῦ,
where π. is insertion for sake of definiteness. Cf. Clem. Alex., 162, 181. — In
𝔐 שַׁלְוַת and שַׁאֲנָן there seems to be a verbal play. — בֶּטַח is adverbial. — רָעָה
פַהַד may mean *disaster of harm,* but פ', = *disaster,* is not elsewhere defined by
a noun of source.

II. **A discourse setting forth the blessings conferred by Wisdom,** the sage (and not Wisdom herself) being the speaker. It
consists of one well-sustained sentence (Ew.), each paragraph
being linked to the preceding by a connective word; the rhythmical arrangement appears to be in quatrains. After the protasis,
stating, as the necessary condition, earnest application to the
teaching of wisdom (v.[1-4]), comes the long apodosis (v.[5-22]), giving
a double result: first, the knowledge of God and its attendant
blessing (v.[5-8], apparently an insertion or a parenthesis); second

($v.^{9-22}$), the comprehension of probity ($v.^{9.\,20}$), and the possession
of wisdom as guide ($v.^{10.\,11}$), which will deliver from evil men
($v.^{12-15}$) and evil women ($v.^{16-19}$), and so lead to the reward of the
upright ($v.^{21}$), in contrast with the fate of the wicked ($v.^{22}$).

1-4. The condition of enjoying the protection of Wisdom.

1. My son, if thou receive my words
   And lay up my commandments with thee,
2. So that thou incline thine ear to wisdom,
   Apply thy mind to discernment,
3. If thou cry to understanding,
   And invoke discernment,
4. If thou seek her as silver,
   Search for her as for hid treasures —

1-4. *Mind*, lit. *heart*, is (as always in OT.) the whole inward
nature, here particularly *intellectual capacity, attention* (so that *thy
heart* substantially = *thyself*). *Discernment* and *understanding*
are synonyms, equivalent to *intellectual perception* and *wisdom*,
here with ethical-religious coloring. It is *unto* (not *for*) discernment and understanding that the pupil is to cry — he calls to her
to come to him and instruct and help him. — The Grk. and Lat.
Vrss. divide the sentence differently from the Hebrew. Grk. :
*If thou receive the utterance of my commandment and hide it with
thee, thine ear shall hearken to wisdom, and thou shalt apply*, etc. ;
Lat. : *If thou receive . . . and hide . . . , that thine ear may hearken,*
etc. (*then*) *incline thy heart*, etc. But it seems clear that the condition includes the whole paragraph, $v.^{1-4}$. — The sage emphasizes
the necessity of earnestness in the pursuit of wisdom — the expressions increase in intensity from *receive, lay up* (*hide*), *incline,
apply*, to *cry, lift up the voice*, and then *seek, search*. Study of
wisdom is represented as an organized discipline requiring definiteness of purpose and concentration of powers. The prophets
demand conformity to the law of Yahweh, and exhort that he
himself be sought ; here attention is directed to a principle and
body of moral and religious knowledge.

1. Synonymous, ternary. The sage speaks on his own authority
(*my words*), appealing neither to a divine revelation to himself,

nor to the teaching of a human master (a trait characteristic of
the Wisdom literature). He is conscious of having words to utter
which it behooves all men to hear. He does not stand apart from
the law of God, but he is an independent expounder of the divine
moral law, having received it into his mind, and comprehending
its nature and effects intellectually and morally. The prophet
speaks in the name of Yahweh, and gives a specific divine
message; the sage speaks in his own name, representing philosophical reflection, the authority in which is the divinely given
human reason and conscience. The term *commandments*, the
same that is used in the prophetical and legal books for the moral
and ritual ordinances of Yahweh, here denotes the sage's own instructions, which in v.² are identified with *wisdom.* — **2.** Synonymous, ternary. Epexegetical equivalent of v.¹, put in Heb. as
purpose (*in order that thou mayst incline*), or, as we more nat
urally conceive it, as result (*so that*). — *Mind* (lit. *heart*) is the
whole inward perceptive nature. The Heb. word is not properly
represented by Eng. *heart*, which conveys to the modern reader
the impression of a particularly emotional element. Physiologi-
cally, the OT. locates emotion in the bowels, and intellect in the
heart; the brain (not mentioned in OT.) was not regarded by
the ancients as having intellectual significance.* — **3.** Synonymous,
ternary. The Heb. begins with a particle (usually = *for*) which
may probably be rendered *yea* (so RV.); it is merely resumptive,
and may be omitted in an Eng. translation. The Syr. reads *and
if;* the Targ., by the change of a vowel, has *and call understanding mother. Invoke*, lit. *lift up the voice to* = *call to*, synonym of
cry to. — **4.** Synonymous, ternary-binary. *Hid treasures*, etymologically *something hidden*, then *treasure*, from the custom, in the
absence of secure places in houses, of hiding valuables in the
earth or in holes in rocks: see Jer. 41⁸ Job 3²¹ Gen. 43²³ (something concealed and unknown), Isa. 45³ (where the word = simply
treasure, the adj. *hidden* being added); cf. Mt. 13⁴⁴; the notion
of something hidden away for safety seems generally to inhere in
the expression; here there is also the suggestion that effort is
necessary to find and secure it.

---

* Of the Semitic languages it is only Arabic that has a word (*dimāg̃*) for *brain*,
the origin of this word is uncertain; the adj. *damīg̃* means *stupid*.

II. 1. אָמַר (poetic word) always in plu. in Pr., דבר being used for sing., 11¹³ al. — **2.** As to the force of ־ and Inf. here cf. Ew., § 280 d; 𝕲 ὑπακούσεται σοφίας τὸ οὖς σου; 𝕷 ut audiat sapientiam auris tua, perh. free translation, perh. taking אזנך as subject, as in Isa. 32³ (Qal Impf.), in which case, though Inf. is possible, we should expect Qal Impf., since אזן never occurs as subj. with Hif. (apparently not in ψ 10¹⁷); 𝕾𝕿 render by the Impf. in continuation of the construction of v.¹, perh. = תקשיב, a good reading, yet it is doubtful whether 𝕲𝕾𝕿 had a text different from that of 𝕳. — The Impf. הטה continues the telic or ecbatic sense of the preceding construction; a ı before it is appropriate but not necessary. 𝕲𝕾𝕿 render it by a Fut., 𝕷 by an Impv. 𝕲 begins the apod. with v.². — v.²ᵇ is given by 𝕲 in double form, first = 𝕳, and then an improbable variation (regarded as genuine by Jäg., Lag.) in which רננך is read instead of לבך, but the introduction of son is pointless, doubtless scribal error. — **3.** כי cannot here = for (𝕲𝕷), nor can כי אם = but (Hitz.), with supposition of a preceding neg. clause. 𝕿 omits כי and inserts ı before אם; 𝕾 has simply יהקרא, perh. free rendering of 𝕳. There is no good ground in ancient authorities for omitting כי, and it must be taken (= yea) as emphatic introduction of the new conditional clause. — 𝕳 אם; 𝕿 אם כי, and so De'R. 874 (379) in Bibl. Erfurt. I.; see Berakoth 57 a, where this clause is cited for the interpretation of a dream respecting one's mother, and cf. Cappel., Crit. Sac. 5. 2. 2. The reading of 𝕿 comes from an old midrash (Norzi), and the omission of כי is a consequence of free citation. — 𝕳 בינה; 𝕲 σοφίαν (instead of φρόνησις), which Heid. takes to be Alexandrian Jewish, and Lag. Christian. — Some MSS. of 𝕲 (Bᵃᵇ ᵐᵍ· ⁱⁿᶠ· A sup ras Cᵃ) and edd. (Comp. Ald. and 𝕾ᴴ obel.) add at end of v.³ τὴν δὲ αἴσθησιν ζητήσῃς μεγάλῃ τῇ φωνῇ, which Jäger considers to be the true 𝕲 text of ᵇ, = ולתבונה תבקש בקל ודל; in favor of this is its divergence from 𝕳. Against its being the true text of Pr. is perh. the parallelism and the occurrence of ברע in the next verse. — Gr. suggests, with little probability, that 3ᵇ may be dittogram of 2ᵇ.

5–8. The consequence of the condition expressed in v.¹⁻⁴.

If wisdom be embraced, then the man will understand the fear of Yahweh (v.⁵), for Yahweh is the source of wisdom (v.⁶), and the protector of the upright (v.⁷·⁸). Apparently an editorial insertion. The proper apodosis to v.¹⁻⁴ is v.⁹ᶠᶠ·: if thou seek wisdom, then (v.¹⁰) wisdom will come to thee. V.⁵⁻⁸ introduce a new thought, and were probably added by an editor who thought that the central idea of these discourses, the *fear of Yahweh*, ought not to be lacking here. See further in notes below.

5. Then shalt thou understand the fear of Yahweh,
   And find the knowledge of God;
6. For Yahweh gives wisdom,
   Out of his mouth come knowledge and discernment;

7. He lays up deliverance for the upright,
   Is a shield to those who walk in integrity;
8. He guards the paths of probity,
   And protects the way of the pious.

5. The fear of Yahweh. Synonymous, ternary. The divine name *God* (*Elohim*) occurs elsewhere in Pr. four times, 2^{17} 3^4 25^2 30^9; the expression *knowledge of God* in OT. only here and Hos. 4^1 6^6 (Nu. 24^{16} *knowledge of the Most High*). In the preëxilian literature *Elohim* is used as proper name only in the Elohistic narrative (Am. 4^{11} Hos. $12^{3(4)}$ seem to be citations from this narrative), not in any prophetic writing except in the passages above mentioned (not in Hos. 4^1 6^6 Mic. 3^7). After the exile it gradually became a proper name (the local, national sense of *Yahweh* disappearing), and in Pr. = *Yahweh*. The change of name here is rhetorical variation. The *fear of Yahweh* (the fear or reverence directed toward him) is equivalent to the *knowledge of God* (the knowledge which has to do with him). The first expression represents the God of Israel as the source of all ethical authority and law, and reverent obedience to him as the principle of life ; the second declares that true learning is concerned with the ethical character of God and the duties which he imposes ; *knowledge* is not only intellectual apprehension, but also communion of soul. Wisdom is thus conceived of as both an attitude of soul and a body of knowledge, all in the sphere of religion. This old-Hebrew point of view stands in the Book of Proverbs in organic union with the human ethical conception of life in this way : the moral content of life is based not on ritual and ecclesiastical law, but on reason and conscience, and these are the gift of God (see next verse). We have here, on the one hand, the recognition of the mind of man as a source of truth, and, on the other hand, the assertion that the moral potency of the mind is the creation of God. This larger conception came to the Jews through natural growth under the stimulus of foreign (mainly Greek) thought. Instead of *shalt* (which implies determination on the part of the speaker, or else is hypothetical) we may write *wilt* (which expresses futurity simply). Cf. note on 1^7. — **6.** Synonymous, ternary. Yahweh the source of wisdom. This is stated as the ground of the affirmation of v.⁵, and brings this paragraph into logical relation with v.$^{1-4}$. He who seeks wisdom will understand the fear or knowledge of God, because all knowledge comes from him. The reference is probably to the whole moral thought and conduct of man — human instincts, the results of experience, the common-law of morality, as well as the ethical prescriptions contained in the Israelitish canonical and oral codes. The stress, however, is laid on man's moral nature, which is represented as a divine gift. — The expression *out of his mouth* (Grk. *from his presence*) means *from him;* he utters his command and man receives wisdom ; the reference seems not to be to his giving a law (the Tora), which would not agree with the general connection. The *mouth* of Yahweh, a frequent expression in the prophets, is found only here in Pr. (Str.) ; here alone God is teacher, elsewhere Wisdom. The expression occurs in Job 22^{22}, and in a few late ψs, 105^5 119$^{72.88}$ 138^4. — **7, 8.** Synonymous, ternary. Yahweh protects the upright. The word rendered *deliverance* occurs, except Isa. 28^{29} and (the textually doubtful) Mic. 6^9, only in Job and Pr. It appears to signify the act or power of establishment or arrangement, and so fertility in expedients, wisdom, and, as result, achievement, help, deliverance. The last sense is the one here naturally suggested by the parallel *shield*. This latter word is to be taken (in the present Heb. text) as in apposition with the subject (Yahweh) of the preceding clause. — The synonymous expressions *the upright* and *those who walk in integrity* indicate right conduct in general ; the *upright* are those who conform their lives to the straight line of moral and religious propriety ; *integrity* is perfectness of life. The reference is to general substantial rectitude, not to absolute freedom from sin or error, or to the inner life of the soul ; cf. Gen. 20^5 1 K. 9^4 ψ 101^2 Pr. 19^1. — **8** presents the same thought in the form of purpose or result (epexegetical equivalent), *so as to guard,* = *he guards* the way, that is, the life and interests, of those who obey him. The expression *guard the paths of probity* is peculiar and difficult ; the verb means either *keep, observe,* or *guard, have an eye on;* in the former sense it is followed as object by the law observed, as in 3^1 5^2 28^7 Dt. 33^9 ψ 119^{33} *al.*; in the latter sense by the person or concrete thing to be defended, as in 2^{11} 4^6 Isa. 26^3 *al.* (once, 22^{12}, by *knowledge*), or by the thing to be watched, as in Job 7^{20}. As

Yahweh is subject, it is the latter sense that appears to be
intended here ; yet everywhere else the *path of probity* (or its
equivalent) is something that is walked in, as in v.[20], not guarded,
though the way of a man is said to be scrutinized (Job 13[27]) or
controlled (ψ 139[3]) by God.   As the text stands, *paths of probity*
must be regarded as a poetical variation of *paths of the upright*
(cf. v.[20]), equivalent to the parallel *way of the pious* (Heb. *his
pious ones*, RV. *saints*).   On *probity* see note 1[3].—The *pious*
man (חסיד) is he who is characterized by *kindness*, *love* (חסד).
The stem seems to signify any strong feeling toward a person,
whether unfriendly, *envy* (as in Arabic), or friendly, *kindness* (as
in Heb.), or both (as in Aramaic, and cf. 14[34] 25[10] Lev. 20[17]).
The substantive is used of kindness shown to man by man (Gen.
24[12]) or by God (Ex. 34[6], often in Pss.), whether of man's acts
toward God (Hos. 6[4. 6] ψ 89[29] 2 Chr. 32[32] 35[26] Neh. 13[14]) is doubtful.   The adj. is used twice of God (Jer. 3[12] ψ 18[25(26)] = 2 Sam.
22[26]), many times of man.   It may be active, = *loving*, or passive,
= *beloved*,   It is the former sense in which it is used of God, and
this seems to be its meaning throughout OT., though the other
is possible, and, in most cases, appropriate ; the deity might be
thought of as the bestower and the worshipper as the recipient of
favors, or the latter might be regarded as bound to his god by a
sentiment of love and devotion, which, at first physical and mer-
cenary, would grow more and more ethically and spiritually pure ;
the active sense is favored by the parallelism in ψ 18[25(26)], *with the
kind* (merciful, good) *thou wilt show thyself kind*.   The adj.
occurs first in the second half of the seventh century (Mic. 7[2] Dt.
33[8] Jer. 3[12]), and elsewhere only in late poetry (1 Sam. 2[9] 2 Chr.
6[41] Pr. 2[8] and Pss.).   When it began to be employed in the sense
of *devoted to God*, *pious* (the rendering *saint* is inappropriate)
can hardly be determined.   In the second century, in the struggle
between Antiochus Epiphanes and the Jews, it appears as a technical term to designate those who strictly maintained the religion
of Israel against the inroads of Hellenism (1 Mac. 2[42] Ἁσιδαῖοι,
Hasidean or Asidean).*   In some Pss. (79[2] 86[2] 116[15] *al.*) it means
pious Israel in contrast with surrounding heathen oppressors or

---

* Cf. Wellhausen, *Die Pharisäer u. d. Saducäer ;* Schürer, *Hist. of the Jew.
People,* II. ii. 26.

apostate Jews. In Pr. it is found only here, in an editorial insertion (perhaps of the second century B.C.) ; it is here a general
term for *pious*.

5. 𝕲[B א A] συνήσεις φόβον, for which Clem. Al., 121, has νοήσεις θεοσέβειαν.
In v.[5b] 𝕲[B] = 𝕳; Cl. Alex. κ. αἴσθησιν θείαν εὑρήσεις (and so Orig.), free ren-
dering, probably original (Lag.). — **6.** 𝕳 פיו ; 𝕲[B] ἀπὸ προσώπου αὐτοῦ =
מפניו, apparently scribal error. — **7.** K וצפן , Q (and some MSS.), better, יצפן
(𝕷 *custodiet*), since the couplets appear to be independent statements;
𝕲 κ. θησαυρίζει, = 𝕳 Kethib (not = צבר), as in 1[18]. — 𝕳 תושיה ; 𝕲 (MSS.)
σωτηρίαν, 𝕷 *salutem*, Cl. Al. βοήθειαν, 𝕿 in MS. (cited by Levy, *Chald.*
Wbch.) רהי, in Bibl. Rab., 1568, סכהי *help*, in Buxt., Lag. שבהיר *glory.* —
𝕳 מגן, rendered by vb. or partcp. in the Vrss.: 𝕲 ὑπερασπιεῖ, 𝕷 *et proteget*,
𝕾𝕿 ובסתר ; 𝕳 is curt poetic construction, instead of the ordinary הוא מ ; we
expect a verb = *protect* (but the stem does not occur in OT. in this sense) or
a noun = *protection* as object of יצפן (but no such noun suggests itself) ; מ
cannot be object of י — 𝕳 להלכי תם ; 𝕲 τὴν πορείαν αὐτῶν = להליכתם (Vog.,
Schleusn.), as in ψ 67 (68)[25]. — **8.** 𝕳 לנצר , equivalent proposition represented
as purpose or result; 𝕾 has ו and Perf., and we may here read Impf.; Gr.
לנצר, but this does not accord with [b]. — 𝕳 משפט is given in all the Vrss., except
that 𝕲 (except Cod. 23) has plu. — K. הסיד sing.; Q and many Heb. MSS.
and all Vrss. have plu., as the context requires; 𝕿 omits the suffix. — Oort, to
secure perfect parallelism, reads : ודרך הסיד ישמרו *and* (*that they may*) *pre-*
serve the way of piety toward him (or, *the way of his kindness*); but this is
not in keeping with the general idea in v.[6-8], in which *Yahweh* is subject, and
דרך הסיד is hard; it would be easier to change משפט to יירם or צדקם (cf. v[20]).

9-22. The proper conclusion to the condition stated in v.[1-4] :
first, the comprehension of righteousness (v.[9 20]), then the guid-
ance and protection of Wisdom (v.[10-19]), with the reward of
goodness and the punishment of wickedness (v.[21. 22]). — V.[20] should
probably be transposed so as to stand next after v.[9]. In its present
position it interrupts the connection between v.[19] and v.[21], while
by its thought it attaches itself naturally to v.[9].

9, 20. Comprehension of rectitude.

9. Then shalt thou understand righteousness and probity,
   ‹ Shalt keep › every path of good,

20. That thou mayest walk in the way of good men,
    Mayest follow the paths of the righteous.

9. The verse is not a poetical couplet in the Heb., which reads
in second line : *and rectitude — every path of good*, giving the first

three nouns in the order in which they occur in 1^3. There the
rhythmical form is proper; here it is defective, and (though it is
possible that the three nouns may have been originally taken from
1^3) it seems better (by an easy emendation) to write the verb
which the parallelism calls for: cf. the expressions *keep* ($=follow$)
the paths in v.^{20}, and *keep my ways* in 8^{32}. On the nouns in first
line see notes on 1^3. — *Path* ($2^{15.\ 18}$ $4^{11.\ 26}$ $5^{6.\ 21}$ ψ 23^3) is lit. *wagon-
road*, then any *way;* the following *good* defines the path as lying
in the domain or leading in the direction of what is (morally)
good. — The *then* attaches this section to v.$^{1-4}$: " if thou earnestly
seek wisdom, thou shalt be morally enlightened, shalt acquire intellectual acumen in ethical questions, and [if the emendation suggested above be correct] the power of right action "; freedom of
choice is implied, and it is assumed that he who fully knows the
good way will follow it.* On the substitution of *wilt* for *shalt*
see note on v.^{5} above. — **20.** Synonymous, ternary. The purpose
that thou mayest walk involves result. The verse thus expands
the second line of v.^{9}. — At the end of first line the Heb. has
simply the word *good* (plural); the parallelism favors the rendering *good men* (not *good things*). *Good* is the general term for
fitness of all sorts, here used of moral fitness and rectitude. —
Follow is lit. *keep.* — The *righteous* or *just* man is he who does
justice, rightness (see note on 1^3). The epithet is applied in OT.
to man and to God, but its significance, depending on the content of the current idea of justice, varies with the different periods
of Heb. history. Yahweh is just to a man or to Israel when he
acts in accordance with natural or legal right. In the earlier
phase of thought Israel's national right was held to be victory over
its enemies, and *justice* came to be equivalent to *victory*, as in
Ju. 5^{11} 1 S. 12^7 Jer. 51^{10}. The purely ethical conception grew
with the general ethical growth of the people; and in the prophetical and later books (see, for ex., Ez. 18) tends to become
predominant, though the primitive idea lingers in places. In Pr.
righteous = morally and religiously good in general; the word
(like *good* and *perfect*) expresses not absolute sinlessness, but general rectitude. In late exilian and postexilian writings it is often

---

* So Plato and the Stoics.

a synonym for the faithful part of Israel (Isa. 53¹¹ 26² ψ 31¹⁸⁽¹³⁾ 94⁽¹
al.). — The Grk. reads the verse as a conditional sentence, an l
connects it immediately with v.¹⁹ : *for if they had gone in good
paths they would have found the paths of righteousness easy;* the
Heb. is preferable. — Bickell omits the verse as marring the
strophic structure of the paragraph ; but this difficulty disappears
in the arrangement here adopted.

**10–19. The moral protection afforded by Wisdom. —Wisdom,
entering the soul (v.¹⁰) and keeping watch over it (v.¹¹), saves
the man from the influence of bad men (v.¹²⁻¹⁵) and bad women
(v.¹⁶⁻¹⁹).**

10. For wisdom shall enter thy mind,
    And knowledge shall be pleasant to thee,
11. Discretion shall watch over thee,
    Discernment shall guard thee,

12. To save thee from the manner of life of bad men,
    From men whose speech is wicked,
13. Who leave the paths of uprightness,
    To walk in ways of darkness,
14. Who rejoice in doing wrong,
    [And] in iniquities take delight,
15. Whose paths are crooked,
    And iniquitous their ways —

16. To save thee from the lewd woman,
    From the harlot with her cajoling words,
17. Who forsakes the friend of her youth,
    And forgets the covenant of God.
18. For her house leads down(?) to Death,
    And her paths unto the Shades;
19. None that go to her return,
    Or attain the paths of life.

10, 11. Wisdom as guardian. — 10. Synonymous, ternary.
The entrance of Wisdom into the soul ; cf. Job 14¹⁶. *Knowledge
= wisdom;* see note on 1². — On *mind* (lit. *heart*) see note on
v.² above. — *Enter* and *be pleasant to* are synonyms, = "become
acceptable to thee, a part of thy intellectual and moral being." —
Thee is lit. *thy soul;* the term *soul* means the principle of life,
and so life or being, and *my soul, thy soul,* are common expres-

sions in OT. for *me* (or, *myself*), *thee* (or, *thyself*). The Heb.
word does not emphasize spirituality of thought, but, being a general term for the principle of life, it may, like its synonym *mind*,
express any intellectual power. —11. Synonymous, ternary-binary.
On *discretion* (or, *insight*) and *discernment* (or, *intelligence*) see
notes on 1^4 and 2^2. — The guardianship (the result of Wisdom's
entrance into the soul) is subjective — the man's security is in his
own reason and conscience, in the law of life which these give ;
the whole is, however, viewed as finally the ordination of God,
though not in the form of an external law. — These two verses
give the ground of the preceding statement (v.$^{9. 20}$) ; understanding will be gained by the entrance of Wisdom into the mind, not
in a forced manner, but so that she shall be acceptable, *pleasant*
to the soul. The man is represented as assimilating wisdom,
coming into harmony with it, following it not through external
pressure, but by inward impulse ; to do right becomes delightful
to him. This is largely because he sees the advantages of rectitude (v.^{21}) ; but there is probably still to be recognized here the
germ of the idea of transformation of nature (a development out
of such conceptions as those of Jer. 31^{33} Ez. 36^{27}). — The Grk.
takes v.^{10} as condition, and v.^{11} as its result : 10. *for if wisdom
enter . . . and knowledge seem beautiful . . .* 11. *good counsel
shall guard thee*, etc. (the same construction may be got from the
Heb. by rendering *when Wisdom shall enter*). This construction
is not decidedly against the context, and gives a good sense ; it
seems, however, to be less natural than the causal construction
(*for*), not because the nouns in v.^{11} are identical in meaning with
those in v.^{10} (such repetition would not be against the manner of
Pr.), but because, as v.$^{9. 20}$ state the result of the condition of v.$^{1-4}$,
we more naturally expect in v.^{10} not a new condition, but a ground
or reason of the preceding statement. The general sense is the
same in the two constructions. There is no need to take v.$^{10. 11}$ as
parentheses ; v.^{12} is logically connected with v.^{11} (see below). —
Bickell, in order to gain an additional couplet (an omission being
indicated, as he thinks, by a discrepancy of gender in the Heb.)
expands v.^{10} as follows : *for wisdom shall enter into thy mind and
knowledge unto thy soul* [*shall come, instruction shall be good to
thy mind, and learning to thy soul*] *shall be pleasant*. This inser-

tion is without support from the Anc. Vrss., and seems not to be
necessary or probable; the text, as it stands, gives a satisfactory
sense and a good rhythm, and the quatrain, which is here desid-
erated, is gained by the transference of v.[20]. On the grammatical
point see critical note.

12–15. First, Wisdom saves from bad men. — **12.** Synonymous,
ternary. Instead of the Infin. *to save,* expressing purpose or result,
we may, by a slight change, read *she will save* (Bickell); the change
does not affect the general sense. — *Manner of life* is lit. *way,* and
whose speech is wicked is lit. *who speak wickedness* (or *wrong* or
wicked things). The Heb. has, in second clause, sing. *man* (apparently used in collective sense); the plu. form accords better in
Eng. with the following verses. Instead of *way of bad* (*men*) we
may render *way of the bad* (*man*), and so in second clause *the
man who speaks;* or *way of evil;* or, possibly, *evil* (or, *wicked*)
way. The concrete form (*man* or *men*) in first clause is favored by
the parallelism, and the plu. is more natural here in English. The
adj. *bad* or *evil* (רע) is used in OT. of any sort of badness, of
body (Gen. 41[3]), of appearance or deportment (Ex. 21[8]), of experience or fortune (Jer. 4[6]), of moral or religious conduct (*passim*);
it describes whatever does not conform to a norm — it is the opposite of the equally general term *good* (טוב); it is here the *morally
bad.* Cf. note on the subst. *evil,* 1[33]. — A *wrong* thing (תהפכות)
is that which is *turned aside* from the path of right; its meaning
is not precisely expressed by *perverse* (which answers to it etymologically), or by RV. *froward* (which = refractory, perverse, obstinate); it may sometimes be properly rendered by *false,* but in
Pr. it is a general term, signifying that which is opposed to the
right (= *wicked, bad*); it occurs in Dt. 32[20] (*they are a generation given to falsities, persons in whom no confidence can be placed*),
and elsewhere only in Pr. — Bad men are here described by their
conduct or *manner of life* (*way*) and their *speech;* the two things
are treated as equivalent each to the other, speech being regarded
as the indication of thought and life. The sage lays stress on the
power of evil association: to avoid bad men is to be saved from
evil suggestion from without, from the reinforcement that sympathy gives to the evil within the heart. He warns against a

malign moral influence, which is not the only one in life, but is
the most obvious, and one of the most powerful.   Rashi says that
the men here referred to are *Epicureans* (that is, heretics in general), who seduce Israel to idolatry and pervert the law to evil.*
— 13. Antithetic, ternary.   Description of the conduct of bad
men. *Uprightness* is a general term for rectitude ; it appears first
in the Deuteronomistic vocabulary (Dt. 9^5 1 K. 9^4 1 C. 29^{17}), and
then only in the Wisdom books; it always has a religious coloring,
except in Job 6^{25}, and, perhaps, Eccl. 12^{10}.   That these men *leave*
(or *forsake*) rectitude does not imply that they had once followed
right paths, but only that they have chosen other paths.   Their
walk is the way of *darkness* in contrast with the light which illu-
mines the way of wisdom, the darkness (as the parallelism suggests) here characterizing the sphere (as in Jno. 3^{19-21}) rather than
the result (as in 4^{19}) ; evil (in contrast with uprightness) seeks
the concealment of darkness.   Such, from the parallelism, seems
to be the sense in this passage, though everywhere else in OT.
where *light* and *darkness* are used figuratively it is the guidance
and safety of the former and the danger of the latter that are indi-
cated (Isa. 2^5 42^6 ψ 27^1 Pr. 4^{18} 6^{23} 13^9 16^{15} Isa. 58^{10} ψ $18^{28(29)}$ Eccl.
2^{14} Pr. 20^{20}), and so it may be here with the term *darkness*.   The
employment of the two terms to express spheres of life characterizes the Mazdean sacred books. — 14. Synonymous, ternary.
A stronger touch.   The connective *and* is inserted in accordance
with the general norm of the couplets. *Iniquities* (lit. *iniquities
of evil*) is the same word in the Heb. that is rendered *wrong
things* in v.^{12}; there the reference was to words, here it is to
deeds — in both cases it is the opposite of *right* that is meant; it
is here (if the text be correct), for the sake of emphasis and
vigor, qualified by the term *evil* (or, *wickedness*). — The *rejoice*
and *delight* are a heightening of the *forsake* of the preceding verse ;
bad men, it is said, not only deliberately choose wicked ways, but
also take pleasure in them.   The sage, in stating this familiar fact,
is probably to be understood not as implying that men delight in
evil as evil, but only as meaning that wrongdoing, interwoven into
life, becomes a source of enjoyment, the enjoyment coming from

---

* On the terms *Epicureans* and *Minim* (Talmudic designations of heretics) see
Buxtorf, *Lex.*, and Cheyne's *Cyclop. Biblica*, Art. "Canon."

the momentary good result, not from the consciousness of committing an unlawful or unrighteous deed. Other things being equal,
men, as a rule, prefer right to wrong. The murderer in 1[11-13] is
represented as committing murder not for its own sake, but to get
gain of goods; his wrong is not in desiring wealth, but in using
improper means to secure it. Wicked men are those whose con-
sciences are not tender and strong enough to prevent their enjoying good things evilly gained. There is a formal resemblance
between this v. and Job 3[22], perh. imitation by our author.* —
15. Synonymous, ternary-binary. Variation of the preceding verses
— description of bad life as departure from the right path. The
Heb. reads (with insertion of a pronoun) *whose paths are crooked
and (they) iniquitous in their ways* (so substantially AV.). Slight
changes in the text give the renderings *who are crooked in their
paths and iniquitous in their ways* (so substantially Oort, RV.),
or *who make crooked their paths* (Dyserinck, Kamphausen) *and
in their ways turn into bypaths* (Kamp.), or *whose paths are
crooked and their ways iniquitous* (so substantially most of the
Ancient Vrss.). Of these the last is simplest, requiring only the
omission of one letter of the Heb.; the meaning is the same in
all. — Two new adjs. are here introduced, synonymous with each
other and with the *iniquities* of v.[14]; they occur in OT. in the
ethical sense only. *Crooked* (עקשׁ) is that which departs from
the right way (allied to *false*); outside of Pr. the adj. occurs in
Dt. 32[5] ψ 18[26(27)] (= 2 S. 22[27]) 101[4], the vb. in Mic. 3[9] Isa. 59[8] Job
9[20]. *Iniquitous* also (נלוז, found, outside of Pr., only in Isa. 30[12])
is that which turns aside into wrong ways, morally perverted,
wrong, false.

16–19. The second class of evil persons from whom Wisdom
delivers men: licentious women. The prominence given in Pr.,
especially in chs. 1–9, to the vice of licentiousness shows that it
was a notorious social evil at the time when the book was written.
In the preëxilian and exilian books comparatively little is said of
it. That there were harlots and adulteresses in Israel from an
early time is shown by such passages as Judg. 11[1] (Jephthah's
mother) 1 K. 3[16] (the two women who appeared before Solomon)

---

* Cf. Strack, *Stud. u. Krit.*, 1896, IV.

Hos. 3¹ (Hosea's wife), by the prophetic denunciations of the
crime (Hos. 4² Jer. 7⁹ Mal. 3⁵), by the laws against it (Ex. 20¹⁴
Dt. 22 Lev. 20¹⁰), and by the employment of the terms harlotry
and adultery (in Pent. Judg. Chr. Ps. Hos. Mic. Jer. Ez.) as designations of religious unfaithfulness. Prostitution was a feature of
the Canaanitish religious cults, and made its way into Israel. If
we exclude the references to this last usage, the mention of the
vice in question in the prophetical books is not frequent; less
stress is laid on it than on the oppression of the poor by the rich.
In a polygamous society and in a country without great cities it
was not likely to grow to great proportions. The case was different when the Jews were dispersed through the world, and lived in
cities like Jerusalem and Alexandria, centres of wealth and luxury,
inhabited by mixed populations. This form of debauchery then
became commoner and better organized. Hetairae flocked to
the cities. Naukratis in the Egyptian Delta was famous under
the Ptolemies for its brilliant venal women. The temptations of
Alexandria are illustrated by the story told by Josephus (*Ant.* 12,
4, 6) of Joseph the son of Tobias. The picture of society given
in Ben-Sira (9³⁻⁹ 19² 23¹⁶⁻²⁶ 25¹⁶⁻²⁶ 26⁸⁻¹² 42⁹⁻¹⁴), based on life in
Jerusalem and Alexandria in the third and second centuries B.C.,
agrees in substance with the descriptions of the Book of Proverbs.
The tone is modern. Instead of the old clan-life of Israel, with
its definite family-ties and local bounds, we have the personal freedom of the Greek period in Syria and Egypt. This tone, most
observable in chs. 1–9, is not wholly wanting in the rest of the
book. The woman is represented as the temptress, the man as
the silly victim.

16. Synonymous, ternary. *To save* may be read (as in v.¹²)
she will save. The terms *lewd woman* and *harlot* are both lit.
strange woman (or, *stranger*). *With her cajoling words*, lit. :
who makes smooth her words (RV. *flatters*, etc.). The reference
is to dissolute women, but the precise sense in which the term
strange is here used is differently understood. The Heb. has two
synonyms, both of which occur in OT. in three significations : one
who is outside the circle of one's family or one's clan ; an alien
to one's nation, = " foreigner " ; one not one's self, = " another."

For the first term (זר) see 1 K. 3[18] Dt. 25[5] Nu. 1[51]; Ex. 30[33] Lev.
22[12]; Pr. 6[1] 11[15] 14[10] 27[2] (this third sense is found only in Pr.).
For the second term (נכרי) see Gen. 31[15] Job 19[15] ψ 69[8(9)] Eccl. 6[2];
Dt. 15[3] 1 K. 11[1]; Pr. 27[2]. Women of this class were doubtless
often non-Israelites, and such might be the sense here (so Siegfr.,
Stade, and, so far as the second term is concerned, De.); but
the general character of the descriptions here and in chs. 5, 7,
9[13-18], and the contrast expressed in 5[19. 20], make it almost certain
that the writer has in mind dissolute women without regard to
nationality, and that the *strange woman* is one who is not bound
to the man by legal ties, who is outside the circle of his proper
relations, that is, a harlot or an adulteress. Rashi: Epicureanism.*
— The smooth, cajoling words are given in 7[13-20]; 7[5] is identical
with our verse, except in the first word — the similarity between
the themes of the two discourses makes the repetition natural. —
The Grk. connects v.[16. 17] not with v.[11], but with v.[15], taking them as
the description of the influence of bad men, and following a Heb.
text very different from ours: 16. *To remove thee far from the right
way and estrange thee from righteous opinion. My son, let not
evil counsel take possession of thee,* 17. *which forsakes the teaching
of youth and forgets the divine covenant.* This is a bit of rabbinical or Alexandrian allegorizing, while in 7[5] the Heb. is literally
translated. — 17. Synonymous, ternary. The strange woman's
social and religious infidelity. The reference is to a married
woman, and the *friend of her youth* is not God (to which sense
the parallelism is supposed by some to point), but her husband.
For the use of the term *friend* (אלוף) see 16[28] 17[9] Mic. 7[5] Jer. 3[4]
ψ 55[18(14)]; the sense *guide, instructor,* is not found in OT. The
expression of our verse is perhaps taken from Jer. 3[2-5], where the
adulterous spouse Israel, charged with her infidelities by Yahweh,
is exhorted to cry to him: *my father, thou art the friend of my
youth,* that is, "the husband of my youth (cf. Hos. 2[7. 15(9. 17)] Ez.
16[43]) whom I have forsaken for others"; but while the infidelity

---

* Cf. Buxtorf, *Lex.*, s. v. ירבי, for the use of *Aramaean woman* as = *foreign
woman* and *harlot.* On the OT. sense of *strange woman* see Kuenen, *Einl.*, iii.
§97; Wildeboer, *Litt. des AT.*, § 23, Anm. 7; Bertholet, *Die Stellung der Isr. und
Juden zu den Fremden,* p. 195.— Cf. the *Maxims* of the Egyptian Any, of the New
Kingdom (Eng. transl. in art. *Egypt. Literature* in *Library of the World's Best
Literature*).

in Jer. is national and ritual, in Pr. it is individual and physical. At the same time, the marriage-obligation is here regarded as a divine law (Ex. 20[14]), and so as an agreement with God to obey him and thus obtain his blessing. The Heb. has *of her God;* the more general form *of God* (as, apparently, in the Grk.) is better. — The conception of the marriage-relation involved in the verse (and throughout the Book) is a high one. The old polygamy or bigamy (the rule up to the exile) is ignored; monogamy is assumed as the established custom. The husband is the trusted friend; the marriage-tie has a divine sanction (cf. Mal. 2[14]). The expression *covenant of God* may refer simply to the general idea of sacredness involved, or it may possibly allude to a religious marriage-ceremony. Of the Israelitish marriage-ceremonies of the pre-Christian time we know little. The old custom was that the woman was brought into the man's dwelling, by that act becoming his wife (Gen. 24[67] 29[23] 1 Sam. 25[40] Dt. 21[12]), purchase-money (*mohar*) being paid the father (Gen. 34[12] 1 Sam. 18[25]); sometimes the man, in the presence of witnesses, affirmed his purpose to take the woman as wife (Ru. 4[10-13]); a feast was sometimes held (Ju. 14[10] Tob. 8[19]), and the bride was led to the husband's home in procession (ψ 45[14. 15(15. 16)] cf. Mt. 25[1-10]).* A trace of a religious ceremony appears in Tob. 7[12. 13(11. 12)], where Raguel takes his daughter by the hand and gives her to Tobias as wife, saying: *according to the law of Moses take her to thy father* (there was also a written contract, Tob. 7[14(16)]); it is not improbable that in this later time it was customary for the father or guardian of the bride to address a word of pious counsel to the newly married couple. No part in the ceremony appears to have been taken by priest or other official person. The modern Jewish marriage, though it differs considerably from the customs of Bible and Talmud, is still essentially a family-ceremony.† — **18, 19.** Synony-

---

* On the view that Canticles is a wedding-poem, consisting of the songs sung by bride, bridegroom, and companions in the marriage-festival, see Wetzstein, in De.'s Comm'y on Canticles; K. Budde, in the *New World*, March, 1894, and in his Comm'y on Cant., in Marti's *Hand-Commentar;* C. Siegfried, *Hoheslied,* in Nowack's *Handkommentar.*

† See the Talm. treatises, *Ketub.* and *Kiddush.*, J. F. Schröder, *Satzungen u. Gebräuche d. talm.-rab. Judenthums,* and I. Abrahams, *Jewish Life in the Middle Ages,* 1896.

mous, ternary.   The fate of those who yield to the seductions of
the adulteress : physical death is their portion.   The meaning is
plain, but the exact rendering of v.[18a] is doubtful.   The Heb., as it
stands, must be rendered *she sinks down to death, her house;* but
death, the *house appointed for all living* (Job 30[23]), would hardly
be called the house of one person ; the rendering *she . . . together
with her house*, that is, with her visitors (Böttch. De. Now.), is not
permissible.   The reading of the Grk. (whose text differed from
our Heb.), *she has set her house by death* (adopted by Bickell),
does not give a satisfactory thought — her house, which is on the
earth, is not naturally represented as being by Death, which is
here the underground-world ; and the Heb. preposition, = *unto*,
must also then be changed to one meaning *near, by*.   The parallelism suggests that *house* is the subject, and a change of the Heb.
accents (not the consonants) gives the possible sense, *bows down*,
or *sinks down*, = *leads down*, for the verb.   The picture presented is of a path which leads from upper earth to Sheol, like
those by which Odysseus and Aeneas descend to Hades (less
probably of a pit through which one sinks into Sheol) ; on this
downward path she and her guests enter, and from the land of
the dead they never return.   A slight change in the Heb. gives a
verb meaning *goes down*, = *leads down* (17[10], used in Job 21[13]
of descent to Sheol), a sense which is perhaps favored by the
similar expression in 5[5]. — *House* (if the text be correct) is the
abode, the place from which goes the path to the Underworld,
with connotation of " household," the woman and those who go
to her house.   *Death* = the realm of death, Sheol (cf. ψ 9[13(14)] Pr.
5[5] 7[27]).   It is not a place of punishment, but the abode of all the
dead.   The punishment referred to in the verse is premature and
unhappy death, which is represented everywhere in OT. as a misfortune, a visitation of God as retribution for wrongdoing (29[1]
ψ 9[17(18)]) ; long life is the reward of the good (3[16]), but the days of
the wicked shall be cut short (10[27]).   This is the old-Hebrew conception, which limits moral-spiritual life to the present world.
Here God, it was held, dispenses rewards and punishments ; when
one has entered Sheol, God no longer takes account of him (only
in Job 14[13] 26[5. 6] is there a suggestion that the power of the God
of heaven may extend to the Underworld).   Death is the physical

event which transfers men from the sphere of activity to that of inactivity, where there is no relation between man and God (Isa. 38$^{18.19}$). This conception seems to be a survival of the early belief which assigned the Underworld to a separate deity (so in Babylonia), independent of the deity who ruled the world, and supreme in his own domain; the subterranean deity vanished from the Israelitish system, but the gap between Sheol and the God of Israel remained. Proverbs retains the old view; its idea of the future life is without ethical elements. — The *Shades* (Rephaim) are the dead, the inhabitants of Sheol.* Earthly conditions, such as distinctions of rank, are represented sometimes as continuing in Sheol (Ez. 32$^{22-30}$ Isa. 14^9), sometimes as not continuing (Job 3$^{13-19}$ ψ 88$^{5(6)}$). The *rephaim* are without mundane power or significance (Isa. 14^{10}), and the pious among them cannot praise God (Isa. 38^{18} ψ 88$^{10(11)}$). Yet they were popularly thought of as being gods, or as possessing supernatural powers (1 Sam. 28^{13} Isa. 8^{19}, a survival of the primitive belief on this point). In Pr. the facts emphasized are that their existence is without happiness, and that they never *return* to live the life of this earth.† — The *paths of life* = the ordinary earthly life, not moral-spiritual life or salvation. The statement that for the victims of the adulteress there is no return to this life is not meant to indicate that for others (the followers of Wisdom) there is return, but only to emphasize the fact that the fate of adulterers (premature death) is irreversible. Pr. has nothing elsewhere on the impossibility of return from Sheol, but it may be assumed that its authors shared the opinion expressed in the other Wisdom Books (Job 14$^{7-12}$ Eccl. 9^6 Ben-Sira 17^{30}).

9. 𝕳 מֵישָׁרִים (1^8 יְשָׁרִים) is rendered as noun (𝕾𝕿 in *stat. constr.* and so Gr.) by all Vrss. except perh. 𝕲, whose κατορθώσεις may be noun = 'ם (so Lag. Baumg.), or verb = *thou shalt establish:* the noun-form occurs elsewhere only once, ψ 96^2 (Heb. 97^2), and then sing. = מכון ; between noun and verb it is hard to decide. The text of 𝕳 presents a serious rhythmical difficulty

---

* Whether the term has any etymological connection with the gentilic name *Rephaim* (Dt. 2^{11} *al.*) is uncertain. Cf. Schwally, in *ZAT.*, 1898, 1. pp. 132 ff.

† In the obscure passage Isa. 26^{19} it is doubtful whether the reference is to a national resuscitation (as in Ez. 37) or to some sort of appearance of the rephaim on the earth.

(in 1³ᵇ, in which the same three nouns occur, the rhythm is good). The difficulty may be removed by writing השכר, from which מערם might come without difficulty, especially if the scribe had 1⁸ in mind. Gr. כיעפט מיש׳.—10. 𝕳 כי; 𝕲 ἐὰν γάρ = כי אם.—𝕳 לבך; 𝕲ᴮ τὴν διάνοιαν, 𝕲ˣᴬ σὴν διάνοιαν.—𝕳 יינעם; 𝕲 καλὴ εἶναι δόξῃ.—The masc. vb. יינעם with fem. subj. דעת is poetic license, as in 8¹⁰ 14⁶ 29²⁵ (where Bi., who here by a long insertion introduces a masc. subj., retains the masc. verb); ד׳ is construed with fem. predicates in Isa. 47¹⁰ ψ 139⁶ Dan. 12⁴, that is, in OT. three times with masc. and three times with fem. predicates. In the former case it appears to be conceived of in a general way as a thing (perh. as the act of knowing) without regard to gender; see other cases of such freedom in Ew., § 174*g*.—11. 𝕳 מזמה; 𝕲 (foll. by 𝕾) βουλὴ καλὴ, to indicate that מ is here used in good sense. Similarly for 𝕳 הבנוה 𝕲 (and so 𝕾) has ἔννοια ὁσία.—On the suff. in תנצרכה see Ew., § 250 *a*, Ols., § 97 *a*; the כה־ is for נכה־, in which ה is vowel-letter, and ג the verb-ending (survival of the Energic form).—12. 𝕳 להצילך; 𝕲 ἵνα ῥύσηταί σε, apparently = 𝕳; 𝕾 יתהפצא, 𝕿 רי ה׳, 𝔏 *ut eruaris*, perh. Impf. instead of ל and Inf., perh. free rendering of 𝕳; Bi. writes הצלך on the ground that this paragraph is not a consequence but an explanation; on this point see notes on v.². רע better taken as subst. defining דרך; the Vrss. render it by adj. Gr. מרע.—? מהפכות; 𝕲ᴮ ˣ ᴬᶜ ᵃˡ. μηδὲν πιστόν (and so 𝕾ᴴ marg.); H-P 23 (= Cod. Venet. San Marco, V) διαστραμμένα (and so 𝕾ᴴ) = 𝕳.—13. 𝕲 begins the v. with ὦ, apparently reading אי, a particle which does not occur elsewhere in Pr., and would not be appropriate here. On the vocalization of the art. (ה) see *Miklol*, 53 *b*, and on the accentuation see Bär-Delitzsch, note on this verse.—In 2 cl. instead of ל and Inf. (ללכת) 𝕾𝕿𝔏 have ו and vb. or partcp. *and walk*, free rendering which gives the sense of 𝕳 correctly, substitution of the coördinate for the subordinate construction. Bi. retains 𝕳. —14. H-P 23, 68 *al.* prefix ὦ.—𝕳 לעשות רע; 𝕲 ἐπὶ κακοῖς.—𝕳 תהפכת, written defect. in some MSS., taken as sing. in 𝕲𝕾𝕿 𝔄r.—The second רע, supported by all Vrss., is somewhat hard. Gr. regards it as dittogram, but the rhythm calls for a word here; Dys. emends to רע, but *the iniquities of another* is hardly possible. Failing a satisfactory emendation, 𝕳 may be retained.— 15. The text of 𝕳 may be rendered *who are crooked as to their paths and perverse in their ways*, or a ב may be prefixed to ארחתיהם, or the ב omitted (so Oort) before מעגלתם; but the order עקשים אר׳ (or נאר׳) is not quite satisfactory (cf. 10⁹ 19¹ 28⁶·¹⁸); Dys. (followed by Kamp.) writes מעקשים (as in 10⁹), a phonetically easy emendation, the מ being supposed to have fallen out through preceding מ, but the order is slightly against this construction also. The simplest reading is that of the Vrss. (except AΘ), which apparently did not have ב before מע׳, *whose paths are crooked and their ways iniquitous;* the order in that case hardly makes a difficulty.—Field suggests that 𝔏 *et infames gressus eorum* may have been influenced by A καὶ θρυλοῦσιν; cf. Job 17⁶ where 𝕲 θρύλημα (or θρύλλημα) = 𝕳 משל *by-word*.—16. 𝕲 has a text wholly different from that of 𝕳: τοῦ μακράν σε ποιῆσαι ἀπὸ ὁδοῦ εὐθείας καὶ ἀλλότριον τῆς δικαίας γνώμης — a consequence attached to v.¹⁵ instead of a new

paragraph. This is not a scribal heterogram of the particular words of 𝔐,
but an independent allegorizing reading of the schools. The next section also
is taken as a description of moral folly, and is introduced by the words υἱέ μή
σε καταλάβῃ κακὴ βουλή (cf. BS 7¹). The connection favors the personal
picture of 𝔐; the reading of 𝔊 illustrates the manner in which the expounders
and scribes, in Jerusalem and Alexandria, sometimes dealt with such ethical
texts as this. — 𝔖 writes Impf. at the beginning (and so Bi.), inserts חכמתא as
subj., omits זרה (for the sake of brevity), and for 𝔐 ההליקה has בהכנא, possibly = ההליפה (Baumg.), though this is generally rendered by אחלף (Pink.).
Bi. omits אמריה on rhythmical grounds, but this seems hardly necessary. —
17. 𝔐 אלוף; 𝔊 διδασκαλίαν (𝔊ᵛ μάθησιν), probably in accordance with its
allegorical conception of the passage (cf. Aram. אולפן), and so 𝔗ᴮᵘˣ· Σ ;
𝔖 מרבינא *rearer, educator,* A ἡγεμόνα, Θ ἡγούμενον, 𝔏 *ducem.* Though no
Vrs. renders by *friend,* this sense is assured in Heb., and is the most appropriate here. The st. = *come* or *bring together,* whence Semitic *thousand,* Heb.
leader (head of clan or tribe), Heb. Ar. *friend,* Arab. *compose* (a book),
Aram. *teach;* the origin of the senses *ox* (N. Sem.) and *ship* (Ass., Aram.) is
not clear. — 𝔐 נרית ארהיה; G διαθήκην θείαν = ב' אלהיב (and so 𝔗 Bi), a
better reading than that of 𝔐. — **18.** 𝔐 שׂחה (mil'el); 𝔊ᴮ ᵃˡ· ἔθετο = שׂתה;
𝔊ᵛ ὥρισεν; 𝔖 *she forgets* (שׂ = שׂכחה, repeated from preceding v.) *the
thresholds* (= שׂפתני) *of her house and the way* (= ארה) *of her paths;* 𝔗,
freely, *whose house is in the depth of death; 𝔏 inclinata est . . . domus eius.*
𝔐 שׂחה, fem., can hardly stand with masc. בית (if ב' were meant as collective,
it would probably have a plur. verb); שׂחה (st. third ה), though it occurs in
Qal only once, and then not certainly (Isa. 51²³), may be taken as = *inclines,
sinks* (Ibn Janaḥ), or we may write שׂחח (cf. ψ 107³⁹); perh., however, we
should read נחת. — 𝔐 אל רפאיב; 𝔊 μετὰ τῶν γηγενῶν (H-P 103 γηΐνων) =
א' ר'; γηγ. is rendering of ר' in 9¹⁸, elsewhere of אדם (Jer. 32²⁰) or בני אדם
(ψ 49²⁽³⁾); in WS 7¹ γηγενοῦς πρωτοπλάστου is Adam. Can γηΐνων *earthy*
be the true reading here and 9¹⁸? cf. γήϊνος, Σ Job 4¹⁹ = בעפר. 𝔊 has the
doublet παρὰ τῷ ᾅδῃ = אל שאול (cf. 9¹⁸). The meaning of the stem in ר' is not
certain, possibly = *weak, powerless* (cf. Isa. 14¹⁰); but this can hardly be the
signification of the gentilic ר'. — **19.** On the ending in ישובון see critical note on
1²⁸. — For v.¹⁹ᵃ 𝔊 has two readings: one, which appears to be the earlier (so
Lag.) takes ישנו as pass., καταλαμβάνονται, and for ארחות has ὑπὸ ἐνιαυτῶν
= שׂנה, or ירהו (cf. 1 K. 8⁵⁹ where εν. = ירה), scribal errors, the latter, perh.,
from 3²; the other is identical with 𝔐 except that for היב it puts εὐθείας (𝔊ᵛ
ἀγαθάς), which may be a moralizing interpretation after the manner of v.¹⁶· ¹⁷, or
perh. (Lag.) a marginal note, or (Baumg.) a familiar term, which has ejected
the original word. Neither of these readings offers any advantages over that of
𝔐. — For 𝔐 ישׂיוו 𝔖 has מתדכרין, *remember,* which in the connection yields
no sense, and is emended by Lag. to מדרכון *attain.* 𝔗 omits suff. in באיה,
and, by way of interpretation, adds בשׂלם after ישובון.

21, 22. Conclusion, stating the consequences of good and bad doing.

> 21. For the upright shall dwell in the land,
>   And the perfect shall remain therein;
> 22. But the wicked shall be cut off from the land,
>   And the transgressors shall be rooted out of it.

21. Synonymous, ternary. The reward of the good stated as motive for right conduct. On *upright* see note on v.[7], on *perfect*, note on 1[12]. The reward of good men is permanent abode in the land; the *remain* = *survive* (or *be left*), implies that certain persons are ejected or destroyed from the land (see next verse), in which in all catastrophes the righteous are maintained. The expression *dwell in the land* (not *earth*) refers to the land of Israel. The ancient Israelitish conception (found also in other peoples) was that gods and men were attached to the soil. The god protected his own land and no other, and the citizen as such enjoyed the benefits of this protection. To leave the land was to lose one's connection with its deity (1 S. 26[19] 2 K. 5[17]) and to give up the rewards which his favor promised. Hence in part the anxiety of the Israelitish law to secure to each tribe family and individual man a possession in the land (Ju. 2[6] Ez. 47[13ff.] Nu. 36[9] Ru. 4[6] and the genealogies in Chron. and Neh.), infringement on which was regarded as a great crime (Mic. 2[2] Dt. 19[14] 27[17] Pr. 22[28] 23[10]). Israel, and not any other nation, was Yahweh's own possession and property (Ex. 19[5] Dt. 14[2] 26[18] ψ 135[4], cf. Tit. 2[14] 1 Pet. 2[9]). Thus the expression *dwell in the land* (ψ 37[3. 11. 29], cf. Mt. 5[5]) came to be equivalent to *enjoy the divine favor and all the blessings of life*, and such is its sense here. Though in later times a large part of the Jews dwelt out of Palestine, the old expression held its own as the symbol of happiness, and with it the hope remained of living and dying in the land with which the divine promises were believed to be connected.* — **22.** Synonymous, ternary. The contrasted fate of evildoers. *Wicked* is employed in Pr. as a general term (along with *foolish*) for those who discard and disobey the divine law of wisdom. The primitive sense is

---

* Much of this feeling still remains in countries in which the Jews are excluded from the rights of citizenship; it has almost completely disappeared in countries in which they have full civil recognition.

doubtful, but in OT. it commonly means *morally bad*. It is also a forensic term (the opposite of *just*), signifying *one whose case in law is bad, wrong*, or *adjudged to be bad* (cf. Ex. 2[13]) ; the Causative of the verb = *adjudge one wrong or guilty in court* (17[15] Ex. 22[9(8)] Isa. 50[9] Job 15[6]). In the prophetical and historical books the noun generally means those who violate the moral law ; in the Pss. it is often used, by a natural transition, as a name for the persecutors of Israel (ψ 17[3] 58[10(11)] 75[8(9)] 119[61] *al.*). In Pr. there is no national limitation ; the wicked are they of all nations who disobey the law of right. — The term *transgressors* or *faithless* is here employed as equivalent to *wicked*. The original sense of the word seems to involve the idea of underhand dealing, faithlessness to an agreement, treachery (Ju. 9[23] Jer. 3[20]), but it is extended to include faithlessness to duty and right in general = *transgressors*. In the Pss. it sometimes means Jewish apostates (ψ 25[3]). — The verbs in the verse express violent extirpation by any means, by the hand of man or God. The first (כרת) is the term used in the legal books to express the execution of intolerable offenders (*that person shall be cut off from his people*, Lev. 7[20] *al.*) ; the second (נסח) is once used (Dt. 28[63]) for the expulsion of the nation from its land. The writer of the verse probably has these half-technical uses in mind, but employs the terms in the broadest sense ; unrighteous persons, he says, shall have no place in the land of promise, no claim, that is, to happiness in this life. Here, as elsewhere, the mode of execution of the punishment is not stated, but the divine judgment is to be understood as coming in the way of natural law (courts of law, failure of plans, sickness, natural death), or through special divine interposition (violent death).

20. 𝕳 דרך טובים; 𝕲 τρίβους ἀγαθάς, according to Lag. false reading of the abbrev. טֹב. — **21.** The Grk. MSS. exhibit two renderings, with a number of verbal variations. The one which appears to be nearer to 𝕳, writing χρηστοί and ἄκακοι, is found (as doublet) in Compl. Ald. and (with obel.) 𝔖[II], in 𝕲[A]𝕲 *𝕲ᵡ ᶜ·ᵃ, H-P 23, 103, 109, 147, 248, 252, 253, 254, *al.*, a group which suggests a combination of the recension of Lucian and some other recension ; the other, writing εὐθεῖς and ὅσιοι, is the text of 𝕲[B], and appears to show the hand of an Alexandrian revisor (see note on v.[19]). — **22.** For 𝕳 ורשעים 𝕲 has ὁδοὶ ἀσεβῶν (𝕲[A] ὁδοὶ δὲ ἀσ.), as in ψ 1[6a] (Jäg.), free or careless transcription of a Grk. scribe, perh. corruption of ὅτι (Heid.). — 𝕳 יֻסְּחוּ, Qal

Impf., must be taken as indef., but the parallelism suggests a Pass., as all Vrss. have it (though this may be free rendering); we may point as Hof. (so Bi.), a form which, however, is not found elsewhere; Gr. ירדו, Hof. of נרח; Oort, Frank., Nif. of פה:. — Bi. omits הָאָרֶץ (as perh. gloss to מִמֶּנָה), which in fact does not appear in the similar passages ψ 37[9. 22. 28. 38]; yet such determinations of כרת by nouns of place occur elsewhere (Jer. 35[19] Ez. 25[7] Lev. 17[10]), and both rhythm and syntax appear to demand a word here, מִמֶּנָה being otherwise left without antecedent.

This chapter states the economical or prudential conception of the good life which is the prevailing view of the book of Proverbs (see note on 1[33]) ; the motive urged for good living is the earthly well-being which attends it.   This sort of eudaemonism, in which the individual actor alone is considered, and the reward of virtue is represented not as inward but as outward (long life, peace, honor, riches, see ch. 3), may seem to us ethically defective in several points.   It does not present the good as an independent ideal, to be pursued solely for its own sake ; it does not hold up the highest well-being of the world as the goal and standard of moral conduct ; it says nothing of a sympathetic community and coöperation of men as the instrument for the development of the moral life ; it makes no direct mention of the function of conscience as moral guide ; and it makes the unmodified declaration that virtue is always attended by outward prosperity.   In this last point Pr. represents the old-Hebrew view, which made no analysis of the inner life, conceived of goodness as obedience to outward law, held that the deity controlled every man's life by occasional and immediate intervention, and so necessarily regarded prosperity as the accompaniment of obedience to divine law.   This view is combated in the book of Job ; but it appears that Job's argument made little impression (perhaps by reason of the absence of an ethical conception of the future life), and that many or most of the sages saw nothing more practically helpful than the old position.   As soon as the idea of future compensation was established (WS. 3), the doctrine of present reward was modified ; in Pr. this idea is not accepted.   See the Introduction, § 5, A, and § 6, 4. — The defects of ethical theory mentioned above are in part explained by the aim of the book.   The sages no doubt recognized the function of conscience, and believed in the value of right in itself.   But they probably held that what men need is not ethical theory, but practical considerations which shall help them to live virtuously.   In this they were right — the mass of men are controlled by their relations to one another in society, and by the hope of reward and the fear of punishment.   It is true also that men's experience has led them to believe that goodness is profitable for this life as well as for the life to come.   Further, an ideal element is introduced by the identification of wisdom with the will of God, which is held to be the absolute right, and by the personification of wisdom (ch. 8) as God's first creation and intimate friend.   The sages, it may be inferred, mean to say that he who connects his ethical law with God is provided with a restraining influence so far as he fears God, and with an elevating influence so far as he loves him.   In certain passages (as, for example, 2^{10}) they appear to reach the ultimate moral conception, namely, the ethical union of man with God conceived of as the moral ideal.   These considerations must modify our judgment of what seems to be a baldly prudential scheme of ethical life.

III. Three independent discourses or paragraphs, introduced each by the address ‹my son,› all more or less fragmentary. The first (v.$^{1-10}$) consists of exhortations to follow the teacher's instruction (v.$^{1-2}$) and observe kindness and truth (v.$^{3.4}$), to trust in Yahweh and fear him (v.$^{5-8}$), and to honor him with one's wealth (v.$^{9.10}$).   The second (v.$^{11-20}$) sets forth the value of divine chastening (v.$^{11.12}$), the preciousness of Wisdom (v.$^{13-18}$), and her function in creation (v.$^{19.20}$).   The third (v.$^{21-35}$) describes the safety which comes from discretion (v.$^{21-24}$) and from the protection of Yahweh (v.$^{25.26}$), enjoins neighborly kindness (v.$^{27-31}$), and sets forth the retribution of the upright and the wicked (v.$^{32-35}$). The third approaches, in parts (v.$^{27-35}$), the form of discourse of chs. 25–27.   The poetical structure of the chapter is distichal, with four-line strophes, though in some places the form is obscure.

FIRST DISCOURSE. V. 1–10.

1. My son, forget not my instruction,
   But keep my commandments in mind;
2. For length of days and years of life
   And peace will they bestow on thee.

3. Let not kindness and faithfulness leave thee —
   Bind them on thy neck [] * —
4. So wilt thou find favor and good ‹ repute ›
   With God and man.

5. Trust to Yahweh with all thy heart,
   And lean not on thine own understanding;
6. In all thy ways acknowledge him,
   And he will smooth thy paths.

7. Be not wise in thine own eyes —
   Fear Yahweh, and turn away from sin —
8. Then will there be health to thy ‹ body ›
   And refreshment to thy bones.

9. Honor Yahweh with thy wealth,
   With the best of all thy revenue —
10. Then will thy barns be filled with ‹ corn ›
    And thy vats will overflow with must.

The teacher exhorts the pupil to remember his instruction, urging the advantage it will bring him. — **1.** Synonymous, ternary. Exhortation. Lit.: *let thy heart* (= mind) *keep* (= guard, preserve) *my commandments*. *Son* = "pupil," as in 1⁸. The content of the *instruction* (law, *tora*) is to be inferred from the precepts of the Book of Pr.; it is almost exclusively moral and religious, never national, but always individual, very rarely ceremonial, never dogmatic. It thus stands in contrast with the *tora* of the prophet, which is national-religious (sole worship of Yahweh and obedience to his will), and with that of the priest (Pentateuch), which is ritual. The sage presents himself as authority and source of moral wisdom; priest and prophet speak only in the name of Yahweh, declaring his word. The prophet, it is said, who shall speak a word not given him by God shall die (Dt. 18²⁰), even though he has been deceived by Yahweh (Ez. 14⁹); the sage finds his word in his own mind — in the prophet this is a crime (Ez. 13². ³). This diversity is the result of the difference of the points of view of different periods of Israelitish history. The sages represent a period of reflection, in which human life is studied for its own sake, and its natural laws investigated. —

---

* The Received Text adds: *Write them on the tablet of thy mind* (lit. *heart*).

2. Single sentence, which may be taken as binary, or as quaternary-ternary. The reward. Long life is considered in OT. to be one of the chief blessings of man's lot (Ex. 20^{12}), including, as it does, the idea of happiness (so that the first line might be rendered : *a long and happy life*). Sheol offered nothing — the longer one lived on earth the greater one's opportunities for work and enjoyment (Isa. 38^{19} 65^{20}).[*] *Peace* is originally *wholeness, completeness of condition*. It is used of bodily health (Gen. 29^6), of political concord (Jud. 4^{17}), of friendly relation between men (ψ 41$^{9(10)}$), of national tranquillity and safety (Jer. 6^{14} 33^6), and, as here, of a general condition of freedom from danger and disturbance.[†] The reference is primarily to outward quiet, though inward serenity is of course involved. This delightful ideal, a long and peaceful life, is the favorite one in Proverbs. It is represented both as the natural product of devotion to wisdom (intelligent uprightness of life), and as the gift of God — two ideas easily harmonized by the conception of wisdom as having its root in reverence for God. — *Bestow on thee*, lit. *add to thee*.

3, 4. An injunction parallel to that of v.$^{1. 2}$, and apparently intended as explanation or definition of it. — **3.** Synonymous, ternary (or, ternary-binary). The verse is perhaps epexegetical of v.^{1}, a description of the law of wisdom as the maintenance of kindness and faithfulness. This combination of qualities (or its equivalent) occurs often in OT. (Gen. 24^{49} Ex. 34^6 Dt. 7^9 ψ 25^{10} 85$^{10(11)}$ Pr. 14^{22} 16^6 20^{28} *al.*) as the expression of perfectly good relations between man and man, or between man and God. *Kindness* is friendly good feeling and the conduct appropriate thereto (see note on 2^8), love of man for man (Esth. 2^{17}) or of man for God (Hos. 6^6). It is not properly *mercy*, compassion, clemency, forgiveness (for which ideas Heb. has other expressions, Dt. 13$^{17(18)}$ Ex. 34^9 Dan. 9$^{9(8)}$). Yahweh is good and kind to Israel because he loves the nation — that is the normal condition of things ; and

---

[*] Cf. Cic. *De Senectute*.

[†] The OT. *shelem* (RV. *peace-offering*) is an offering which completes one's duty to God or makes one whole with him by the fulfilment of a vow or by a free gift of gratitude for favors received. Arabic *Islam* ("submission, resignation") is the putting one's self in a position of soundness with God by faith, obedience, and submission.

even when his kindness is brought into connection with the removal of transgression, as in ψ 103, it still remains simple kindness. —*Faithfulness* (*firmness*) is steadfastness, fidelity to one's word and to the obligations which spring from one's relations with men. It is thus sometimes equivalent to *truthfulness* (ψ 15²) or to *truth* (1 K. 10⁶ Dt. 13¹⁴⁽¹⁵⁾), but has usually, as here, a wider signification. — The two qualities together, complementing each other (love being thus saved from feebleness, and fidelity from harshness), may be said to form a perfect moral character. They are to be attached to the neck not as an amulet to ward off evil (though such ornaments may originally have been amulets),* but, as the general connection indicates, as a necklace (1⁹) or a seal-chain (Gen. 38¹⁸, possibly as bearing a seal-ring), that one may carry them with him always, and have them in remembrance. — The Heb. adds the parallel line : *write them on the tablet of thy mind*, a form of expression which occurs only here and in 7⁸ Jer. 17¹, but the same idea is found in Dt. 30¹⁴ Jer. 31³³. The allusion is to the tablets of the decalogue, and to the command (Dt. 6⁸·⁹) to write the divine precepts on hands and forehead, doorposts and gates (the later phylacteries, etc.)† ; cf. the Arab. expression *to write a thing with a needle on the inner corner of the eye*. The moral law is not only to be accepted as an external code, but also to be received into the mind and form part of the man's nature (cf. Jer. 31³³). — This third clause is lacking in some Gk. Mss., and is probably not original — the verse is complete without it, and it mars the symmetrical distichal form of the paragraph ; it may have been inserted by a Heb. scribe from 7³, where it is in place. — The general idea of *kindness* tended to pass into that of *pity* for the poor and *almsgiving;* so the Lat. Vulg. here has *misericordia*, and the Grk. a word (ἐλεημοσύναι) which was later employed for *alms* (BS. 3¹⁴ Mt. 6² Lu. 11⁴¹ Diog. Laert. 5, 17), and has given us our word *eleemosynary*, though here it seems to mean *pity, mercy.* — **4.** Single sentence, ternary. The recompense.

---

* The preëxilian Israelites wore amulets called *saharon* (Isa. 3¹⁸, cf. Jud. 8²¹·²⁶) and *laḥash* (Isa. 3²⁰) ; apparently also earrings served as amulets (Gen. 35⁴, cf. Hos. 2¹³⁽¹⁵⁾). How long this practice continued is uncertain. The *thummim* (*tummim*, sometimes improperly identified with Arab. *tamima*) was not an amulet.

† Such legends also appear to have been originally of the nature of amulets.

The Heb. reads: *And thou wilt find* [lit. *and find*] *favor and good understanding in the sight of God and man*, in which the term *understanding* is unsatisfactory, since *good understanding* (or, *intelligence*) is not of the nature of recompense, parallel to *favor*, but is rather the cause of the latter (so 13[15] *good understanding gives favor*). Most of the Vrss. have found difficulty with the expression. The Grk. attaches the first part (through the word *favor*) to v.[3], and then renders: *and devise excellent things in the sight of the Lord and of men* (so quoted freely in Rom. 12[17] 2 Cor. 8[21]) ; but this does not agree with the connection, from which we expect the statement of the result of acting as v.[3] enjoins. The Peshitta Syriac has . . . *favor and good and understanding*, and the Targum . . . *favor and understanding and good*. A slight change in the Heb. gives *name* instead of *understanding;* the expression *favor and good name* (cf. 22[1]) expresses the recompense required by the connection. — On *favor* see note on 1[9]. To *find favor* is to be acceptable, approved, well thought of (Gen. 6[8] Ru. 2[10]) ; a kind and faithful character, says the sage, will be acceptable both to God and to men (so Lu. 2[32]) ; *in the sight of* = " on the part of," " with " ; the same isolation of moral qualities as the condition of the divine favor is found in Isa. 1[18] [19] 66[2] ψ 24 *al.*, but is more complete and persistent in Pr. than in any other Biblical book. The *good reward* of right doing (if we accept this reading) is this favor and the benefits (friendship, protection, aid) which naturally flow from it.

5-10. The blessing attendant on trusting and honoring God. Exhortation to trust (v.[5]), acknowledge (v.[6]), and fear him (v.[7]), the result of which will be health (v.[8]). Exhortation to honor him in the use of wealth (v.[9]), the result of which will be abundance of wealth (v.[10]). — The preceding paragraph (v.[1-4]) deals with the ethical side of life, this with the religious side.

5-8. Benefit of dependence on God. — 5. Synonymous, ternary, or ternary-binary. The Grk. has *God* instead of *Yahweh;* the interchange of divine names seems not to be significant in Proverbs, but the Grk. preference for *God* may indicate the later Jewish feeling. To *trust to* God is, from the connection, to regard him as the source of wisdom and power, the guide in the moral life

and in all other things, to obey his law, and have confidence in
him ; see note on 1^7. We may render *trust in*, understanding this
expression in the sense indicated. *With all the heart* = with the
whole conviction and force of the mind, absolutely. — Opposed to
this posture of mind is the *leaning on one's own understanding*
(insight, wisdom) as on a prop or staff (2 S. 1^6 Mic. 3^{11} Job 24^{23}).
The assumption is that man's intellect, apart from God, will not
guide him aright. This assumption is founded not on any theory
of man's native depravity (such a theory does not exist in OT.),
but on observation of life. Man is often blinded by passion and
at the mercy of temptation ($1^{10\text{-}14}$), but he may avoid sin by his
own will (1^{10}) if he will give heed to God's law, which is a fixed
rule of conduct unaffected by the mutations and perversions of
human passion. Man, further, is fallible, and does not always
know what is best to do — he must have confidence in a higher
wisdom if he wishes to feel secure and be free from anxiety. This
sense of security and peace is involved in the term *trust* (cf.
Ju. 8^{11}). The sage probably does not mean to exclude human
thought and effort. In times of great national distress prophets
and psalmists sometimes represent the military strength of nations
as nothing when compared with the absolute power of the God of
Israel (Hos. 1^7 Isa. 2^{17} 10. 31 ψ $20^{7(8)}$ $118^{8.9}$) ; but here, as generally in OT., the idea seems to be that human wisdom and strength
must be guided and sustained by God. — **6**. Single sentence, ternary. Repetition of the injunction, with statement of the result
of obedience. *Acknowledge* = *know, have intimate acquaintance
with*, that is, know and obey the divine law, recognize its suprem-
acy and take it as guide. To *smooth* is to *make level;* the metaphor is derived from the preparation of a highway, as in Isa. 40^3.
The usual way of human life, the sage intimates, is full of inequali-
ties and difficulties, but he who has in mind the law of God will
find these hindrances removed and his path made easy. The
reference is not to nice moral problems which shall be solved by
the divine law, but, as the context indicates, to external difficulties
and dangers, such as poverty, sickness, enmities, evil allurements.
The *paths* are all a man's ways, social, commercial, political,
religious ; he has only to do right and trust in God, and affairs
will be made easy for him — he will enjoy prosperity in the sense

of v.[10. 16. 24. 25] ; it is the old doctrine of the prosperity of the righteous. — At the end of the verse some Grk. MSS. add *and thy foot
shall not stumble*, a scribal insertion from v.[23]. — **7**. Synonymous,
ternary, or, ternary-quaternary. Repetition of the warning against
self-confidence. Progressive parallelism. The holding one's self
wise is represented as the contrast to or negation of fearing God,
an antithesis similar to that of v.[5] — it is assumed that to trust to
one's own wisdom is to follow another law than that of God,
ordinary human standards of judgment being different from the
divine standard ; a somewhat different view of conceit of wisdom
is given in Eccl. 7[16]. The *fear of Yahweh*, which is assumed to
be the true wisdom (as in 1[7]), is defined as turning away from
sin (lit. *evil*). The *evil* in this case cannot = *misfortune*, escape
from which would then be the result of fearing God (as in v.[6b]),
for the verb means a voluntary avoidance, and expresses moral
character (as in Job 1[1] Pr. 16[6]). The fear of Yahweh, it is
implied, gives the proper ethical norm of life, and *wisdom*, as
generally in chs. 1–9, is understood to involve a religious element.
Clem. of Alex. (*Strom.*, 155) has *fear God who alone is mighty*, a
free expansion, perhaps suggested by Mt. 10[28] (Lag.). — **8**. Synonymous, ternary-binary. The reward. The first line may be read :
it (the fearing Yahweh and departing from sin) *will be*, etc., but it
is better to take *health* as subject of the verb ; and *then* may be
inserted (after the Grk.) as giving a better syntactical connection
with the preceding verses. Instead of *body* the Heb. has *navel*, an
improbable reading, since elsewhere (Ez. 16[4], and a similar term
Cant. 7[2]) the term is not used for the whole body and being. A
slight change in the Heb. gives the word for *body* (so the Grk.
reads) or the word for *flesh*. The latter term occurs in 11[17] for
the whole man ; the combination *body and bone* (= *flesh and
bone*) is found, in this sense, in Gen. 29[14] 2 Sam. 5[1] Job 2[5] (and cf.
Job 21[24] 30[30]). Each of these terms is used as = *self* (designation
of the spiritual from the physical), as in Neh. 9[37] ψ 16[9] 35[10] 63[1(2)],
and we may here render : *thou wilt have health and refreshment*.
Of these two words the first is properly an abstract noun of action,
healing (deliverance from disease), and the second, *refreshment*, is
that which refreshes (lit. *drink*, as in Hos. 2[7] ψ 102[10]). The sense
of the verse is that obedience to the law of God secures for a man

a thoroughly healthy and happy condition of being. The happiness is primarily freedom from bodily and other outward ills, but necessarily involves inward peace.

9, 10. Religious use of wealth. — 9. Synonymous, ternary-binary (or, ternary). The word here rendered *revenue* (RV. *increase*) commonly refers to agricultural produce, and this sense is indicated by v.[10]; elsewhere in Pr. (as, for example, in 16[8]) the word appears to have a wider meaning. The reference in the injunction seems to be rather to a general righteous employment of riches than to the payment of the legal tithes. There is elsewhere in this part of the book (chs. 1–9) no reference to the ceremonial law as obligatory (in 7[14] sacrifice is mentioned as a popular observance), and the immediate context favors the more general interpretation. The term here rendered *the best* (ראשׁית) is so used in Am. 6[1] ψ 78[51] 105[36] (of persons) 1 Sam. 2[29] Am. 6[6] (of things). See the injunction to give freely in v.[27], and compare the similar injunction in Ben-Sira 29[9. 11]. God would thus be honored by obedience to the commands respecting the care of the poor and other general moral precepts. — The sense will, however, be substantially the same if we translate *with* (or, *out of*) *the first-fruits of all thy revenue*, the reference then being to the triennial tithe for the poor (Dt. 14[28. 29]) and the annual tithe for the temple-ministers (Dt. 18[12. 13] Nu. 18[12. 13]). These were doubtless regarded as obligatory by all pious Israelites, though in Prov. they are elsewhere silently passed over as part of the acknowledged routine of religious life, observance of which did not necessarily argue a genuine spirit of obedience to the moral law. — *With* is lit. *out of*, a form of expression which is meant to indicate that it is a portion of one's wealth that is to be thus used. The verse reads in the Grk.: *Honor the Lord out of thy righteous labors, and give him the first of thy fruits of righteousness,* which appears to be a scholastic paraphrase or interpretation of the Hebrew. — **10.** Synonymous-ternary. Statement of the reward of such use of wealth. Our Heb. text reads: *thy barns will be filled with plenty;* but this last term is elsewhere always adverbial (Gen. 41[29] Eccl. 5[12(11)]), and never a thing with which something may be filled; an easy emendation (suggested by the Grk.) gives *corn*, parallel to *must*. *Corn* is a general term for cereals. *Must* (תירוש, which the Vrss. here all render by *wine*) is the wine-crop, the grape-juice expressed and gathered into vats; it is frequently mentioned, along with corn and oil, as one of the main crops of the land of Canaan (Dt. 7[13] Neh. 5[11]). Apparently it was not commonly drunk till it was fermented; it is spoken of as exhilarating (Ju. 9[13]) and intoxicating (Hos. 4[11]). The reward of honoring Yahweh is here physical, in keeping with the old-Hebrew idea. The agricultural life contemplated suits the Palestinian Jews throughout the whole of the OT. period; abundance of the standard crops, corn and wine, was a synonym of prosperity down to the final dispersion of the people (A.C. 70). So *wealth*, in v.[9], = "agricultural revenue."

III. 1. 𝔊 νομίμων (H–P, 68 *al.* νόμων) takes תורת as plu., possibly (Heid.) a Pharisaic reading to include the oral tradition, more probably induced by the plu. in ᵇ; Cl. Alex. θεσμῶν, perh. from memory (so the Draconian laws were called). — 𝔊 ῥήματά for 𝔐 מצוה is rhetorical, untechnical rendering, not reference to the decalogue. — נצר is properly *preserve, keep safe* (and so substantially = *remember*), though "keeping in mind" may be practically equivalent to "observing, obeying" (ψ 25[10] 78[7]). — **3.** Jäger gets rid of the triplet form by attaching ᵃ to v.² (changing אל to לא), but this clause belongs by its content to v.³. It is better to omit ᶜ, which is lacking in 𝔊ᴮ ᵃˡ. (found in 𝔊ᴬ ᵃˡ. ΘΣ Compl., Ald., Cl. Al., Proc., 𝔖ᴴ *sub ast.* 𝕷𝔖𝕿); see note on 7³. The different positions given the clause in Grk. MSS. suggest that it is a gloss (Lag.). — 𝔊 ἐλεημοσύναι (for חסד) here = *kindness, mercy*, as in Gen. 47[29], not *alms*. — **4.** For 𝔐 Impv. מצא Bi. writes תמצא, which, however, is unnecessary, the Impv. being not uncommon in prot. and apod. of a conditional sentence (6⁶ 8³³ 9⁶ *al.*). — 𝔐 שכל is taken by 𝔊 as Impv., προνοῦ, against the connection; 𝕷 *disciplinam*, a meaning which the word will hardly bear; as שכל (perhaps occasioned by 13[15] ψ 111[10]) here affords no satisfactory sense, we may emend to שׂים, which suits the connection, though it is without support from MSS. or Vrss. — 𝔖𝕿 take טוב as subst, inserting ו before it, 𝕿 following the order of 𝔐, 𝔖 transposing ·· and ··. This latter fact may seem (Baumg.) to indicate that 𝔖 here follows 𝕿, only introducing an error; but elsewhere 𝕿 seems to be dependent on 𝔖, though it sometimes shows a correction after 𝔐. — **5.** 𝔐 אל (twice); read על (so 𝔊 in second occurrence); throughout OT. we should probably emend אל after בטח to על. — 𝔐 יהוה; 𝔊 θεῷ. — **6.** 𝔐 ירשרו; 𝔊 αὐτήν, *scil.* σοφίαν, against the connection; 𝔊 takes ᵇ as telic. — **7.** 𝔐 יהוה 𝔊 τὸν θεὸν. — **8.** In רפאות רהי it is doubtful whether the subject of רהי is רי or the statement in v.⁷ᵇ; in the latter case we should expect היא after רי, in the former case a connecting particle, as in fact 𝔊 introduces the verse with τότε, and 𝔖 with telic רי; a connective seems preferable: *so will there be* or *that there may be*. רפאות is an Aramaic form. — 𝔐 שר *navel*; 𝔊 σώματι, and so

𝔖ᴴ; 𝔖 ‎בסר‎; 𝔏 = 𝔚; 𝔗 ‎כּוּנִישׁר‎ (Lag.) or ‎כּוּנְשׁר‎ (Buxt.) = 𝔚 (the word, in Syr. ‎כּוּנְרְשׁר‎ or ‎כּוּנְשׁר‎, seems to be a compd. of ‎שׁר‎, but the force of the first element is doubtful). Read ‎כְּשׁר‎, with 𝔊, Cler., Bi.; or, with Vog., Schl., Ew., Hi., Oort, Kamp., ‎שְׁאֵר‎. — On 𝔊 ἐπιμέλεια as rendering of ‎שׁקוי‎ see Schleusner's note; Procop. ἐπιμένεια *stability*; 'A ποτισμός, of which Deissmann (*Bibelstudien*, p. 152) finds an example as early as B.C. 240. — **9.** 𝔊 renders ‎הון‎ by δικαίων πόνων, a homiletical expression intended to warn against the unjust acquisition of wealth; for a similar use of π. see BS. 14¹⁵ 28¹⁵, and for the idea Pr. 10¹⁶; *labor = wealth* Eccl. 2²² *al.* 𝔊 similarly defines ‎הבואת‎ by δικαιοσύνης, and further omits ‎כל‎, which term, here unnecessary though not out of place, may have been lacking in the Heb. MS. of 𝔊. — **10.** 𝔚 ‎שֶׂבַע‎; 𝔊 πλησμονῆς σίτου (so rightly Procop.; the text has σίτῳ by scribal error, or, if πλ. did not originally stand in the Grk. the Dat. σίτῳ might have been used after the vb. πίμπληται); but a marg. note in 𝔖ᴴ (which = 𝔚) states that the σ. is found neither in the Heb. nor in the Grk., from which it may be inferred that the Grk. MSS. here varied. The text of 𝔊 presents a conflation of two readings, πλ. = ‎שׂבע‎ and σ. = ‎שֶׂבֶר‎, of which the latter is more likely to be original, and the former a correction after Heb. The reading ‎שׁבר‎ suits the context and is adopted by Oort, and regarded as original by Frankenberg; it is perh. against it that in the combination *corn and wine* in OT. it is always ‎דגן‎ and never ‎שׁבר‎ that is used, though this is not decisive, and ‎שׁבר‎ seems to be required by the parallelism; for its use see Gen. 42¹ *al.* Am. 8⁵ Neh. 10³².

11, 12. A separate paragraph (a quatrain) on **the benefit of divine chastening**, possibly here placed as a modification of the preceding paragraph, to explain cases in which worldly prosperity does not follow rectitude. It would then be of the nature of an editorial insertion.

> 11. Reject not, my son, the instruction of Yahweh,
> And spurn not his reproof,
> 12. For whom ‹ he › loves he reproves,
> And he afflicts ‹ him › in whom he delights.

11. Synonymous, ternary- (or, quaternary-) binary. Instead of *reject* we may render *despise* (the general sense is the same in the two renderings), and instead of *spurn* (lit. *loathe*) the nearly equivalent *be wearied out with, weary of* (so RV.), as in Gen. 27⁴⁶; The Grk. has *faint not* (so quoted in Heb. 12⁵), = " give not up thy self-command and endurance," which may be an interpretation of our text, or may represent another Heb. term. — **12.** Synonymous, ternary (in the emended text). In the first line the Heb. has *Yahweh* (*Yahweh loves* instead of *he loves*), which is a scribal insertion (*explicitum*) for clearness. — The second line reads, according to the Masoretic pointing, *and* [= *yea, reproves him*] *as a father* [*reproves*] *the son in whom he delights*, or *delights in him as a father in his son*. These renderings, though possible, are hard, and the suggested representation of God as father would perhaps make a difficulty, since it would be unique in Proverbs. The translation *afflicts* given above (which the Heb. consonants permit) is supported by the parallelism, by the Grk., and by Job 5[18]. The parallelism naturally suggests (though it does not absolutely require) an explicit reference to disciplinary suffering. The Grk. has *for whom the Lord loves he reproves, and scourges every son whom he receives* (so quoted in Heb. 12[6]), in which *scourges* = *afflicts*. Job 5[17. 18] reads :

> Happy is the man whom God reproves,
> Therefore despise [or, reject] not the instruction of Shaddai,
> For he wounds and binds up,
> He smites and his hand heals.

The similarity between the passages in Job and Prov. makes it probable that one is an imitation of the other, or that the expressions used were current in the schools.* — The word *son* in second line should be changed to *him*, so as to secure a better parallelism. — Whichever translation be adopted, the sense is the same : the suffering of a good man is to be regarded as a divine chastening dictated by love. The thought is found in Job 4. 5 (Eliphaz) and 33 (Elihu), but only here in Proverbs. The sages of Prov. elsewhere adopt the old view (defended by the three friends in Job) that suffering is always the punishment of sin ; the author of our passage (following the school of Eliphaz and Elihu) considers the exception to the rule, and finds the explanation of the suffering of the righteous in the disciplinary love of God, which is also the NT. view (it is suggested in OT. in such passages as Am. 4[6-11]). Though hinted by the earliest of the Israelitish ethical writers (Amos), it appears to have made no lasting impression till after

---

* Recent writers are divided in opinion on the question of priority between Job 5 and Pr. 1-9. As Pr. agrees, in the point of view under discussion, with Ben-Sira, it should probably be regarded as the later, unless Job be put very late (in the second or first century B.C.). In both Pr. and Job it is individual rather than national suffering that is contemplated.

the acceptance (in the second or first century B.C.) of the doctrine of ethical immortality.*

11. For various unimportant var. lect. of 𝔊 in v.[11. 12] see H–P. 𝔐 רְנִי should probably be omitted as (early) scribal insertion. — **12.** אֶת without Makkef, as in ψ 47[5] 60[2], probably a scribal accident. יהוה in v.[12] is sustained by all Mss. and Vrss., but may be omitted (as *explicitum*) with advantage to the rhythm. For 𝔐 וּכְאָב read Hif. יַכְאִב, after 𝔊 μαστιγοῖ, and as in Job 5[18]; Pi. כאב (Dys., cf. Cappell.) is possible, but does not occur in OT. — 𝔐 אֶת בֶן; 𝔊 (exc. H–P 106) πάντα υἱόν, adopted by Bi.; the π. is natural, and may be rhetorical explanation; the universality indicated by 𝔐 in ⁱ is involved in the Heb. of ᵇ. The בן, found in all texts, probably suggested the pointing כְאָב, and must be early; yet it is not appropriate here (it probably has no connection with the common address בני of v.[11]); we expect אשר or כל אשר, and this reading may be adopted as the most probable. — 𝔐 ירצה; 𝔊 παραδέχεται, free rendering of 𝔐, as in Mal. 1[13]; 𝔖𝔗 רדי seems to be repetition from preceding cl., or, instead of ירצה they perh. read ירצה or יררה.

13-20. Excellence of wisdom. — A group of 8 couplets, v.[19. 20] forming a separate sub-paragraph.

13. Happy the man who finds wisdom,
    And the man who gains understanding;

14. For the profit she brings is better than [ ] silver,†
    And the revenue she bestows than gold.

15. She is more precious than corals —
    No treasures [ ]‡ can compare with her.

16. Long life is in her right hand,
    In her left hand riches and honor.

17. Her ways are ways of pleasantness,
    And all her paths are peace;

18. She is a tree of life to those who grasp her —
    Happy are they who hold her fast.

19. Yahweh by wisdom founded the earth,
    By understanding established the heavens.

20. By his knowledge the waters well forth,
    And the clouds drop down dew.

13. Synonymous, ternary, or, quaternary-ternary. The Grk. and Syr. Vrss. have two terms for *man* (*human being . . . mortal*),

---

* On the doctrine of the Talmud, see Weber, *Theol.* § 69.

† Heb.: *better than the profit of silver.*

‡ Heb.: *no treasures of thine.*

and it is not improbable that the Heb. originally had such a variation, perhaps = *homo* . . . *vir*, or two equivalent words = *homo*. Whether wisdom is acquired by one's own effort or received as a gift from God, is not said ; the two points of view were probably not distinguished by the writer.   The beatitudes of Prov. all (with the exception of 16^{20}) relate to the individual moral life, standing thus in contrast with those of the legal and historical books (and ψ 32^{12} 146^5 Eccl. 10^{17}) which refer to national life, and to those of the Psalter, which, with a few exceptions, have a personal-religious tone.*—14. Synonymous, ternary-binary (in the emended text). Literally : *for her acquisition is better than the acquisition of silver, and her revenue than gold.*   The expression rendered *her acquisition* may mean *the acquiring her*, or *what she acquires* (*her gain, profit*), or *what she produces* (= *the gain that one gets from her*), or *her trade*, or *trading in her* (= RV. *the merchandise of it*, the word *merchandise* being used in the now obsolete sense of *commerce*).   The meaning seems to be fixed by the second clause, in which *her revenue* must signify either *what comes to her* (*her income*), or *what she yields* to her possessor (*the income from her*) ; the second of these senses is supported by the connection, in which the topic is the advantage that man derives from wisdom, and by the similar passage 8^{19} *my fruit is better than gold and my revenue than silver*, that is, as v.^{17} suggests, what she has to offer to her followers.   From the parallelism we may conclude that *her acquisition* or *gain* signifies *the profit she brings*. The translation *for to acquire her is better than to acquire silver and to gain her* (*is better*) *than gold*, though intelligible and not out of keeping with the context, is hardly allowed by the Hebrew. Grk. : *for it is better to traffic for her than for treasures of gold and silver;* cf. Mt. 13$^{44-46}$.   Latin Vulgate : *for the acquisition of her is better than traffic in silver and her fruit is of best and purest gold.*   Peshitta Syriac and Targum : *for traffic in her is better than traffic in silver and her fruit than pure gold.*   These various translations give the same general idea.   The parallelism here and 8^{19} suggests the omission of the second *profit* (or *acquisi-*

---

* The Psalmist, however, often speaks as a member of the nation; his individual experience is the common one.

tion) in first line. — In ψ 19¹⁰ ⁽¹¹⁾ similar praise is given to the
Tora ; the points of view of the sage and the psalmist are different.
— **15.** Synonymous, ternary. The Heb. has *all thy treasures cannot* (= *none of thy treasures can*) *compare with her ;* the Possess.
Pron., which is inappropriate, is better omitted with all the ancient
Versions. The meaning of the Heb. noun in first cl. (פנינים) is
uncertain. It was unknown to the ancient Vrss.: Grk., Syr.,
Targ., here have *precious stones*, Lat. Vulg. has *all wealth ;* elsewhere Lat. has a number of other renderings ; in Job 28¹⁸ Targ.
has *pearls.* The rendering *corals* is based on Lam. 4⁷, where the
word is used to indicate ruddiness of complexion. There and
here RV. has *rubies* in the text, and *corals* in the margin (see
Job 28¹⁸) ; the ruby would be appropriate in Lam. 4⁷ by its color,
but the word here employed never occurs in lists of gems (such
as Ex. 28¹⁷⁻²⁰ 39¹⁰⁻¹³ Ez. 28¹³), but only in poetical books (Lam.,
Job, Prov.). The coral was highly valued by the ancients (Plin.,
H.N., 32, 11), and, as it was found on the coast of India and in
the Red Sea, might well have been known to the Jews. The rendering *pearls* (Bochart, Ewald, Reuss, Noyes, Strack, *al.*) would
suit if the complexion in Lam. 4⁷ could be understood as pearly ;
corals is favored by Gesen., Fleischer, De., Kamphausen, and
others. *Treasures* is lit. *what is desired, desirable, precious.*
Wisdom is a source of gain (v.¹⁴) and is thus precious. — Between
the clauses of the Heb. text the Grk. inserts *nothing evil shall
resist her, she is well known to* (or *easily recognizable by*) *all who
approach her ;* the first of these added clauses may be a corrupt
form of the Heb. second cl. (perhaps for *nothing desirable can be
set over against her*), and the second may come in like manner
from Heb. first clause. The addition is an interruption of the
connection, and its meaning is obscure. — **16.** Equivalent clauses,
ternary. At the beginning of second cl. *and* may be inserted, with
the Grk., and after the prevailing norm of the couplets. The preceding description of the excellence of wisdom is figurative —
nothing is said of the precise nature of the benefits she confers.
Here we have an explicit statement of the material rewards that
attend her ; see n. on v.² *Long life* is lit. *length of days.* The
riches and honor, here mentioned in addition to *long life*, are to be
taken literally. The sage's point of view seems to be twofold.

On the one hand, his conception of wisdom includes prudence and sagacity, qualities that usually secure both wealth and the esteem of men; cf. such passages as 10^4 11^{26} 12^{11} 14^{31} 19^6 21^{22} 22^{29} 24^{3-6} 27^{23} 31^{10-31} — this idea runs through the whole book. These qualities do not exclude the higher side of the conception of wisdom which appears elsewhere in the book. On the other hand, there is the idea that God, by some direct intervention or according to the general laws of his government of the world, bestows prosperity on those who obey the precepts of wisdom. — After this verse the Grk. adds: *out of her mouth proceeds righteousness, and law and mercy she bears on her tongue;* cf. Isa. 45^{23} *out of my mouth proceeds righteousness* (Yahweh is the speaker) and Pr. 31^{26} *and the law of kindness* [= *kindly instruction*] *is on her tongue* (said of the good housewife). This couplet, which is not in keeping with the context, is the addition of an annotator who felt that the passage should contain not a Pharisaic glorification of the Tora (Heid.), but a recognition of the ethical elements of wisdom. Our present Grk. text of $31^{26\,b}$ (on which see note) is different from the clause here cited, and the latter must have been translated from the Heb. or from a Grk. text which followed the Hebrew; the Grk. should probably here read: *the law of kindness*, etc. The ethical element introduced by the Grk. lies outside the idea of the Heb. sage, whose purpose is simply to describe wisdom as the *summum bonum*. — **17.** Synonymous, binary, or ternary. The *pleasantness* and *peace* are to be interpreted according to v.^{16}: a life controlled by intellectual and moral wisdom will be free from disturbances and cares. Cf. Job 5^{24} where peace is the reward of the man whom God instructs. It is outward peace that is primarily meant, but this would doubtless be accompanied, in the view of the writer, by serenity of mind; the Heb. conception of life, as is apparent throughout the Book of Proverbs, was distinctly objective, but it necessarily included, as all human thought does, the posture of soul. *Peace!* is the common salutation among men in OT. (as now among the Arabs), a general expression, covering all the outward conditions of life; the distinctively inward application of the term does not appear in OT. Cf. Jno. 14^{27} 16^{31}. — **18.** Synonymous, probably ternary-binary. *Tree of life* is a figurative expression (probably a commonplace of the poetical vocabulary), equivalent (as appears from 11^{30} 13^{22} 15^4) to *source of long life and peace;* the statement of this verse is thus identical in meaning with that of v.$^{16. 17}$. The poetical image of lifegiving fruit (found also Ez. 47^{12}, and cf. the *fountain of life*, Pr. 10^{11} *al.*) is probably connected with the conception of a primitive sacred tree of life, and it is not unlikely that the allusion here is to the tree of Gen. 2. 3; if this be so, it is the only such allusion, besides that of Ez. 47^{12}, in OT. (the description of the garden of God in Ez. 28 has no mention of this particular tree). In Genesis the *life* is physical; the man, it is said, would have lived forever if he had eaten of the fruit of the tree, even after he had violated the command by eating of the other tree (Gen. 3^{22}).* Here also the *life* is physical, as appears from v.^{16}; there is no reference or allusion to existence beyond the grave. But the sage departs from the account in Gen. in that he attributes long life to a quality of mind.

19, 20. A separate paragraph. **From a description of the blessings which wisdom confers on man, the sage goes on to exalt it as a guiding principle of God in the creation and maintenance of the physical world;** the same conception is found in 8^{18-31} (and cf. Job 28^{20-28}), BS. 1^{24} WSol. 7. This view is characteristic of the Wisdom books, while in the Prophets (Am. 4^{13} 5^8 9^6 Isa. 40 — there are no such references in preëxilian writings) and the Psalms (89. 104. 139) God's works are cited as illustrations of his greatness and his care for his people. The cosmical conception, which dwells on the order of the world for its own sake, belongs to the post-prophetic period and indicates an influence of Greek thought.† This paragraph obviously connects itself with the preceding and not with the following (which is an exhortation to obey the laws of wisdom) ; whether it originally formed part of a larger section is uncertain. — **19.** Synonymous, quaternary-ternary. Wisdom as primeval attribute of the Creator.

---

* On the tree of life in Gen., see Dillmann, *Genesis;* Budde, *Bibl. Urgeschichte;* Cheyne, *Job and Sol.*, p. 123, and *Bampton Lect.*, p. 441 f.; Schwally, *Leben nach d. Tode*, p. 118.

† There is perhaps a trace of Persian thought also; cf. Cheyne, *Jew. Relig. Life after the Exile*, pp. 151, 208. Whether the sages were affected by Egyptian cosmogonic ideas is uncertain.

It is the skill shown in the creation that is had in mind (as in Job 28 Pr. 8); contrast the national point of view of the prophets and the psalmists, the social interest of Gen. 2, and the statistical form of Gen. 1. Wisdom here seems to be simply an attribute, with no approach to hypostatization. — The expressions *founded* and *established* belong to the old-Hebrew cosmogonical ideas. The earth was conceived of as a plane mass, resting on an ocean (ψ 24² 136⁶), as having foundations (Isa. 51¹³ ψ 104⁵ Pr. 8²⁹) and as supported by pillars (Job 9⁶ ψ 75³⁽⁴⁾); Sheol was apparently supposed to lie beneath the subjacent ocean (cf. Am. 9². ³). Above the earth the heaven or sky was thought of as a material expanse (Gen. 1²), fixed in its place by God and supported by pillars (Job 26¹¹ ψ 18⁷⁽⁸⁾), by which we are probably to understand the mountains. The plu. *heavens* represents the sky as made up of contiguous parts; the expression *heavens of heavens*, elsewhere used of the celestial abode of the deity (Dt. 10¹⁴ 1 K. 8²⁷ ψ 148⁴) conceives of it as including different planes. The three divisions of the world are given in Ex. 20⁴: the heaven above, the earth beneath, the water under the earth.* — The monotheistic view of creation is here assumed as generally held (while Isa. 40 contains a polemic against polytheism). — **20**. Parallels, ternary. Wisdom in the divine direction of the material world. The verbs are better taken as Present; v.¹⁹ deals with the creation of the world, here we pass to its present guidance; if the verbs be rendered as Past, the reference will be to the original arrangement. Lit. *the deeps are cleft*, that is, the subterranean structure is broken up so that the water may flow. The *waters* include all bodies of water that issue from the ground, namely, springs and rivers, and also the sea; these come from the subterraneous ocean. Along with them is mentioned the water that is held to come from the other great aqueous supply: the *dew* is supposed to fall from the *clouds*, and the term is probably meant to include rain (cf. Job 28²⁵. ²⁶ 36²⁸); the reference is to an ocean above the sky. Cf. (Gen. 7¹¹) the double process by which the flood is produced: the fountains of the great deep

---

* For later Jewish cosmogonic ideas see *Secrets of Enoch*, ed. R. H. Charles; Weber, *Theol.*, § 44. On Babylonian ideas cf. Jastrow, *Relig. of Bab. and Assyria*, pp. 112 f. 489.

burst forth (that is, water rises from the subterranean ocean), and
the windows of heaven are opened (that is, openings are made in
the sky through which the water of the celestial ocean may fall).
Apart from any scientific conception of method the verse declares
that the divine wisdom appears in the distribution of water in the
world.   It is possible that in the original form of the section other
illustrations of God's wisdom followed.   Cf. 8²²⁻³¹.

13. 頂 ארכ ... אדב; 𝕲 (followed by 𝕾) ἄνθρωπος (ἀνήρ) . . . θνητὸς;
we should perh. read אונ or איש (so Kamp.) instead of second א; 𝕷 omits
it. — 頂 יפיק; 𝕲 εἶδεν, Cl. Alex. Migne I. 357 εὗρε (but 552 οἶδε), assimilation
to vb. of ᵃ; Saadia יפה. — **14.** סחרה; 𝕲 αὐτὴν ἐμπορεύεσθαι (Cl. Al. ἐμπορευ-
θῆναι, Ped. 91); 𝕲ᵇ ἢ χρυσίου κ. ἀργυρίου θησαυρούς, prob. free rendering of
頂, cf. 31¹⁸ where ס is rendered by ἐργάζεσθαι; 𝕾 follows 頂, only inserting
מיניה (= כב), before last word. — **15.** The tone in יקרה is drawn back for the
sake of the rhythm. — K פניכ, scribal error for Q. פנינים; a similar error in
Lam. 4⁷ was perh. the source of 𝕷 ebore antiquo. — For 頂 חפציך read with all
anc. Vrss. חפצים (so Oort, Bi.), the restrictive suff. being out of keeping with
the context. — 頂 ישוו; 𝕲 ἄξιον, and, in the doublet, ἀντιτάξεται (אᶜ·ᵃ A ἀντιτάσσεται).   𝕲 doublet πονηρόν (חמ), perh. for ποθητόν (Jäg., Grabe, cited
by Schl.).   𝕲, second doub. εὔγνωστός ἐστιν πᾶσιν τοῖς ἐγγίζουσιν αὐτῇ
(Proc. by scribal error ὀργίζουσιν, 𝕲ⱽ ἐφαπτομένοις) perh. = נידרה היא [יכר]
קרוביה or נ:ה לאיר לפניה; in any case not original. — For 頂 בה Oort would
rather read לה; the Prep. after כיה (= like, equal) is ר or אל except here
and 8¹¹ Esth. 7⁴; the כ may introduce the noun of estimation. — **16.** After
ארך ימים 𝕲 adds καὶ ἔτη ζωῆς, apparently from v.²; the addition mars the
rhythm.   𝕲 also introduces the v. by γὰρ (adopted by Bi.), but the causal
form does not agree with the context. — On the couplet inserted by 𝕲 see
what is said above, and cf. notes of Lag. and Heid.   In ᵇ we should perh.
read νόμον δὲ ἐλέου. — **17.** 頂 שלום: 𝕲ᴮ ᵃˡ. ἐν εἰρήνῃ, 𝕲ⱽ ᵃˡ. μετ' ειρ., 𝕲ᴬ omits
prep.; 頂 is to be retained. — **18.** In ᵃ, as often elsewhere (rhetorical expansion), 𝕲 prefixes πᾶσι to the Part. (מחזיקים). — Instead of בה the suff. might
be attached to the Partcp. — In ᵇ 頂 has sing. pred. מאשר with plu. subj.
תמכיה.   𝕷 (and so Bi.) makes subj. sing., and 𝕾𝕿 pred. plu., but these renderings do not necessarily indicate the precise form of the Heb. text of the
Vrss., since they might in any case make their translations conform to grammatical rules; in the construction of 頂, which occurs elsewhere (Gen. 27²⁹
Ex. 31¹⁴ al., see Ew. § 319 a), the sing. pred. is distributive or individualizing, or it is a simplified (unitary) form similar to initial sing. vb. followed by
plu. subject.   The vb. אשר = make or call happy seems to be Denom. —
Clause ᵇ stands in 𝕲ᴮ καὶ τοῖς ἐπερειδομένοις ἐπ' αὐτὴν ὡς ἐπὶ κύριον; 𝕲ᴮ ᵃᵇ
adds ἀσφαλή and 𝕲 ⁱ ᶜ·ᵃ· ᴬ ἀσφαλής, and so 𝕾ᴴ Proc. Hil.; ασφ. = מאשר
(taken as Pi. Part. = guide or as Pu. = guided, and perh. read מאשות), is
understood as referring to wisdom; ὡς ε. κ. apparently = כיה, repetition out

of המכיח (Lag., Oort). The Heb. text of 𝕲 = 𝔐, only with Prep. ל before
ה.— 19. 'Εν (= ב) is prefixed to σοφίᾳ by several Fathers, and to φρονήσει
by 𝕲 ℵ o. a. A many curss. and several Fathers (see H-P), probably a scribal
variation. 𝕾𝕿 attach 3 sing. masc. suff. to the second noun, 𝕾 to the first
also. — 20. Suff. in רעתו omitted by 𝕲BA, inserted by 𝕲 ᶜ ᵉ·ᵃ H-P 69 al. Comp.
Ald. — The precise sense of the expression תהלות נבקעו is not quite clear; we
expect: "the rock (or, the earth) was cleft, and the waters issued," as in ψ 78¹⁵.
The construction in Pr. is supported, however, by Gen. 7¹¹ ψ 74¹⁵; the latter
passage can hardly be rendered: *thou didst cleave a way for fountain and
brook*. Apparently the subterranean רהב is regarded as a mass, lying motionless, and requiring to be cleft in order that its waters may move. Instead of
ירעפו 4 MSS. have יירפו with same meaning (cf. Dt. 32²), perhaps scribal
error, or euphonic variation; on transposition of radicals in stems see Böttch.,
Lehrb., I. § 265–267.

21–26. A separate section (parallel to but distinct from the
preceding), **exhorting to the practice of Wisdom on the ground
that it will give security to life.** Hitzig's reasons for regarding
the section as an interpolation (namely, that the repetition of the
promise of reward is unnecessary, that the vocabulary contains
late expressions, and that the omission of these verses secures a
division of the chapter into paragraphs of ten verses each) are
now generally rejected. The whole section, chs. 1–9, is not early,
but late; it is made up of sub-sections, in which there is necessarily repetition; and the hypothesis of decimal division is arbitrary.

21 b. My son, keep [with thee] wisdom and discretion,
21 a. Let them not depart from thy sight;
22. They will be life to thy being,
    Adornment to thy neck.

23. Then wilt thou go thy way securely;
    Thy foot will not stumble;
24. When thou ‹sittest down›* thou wilt not be afraid,
    Thou wilt lie down, and thy sleep will be sweet.

25. Thou wilt not fear the calamity that befalls the ‹foolish,›†
    Nor the storm that strikes the wicked;
26. For Yahweh will be thy protector,
    And will keep thy feet from snares.

21. Synonymous, ternary, or, in the emended text, quaternary-
binary. The present Heb. text reads: *my son, let them not*

---

* Heb.: *liest down.*　　　† Heb.: *Fear not sudden calamity.*

depart (or, *swerve*) *from thine eyes, keep wisdom* (or, *sagacity*) *and discretion*.   But the subject of the first cl. is lacking.   The antecedent of *them* cannot be supplied from v.[19. 20] (where *wisdom, understanding*, and *knowledge* are attributes of God, and in any case such reference to them would be too abrupt), or from the second cl. (which would be against Heb. usage).   A similar objection applies to the rendering (obtained by a slight change in the Heb.) *let it* [wisdom] *not swerve:* the reference to *wisdom* is abrupt, and the sing. does not agree with v.[22].   The Vrss. are unsatisfactory.   Grk. (the text of which may be corrupt) : *my son, do not escape* (lit. *flow away*) ; Lat. : *let not these flow away from thine eyes;* Syr. Targ. : *let it not be despicable in thine eyes.* The beginning of the paragraph, which contained the antecedent of *them*, may have fallen out ; it may perhaps be supplied from the closely parallel passage 4[20-22].   We may either insert a verse similar to 4[20], or supply a single word and read *let not my words* (or, *let not wisdom*) *swerve*, etc.   The term *swerve, turn aside*, seems strange in this connection, and the Vrss. assumed different stems.   We expect one of the usual words for *depart*, as in 27[22] or 17[13], or else, with inversion, *turn not away from my instruction.* A proper form may be got by transposing the clauses : *my son, preserve sagacity and discretion, let them not depart from thine eyes* (Umbreit), which is without Versional support, but seems to be the simplest solution of the difficulty of the first clause.   On the terms *sagacity* (= *wisdom*) and *discretion* see notes on 2[7] and 1[4], and on *keep* see notes on 2[20] 3[1]. — **22.** Synonymous, ternary-binary.   The reward (the description of which goes through v.[25]). Instead of *will*, here and throughout the paragraph (simple statement of result), we may render *shall* (authoritative statement). — Grk. *in order that*, but the verse is better understood as expressing result.   The *life* is physical, as in 3[2. 16].   *Being* is here better than *soul* (as rendering of שׁפֶנ), since the latter term conveys to us a spiritual sense not contained in the Hebrew ; we might translate *they will* (or, *shall*) be *life to thee*, that is, they will (or, shall) confer on thee long life, a supreme blessing.   *Adornment* is lit. *beauty, grace of form* (see note on 1[9]), and so an ornament as a thing of beauty, and as a lasting possession ; see notes on 1[9] 3[8]. True sagacity, it is declared, will bring its possessor not only long

life but also loveliness and graciousness, the reference being to
the attractiveness of a character moulded by a high, Godfearing
intelligence, beautiful in itself and attractive to men. — The Grk.
here inserts v.[8], with a slight variation (*flesh* instead of *body*). —
23. Synonymous, ternary. Security in walk. The second cl. (which
reads lit. *and shalt not strike thy foot*) occurs in ψ 91[12] with the
addition *against a stone;* there the guidance is referred to angels,
here to wisdom; the whole psalm is parallel to our section, and
shows the difference between the points of view of psalmist and
sage. — A slight change in the Heb. gives the reading *thy foot
will* (or, *shall*) *not stumble* (so Grk. RV.) ; the sense is the same
in both renderings. The expression was probably a common one
to express safety; it is unnecessary to suppose that Pr. took it
from ψ, or ψ from Pr. — **24.** Parallels, ternary. Security at home.
The Heb. text reads : *when thou liest down thou wilt* (or, *shalt*)
not be afraid, yea, thou wilt (or, *shalt*) *lie down and thy sleep
will* (or, *shall*) *be sweet.* The repetition of the verb is somewhat
strange, though it is defensible on rhetorical grounds. The Heb.
vb. has the two senses *lie down* and *sleep*, and Schultens thinks
that the first of these is to be understood in first cl., and the
second in second cl.; but this is not permissible. Grk., in first
cl.: *when thou sittest down;* Targ.: *when thou liest down and
sleepest;* Syr.: *and thou shalt sleep;* Lat.: *if thou sleep thou shalt
not be afraid, thou shalt rest,* etc. In ψ 3[5(6)] 4[8(9)] the expression is
lie down and sleep; in Dt. 6[7] we have the pairs *sit down, walk,*
and *lie down, rise.* We might retain the Heb. text, and understand it to refer to sleep undisturbed by attacks of robbers and
murderers; but a more natural form is obtained by changing the
first *lie* to *sit.* — **25.** Synonymous, ternary. Security from calamity. Lit. *terror* (or, *calamity*) *of the foolish* and *storm* (or, *desolation*) *of the wicked.* The Heb., instead of *terror of the foolish*,
has *sudden terror*, which gives a good but less appropriate sense ;
the parallelism favors a reference to a class of persons, and this
reading is supported by 1[26. 27]. The translation *foolish* requires no
change in the consonants of the Hebrew. At the end of second
line the Heb. has *when it comes*, an addition to complete the
rhythm, but unnecessary to the sense. — The declarative rendering *thou wilt* (or, *shalt*) *not be afraid* is required by the connec-

tion; the imperative *be not afraid* is here out of place. The
wicked will be visited with storms of calamity, but when these
come the man who is guided by the divine wisdom need not fear
— they shall not reach him. Cf. the similar statements in Job 5[21]
ψ 91[5-8]. — **26.** Progressive, ternary. The ground of hope. *Protector* is lit. *confidence* = ground of confidence; cf. Job 8[14] 31[24].
The specifically religious theistic point of view (as in Job 5[17-26]
ψ 91) is here introduced — wisdom is identified with trust in God,
according to the fundamental principle stated in 1[7].

21. If יָלוּז be referred to st. לוז, this use of the word (= *depart*) must
probably be regarded as peculiar to the Hokma diction. 𝔊 (παραρυῇς = תוּר)
and 𝔏 (*effluant*) appear to have taken it from נוד *flow*, 𝔖𝔗, foll. by
Prep. ב) from זלל *despicable*. In 4[21] 𝔊 has ἐκλίπωσίν, 𝔖𝔗 נוזן (from זלל),
𝔏 *recedant* (from לוז or נוז). Lag. supposes that παραρρυῇς (as he writes the
word, but apparently without MS. authority) comes from preceding ἐρρύησαν
by erroneous repetition of ρρυῃς, and he thinks it impossible to restore the
verb. 𝔊 (which omits מֵעֵינֶיךָ) must be rendered *do not slip away* (that is,
from my instruction, or, *from wisdom*), a strange reading, and 𝔖𝔗𝔏 are
equally unsatisfactory. There seems to be nothing better than to retain 𝔥;
on the construction of the verse see note above. Bi. reads תלוּז, 3 sing. fem.,
understanding *wisdom* as subject; Oort יָזוּר (cf. the stem אזר). The reading
of 𝔖𝔗 is found in Kenn. 95, 150, and is adopted by Houb., and the form
יליזו (as in 4[21]) occurs in some printed edd. (see De' Rossi). — In ᵇ 𝔊𝔖 attach
I pers. suff. to the nouns, and 𝔖 treats נצר as Inf. Heid.'s remark that 𝔖𝔗
reverse the order of the nouns is not correct (cf. Pink.). — **22.** 𝔊 ἵνα ζήσῃ
ἡ ψυχή σου (or σὴ ψυχὴ H-P 23, 252) is free rendering of 𝔥. — **23.** 𝔊 πεποιθὼς and ἐν εἰρήνῃ, doublet; πάσας, rhetorical insertion. — 𝔥 תגוף; the Qal is
regularly trans., and is so rendered ψ 91[12] by 𝔊𝔏; here intrans. by 𝔊𝔏 and
apparently by 𝔖𝔗; Saadia בַּיֵי ולא הצרם רגלך, in which the verb may be taken
either as trans. or as intrans., *and thy foot will not strike* (or, *thou wilt not
strike thy foot*) *against anything* (rendered intrans. by Derenbourg and Lam-
bert). There is no reason for abandoning the ordinary sense of the word. —
24. 𝔥 has שכב in both clauses, Impf. and Perf., rhetorical variation; a better
reading is given in ᵃ by 𝔊 (foll. by 𝔖ᴴ), κάθῃ = יֵשֵׁב (referred by Hitz., Heid.
to influence of Dt. 6[7]), adopted by Bi. on the ground that 𝔥 is intolerably
tautological. The Vrss. all vary the expressions: 𝔊 κάθῃ and καθεύδῃς;
𝔗 השכב והרדמך in ᵃ and תֵי׳ in ᵇ; 𝔖 תרי׳ in ᵃ, תֵי׳ in ᵇ; 𝔏 *dormieris* and *quiesces;* and so Saad. *lie down* and *sleep.* These renderings may be rhetorical
variations of 𝔥. In 𝔗 the וּשׁי is explanatory addition to וּהרי׳ (𝔖). — **25.** 𝔥
אַל may be changed to לא, after the norm of v.[24], or perhaps may be taken
as declarative, which force it possibly sometimes has in poetry (Job 32[21]) and
elevated prose (Jer. 14[17]), though in these passages it may be scribal error.

— For פחד Gr. proposes חיד, referring to 1²⁶·²⁷ where 𝔊 has ὄλεθρος and θόρυβος; yet these may be understood as free translations of פחד taken as = *cause of fear;* 𝔊 here has πτόησιν ἐπελθοῦσαν, in which π. = כחד, and ἐπ. is repetition from ᵇ or represents פ־אב read as some form of בוא. The *terror and storm* of 𝔐 are understood by 𝔊, against the connection and against the suggestion of 1²⁶·²⁷, as an attack made on the righteous by the wicked. — 𝔐 פְּ־אָב; point פְּרָאָב (Oort). — 𝔐 כי הבא; cf. בבא 1²⁶·²⁷. — **26.** On the *Beth essentiae* in בְּנְסֵרֵךְ (so Ex. 18⁴ Isa. 40¹⁰ ψ 146⁵) see Ges.²⁶, § 119 *i*, Ew., § 229 *b*, and cf. 𝔗 בנס;רֵךְ; on the similar Arab. construction see Casp. ed. Wright, II. § 56 *a* and Rem. *a*, ed. Müller, § 423, 2 *a*; 𝔏 *in latere tuo* and 𝔖 עמך take כ as = *loin, flank;* 𝔊 ἐπὶ πασῶν ὁδῶν σου = בבסרֵךְ. — 𝔐 רֵכֵר ἀπ. λεγ.; Oort suggests that it may be pointed as Qal Inf. or written Nif. Inf. הלכר; 𝔊ᴮ ᵃˡ σαλευθῇς (= מוט or נוף?), which Semler would change to ἀγρευθῇς (so H-P 23, 252ᵐᵃʳᵍ·, and 𝔖ᴴ תהציר), and Lag. to συλληφθῇς.

27–30. A detached group of sayings, **enjoining kindness to one's fellowmen.** They are prosaic in style, roughly formed couplets, with scarcely perceptible rhythm. In their homely character they resemble rather some of the aphorisms of chs. 10–29 than the discourses of chs. 1–9, and seem out of place here. Their presence appears to indicate that these two divisions of the Book were finally edited about the same time. Cf. 6¹⁻⁵· ⁶⁻¹¹· ¹²⁻¹⁹ 9⁷⁻¹² Eccl. 7¹⁻⁹.

> 27. Withhold not good from thy ‹neighbor›
>   When it is in thy power to do it;
> 28. Say not to thy neighbor: "Go and come again,
>   And tomorrow I will give," when thou hast it by thee.
>
> 29. Devise no injury to thy neighbor,
>   Seeing he dwells in confidence by thee.
> 30. Strive not with a man without cause,
>   If he have done thee no harm.

27, 28. Two nearly identical exhortations to beneficence. In v.²⁷ the Heb. has *from its possessors,* which cannot mean *from the poor* (Grk.), as if they were lawful owners of alms, or *from them to whom it is due* (RV.); nor can we render, with Lat. Vulg.: *Restrain not him who can from doing good; if thou art able, thyself do good.* The connection (v.²⁸· ²⁹) suggests some such word as *neighbor,* which may be got by a not very difficult change of the Hebrew. The word is wanting in Peshitta and Targum, which have the general precept *refrain not from doing good,* but the connection favors the reference to the "neighbor." The term means *associate, clansman, neighbor, friend*, but seems here to be employed in the wider sense in which it is used in Dt. 15^2 Lu. 10$^{27.\ 29.\ 37}$ (taken from the Grk. of Lev. 19^{18}). Similar injunctions are found in 11$^{24.\ 26}$ 14$^{21.\ 31}$ 17^{17} 21^{26} 27^{10} BS. 29$^{1.\ 2.\ 20}$. In all these the tone is one of broad human sympathy. — **28** enjoins prompt and hearty help, as in our proverb: "who gives quickly gives twice"; there is no ground for restricting the injunction to paying a hired man his wages (see Rashi). The first cl. may be understood as quoting two equivalent speeches of the man who puts his neighbor off: *Go and come again* and *Tomorrow I will give*. Grk. omits *to thy neighbor*, perhaps by scribal error; the expression is possibly an insertion of the Heb. scribe for the sake of clearness, certainly not (as Lag. thinks) to restrict an injunction which was thought to be too general. Cf. the omission of the similar expression of v.^{27} by the Aramaic Vrss., which likewise seems to be scribal abridgment or inadvertence. At the end of the verse Grk. adds *for thou knowest not what the next day will bring forth*, a not very appropriate gloss, taken from 27^1. — **29.** Single sentence, ternary. Against malicious conduct. *Seeing he dwells in confidence by thee*, that is, *dwells unsuspecting*, or, as the Grk. has it, *seeing he dwells by thee and trusts in thee*. Trustful feeling, here stated as the ground of obligation of kindness, is the basis of social life; to a generous mind the plea is a strong one. — **30.** Single sentence, ternary. Against groundless quarrelling. The verb in first cl. means *contend*, in general, and in this sense is found in proper names, as Jerubbaal, = "Baal [that is, Yahweh] contends [for me]." It is a common term for litigation, but is here used for any (unfriendly) disputation. The verse is tautologous, the second cl. merely repeating the *without cause* of the first clause. One or the other of these might be omitted without detriment, and in fact Syr. omits second cl., probably for simplification; but the repetition may be retained as rhetorical fulness. The Grk. has, in second cl., *lest he do thee harm*, a suggestion similar to that of 6$^{1-5}$ 14^{17} 20^3 22$^{24.\ 25}$, but here not in keeping with the context, which contains merely injunctions without statement of consequences. The meaning of the verse is that while contention is sometimes right and necessary, it must always be for good cause.

27. In expressions of position or quality בעל always signifies one who employs or controls the thing in question : *husband* = owner of a wife; *ally*, Gen. 14[13] = one who enters into and employs a treaty; *dreamer*, Gen. 37[19] = one who has and employs dreams; *archer*, Gen. 49[23] = one who uses arrows; a *man of affairs*, Ex. 24[14], conducts his affairs; *creditor*, Dt. 15[2] = one who makes and controls a loan; the hair of a *hairy man*, 2 K. 1[8], belongs by nature to him; a *legal adversary*, Isa. 50[8], is one who conducts the prosecution; one who is *sworn*, Neh. 6[18], makes an oath; a *bird*, Pr. 1[17], uses its wings; a *waster* effects waste; an *angry* man, 22[24] 29[22], feels and shows anger; a *glutton*, 23[2], has appetite; a *rogue*, 24[8], makes mischief; a *babbler*, Eccl. 10[11], uses his tongue. There is thus no authority in Heb. usage for the statement (made by Schult., De., and others) that בעל טוב may here mean not him who does good but him to whom good is done; and further, the sense actually given by them is something still different, namely, him who stands in need of good or deserves it. Nor does Aram. permit such a rendering. The word must be either, with 𝔖𝔗, omitted, or else changed; a corruption of רעיך into בעליו offers no great graphic difficulty. From 𝔊 ἐνδεῆ Gr. suggests שׁאליו, and Oort sees nothing better than אביון; but 𝔊 is probably free rendering of 𝔐. — K ידי is possible, but marginal reading יד is the common form and is found in many MSS. of Kenn. and De'R.; Rashi gives two explanations, one = 𝔐, one = 𝔊. — **28.** 𝔐 רעיך is sing., the Yod being third rad.; the omission of this letter, as in margin, is unnecessary, though it is omitted in many Span. MSS. As the next word is רך, the omission of רעיך in 𝔊 may be due to homoeoteleuton, or possibly to homoeoarkton, especially if it were written in the abridged form רר. — 𝔖, probably by scribal inadvertence, transfers ויש אהך from end to beginning of the verse. On the addition in 𝔊 see note on this verse above. — **29.** 𝔐 הרשׁ ; 𝔊 τεκτήνῃ; BS 7[12(13)] ἀροτρία; the figurative sense *devise* comes more naturally from *carve*, but possibly also from *plough*. — **30.** 𝔐 אב לא; 𝔊 μή, perh. taking 𝔐 as = פן, or perh. reading אשׁר לא or אשׁ' לא. — It was hardly on moral grounds that ᵇ was omitted in 𝔖.

31-35. Comparison between the fortunes of the wicked and the righteous — a separate group of aphorisms, similar to the religious aphorisms of chs. 10-22, having a general connection with the preceding paragraph. It is a warning against the seduction of the apparent prosperity of wickedness.

31. Envy not the man of violence,
    And take no pleasure in his ways;

32. For a bad man is an abomination to Yahweh,
    But between him and the upright there is friendship.

33. The curse of Yahweh is on the house of the wicked,
    But the habitation of the righteous he blesses.

34. Scoffers he scoffs at,
But to the pious he shows favor.

35. Wise men obtain honor,
But ignominy is the ‹portion› of fools.

31. Synonymous, ternary. The warning. The second line may be rendered : *take pleasure in none of his ways* (lit. *take not pleasure in all his ways*). The parallelism calls for *take pleasure* (1^{29} Gen. 6^2) rather than *choose* (which, however, gives a good sense). The *violence* is highhanded, unlawful procedure of any sort ; *man of violence = wicked man ;* the " violence " was generally practised for purposes of pecuniary or political gain ; cf. 10^6 16^{29}. It is assumed that there is something in the fortunes of such a person which one might be tempted to envy, and so to be pleased with (or, choose) ; for the explanation see ψ $37^{3ff.}$. It is the problem of the Book of Job, which is here solved in the old way ; see next verse. — Grk. reads *procure not the reproaches of bad men, and covet not their ways,* in which first clause comes from scribal error, but second clause is favored by the parallelism and by 24^{19} ψ 37^1. On the other hand our text is supported by 24^1, and gives a good sense. Lat. *do not imitate his ways,* which represents the Hebrew. — **32-34.** The reason for the warning is here found in the way in which God deals with the righteous and the wicked. The rewards and punishments are earthly and external ; there is no recognition of ethical immortality, and life is regarded on the side of its outward experiences. — **32.** Antithetic, ternary-binary. This form is common in chs. 10-22, but not in chs. 1-9. The term *abomination* is used in the earlier historical, the prophetical, and the legal literature of what is contrary to a religious cult or usage, Israelitish or foreign, as in Gen. 43^{32}, K. 14^{24}, Dt. 14^3, Ez. 5^9, etc. ; in later books it is extended to include moral offences, as here ; it means something which is incompatible with the nature of Yahweh. The *bad* (or *iniquitous*) man (for the term see note on 2^{15}) is as abhorrent to Yahweh as an idol or other abomination, but with the *upright* he sits as with familiar friends (lit. *with the upright is his friendship*). The word rendered *friendship* means private, intimate converse and friendly relation, then the assembly or persons who thus converse together,

and finally the secret counsel they take and the design or plan
they form. The connection must decide in any given case which
of these significations is most appropriate. With this passage cf.
Job 29[4.5] ψ 25[14] (and ψ 55[14(15)]), in which the sense is clearly
friendship. The ground for avoiding the ways of the wicked
(v.[31]) is that Yahweh is hostile to him and friendly to the righteous; what this friendliness secures is stated in the next verse. —
33. Antithetic, quaternary-ternary, or ternary (as in chs. 10–22).
We may render *on the house* or *in the house*. The value of Yahweh's
friendship is here said to be the (external) prosperity it brings; no
reference is made to the moral benefit of communion of soul between God and man — this latter is rather regarded as the ground
of the blessing. A *curse* in the mouth of God is a sentence or pro-
nouncement of evil; in the mouth of man it is an imprecation, an
invocation of divine punishment. Similarly God *blesses* by pro-
nouncing good, man by invoking good from God.* — Lat. *poverty
from the Lord* is an interpretation of *curse of Yahweh* suggested
by second clause. — **34.** Antithetic, ternary (or, ternary-binary).
The *surely* of RV. is incorrect; see critical note below. Nor is
the hypothetical rendering satisfactory: *if* (or, *though*) *he scorns*,
etc., *yet he shows*, etc., the preceding and succeeding verses being
declarative. Still less can v.[34] be protasis and v.[35] apodosis. A
variation of the preceding statement. On *scoffers* see note on 1[22].
For the conception of reciprocity in first cl. cf. ψ 18[25(26). 26(27)]; the
representation of God as acting toward men as they act toward
him rests on an ancient anthropomorphism, which in Pr. is probably purified by the conviction that God, as just, must be hostile to
evildoers; but the thought never rises to the point of conceiving
of him as merciful to fools and sinners. — The word here translated *pious* (עניים) is that which is variously rendered in RV.
by *poor, afflicted, humble, lowly, meek*. Its primary sense seems
to be *one who is bowed, bent,* or *one who bows himself* (under or
before a hostile force); it thus comes to signify one who suffers
from financial poverty (Am. 8[4] *al.*), one who is oppressed by the
strong, particularly the nation Israel in the time of national afflic-

---

* The Heb. term for *bless* never means *curse, blaspheme,* or *renounce;* in Job 1[5. 11]
2[5. 9] the Heb. word is to be changed so as to read *curse*.

tion (ψ 74^{19} *al.*), or, one who afflicts himself by fasting or is
humble before God, and so in general the *Godfearing, pious* (so
used of Moses, Nu. 12^3, and so ψ 37^{11}, quoted in Mt. 5^5). This
last is the sense suggested by the parallelism here, though *lowly,
humble*, is also appropriate. — Grk.: *the Lord resists the proud,
but shows favor to the humble*, quoted, with slight variations, in
Jas. 4^6, 1 Pet. 5^6. — Bickell omits the verse as an interpolation
which breaks the connection between v.^{33} and v.^{35}; it is, however,
closely parallel to v.^{33}, and, if any verse is to be omitted as irrelevant, it should rather be v.^{35} (see note on this verse below). —
For the sentiment cf. 16^{19}. — **35.** Antithetic, ternary. The first
cl. = *honor is the portion of wise men*. The thought is that of 11^2
12^8 13^5 14^{19} 22^{29} *al.*: men of integrity and insight will receive
recognition at the hands of their fellowmen — the approbation
of society is presented as a motive for rightdoing — a powerful
inducement. The term *wise* doubtless includes moral and religious as well as intellectual elements, and so *fools* in the second
clause. The verb means primarily to *have or obtain possession* (as
in Jos. 14^1), and secondarily to *inherit*, a sense which is here not
appropriate. *Honor* is the respect or high recognition accorded
by God to man, or by man to God or man (1 K. 3^{13} Gen. 45^{13}
1 Sam. 6^5); opposed to it is the *shame* of the second cl., slight
estimation, contempt. — The translation of the second cl. is doubtful, one word being apparently corrupt. This word, as it stands,
may mean *lift up* (from the ground, 2 K. 2^{13}), *exalt* (ψ 89^{20}), *take
away, remove out of the way* (Hos. 11^4 Isa. 57^{14}), *offer* as gift or
sacrifice (that is, lift up before the deity, Ex. 35^{24} Lev. 4^8). None
of these senses are here suitable: fools do not exalt or remove or
offer ignominy, nor does ignominy do these things to fools. No
satisfactory translation of the clause has been made. Grk.: *the
godless exalt dishonor;* Lat. (followed by RV.): *ignominy is the
exaltation* (or, *promotion*) *of fools* (lit. *shame exalts fools*), and
so Schult.: *the brand of infamy gives notoriety to fools;* Syr.
Targ.: *fools suffer* (lit. *receive*) *shame,* which is not a translation
of the Heb., the word in Heb. meaning not "to take away for one's
own benefit or use," but "to take out of the way, do away with,"
and, in the ritual, "to take a portion not for one's self but for
God." A slight change of text, with an insertion, gives the ren-

dering *fools change [their glory] into shame* (cf. Hos. 4[7] Jer. 2[11]
ψ 106[20]), but the insertion is improbable, and the resulting sense
not clear or appropriate. Another slight change gives *fools increase shame* (cf. Isa. 40[29] Eccl. 6[11] 10[14]), a good and natural
sense ; and a similar rendering is appropriate in 14[29]. But an
equally easy and more probable emendation gives the verb *possess,
get possession of* (= *obtain*). In any case the meaning of the
second cl. is *ignominy is the portion of fools*, that is, of those who
are not wise enough to see that it is their duty as well as their
interest to obey the divine law. The ignominy and the honor, it
is to be supposed, are assigned by God. The couplet appears not
to belong with the preceding quatrains, from which it differs in
tone ; it is probably the addition of an editor.

31. ⅏ μὴ κτήσῃ [תְּקְנֶה] κακῶν ἀνδρῶν ὀνείδῃ, in which ὀν. may = ﬡ חמס
(Baumg.) as in 26[6] Job 19[7], κ. being epexegetical; Lag. suggests that κ. α. ο.
is simply poetical expression of κ. α., like μέγα σθένος Ἠετίωνος = Ἠετίων. —
ζηλώσης may = ﬡ תבהר; according to Oort, it = תחחר, which seems unnecessary.* — 32. ⅏ seems to make παράνομος (נלוז) subj. of [b] ἐν δὲ δικαίοις οὐ
συνεδριάζει, but doubtless οὐ is scribal error, repetition of following συ (Lag.),
and κύριος is subj. — Heid., noting that ⅏ has παρ. instead of σκολιάζων (14[2])
and ἀκάθαρτος instead of the usual βδέλυγμα, sees in this v. a Pharisaic attack
on the Sadducees, the paranomists, and regards συνεδριάζει as an allusion to
the Sanhedrin. This is possible, but not necessary, and the supposed allusion
in συνεδ. vanishes with the disappearance of οὐ. — 33. ﬡ יהוה; ⅏ θεοῦ. All
following nouns are plural in ⅏, perh. stylistic variation of the translator,
perh. representing variations from our Heb. text; so 𝔖𝔗 Saad. have plu. in [a],
𝕃 in [b], and in ⅏𝕃 the vb. in [b] is Pass. plu. — 34. אם ללצים cannot here mean
when he deals with scorners (Lag., De., Kamp.) as separate protasis (with
הוא יליץ as apodosis), nor can אב = *surely* (RV.), since, in asseverations, this
word has negative force. Gr., Oort, change אב to אלהים (after Jas. 4[6] 1 Pet. 5[5]),
and Oort omits pref. ל; but יהוה is the divine name used above in the paragraph, and the הוא further must then be omitted. Dys.'s emendation to עם,
with omission of pref. ל (which may easily be doublet) is simpler, bringing
the sentence into the norm of ψ 18[26]. Or, we may, with ⅏ κύριος ὑπερηφάνοις
ἀντιτάσσεται, omit אם (so 𝔖𝔗𝕃), though this is graphically not so easy.
⅏ κύριος may represent יהוה, or may be *explicitum*. — K. עניים; Q ענוים, for
which 𝔖 has תכימא. For יליץ 𝔖𝔗 have נסחוף *casts down*, free rendering. —
35. ﬡ ירים; ⅏ ὕψωσαν; 𝔖𝔗 נקבלון; 𝕃 *stultorum exaltatio*, apparently taking
קלון as subj.; Dys. emends to מֵמִירִיב, Gr. better to מרבים, but we should probably read הֲרִים or ירץ.

---

* Heid., by oversight, quotes Procop.'s comments as additions to the Grk. text.

IV. Three exhortations ($v.^{1-9}$, $v.^{10-19}$, $v.^{20-27}$), the theme of all three being the excellence and beneficent power of wisdom. — They are like those of chs. 2. 3 in that the advice is of a general nature, while in chs. 5. 6. 7 it is directed against a particular sin.

1–9. The sage cites the instruction given him by his father. The text is, in parts, in such condition that we cannot be sure of the exact sense. The Vatican Grk. makes the teacher's instruction (and not wisdom) the subject of praise.

> 1. Hear, O children, the instruction of a father —
>   Give heed that ye may comprehend wisdom.
> 2. For good counsel I give you —
>   Forsake ye not my teaching.
>
> 3. When I was of tender age, []
>   Beloved by my ʻ father,ʼ
> 4 *a*. He used to teach me and say to me :
> 4 *b*. " Let thy mind retain my words.
>
> 4 *c*. Keep my commandments and live ;
> 5 *a*. Get wisdom, get understanding.
> 6. Forsake her not, and she will preserve thee,
>   Love her, and she will keep thee.*
>
> 8. Prize her, and she wilt exalt thee,
>   She will honor thee if thou embrace her ;
> 9. She will encircle thy head with a chaplet of beauty,
>   Bestow on thee a crown of glory."

1. Extensive or exegetical (the second cl. repeating first cl. and giving the reason for it), ternary. Exhortation to hearken. The sage (by the plu. *children* or *sons*) addresses himself to a circle of hearers, a school, though the difference of number is not significant ; when the sing. is used, the address is to a class of persons, young men in general. *Father* is not here used in the stricter (family) sense of the word, but with the wider connotation of *teacher ;* see note on 1^8, and cf. $v.^3$ below. On *instruction* and *wisdom* (the term usually rendered *understanding*) see notes on 1^2. The word rendered *give heed*, = *hearken, attend*, is a synonym of *hear* ised only in poetry and solemn prose. *Compre-*

---

* On the omission of $v.^{5b. 7}$, see note on these verses below.

hend = know (1²). The source of authority of the teaching is the experience of the teacher. — **2**. Continued thought, ternary- (or, quaternary-) binary. The ground of the sage's claim to be heard. The sage speaks with conviction and authority ; he believes that his teaching is sound and important, and the *teaching* or *law* that he gives is his own, that is, is grounded in his own soul, though derived from divine teaching ; the prophet, on the contrary, never speaks in his own name. *Counsel* or *instruction* (RV. *doctrine*), with which *law* is synonymous, is here given to others ; in 1⁵ (on which see note) it is received from others. Grk. *gift* = something received. Lat. *I give you a good gift* (omitting *for*, which, though not necessary, is appropriate, nearly = *namely*). — **3**. The sage refers to his own childhood. The Heb. reads : *For I was a son to my father* [or, *my father's son*], *tender* [= *of tender age, weak*] *and an only child in the presence of* [= *with*] *my mother*. Grk.: *I also was a son, obedient to a father, and beloved in the presence of a mother*. The first cl. is strange — it seems unnecessary and unnatural to describe a boy as the son of his father, and it is not probable that any writer would use such an expression ; we expect a word descriptive of the son's relations with the father (as the relations with the mother are described in the second cl.). The *obedient* of the Grk. seems to be free rendering of our Heb. (instead of *tender*), though it may represent a different Heb. word ; something like this would be possible, but is not particularly appropriate ; it would require a change in the order of the words. The *only child* also is improbable ; an adj. like the *beloved* of the Grk. would be appropriate ; but this sense (RV. *only beloved*) does not properly belong to the Heb. word here used ; the expression *as an only child* would be in place. After calling on his pupils to give heed to his instruction, the writer (in order to give the weight of tradition to his words) might naturally say *for I myself was a son, under the authority of a father, and beloved by a mother*. But, as only the father is referred to (in the Heb. text) in the following couplet, it seems probable that the mention of the mother here does not belong to the original form, and that *my mother* took the place of *my father* in the second line after the expression *to my father* had been introduced, by scribal error, into the first line. If, with this

correction, we substitute *beloved* for *only son*, we have a simple
and clear sentence. — The verse suggests an interesting picture of
the family-training of the time (probably the third century B.C.).
The father is the authoritative guide of the children.* The instruction is oral — there is no reference to books; books were
rare, and were probably used only by advanced students, though
children of the better families may have been taught to read at
home. There is no sign of the existence of children's schools at
this time.† — **4–7**. It is not easy to determine the precise connection of thought in this passage. V.$^{4a. b}$ and v.^{6} are plain; the
difficulty lies in v.$^{4c. 5. 7}$. The following considerations may help to
fix the wording. V.^{7}, since it interrupts the connection between
v.^{6} and v.^{8}, is syntactically confused, and is not found in the Grk.,
may be omitted (see note on this verse below). V.^{5b} also interrupts the connection between v.^{5a} and v.^{6} (this last verse supposing
a preceding reference to wisdom), and should be omitted. We
shall thus have to form a couplet out of v.^{4c} and v.^{5a}. The resultant
paragraph is not free from difficulties; but it follows the indications of the Heb. text, and affords a clear sense. — **4**. The two
first clauses make a couplet, continuous, ternary. The father's
address, beginning with the second clause, appears to extend
through v.^{9}. The father alone is here cited, in the Heb., as
teacher (see note on preceding verse). Grk. (reversing the order
of the verbs): *they said and taught me*, thus including the mother;
in v.^{5}, however, it makes the father alone the speaker, and so, probably, it should be throughout, in accordance with the manner of
the rest of the section, chs. 1–9. — On *mind* (lit. *heart*) see note
on 2^2. *Retain* = grasp, hold firmly in hand, hold fast. — The
third line of the verse is identical with the first line of 7^2, and is,
for this reason, here thrown out by some critics as a scribal insertion; but such repetition is possible (for ex., 1^{8b} = 6^{20b}). Grk. has
only the first half, omitting the words *and live;* but for this omission there is no good reason. In the present state of the text there
seems to be nothing better than to attach the line to the first line

---

* The mother also was doubtless the instructor of the child (see 1^8), whether or
not she is mentioned in this verse.

† On the education of children see Nowack, *Heb. Arch.*, I. p. 172; Schürer,
Gesch. (= *Hist. of the Jew. People*, II., 2, § 27), and the literature therein named.

of the next verse, though it is an objection to this construction that the resultant couplet does not present a satisfactory parallelism — we expect a whole couplet devoted to wisdom, preparatory to v.[6]. No arrangement of the lines, however, is entirely free from objections. — *And live = that thou mayest (by them) live*, that is, "that they may secure the happiness of a long earthly life;" for the idea see 3^2. — **5.** The present Heb. text reads: *get wisdom, get understanding, forget not, and turn not away from the words of my mouth*. If the wording be genuine, the iteration expresses the earnestness of the sage, who identifies his instructions with wisdom. But the present form is hardly original. The second line (*and turn*, etc.) belongs naturally with v.[4c]; and the expression *forget not* should properly follow not *get wisdom*, etc., but *keep my commandments*. The former phrase is omitted in the Grk., which reads: *keep commandments, forget not, and neglect not the discourse of my mouth;* this is in itself clear, but it makes the teacher's *discourse* the antecedent of v.[6] (*forsake it not*), whereas the tone of v.[6. 8. 9] almost forces us to regard *wisdom* as their subject. It is, therefore, better to omit the second clause (*and turn*, etc.) as a gloss on v.[4b. c], and also the *forget not*, and retain the rest as an introduction to v.[6]. — Other proposed constructions are: *forget not to acquire wisdom, and swerve not from the words of her mouth* (Graetz), which has the advantage of offering only one subject (as in v.[6]), but is open to the objection that Wisdom's "mouth" is nowhere else mentioned; Oort also would omit *get understanding* (as gloss on *get wisdom*), and add to *forget not* some such expression as *my law* (as in 3^1), but thinks that the whole verse is probably a scribal insertion; *get wisdom, get understanding, forget not* [*the instruction of my lips*], *and swerve not*, etc. (Bickell). While the general sense is plain, the original form can hardly be recovered. It seems probable that in v.[5] the writer passes from reference to his own "instruction" to the praise of "wisdom." If the Grk. reading of v.[4c. 5] be adopted (see above), we must probably suppose a break at the end of v.[5], the following paragraph (v.[6. 8. 9]) having lost a couplet in which *wisdom* was introduced. — **6.** Synonymous, binary. In the Heb. the subject of the discourse is *wisdom* or *understanding* which preserves its followers, as in 2^{11}; in the Vat. Grk. the subject is

the utterance or instruction of the sage, the function of which is
the same as in $3^{1.2}$; the essential thought is the same in both.
The verb *love*, used in the ethical sense, with man as subject, here
has the abstract *wisdom* as object (in 1^{22} its opposite, *ignorance*) ;
in the Prophetical books (Am. 5^{15} Mic. 3^2 *al.*) the object is generally right conduct, in the legal books (Dt. 6^5 Lev. 19^{18} *al.*)
Yahweh and man, in ψ (26^8 119^{97} *al.*) Zion and the Tora. — The
sing. *her* appears to point to one antecedent in v.⁵, whereas Heb.
there has two terms. — **7.** The text is corrupt, and the verse
should probably be omitted.   The Heb. reads : *the beginning of
wisdom — get wisdom, and in all thy substance get understanding,*
or *buy wisdom, and, with all that thou hast gotten, buy*, etc., that
is, buy wisdom at the price of all thy property, cf. 23^{23} Mt. $13^{45. 46}$,
or, *along with all*, etc. (AV. *with all thy getting* is incorrect).
The rendering *wisdom is the principal thing* (RV. Zöckler, in
Lange) is here out of the question ; the word (ראשית), in the
sense of *best, chief, principal,* never occurs undefined (only twice
in OT. undefined, Isa. 46^{10} and the doubtful Gen. 1^1, both times
in the sense of *beginning*), and here we obviously have the familiar
expression *the beginning of wisdom*.   This expression cannot be
brought into intelligible connection with the rest of the verse.
The statement *the beginning of wisdom is "get wisdom,"* if syntactically possible (which is doubtful), involves an intolerable tautology, and the same objection holds to the rendering (obtained
by changing Impv. to Inf.) . . . *to get wisdom*.   Bickell, to avoid
the tautology, reads *the beginning* (or, *chief*) *of thy wealth is*,
etc., which is out of keeping with the tone of the paragraph, is
without Versional support, and is an unnatural form of expression.
— The resemblance between v.⁷ and v.⁵ᵃ is obvious ; the former is
expansion of the latter, or both are corruptions of the same original.   In any case v.⁷ interrupts the connection between v.⁶ and
v.⁸, and is probably a gloss.   Possibly the expressions *get wisdom*
and *get understanding*, written in the margin as a summary of v.⁴⁻⁹,
got into v.⁵, and then in expanded form were inserted as v.⁷ ; this,
if it happened, must have happened after the Vat. Grk. Vrs. was
made — the omission of such passages by the Grk. translator is
not probable.   See note on v.⁵. — **8.** Synonymous, binary.   The
meaning of the first vb. is not quite certain.   It may signify *cast*

up an embankment against a thing, or (Grk.) around a thing,
so as to protect it; or, *make a rampart* of a thing (Jäger),
surround one's self with a thing as a protection; or *cast up* as a
highway (cf. 15[19] Isa. 57[14]), and so make plane and firm; or, perhaps, simply *raise up, exalt, esteem highly, prize* (cf. the similar
form in Ex. 9[17]). This last agrees with the parallel *embrace*, and
is adopted by most expositors. Syr. Targ. have freely *love her;*
Lat. Rashi: *lay hold of her;* Saad.: *give thyself up to her.* A proposed emendation is: *despise her not* (Frankenberg), which gives
a good sense but not a perfect parallelism. — **9.** Synonymous, ternary. Lit. *give to thy head a chaplet.* *Beauty* (or, *grace*) and
glory are physically descriptive terms — the sense is *beautiful
chaplet* and *glorious* (or, *splendid*) *crown;* cf. 1[9] BS. 6[29-31] 25[6].
The expression may be suggested by a custom of wearing chaplets
and crowns at feasts, or on other joyful occasions, as weddings;
cf. Ez. 16[12] 23[42] Isa. 28[1] Job 19[9] BS. 32[2]; how far such a custom
existed among the earlier Hebrews the OT. does not inform us,
but it may easily have been borrowed at a later time.[*]

1. 𝕾 takes דעת as subst., and connects it by ו with בינה.—**2.** 𝔐 לקח;
𝕲 δῶρον, 𝔏 *donum*.— 𝔐 יורי; H-P 68. 161. 248 Comp. Ald. τὸν ἐμὸν λόγον,
which hardly represents a different Heb. text from ours — not necessarily
Christian correction (Lag.), more probably rhetorical variation. — **3.** 𝕲 ὑπήκοος
may be rendering of 𝔐 רך taken as = *soft, submissive;* Lag. holds it to be
rendering of כַּד *poor* (Lev. 25[25 al.]); Heid. of יָד *oppressed* (26[28] ψ 10[18] al.),
neither of which terms is here appropriate, or likely to be rendered by ὑπήκοος.
The connection in 𝔐 requires a descriptive term between בן and לאבי; רך
might be transposed so as to stand before יחיד or before היית, but the signification would still make difficulty unless it could be understood as = *petted*
(𝔗 מפנק), parallel to *beloved* in [b]. Read יחיד רך ויקר לפני אבי כי בן הייתי.— The
κἀγὼ of 𝕲 is probably inserted to bring out the proper emphasis. — 𝔐 יחיד;
read יחיד; 𝕲 here has ἀγαπώμενος; יחיד is rendered by ἀγαπητός Gen. 22[2. 12. 16]
(𝕲[B] does not contain these passages) Am. 8[10] Jer. 6[26] Zech. 12[10], by μονογενής
Ju. 11[34] (𝕲[A] adds ἀγαπητή) ψ 22[21] 25[16] 35[17], and by μονοτρόπους ψ 68[7]; יחיד is
always rendered by some form of ἀγαπ.; we cannot, therefore, determine 𝔐
from 𝕲; but in any case יחיד must here mean *only child*, and this in the
connection is inappropriate. On the MS. reading רבני instead of לפני see
De' Rossi's note. — **4.** In [a] the vbs. might be read as sing., as in 𝔐, or plu.,
as in 𝕲.—Ἐρειδέτω may represent 𝔐 יתמך taken as Nif. (see Concord. of

---

[*] Cf. Nowack, *Heb. Arch.,* I. p. 185 f., and for the Grk. and Rom. customs, Becker,
Char., Exc. I., *Gall.,* Exc. I., and the refs. in the Dicts. of Antiqs.

Grk.), or perh. יסר (De.). — ὁ ἡμέτερος λόγος, = נדרני, hardly original, probably rhetorical interpretation of Grk. translator. — 𝔐 חיו, lacking in 𝔊^B (𝔖^H ast., retained by Proc.); the clause was perhaps introduced from 7², where it is natural (𝔖 adds 7^{2b} at end of v.); according to Lag. והי comes from the half-obliterated המד of a gloss (see note on next verse). — After ה 𝔗 inserts יהוה, so as to express divine authority for the teaching, or it = ו, erroneous repetition of the two ו in חי ורבמן (Pink.). — 5. 𝔐 קנה חכמה קנה בינה, lacking in 𝔊^B (𝔖^H ast); Gr. reads קנה ה as obj. of אל תשכח, and omits ק' ב' as gloss, but ו as obj. of ה does not occur elsewhere and is not a natural construction. The whole expression (together with יהיה) interrupts the connection between בו (v.⁴) and אל הם, and if v.^{5b} be retained must be regarded as a gloss; it may be retained if v.^{5b} be thrown out; see note on v.⁷. — 7. Lacking in 𝔊^B (𝔖^H ast.); it interrupts the connection between v.⁶ and v.⁸, is syntactically and lexicographically difficult, and must be regarded as scribal insertion. Lag.'s explanation of v.⁷ and v.^{5a} is as follows: v.⁷, in distichal form, stood in the margin of some Heb. MS., and was incorporated into the text in two places by two different scribes; one inserted it after v.⁶, writing חכמה for an illegible word which followed ראשית (the word should be a synonym of קנין, and Bi. writes חיל); the other found ו and ובכל קנינך illegible, and omitted them, made וחיה out of the first ה, and attached the resulting sentence to v.⁴. This ingenious and complicated reconstruction still leaves an unsatisfactory couplet *the best of wealth is get wisdom and*, etc. As ר' ה' cannot be brought into syntactical relation with the rest of the sentence, it may be better to regard it as a fragment of a distich similar to 1⁷, and to take the rest of the verse as a fragment of another distich similar to 23²³, though it is hard to say how the text assumed its present shape. — 8. 𝔐 סלסל; 𝔊 (and so 𝔖^H) περιχαράκωσον; 𝔖𝔗 הביב; 𝔏 *arripe*. The vb. may be denom. from סללה or מסלה; but, as from these nouns it may be inferred that the st. = *lift up* (so here Aben Ez. Qamhi), it may here be rendered, in general accord with the rest of the v., *prize*. For other renderings see Schultens' note. Frank. proposes to emend to אל תסליה, from Aram. סלה, = Heb. נסה, on which see note on this v. above. — In ᵇ 𝔊, not so well, takes כבד as Impv. with 3 sing. fem. suff., attaches 2 sing. suff. to תה, and connects by ἵνα (𝔐 כי). 𝔖𝔗 reverse the positions of the vbs. — 9. 𝔐 לויה occurs only twice in OT., here and 1⁹; the stem in Heb. and Aram. = *be attached to, accompany*, in Arab. and Eth. *twist, wind* (so perh. also in Heb. לויה), which is the meaning in לויה. Gr. (as in 1⁹) reads בכלילת; — 𝔐 תמונך; 𝔊 ὑπερασπίσῃ, but stem מגן (= *give, give up* Gen. 14²¹ Hos. 11⁸) is not connected with מגן *shield*, which appears to come from גנן *enclose, protect*. Gr. proposes תענדנ *bind* (see 6²¹) which is hardly better than 𝔐.

10–19. A separate discourse, consisting of **exhortation to obey the sage's instruction** (v.^{10-13}), **and to avoid the way of the wicked in view of their character** (v.^{14-17}), **with a description**

of the paths of the righteous and the wicked (v.[18. 19]). The order of verses in the second half is unsatisfactory, and is variously changed by commentators. Hitzig omits v.[16. 17] as interpolation, inverts the order of v.[18. 19], and before the latter inserts *for;* Delitzsch, Nowack, Strack, Graetz simply invert the order of v.[18. 19]; Bickell places v.[16. 17] after v.[18. 19]. The inversion of the order of v.[18. 19] seems to be all that is needed to secure a natural sequence.

10. Hear, my son, and receive my words,
And the years of thy life will be many.
11. In the way of wisdom I instruct thee,
Lead thee in the paths of uprightness.

12. When thou walkest, thy steps will be unimpeded,
And if thou run, thou wilt not stumble.
13. Hold fast ‹my› instruction — let it not go —
Keep it, for it is thy life.

14. Enter not the path of the wicked,
Walk not in the way of bad men;
15. Avoid it, traverse it not,
Shun it, and pass on.

16. For they sleep not unless they have done harm,
Nor slumber unless they have made some one stumble;
17. They eat the bread of wickedness,
And drink the wine of violence.

19. The way of the wicked is like darkness —
They know not at what they stumble.
18. But the path of the righteous is like the light of the dawn
Which shines ever brighter till the full day comes.

10. Protasis and apodosis, ternary, or quaternary. Lagarde (by a slight change of text) reads : *hear, my son, the instruction of my words*, etc., but elsewhere *instruction* is ascribed not to *words*, but to a person, and the verb *receive* is favored by 2[1]. The form of address is similar to that of v.[1]; on sing. *son*, instead of plu. *sons*, see note on that verse. The reward — long life — as in 3[2. 16]. It is again the sage that is the source of instruction. — **11.** Synonymous, ternary. The sage (as in v.[2]) characterizes his instruction. Not (RV.) *have taught* (or, *instructed*) and *have led;* the reference is to the present instruction. *Wisdom* is here parallel to *uprightness*, practical moral goodness. There is no mention of a divine law ; this, no doubt, is taken for granted, but the teacher's present interest is the practical guidance of life. — **12**. Synonymous, ternary-binary, or ternary. The inducement. For the expression of first cl. cf. Job 18[7] ; lit. *thy step will not be straitened*. The life of a good man is likened to a journey on a well-made road — there will be no narrow and difficult ways, nor any stones or other occasions of stumbling, even when one runs ; cf. 3[6. 23]. — **13**. Synonymous, ternary. Repetition of exhortation. The *my instruction* (after the Grk. — the Heb. has simply *instruction*) is in accordance with v.[10. 11], in which the teacher offers his own words for the guidance of the pupil. The *it* is fem. in the Heb., though the word for *instruction* is masc. ; the writer in thought identifies the latter with wisdom ; cf. 2[1. 2] 3[1. 2. 21. 22]. *Life* is to be understood as in v.[10] ; it includes not only length of days, but also all else that is desirable ; while the reference is not primarily or chiefly to the inner life, this is probably involved in the writer's scheme — moral enlightenment, he means to say, is the essence of life (cf. Eccl. 12[13]), and is to be resolutely grasped and held. Grk. : *keep it for thy life*, the same idea as in the Hebrew.

14-17. Warning against association with bad men on the ground of their moral character. — 14, 15. Synonymous ; v.[14] is ternary, v.[15] is binary (curt, sharp injunction). Warning. Emphatic iteration. In v.[14b] the sense is not *even if thou enter, continue not to walk* therein. On *walk* see critical note. — **16, 17**. Synonymous ; v.[16] is quaternary, v.[17] ternary. Characterization of the manner of life of the wicked. Hyperbolical expression of their life as one of violence (legal and illegal unkindness, oppression, robbery, murder). The type of character portrayed is an extreme one, reckless violence ; no account is taken of those whom moral evil has only slightly touched. The writer may have in mind the foreign and native oppressors of the Jews in the fourth and third centuries B.C., as in ψ 14. 53. 64. 74, etc. ; more probably he is thinking of a class of men that was numerous in the great cities of that period, unscrupulous government agents, revenue farmers, grasping and desperate men of all sorts, some of whom are described by Josephus. The conditions of the society of the time were favorable to violence and oppression, and it is on these conditions that the writer bases his description, which must thus be taken as a local picture of life. His division of men is simple : they are wholly good, or wholly bad, or ignorant and stupid ; he does not recognize the nicer and more complicated experiences of the soul. There is a certain justification for this general point of view : evil, it may be said, whatever its degree, is always evil, and therefore to be avoided ; dallying with transgression of assured moral rules is dangerous. This is the sharply defined, objective old-Hebrew view, which stands in contrast with the modern disposition to distinguish and divide, to recognize good and evil in all things. — The defining terms *wickedness* and *violence* (v.[17]) may express substance or origin ; the meaning may be that these are the food and drink of the wicked (cf. Job 15[16] 34[7]), or that the latter procure the necessaries and goods of life by these means (cf. 9[17]), and both these senses are permitted by the general connection and by the parallelism of v.[16] ; the first interpretation is favored by Procopius, Schultens, Umbreit *al.*, the second by C. B. Michaelis, De., Zöckler, Strack, Nowack. The general sense is not affected by this difference of interpretation ; the first sense appears to suit the context better. — The last word of v.[16] *cause* (*some one*) *to stumble* presents a difficulty : the object is not expressed in the Heb. (the form in the text is intrans., the trans. form is given in the margin), and the Syr. has *till they do their desire ;* the Heb. may be corrupt, but no satisfactory emendation is obvious. — Hitzig omits v.[16. 17] on the ground that they have no logical connection with v.[15], but the relation between the verses seems clear.

18, 19. Contrasted fortunes of wicked and righteous, presented as a motive for living righteously. As v.[19] connects itself by the sense with v.[17], and the initial *and* (*but*) of v.[18] more naturally indicates a contrast with v.[19], it is better to transpose the two verses. — **19.** Progressive, ternary. The characterization of the life of bad men as uncertain and perilous follows fitly on the preceding description of their moral character. The figure is that of a man stumbling on in darkness — so the wicked is exposed to perils of fortune. These pertain not to his inward moral and

religious experiences, but to his outward fate; the reference, as
the context shows, is not to the darkening of the intellect and the
hardening of the conscience by sin, but to outward uncertainty
and misfortunes, such as sudden death and the loss of worldly
goods (cf. $1^{19. 32}$ 2^{22} etc.).— Instead of *as darkness* some Heb.
MSS. have *in darkness*, and the ancient Vrss. *dark;* our text is
favored by the *as* of v.[18]. The noun, used only in poetry and
solemn prose, means deep darkness and gloom; so in Ex. 10^{22}
Dt. 28^{29} Joel 2^2 etc., and cf. the similar term in Job 3^6 10^{22} ψ 91^6.
— **18.** Comparison, quaternary. From the connection the refer-
ence is not to the glory of the righteous life, but to its security.
The good man walks in safety — his path is clear, and not beset
with dangers; the explanation is given in 3^{1-26}. It is happiness
and security from outward evils in this life that is meant. Such a
conception of the perfect well-being of the righteous may have
paved the way for the later doctrine of immortality, though this
doctrine is not hinted at in Proverbs. — The rendering *dawn* is
not certain. Grk., taking the word as verb: *the ways of the
righteous shine like light* — grammatically good, but not favored
by the form of v.[19], in which the standard of comparison is a noun
(*darkness*). The rendering of the Lat. Vulg. (and so Syr. Targ.
RV.), *shining light* (obtained by a change of vowels), is not
probable, as this expression (light defined by its brightness) does
not occur elsewhere. The term *brightness* is used in a general
way (Ez. 1^4 Isa. 62^1), and with reference to the light of fire
(Isa. 4^5), of the moon (Isa. 60^{19}), the stars (Joel 2^{10}), the sun
(Am. 5^{20} Isa. 60^3 Hab. 3^4 2 Sam. 23^4); here, as in Isa. 60^3, it
seems to be the light that precedes the full day. — The last expression in the v., lit. *till the day is established* (or, *certain*), probably
means the coming of full day in contrast with early light or dawn
(see critical note). Many expositors, however (Rashi, Schult.,
Fleisch., De., Reuss, *al.*) understand it to signify *noon*, when the
day reaches its height, or (De.) when the sun appears to stand
still in the zenith, or (Fleisch.), in a figure taken from scales,
when the tongue of day is vertical. The *perfect day* of the Lat.
(adopted by RV.) lends itself to either interpretation, and is perhaps preferable for that reason. Ewald, who takes the reference
to be to the forenoon sun, thinks that the figure is derived from

Ju. 5³¹ (the rising sun dispersing darkness). — However the doubtful terms be rendered, the general sense is plain : the God-fearing
man walks in a light (divine guidance) which, so far from growing
less, continually increases, and shields him from all harm.

10. Instead of 韭 וְיֵ֫רַע the noun רֵעָה is read by Lag., who objects to the
obj. after two Imps.; שׁ֫מַע, he thinks, cannot well be taken as isolated exhortation, and elsewhere in this series of paragraphs (4¹·²⁰ 5¹) the initial vb. of hearing or heeding is followed by its own noun (some word signifying utterance or
teaching). On the other hand, see note above on this word; 𝕲 = 韭. In ᵇ 𝕲
has two renderings, one = 韭, while in the other אֹרְחֹת or דְּרָכֶי stands instead
of שָׁמַע, or (Heid.) less probably, שְׁבִיתָה (שְׁבִירִי?), which does not occur elsewhere in Pr. The second rendering, as freer, is prob. original (Jäg., Lag.),
only ὁδοί, which is unnatural, seems to be scribal error, through incorrect hearing of the copyist (itacism), or through ὁδούς in next v., or through corruption
of the Heb. — 𝕿 שׁ, error for דַּי .. — **11.** The vbs. are Pres. Perfs. — 韭 יֵרֶד;
𝕲 ὁδούς (and so 𝕾𝕿), which agrees with plu. in ᵇ, and may be rhetorical
assimilation, or original Heb. reading. — **12.** 韭 צַעַד, poetic and elevated term
for step, walk; plu, by natural usage of language, in 𝕲𝕾𝕷 and RV. —
𝕾 יֵנּוּ shaken, free rendering of 韭 יֵצַר. — **13.** Read סוּר, with 𝕲 ἐμῆς
παιδείας, as the connection requires. In ᵇ 𝕲 has free rendering of 韭. —
14. 韭 רָאִשֵּׁר (st. as in יֵשֶׁר, and Arab. סר); the Pi. occurs elsewhere only in
caus. sense = lead, or call happy, and, as the connection (parallel הבא) here
suggests the meaning go forward, walk, it is better to point as Qal, as in 9ᵇ;
Lag. writes יֵשׁוּר (for הָאִשׁוּר), which perh. gives an easier rhythm. The Vrss.
translate by regard as fortunate (desirable), be pleased with, envy, 𝕲 ζηλώσῃς,
ΑΘ μακαρίσῃς, 𝕾𝕿 דְּרֵיכ, 𝕷 tibi placeat (and in ᵃ 𝕷, by assimilation, has
delecteris). — **15.** 韭 רְגָלֶהוּ is sustained by parallel שֵׁבֶה; 𝕲 (foll. by 𝕾) ἐν
ᾧ ἂν τόπῳ στρατοπεδεύσωσιν, perh. = הָרְגֵּיהוּ (Jäg.) or יֵרֶצוּם (Lag.), or מִרְעֵהֶם
(Oort) their pasture-ground or camp, though the word occurs in OT. only of
flocks; Heid. suggests the improbable כְּרָד district (only Neh. 3⁹ ⁽ᵃˡ⁾ 𝕲 περί-
χωρος); Schult., after the Arab., disturba seriem ejus, " give up association
with them; " 𝕿ᴸᵃᵍ שׁ שׁ (Buxt. א Ɑr. אֲדִי), heed not, pass over, without
suff., and following suffs in plu. — יֵעַד is perhaps Aramaism. — **16.** 韭 K
יֵעֵירוּ, Q better יֵעֵירוּ (so 𝕿), though without obj. expressed (see Ew., § 303 c);
𝕲 κοιμῶνται (writing שׁ instead of אם) = יֵשְׁכְּבוּ (Schleusn., Lag.) or שׁכבוּ
(Oort), less prob. שׁ (Heid.); 𝕾 יֵעֲבְרוּן צִבְיוֹנֵהוֹן do their will, not = יַבְשִׁילוּ
cook, mature (Umbr.) or יֵעֵירוּ get control of (Heid.), but free rendering or
interpretation of 韭 = do harm, work their wicked will on (𝕿 work fall or
destruction). Oort proposes to read יֵחֲרִיבוּ destroy, of which, he suggests, the
יֵשְׁרוּ of v.¹⁷ may be mutilation. Bi. regards 韭 as scribal erroneous copy of
last word of v.¹⁹ (which v. he puts immediately before v.¹⁶), and reads יָלִינוּ
murmur, speak blasphemously, which 𝕲, he holds, took wrongly in its other
sense of lodge. These readings offer no advantage over 韭. — **17.** 韭 חַכְסִים;

𝔊 παρανόμῳ = 𝔐 — 𝔐 ישׁרי; 𝔊 μεθύσκονται = יעכרו or יׁכרו, which Oort thinks may be the true reading of 𝔐, the ישׁרו being then corruption of יׁחיחו (see n. on v.[16]). 𝔖𝔗 *their bread* (ː ־ ׁ) *is the b. of wickedness* (𝔗 *of the wicked*), which is not favored by [b]. — **19.** 𝔐 יֱאֱרֶׁך; 15 MSS. and Bibl. Brix. have ב instead of ׃, and so 𝔊𝔖𝔗𝔏 have adjs. = *dark*, a reading which agrees well with [b], giving explicitly the reason why the wicked stumble — their way is *in darkness*: on the other hand 𝔐 is favored by the ב of v.[18] — the way is dangerous, *like darkness.* — Instead of בַּֽנַּה יכׁׁרו Bi. (on what ground he does not state) reads בֱמֱׁכׁׁׁרֶׁי [*they do not perceive* or *take note of*] *its stumbling-blocks*, which does not appear to be rhythmically or otherwise better than 𝔐. — **18.** 𝔊 takes נוׁה הׁׁׁךׁ and ׀ א as preds. of ארח (which it reads as plu., ὁδοί); this is hardly possible so far as regards the two last, which naturally refer to the noun אור; the first may be understood as Partcp. agreeing with אׁׁר (so 𝔖𝔗𝔏 and RV.) or, less probably, with ארח (in which case it must be fem. — so perh. 𝔊), or as vb. (Oort) referring to ארח (so perh. 𝔊), or as subst. defining אור. In this last case it must mean *dawn, early light*, and this rendering is favored by the fact that it offers a contrast to the *full day* of [b]. The pointing as Partcp. agreeing with אׁׁר, while grammatically good, is rhetorically not probable; light is said to shine (Isa. 9[2(1)] Job 18[5] 22[28]), and the moon is said (Isa. 13[10]) to cause its light to shine, but light is not elsewhere described as a shining thing; if the epithet were employed, the expression would naturally be defined by the name of the luminary or source of light. נׁיׁח does not elsewhere in OT. certainly occur in the sense of *dawn* (possibly in Isa. 62[1], cf. 2 Sam. 23[4]); but cf. 𝔖 נׁׁוׁרׁא BS 50[6], where 𝔊 has ἀστὴρ ἑωθινὸς and 𝔏 *stella matutina.* — 𝔐 יׁׁכׁׁן, an impossible pointing, since the word is not a subst.; point נׁׁׁכׁׁן, Perf. Nif. The OT. meaning of the word is simply *fixed, firm*, which may here refer either to full day or to noon; on the expressions τὸ σταθερὸν τῆς ἡμέρας, ἡ σταθερὰ μεσημβρία, Arab. אׁלׁנׁהׁאׁר קׁׁׁׁׁׁׁׁׁׁתׁ, = *noon*, see Schult., Ges. (*Thes.*) Fleisch, De., and cf. Lucan, *Phars.*, ix. 528, 529.

20-27. A paragraph similar to the three preceding, containing injunctions to give heed to the teacher's instructions (v.[20-23]) and to practise rectitude (v.[24-27]).

20. My son, attend to my words,
    To my instructions lend thine ear.

21. Let them not depart from thee,
    Keep them in mind.

22. For they are life to those who find them,
    Health to their whole being.

23. With all vigilance guard thou thyself,
    For thus wilt thou gain life.

24. Banish from thee wickedness of mouth,
    Sinfulness of lips put far from thee.

25. Let thine eyes look straight forward,
    Thy gaze be directed straight before thee.

26. Let the path of thy feet be smooth,
    Let all thy roads be firm.

27. Turn not to right nor to left,
    Keep thy feet away from evil.

20, 21. The exhortation. — **20.** Synonymous, ternary. *Instructions* and *lend* are lit. *sayings* (or, *words*) and *turn* (or, *incline*). See notes on 3^{21} $4^{1.\ 10}$. — **21.** Synonymous, binary-ternary. Lit.: *Let them not depart from thine eyes, keep them in thy mind* (lit. *heart*, the inward being), = keep them in mind. On *depart* see note on 3^{21}. Syr. and Targ. have the improbable reading *let them not be despicable in thine eyes.* — **22, 23.** Ground of the exhortation. — **22.** Synonymous, ternary (or, binary). The grammatical number is uncertain. We may read: *for they are life to those who find them and health* (or, *healing*) *to all their being* (lit. *flesh*), or . . . *to him who finds . . . all his. Life*, as in 2^{21} $3^{2.\ 22}$ 4^{13}, = long life or preservation of life, which comprehends all outward earthly blessing. The synonym *health* (or, *healing*), involves deliverance from the evils of life; cf. 3^8. *Flesh* stands for *body*, and so = *being;* cf. *bones* and (in the corrected text) *body* in 3^8. The terms *flesh, heart, soul* often = *self.* The Gk. here has *all flesh,* = *all men*, as in Gen. 6^{12}, etc. — **23.** Single sentence, ternary. Vigilance as source of life and happiness. The Heb. in first line reads: *more than all guarding* (= " with more vigilant guarding than in any other case ") *watch thou over thy heart,* = " watch thy heart (or, thyself) more than anything else " ; the same general sense is given by the rendering: *above all that thou guardest,* etc. (De., RV. marg.), but this signification (" the thing guarded ") the word has not elsewhere in OT. In this interpretation the object of the comparison (between the heart or self and other things) is not clear, and is not found elsewhere in Proverbs. A better sense is given by the Greek reading: *with all watching guard* etc., that is, in every way, with all possible vigilance and diligence (so AV., RV.). — The second line is lit.: *for from it are the outgoings of life,* that is, the beginning or origin (usually the " border " or " boundary," Ez. 48^{30}, once, apparently, " escape," ψ $68^{20(21)}$). The *it* may grammatically refer to *heart*, but Prov.

everywhere else (as in $3^{2.7.8.21.22}\ 4^{4.10.13}\ 6^{23}\ 8^{35}$) represents *life* as
the result of acceptance of wisdom and obedience to instruction;
we should probably, therefore, take the *it* to refer to the " guarding " of first line : " therefrom (= from thy diligent obedience)
proceeds life." * The word *heart* is to be understood as = *self*,
and not as indicating a contrast between inward and outward life;
such a contrast is not found in Prov. — the outward life is treated
as the expression of the inward self. — *Life* = prosperity. The
sense of the couplet is : with utmost care guard thyself from sin
— thus wilt thou be happy. The use of *heart* as = intellectual
being does not rest on a belief that the heart is the centre of the
physical life. The blood was held, by common observation, to be
the life (Dt. 12^{23}), but the function of the heart in the circulation
of the blood was unknown to the Hebrews, and, whatever importance they may have attached to this physical organ as prominent
in the cavity of the body, no less importance was attached to
other organs, as the bowels and the kidneys (and perhaps the
liver, but not the brain). The ground of their assignment of particular mental functions to various physical organs is not known to
us. — **24, 25.** Against wicked speech. — **24.** Synonymous, quaternary. *Wickedness* and *sinfulness* (RV. *froward* and *perverse*)
mean departure (turning aside) from truth and right, contrariness
to good ; cf. notes on $2^{15}\ 3^{32}$. The man's utterance is understood
to express and be identical with his thought and purpose ; so that
the precept is equivalent to " think no evil." There is perhaps
also the implication that evil thought, when embodied in words,
acquires greater consistency, and goes on its bad mission beyond
the thinker's control. — **25.** Synonymous, ternary. Uprightness
of conduct symbolized by straightforwardness of look, in contrast
with the devious and crooked ways of wickedness (v.^{24}). The
serious man fixes his gaze on the goal and suffers nothing to turn
it aside. The rendering in first line : *look to the right* (= *righteousness*) (Frank.) is unnecessary, and is not in keeping with the
figurative form of second line and v.$^{26.27}$. — **26, 27.** The path of
rectitude. — **26.** Synonymous, ternary-binary (or, perhaps, ternary). That is, " make thee a plane, solid road in life." The

---

* This seems to be the interpretation of Saadia and Rashi.

figure is taken from the preparation of a highway for a king or an
army (Isa. 40$^{3.4}$) — hills are cut down and valleys filled, crooked
roads are made straight and rough places smooth, so that there
shall be no need to turn aside from the highroad. Even so a man
must arrange his path in life, walking in the straight and smooth
way of rectitude. — The word *make level* occurs in 5$^{6.21}$ Isa. 26^7,
ψ 78^{50}; the sense *weigh, ponder* (denom. from *scales*, ψ 58$^{2(3)}$) is
not here appropriate. The second verb is equivalent to the first,
meaning *put in good condition of stability and security*, not *mark
off, lay out*, though these terms, like *ordered* and RV. *established*,
involve the same general idea; like the first it has the general
sense of preparedness (Ex. 19^{11} ψ 7^{14}). Grk.: *make straight
paths for thy feet* (so freely Heb. 12^{13}) *and make thy ways
straight*, which agrees in sense with the Heb., though it is not
verbally accurate; evil is crookedness (v.^{24}) and good is straightness. — The plane and solid way in life is to be secured (v.$^{20-22}$)
by accepting the instruction of the sage, that is, of Wisdom. —
27. Synonymous, ternary. The straight way. Duty consists in
walking unswervingly in the path so prepared (v.^{26}) — to swerve,
the second cl. explains, is to fall into *evil*, physical and moral. —
Grk. appends the quatrain: *For the ways of the right hand God
knoweth, but distorted are those of the left. And he himself will
make straight thy paths, and guide thy goings in peace.* The conception here differs from that of v.$^{26.47}$ in two points (Hitz.):
right and *left*, instead of representing both of them divergencies
from the straight path of rectitude, express the one the good way
and the other the bad, and the ways are made straight not by the
man but by God. The insertion (which is the expansion, by
the addition of the second and fourth lines, of a modified form
of 5^{21}) was made by some one who felt that the fact of divine
supervision ought to be strongly brought out. Lagarde thinks
that it does not go back to a Semitic original, but is the work of
a Greek-speaking Christian of the primitive period; he refers to
the numerous dissertations on the two ways in life.* On the
other hand, De. shows that it can be naturally expressed in Hebrew. It is hardly possible to determine whether it is due to a

---

* Plato, *Laws*, iv, 717, referred to in Plut., *Isis*, 26.

Jew or to a Christian, but in any case it bears witness to the freedom, in dealing with the text, which copyists or editors allowed
themselves. — Hitzig regards the Heb. v.[27] as a superfluous scribal
amplification ; however, it adds something to the thought of v.[26],
is not out of keeping with the tone and manner of the section,
and is found in all Ancient Versions.

21. 頁 יריו Hi., only here; we should perh. read Qal (as in 3[21]), so Bi.
𝔊 ὅπως μὴ ἐκλίπωσίν σε, perh. reading יזו, from יר ; cf. note on 3[21].   For
頁 מֵעֵינֶיךָ 𝔊[AB] have αἱ πηγαί σου (= מַעְיָנֶיךָ) and 𝔊[23. 252. 254. 297] αἱ π. τῆς
ζωῆς σου (𝔊[95] omits σου); Lag. regards the latter (which Procop. also has)
as the original; but as the reading of 𝔊[AB] has no meaning, the words
τ. ζ. σ. may have been added by a Grk. scribe to make sense.   Nor is there
probability in Lag.'s view that the διὰ παντὸς (= נכר עָ ם) of 𝔊[254. 297] (inserted
after רבנך) belongs to the Heb. original; cf. 𝔊 6[21].   Heid. suspects in 𝔊 provision against a possible Pharisaic interpretation of the cl. as a reference to
the frontlets of Dt. 6[8] ! — 𝔖𝔗 בעינך (Lag. ניזרן), from ילל, as in 3[21], on
which see note. — **22.** As the suffs. in בצאתהכ and בשרו are inconcinnate, one
of them must be changed; the sing. ו cannot be retained as individualizing;
𝔖𝔗 write the first as sing; 𝔊 here has plu., but in [b] 𝔊[B א*] 𝔏 omit suff.
(giving an improbable reading), αὐτοῦ is added in א[c.a.] A 23, 254 𝔖[H] and
αὐτῶν in 109, 157, 252, 297; these all go back to 頁, and show that its form is
early. — The πᾶσι of 𝔊[161 al.] before τοῖς εὑρίσκουσιν may be a part of the Grk.
original, but does not call for the insertion of כר in 頁.   The αὐτήν in [a] seems
to have ῥῆσις (v.[2]) in view. — **23.** 頁 מכל כשמר; the prep. is מן in 𝔗 and ΑΘ
(ἀπὸ παντὸς φυλάγματος), ב in 𝔖 and apparently in 𝔊 (πάσῃ φυλακῇ), and
𝔏 (omni custodia); the latter is adopted by Oort, Bi., Frank., RV., and
seems preferable; מ means properly the act of watching, hardly the thing
watched — the two interpretations give the same general sense. — The τούτων
of 𝔊 in [b] appears to refer to the λόγοις of v.[20] (so Procop. understands it);
the pronouns in the section are strangely varied in 𝔊. — **24.** The Vrss. except
𝔗, render by various adjs. the substs. which in 頁 are defined by פה and
שפתים (so RV.) 𝔖 עמיקא deep, representing 頁 עקשות, is apparently miswriting of א עיקורא (𝔗 עיקורא); cf. 𝔖 22[4]. — On לוז see Ew., § 165 b, Stade, § 304 c,
Preuschen, in ZAT., 1895, and De.'s note; the regular form of stat. const.
(from רוז) would be רז — this seems to be poetic variation, unless it be from
an otherwise unknown st. לזה, like שבות שבות from שבה. The forms in גת
appear to be Aramaisms. — **25.** Both terms of direction לנכח and נורך are
improperly understood by 𝔊 in an ethical sense, ὀρθὰ and δίκαια (and so 𝔖[H]
Procop.), and the first by 𝔖𝔗𝔏 (not by ΑΘΣ); cf. ψ 17[3]. — **26.** 頁[a] is paraphrased by 𝔖𝔗 keep thy feet (lit. make t. f. pass by) from evil ways (as in
v.[2]).   𝔏 dirige for פרס. — 頁 כר ג is omitted by 𝔊 (in reversal of its custom,
which is to insert a כר in such statements), except H-P 296 (correction after
頁).   יבנו is taken as active by 𝔊ΑΣΘ. — For variations of patrist. writers see

H-P. — 27. הרע ; 𝔊 ἀπὸ ὁδοῦ κακῆς, as in 2¹². — On the added quatrain
in 𝔊 see note above.

V. A discourse against sexual licentiousness in men. — After
the usual introductory exhortation to give heed to instruction
(v.¹·²), the deadly influence of the harlot is described (v.³⁻⁶), the
pupil is cautioned to avoid her lest loss of wealth and destruction
come on him (v.⁷⁻¹⁴), and is urged to conjugal fidelity (v.¹⁵⁻²⁰), the
motive presented being the fate of the wicked (v.²²·²³).* Cf.
BS. 23¹⁷⁻²⁶ 42⁹⁻¹⁴.

THE DEADLY POWER OF THE HARLOT. V.¹⁻⁶.

1. My son, give heed to [] wisdom,†
   To [] understanding † lend thine ear,
2. That discretion may watch ‹over thee,›
   That knowledge [] may preserve ‹thee,›
   [To save thee from the harlot,
   The woman of enticing words.]

3. For the lips of the harlot drop honey,
   Her words are smoother than oil;
4. But at the last she is bitter as wormwood,
   Sharp as a two-edged sword.

5. Her feet go down to Death,
   Her steps lead down to Sheol;
6. ‹No› well-built highway of life she walks,
   Uncertain her paths and not ‹firm.›

1, 2. The general exhortation. — 1. Synonymous, ternary. The
Heb. (in this followed by all Anc. Vrss.) has the poss. prons. *my
wisdom* and *my understanding;* but the sage, while he speaks of
his own *words, commandments, law, instruction,* never elsewhere
claims *wisdom* (= *understanding, knowledge, insight,* or *discretion*)
as his own, but represents it as the goal to which his instruction
leads; see 2¹⁻³· ⁹⁻¹¹ 3¹· ²¹ 4¹· ²· ¹⁰· ²⁰; for the meanings of the terms see
note on 1²⁻⁴. — **2.** The text is in disorder, and can be only conjecturally restored; and the connection between v.² and v.³ is not
expressed. The Heb. (followed substantially by all Vrss. except

---

* On v.²¹ see note on that verse below.
† Heb. : *my wisdom* and *my understanding.*

Grk.) reads *to preserve* [= *that thou mayest preserve*] *discretion* [= *sagacity, insight*], *and that thy lips may keep knowledge*. But the reference to the *lips* of the pupil, proper in 4^{24}, is out of place here; lips *utter*, but do not *keep;* we should rather expect *thy mind (heart)*, as in $3^1 \, 4^4$, or simply *keep thou*, as in $4^{13} \, 7^2$, if the point is the inward acceptance of wisdom or instruction. The mention of the *lips of a strange woman*, in v.^{3}, might suggest, as contrast, *my lips;* so Grk.: *and the knowledge of my lips is enjoined* [or, according to another reading, *I enjoin*] *on thee*. This is so far better than the Heb. as it refers to the utterance of lips, but it is syntactically not in accord with the preceding (in which the pupil is the subject), and the expression is strange — the lips of the teacher are nowhere else described as the possessors of knowledge, though they are said (15^7) to *scatter knowledge*, that is, by words. These considerations are unfavorable to the emendations *that the knowledge of my lips may be preserved for you* (Oort), and *that my lips may enjoin knowledge on thee* (Bickell). It is hardly possible to construe the expression *thy lips* (or, *my lips*), which appears to have been introduced by an early scribe from the next verse. Dyserinck, omitting this expression, and seeking a connection between v.^{2} and v.^{3}, reads : *that thou mayest keep discretion and knowledge, that they may preserve (thee) from the strange woman* (cf. 7^5). Some such form as this is required by the connection. The resemblance between this passage and $2^{11.\,16} \, 7^{1-5}$ is obvious, and we should probably here introduce a couplet like $2^{16} \, 7^5$, and read : *that discretion may watch over thee and knowledge preserve thee, to save thee from the strange woman*, etc. (as in the translation given above).

3–6. Description of the harlot; cf. $2^{16-19} \, 7^{5-21.\,26.\,27}$. The description follows abruptly on the exhortation, while elsewhere there is an easy transition from the appeal (*hear, attend*) to the subject-matter of the instruction. Before v.^{3} the Grk. inserts *give no heed to a worthless woman* (Lat. . . . *to a woman's deceit*) ; but this destroys the distichal form of the verse ; it is a scribal effort to secure connection between v.^{2} and v.^{3}, but it is not in the manner of similar passages, and probably does not represent a Heb. text. On other proposed transitional expressions see note

above; some reference to the *strange woman* must have preceded
v.³, but it was early lost. — The warning is addressed only to men ;
nothing is said of the danger to women from the seductions of
men. This silence may be due in part to the belief that women
were more hedged in and guarded by social arrangements, and
less exposed to temptation than men ; but it is chiefly the result
of the fact that in the OT. (as in most ancient and modern works
on practical ethics) it is only men that are had in mind, the moral
independence of women not being distinctly recognized. The
only addresses to women as such in OT. are the denunciation of
the luxurious ladies of Jerusalem in Isa. 3¹⁶–4¹ (connected with
the nation's defection from Yahweh), and the similar sarcastic
prediction of Am. 4¹⁻³, directed against the great ladies of Samaria.
Ez. (13¹⁷⁻²³) denounces the prophetesses in their official capacity.
Ben-Sira (25²⁵. ²⁶ 26¹⁰ 42⁹⁻¹¹) directs the husband how to deal with
his erring wife, and the father how to manage his daughter, but
addresses no word of advice to women. In our chapter the man
who is warned is thought of as married (v.¹⁵), and, if we may conclude from 7¹⁹, the woman against whom he is warned is married.
The married state is regarded as the normal one; in ancient life,
men, as a rule, were married at an early age. — **3.** Synonymous, ternary. On *strange woman*, = harlot, see note on 2¹⁶. The specious,
soft-speaking lips are compared to a honeycomb, and are said to
drop honey (the word means the honey of the comb), an expression
which in Cant. 4¹¹ denotes not sweet speech but bodily sweetness.
Bickell judges, from the parallelism, that the verb *drop* does not
belong here, but has been introduced from Cant. 4¹¹, and that we
should read *the lips . . . are honey;* the emendation hardly improves the rhythm of the Heb., and is otherwise improbable —
the sweetness of honey is a standard of comparison in the Bible
(Ju. 14¹⁸ Ez. 3³ Rev. 10⁹. ¹⁰ ψ 19¹⁰ 119¹⁰³), but neither mouth nor
lip is called honey; we might, perhaps, say *are sweet as honey*, or,
are as honey, though, while *words* are called *honey* (16²⁴), the
mouth or the lip is rather the source from which the honey drops
or flows. — The term rendered *words* (RV. *mouth*) is properly
palate (roof of the mouth), to which the tongue cleaves from
thirst (Lam. 4⁴) or from emotion (Job 29¹⁰), the result being
sometimes dumbness (Ez. 3²⁶) ; it is the organ of physical taste

(Job 12^{11}), and thence comes to express intellectual discernment (Job 6^{30}) ; and it is used, as here, for the vocal cavity as the seat of speech (8^7 Hos. 8^1) ; its *smoothness* denotes flattery (29^5) or hypocrisy (ψ 5^{10}) ; so Eng. *smooth* and *oily*. — The woman is described as mistress of cajoling, enticing words ; see the specimen of her persuasions given in 7$^{14-20}$. Rashi and other Jewish expositors explain the figure of the woman as Epicureanism (philosophical scepticism, irreligiousness), or as heresy in general (including idolatry) ; and it was similarly allegorized by some early Christian writers. — 4 Synonymous, ternary. Lit. *the end* (RV. *latter end*) *of her is bitter*, etc., that is, the final outcome or result of relations with her ; the term *end* (Heb. *aḥarith*) always involves the idea of final judgment. In contrast with the sweetness and smoothness of the woman's speech and demeanor is put the bitterness and sharpness of the doom she brings on men (v.^{5}). *Wormwood* is a symbol in OT. of suffering, as the result of man's injustice (Am. 5^7 6^{12}), or as divine punishment (Dt. 29$^{18(17)}$ Jer. 9$^{15(14)}$ 23^{15} Lam. 3$^{15. 19}$) or, as here, as the natural outcome of man's sin. The plant meant is some species of *Artemisia**; the word is probably here used in a generic sense ; Grk. *bile*, the other Vrss. *absinthium*. — **5.** Synonymous, ternary. See 2^{18}. *Death* is here a place, = *the realm of death*, = *Sheol*. — *Lead down to* is lit. *take hold on* (as in ψ 17^5) = *cleave to, follow* (or, *keep*) *the path to*. On *Sheol* see note on 1^{12}. The woman's manner of life is represented as fatal to earthly well-being — to enter into relations with her is to go the way that shortens one's days ; the purely moral side of the procedure is not referred to. This is part of the general representation of the Book that wickedness brings death, that is, premature and unhappy death ; so 2$^{19. 22}$ 4^{19}. Whether in the present case death comes from the weakening of bodily strength or by direct intervention of God is not said. The connection does not suggest a reference to legal punishment. — Grk. : *for the feet of folly* (perh. a philosophical abstraction) *lead her associates with death to Hades, and her steps are not firmly fixed*, paraphrase, *with* instead of *to*, incorrect division of the verse, and consequent inser-

---

* See Celsius, *Hierobotanicum ;* Tristram, *Survey ;* J. H. Balfour, *Plants of the Bible.*

tion of the negative.   Lat., second cl.: *her steps penetrate unto
the Underworld* or *the dead* (*ad inferos*). — **6.** Text and translation are uncertain.   The Heb. reads: *the path of life lest she* [or,
thou] *make level, her ways are unstable* [*totter, reel, wander aimlessly*], *she knows not* [or, *thou knowest not*]; that is, *her ways
are unstable in order that she may not* [or, *that thou mayest not*]
prepare the paths of life; but in sentences in which the protasis
is introduced by *lest,* the apodosis always states that which is
done in order that something else may not happen (the two
things must, of course, be different), while here the two clauses
are identical in meaning — to say that her paths are unstable in
order that they may not be stable, or, in order that thou, if thou
walk in them, mayest not be stable (cf. 4[26]), gives no sense, and
could not have been written by the Heb. author.   The Anc. Vrss.
take first cl. as an independent affirmation parallel to second cl.,
and have *not* instead of *lest,* and this no doubt gives the proper
general form (but RV. *so that . . not* is impossible).   The connection indicates that it is the woman (and not the man) that is
spoken of throughout the verse; the verb in first cl. means *make
plane,* and not *enter on, walk in* (Anc. Vrss.), or, *ponder* (Schult.
RV. marg.).   The last phrase of the verse, *she knows not,* is
strange, whether it be taken to mean that she knows not that her
ways are unstable, or that she knows not whither her ways wander
— the point indicated by the connection is not her ignorance (in
9[13] ignorance is appropriately introduced, and cf. ψ 35[8]), but the
evil character of her paths.   Our verse is clearly intended to
express the contrast to 4[26]: there *make level the path of thy feet,*
here *she does not make level the way of life;* there *let all thy ways
be made firm,* here *her paths are unstable and,* after which we
expect an expression = *not firm.*   There might seem, further, to
be tautology in the terms *way of life* and *make level,* since a way
that leads to life must of necessity, according to OT. usage, be
level; but *life* here appears to stand as contrast to the *death* of
the preceding verse, and the verb may be retained in the sense of
prepare, or may be changed to one meaning *tread* or *enter,* as in
the Versions.   We may, with probability, read: *she prepares not
a highway of life, her paths wander and are not firm.* — Notwithstanding the uncertainties of the text, the general sense of the

verse is clear: the path of the harlot is unstable and does not lead to life — the verse states negatively what v.[5] states positively, that is, she and her associates are doomed to a premature and wretched death.

1. Drop the ı pers. suffs.; see note above. — 𝕲 writes ᵇ as in 4[20], λόγοις (so 𝕾, only sing.), exc. H-P 23, 252, which have φρονήσει. 𝕾ᴴ has doublet, first = 𝕲ᴮ ᵃˡ· (with obel.), second = 𝖍𝕲[23. 252], the latter being correction after 𝖍. Between 𝕲ᴮ and 𝖍 it is not easy to decide; 𝖍 is perh. favored by the parallelism. — **2.** To דיבר Bi. appends suff. ך, which is proper (as subj.), though not necessary in poetical style. 𝕾𝕿, taking מ as subj., render לש by Pass. Impf. and insert ב before מ. — 𝖍 מזמות; 𝕲 ἔννοιαν ἀγαθήν. — In ᵇ 𝕲ᴮᴬ*(vid) αἴσθησις δὲ ἐμῶν χειλέων ἐντέλλεταί σοι = יצוו לך שפתי ור׳ (Jäg., adopted by Bi.); the other MSS. of 𝕲 αἴσθησιν . . . ἐντέλλομαί σοι = אצוה . . .; on the objection to this reading and that of 𝖍 see note above. The passage should perhaps stand as follows (cf. 2[11. 16]):

תשמרך מזמה ודעת ינצרך
להצילך מאשה זרה מנכריה אמריה החליקה

Or, the first half only of second line may be inserted, and we shall then have a couplet quaternary-ternary. — **3.** 𝕲 (and so substantially 𝕃) prefixes μὴ πρόσεχε φαύλῃ γυναικί, = אל תקשיב לאשה אוילה, against which the objection based on the rhythm seems decisive, though some such connecting phrase (see note on v.[2] above) is necessary. — 𝖍 זרה; 𝕲 πόρνης, = זנה, or free rendering of 𝖍. — 𝖍 חלק; 𝕃 *nitidius* (= *more shining* or *sleeker*), free trans. of 𝖍, or perh. from some form of הרל. — 𝖍 מְשֶׁמֶן; 𝕲 πρὸς καιρὸν apparently (Lag.) for πρὸ ἐλαίου; ΣΘ ὑπὲρ ἔλαιον; for σὸν read τὸν (Jäg.). — Bi. improperly omits תשפנה, which is required by the usage of language. — The primitive sense of חך (for חנך) *palate* is uncertain, perh. a *narrow* aperture or passage (Ges. *Thes.*, Dillm. *Lex. Ling. Aeth.*, cf. חנק, ענק); the vb. is denom., = in Arab. *to rub a child's palate* (with chewed dates, etc.) when it is named, probably by way of dedication to the clan-deity (W. R. Smith, *Kinship*, p. 154), and hence perh. *initiate, dedicate, educate;* in Heb. *train* a child (22[6]), *dedicate* a private residence (Dt. 20[5]) or a temple (1 K. 8[63]); cf. note on 22[6]; the proper name חנוך (if it be Heb.) may, like Arab. חניך, mean a man of experience or wisdom. Cf. Lane, *Lex.;* BDB. — On 𝕿 see Lag., Pink. — **4.** Instead of 𝖍 *as* (כ) 𝕲 has *than* (מ = מן); cf. Heb. 4[12]. 𝕾 has מן in both clauses, 𝕿 in ᵇ only; there was confusion between כ and מ in the Heb. MSS. (easy in either the old or the square script). — At end of ᵃ 𝕲 rhetorically adds εὑρήσεις, and 𝕾 makes suff. to אחריה plu., referring to its *words* in v.[3] (𝖍 חך). — **5.** On the paraphrasing text of 𝕲 see notes of Jäg., Lag.; it paraphrases suff. in רגליה, takes ירדות as Hif., has את before מות, and Nif. of תמך, before which it inserts neg.; 𝕾𝕿 Gr. סמך; 𝕃 *penetrant;* 𝕾ᴴ סתח (= 𝕲); Bi. writes יה׳ ׳צ sing.; there is no reason for changing 𝖍, unless, as in 2[18], preps. be inserted before מות and

שאול, though these may stand as objectives without preposition. — **6.** 𝕳 פן is unintelligible; the connection requires a neg. (perh. בל), as all Anc. Vrss. take it. Succeeding interpretations have been various. Talmud, *Moed Katon*, 9 *a*: *do not ponder the path of life* (that is, to discover the precepts, obedience to which is most rewarded by God); Rashi: *do not ponder the way of the life* of the woman, for all her paths lead to death; Schultens (connecting it with 5ᵇ): (she plunges into Sheol) *lest perchance she should ponder*, etc., and possibly repent (a result which she wishes to avoid); C. B. Mich.: (her ways wander) *lest thou ponder*, etc.; Ew. *al.: lest she ponder ;* Nowack, Strack: *that she may not enter on ;* Kamp.: *that she may miss ;* De. (adopting an untenable translation of פן): *she is far from entering;* Noyes: *she gives no heed to;* Frank. omits the line as incapable of satisfactory translation, but thinks that 𝕲 gives the sense properly. The objections to פן are first its position (not at beginning of clause), and secondly, the identity of content of the two clauses; on the supposed similarity in this last respect of 15²³ (למען, cited by Now.), see note on that verse. — 𝕳 ארח; 𝕾 ארעא, miswriting of אורחא (Vogel). — 𝕳 תפרס; 𝕲 freely ἐπέρχεται (and so 𝕾𝕿); 𝕷 *ambulant*, referring to *pedes* v.⁶, or to *gressus* v.⁶; Gr. תסלף *subvert*. 𝕳 may be retained. — 𝕳 לא תדע is omitted by Bi. as marring the parallelism; it is rhythmically and in sense inappropriate. The Vrss. represent 𝕳; 𝕲 (foll. by 𝕾𝕷) καὶ οὐκ εὔγνωστοι (referring to τροχιαί), = *she knows them not;* 𝕿, reproducing 𝕳 exactly (only pref. ו) ולא ידעא; Schult. *haud curat*, and so most later expositors (as RV.) *she knows* (or, *observes*) *it not;* C. B. Mich.: *so that thou knowest not* (where thou art). Some expression here seems required by the rhythm, and we may doubtfully emend to יבנו (4²⁶).

7-14. After this general description of the perils of association with the harlot, **the discourse repeats the warning against her** (v⁷·⁸), **basing it on the suffering she brings, namely, loss of wealth** (v.⁹·¹⁰)**, and closing with a picture of the victim's useless regret** (v.¹¹⁻¹⁴).

7. Now, therefore ‹ my son,› hearken to me,
   And depart not from the words of my mouth.

8. Keep thy path far from her,
   Go not near the door of her house;

9. Lest thou give up thy ‹ wealth › to others,
   The (toil of) thy years to ‹ aliens,›

10. Lest strangers enjoy thy substance,
    And thy labors (go to) an alien's house;

11. And thou groan at last,
    When thy body and flesh are consumed,

12. And say: "Alas! I have hated instruction,
    And guidance I have despised;

13. I have not listened to the voice of my teachers,
    Nor hearkened to my instructors;
14. I had wellnigh come to complete grief
    In the congregation and the assembly."

7, 8. Synonymous, ternary. Exhortation : " seeing she is as I have said, avoid her." The Heb. has plu. *sons*, but the sing. is called for by the rest of the address, and is found in the Grk. and the Latin. The woman (probably married, but whether married or unmarried) has her own house.

9, 10. Synonymous ; v.[9] is ternary-binary ; v.[10] is ternary. More particular statement of the loss she inflicts. Our Heb. text reads : 9. *Lest thou give up thine honor to others and thy years to the cruel* [or *to a cruel one*], 10. *lest strangers be filled with thy strength, and thy labors* (*go*) *into an alien's house*. The *strength* of v.[10] = *wealth*, as in Job 6[22] (RV. *substance*). In v.[9] (which seems intended to express the same thought as v.[10]) the parallelism suggests the reading *wealth* (or perhaps *life*, as in the Grk.) instead of *honor*, and the meaning will then be that all the outcome, the earnings, of the man's life pass into the hands of others. If the reading *honor* be retained, this word must be interpreted similarly, as equivalent to *years*, that is, the *labor of years*, *wealth*, called *honor* because it gives a man an honorable position among men. The two clauses of v.[9] must be taken as synonymous ; we cannot understand *honor* as expressing the freshness and grace of youth, and *years* the dignity of age. The term *cruel*, if it be the right reading, is parallel and equivalent to *others, strangers, aliens*, and is to be understood as describing the pitiless character of these persons (creditors, sharpers, the woman and her friends, including, perhaps, the husband) who get possession of the victim's money. It is, however, a surprising term in this connection (the general reference being simply to the fact that the man loses his property), and seems to be scribal error for the word meaning *alien* (as the Targ. has it). The quatrain appears to give a complete double set of synonyms, four words signifying " wealth," and four signifying " other persons." — In any case the penalty predicted for the debauchee is loss of worldly wealth, as, on the other hand, riches is the reward of the wise (3[16] 8[18]). The reference (cf.

v.⁵) cannot be to the punishment of death for adulterers ordained in the Israelitish law (Ez. 16⁴⁰ Lev. 20¹⁰), since there is here no hint of such a fatal ending or of legal procedure (cf. note on v.¹⁴), but the intimation is that the punishment, loss of wealth, comes from ordinary social causes. Still less is it meant that the offender may be emasculated and become the slave of the injured husband (Ew.) ; no such provision exists in the OT. law. It is simply that the licentious man, careless and prodigal, is preyed on by others (chiefly the woman and her husband and lovers), and thus sacrifices his years to aliens. This is the sting of his doom, that his toil goes to build up not his own house but another's, and his life thus becomes a failure. The point of view is external — there is no reference to corruption of soul ; that is no doubt assumed, but the moralist uses what he thinks the most effective deterrent argument, the social destructiveness of the vice in question.

11-14. The man's lamentation over his broken life. — **11.** Progressive, binary-ternary. *At last* (lit. *in thy aftertime* or *at thy end*) = when the results of thy action show themselves ; the reference may be to the period immediately succeeding the loss of wealth or to the end of life. *Body and flesh* (= the being, personality) are *consumed*, worn out, the allusion being not to the physical results of sexual indulgence (the point is not excess, but illegality and immorality), but to the loss of social position and power, in general to the failure of the man's life. The picture is identical in substance with that of v.⁹· ¹⁰, loss of wealth involving or expressing loss of all that makes life enjoyable. — Grk. : *and thou repent at last when the flesh of thy body is consumed*, a reading which represents slight modifications of our Heb. text : *groan, mourn, repent* are practically equivalent, *groan* being the strongest ; the rhetorical repetition *body and flesh* is more effective than the preciser *flesh of body*. — **12, 13.** Synonymous, ternary. Lit. *my heart* (= myself) *has despised* (v.¹²), and *lent* (lit. *inclined*) *mine ear to mine instructors* (v.¹³). The Heb. prefixes *how* to the whole quatrain, the sense being : *how have I hated . . . despised . . . how have I not listened . . . and not inclined !*, an awkward form of expression in English (RV. has an ungrammatical sentence in v.¹²ᵇ, and drops the *how* in v.¹³). Heb. employs this *how* as in-

troduction to laments (2 Sam. 1^{25} Zeph. 2^{15} Ez. 26^{17} Isa. 14^4 1^{21}
Lam. 1^1 2^1 Jer. 48^{17}) with the sense *how lamentable the case!*, here
how foolish I was!, a meaning which is expressed by *alas!* Instead of the Perf. *have hated*, etc., we may render by the Pret.
I hated, etc. On *instruction* and *guidance* see notes on 1$^{2.23}$.—
The sage here reaches the gist of his discourse — obedience to
instruction would have saved the man from this unhappy fate.
The *teachers* are wise men, fathers of families and heads of
schools. Here, as elsewhere in the book, it seems to be assumed
that more or less organized schemes of moral instruction for young
men existed — incipient universities such as appear in the second
century B.C. — **14.** Progressive, ternary. Lit.: *had wellnigh fallen
into all evil.* If the *evil* be moral, the *congregation* (or, *assembly*)
is the crowd of bad companions who lead the man astray, or the
community which witnesses his downfall; but this interpretation
does not agree with the connection — he declares (v.$^{12.13}$) not that
he came near descending, but that he did descend into the depths
of moral evil, and he reflects that he has barely escaped something else, namely, crushing suffering. This sense of the term
evil occurs in 13^{17} ψ 10^6 27^5; here it appears to mean official punishment. *Congregation* and *assembly* (synonymous terms) signify
first any mass of persons gathered together, and then particularly
a community (sometimes the whole body of Israelites) in organized political or judicial form, here the official gathering of the
man's community to take cognizance of offences against law. In
the early time every Israelitish community appears to have exercised judicial and executive powers (Dt. 17^7 21 Lev. 24^{16}.) In
the Roman times also the Jewish communities all over the empire
seem to have had the right of jurisdiction over their members, and
this was probably the case in the Grk. period in Palestine and
Egypt.* The adulterer might, perhaps, have been sentenced to
death (but see notes on 6$^{33\,ff.}$) ; he sees that he came near losing
his life or suffering some other overwhelming punishment; cf. Ben-
Sira 23^{21}. It is obvious that the point here is different from that
of v.$^{9.10}$, and that in v.^{5} also the reference is general, not particularly to legal punishment. The stress here laid on the verdict of
the community is to be noted.

---

* Cf. Schürer, *Jewish People*, 2, 2, § 31.

7. 𝔐 בנים; 𝔊 *vié*; read בני, as in v.[1. 20], and make the vbs. sing. —
8. 𝔐 חעליה; 𝔊 ἀπ' αὐτῆς; Bi. unnecessarily מפנה. — 𝔐 פחה and בית written
by 𝔊 (in several different forms) plu., by Heb. or Grk. scribal inadvertence.
— 9. 𝔐 הוד; 𝔖𝔗 חיל; 𝔊 ζωήν, which may perh. represent הד taken (like רכב,
see Dillm.'s note on Gen. 49[6], Geiger, *Urschrift*, p. 319) as = *soul* (Lag.), but
more probably is rendering of חיי, which is favored by the parallel שנת, 𝔊 βίον;
Oort הין, which Gr. regards as the Heb. text of 𝔖 (cf. Pink.), and it should
probably here be read instead of 𝔐 הד. — 𝔐 אכזרי, emend to וכדי; 𝔊 ἀνελε-
ήμοσιν (and so 𝔖𝔏); 𝔗 here and 11[17] נוכראין (= Heb. וכרי), regarded by Vog.
as scribal error for אכזראין, by Baumg. for נכזריא (so 17[11]); the connection
favors 𝔗. — 10. 𝔐 פן (lacking in 𝔊[A. 103]) is omitted by Lag. as bad Heb.,
since the force of the part. in v.[9] may extend through v.[10]; but such repetition
is rhetorically permissible. — The Vrss. properly supply a vb. in [b]; 𝔐 is poetically concise. With use of כח as = *wealth* cf. similar use of חיל. — 11. 𝔐 נהמת;
𝔊 (followed by 𝔖), not so well, μεταμεληθήσῃ, = נהמת. — 𝔐 באחריתך; Clem.,
Strom. 122, ἐπὶ γήρως (and so 𝔖), regarded by Lag. as the genuine text of 𝔊,
ἐπ' ἐσχάτων being revision. — The σάρκες σώματός σου of 𝔊 (adopted by Bi.)
is rhetorically not so good as 𝔐. Geiger, *Urschrift*, p. 418, supposes that the
original text had כלה instead of כלה. — 12. The diff. between 𝔐 תוכחת and
𝔊 ἐλέγχους is one of pointing (in 6[23] 𝔐 has plu. and 𝔊 sing.), and there is
little choice between them. 𝔊[23. 252. 297] Constitt. 9[8] Arab. but not Aeth. (Lag.).
add δικαίων, an addition natural but not found elsewhere. — 13. In ולא omit ו,
with 𝔊. Instead of בכור a number of MSS. have לקול, which is perh. better. —
Lag. points out that the reading of 𝔊[B al.] παιδεύοντός με καὶ διδάσκοντός με is
the original Grk. (though not the translation of the original Heb.), and that
of 𝔊[23 al.], conformed to the Heb., a correction. — 14. 𝔐 כמעט; 𝔊 παρ' ὀλίγον;
A ὡς ὀλίγον; Schol. ἐν βραχυτάτῳ; 𝔏 *pene*; 𝔖𝔗 עד כליל *wholly*; Gr. emends
to נמאס *despised*. — 𝔖𝔗 בישין takes רע as plural.

15–20. Exhortation (couched in erotic terms) **to avoid harlotry and observe conjugal fidelity.** The sacredness and social
value of the family are implied. It is assumed that men are married, and the exhortation indicates that conjugal infidelity was a
crying evil of the time. The paragraph consists of two parts, the
first (v.[15–17]) figurative, the second (v.[18–20]) the literal interpretation of the first. The terms *cistern, waters*, etc., are used figuratively, but the allegorical interpretation of the *wife*, as = *wisdom*,
etc., is excluded by the connection.

15. Drink water from thine own cistern,
    Running water from thine own well.
16. Should thy springs be scattered abroad?
    Thy streams of water in the streets?

17. Let them be for thyself alone,
    And not for others with thee.

18. Let thy fountain be ‹ thine own,› *
    Get thou joy from the wife of thy youth;

19. [] Let her breasts intoxicate thee always,†
    Be thou ever ravished with her love.

20. Why shouldest thou [] ‡ be ravished with a stranger,
    Embrace the bosom of another woman?

15. Synonymous, binary-ternary. The *cistern* is a receptacle (often hewn out of the rock, Jer. 2[13]) into which water falls or flows from without and in which it remains motionless; in the *well* (Nu. 21[17, 18]) the water rises from beneath and has movement, life (so here *running water* is not spoken of in connection with the *cistern*); the two terms are rhetorical variations of expression for a supply of drinking-water. The figure appears to be a general one : let thy own wife be thy source of enjoyment, as refreshing as water to a thirsty man. The enjoyment meant is sensual, but there does not seem to be a comparison of the female form to a cistern or well, or a designation of the wife as the source of children (cf. Ex. 21[10], Koran 2[223]); there is no reference to children in the paragraph. The basis of the figure is given in Isa. 36[16] where drinking from one's (literal) cistern is the symbol of enjoyment of one's home. The general idea of origin is expressed in Isa. 51[1] : Abraham is the rock whence was hewn the stone for the building of the nation, Sarah the rock-pit (the same word that is here used for cistern) whence the nation was dug; in this there seems to be no pictorial allusion to the mother's womb — father and mother are spoken of in the same way. In Eccl. 12[6] also *cistern* stands in a general way for life. § A close approach to the wording of our verse is found in Cant. 4[15], in which the heroine is called *a garden-fountain, a well of living water, of streams from Lebanon* (and cf. v.[12]), that is, a source of refreshing and enjoy-

---

* Heb.: *blessed.*

† On the omission of first line of v.[19] see note on this verse below.

‡ Heb. inserts *my son.*

§ In Eccl. 12[1] the emendation *cistern* (בור) or *well* (באר), = *wife*, instead of *creator* (בורא), is not favored by the connection, and is, on rhetorical grounds, extremely difficult if not impossible; probably 11[10b]. 12[1a] is orthodox scribal insertion.

ment (the similarity of expressions in Pr. and Cant., here and elsewhere, suggests that one of these books drew from the other). — Grk., by a slight change of text, has *drink waters out of thine own vessels* (ἀγγείων), and in NT. (1 Th. 4⁴ 1 Pet. 3⁷) *vessel* (σκεῦος) = *wife;* the latter term represents the body as the locus or instrument of the soul or of service, and often = *person,* but the Grk. term here means *drinking-vessels.* — Our Heb. text introduces the wife not as child-bearer, but as source of pleasure. For the general figure cf. BS. 26¹². — **16.** Synonymous, ternary-binary. It is a question whether the infidelity here referred to is that of the husband or that of the wife. The connection clearly favors the former interpretation; the reference in v.¹⁵ and in v.¹⁸⁻²⁰ is obviously to the man, and it is not likely that the discourse would be interrupted by the introduction of a topic which is mentioned nowhere else in the chapter; and v.²⁰, further, appears to give the literal meaning of v.¹⁶·¹⁷, as v.¹⁸ gives that of v.¹⁵. The sense is: seek not thy pleasure in the streets (from harlots, see 7¹²), from all sorts of sources (*scattered abroad*). *Springs* and *streams* symbolize sources of enjoyment, and particularly such as are commonly outside of one's house-land; while *cistern* and *well,* v.¹⁵ (also sources of enjoyment) are properly attached to the house. — The interrogative form (which may be rendered by a negative), though not given in the Heb., is permissible, and is demanded by the connection. The declarative or the jussive form (*thy streams will be* [or, *let thy streams be*] *spread abroad*), adopted by a number of expositors (from Aquila and Saadia on), is held to mean "thou shalt have numerous descendants" (Schult.), or "let thy generative power act freely within the marriage-relation" (De.); but these interpretations are not favored by the context. The terms *springs,* etc., cannot naturally be taken to mean "generative power" (Ew., De., *al.*); the connection shows that they signify "sources of pleasure" (here sensual pleasure). — Those who make the woman the subject interpret: "let not thy wife stray abroad" (as a result of thy infidelity). — Grk.: *let not thy waters overflow,* etc. (the negative is involved in the interrogative form). — Others: "do not squander thy virile strength," which is correct in general sense (see above), but incorrect in form. — **17.** Synonymous, ternary, or binary. Repetition of the exhorta-

tion of v.[16], = "let thy pleasures belong to thyself alone (that is,
be derived from thine own wife), and not be shared with others
(as they must be, if thou consort with harlots)." — On the less
probable interpretation : "let thy wife be for thee alone, and not
for others with thee " (= let not thy wife become a harlot) see
note on preceding verse. — **18–20.** This group repeats and interprets the exhortation of the preceding in literal terms — the erotic
expressions (cf. Canticles) are partly explained by the fact that
women did not in ancient times form part of the audiences addressed by men, or of the public for which books were written.*
— **18.** Synonymous, ternary. *Fountain,* parallel to *water, springs,
rivers* of v.[15. 16], is explained in second cl. as = *wife,* as source of
physical pleasure. The Heb. reads : *let thy fountain be blessed.*
The " fountain " may be regarded as *blessed* when it is enjoyed
in accordance with the laws of God and man, that is, in the marriage-relation, in contrast with the pleasures of illicit love ; as
appears from the connection, there is no reference to the blessedness of children born in wedlock — the wife is viewed not as child-
bearer but as pleasure-giver. The term *blessed* is, however, not
what we should expect ; the section contrasts the wife as *one's
own* with the harlot as *stranger,* and there is probability in the
Grk. reading *let thy fountain be thine own* or *for thee alone*
(which represents a slight modification of our Heb. text) (cf.
v.[17]). The *fountain* of Lev. 12[7] 20[18] refers to the blood of child-
birth and menses and has nothing to do with our passage. The
joy of second cl., as appears from the following context, is sensual. — Among ancient peoples marriage was considered a duty,
and early marriage appears to have been the general custom ;
such a custom is assumed in the expression *wife of thy youth,* and
the writer probably had in mind its value as a guard against
debauchery. It has been suggested † that the astonishing vitality
of the Jews is due in part to their maintenance of early marriage
(a custom which they have always kept up except when, as now to
some extent, they have fallen into the habits of other peoples). —
19. Synonymous, ternary (the first line of the Heb. being omitted).

---

* Cf. the Idyls of Theoc., Bion, Moschus.
† For ex., by Leroy-Beaulieu, *Israël chez les nations,* Ch. VII.

Expansion of second line of v.[18]. As first line of v.[19] the Heb. has: *Lovely hind, charming wild goat* — an expression which, if it be retained, must be regarded as a parenthetical exclamation, whether it be attached to this verse or to the preceding; but it interrupts the discourse and destroys the distichal form, and is doubtless the insertion of a scribe, a gloss on *wife*. Bickell, inserting one word, writes the verse as a quatrain: *Lovely hind, charming wild goat, Let her breasts intoxicate thee, Let her always make thee quiver, Be ever ravished with her love;* but the inserted word is doubtful and improbable. — The *hind* is some variety of deer (Dt. 12[15]), probably red or fallow. The *wild goat* (1 Sam. 24[2(3)] Job 39[1] ψ 104[18]), an inhabitant of the rocks, is gray in color, and of great agility and grace; it is said to be still found at Engedi, where David's men may have hunted it; the renderings *roe* (RV.) and *gazelle* (Strack, Kamph., *al.*) are hardly allowable.* This is the only place in OT. where a woman is compared to an animal as type of beauty (Cant. 4[1. 2. 5] are not properly exceptions), though such comparisons for men are not rare. — A change in the vowels of the Heb. gives in first line *love* instead of *breasts*, but the latter reading is favored by the *bosom* of v.[20]. — The Targum interprets the *wife* as = the *law: wisdom learn thou always, and to love of it ever strenuously apply thyself.* — **20.** Synonymous, ternary. This verse is naturally taken in connection with the preceding exhortation. The question is asked: why seek another woman? the answer expected is: there is no reason for so doing, seeing thy wife is sufficient; the appeal is based on the foregoing section. If the verse be connected with what follows, it should be rendered: *why wilt thou be ravished with* (or, *fascinated by*), etc.?, that is, seeing thou wilt certainly be punished for such conduct (v.[21], but see note on that verse below). — The address *my son* in the Heb. is rhythmically hard, is not found in the Grk., and is better omitted. — With this section cf. BS. 9[1-9]. The sage of Prov. combating a particular vice, here treats the wife not as intellectual companion of the husband or as mother of the family, but as satisfaction of bodily desire — he sets lawful over against unlawful passion; but, of course, it is not thence to be inferred that the

---

* See Tristram, *Fauna*, etc., in *Survey of West. Pal.*

teachers of the time did not take the higher view of the marriage-relation; cf. 31^{10-31}, BS. $26^{1-3.\ 13.\ 14}$ $36^{23(28)}$.

21–23. General concluding reflection, similar to what is found at the end of chs. 1. 2. 3, without special bearing on the body of the chapter, perhaps the addition of the final editor.

> 21. For the ways of a man are before the eyes of Yahweh,
>   And he weighs all his paths.
> 22. His iniquities shall catch him [], *
>   And in the net of his sins he shall be taken.
> 23. He shall die for lack of instruction,
>   And ‹ perish › † through the greatness of his folly.

21. Synonymous, ternary. The universal supervision of God is cited as a general reason for carefulness in conduct; the principle applies to all men, not especially to adulterers. In second cl. the parallelism favors the rendering *weighs* — God has his eye on, estimates and judges human actions (Grk. *observes*, Targ., Syr., *all his ways are uncovered before him*). We may also translate *makes plane* (see note on 4^{26}), understanding this expression to mean *arranges, makes possible*, that is, God so ordains life that the bad man may run his course and meet his punishment, man is free (De., Now., Str.); but here, as in $1^{31.\ 32}$, it seems to be the judgment of God rather than the freedom of man that the writer has in view. The way in which the divine government shows itself is explained in the following verses. — Such must be the course of thought if the present text be correct. But the connection between v.^{21} and the following verses is not clear. V.^{21} regards all men, good and bad, v.$^{22.\ 23}$ regard bad men only. The insertion of the words *the wicked*, in v.^{22}, appears to show that the reference in the *him* was thought to need explanation; and it is natural to suppose that, when the verse was written, the reference was clear, that is, that the antecedent of *him* had been expressed. The same thing is true of the *his* in first line of v.^{22} — it has now no expressed antecedent. It follows either that v.^{21} originally referred to the *wicked* (a supposition with which the general verb *weigh* does not agree), or that some passage (perhaps a couplet)

---

* Heb. inserts *the wicked*.   † Heb.: *go astray*.

referring to the "wicked" has fallen out, or that v.[21] is the insertion of an editor.   The last construction would still require a
modification of v.[22] (see note on this verse below). — **22.** Synonymous, binary-ternary (in the emended form of the couplet).
In first cl. the Heb. has *shall catch him, the wicked*, in which both
objects cannot be original, and it is more probable that the
explicit term *the wicked* is an old scribal explanation (found in
Targ., Syr., Lat., but not in Grk.).   The rendering (obtained by
changing the text) *his own iniquities shall catch the wicked* is possible but syntactically hard.   Possibly we should read : *the wicked
shall be caught in his iniquities*, or, less probably (with Grk.) :
iniquities shall catch a man. — The figure is that of an animal
caught in a net, the man is caught in his own wrongdoings (the
plu. *sins* is given in most of the Anc. Vrss.).   This is the dispensation of God, and it is implied that it is also the natural course
of things.   *Net* is literally *strings* or *threads.* — **23.** Synonymous,
ternary.   The thought is that of 1[30, 31] — sin is the result of lack of
instruction, of the guidance of divine wisdom as given particularly
in the teaching of the sages ; see the preceding sections *passim.*
Further, death is the outcome of sin, see 1[32], etc.   The parallelism, with comparison also of such couplets as 1[32], seems to require
the sense *perish* in second cl. (so one reading of the Grk.).   The
Heb. has *go astray*, an expression so weak alongside of the *die* of
first cl. that those who retain it have to interpret it as = *stagger* or
fall into the grave or *into utter ruin* (Noyes, Reuss, De., *al.*), a
sense which the Heb. verb nowhere else has, or *wander from the
path of life* (Wild.), for which pregnant sense there is no authority. — V.[21-23], as regards the idea, constitute a separate paragraph,
which, however, does not give the expected quatrain-form ; some
critics, therefore, attach v.[21] to v.[20] (with which it is not logically
connected).   The chapter, as it stands, has an uneven number of
couplets, and, consequently, at least one defective quatrain.   This
defect may be removed by changes of text, as by the omission of
a couplet (*e.g.* v.[2] or v.[7] or v.[21]), or by the expansion of one couplet
into two (see note on v.[19]).   Failing a satisfactory emendation of
this sort, we have to accept a formal irregularity in this chapter,
with the possibility that the writer allowed himself a certain
license in the construction of quatrains and paragraphs.

15. אֵת as בֹּ, and so 𝔏 in ᵃ; in ᵇ 𝔊, followed by 𝔏, substantially = בֹּ. —
בֹּור; 𝔊 ἀγγείων, which may be free rendering of בֹּ, giving the sense
drink from thy drinking-vessel, or may represent ס ־, hardly = כְּלִי (Heid.),
which would be graphically hard; Lag. refers 𝔊 to Syr. כּוּר, graphically easy,
and in Geopon. 23¹⁴ *al.* = ἀγγεῖον (and cf. Payne-Smith, *Thes.*, *Syr.*); the
usual sense of the Aram. word is *hive* (of bees), but Jewish Aram. כורת occurs
with the more general meaning *box*, *pot* (see the references in Buxt., Levy,
Jastrow). — **16.** Of 𝔊 MSS. B alone inserts μή before the vb. in ᵃ; the sense
thus obtained is correct, but the insertion of the neg. in בֹּ is unnecessary (see
note on v.¹⁶ above). Whether μή belongs to the Grk. original is doubtful;
Lag. thinks that μὴ ὑπερεκχείσθω represents a single Heb. word (a view not
supported by the οὐκ ἐρείδεται of v.ᵇ). — The insertion of ὕδατα in ᵃ was made
necessary by the reading of מ in מַעְיָנֹתֶיךָ as prep.; in ᵇ פלגי was understood
as vb. — **18.** בֹּ בָּרוּךְ; 𝔊 ἰδία (whence Chrys. v. 98 *al.* μόνῳ), probably = לְבָרֵךְ
(Vog.), as in v.¹⁷, after which בֹּ should probably be emended; Heid. improbably בְּיָדְךָ, out of בּוֹרֵךְ; Bi. emends בֹּ to בְּרֵךְ, after v.¹⁵; Oort thinks it probable
that the Grk. transl. read בְּרֵךְ (*let thy fountain be thy cistern*) and gave a free
rendering; Oort's own reading בָּרֵךְ *beneficent* hardly suits the idea of the paragraph, in which the soleness of the wife is the theme. — בֹּ מֵאֵשֶׁת, for which
12 Heb. codd. and one cod. of 𝔗 (De' Rossi) have בָּא, 𝔊 μετά and so 𝔖𝔏
Arab., the commoner construction, and possibly the right reading here and
elsewhere (Eccl. 2¹⁰ 2 C. 20²⁷); Midr. Mishle has מ, *Shohar Tob* ב. —
19. יְרַוֻּךָ is the reading of the Occident. recension, and the Q of the Orient.,
which as K. has ירויך (Ginsb.). For השנה 3 codd. of De' Rossi have רשנה
increase, prob. scribal error. The Vrss. find difficulty in construction and
sense. 𝔊 fills out ᵃ with ὁμιλείτω σοι, in ᵇ has ἰδία (לברך?) for רָדֶיהָ, and ἡγεί-
σθω (יויר?) and συνέστω (ירעו?) for יָרַו (Lag.) (but these terms may be
merely allegorizing paraphrases), in ᶜ renders הציר by πολλοστὸς ἔσῃ. 𝔖
writes אורחתה in ᵇ, either allegorizing or reading דרכיה for רדיה. 𝔗 allegorizes
throughout; only ΑΣ (and doubtless Θ) 𝔏 Arab. follow בֹּ literally. Bi., taking συνέστω σοι as = רעיך, inserts רֵיעֶךָ before בכל עת, thus gaining an
additional line, parallel to the ᶜ of בֹּ, an attractive emendation if the sense
required (*intoxicate*) could be shown to belong to Hif. of רעל; see note on
this verse above. The text of בֹּ is to be retained in ᵇᶜ, but it is doubtful
whether ᵃ formed part of the original Heb.; see n. on this v. above. The
emendation רדיה for רָדֶיהָ (Hitz., *al.*) is not necessary; cf. Geiger, *Urschrift*,
397 ff. — **20.** בֹּ השנה, in 3 codd. תש; 𝔊 πολύς, = Aram. תשנה; cf. BS. 9⁴.
𝔗 תשרגו *lead astray*, 𝔖 תמעא *go astray*. — הֵק is omitted in B-D by typo-
graphical error. — **21.** הוא should be inserted before מפלס. — **22.** Omit את
הרעע as scribal explicitum, with 𝔊; the termination of the vb. יל is נ־, not
נו־. 𝔊 ἄνδρα, whence Bi. האש, which is not probable; ἄνδρα seems to be
merely explicit expression of the Heb. suffix. Possibly we should read: בְּעֵינֵי
ילכד הרשע (cf. 6² 11⁶ Eccl. 7²⁶). — **23.** הוא, supported by the Vrss., gives unnecessary emphasis, and has perh. got into this place by scribal transposition
from v.²¹. — 𝔊 μετὰ ἀπαιδεύτων, perh. error for διὰ ἀπαιδευσίαν, as 𝔖 has it. —

יְשׁוּה, weak and inappropriate, perh. scribal repetition from v.²⁰ — we expect a vb. like שׁחת or אבד or better יגע, which occurs along with מוה in Job 3¹¹ 4¹⁰; the change of יגוע into ישׁוה is graphically not very difficult. 𝕲 ἐξερίφη perh. = יְשַׁרֵך or ינרשׁ. For its βιότητος (which stands in the place of אַוַלְתּי) Schl. suggests ἠλιθιότητος. 𝕲 adds the line καὶ ἀπώλετο δι᾽ ἀφροσύνην, which Jäger, Baumg., take as rendering of ᵃ, Schl., Lag., more probably as rend. of ᵇ (Schl. writes διὰ πολλὴν αὐτοῦ ἀφρ.), and the vb. ἀπ. sustains the change of text above proposed.

VI. The second half of the chapter (v.²⁰⁻³⁵) is **a discourse against adultery,** similar to that of ch. 5. — The first half consists of four short sections wholly different in style from the rest of this Division (chs. 1–9) ; while the other discourses are general praises of wisdom, or warnings against robbery and debauchery, conceived in a broad and solemn way, these are **homely warnings against petty vices,** with one arithmetical enumeration of sins. V.¹⁻⁵ : against going security for others ; v.⁶⁻¹¹ : against sloth ; v.¹²⁻¹⁵ : against mischief-making ; v.¹⁶⁻¹⁹ : against seven sins. In tone these closely resemble 22¹⁷–24³⁴ and 30¹¹⁻³¹, with which they obviously belong. Since they interrupt the course of thought in chs. 1–9, it is not likely that they were here inserted by the author of this Division ; they were probably misplaced by an editor or scribe, and at an early period, since they occur here in all the Ancient Versions. The metrical unit is the couplet, most of the lines being ternary ; a division into quatrains is not always recognizable.

1–5. In eager, semi-humorous fashion men are cautioned against pledging themselves pecuniarily for others — a thrifty, self-regarding, prudent injunction, sound from the point of view of social-economic justice and kindness, though the author would probably not deny that there are times when such prudential maxims must be thrown to the winds. Cf. 11¹⁵ 17¹⁸ 20¹⁶ 22²⁶ 27¹³, BS. 29¹⁸· ¹⁹ ; in favor of suretyship is BS. 29¹⁴⁻¹⁷. Commercial lending is to be distinguished from lending to the poor and unfortunate (Ex. 22²⁵⁽²⁴⁾ ψ 37²⁶), though borrowing is regarded in 22⁷ as a misfortune.

> 1. If, my son, thou hast become surety for thy fellow,
>   Hast pledged thyself for another,
> 2. Hast snared thyself by thine own ‹ lips,› *
>   Trapped thyself by the words of thy mouth,

---

* Heb.: *the words of thy mouth.*

3. Then do this, my son [] * —
   For thou art come into thy fellow's power —
   Go in hot haste,
   And beset thy fellow,
4. Give not sleep to thine eyes
   Nor slumber to thine eyelids,
5. Free thyself as a gazelle from the ‹ snare,› †
   And as a bird from the hand of the fowler.

1, 2. Synonymous, v.[1] ternary, v.[2] (as emended) binary. The earnest, eager tone suggests that the writer has experienced or observed the predicament which he describes — it is a business-man advising his friend. The address *my son*, with which the Heb. begins, here not inappropriate, is by some critics omitted on rhythmical grounds. *Pledged thyself*, lit. *struck thy hand*, refer-ence to a legal procedure for concluding a bargain (cf. 2 K. 10[15]). In v.[2a] *lips* (instead of the *words of thy mouth* of the Heb.) is taken from the Grk., and is in accordance with the usage of the context, in which synonyms and not repetitions are employed. *Fellow* and *another* (RV. *stranger*) here mean any person with whom one has dealings — the terms are not contrasted, but synonymous; for the first see Gen. 11[3] Ex. 2[13] 20[16] Pr. 6[29], etc., for the second 1 K. 3[13] Job 15[19] Pr. 5[10], etc. The figure of the couplet is taken from hunting — the unwary surety is an animal caught in a trap. — **3–5.** The rest of the section urges the surety to get out of his difficulty as quickly as possible. — **3.** Probably a quatrain (as in the Grk.), though the text is not quite certain; the first couplet may be taken as ternary, the second couplet as binary. *This* refers to what follows. The expression *and free thyself*, added in the Heb. at the end of the first line, is anticipatory, unnecessary, and inter-ruptive; it was probably inserted by a scribe from v.[5]. The second line is parenthetical, and states the reason for prompt action; *power* is lit. *hand;* the commoner expression is *to fall into one's hand* (2 S. 24[14] Lam. 1[7], cf. Nah. 3[12]). The verb in third line is doubtful in form and signification. It is taken by some to mean *tread, stamp, crush thyself down, demean, humble thyself* (RV.); by others, as denominative from a word meaning *mire*, in the equiv-alent sense *get down into the mire* (see Ez. 34[18], and cf. Pr. 25[26]).

---

* Heb. adds (probably from v.[5]): *and free thyself*.   † Heb.: *hand*.

The connection favors the meaning *violently bestir thyself* (RV. marg. *bestir thyself*), *act impetuously* or *move quickly* (so the Vulg.). Grk. : *Do, my son, what I bid thee, and save thyself — for thou art come into the hands of bad men on thy friend's account — be not slack, but sharply assail thy friend also for whom thou hast pledged thyself* — the same general meaning as that of the Heb. : no time is to be lost and no soft words to be used — go and insist on being released from your pledge. *Importune* (RV.) is hardly strong enough ; *beset, besiege,* or *assail* better express the impetuosity involved in the Heb. term. *Then* (RV. *now*) is illative, not temporal ; so in Ex. 33^{16} Job 9^{20} 17^{13} *al.* — **4, 5.** Synonymous, v.^{4} ternary-binary, v.^{5} ternary. Continuation of exhortation. In v.^{5a} the Heb. has simply *from the hand* (so Vulg.), and RV. (as AV.) supplies, by conjecture, *of the hunter;* this is a natural construction, and it is possible that the defining word may have fallen out of the Heb. ; but it is simpler to read *snare* or *trap,* with Grk., Targ., Syr. ; see this expression in BS. 27^{20}. — The animal named in v.^{5a} is a deer (Dt. 12^{15}), swift, an inhabitant of the plain (2 S. 2^{18}) and of the mountain (1 C. 12^8, perh. 2 S. 1^{19}), a symbol of masculine beauty (Cant. 2^9 8^{14}), and so is generally understood to be the *gazelle* (*Tabitha*, Acts 9^{36}, is the fem. form of the equivalent Aramaic word).*

Of the details of the old Heb. law of suretyship or endorsement we have no information. Besides the procedure of Judah in pledging himself for Benjamin (Gen. 43^9), and a couple of allusions to the practice (Job 17^3 ψ 119^{122}), we find in OT., outside of Pr., only one description of a business-transaction involving personal security (Neh. 5$^{1-11}$), and this is rather of the nature of a mortgage given by a man on his children regarded as his property. The allusions to personal endorsement all occur in postexilian writings ; it is probable that the custom (for which there was no ground in the commercially simple preëxilian life) sprang up when the Jews were scattered through the Persian and Greek empires and entered on their real commercial career. On the law of pledges of things see Ex. 22$^{25-27}$ Dt. 24$^{10-13}$. — The surety was sometimes financially ruined by having to meet the obligations of

---

* See Tristram, Wood, Nowack.

the debtor (BS. 29$^{18. 19}$), and was thus at the mercy of the latter, who might throw him into the hands of the creditor; the *bad men* of the Grk. in v.^{3} appear to be creditors. Probably all of a man's property might be pledged for debt; whether there was a homestead-exemption law is uncertain, nor does it appear whether the debtor could be sold as a slave.

6–11. Against sloth. The example of the ant is adduced, and the sluggard warned that poverty will overtake him. The tone is perhaps satirical; the passage is a specimen of the popular teaching of the sages. — The parallel passage, 24$^{30-34}$, does not adduce the ant, but describes the neglected condition of the sluggard's field, and has the same conclusion as our section: 24$^{33. 34}$ = lit. 6$^{10. 11}$. The two paragraphs are variations on the same theme; both have taken the ending from the same source (some familiar expression, or some earlier collection of aphorisms, now lost), or one has borrowed from the other. In either case our passage has a clearer unity than that of ch. 24, in which our v.^{9} must be introduced before v.^{33} in order to connect the conclusion with what precedes. Bickell so transfers v.^{9}, and omits v.$^{10. 11}$ as identical with 24$^{33. 34}$; but both sections must be retained entire as parallel passages, with the possibility that one has borrowed from the other. Obviously our section does not belong in its present place, though when and how it was misplaced we cannot say; the change was made early, since the Versions here accord with the Hebrew. Cf. BS. 22$^{1. 2}$.

6. Go to the ant, thou sluggard,
   Consider her ways and be wise.
7. She, having no chief,
   Overseer, or ruler,
8. Provides her food in summer,
   Gathers her provision in harvest-time.

9. How long wilt thou sleep, O sluggard?
   When wilt thou rise from thy slumber?
10. A little sleep, a little slumber,
    A little folding of the hands to rest —
11. So shall thy poverty come as a highwayman,
    And thy want as an armed man.

6. Progressive, ternary. Cf. 30^{25}. On the ant in proverbial literature see Malan on this verse.* On the habits of the animal see *Encyl. Brit.*, Darwin in *Journ. of Linnaean Soc.* VI. 21, Lubbock, *Ants, Bees, and Wasps.* What particular species is here meant is uncertain; cf. Tristram, *Nat. Hist. of the Bible.* — The term *sluggard* appears to belong to the parenetic vocabulary of OT.; it occurs only in Proverbs. But the observation of the habits of the ant and its use as an example of industry may be old; cf. 1 K. 4^{33} (5^{13}). — **7.** Synonymous, ternary-binary. The three terms employed are here used as synonymous, though they have their different shades of meaning. The first is employed in OT. of both civil and military leaders (Ju. 11^6 Isa. 3^6); the second denotes a sort of roll-officer, who keeps a list of names and superintends the men at their work, in peace or in war (Ex. 5^6 Dt. 20^5 2 Chr. 19^{11}); the third is a general term for ruler, royal or other (1 K. 4^{21} [5^1] Isa. 16^1 Jer. 51^{46}). — Ants are said by recent writers to have an elaborate social organization, sometimes with king and queen, sometimes with a slave-class acquired (as by the *termites* or white ants) by capture and forced to do the work of the community. This organization seems to have been unknown to the ancients (Aristotle, *De Anim.*, I. 1. 11, calls them anarchal, without government), though Aelian (in his History of Animals, third cent. of our era) speaks of their leaders and nobles. — This verse is omitted by Bickell as a prosaic gloss, which weakens the comparison and introduces the irrelevant consideration of governmental direction — irrelevant because men are industrious not by pressure of rulers, but from regard to their private interests. The second and third points are not well taken: social organization certainly helps human industry, and our writer says that ants, without this advantage, set men a good example. The argument from lack of poetic form has more weight, — the verse is not a complete couplet, — but we can hardly throw it out on that account. Grk. makes it a triplet, and possibly some word or phrase has fallen out of the Heb. text. — **8.** Synonymous, ternary. The vbs. *provide* (lit. *establish, prepare*) and *gather* here amount to the same thing, and the nouns *food* and *provision* are synonyms. The word ren-

---

* De. mentions also Goldberg, *Chofes Matmonim*, and Landsberger, *Fabulae aliquot Aramaeae.*

dered *summer* is sometimes used for the warm season in general, as opposed to *winter* (Gen. 8²² ψ 74¹⁷), extending apparently through harvest-time (Jer. 8²⁰), sometimes for the latter part of the fruit-season (Isa. 28⁴ Jer. 40¹⁰). *Harvest* also is temporally indefinite, varying with the crop, from March (barley, 2 S. 21⁹) to September (grapes, Isa. 18⁵). The two clauses are identical in meaning; the sense is not that the ant does one thing in summer and another in harvest-time. Nor is it intended to express progress in the action (by the different Heb. verb-forms) : *begins to provide in summer, completes the gathering in autumn.* The structure of the other verses of the section points to an identical parallelism here. — As to the industrial habit spoken of in the verse, the latest authorities hold that some species of ant are graminivorous and store up food ; for the modern opinion see the works cited above, and for ancient statements see Malan. — Grk. adds : *Or, go to the bee and learn how diligent she is and how seriously she does her work — her products kings and private persons use for health — she is desired and respected by all — though feeble in body, by honoring wisdom she obtains distinction.* The addition comes from a Grk. scribe (it is probably a gloss which has got into the text) who thought that the other industrious insect ought not to go unmentioned. Elsewhere in OT. (Isa. 7¹⁸ Dt. 1⁴⁴ ψ 118¹²) the bee is introduced as hostile to man ; the word does not occur in the Heb. text of Proverbs. — **9.** Synonymous, ternary. It is agricultural life that the description is dealing with (cf. 24³⁰), in which early rising is a necessity.* Cf. the Eng. *early to bed and early to rise*, etc., and many such popular sayings ; Persius v. 132–134 resembles our passage in form. — **10.** Synonymous (or, continuous), binary (or, binary-ternary). The sluggard's reply, or continuation of the remonstrance of the sage. The repetition of *a little* is perh. intended to give a humorous coloring, but may be meant simply as a serious description. Cf. the babbling words put into the drunkards' mouths in Isa. 28¹⁰. The second clause is lit. *a little folding of the hands to lie*, that is, to lie comfortably, to compose one's self to sleep. The same phrase in Eccl. 4⁵ signi-

---

* Early rising was, however, the general rule in ancient life; see Plato, *Laws*, vii. pp. 807, 808 ; Arist., *Econ.* i. 5 ; Juv., vii. 222 ff.

fies stupid inactivity. — **11.** Synonymous, ternary. *Highwayman* is roadster, wayfarer, the implication being that his purpose is bad ; the term. like Eng. *highwayman*, belongs to a time when travelling was not safe, when men who frequented the public roads were likely to be *robbers* (cf. RV.). *Armed man*, lit. *man with a shield*, perhaps a wandering soldier out of service (Oort), more probably simply a dangerous assailant. Poverty, properly (as result of sloth) a negative thing, lack of goods, is personified as a powerful and ruthless enemy who destroys or carries off one's substance. — Instead of *shieldman* Grk. has *swift runner* (apparently representing a different Heb. text from ours), which offers a formal but not a real parallel to the *wayfarer* of first clause. Grk. (followed by Vulg.) further adds : *but if thou be diligent, thy harvest will come as a fountain, and want will depart as a bad runner* — the contrast to the preceding statement, and probably from a Grk. hand.

12-15. The mischief maker — rebuke of mischievous talk and hints. — The tone is curt and sharp, the rhythm irregular ; the vocabulary perhaps points to a late period.

12. A wicked man, a bad man
   Deals in false speech,

13. Winks with his eyes, scrapes with his feet,
   Signs with his fingers,

14. Devises mischief in his mind,
   Is always sowing discord.

15. Therefore of a sudden shall calamity strike him,
   Suddenly shall he be crushed, and that without remedy.

In this translation the second line of v.[14] appears as merely one item in the indictment, but the paragraph may also be translated : *a wicked man . . . dealing with . . . winking . . . scraping . . . signing . . . devising . . . is always sowing discord*, the last expression giving the result of the preceding acts ; this construction does not modify the general sense.

12. Parallels, ternary. The two adjectives are synonymous, expressing general depravity ; the first (Heb. *man of belial*) occurs in 16[27] 19[28], the second (Heb. *man of badness* or *iniquity*) in 6[18] 10[29] 17[4], etc. The term *belial* usually means *deep depravity* (not merely *worthlessness*) ; in two passages, ψ 18$^{4(5)}$ 41$^{8(9)}$, apparently *utter ruin* (cf. Cheyne, *Psalms*). Instead of *son of Belial* (Ju. 19^{22}, etc.) the rendering should be *wicked man*. *Speech* is lit. *mouth* — the fault denounced is evil talk. Grk. and Syr., however, omitting *mouth* have *walks in ways that are not good*, and this may be the right reading ; the *false* of the Heb. would then be defined in v.$^{13.14}$; cf. 4^{24}. *Mouth* may be understood as expressing the man's whole thought. The first line is by some expositors (Saadia, Zöck., *al.*) taken as a separate sentence : *a worthless* [properly *wicked*] *man is the deceiver*, which is possible, but does not agree so well with the structure of the paragraph. — **13**. Three binary clauses. Gestures indicating the spirit of malice and mischief. Movement of the *eyes* occurs in 10^{10} BS. 27^{22} as sign of mischief, in ψ 35^{19} as sign of exultation; cf. the Arab. saying (attributed to Ali) *O God, pardon us the culpable winking of the eye* (De.), and see other parallels in Malan. The second verb is rendered in the Grk. by *gives signs*, in Targ. and Syr. by *stamps*, in Aq., Sym., Vulg. (in accordance with a Talmudic use of the word) by *rubs* (*scrapes, shuffles*) : in any case the movement is a mark of enmity, perhaps a sign to a confederate ; the rendering *speaks* (RV.) is here inappropriate, though the verb elsewhere has that meaning. *Signing* (lit. *teaching*) with the *fingers* is a universal gesture, of various import, here mischievous, contemptuous, etc.; for the sense *show* see Gen. 46^{28} Ex. 15^{25}. For other inimical movements of the body see Job 16$^{9.10}$. The verse is a lively description of the silent, underhand procedures of mischiefmakers, the hints, suggestions, provocations, and signals that are effective in hatching quarrels or giving insults. — **14**. Synonymous, ternary. A direct statement of what is implied in the preceding verses. The man occupies himself with devising mischievous schemes, in private and public relations; in second cl. Grk. has *makes disturbances in the city*, a fuller statement of what the Heb. suggests. In the Heb. text the verse reads : *Evil is in his mind* [lit. *heart*], *he devises mischief continually, he spreads strifes*, a triplet which may be reduced to a couplet by the omission of one word (*mischief*) ; the change does not affect the sense. *Evil,* = *mischief*, is in the most general sense departure from good ; see note on 2^{12}, *evil* and *wrong*. — **15**. Synonymous, quaternary. The penalty. The writer's sense of the seriousness of the vice described is indicated by the abrupt, vehement, almost fierce, declaration of punishment. On *calamity*, see note on 1^{26}. The two Heb. terms for *sudden* are synonyms; the first occurs in 24^{22} (it is better omitted in 3^{25}), the second in 29^{1} (the second cl. of which is identical with second cl. of our verse — note the difference between the offences in the two verses). *Crushed* is lit. *broken,* = *destroyed;* see Jer. 17^{18} Ez. 32^{28} Lam. 1^{15} Dan. 8^{25}. The blow is irremediable, that is, it is death. The agency of destruction is not stated; the writer's view doubtless was that it might come from God directly, by sickness, etc., or indirectly, through the enemies, private and public, that a mischief-maker naturally raises up against himself. Sudden death was regarded as a great misfortune, and as a sign of divine anger, since it sent the man irretrievably to Sheol (see 2^{19}), where he could never gain a position of favor with God.

16–19. A list of seven things hateful to God. — The section is similar to those in 30^{11-31} in its arithmetical enumeration, and to 6^{12-15} in its subject-matter and rhetorical form (absence of comparisons); by the nature of its contents it appropriately follows v.$^{12-15}$. The things enumerated belong all together; they portray the character of the man who schemes to despoil and ruin his fellows.

16. There are six things that Yahweh hates,
    Yea, seven are an abomination to him:
17. Haughty eyes, a lying tongue,
    And hands that shed innocent blood,
18. A mind that devises wicked schemes,
    Feet that make haste to do harm,*
19. A false witness who utters lies,
    And he who sows discord among brethren.

16. Progressive (substantially synonymous), ternary. The sequence *six, seven* does not imply that the seventh thing is an afterthought, or inferior in importance to the others; it is a rhetorical form, equivalent to our *six or seven,* arithmetically indefinite, implying that the enumeration does not exhaust the list of things

---

* Heb.: *make haste to run to harm.*

coming under a particular category ; cf. notes on $30^{7. 15}$. Between
the expressions *Yahweh hates* and *abomination to him* there is no
difference of meaning; on *abomination* see note on 3^{32}. The
sense of the verse is : *God hates and abominates a number of
things, namely.* — **17**. Parallels, ternary. *Haughty eyes;* so 30^{13}.
Haughtiness is naturally expressed by the eyes (cf. Lat. *super-
cilium*); see ψ 131. In ψ $18^{27(28)}$ the expression characterizes
Israel's proud and oppressive enemies, whom Yahweh will bring
down. More generally in Isa. 2^{11-17} 10^{33} Job 21^{22} 38^{15} all lofty
things are conceived of as standing in antagonism to God and
therefore destined to be overthrown (cf. the Greek representation
of the deity as jealous of powerful men, Prometheus and Poly-
crates of Samos, and the Hindu stories of Indra's fear of certain
Munis). This national point of view remains to the end of OT.
(Daniel), in Apocryphal books (Ben-Sira, Macc., etc.), and in the
Talmud, but does not appear in Pr. ; in our verse it is individual
moral feeling that is spoken of — haughtiness, put alongside of
falsehood and murder, is to be understood as implying disregard
of human rights and divine laws — it is excessive conceit of and
regard for one's own person. — Instead of *innocent blood* we
might render by *the blood of the innocent* (or, *righteous*) as in
Dt. 19^{10} Jer. 19^4; the meaning is the same. — **18**. Parallels, ternary. The expression *wicked schemes* might be understood in a
wide sense as including all plans and plots that are opposed to the
right, but here refers particularly to harmful plots. The Heb., in
second line, reads : *make haste to run*, which means not swiftness
in running (RV. after the Vulg.) but haste in beginning to run,
eagerness to seize on every opportunity to engage in wickedness ;
the picture of eagerness contained in the word *haste* is heightened
by the term *run* (instead of *walk*) ; cf. ψ 147^{16}. The Grk. omits
run, reading *feet hastening to do ill;* cf. 1^{16}, where only one verb is
employed in each clause ; as the *run* is unnecessary, the Grk. text
is probably to be preferred. — **19**. Parallels, ternary. The second
cl. is identical in meaning with v.^{14b}, *brethren* being taken as =
friends or *associates*, members of the same circle — the suggestion
is that there is no occasion or temptation to sow dissensions except
among persons whose mutual relations are amicable.— The meaning of first cl. is plain, but its form is doubtful. In 14^5, where the

Heb. text recurs, it is properly rendered *a false witness utters lies* (and so the Grk. here), but this is out of keeping with the syntactical form in the other verses — we expect a subject defined by following words. Similar objections hold to other translations of our Heb. text : *he who utters lies is a false witness* (cf. for the construction Eccl. 1[18], but here the resulting identical proposition is out of the question, and the declarative sentence is out of keeping with the context) ; *he who utters lies as a false witness* * is hard and improbable, and so the appositional rendering *he who utters lies, a false witness*, and *he who utters lies, false testimony*. The cl. is not in proper shape, and it seems better, with Syr. and Targ., to invert the Heb. order and translate by *a false witness who utters lies*, † which accords in form with the rest of the section. For the thought cf. 12[17] 14[5. 25] and 19[5. 9] 25[18] ; for laws against false testifying see Ex. 20[16] (= Dt. 5[20]) Dt. 19[18] Lev. 6[3] (5[22]). The expression *witness of falsity* (as the Heb. reads) is parallel to *tongue of falsity* in v.[17].

1. 𝕸 בני, attested by all Vrss., omitted by Bi., as marring the rhythm; without it we have only two ictus in the line. — The force of the אם, which extends to end of v.[2], is confined by 𝕲 to v.[1a]. — 𝕸 plu.; כפי; read sing., with 𝕲𝕾𝕿𝕷, as the sense requires. — **2.** Taken by 𝕲 as ground (γάρ) for the statement of v.[1b] (παραδώσεις), and written in 3 pers. — a divergent text which does not agree with the context so well as 𝕸. — The repetition of אמרי in 𝕸 is strange, and so also the similar repetition, χείλη, χείλεσιν, in 𝕲; as the χείλη prob. had a Heb. basis, it is better to write שפתי in second line of 𝕸; ῥήμασι inst. of χείλ., is given in H-P 147 (161 suprascript.), 252, 297, and Compl. (and λόγῳ in Arm.), which may be a correction after 𝕸, or a rhetorical variation. On ἰδίου = ἑαυτοῦ see Deissmann, *Bibelstud.*, pp. 120 ff. — **3.** 𝕸 ורגל, see note on v[1]. — In ᵃ 𝕲 ἃ ἐγώ σοι ἐντέλλομαι seems to be free rendering of 𝕸 זאת אפוא, hardly = אצרך; εἰς χεῖρας κακῶν in ᵇ, = בכף רעים, is prob. doublet (possibly the orig. Grk. reading), the 𝕸 text being represented by διὰ σὸν φίλον; ἴσθι (in ᶜ) is perh. scribal error for ἴθι, which reading is found in codd Bᵃᵇ A (see Lag.'s n.). — 𝕸 התרפס; 𝕲 μὴ ἐκλυόμενος, 𝕷 *festina*; 𝕾𝕿 render the two vbs. of 𝕸 freely by גרג הכיל *arouse therefore*, apparently giving no separate word for 𝕸 ה'; and in ᵃ אפוא is not rendered at all. ר'ך and ר'יך, difference of orthography. To make the reference in ר'יך clear 𝕲 adds ὁ ἐνεγυήσω. — **4.** Gr. suggests 3 pers., instead of 2 pers., for the suffix. — **5.** 𝕸 כ'יר, here impossible (used in rabbin. Heb. as = *offhand, immediately*); the expression occurs isolated elsewhere only 1 K. 20[42] where it is error for

---

* Ew., De., Now., Zöck., Str., Kamph.   † RV. Noyes, Reuss.

מידך (see 𝔊); here we must either supply a word, as ציד (RV., Bött.) or פח
(Gr., Str.), or better, with 𝔊𝔖𝔗, Oort, Bi., write פח for יד; Kamp. transfers
the ו of וכצפור to יד, . . . *as a gazelle from his hand, as a bird*, etc., which is
simple, but does not account for 𝔊 βρόχων or secure parallelism with יקוש;
this last is omitted in 𝔊𝔖𝔗, but is favored by the rhythm. For the second יד
several Heb. codd. have פח. — **6–11.** The style of 𝔊 in this section is freer
than in most other passages; the text is often rather a paraphrase than a
translation — a result perh. of the secular and homely nature of the subject-
matter. — **6.** 𝕳 נמלה, 𝔊 μύρμηξ, 𝔗 שומשמן or שושמן, 𝔖 שושנא (Arab. סמסם);
the origin of the Heb. word is unknown. — The ζῆλωσον and ἐκείνου σοφώτε-
ρος of 𝔊 are rhetorical expansion. — 𝕳 לך; 𝔖𝔗 paraphrase by התרמא *imitate*.
𝔖 omits 𝕳 עצל, and transfers וחכם to next verse. — **7.** 𝕳 קצין; 𝔊 γεωργίου, not
= Aram. קטין (Lag.), but free rendering of קציר (which 𝔖𝔗 read instead of
קצין). — 𝕳 שטר; 𝚺 γραμματέα. — **8.** The variation of vb.-forms is rhetorical.
— On the terms in the addition in 𝔊 see Lag.'s note. — **9.** 𝕳 תקום; 𝔊ᴬᴮא ᵃˡ.
ἐγερθήσῃ, as in Ju. 2¹⁶·¹⁸, perh. = תקיץ, cf. Pr. 6²². — **10.** Oort suggests that
לישכב is dittogram from ל תשכב of preceding verse, but the word is in sense
and rhythm appropriate; it was perh. lacking in Heb. text of 𝔊, hardly (Oort,
Baumg.) read לשׁרים (στήθη); cf. Pinkuss' note. — 𝔊 makes the v. an address to the sluggard, and in ᵃ has an additional cl., ὀλίγον δὲ κάθησαι, = מעט
שכב, probably expansion of Grk. scribe (the Heb. rhythm is against it) or here
introduced by error from ᵇ (cf. remark above on לישכב). — **11.** H מהלך, written מתהלך in 24³⁴. — ראש (ריש), a favorite word in Pr., though עני (גו),
דל, אביון, also occur a number of times. — The v. is variously rendered in the
Vrss. H מהלך is explained in 𝔊 as κακὸς ὁδοιπόρος, and is taken by 𝔖𝔗,
against the parallelism, as vb., ותידרכך *will assault thee;* 𝕳 איש מגן, 𝔊 ἀγαθὸς
δρομεύς (and in the added couplet κακὸς δρομεὺς), 𝔖𝔗 גברא כשירא *a quick
(alert) man*, = איש נמר (Lag., Oort) or better איש מחר (Baumg.), neither of
which readings seems preferable to that of 𝕳 (with which 𝔏 agrees). The
additional couplet in 𝔊 is doublet of 𝕳; on its Heb. text see Hitz., Lag.,
Baumg. In 24³⁴ 𝔊 (like 𝔖𝔗) renders מ by προπορευομένη, and in ᵇ 𝔖𝔗 have
טבלרא *tabellarius, courier* (= δρομεύς). 𝕳 appears to have in mind the violence of the armed robber, 𝔊𝔖𝔗 the swiftness of the traveller or courier. —
12. 𝕳 אדם is not elsewhere followed by defining subst., and De., Str., therefore
take בליעל as adj. (cf. constr. in 11⁷), but, as this is hardly allowable, we must
either write איש, as in 16²⁷, or accept this phrase as proof that אדם may be followed by defining subst. — 𝕳 בליעל; for the two defining terms (of 𝕳) 𝔊 has
ἄφρων and παράνομος (103, 253: παράν. and ἄφρων), and ב may here be represented by the latter (which is its more usual representative); 𝔖 סכלא *folly;*
𝔗 טלמא *oppression;* 𝔏 *apostata* (so elsewhere Aq.). בליעל occurs 27 times
in Mas. text of OT., and further apparently, according to 𝔊, in 1 Sam. 29¹⁰,
perhaps also (Cheyne) in ψ 52⁶ (always as subst.), and = *wickedness* everywhere except Nah. 1¹¹ 2¹ ψ 18⁵ (= 2 Sam. 22⁵) 41⁹, where it = *ruin, destruction* (= *death*). The origin of the word is doubtful. It has commonly been
regarded as a compound, the first element being the neg. בלי, the second ele-

ment being עִיל, or some form of עָלה or יִעֵל. An early Jewish explanation is reflected in the *apostate* of Aq. 𝕃, = בְּלִי עֹל *without yoke, disobedience* (so *Sanhed.* 111 *b*). From עָלה: *one does not ascend*, = moral lowness (Kimchi); or, *one does not rise* (or, *emerge*), = ruin (so Lag., *Proph. Chald.* XLVII, on ψ 41⁹: [sickness] *from which one does not rise*, suggesting דֶּבֶר instead of דְּבַר); and, more generally, [the depth] *from which one does not come up* (Cheyne, *Expositor*, June, 1895, Baethgen, Halévy), = Sheol (JDMichaelis). From יִעֵל: *no profit*, = *worthlessness* (like בְּרִי רַעַת *ignorance*, and בְּלִי שֵׁם *namelessness*, and cf. לֹא יִעֵל, Jer. 2¹¹, = *worthless* [foreign] *god*), in moral sense, like אָון (Gesen. and most modern expositors). The word is possibly not a compound. It has been proposed to connect it with Babylonian *Bilil*, a goddess of the Underworld * (Cheyne, *Expos. Times*, June, 1897); נחלי בְּ (ψ 18⁵) would then = *streams of Sheol*, and אנשי בְּ = *servants of Bilil*, = "bad men." This last rendering cannot be accepted, since the Underworld and its deities had no ethical significance for the ancient Semites; but it is conceivable that in ψ 18⁵ (if the ψ be postexilic) an original בְּלִיל *Bilil* (= Sheol) was changed by an editor into the familiar בְּלִיַּעַל purposely or by error. Yet the meaning *ruin* (= death) accords satisfactorily with the parallel terms in the ψ, and the character of the deity *Bilil* is at present too uncertain to rest an argument on. Cf. Mich., *Supplementa*, s.v. יִעֵל; Baudissin in Herzog, *RE*³., and in *Expos. Times*, November, 1897; Cheyne in *Expos. Times*, December, 1897, May, 1898; Moore, *Judges*, on Ju. 19²². The derivation from the noun יִעֵל appears to be the most probable; the two elements came to be written as one word, like צַלְמָוֶת. Cf. the various combinations with negatives in Heb. (לֹא עַמִּי, לֹא רֻחָמָה), and the use of the Ass. *balū*, as noun = *nonentity*, as prep. = *without*. — Bef. עִקְּשׁוּת ins. בְּ (so Bi.). — 𝕳 פֶּה; 𝕲 ὁδοὺς οὐκ ἀγαθάς, perh. after 16²⁹ (Jäg.); פה is omitted in 𝕾, and Oort for פ writes זה, which he transfers to next v. to represent 𝕲 ὁ δ' αὐτὸς. The stem עִי, subst. or adj., occurs in 𝕳 with *way* in 2¹⁵ 28⁶, with *heart* 11²⁰ 17²⁰, with *lip* 19¹, with *mouth* here and 4²⁴; דרך would here agree well with the following context, but no serious objection in this regard can be made to פה; 𝕲 and 𝕳 represent parallel texts. — **13.** K. עַיִן and רֶגֶל, sing., and so 𝕲; Q plu., perh. better; 𝕃 strangely *oculis, pede*, and *digito*. — 𝕳 מֹלֵל, 𝕲 σημαίνει, 𝕾𝕿 רכס, 𝕃 *terit*, A τρίβων, Σ προστρίβων; the most appropriate sense is *rub, stamp, scrape*, not found elsewhere in OT., but well attested in Talm.; whether there is any connection between this and the sense *speak* is uncertain. — 𝕳 מוֹרֶה, 𝕲 διδάσκει, 𝕾𝕿 רמז; *teach* = *show, give indications* (on relation between senses *teach* and *throw* in ירה see SS., BDB.). — **14.** 𝕳 is supported by the Vrss., exc. that 𝕲 adds

---

* As Underworld deity she appears only in a mutilated passage in the *Descent of Ishtar*, where she seems to be the sister of Ishtar (cf. Jensen, *Kosmologie*, p. 225). The form *Bilili* occurs in a list of gods in pairs, who are invoked thus: "in the name of Alala and Bililu may it be conjured away!" Otherwise only the fem. form *Bililitum* is found (G. A. Reisner); cf. M. Jastrow, *Relig. of Babylonia and Assyria*, pp. 417, 589.

at end of ^b πόλει (H-P 106 πολλάς), perh. expansion of Grk. scribe, less probably = במדינה (after 翟 מְדִינַם) or עָר (from foll. עָר).— As ^b ends with Partcp.,
there is some ground for so ending ^a and omitting רע, which here produces
rhythmical limping (so Bi.) and is not necessary for the sense; cf. the bal-
anced phrases in the similar v.¹⁸.— Saadia (ed. Derenbourg) takes תהפכות in
sense of *change* of mind.— K. מְדָנִים, Q מִדְיָנִים; sing. is always written מדון,
plu. 3 times מדנים (twice 6¹⁹ 10¹², without Q), elsewhere K. מדונים, Q מדינים
(a late, probably academic, attempt to bring out the Yod of the stem); on
Mas. text see notes in B-D on 6¹⁴ 25²⁴, and on the form Ew., § 54 *d* 160 *d*,
Ols., § 203 *b*.— For יצלח Gr. reads יָלחש, *whispers.*— 15. 𝕲 takes פתע and
ישבר as substantives; in OT. פ occurs as subst. only with prep. and in sense
of *a moment.*— 16. הֵנָה cannot be Dem. adj. (*these six* or *those six*), but is
(cf. 30¹⁸· ²⁴· ²⁹) either pred., *six things are those*, with following rel. cl. (so
apparently 𝔖𝕿𝕷), or as subj., *six — they are what Y. hates;* in ch. 30 the pron.
is better taken as appositional subject.— For שֶׁי 𝕲 read שָׂשׂ (Jäg.), χαίρει,
and ישבר (Lag. = וְשֹׁבֵר) or נשבר, συντρίβεται, for שבע (or וְשֹׁבַע).   Read sing.
תּוֹעֲבַת, as in marg.— 18. 翟 לרוץ, lacking in 𝕲, is omitted by Lag. as scribal
error (לרץ wrongly written for לרע), and by Bi. as tautological; it is not
necessary, and is probably error (though the combination of מהרה and רץ is
found in ψ 147¹⁵, and לרץ may easily have fallen out of the Heb. text of 𝕲).—
19. פיה, as to its form, might be taken as subst. and pointed as in stat. const.;
but common nouns made by pref. Yod are rare, the resulting sense (*a breather
of lies, a false witness*, so 𝕷), though possible, would not accord very well with
the context (in the other cases mentioned the appositional construction does
not occur), and the Vrss. (exc. Saad. who apparently understands it as Inf.)
take יח as vb. The cl. seems to be taken from or assimilated to 14⁵ (where it
is in good form), and should here be inverted, as in 𝔖𝕿; cf. 12¹⁷. עֵר is taken
as abstr. by Saad. Gr. The omission of עֵר שקר would leave an unsatisfactory
sentence.— ⸰ is well rendered in 𝕲^{AB al.} by ἐκκαλεῖ (H-P 103 ἐκχέει).— משלח,
Gr. מלחש, as in v.¹⁴.— מדנים, see note on v.¹⁴; it is lacking in 𝖲.

20–35. Warning against the adulteress.

— We here return
to the material proper to this Division (chs. 1–9). This subsec-
tion connects itself immediately with ch. 5, having the same general theme.— First comes commendation of parental instruction
(v.²⁰· ²¹), then apparently of wisdom (v.²²· ²³), especially as safeguard
against the adulteress who brings misfortune to her victim (v.²⁴⁻²⁹),
he getting only wounds and dishonor (v.³⁰⁻³³) through the outraged
husband's anger (v.³⁴· ³⁵). The section is similar to 2¹⁶⁻¹⁹ 5. 7. 8¹³⁻¹⁸.
These may all have been composed by one man (since there is
great resemblance between them), or they may have been collected from various sources by an editor.

20, 21. Commendation of parental instruction. — See note on 1[8. 9].

> 20. Keep, my son, the precept of thy father,
> And reject not the instruction of thy mother.
> 21. Bind them continually to thy heart,
> Hang them around thy neck.

20. Parallels, quaternary-ternary.　Parental instruction is identified with the teaching of the sages; it is assumed that in the well-ordered household father and mother will be wise; the same assumption is made in all commands to honor and obey parents. *Instruction* represents the Heb. word (*tora*) usually rendered *law*. The Grk. has plu. in both clauses, *laws, ordinances;* the Vulg. *precepts, law. Cast away* (the proper sense of the Heb.)=substantially *forsake* (RV.), but is more forcible, = *reject.* — **21.** Synonymous, ternary-binary.　In 3[3] the teacher's law is to be written on the tablets of the heart; here, with a change of figure, it is to be firmly attached to the heart, which is the seat of thought and moral and religious life.　The figure of second cl. is found in 1[9] 3[3. 22], etc. — The term *continually* is used of perpetually recurring or repeated acts (as the daily offering in the temple), and so = *constantly, always, all the time;* see Isa. 57[13] Jer. 52[3] ψ 16[8]. The plu. *them* may refer to *precept* and *law* (v.[20]) taken as different things, or these terms may have been plu. in the original Heb. text (as they are in the Greek).

In the remainder of the chapter the wording and arrangement present difficulties.　The sing. pronoun in v.[22] points to *wisdom* (or one of its synonyms) as antecedent, as, in fact, in chs. 1–9 only "wisdom" watches over and leads (2[11. 21-24] 4[6] 7[4. 5]); but, as the text stands, the *it* (or, *she*) of v.[22] has no such antecedent. We might (with Bickell) insert, at the beginning of v.[22], some such line as *wisdom will keep thee;* but this would still leave the connection between v.[23] and v.[24] unsatisfactory, for elsewhere (2[16] 7[5]) it is not *precept* or *instruction* but *wisdom* or *discretion* that saves from the harlot and other destructive persons.　Further, while the normal arrangement in chs. 1–9 is in quatrains, we here have two natural sextets, v.[24-26] and v.[27-29]; Bickell gets rid of the latter of these by omitting v.[29], and of the former by attaching v.[24] to v.[23] (the objection to this procedure is stated above), making v.^{22} a quatrain. — A better emendation would be to omit the doubtful couplets v.$^{26. 29}$, and make v.^{22} a couplet by the omission of third line ; and v.^{23}, which obviously connects itself with the first couplet, should be transposed before v.^{22}.

22–25. Wisdom as guide, and as guard against the harlot.

23. For precept is a lamp, and instruction is light,
   And the guidance of admonition is the way of life.
22. When thou walkest she [Wisdom] will lead thee,
   When thou liest down she will watch over thee.*

24. To preserve thee from the ‹alien› † woman,
   From the wiles of the stranger's tongue;
25. Desire not her beauty in thy heart,
   Let her not captivate thee with her eyes.

23. Synonymous, quaternary. The discourse here turns from parental instruction to the idea of instruction and law in general (retaining the two terms of v.^{20}) ; the two categories were probably considered to be identical. *Precept* and *instruction* (synonyms) represent the teaching of the sage (cf. 4^2), held to be based on the divine law. *Guidance* (RV. *reproofs*), plu. in our Heb. text, is sing. in Grk. Syr. Targ. Lat., and a number of Heb. MSS., and throughout Pr., except here and 29^1 ; for the meaning see note on 1^{23} ; and on *admonition* see note on 1^2. *Way of life* is the course of a long and prosperous earthly life, and the conduct that secures it ; see 2^{19} 3^2 5^6 and ψ 16^{11}, and for similar expressions see Job 28^{13} ψ 27^{13} 36$^{9(10)}$ Pr. 10^{11} 13^{14} 15^4 *al.* The Syr. and Targ. have *guidance and instruction;* Grk., *for the precept of law is a lamp, and a light is* [or, *is a lamp and a light,*] *a way of life and guidance and instruction;* the Heb. (taking *guidance* as subj. in second cl.) gives a more natural construction. — **22.** Parallels, ternary. Similar imagery in 3$^{23. 24}$ 4^{12} ; in ψ 91 the guidance, here referred to law and instruction or wisdom, is ascribed to God. The *she* (RV. *it*) can hardly be understood to refer to the *instruction* of v.^{23} (see remark above) ; the writer

---

* Heb. adds : *when thou wakest, she will talk with thee ;* see note on this verse below.

† Heb. *bad* (or, *evil*).

passes silently to *wisdom* as subject, or else something (a line or a
couplet) has been lost from the text. — Some commentators, maintaining the order v.[22. 23], gain an antecedent for *she* by inserting a
line as first line : *wisdom will* (or, *shall*) *guide thee* (or, *keep
thee*), or, *seek wisdom, forsake it not*, or, as second line : *when
thou runnest, she will keep thee;* these additions make a quatrain
of the verse.   The present unsymmetrical form may also be got
rid of by omitting the third line, *when thou wakest she will talk
with thee*, which, while it gives an intelligible thought in itself,
seems unnecessary, since walking and lying down include all of
one's time (cf. $3^{23. 24}$).   The addition may have been made by a
scribe who, taking *liest down* (which is really contrast to *walkest*)
as = *sleepest*, thought it proper to complete the picture by introducing *awaking*.   The verb *talk* is here strange ; we expect a synonym of *lead*. — If we keep the triplet, the meaning is : wisdom
will guide thee in thy active life of the day, guard thee while thou
liest helpless in sleep, and at thy awaking be with thee to utter
words of advice. — **24.** Synonymous, ternary.   The special theme
of the section : the adulteress is the peril against which the aid of
wisdom is particularly invoked.   In first cl. the Heb. has *evil
woman*, an appropriate description, but the parallelism suggests
the reading *the wife of another* (requiring the change of one
vowel), as in the Grk. (*married woman*), and v.[20]; or the sense
alien (as in 2^{16}) may be got by a slight change of consonants.
Stranger, as in 5^3 7^5, = " wife of another man " ; see note on 2^{16}.
The *harlot*, the unmarried licentious woman (or the professional
prostitute), is mentioned in 6^{26} 7^{10} 23^{27} 29^3, but is to be distinguished from the unchaste married woman (called *adulteress*, 30^{20},
and *stranger*), against whom, as the more dangerous person, a great
part of chs. 1–9 is directed.   She is the more guilty of the two
because she violates the marriage-vow (2^{17}) ; the danger from her
is described below.   See note on $2^{16. 17}$.   The social evil here portrayed is more particularly appropriate to the postexilian period ;
the preëxilian shrine-prostitute (Gen. $38^{21. 22}$ Hos. 4^{14} Dt. $23^{17(18)}$)
belongs to a very different sort of Israelitish society. — **25.** Synonymous, ternary-binary.   The Heb. connects the two clauses by
and, and at end of the verse has *eyelids* instead of *eyes*, perhaps
with allusion to the seductive play of eyes (winks, etc., Vulg.,

nods), but the term is generally simply equivalent to *eyes*, Jer. $9^{18(17)}$ Job 16^{16} ψ 11^4 Pr. 4^{25} 6^4, cf. 30^{13}. — Vulg. *let not thy heart desire*, etc.; the Grk. interprets first cl., and writes second cl. in twofold form: *let not desire of beauty overcome thee, neither be thou caught by thine eyes nor captivated by her eyelids.*

26. Our Heb. text next gives a couplet of which the second cl. (lit. *the married woman hunts for the precious life*) presents no difficulty; for the expression of the predicate cf. Ez. $13^{18.\,20}$. There is difference of opinion among expositors as to whether the *harlot* of first cl. is synonymous or contrasted with the *married woman* of second cl.; the latter view (which is that of the Anc. Vrss., Ew. *al.*) is favored by the fact that the two terms are distinctly contrasted in 7^{10}, and elsewhere in chs. 1–9 it is always the *stranger* (that is, *married woman*) against whom men are warned. If this view be adopted, the verse does not condone association with harlots (Now.), but simply lays stress on the greater harmfulness of the other class of unchaste women (cf. the contrast between the thief and the adulterer, v.$^{30-32}$). — Text and translation of first cl. are doubtful. The Heb. reads either *for on behalf of a harlot to* [= *as far as*] *a loaf of bread*, or, *for in exchange for a harlot*, etc. The first form is adopted by the great mass of expositors, who then take *on behalf of* as = *on account of* or *by means of*, and supply the expression *one* [or, *a man*] *is brought down* [or, *comes down*].* The objections to this interpretation are that the prep. does not mean *on account of* or *by means of*, and that the assumed omission of the verb is hard and improbable; the prep. may be changed (Gr., Oort), but the difficulty of the verb is not thereby removed. The second form appears to have been adopted by the Anc. Vrss. (Grk. Syr. Targ. Vulg. and also Saad.), which translate substantially : *for the price of a harlot is a loaf of bread*, = *in exchange for a harlot* [*one gives*] *a loaf of bread*, in which the insertion makes a difficulty as in the other form, and the sense given to the prep., though found elsewhere (Job 2^4), is here unnatural and improbable; this rendering of the line may, however, be obtained by a change of text. The

---

* So Rashi, Aben Ezra, Schult., Hitz., De., Now., Reuss, Zöck., Noyes, Str., Kamp., RV.

first translation declares that the harlot brings a man to poverty, while the married woman seeks his death ; the second, that one pays a small price for the one, a great price for the other. Either of these senses of first cl. is intelligible ; the first agrees better with the context, in which the theme is the harm wrought by unchaste women. Poverty, it is true, is usually indicated by *morsel* (of bread) instead of *loaf* (17^1 28^{21} Oort), but in 1 S. 2^{36} the two terms appear to be used as synonymous. A slight change in the Heb. gives the same verb in the two lines : *for a harlot hunts just* (or, *only*) *a piece of bread*. This gets rid of some of the syntactical and other difficulties, and the resulting form has the directness and homeliness of a practical aphorism : the ordinary harlot is after subsistence, will deprive a man of his money, but not ruin him ; the unchaste married woman brings on him destructive social (and possibly legal) punishment. That concubinage did not bring great social discredit among the Jews of the third century B.C. may be inferred from the story in Jos. *Ant.* 12, 4, 6 ; and adultery is here denounced as by far the more dangerous evil. The retribution attending it is loss of physical *life*, either at the hands of the outraged husband, or by the operation of law — there seems to be no allusion to loss of property, or to destruction of bodily powers by dissipation ; see notes on v.$^{32-35}$ (and cf. Geiger, *Urschrift*, p. 241). — The couplet, however, in whatever way it be taken, remains obscure. It is not clear whether the two clauses describe two classes of women or only one class ; and it is difficult to give a satisfactory translation of the first clause. The verse has the appearance of an editorial or scribal addition (gloss). We may conjecturally translate :

> For the harlot seeks a morsel of bread,
> But the adulteress hunts the precious life;

or :

> For the price of a harlot is a morsel of bread,
> But the adulteress hunts the precious life.

The rest of the chapter deals with the perils which beset the adulterer : first an illustration (v.$^{27-29}$), then a comparison with another crime (v.$^{30-33}$), finally the ground of the peril (v.$^{34.35}$). While in ch. 2 the sage describes death as the punishment of this sin, and in ch. 5 loss of wealth and of social position, he here dwells on the revenge taken by the husband of the woman. The moral wrong of adultery is of course assumed; the practical moralist lays stress on the penalty as the best way of deterring men from the commission of the crime in question.

27–29. Illustrations of the peril of adultery.

> 27. Can one take fire in his lap
> And his clothes not be burned?
> 28. Or, can one walk on hot coals
> And his feet not be scorched?
> So with him who has commerce with another man's wife —
> Whoso touches her will not go unpunished.

27. Question, ternary. The same term is used in Heb. of the *breast* or *bosom* of the body (5^{20}) and of the middle portion of the outer garment in which things were kept and carried and on which they were laid (so now in Syria and Egypt); here the reference is not to the bosom (De., who improperly cites Isa. 40^{11}), but to the *lap* of the garment; so in 16^{33} the lot is cast into the *lap.* — **28.** Question, ternary. For *coals* see 25^{22} 26^{21}; they were of wood (cf. ψ 120^4); in Isa. 6^6 a different word is used (*hot stone*). — **29.** Single sentence, ternary. *Go unpunished* or *be held guiltless* or *free*. Though the statement is general in form, the special reference, as appears probable from v.$^{30-35}$, is to legal punishment, or to the husband's vengeance; here, as in the preceding paragraph, there does not seem to be any allusion to the enervating effects of adultery on body and mind, or to an immediate divine interposition. It is implied that the law is so strict, or the husband so determined, that no plea offered by the offender, such as provocation, seduction (v.^{24}), or the notorious character of the woman, will be accepted. The character of tribunal and punishment is not stated.* — The couplet gives a natural exposition of the illustrations of v.$^{27. 28}$, but it may be omitted without detriment to the sense, the consequence being stated in v.^{32}.

30–35. Another illustration of the folly of adultery, derived from a comparison between the adulterer and the man who steals

---

* See note on 5^{14}.

to satisfy hunger. The latter may get off by a private money-payment (v.30. 31), the former, by reason of the husband's jealousy, cannot make such compensation, is forever disgraced (v.32-35), and apparently falls into the hands of the law.

> 30. Men do [it is true] despise a thief if he steal
>   To satisfy his appetite when he is hungry;
> 31. And, being caught, he must restore sevenfold,
>   Must give all the effects of his house.
>
> 32. But he who commits adultery is devoid of sense,
>   He destroys himself who so acts.
> 33. Blows and disgrace he will get,
>   And his ignominy will not be wiped away.
>
> 34. For jealousy is fury in a man,
>   And he will not have pity in the day of vengeance;
> 35. He will not accept any ransom,
>   Nor be content though thou give many gifts.

30, 31. The first couplet is a single sentence, ternary; the second is synonymous, ternary. The Heb. reads : *men do not despise the thief if he steal*, etc. This has been understood to mean that one who is driven by hunger to steal is pitied but not despised — his offence is not condoned, but he does not of necessity lose social position, and (v.31) he recovers legal standing by making compensation.* No doubt moralists are disposed to make allowance for such cases of theft; but there is no trace of this leniency in OT. (in Jer. 2²⁶ the thief is disgraced), and moreover, the sage here (v.31) forgets or ignores the thief's poverty, and represents him as a man of property. To avoid this discrepancy some commentators (Now., Str.) regard the two couplets as describing two different cases, that of the hungry thief, who is not despised, and that of the ordinary thief, who has to make restitution, the two categories corresponding respectively to v.32. 33 (disgrace) and v.34. 35 (no money-compensation). We should thus have the contrast : " a thief may escape disgrace, or may get off by payment of money; an adulterer does not escape disgrace, or get off by such payment." This contrast is not expressed in the text — there is no change of subject in v.30. 31; and there is, further, the doubt

---

* Cf. Loewenstein, *Die Proverbien Salomos* (1838), on this verse.

whether this lenient view of the hungry thief is probable. — The
first couplet may be read as a question (Hitz., Frank., *al.*) : *do not
men despise*, etc. ?, = *men despise*, etc.   The contrast will then be :
"a thief suffers disgrace, but escapes with loss of money ; an
adulterer gets disgrace and blows, and no money-payment atones
for his offence." This seems to be the better interpretation of
the contrasted fortunes of thief and adulterer. The discrepancy
between v.[30] and v.[31] remains ; it must be regarded as an oversight of the author, or the Heb. text must be so changed as to
indicate the two classes of thieves referred to above. — The rendering : *men do not overlook a thief though he steal*, etc. (Ew.,
Zöck., Noyes) is not warranted (the verb does not mean *overlook*),
and loses the main contrast of the paragraph. — The similar phraseology in Cant. 8[7], *if one should offer to give all the substance of
his house for love, he would be utterly despised* (that is, his offer
would be rejected with contempt), might suggest the translation :
men do not contemptuously repulse (= *reject the offer of*) *a thief if,
stealing to satisfy appetite and being caught, he offer to restore*, etc. ;
but this is hardly a natural rendering of the Hebrew. — In the
earliest law-book the rule is that the thief, when caught, shall pay,
according to circumstances, double, fourfold, or fivefold (Ex. 22[1. 4. 7]
[21[37] 22[3. 6]]), and there are similar rules for fraud (Ex. 22[9(8)]
Lev. 6[1-5] [5[20-24]]) ; on payment of the mulct the thief recovered
legal standing.   The *sevenfold* in our passage points, perhaps, to
a change in the law, but it is more probable that the reference is
not to a legal penalty, but to a private arrangement with the
injured person, and that the *seven* is a round number, = *very
large ;* the "sevenfold restitution " is then explained as possibly
amounting to *all the effects* (or, *substance*) *of his house.* — The
phrase *when he is hungry* is omitted by Bickell as a gloss ; it is
not logically necessary, but is a not unnatural poetical expansion.
— The Heb. terms rendered *steal* and *thief* involve secrecy and
not violence or malignancy (2 Sam. 19[6(4)] Hos. 7[1] Joel 2[9] Job 4[12]) ;
for violent procedure other words * are employed. — V.[31a] is rendered in Grk. Syr. Targ. *it is not wonderful if*, etc. ; Vulg. *it is
no great offence*, etc. ; these translations may be free renderings of

* גזל, פרץ.

our Heb. text. — **32–35**. The folly of the adulterer in provoking the wrath of the injured husband. — **32**. Synonymous, ternary. He is a fool (*devoid of sense*, lit. *of mind* or *heart*) because he *destroys himself;* how this is done is indicated in the following verses. The rendering *destroys his own soul* (RV. *al.*) conveys a wrong impression by suggesting moral and spiritual depravation and destruction — an idea correct in itself, but not here expressed. The writer doubtless held adultery to be a crime against society and against the adulterer's own moral being ; but, instead of speaking of the necessity of preserving the purity of the family and the individual (considerations which generally have little force against passion), he employs what he regards as the most effective argument — the appeal to self-interest : an adulterer, he says, is (even compared with a thief) a fool. — The second cl. may be rendered (but not so well) *he who would destroy himself so acts* (Targ., RV.), or, with slight change of text, *he works destruction for himself* (Grk. Vulg.). — **33**. Synonymous, ternary. The retribution follows. According to the old law the punishment of adultery was death for both parties (Dt. 22$^{22-24}$ Lev. 20^{10} ; cf. Ez. 23$^{45-47}$ — the character of the penalty in the old ordeal of Nu. 5$^{11-29}$ is doubtful). Later the rigor of the law appears to have been relaxed ; in Ben-Sira 23$^{18-26}$ nothing is said of death, and Jno. 8^5 seems to recognize the possibility of other than capital punishment (as in fact the woman goes free). In our verse (as in v.^{31}) it may be that it is not legal punishment that is meant. The outraged husband might prefer not to parade his wrong in the courts — he might deal with the offender himself by the simple method of bodily chastisement (*blows*), though this was possibly a public form of punishment (cf. BS. 23^{21}). In any case, as the thing became known, the criminal would suffer indelible *ignominy*. — As the paragraph is dealing particularly with the male offender, there is no reference to the penalty which might be inflicted on the woman. In later times divorce, either public or private (cf. Mt. 1^{19}), lay within the power of the husband, and it is probable that this mode of redress existed when our chapter was written, and is here assumed as possible. But the moral interests of the unchaste woman are not considered in chs. 1–9 ; she is treated simply as an evil to be avoided, and was in law largely a chattel of

the husband.   In the regard of showing no sympathy with the
unchaste woman Prov. is not peculiar—it has been the general
rule in most communities up to the present day.   The feeling
underlying it apparently is that such a woman is merely a tempter,
and must be utterly depraved.   Somewhat higher ethically is the
sympathy expressed by Ptahhetep, *Instructions*, § 37 (see Art.
Egypt. Literature, in *Library of the World's Best Literature*).—
34. Synonymous, binary (or, binary-ternary).   The sense of first
cl. is : *jealousy enrages a man* (or *husband*) ; Grk. : *the fury* (or,
spirit) *of her husband is full of jealousy ;* Vulg. : *jealousy and a
man's fury* (or *a man's jealousy and fury*) *will not spare*, etc.   On
the power of jealousy see 14^{30} 27^4 Cant. 8^6.   The *day of vengeance*
may be either private or legal.   The sage uses the common fact
of the husband's rage as a warning.   On the ordeal of Nu. 5 see
note on preceding verse.   On the power of the Jewish congregation see note on 5^{14}. — **35.** Synonymous, ternary.   It is assumed
that the adulterer (like the thief, v.[31]) will attempt to escape punishment, public or private, by the payment of money as compensation or bribe—either the law allowed such compensation at the
time, or it is supposed that the husband will not go to law.   *Ransom* (lit. *covering* of a fault) is the general term for anything
offered or prescribed in lieu of punishment, whether as legal satisfaction (Ex. 21^{30} Nu. 35^{31} Job 33^{24} Pr. 13^8 21^{18}) or as bribe
(Am. 5^{12}).   The second cl. explains that the compensation here
meant is in money or its equivalent.   The general case is here
stated ; there might be exceptions, but ordinarily the husband
would be relentless, and the adulterer is a fool to run such a risk
—the thief may escape, but not the adulterer.

20, 21. Between the Heb. sing. nouns and the Grk. plu. in v.[20] there is
little to choose.— 𝕳 לֵב, 𝕲 ψυχῇ. — **22.** On the inversion of v.[22. 23] see note
above on v.[22-24]. 𝕳 תַּנְחֶה אֹתָךְ; 𝕲 (followed in part by 𝕾) ἐπάγου αὐτήν κ.
μετὰ σοῦ ἔστω, = תִּנְחֶךָ אֹתָךְ (Jäg.), or the second part is doublet, = תִּהְיֶה אִתָּךְ.
𝕷 *gradiantur* and *custodiant*, to conform the number to that of v.[21].   Bi.
inserts at beginning וחכמה גם הֵא הַצֹּרֶךְ; see note above on v.[22].   In third line
𝕮 is free rendering of 𝕳. — For 𝕳 תְשִׂיחֶךָ Gr. suggests תּוּשִׁיתֶךָ. — **23.** 𝕳 plu.
תּוֹכֵחוֹת; read sing. with 𝕲 ἔλεγχος, but וּ (𝕲 καὶ) should not be inserted before
מוּסָר; Cl. Al. 154[19] (cited by Lag.) has ἐλέγχει.   𝕮 makes two clauses instead
of three : ὅτι λύχνος ἐντολὴ νόμου, καὶ φῶς ὁδὸς ζωῆς καὶ ἔλεγχος καὶ παιδεία;
𝕳 is preferable on grounds of sense and symmetry.   Gr. מִצְוַת אָבִיךָ and תּוֹרַת

אפך.—**24.** 鬼 רע, ⑤ ὑπάνδρου, = רֵעַ (Vog.), adopted by Gr., Bi.; to this
Baumg. objects that the word, used as = *another*, always has the suffix, as in
v.²⁹; read זרה.—**25.** In ᵃ ⑤ gives free rendering, and in ᵇ has doublet, the
original having ὀφθαλμοῖς, the revision βλεφάρων to agree with 鬼 (Lag.).—
𝕃 takes לבבך as subj.—**26.** 鬼 בעד, probably taken as prep. *in exchange for*,
and rendered freely in all Vrss.: ⑤ τιμή, 𝕃 *pretium*, ℭ רמיא (for רמין *price*,
Oort) with מלהא added as explanation, Ꮥ דומיה, for רביא *price* (but cf. Nöld.,
in Pink.); Oort, doubtfully, ביד; read הצד or צדה *hunts*.—鬼 עד, omitted by
Bi. (who also omits אשת), read אך by Ew., Gr., and one or the other of these
emendations should be adopted.—Frank.: כי ערך אשת זנה ערך ככר לחם, an
appropriate emendation, after ⑤𝕃 (though it would be better to omit the
second ערך), but graphically not so easy as the one above proposed.—
29. Omitted by Bi. without explanation, apparently to gain a simple quatrain
(v.²⁷·²⁸), he having above (v.²²) expanded a verse (triplet) into a quatrain;
v.²⁹ is a natural, though not necessary, conclusion to v.²⁷·²⁸; it might be
omitted without loss, and its naturalness might account for its insertion as a
gloss.—The form of 鬼 is substantially supported by the Vrss.—**30.** The
Vrss. suggest no emendation of 鬼, of which they give free translations; see
note on this verse above.—**31.** שִׁבְעָתָיִם is in form dual of the fem. (as in the
second numeral), lit. *two sevens*, but used in the sense *sevens*, = *sevenfold;*
for a different view see M. Heilprin, *Histor. Poetry of the Anc. Hebrews*, Vol. I.
note A. 鬼 יִתֵּן; ⑤, interpreting correctly, δοὺς ῥύσεται ἑαυτόν.—**32.** 鬼 reads
lit. *he who destroys himself* (ℭ *who wishes to destroy*, etc.) *he does it*, or better
he destroys himself who does it (taking הוא as in apposition with משחית).
⑤ (followed by 𝕃) appears to render freely, so that its Heb. text can hardly
be conclusively made out. It improperly takes the verse as a single sentence,
writes δι’ ἔνδειαν (= בחסר?), makes כי (or משחת) obj. of the verb in which it
omits suff. (περιποιεῖται), and apparently omits הוא (omitted by Bi.). 鬼
gives a good sense as it stands, but becomes easier if we omit הוא and take
יעשנה as rel. clause.—**33.** 鬼 ימצא, ⑤ ὑποφέρει, which Lag. emends to ἀποφέ-
ρει, prob. = 鬼, not ישא (cf. the different rendering of ישא in v.³⁵).—At end
⑤ adds εἰς τὸν αἰῶνα, probably rhetorical expansion, but Lag. holds that לעולם
stood in 鬼 and has fallen out by similarity to following לא תמחה; the addition
is possible, but is not favored by the rhythm; Baumg. compares the אל חמח of
ψ 109¹⁴.—**34.** 鬼 כי קנאה חמת גבר; the subj. (as the connection shows) is קִ׳
(as in Cant. 8⁶ קָשָׁה כשאול ק׳), and we should perhaps expect that ג would be
attached to it and not to ח, though the present form is intelligible. ⑤, badly,
μεστὸς γὰρ ζήλου θυμὸς ἀνδρὸς αὐτῆς, taking ח as subj. ℭ = 鬼; Ꮥ follows
⑤, only inverting the order of the words, and omitting αὐτῆς: *the fury of a
man, because it is full of jealousy, will not spare*, etc.—**35.** ⑤ and 𝕃 render
鬼 freely, and independently each of the other.

VII. Warning against the adulteress.—A more elaborate
treatment of the subject of 2¹⁶⁻¹⁹ 5, 6²⁰⁻³⁵, and similar in arrange-

ment to these subsections. The number of these closely similar
addresses suggests that the section chs. 1–9 is a compilation. —
The writer counsels obedience to his word (v.$^{1-3}$), that is, to wisdom
(v.^{4}), that it may preserve the pupil from the adulteress (v.^{5}),
whose fatal wiles are described (v.$^{6-23}$), and concludes with an
appeal to avoid her (v.$^{24-27}$).

1–5. Wisdom the preserver against the adulteress.

1. My son, keep my words,
   And lay up my commandments with thee.
2. Keep my commandments and live,
   And my law as the apple of thine eye.
3. Bind them on thy fingers,
   Write them on the tablet of thy mind.
4. Say unto Wisdom: "Thou art my sister,"
   And call Understanding kinswoman.
5. That she may keep thee from another's wife,
   From the adulteress with her enticing speech.

1, 2. Both couplets are synonymous, ternary. One form of the
standing introductory summons; see 3^1 4^1, etc., Ben-Sira 3^1.
Words, commandments, law are synonyms; the Impv. *and live* =
and thou shalt live, or *so that thou mayest live* (that is, live long
and happily). *Apple of the eye*, = pupil of the eye, symbol of
most delicate and precious things, here and in Dt. 32^{10} ψ 17^8; in
Pr. 7^9 20^{20} = centre, core; in Lam. 2^{18} *daughter of the eye* is
equivalent to *eye*. — Between our v. and v.^{2} Grk. has *my son, fear
the Lord and thou shalt be strong, and beside him fear no other*, in
general accordance with $3^{7.9}$ 14^{26} (cf. Eccl. $5^{7(6)}$), but out of keeping with the context here, in which the point is obedience to the
teacher himself; it is the addition of a scribe or an editor who
thought that a distinctly religious exhortation should be here introduced. Cf. Racine, *Ath.* I., 1 : *je crains Dieu, cher Abner, et n'ai
point d'autre crainte.* — **3.** Synonymous, binary (or, perhaps, ternary). Nearly identical with 3^3 6^{21}. As the hands are always in
sight, the finger is a fit reminder-place ; so in Dt. 6^8 11^{18} Ex. 13^{16},
which our verse may have in mind. It is uncertain how long
before the beginning of our era the custom existed of winding
prayerbands (*totafoth, tefillin,* phylacteries) around the finger and

arm ; the earliest reference to them is in NT. (Mt. 23^5) and Josephus (*Ant.* 4, 8, 13). From 1^9 3^3 6^{21} it would seem more probable that the allusion here is to a ring, probably the seal-ring (Gen. 38^{18} Jer. 22^{24} Cant. 8^6) which appears to have been commonly worn by men ; the same verb *bind* is used in 3^3 of a necklace. In second cl. the allusion is probably not to the command (Dt. 6^9) to write the law on doorposts and gates, but to the tablets of the law, or to inscribed tablets in general. In any case it is inward recognition of law that is enjoined, and the law is that not of Moses, but of the sage himself.* — **4.** Synonymous, ternary. Expression of closest intimacy. *Kinswoman* involves the idea of intimate friendship ; in Ru. 2^1 3^2 (the only other places in which the term occurs) the point is the obligation of kinship. Grk. : *say that Wisdom is thy sister and gain the friendship of Understanding* (lit. *gain Understanding as friend*), in which the parallelism (*say . . . gain*) is not so good as in the Heb. — **5.** Synonymous, ternary. The woman is described in both clauses in the Heb. as *stranger*, that is, another man's wife, and therefore, in this connection, an adulteress. The final clause is lit. *who makes smooth her words*, = "uses enticing words." The verse is substantially identical with 2^{16} 6^{24} (on which see notes), and is on that account omitted by Bickell ; but, though not necessary, it gives a natural and desirable connection between the exhortation (v.$^{1-4}$) and the description (v.$^{6-23}$). It is possible that these two paragraphs were composed independently of each other — in that case v.^{5} is the insertion of the compiler, and should therefore be retained.

6–23. Detailed description of the seductive arts of the adulteress, and of their fatal result. — A thoughtless young man, wandering through the streets at night (v.$^{6-9}$), is accosted by an impudent woman, a frequenter of the streets (v.$^{10-13}$), who invites him to go to her house, saying that she has prepared a feast with all pleasant accompaniments, and that her husband has gone away on a long journey (v.$^{14-20}$) ; he yields, and goes unconsciously to destruction (v.$^{21-23}$). The description differs from that of 2^{16-19}

---

* Inscribed objects attached to the person were, perhaps, originally amulets or talismans ; cf. notes on 1^9 3^8.

(which merely states that death is the result of a licentious course) and from that of 6^{24-35} (which dwells on the folly of this sin) in the detailed picture it gives of the woman's wiles. Literary skill is shown in the vivid contrast between her attractive home, the scene of luxurious carousal, and the wretched death that follows. The description shows acquaintance with the later city life. Cf. Ben-Sira 9^{3-9} 19^2 26^{9-12} 42^{12}.

6–9. The young man.

6. For at the window of my house
   Through my lattice I looked forth,
7. And saw among the youths,*
   A young man void of sense,
8. Passing along the street near her corner,
   Walking in the way that led to her house,
9. In the evening twilight,
   [Or] in the darkness of the dead of night.

6. Continuous, ternary. The *for*, introducing the illustrative case, follows naturally on v.^{5}, less well on v.^{4}. The case put is represented as typical — the suggestion is: one may any evening look out and see, etc. — In first line we should perhaps read: *through* (or, *out of*) *my window I looked*. — The windows of Oriental houses (like those of Europe some centuries ago) are not enclosed with glass, but have trellis-work of wood or metal, through which a person standing within may see the street without being seen from without;† the window was a favorite place of observation (so in *Thousand and One Nights* frequently). — Grk. represents the woman as the observer: *from her house she looks out of a window into the streets*. The picture of her as on the watch for her prey is natural and effective in itself, but hardly agrees with v.$^{10-12}$ in which she is already in the street; if she is indoors in v.$^{6-9}$, we should expect to have in v.^{10}: *she came forth and met him;* the woman appears to be introduced as a new personage in v.^{10}. — **7.** Single sentence with peculiar rhythm, the first line consisting of two parallel clauses, with their completion in second

---

* Heb.: *and saw among the simple, observed among the youths.*

† Ju. 5^{28} 2 S. 6^{16} 2 K. 9^{30} Cant. 2^9; Aristoph., *Thesmoph.*, 797; Livy, 24, 21; Vitruv., v. 6, 9.

line, or (if the second line be begun with *perceived*) the second
line giving a parallel to first line, and adding the completing
phrase. The expression of the Heb., *saw among the simple*, which
introduces a tautology (*simple = void of sense*) should be omitted ;
the couplet will then be a single sentence, binary. — *Simple =
void of understanding;* see note on 1⁴. — **8.** Synonymous, ternary.
A corner, as in Grk., is hardly better than Heb. *her corner;* the
latter expression denotes not the particular place at which she
stands (in v.¹² she does not confine herself to one spot), but the
corner near which her house is. — The young man is not represented (as RV. suggests) as going to her house, but only as following the road that led thither ; he is strolling aimlessly within
her domain, and so meets her ; Ben-Sira 9⁷ warns young men
against such nocturnal strolling. — The *her house* implies that she
has already been mentioned ; the reference, according to the Heb.
text, is to v.⁵, but in the Grk. text more naturally to v.⁶ (see note
above). — **9.** Parallels, ternary. The two clauses, as they stand
in the Heb., giving different parts of the night, must be connected
by *or* or *and;* Grk. : *in the evening-gloom, when there is quiet of
night and of darkness* (different text, or free rendering), which
has the advantage of giving unity of time to the two clauses. *Twilight*, the dim light near sunrise or sunset, is defined by *evening*.
The second cl. is lit. *in the pupil* (= centre, middle) *of the night
and darkness*. The intention of the Heb. text seems to be to
indicate the whole period of darkness during which people were
accustomed to walk in the streets : from twilight to midnight one
may see young men traversing the streets. The second line may
perhaps mean : *in the darkness of complete night* (so RV.), that is,
any time after twilight. — In the early evening or in bright star-
light or moonlight figures without might be visible from a window,
and torches and lanterns were sometimes carried, though hardly
by the persons here described ; for the rest the description is im-
aginative, though no doubt based on personal observation. Roman
youths at such times sometimes wore masks (Juv. 6, 330).

VII. 1. On the added v. in 𝔊 see note above on v.¹ The fact that it
appears in no other Vrss. exc. 𝔖ᴴ throws no light on its date; such additions
were natural for a long period. Ew., without giving reasons, regards the v.
(which he renders into Heb.) as genuine. — **2.** Segol with Athnaḥ in חַיֶּה

bears witness to the phonetic force of this vowel. — אישון, = Arab. *insân*, apparently a *human* (or *manlike*) *thing;* the ending *on* (*ân*) is elsewhere in O.T. not dimin. but general-relational; Aram. *ûn* is diminutive.   א׳ עין is parallel in ψ 17[8] to בַּת עַיִן (perhaps = the centre or principal part of the eye); the Aram. Vrss. here render א׳ by בבחא *gate;* cf. Ges., *Thes.*, BDB. — תורתי; 𝕲 τοὺς δὲ ἐμοὺς λόγους, as if it read רברי, or אמרי, as in 4[10]; between such variants there is no ground of choice. — **3.** For 𝕳 אצבעה 𝕾, by scribal inadvertence, has צור, as in 3[3]. — **4.** 𝕳 חקרא; 𝕲 περιποιήσαι, = תקנה (Jäg.); whether 𝕲 had הבינה (Jäg.) or took ל in 𝕳 לבינה as sign of accus. (Lag.) can hardly be determined. — For מֹרָע Oort suggests fem. מרעה, but this is not necessary. — **5.** 𝕲 πονηρᾶς, apparently miswriting of πόρνης (Lag.); cf. 𝕲 in 2[16]. — **6, 7.** On the 1st pers. in the vbs. in 𝕲 see note on these vv. above.   Oort suggests הבכתי for ביתי, to secure fuller parallelism, and Gr. the insertion of ורנה before נער; 𝕾 has 3d pers. plu. — **8.** 𝕳 מנה; the masc. form of the noun is found only here and Zech. 14[10]. — נָשׁוּק is omitted in 𝕲, יצער in 𝕾 (by free translation or inadvertence).   For יצער 𝕲 has λαλοῦντα, error of Grk. scribe; for proposed emendations see notes of Lag., Baumg., and on 𝕿 cf. Pink. — **9.** The Heb. text appears to offer an inverted parallelism (cf. Schult.) : נשף (degree of light), ערב (part of the day), אישון לילה (part of the night), אפלה (degree of darkness); we should probably, in accord with the preceding expressions, read כאמלה.   𝕲, however, makes two phrases of the v.: ἐν σκότει ἑσπερινῷ, = בני׳ ערב, and ἡνίκα ἂν ἡσυχία νυκτερινὴ καὶ γνοφώδης, = 𝕳, except that for אישון it seems to have had some form of ישן *sleep* (Schl.), or possibly of שקט *repose*.   With such twofold division 𝕳 would read: *in the twilight of evening, in the depth of black night.*

10-12. The woman.

> 10. And lo, ‹the› woman comes to meet him,
> In harlot's dress, and wily (?) of heart.
> 11. She is boisterous and a ‹gadabout› —
> Her feet rest not in her house —
> 12. Now she is in the street, now in the squares,
> And she lurks at every corner.

10. Continuous, ternary.   As the woman is referred to above (v.[8]), the def. art. (as in the Grk.) is preferable to the reading of the Heb. (*a woman*).   She *comes to meet him* by design, not simply *meets* (or, *met*) *him* (RV.).   Instead of *dress* (or, *ornament*) Grk. has *form, appearance*, a sense (= mien) which perhaps better suits the context, in which the woman's character is described.   Whether harlots at this time wore a distinguishing dress is uncertain (in Gen. 38[15] it is the veil that is characteristic) ; the reference is perhaps to the style of attire.   In this expression the

woman here described (the married woman) is technically distinguished from the harlot proper (who was unmarried). — The
translation *wily* (RV.) is conjectural; other proposed renderings
are *false* (Schult.), *malicious* (Ew., Now., Kamp., etc.), *secret*,
hypocritical (Berth., Str., Stade), *excited* (Frank.), *subtle* (AV.,
De.); in Isa. 48⁶ the Heb. word appears to mean *hidden*, *secret*,
and here, if the reading be correct, some such sense as *wily* suits
the connection. Grk.: *causes the hearts of young men to fly away*
(or, as emended by Lag., *causes young men to lose their heads*);
Vulg.: *prepared to catch souls.* These renderings may represent
our Heb., or may rest on a different text; they do not suggest
any satisfactory emendation. — **11.** Synonymous, ternary. Here
also the adjectives are doubtful. The first (which occurs again in
9¹³) usually expresses excited movement and noise (1 K. 1⁴¹ Isa.
22²), and may here refer to the woman's free, boisterous manner
of talking, or to her unrestrained actions, or to both of these;
proposed renderings are *garrulous* (Vulg.), *loud, clamorous,
excited, vehement, passionate, boisterous,* of which the last appears
best to reproduce the Heb. term. The second word, as it stands
in our Heb. text, means *rebellious, selfwilled, wilful,* which may
be understood as expressing her attitude toward her husband, her
refusal to obey him and stay at home; a slight change of letters,
however, gives the sense *going about, gadding about* (Vulg. *strolling,* cf. Cant. 3²·³, where the maiden and the watchmen go about
the city), and this is in keeping with the following clauses. The
older Greek laws forbad free women to leave their houses after
sunset,* but it appears from this passage and from Cant. 3² and
Ben-Sira (26⁸·¹⁰) that at a later time women had no little liberty
of movement, and part of the duty of a careful husband or father
was to keep his wife or daughter indoors (Ben-Sira 25²⁵, cf. 1 Tim.
5¹³ Tit. 2⁵). — **12.** Synonymous, binary- (or, quaternary-) ternary.
Licentious women showed themselves freely in the streets and in
the squares or open places at gates and elsewhere (see note on
1²⁰·²¹), choosing corners particularly as convenient places for
seeing and being seen. The paragraph is a vivid description of
the city manners of the later time (probably third cent. B.C.).
V.¹¹·¹² are of the nature of a parenthesis.

---

* Becker, *Char.* 468 f.

10. The Art. before אשה (found in 𝔊) has dropped out by reason of preceding ה. Before לקראת there is usually a vb. of going, but this is sometimes omitted, as in I S. 10[10] *al*. — The signification *dress* for שית seems to be assured by ψ 73[6]; after 𝔊 εἶδος Hitz., Oort suggest a form of שוה (8[11] 26[4] 27[15]). If the text-word be retained, prep. ב should perh. be inserted before it. — 𝕳 נצרת לב; 𝔊 (foll. by 𝔖𝕿) ποιεῖ νέων ἐξίπτασθαι καρδίας (the νέων is explanatory insertion), as if from נדר (cf. 27[8]); Lag. emends to ἐξίστασθαι (Eur. *Bacch.* 850) *lose one's senses*, and thinks that 𝔊 had מצירת *producing a whirl*, after Syr. צורן (Castel. 755), but such a sense is proved neither in Heb. nor in Aram.; 𝕷 *ad capiendas animas*, apparently from ציד (Berth., cf. Ez. 13[20]). There is no satisfactory derivation for the text-word; that from נצר (*hidden, wily*, cf. Isa. 48[6]) seems least objectionable. There is perh. scribal error; we expect some word like נעקש (28[18]) or נפתל (8[8]) or ערם (but this stem is employed elsewhere in Pr. only in good sense), and see the expressions in Eccl. 7[26]. Schult., *fictu cordis*, from צור, in sense of Arab. צּור. — **11.** 𝕳 סוררת *headstrong*; 𝔊 ἄσωτος *profligate* seems to represent 𝕳 (Lag. improbably, from סרח); read סובבת (cf. Cant. 3[2. 3]), 𝕷 *vaga*, 𝕿 פרידהא. — **12.** 𝔊, less well than 𝕳, divides the v. at בחוץ, after which it inserts, to complete the parallelism, the vb. ῥέμβεται *roams*.

13–20. Her invitation: she assures him that she has made special preparations to receive him.

13. So she seizes him and kisses him,
   With impudent look says to him :

14. "A vow-offering was due from me —
   To-day I have paid my vows —

15. So I came out to meet thee,
   To seek thee — and I have found thee.

16. I have spread my couch with coverlets,
   With striped cloths of Egyptian yarn.

17. I have perfumed my bed with myrrh,
   With aloes and with cinnamon.

18. Come, let us, till morning, take our fill of love,
   Let us take our pleasure in love.

19. For my husband is not at home,
   He is gone on a long journey;

20. He took a bag of money with him,
   He will come home at full-moon feast."

13. Continuous, binary-ternary. This free procedure may have taken place in a retired spot, else it would probably not have escaped the attention of the police ; though women at this period had, as we have seen (note on v.[11]), some liberty of movement, it would appear from Cant. 5^7 that the night-watchmen sometimes arrested strolling women, though under what circumstances does not appear. Watchers on city-walls no doubt existed from of old (Isa. $21^{11.\ 12}$ 62^6 ψ 127^1), but the relatively modern night-patrol is mentioned only in Cant. 3^3 5^7. — The expression *with impudent* (or, *wanton*) *look* (lit. *puts on a bold face*, so 21^{29}) does not intimate that the woman assumes an attitude not natural to her, but simply describes her meretricious boldness. — **14.** Protasis and apodosis, ternary. Of course the observer at the window does not hear the long and probably whispered speech that follows (v.$^{14-20}$) ; the writer describes a common scene. — The woman (who thus appears to be an Israelite) begins by telling the young man that her payment of a vow-offering enabled her to provide special entertainment at this time; the feast is not mentioned, but, as the invariable accompaniment of the sacrifice, is taken for granted ; we might, therefore, render : *I have a sacrificial feast at my house.* The Heb. term here rendered *offering* (*shelem*, RV. *peace-offering*) is a general one comprehending several varieties. It signifies primarily *wholeness, soundness,* and so security, friendly, peaceful relations with the deity, or the payment of one's obligations to the deity so as to secure his friendship.* As a technical sacrificial term it denotes the ordinary offerings made freely to gain favor, or presented in gratitude for favors bestowed or in fulfilment of a vow (see the different sorts in Lev. 7^{11-21}). It consisted always of flesh, to which (at least in the later ritual) was added flour, oil, and wine (Nu. $15^{9.\ 10}$) ; and of the animal presented only the blood and the fat of the intestines was offered on the altar, the rest was eaten by the worshippers. The *shelem* thus differs from the *holocaust* (Heb. *ola*, RV. *burnt-offering*) which was wholly consumed on the altar. It is in fact the old sacrificial meal of the family or clan, which was of a festive character (Am. 5^{21-23}). In the present instance its occasion is a vow which has just been fulfilled (*to-day*) ; the law required that the flesh should be eaten on the day of offering (Lev. 7^{16}). The woman, not inattentive to her religious duties (and there is no reason to suppose

---

* The same stem is found in Arab. *Islam*, = the establishing of sound relations with God by *submission, resignation ;* and *Moslem* = one who is resigned to God's will, a professor of Islam.

that she herein acted otherwise than in good faith), having discharged her vow and prepared the feast, goes out to seek a companion, and pretends to the youth (it seems probable that it is a pretence) that she has come expressly to find him.   If the sacrifice was offered on an altar, the scene of the incident is doubtless Jerusalem ; but it is possible that the Egyptian Jews, before the building of the Onias-temple (B.C. 149), maintained customs of vows at home, dedication being substituted for actual sacrifice. From the plu. *vows* it may perhaps be inferred that vows were suffered to accumulate, so that a number were paid at one time ; and from Eccl. 5⁴⁻⁶ we gather that there was sometimes undue delay in paying, so that it became necessary for the priests or other officers to send messengers to demand payment.* — **15.** Continuous, ternary. The *so* (or, *therefore*) refers to the festive character of the occasion : " as I have prepared an excellent table, and do not wish to enjoy it alone, therefore I have come," etc. *To seek thee*, lit. *to seek thy face.*   The reading proposed by Bickell, *that I might find thee*, is feeble and improbable. — The two next verses describe the luxurious appointments of the woman's house, whence (and from v.¹⁹·²⁰) it may be inferred that her husband was a man of substance, and she of good social position. — **16.** Synonymous, ternary.   *Couch* is properly *bedstead* (Dt. 3¹¹ ψ 132³), elsewhere (Job 7¹³) used also for the whole of the sleeping-furniture, but here apparently for the structure on which bed-clothing is spread. The uncertainty of the term here rendered *coverlets* appears from the diversity of the translations given it : Grk., Vulg. *cords ;* Syr. Targ. *beds* or *mattresses* (or perh., *cushions, pillows*) ; Aq., Theod. *spreads ;* and these renderings (except the first) are variously adopted by modern commentators.   The word occurs elsewhere only in 31²², where it seems to mean some sort of cloth-work (Grk. is here doubtful, Aq., Th., Vulg. *spreads,* Sym. *carpets shaggy on both sides*).   AV. *coverings* probably gives the sense of the term (RV., not so well, *carpets,* marg. *cushions*), but the addition *of tapestry* (= embroidered) is without support.   AV. *decked* = *covered, spread.* — The terms in second cl. must also describe some sort of bed-clothing : the first is in Grk. *carpets shaggy on*

---

* On the later regulations respecting delay see commentary on Dt. 23²¹⁻²³ in *Rosh ha. Shanah,* 5 *b.*

both sides; Syr. Targ., *spreads* or *carpets;* Vulg. *embroidered carpets;* recent commentators generally *striped* (or, *party-colored*)
spreads or *cloths.* The second term represents some kind of material, *stuff,* or, as the word signifies in Aram., *yarn;* it is left
untranslated by the Anc. Vrss. (or they may have had a different
word), except that Theod. has *marked with Egyptian paintings.*
— Across the ancient Greek bedstead (which was usually of wood,
sometimes of bronze) were stretched girths (cords) which supported a mattress, and on this were spread coverlets, which were
sometimes colored. There was a headboard, and sometimes a
footboard; at the former were placed cushions or pillows. This
is the general arrangement here referred to, though the precise
significations of the various terms are doubtful. — The mention of
Egyptian material may indicate that the section was not written in
Egypt; commercial intercourse between Egypt and Palestine had
existed since the time of Solomon, and became more frequent
after the settlement of the Jews in Alexandria. — **17.** Continuous,
ternary-binary. After the bedstead was spread with costly coverings, the *bed,* thus prepared, was *perfumed* (lit. *sprinkled*).
The aromatic substances here named are frequently mentioned in
OT. (e.g. Cant. 4^{14}). *Myrrh* is a gum-resin which exudes from
the *Balsamodendron Myrrha,* a shrub growing in Arabia and
Abyssinia; it is reddish brown in color, has an agreeable odor
and an aromatic-bitter taste; a liquid form of it appears to be
mentioned in Ex. 30^{23} Cant. 5^5; for its use in the preparation of
the temple-oil see Ex. 30^{22-25}. *Aloes* is the fragrant resin-gum of
Aloexylon and *Aquilaria ovata* of Malacca and *A. agallochum*
of Bengal. *Cinnamon* is the aromatic bark of a Ceylonese tree;
it was an ingredient of the sacred oil of the Jews (Ex. 30^{22-25}).
The description indicates a high degree of luxury. Among the
Israelites ivory couches (or divans) were used by the rich as early
as the eighth cent. B.C. (Am. 6^4), but the perfumes here mentioned appear only in postexilian writings (Ex. 30, Esth., ψ 45,
Cant., Pr.); they seem to have become known to the Jews
through late intercourse with foreign peoples. — **18.** Synonymous,
quaternary-binary. The vbs. express fulness of enjoyment. The
first (*take our fill*) means to be filled, saturated with water (Isa.
55^{10}), with blood (Isa. 34^7 Jer. 46^{10}), with love (here and 5^{19});

the second means to enjoy one's self, Grk. *to roll in*, Targ. *give one's self up to*, Vulg., Syr. *embrace*.—**19**. Synonymous, ternary. In first cl. the Heb. reads *the man*, an expression which is perhaps used by the woman in a slighting way instead of the friendly *my husband*, as if she would say: the man who owns the house, whom I happen to be bound to but do not care for. But such a refined sneer does not seem very probable, and, as Grk. has *my husband*, we should rather so read, or with RV. write *the goodman*. The master of the house appears to be a rich merchant, called on to make long journeys, as was the custom with merchants (Tob. 5³ 9² Mt. 13⁴⁵).—**20**. Continuous, ternary. Time is reckoned by feasts, and these by the phases of the moon (so now frequently in rural communities, even where the solar year exists). *Fullmoon-feast* (ψ 81³⁽⁴⁾) is the middle of the month—the scene occurs in the first half of the month, and the intimation is that some days must elapse before the husband can return. There was no fixed day for paying vows. The festival referred to may be Passover or Tabernacles.

13. On the ı *rafatum* of הֵעֻזָּה (a local peculiarity of Masoretic pronunciation) see De.'s note in B-D. פָנֶיהָ is unnecessarily omitted by Bi., apparently on rhythmical grounds.—**14**. 𝕳 שְׁלָמִים; plu. everywhere except Am. 5²² (where it is perh. scribal error). זֶבַח often = שֶׁלֶם (Ex. 24⁵, cf. Ez. 44¹¹ with 45¹⁵), here = *slain offering*.—**15**. The Vrss. have free renderings of 𝕳. On 𝕾𝕿 see Pink.—**16**. 𝕳 מַרְבַד, רְבִד, of uncertain meaning, the vb. only here, the noun here and 31²²; 𝕲ᴮ κειρίᾳ (𝕲ᐟᶜᐧᵃᐧᴬ plu.) τέτακα, in which the noun = *girths*, suggests the sense *bind* for the vb. (as in רָבִיד *chain*, Gen. 41⁴² Ez. 16¹¹, and in Arab.), but in 31²² 𝕲 has χλαίνας *mantles*, which favors the rendering *coverlets* here; 𝕾𝕿 have stem שׁוי, Αθ περιστρώννυμι, *spread* in vb. and noun; 𝕷 *intexui funibus*, the noun being after 𝕲, but the vb. *weave*, appropriate in 31²², is here out of place. The weight of authority appears to favor the sense *spread*.—חֲטֻבוֹת, cf. Arab. חטב. Oort, taking it as rendered by 𝕲 ἔστρωκα, emends to הִשַּׁתִּי, but the Grk. word rather represents 𝕳 אֵטוּן, read as הִשַּׁתִּי or אֵפָה.—אֵטוּן, found here only, is possibly a foreign word (but ὀθόνη *linen* may be a loan-word from Sem.); in Jew.-Aram. it = *thread*, a possible sense here, but 𝕿 has another term, קרמא *carpet*, perh. = *stuff woven of thread*. On the form see Ols., p. 335; it seems unnecessary to regard it as Aram.—**17**. 𝕳 נַפְתִּי *sprinkle*, Qal only here; Bi., Hif. הִנַּפְתִּי (cf. ψ 68¹⁰), Oort נִטְּפָתִי (cf. Cant. 5⁵); Gr. נָפְתִּי, from נפת.—מֹר is Semitic, אֲהָלִים (cf. Hind. *aghil*, Sanscr. *aguru*) East Indian, and קִנָּמוֹן, though its origin is uncertain, is probably foreign.* —

---

* Cf. H. Lewy, *Semit. Fremdwörter im Griech.*; C. P. G. Scott, *Malayan Words in Eng.*, in JAOS., Vol. 17.

18. The plu. דדים and אהבים are used always of sensual love. Geiger, *Urschrift*, p. 398, reads דַּדִּים (see 5¹⁹), but the Mas. form is better. 𝕳 נתעלסה; 𝕲 ἐνκυλισθῶμεν, after which Oort unnecessarily emends to New-Heb. נתעגלה *let us wallow.* — Bi., to complete his scheme of quatrains, adds the couplet וספל ענים אהבת רע וימהקו העננים גנבם — the woman, he holds, according to v.²¹, employed argument (לקה) and it must be introduced here; but her persuasions are sufficiently given in v.¹⁴⁻²⁰. — 20. כֶּסֶא, only here and ψ 81⁴ (כסה). Here 𝕿 has עירא *feast* (Rashi: the time fixed for the feast), 𝕾 = 𝕲, 𝕲 δἰ ἡμερῶν πολλῶν (perh. free transl. — Lag. suggests that δἰ ἠμ. = διχομήνη), 𝕷 *plenae lunae* (and so Bar Ali, cited in Ges. *Thes.*), Saad. *day of sacrifice*, Aben Ezra *new moon;* in ψ 81⁴ 𝕿 has ירהא דמתכנסי, 𝕾 כֵּסֵא, 𝕷ᵛ *in medio mense*, 𝕲 εὐσήμῳ *favorable* (apparently a guess). And since in 𝕾 כסא stands for the 15th day of the month in 1 K. 12³² and for the 23d in 2 C. 7¹, the word appears to mean either the week of the feast from the middle of the month on, and so either the feast (either Passover or Tabernacles, here perhaps the latter, 𝕿 ψ 81⁴ appears to interpret it as the former), or its first day. On the form see Ols. p. 256, 282. The word seems to be Aramaic, but its etymology is uncertain — prob. not from stem = *cover* (Ges., De., "the disk of the moon is covered with light"), perh. related to Arab. נכא *latter part*, and = second half of the month, and so the festival of that time; 𝕿 מרהכס may be denom. (*the month of*) *the* כסא, but prob. = *covered* (so *Rosh ha. Shanah* 7 *b*. 8 *a*). Aben Ezra's interpretation is against this derivation, but his rendering is opposed to that of earlier authorities. The word, however, may mean simply *feast*. BDB. compares As. *kuseū* (see De., *Ass. Handwb. s. v. kuseū, aqū*), *full moon* (as *tiara* of a deity).

21–23. The youth yields to her persuasions, and thus goes to his death.

21. With much fair speech she persuades him,
    By the blandishment of her lips seduces him.

22. So enticed he follows her,
    Like an ox that goes to slaughter,
    Like a ‹ calf that is led to the stall,›

23 b. Like a bird that hastes to a net,
   c. Knowing not that it concerns its life,
   a. Till an arrow cleaves its liver.

21. Synonymous, ternary. *Fair speech* is lit. *teaching, instruction* (see note on 1⁵) — designation of the woman's enticing description as a didactic discourse or argument. *Persuades*, lit. *causes to yield; blandishment of her lips*, lit. *smoothness of her lips;* see 2¹⁶ 5³ 6²⁴ 7⁵. *Seduces*, lit. *carries off* (or, *away*). The two verbs are employed in OT. to express the leading away of Israel after other gods than Yahweh, the first, for ex., in 1 K. 11², the

second in Dt. 13⁵⁽⁶⁾. The two clauses do not involve a climax, but are identical in meaning. — **22, 23**. The text is corrupt in individual words, and there is probably a displacement of clauses. The three lines of v.²³ should probably stand in the order *b c a*; in v.²² Bickell further follows the order *a c b*. The two verses form three couplets, and should probably be divided into three verses, in the order ²²ᵃ·ᵇ·, ²²ᶜ·²³ᵇ·, ²³ᶜ·ᵃ·. The difference of length of lines in the Eng. translation does not exist in the Heb. — **22**. Comparisons, ternary. The Heb. reads: *he follows her suddenly, as an ox that goes to slaughter, and as fetters to the chastisement of a fool,* in which *suddenly* is inappropriate, and third cl. yields no sense; Luther's *as to the fetters where fools are chastised* is not allowed by the Heb., and lacks the fatal character which the connection requires; the latter objection applies to the inversion of AV. (adopted by De., Now., Str.) *as a fool to the correction of the stocks* (or, *the chastisement of fetters*); the rendering *one in fetters* (Noyes, RV. marg.) is impossible, and there is no sufficient evidence that the Heb. word (עֶכֶס) means *fetters* — in the only other place in which it occurs in OT., Isa. 3¹⁸, it is used in the sense of *anklets* (and in Isa. 3¹⁶ the verb *shake the anklets* occurs), from which can be inferred only that the sense *fetters* is possible (Schult.: *as it were, with head bound to feet*). The parallelism suggests the mention of an animal, and so Grk. Syr. Targ. *as a dog to bonds;* Vulg. *as a frolicsome lamb, not knowing that a fool is led to bonds.* The rendering *as a calf that is led to the stall* is obtained by a few changes in the Heb. consonants; the stalled calf was kept for slaughter (Am. 6⁴ 1 Sam. 28²⁴, cf. Pr. 15¹⁷). — Instead of *suddenly* read, with Grk., *enticed* or *deceived* or *persuaded*, according to the stem in 1¹⁰ 16²⁹ 20¹⁹ 24²⁸ 25¹⁵ Jer. 20⁷ Job 31⁹, cf. Hos. 7¹¹ Job 5². — The verse is a picture of the brute-like stupidity with which the man goes to his unforeseen fate. The death (which is physical) is apparently represented as coming not by violation of the laws of temperance, but by general dispensation of God in social and legal penalties; cf. 1³² 2²², etc. There is no reference to the mode of death; the description resembles that in ch. 2 (v.¹⁶⁻¹⁹) more than those in chs. 5 and 6. — **23**. Comparison and consequence, ternary. As the text stands, v.²³ᵃ is connected with the preceding context ("he follows her as an ox, etc., till an arrow cleaves his liver "), and a new comparison, to a bird, is added. We gain simplicity by transferring the third line to the end of the verse (so Hitz., De., Bi., Frank.), and dividing v.$^{22.23}$ into three verses so as to read according to the translation given above. The Heb. order is given in the Anc. Vrss., only Grk. Syr. Targ. have in first line *as a stag shot in the liver with an arrow* (in which *stag* represents the last word of v.^{22} of the Heb.). The third couplet, in the order given above, appears to refer to the bird, which is shot as it approaches the net or after it is entrapped; a similar reference to the ignorance of birds is made in 1^{17}. — *Liver*, as seat of life, is found only here and Lam. 2^{11}, elsewhere only in ritual procedures. It is common in Bab.-Assyrian. Possibly in some passages, as ψ 16^9, in which *my glory = myself*, we should read *my liver* (parallel to *my heart* or *my soul*).

24–27. Concluding exhortation against the woman, based on her fatal influence; so 2$^{18.19}$ 5^8 9^{18}, cf. 6$^{32-35}$.

24. Now, therefore, ‹my son,›* hearken to me,
And attend to the words of my mouth.

25. Turn not aside to her ways,
Go not astray in her paths.

26. For many are the dead she has cast down,
And numerous they she has slain.

27. In her house are ways to Sheol,
Going down to the chambers of Death.

24. Synonymous, ternary-binary. The Heb. has plu. *sons*, without possess. pron., in this verse, and sing. in v.^{25a}; the change of number is possible, but is here not probable; the Grk. has the sing., and this, in any case, is better in an English translation. — Here, as elsewhere, the sage is his own authority. — **25.** Synonymous, ternary-binary. Lit. *let not thy mind* [*heart*] *turn aside*, in which *thy mind* (like *thy soul* elsewhere) = *thyself*. *Turn aside* (found elsewhere only in 4^{15} Nu. 5$^{12.19.20.29}$, noun in Hos. 5^2) is declining from the right way, = *go astray*. — Many Heb. MSS. connect the two lines by *and*. Grk. omits second line,

---

* The Heb. has *ye children* (or, *sons*).

probably by scribal error; it is necessary for the symmetry of the
verse. — **26.** Synonymous, ternary-binary. The first cl. may also
be rendered: *for many she has cast down dead;* the translation
given above is favored by the parallelism. The form of RV.: *she
has cast down many wounded* is not permitted by the Heb., and the
slain of second cl. requires *dead* instead of *wounded.* — In second
cl. AV. has *yea, many strong men have been slain by her,* RV.,
better, *yea, all her slain are a mighty host.* The reference is not
to the strength of the victims (with the implication: if she has
slain strong men, how can the ordinary man expect to escape?),
but, as appears from first cl., to their number. The Heb. word
has the meaning *numerous* in Am. 5^{12} Zech. 8^{22} ψ $40^{5(6)}$ *al.* Second
cl. reads in the Heb.: *and numerous are all her slain,* in which
the *all* is not agreeable to Eng. idiom, and probably does not
belong to the original Heb. text. — **27.** Synonymous, ternary-
binary. Heb. lit. *her house is ways to Sheol* (so Schult., Ew.,
Frank.), rendered by AV., RV. *her house is the way,* etc., by
Reuss *is in the way,* by Hitz., De., Str. *is a multiplicity of ways,*
by Now., Kamp. *is full of ways.* The sense appears to be that
many paths, leading to the Underworld, issue from her house (cf.
12^{28} 14^{12}) — there are many chances of death from association
with her. The penalty referred to is premature physical death,
as in 1^{32} 2^{22} 5^{23}, not moral depravation, and not punishment after
death; see note on 1^{12}. *Chambers of Death* = simply *Sheol,* not
the private rooms of the Underworld, its most distant and painful
parts. The distinctions in Sheol are not moral, but ritual or
social: the uncircumcised and those who descend without proper
burial-rites are assigned to remote, socially inferior, corners (Ez.
32^{18-32} * Isa. 14^{15}), kings and great warriors sit on thrones or occupy
other prominent positions (Isa. 14^9). In the Babylonian Underworld there seems to be some sort of sevenfold division (see
Descent of Ishtar), the significance of which is not known. No
such division appears in OT. (not in Dt. 32^{22} ψ 86^{13}) — there is
mention of gates (Isa. 38^{10} ψ $9^{13, 14}$ 107^{18} Job 38^{17}), as in Babylonian,† but not of courts, streets or houses. The word *chamber*

---

* Emended text in Haupt's *Sacred Books of the Old Testament.*
† The *bars* of Job 17^{16} is doubtful — see note in Budde's *Hiob.*

does, indeed, generally stand in contrast with the space outside
the house (court or street), and in earthly life implies privacy
(Ju. 3²⁴ 2 K. 6¹²) ; but in poetical usage it appears to stand (sing.
or plu.) for the whole of a given place or space (Job 9⁹ 37⁹).   If,
however, the term be here understood to imply divisions in Sheol,
these (as OT. usage shows) are not connected with moral differences in the inhabitants.

22. 𝕳 פְּתָאֹם, not *headlong* (Schult.) but *suddenly ;* 𝕲 κεπφωθείς *cajoled*
(like a simpleton, κέπφος), as from stem פתה; some form of this stem is required by the connection, perh. יִפָּתֶה; cf. Job 31⁹ אִם נִפְתָה לִבִּי עַל אִשָּׁה; graphically נ might easily pass into ת, especially if נ in latter was marked by a line
(פ.א.).— פֶּם, here yields no sense; 𝕲 κύων, = כֶּרֶב; 𝕷 *agnus*, = כֶּבֶשׂ; read
רֶגֶל.— מוּסָר *correction ;* 𝕲 δεσμούς, = סֹר ., better than 𝕳, but not wholly appropriate, since it does not naturally correspond to the parallel מֻכָּה; it may
therefore be better to read בְּרֶבֶק *stall* (see note on this v. above), though
the reading of 𝕲 is intelligible. — אֱוִיל must be taken as vb., some such form
as יוּבַל (Gr.).   It is read אַיִל by 𝕲 and transferred to next v.: ὡς ἔλαφος τοξεύ-
ματι πεπληγώς. — **23.** On the inversion of clauses see note on this v. above.
The order of 𝕳 is retained by the Vrss. — **24.** 𝕳 בָּנִים; 𝕲, better, *υἱέ.* —
25. On יֵשְׁטְ see Stade, § 489 b, and cf. Ew. § 224 c. — Cl. 2, lacking in 𝕲ᴮ, is
given in 𝕲ˢ ᵉ· ᵃ· ᴬ, H-P. 23, 68, 106 al., Compl., Ald., and, according to 𝔖ᴴ,
belongs to ϴ; the omission in B is inadvertence. — **26.** 𝕳 חֲלָלִים; 𝕲 freely
τρώσασα.   It may be also by freedom of translation that 𝕲 does not render
כָּל; but this word, though syntactically possible, and not unaccordant with the
rhythm, is not necessary, and is in any case naturally omitted in an Eng.
translation. — **27.** In cl. 1 𝕳, reproduced by 𝕲𝕿𝕷, is possible though hard;
𝔖's insertion of אֹרְחָה, = רְנִי, before בֵּיתָהּ is no doubt explanatory addition.
Insertion of ב is easy, but perh. unnecessary. — 𝕳 יְרֵדוֹת; 𝕲 κατάγουσαι, free
rendering, or = מִ רִיוֹת (Lag.).

VIII. Exalted function of Wisdom. — A separate discourse (cf.

1²⁰⁻³³), consisting of two closely related sections (v.⁴⁻²¹ and v.²²⁻³¹)
with introduction and conclusion.   After the description of Wisdom as public exhorter (v.¹⁻³) comes her address, in the first section of which (v.⁴⁻²¹) is set forth her high character and honorable
function among men (she utters truth, v.⁴⁻⁹, and confers knowledge,
riches, and honor, v.¹⁰⁻²¹), and in the second (v.²²⁻³¹) her position as
cherished companion of Yahweh in the beginning ; the conclusion
states the happiness of those who obey her and the evil fate of
those who reject her (v.³²⁻³⁶).   With this hymn to Wisdom cf. the
hymns to Yahweh, ψ 104. 107, and the praise of Wisdom in Job 28,

Ben-Sira 1[1-21] 24, Wisd. Sol. 7[8]-8[21]; it most resembles the last two passages in its personification, being in this point more advanced than the description in Job.

1-3. Wisdom stands in places of concourse, and cries to men.

1. Does not Wisdom call?
   And Understanding utter her voice?
2. At the head of thoroughfares, on the road,
   In the streets she takes her stand.
3. Beside the gateways, at the portal of the city,
   At the entrance of the gates she cries aloud.

The phrases are nearly the same as in 1[20. 21], only Wisdom is here dramatically described as taking her stand. — 1. Synonymous, ternary (or, binary-ternary). *Wisdom* and *understanding* are identical in meaning; see note on 1[2]. — 2. Synonymous, ternary. The Heb. reads: *at the head* (or, *on the top*) *of high places on* (or, *by*) *the road* (or, *way*); the *high places* might be supposed to be the walls and battlements of the city, or benches on the streets, or the platforms of the shops, which in Eastern cities are slightly elevated above the street, and would permit a speaker to make himself visible to the throng of bypassers; but we know of no such custom, and comparison with 1[21] makes it probable that the term here = *thoroughfares;* cf. 9[3. 14]. As thoroughfares are called *noisy places* and *broad places* (1[20. 21]), so they may be called *high places* or *highways*, as in 16[7] (where, however, another word is used); cf. Ju. 5[20]. Parallel to this is the expression *in the streets* (not, as RV., *where the paths meet*). Grk. omits *on the road*, rendering v.[2]: *on the lofty summits she is, amid the ways she stands;* the omitted phrase may be a gloss on the preceding expression, but something seems necessary here, and, in the absence of anything better, this phrase may be retained. — 3. Synonymous, binary. While v.[2] thus mentions one sort of public place (the street), v.[3] gives the other sort, the city-gates, which were common meeting-places for citizens, like the Greek agora and the Roman forum; see, for ex., Ju. 9[35], 2 Sam. 15[2], Dt. 22[15], Jer. 17[9], ψ 69[12(13)]. The three expressions here used are merely varied ways of describing the space at the gates where men met to talk. For the second the Heb. has *the mouth* (RV. *entry*) *of the city;* we should perhaps read *in front of the city*. The *gates* (lit. *doors*) are the openings in the *gateways*, the latter being elaborate structures, covered ways with a door at each extremity; for the full phrase *door of the gateway* see 1²¹, Jos. 8²⁹, 1 K. 22¹⁰, Jer. 1¹⁵, Ez. 8³. The couplet, thus, does not mention three different spots (on this side, on that side, and within the gateway), but gives only one place. Wherever men throng thither Wisdom goes. Instead of the immediate word of Yahweh, which the prophet announces, the sage proclaims man's own conviction of rational life, which, however, he identifies with the will of God. — Bickell omits v.²ᵃ· ³ᵃ as glosses, and thus makes one couplet out of v.²· ³, and this was perhaps the original form:

> Does not Wisdom call?
> And Understanding utter her voice?
> In the streets she takes her stand,
> At the gateways cries aloud.

4–21. The teaching and the rewards of Wisdom. — After an introductory appeal to men (v.⁴· ⁵), the section falls naturally into two main parts, first (v.⁶⁻¹¹), Wisdom's ethical excellence (her instruction, v.⁶⁻⁹, her superiority over silver, etc., v.¹⁰· ¹¹), and second (v.¹²· ¹⁴⁻²¹, omitting v.¹³ as scribal insertion) her intellectual eminence (she enables kings to rule well, v.¹²· ¹⁴⁻¹⁶, and dispenses riches and honor to those who love her, v.¹⁷⁻²¹). Cf. Job 28¹⁵⁻¹⁹, Ben-Sira 1¹⁷· ¹⁹, Wisd. Sol. 7⁹· ¹⁴ 8⁵.

4, 5. The appeal.

> 4. To you, O men, I call,
> And my appeal is to the sons of men.
> 5. Learn, O ye simple, to know understanding,
> And, ye fools, to understand wisdom.

4. Synonymous, ternary. The terms *men* and *sons of men* appear to mean *all classes of men*, and to indicate the writer's view of the universality of the mission of Wisdom, who seeks her disciples among Jews and Greeks, learned and unlearned. *Appeal* is lit. *voice*. — **5.** Synonymous, ternary. Lit.: *comprehend, ye simple, discretion, and, ye fools, comprehend wisdom*. Wisdom is the sage's ideal scheme of life, to be sought by those who have it not; they must set themselves to comprehend its nature. On *simple* and *fool* see notes on 1⁴· ²². The Heb. word here translated

by *understanding* is that which in 1⁴ is rendered by *sagacity* (*orma*);
it means true knowledge of the principles of life. The signification of the corresponding term in cl. 2 (lit. *heart*) is given in
Hos. 7¹¹ : *Ephraim is like a silly dove, without sense.* The couplet may be rendered : *Ye inexperienced, acquire intelligence — ye
thoughtless, embrace wisdom.* — The Latin here has simply *ye fools,
give heed* (= *set your mind on*), which does not maintain the parallelism of terms. The rendering of RV., *be ye of an understanding heart*, does not give the sense of the Hebrew, in which the
exhortation is not *understand in your mind*, but *apprehend and
appropriate the idea of wisdom.* The writer accordingly goes on
to tell what wisdom is.

6–9. Wisdom declares her moral excellence.

> 6. Hear ye, for I speak ‹ verity, › *
>   And the utterance of my lips is right.
> 7. Yea, my mouth discourses truth,
>   And ‹ false lips are my abomination. › †
> 8. All the words of my mouth are just,
>   In them is nothing false and wrong.
> 9. They are all true to those who understand,
>   And right to those who find knowledge.

These verses form a group of aphorisms, all saying substantially
the same thing, with variations of phraseology. — 6. Synonymous,
ternary. Instead of *verity* (lit. *verities*) the Heb. has *princes*, or
perhaps *princely* (*noble*) *things* (RV. *excellent things*), a term here
out of place ; a slight change of letters gives the word used in v.⁹ᵃ,
straightforward, honest, true things, corresponding to the *right* or
right things in the second clauses of v.⁶ and v.⁹. *Utterance* is literally *opening.* — 7. Synonymous, ternary. The initial particle,
sometimes = *for*, is here better taken as asseverative ; v.⁷ is parallel to, not explanatory of, v.⁶. In cl. 2 our Heb. has *and wickedness is an abomination to my lips*, in which the lips are poetically
described as rejecting wickedness with horror ; but a more natural
reading is suggested by 12²², *false lips are an abomination to
Yahweh* (cf. 16¹³), and Grk. here has *false lips are an abomina-*

---

* Heb. : *excellent things* (?).

† Heb. : *wickedness is abomination to my lips.*

tion to me; the change of sense requires no great change in the Hebrew. — **8**. Synonymous, binary-ternary (or, ternary). *Just*, lit. *in justice* (RV. *in righteousness*) = *in accordance with right* (see notes on 1³ 2⁹·²⁰), in contrast with the *false* and *wrong* of the second clause, synonymous terms whose original, physical sense is *twisted* or *crooked;* the first occurs in Pr. only here (cf. Job 5¹³); on the second see note on 2¹⁵. — **9**. Synonymous, ternary. The sense *right, true* for the adj. in first cl. is assured by 2 Sam. 15³ Am. 3¹⁰ Isa. 30¹⁰ Prov. 24²⁶, and the second adj. is identical in meaning with that of v.⁶ᵇ. What the verse says is not that Wisdom's words are clear, intelligible, simple to the instructed,* but that they commend themselves as true; RV. *plain* is ambiguous, being = either *level* (as in RV. Isa. 40⁴) or *clear*, but neither of these senses is correct. — The verse is an appeal to the moral consciousness of men, affirming that he who *understands* the true relations of life, who *finds* (attains) moral *knowledge*, will recognize the truth of Wisdom's words. This affirmation stands almost alone in OT. In Ez. 18²⁵ there is the assumption that the people know in their hearts that Yahweh's moral procedure is right; here we have a direct recognition of the insight of the conscience. How a man comes to understand the truth the sage does not say. His picture is objective and stative: the world is divided by him into the two classes of the wise and the fools, and it depends on the man's will to which of these he shall belong. In the NT. the nearest approach to this conception of moral classes is found in the Fourth Gospel.

10, 11. The sage declares the preciousness of wisdom.

> 10. Take ye instruction and not silver,
>   And knowledge rather than choice gold.
> 11. For Wisdom is better than corals,
>   With her no treasures can compare.

The same thought is found in 3¹³⁻¹⁵, on which **see notes**; 8¹¹ is substantially identical with 3¹⁵. There (and so 8¹⁹) **the revenue** or outcome of wisdom is extolled, here wisdom itself. — **10**. Synonymous, ternary. The Hebrew has *my instruction*, but the simple

---

* Kamphausen, and, in part, Delitzsch.

noun (as in the Grk.) answers better to the *knowledge* of second cl.,
and to the *wisdom* of v.^{11}. The speaker is not Wisdom, but the
sage : the most desirable thing in life, he says, is the insight which
enables one to order one's life by the standard of truth — the
point of view is that not of the prophets and psalmists, but of the
younger school of Jewish thinkers. Cf. 4$^{5-9}$. *Choice gold* is doubtless the same as the *fine gold* of 3^{14}, gold valuable by the goldsmith's standard. The word rendered *choice* is found, in OT., only
in Proverbs.* — **11.** Synonymous, ternary. On *corals* see note on
3^{15}. *Treasures* is literally *desirable things* (as, for ex., in Hag. 2^7),
a general term including all things held to be valuable. Instead
of *can compare with* we may render *are equal to*.

13. This verse is not here in place, but it is not clear where it
is to be put. It not only interrupts the connection between v.^{12}
and v.^{14} (in which the intellectual excellence of wisdom is the
theme), but its tone is not that of the rest of the chapter. It
differs from the paragraph v.$^{6-9}$ (which it resembles in a general
way) by the use of the expression *the fear of Yahweh;* in this
paragraph it is with moral insight, and not with religious fear, that
the writer is dealing, and elsewhere in Proverbs the *fear of Yahweh*
is defined only in general terms (as = wisdom, 1^7 9^{10} 15^{33}, or as
source of blessing, 10^{27} 14$^{26.\,27}$ 19^{23}), not by a specific moral content (in 16^6 men depart from evil *by the fear of Yahweh*). Elsewhere in this chapter Yahweh is spoken of only in his relation to
Wisdom, either as her friend (v.$^{22-31}$), or as granting favors to her
friends (v.^{35}). The first clause of the verse is a general declaration which (apart from the difficulty stated above) might stand
anywhere in the section 10^1–22^{16}; it is omitted by Bickell as a
gloss summing up the content of the verse. But even with this
omission it is impossible to find a natural place for the verse in
this chapter. In the section v.$^{6-9}$ the theme is the truthfulness
of the instruction of Wisdom, and the mention of *pride* is out of
place, and its thought has no special relation to that of v.^{17}, after
which it is put by Bickell. We must therefore conclude that the
verse, though found in all the Anc. Vrss., is a scribal insertion.

---

* On ancient Semitic methods of preparing gold, cf. Rawlinson, *Phœnicia*, Ch. 10.

Many such aphorisms were doubtless in circulation among the learned, and were occasionally inserted out of place. Heb.:

> The fear of Yahweh is hatred of evil.
> Pride and arrogancy,
> The way of evil and the mouth of falsehood
> Do I hate.

Or, omitting the first line:

> Pride and arrogance and sinful life
> And the mouth of falsehood I hate.

The inconcinnity of the two parts of the verse, as it stands in the Heb. text, is obvious: the first part is the sage's statement of the relation of religion to evil; the second part is, in the connection, Wisdom's statement of her attitude toward evil. The rhythmic arrangement is bad, and is not bettered by Grk.: *the fear of the Lord hates unrighteousness and insolence and pride and the ways of wicked men, and I hate the corrupt ways of bad men.* On the omission of first line see above. The sentiment of the verse is a familiar one in Proverbs; see 2¹² 6¹²⁻¹⁹ 11² 16⁶. *Pride* and *arrogancy* are identical in meaning; the first occurs only here in OT., the second is found in 16¹⁸, and in OT. often elsewhere. On *falsehood* (lit. what is turned away, that is, from truth) see notes on 2². ¹⁴ 6¹⁴.

VIII. 1. 𝕳 (which 𝕷 follows exactly, and 𝕿 with one variation) is supported by the context. 𝕲ᴮᴺᴬ σὺ . . . κηρύξεις and ἵνα . . . ὑπακούσῃ (for תהן קולה); Procop., with H-P 23, 109, 147, 157, 295 Ald., διὸ σὺ . . . κήρυξον, and 𝕿 has מטול היכנא, = לכן, = διό. Since this is a separate discourse, a connecting לכן is improbable. The natural subject in ᵇ is Wisdom's utterance, and the תשמע אותך of 𝕲 is doubtless scribal error. — **2.** עלי דרך is omitted by 𝕲, but the rhythm requires some word here, and nothing better offers itself. Bi. omits these and the two preceding words, and v.³ᵃ, reading (v.². ³) בית נתבת נצבה מבא פתחם הרן; the maintenance of the full form of 𝕳 is favored by 𝕴²⁰. ²¹. The difficult מרמים is better taken as the equivalent of its parallel נתיבות of second cl. 𝕳 בראש מ, 𝕲 ἐπὶ τῶν ὑψηλῶν ἄκρων, 𝕷 *in summis excelsis que verticibus.* 𝕳 בית is scribal error for בתוך (v.²⁰), or possibly Aramaism. — **3.** 𝕳 לפי קרת; 𝕲 δυναστῶν, perhaps for ἀστέων (Jäg.). פי is used of the mouth of a well (Gen. 29²) or of the Underworld (ψ 69¹⁵⁽¹⁶⁾ 141⁷) or of the earth (Gen. 4¹¹), but never elsewhere of the entrance to a city. 𝕷 *juxta portas civitatis,* free rendering, possibly reading לפני ק. לפי ק is parallel to בעיר in 1²¹ (on which see note), and may be a gloss; Oort suggests קראה as pos-

sible emendation. The two passages, 1[20. 21] 8[1-3], have probably affected each
other, and it is difficult to restore the true text. מבוא may be taken as
locative, without preposition. — **4.** 𝔐 איׁׁיׁ (elsewhere only Isa. 53[8] ψ 141[4])
here = בני ארם, = ἄνθρωποι; the distinction which seems sometimes to be
made (ψ 49[2(3)] 62[9(10)], cf. Isa. 2[9]), between ב׳ ארם and ב׳ איש, is not contemplated here. — **5.** 𝔐 הבינו לב, 𝔊 ἔνθεσθε καρδίαν, = הכינו לב, to which the objection is not so much that the remote object is not expressed (for the שית לב
of 1 Sam. 4[20] offers support for such a construction) as that it destroys the
parallelism of the verse — לב corresponds to ערמה. — **6.** 𝔊 εἰσακούσατέ μου. —
𝔐 נגידים, as adj. ἀπ. λεγ., possibly (cf. נָנֶר נֶגֶר) *visible, clear* (see Schult.'s
note), but probably (from נגיד) *princely*, a sense here inappropriate; read
נכחים, as in v.[9a] (so Grätz); 𝔊 σεμνά; 𝔖𝔗𝔏 as 𝔐. — 𝔐 מפתח, elsewhere *key*,
here *opening* (abstract noun of action); 𝔊 ἀνοίσω, apparently Pi. Part., not
so well; Oort מפתח, *from the door*, referring to Mic. 7[5], where, however, the
phrase is different. — **7.** 𝔐 הׁוׁעבת שפתי רשע; 𝔊 ἐβδελυγμένα ἐναντίον ἐμοῦ
χείλη ψευδῆ; read ה׳ לי שפתי ר׳ (or תועבתי), in accordance with 12[22]. — Before
אמת Bi. inserts דברי, a doubtful betterment of the rhythm. — **9.** 𝔐 has Part., in
first cl. sing., in second cl. plu.; 𝔊, better, plu. in both. — **10.** מוסרי; omit suff.,
with 𝔊, in agreement with רעת in second cl. — 𝔐 אל (and not לא) on account
of the injunction involved; see Ges.[26], § 152, 1 *b*, Anm. 1. — In [b] several different Grk. readings are found: 𝔊[B] = 𝔐; 𝔊[Bb(vid.)] has, as doublet, ἀντε-
ρείσθαι (Clem. Al., Procop. ἀντερείδεσθε, read ἀνθαιρεῖσθε) δὲ αἰσθήσει χρυσίου
καθαροῦ, 𝔊[A], as doublet, ἀνταναιρεῖσθαι (read ἀνθαιρεῖσθε) αἴσθησιν χρυσίου
καὶ ἀργυρίου; the readings which differ from 𝔐 are probably nearer the Grk.
original (Lag.). The verb was inserted, by the translator, to secure symmetry, or (Lag.) he read נבחרה as pred. of רעת; 𝔐 is to be maintained.

**12, 14–16. The function of Wisdom in the guidance of the
rulers of the world through her control of intelligence.** — With
this prominence given to political leaders may be compared the
references to kings in other parts of the Book (14[28] 16[10-15] 19[10. 12]
22[29] 24[21] 25[1-7] 29[4. 14] 30[31] 31[4] *al.*). After the remark of the sage in
v.[10. 11] Wisdom now resumes her discourse.

12. I, Wisdom, ‹ possess › * intelligence,
    I have knowledge and insight.

14. With me is counsel and skill,
    With me understanding and might.

15. By me kings do reign,
    And rulers administer justice.

16. By me princes govern,
    And sovereigns ‹ rule › † the earth.

---

* Heb.: *dwell in.*   † Heb.: *all the rulers* (or, *judges*) *of.*

12. Synonymous, ternary. *Possess* is emendation of the Heb. *inhabit*, which is here unnatural. The statement of the Heb. is not that Wisdom dwells, in friendly alliance, *with intelligence*, but that she dwells *in intelligence*, an unexampled form of expression.* V.$^{12.\ 14}$ obviously set forth the resources of Wisdom ; the predicates all state what she has at command. The connection calls for a word expressing ownership, and the Peshiṭa and the Targum have *create*, which is apparently the rendering of the Heb. verb (see v.^{22}) which means both *create* and *possess;* the latter term fits the connection. Another emendation is *am acquainted with* (cf. ψ 139^3). In second cl. the verb, lit. *find*, = *come upon, come into possession of* (so in v.^{35}). On *intelligence* (or, *sagacity*) see notes on 1^4 8^5. In second cl. the *and*, lacking in the Heb., is properly supplied by RV.; the combination occurs in 1^{4b}. The three predicate nouns are synonyms. — **14.** Synonymous, binary-ternary, or binary. In second cl. *and* is lacking in the Heb. before the second noun ; this being supplied, the translation is : *I, understanding is mine and might.* The rendering of RV. *I am understanding* is out of keeping with the context and with the usage of the whole Book. *Counsel* is advice, and the knowledge which enables one to advise profitably. *Skill* is the ability so to arrange things as to lead to the desired result ; see note on 2^7. *Might* is power of thought, and, by consequence, of action ; see Isa. 11^2 and Job 12^{13}, passages which stand in some relation to this. — The predicates in v.$^{12.\ 14}$ are synonyms of wisdom ; but the latter conception is here personified, and endowed with all the qualities that are connected with it. — **15, 16.** Synonymous, ternary. The rendering above given of 16^b (which is after the Grk.) has the advantage of gaining symmetry of clauses. The Heb. reads *and sovereigns* (or, *nobles*, or, *magnates*), *all the judges of the earth.* A similar sequence occurs in ψ 148^{11} : *kings of the earth and all peoples, princes and all judges of the earth;* in the psalm it is natural, v.$^{8-12}$ being composed entirely of groups of nouns, with the verb in v.^{7}. In our passage the arrangement is different : v.$^{15a.\ 15b.\ 16a}$ consist each of subject and predicate ; the predicate is simply verb in v.$^{15a.\ 16a}$, in v.^{15b} it is verb and noun, and this form we expect in v.^{16b}. The

---

* Cf. the appropriate expression of 1 Tim. 6^{16}: [God] *dwelling in light unapproachable.*

Heb. text seems here to have been assimilated to that of the psalm. — *Administer = decree.* — Instead of *earth* some Vrss. and Heb. MSS. have *justice*, which is probably repetition, by scribal error, from end of preceding verse. — The rulers of the world are here conceived of ideally as governing by wisdom. The writer's tone is friendly; it is that of a man who looks on governments broadly, as institutions of life to be controlled by the laws of human knowledge and discretion. He thus stands in contrast with those psalmists who regard the kings of the earth as hostile to Israel (as ψ 149[8]), and with such passages as Eccl. 10[20], in which the king is spoken of as a dread personage to be cautiously dealt with. Throughout Proverbs the source of royal success is wisdom; in the Psalms it is Yahweh who guides the earthly rulers of Israel (ψ 144[10]), and is indeed himself Israel's king (10[16] 29[10] *al.*).

17–21. The first half of the chapter concludes with a description of **the earthly rewards of Wisdom.** Whatever men seek, riches and honor, is supplied in abundance by Wisdom — men will consult their interests in seeking her. The sage appeals to dominant human motives, and teaches men how to make life a success in the worldly sense. Cf. 3[10. 16-18]. V.[17] belongs rather to this paragraph than to the preceding.

> 17. I love those who love me,
>   And they who seek me find me.
> 18. Riches and honor are with me,
>   Lordly wealth and prosperity.
> 19. My fruit is better than finest gold,
>   And my produce than choice silver.
> 20. In the way of equity I walk,
>   In the paths of justice,
> 21. To endow my friends with wealth,
>   And fill their treasuries.

17. Synonymous, ternary-binary. On the rendering *seek*, instead of *seek diligently* (or, *early*), see note on 1[28]. — The reciprocity expressed in first cl. is not real (like that of ψ 18[25. 26(26. 27)]), but only formal, the sense being that, by a natural law of mind, only those who earnestly desire Wisdom can come into intimate relations with her. The first clause states the attitude of mind, the

second the consequent effort — the two are mutually complementary. It is assumed that men may naturally desire wisdom, and
that search for it is always successful. The sage recognizes to the
full the moral responsibility and potency of man; the highest gift
of life is within every man's grasp. His thought is an expanded
and refined form of the old-Hebrew idea (Ez. 18[4]). Similar
stress is laid in the Fourth Gospel on the power of the human
desire and will (Jno. 5[40] *ye do not wish to come to me*) and on the
attitude of mind here expressed by the word *love* (Jno. 3[19] *men
loved the darkness rather than the light*). Cf. note on v.[9]. —
18. Synonymous, ternary. The connection shows that the reference is to earthly honor and wealth (as in v.[21] 3[10] *al.*). *Honor* is
good repute in the eyes of men. *Lordly = splendid*, or, in general,
great, Grk. *abundant*, Lat. Vulg. *superb*, RV. *durable*, margin
ancient (that is, *inherited from ancestors*) ; the word appears to
mean *advanced, eminent,* and some such superlative adjective is
suggested by the connection, but the sense *inherited* (Stade) is
not appropriate. — The term here translated by *prosperity* (צדקה)
is usually rendered by *justice* or *righteousness.* It signifies primarily that which is *right, true,* as quality of a fact or of the soul
(the English *justice* has the same double sense). In its most
general meaning, *in accordance with propriety* or *with the facts in
the case,* it occurs in 1 Sam. 26[23], where Yahweh is said to give
every man his *due,* and in Joel 2[23], where Yahweh gives rain in *just
measure.* It thus comes to mean the *just measure of fortune* which
is meted out to a man, for example, by God, and then, by a natural transition, the good decision in his favor, the *good fortune*
awarded him — sometimes a legal decision by a judge (and the
judge may be God). It expresses Yahweh's interpositions on
behalf of Israel (Ju. 5[11]), that is, his (just) decisions in their
favor, and the good fortune which his protection insures : *every
tongue that enters into a legal contest with thee thou shalt get the
better of* [= procure a sentence of condemnation on] — *this is the
lot of the servants of Yahweh, and their fortune awarded by me,
says Yahweh* (Isa. 54[17]). This signification comes out clearly in
ψ 112, which is a description of the happiness of the man who
fears Yahweh ; his happiness is based on earthly prosperity, and
it is said of him, among other things (v.[3]) : *wealth and riches are*

in his house, and his good fortune lasts for ever (that is, is continued in his descendants). So the word must be taken in 21²¹ᵇ, if
it be retained in the text (it is lacking in the Grk.), and this sense
is required by the connection of our verse; the sage ascribes to
Wisdom the bestowal of well-being which the psalmist ascribes
to Yahweh. — **19.** Synonymous, ternary. *Fruit* and *produce*
(= *product, crop, revenue*) are synonymous agricultural expressions of blessing and prosperity. As in the preceding verse,
the blessing is external. The comparison affirms not that Wisdom's reward is different in character from gold (namely, moral
and spiritual), but that it is more splendid and desirable than the
most precious metals. — In first cl. the Heb. has two terms, generally rendered by *gold* and *fine gold;* their precise meanings are
uncertain, but their combination may be represented by *finest
gold.* Cf. note on v¹⁰. — **20, 21.** Both couplets are synonymous;
v.²⁰ is ternary, v.²¹ ternary-binary. Wisdom sums up her promises
of reward in the declaration that she deals equitably and justly
with her friends. *Equity* and *justice* are synonyms. The former
term represents the Heb. word rendered by *prosperity* in v.¹⁸;
here it is a quality of action (= right decision), there it is the
result of this action. The statement of v.²⁰ is simply *I deal justly.*
Friends, lit. *those who love me,* as in v.¹⁷; *wealth* = *possession,
property* (RV. *substance*). The initial particle in v.²¹ expresses
purpose (*in order that I may*), and this is here equivalent to
result (*so that I do*). Wisdom's justice is guarantee that she will
properly reward those who devote themselves to her; the two
verses may be thus paraphrased: *Since I am just, my friends will
be properly rewarded.* The rendering *righteousness* (instead of
equity) in v.²⁰ is misleading; it conveys to us the idea of obedience to religious law, or moral and religious purity; but these
qualities, though they belong to Wisdom, are not here in question;
the writer, as the connection shows, has in mind simply the justice
which assures to every man his due. — At the end of v.²¹ Grk.
adds, as introduction or transition to the following section, the
words: *If I declare to you the things of daily occurrence, I will remember to recount the things of old* — that is, I now pass from our
present life to the history of the primeval time — an explanatory
note by a scribe, not a part of the original text.

12. שָׁכַנְתִּי, an improbable expression; 𝔊 κατεσκήνωσα; 𝔖𝔗 ברית *create* (cf. Pink); read הַסְכַּנְתִּי *understand*, or קִנְיָתִי, which is graphically not hard, if the שׁ of שׁכנתי may be miswriting of preceding ה (in חכמה). Before מזמות insert ו. 𝔐 אמצא; 𝔊 ἐπεκαλεσάμην, for ἐπεκτησάμην (Jäg.). — 13. 𝔐 שֹׂנֵאת רָע; on 𝔖𝔗 cf. Pink.; on an apparently personal interpretation of רע (= *bad man*) in Talm. see H. Deutsch, *Spr. Sal.*, p. 68. — 14. In ᵇ we must either take אני as preposed subject, and insert ו before וגבורה, or, what is simpler, following 𝔊, change אני to לִי. — 16. 𝔐 כָּל שֹׁפְטֵי ארץ; 𝔊 τύραννοι κρατοῦσι γῆς; read ישפטו א׳. — For ארץ 𝔖𝔗𝔏 and many Heb. MSS. and printed Edd. give צדק (see De' Rossi), which seems to be scribal repetition from end of preceding verse; after שפט we expect ב before צדק, as in ψ 96¹³ 98⁹. — On 𝔖𝔗 see Pink.'s note. — 17. Read Qeri אֹהֲבַי (so 𝔊); Bi. אֲהֵב יה אֹהֵב *I love him who loves Yah*, an improbable reading. — 18. 𝔐 יְהֵק; 𝔊 πολλῶν, perhaps for παλαιῶν (Grabe, cited by Lag.); 𝔗 וּמְזוֹלִיא *and riches;* 𝔖 = 𝔐; 'Α μετ' εἰρήνης; Σ (and Θ) παλαιός; 𝔏 *superbae.* — 20. At the end 𝔊 adds ἀναστρέφομαι, to correspond with the vb. of first cl., but against the rhythm. — 21. 𝔐 יֵשׁ; 𝔊 ὕπαρξιν; 𝔗 שְׁנִיא סַנִיאָהא *many years;* 𝔖 סבָרא *hope;* 𝔏 *ut ditem.* On the form cf. Ew., § 146 d, Stade, § 370 b, and on the meaning BDB. On the couplet added in 𝔊 (the style of which differs from that of the context) see notes of Jäger, Lag., Baumgartner.

22–31. Wisdom's primeval life with Yahweh. — A section distinct from, but allied to, the preceding. The statement of Wisdom's rewards is followed by a description of her creation and her intimate relations with Yahweh; the picture is similar to that in 3¹⁹·²⁰, but is more detailed, with distincter personification, approaching but not reaching hypostatization. Wisdom was brought into being before Yahweh began the work of creation (v.²²⁻²⁶), was present when he established heavens, sea, and earth (v.²⁷⁻²⁹), rejoicing in all his work (v.³⁰·³¹). This is the culmination of the portraiture, in Proverbs, of Wisdom's function in the world: she is the source of sound knowledge in life (v.⁵⁻¹¹), she conducts the government of society (v.¹²⁻¹⁶), and confers the noblest rewards (v.¹⁷⁻²¹), she antedates human experience, having been present at the construction of the world (v.²²⁻³¹). The description is completely non-national and universal, and thus stands in contrast with the similar passage in Ben-Sira (ch. 24), in which Wisdom dwells in Israel and is identified with the Jewish Law. From the more vivid and human picture of Wisd. Sol., ch. 7 it differs in its architectural simplicity and solidity, while Philo's Wisdom is more philosophical in form and comes to the very verge of hypostasis.

In Job 28 the representation of Wisdom is ethical, not cosmogonic : eluding man's search she is declared by God to be identical with righteousness.   Proverbs offers the earliest surviving
form of that Hellenized conception which finally took complete
shape in Philo.   The sage of Proverbs is thoroughly Israelitish,
but his idea of the unity and order of the world has been formed
in an atmosphere pervaded by Greek thought.   His Wisdom is
the creature of Yahweh, God of Israel and of the whole earth, but
is at the same time the highest intelligence, conceived of as
present with God in the creation of the world, and directing all
human life — a conception which thus combines philosophic universality and Jewish theistic belief.

With the picture of creation here given cf. that of Gen. 1, that
of Job 38^{4-11}, and the Babylonian cosmogonic epic.*   Our poem
divides itself naturally into four parts : Wisdom's primeval origin
$(v.^{22.23})$; her birth before the world $(v.^{24-26})$; her presence at the
creation of the world $(v.^{27-29})$; her joyous existence in the presence of God $(v.^{30.31})$.   The third division seems to refer in a general way to the second : $v.^{28.29a}$ have the same material as $v.^{24}$, and
$v.^{29b}$ has the same as $v.^{25.26}$; $v.^{27}$ has no antecedent, unless there
be in $v.^{22.23}$ an implication of the creation of the heaven (cf. Gen.
1^{1}).   The paragraph consists of ten couplets, and might be
written as five quatrains (so Bickell), but the logical division
would thus be abandoned.

> 22. Yahweh formed me as the beginning of his creation,
>   The first of his works, in days of yore;
> 23. In the primeval time was I fashioned,
>   In the beginning, at the origin of the earth.
>
> 24. When there were no depths was I brought into being,
>   No fountains full of water;
> 25. Before the mountains were sunk,
>   Before the hills was I brought into being,
> 26. When he had not yet made the earth, [] †
>   Nor the first of the clods of the world.

---

* See Delitzsch's edition of the poem, and the discussion of it in M. Jastrow's
Relig. of Babylonia and Assyria, ch. 21.

† Heb. adds : *and the fields*.

27. When he established the heavens I was there,
　　When he marked off the vault on the face of the deep,

28. When he made firm the clouds above,
　　‹ Fixed fast › the fountains of the deep,

29. When he set bounds to the sea, [] *
　　When he laid the foundations of the earth.

30. And I was at his side, as his ‹ ward, ›
　　Full of delight day by day,
　　Sporting in his presence continually,

31. Sporting in his world.　[] †

22, 23. Wisdom's primeval origin.

22. Synonymous, quaternary-ternary. Instead of *Yahweh* Targ. has *God.* — The rendering *formed* (= *created*) is supported by the parallel expressions in v.²³. ²⁴. ²⁵ (*made* or *ordained* and *brought into being*) ; the translation *possessed* (RV.) is possible, but does not accord with the context, in which the point is the time of Wisdom's creation. — The Hebrew, all the Greek Versions, and the best MS. of the Vulgate (Cod. Amiatinus) have *as the beginning*, Clementine Vulgate, Syriac, Targum *in the beginning* (so RV.) ; the two readings are substantially identical in meaning, but that of the Hebrew is favored by the form of second cl. (*first*), and by the similar phrase in Job 40¹⁹, where Behemoth is described as the *chief* (lit. *beginning*) *of the creation of God.* ‡ — *Creation* is lit. *way*, = *procedure, performance* (Job 26¹⁴ 40¹⁹) ; Grk. has plu. *ways*, which is perhaps favored by plu. *works* of second cl. — *First* (RV. margin) is the more natural rendering of the Hebrew ; *before* (RV. and some Anc. Vrss.) is hardly allowable. — Cf. *the beginning of the creation of God* (Rev. 3¹⁴), and *the firstborn of all creation* (Col. 1¹⁵). — *In days of yore* (RV. *of old*) = " in remotest antiquity " ; see note on the parallel expression in next verse. — **23.** Synonymous, binary. While v.²² describes Wisdom as the first of Yahweh's works, v.²³ gives the time of her creation in general terms. The Hebrew prepositions introduce the point of time not *before* which (RV., some Anc. Vrss.) but *at* which the creation took place. *Primeval time* (usually *everlasting* in RV.)

---

* Heb. adds : *that its waters should not transgress his command.*

† Heb. adds : *and my delight was with mankind.*

‡ See Budde's note, in Nowack's *Handkommentar.*

is time hidden by distance, remote, dim, in the past or in the
future; in Mic. $5^{2(1)}$ it is used to express the remote origin of the
Davidic house: *a ruler in Israel whose origin is long ago in the
distant past.* The familiar expression *from everlasting to everlasting* gives the two termini of a long period, = from a remote past
to a remote future; so in ψ 90^2, where the termini, applied to
God, are indefinitely remote, though the Hebrew word has not
the modern sense of the temporally infinite. — The rendering
fashioned is favored by the *formed* of v.[22] (see also the verbs
expressing *birth* in v.[24. 25]). It seems, however, to be forcing the
terms when it is held (Frank.) that v.[22. 23] refer to Wisdom's conception in the womb, and v.[24–26] to her birth; both paragraphs
relate to her birth, the difference between them being that the
first is general, the second specific. The rendering (see ψ 2^6)
ordained, established (RV. *set up*), = *placed in position*, is permitted by the connection, but is less apposite. — *The origin* (lit.
first times) *of the earth = the beginning* of Yahweh's work. —
Wisdom, though coeval with the beginning of the divine activity,
is created at a definite point of time, and thus differs from the
Logos of Philo and the Fourth Gospel. The date and occasion
of the beginning are not defined (though Wisdom precedes the
physical world), and nothing is said of the existence of Wisdom
or of the nature of the life of God before the creative work
begins.

24–26. Wisdom anterior to the physical world.

The physical world is described by its parts: in v.[24] the waters,
in v.[25] the mountains, in v.[26] the soil. — **24.** Synonymous, binary.
Depths are the great masses of water, seas and rivers, including
probably the subterranean ocean whence *fountains* spring; see
note on 3^{20}. *Brought into being*, lit. *brought forth;* the same
figure is used of the earth in ψ 90^2, and of the sea in Job 38^8;
here it seems to be a pure figure of speech (parallel to *formed,*
v.[22]), with no reference to physical begetting; Wisdom is the
creature, not the child, of Yahweh. In the Hebrew of second cl.
the *fountains* are described by a term usually understood to mean
heavy, heavy-laden, and so *abounding* (RV.) or *rich* (*in water*);
the word occurs nowhere else in this sense, and is not found in the

Grk.; a slight change of the Heb. gives the meaning *full*, but the word should perhaps be omitted. — **25.** Synonymous, ternary. The word *sunk* refers to the ancient view that the mountains were solid structures resting on foundations sunk deep in the earth down to the floor of the subterranean ocean; so ψ 18[7(8)] *the foundations of the mountains shook* (in an earthquake), and Jon. 2[6(7)] *I went down to the bases* (or, *extremities*) *of the mountains* (the level of the bottom of the sea).* — **26.** Synonymous, ternary. The Hebrew reads : *the earth and the outside places.* The expression *outside places* is difficult. To understand it as referring to the heavenly spaces (for which it would be a strange and improbable term) seems forbidden by the parallelism, second cl. speaking of the earth alone. The word must mean *fields*, as in Job 5[10]. To obtain a contrast some expositors take *earth* as = *cultivated land*, and *fields* as = *uncultivated land*, but this does violence to the language. It is difficult to regard the two terms as synonymous, as in Job 5[10]; in Job they occur in different clauses in proper parallelism, while here they stand together connected by *and* (which can hardly be taken as = *namely*), and, even if the synonymity were allowed, we should have to suppose a whole to be put in apposition with some of its parts. This is obviously different from the common expression *the earth and all that it contains* (*the earth and the fulness thereof*). We get no light on the verse from the Anc. Vrss. Grk.: *the Lord made countries and uninhabited tracts and inhabited summits of the region under the heavens*, which follows the Heb. in a general way, but yields no sense. Syr. Targ. Lat. have *rivers* instead of *outside places;* Aq. and Sym. have *exits*. Either these renderings are guesses, or they represent forms of text different from ours. It seems impossible to fix the Heb. original, but, in any case, both clauses refer to the creation of the earth, and the expression *outside places* may be omitted without detriment to the thought. For Heb. *first* (or, *mass*) *of the clods* (or, *dust*) Lat. has *poles;* the chronological rendering *first* (instead of *mass*) is favored by first line (*not yet*).

---

* Cf. the Babylonian view, given in Jastrow's *Relig. of Bab. and Ass.,* p. 443, 488 f.

27–31. Wisdom present at the construction of the universe.

27–29 describe the creation of the physical world (omitting
heavenly bodies and animate things), probably selected on account of its obvious grandeur ; the wonderfulness of man is rarely
spoken of in OT. (ψ 8. 139). Cf. Job 38[4-11]. — **27.** Synonymous,
ternary. The *heavens = sky*, thought of as a solid expanse
(Gen. 1[6]) to be fixed in its place. To the eye it appears as the
interior of the dome, a circle, sphere, *vault*, on which God is said
to walk (Job 22[14]) ; this vault descends on all sides to the terres-
trial expanse, forming a circle (the horizon), and is said to rest on
the *deep*, that is, the ocean which not only underlies but also flows
round the world (Gen. 1[2] ψ 104[6-9]). This conception (to which
that of the Babylonians and Greeks is similar) * rests on the
simplest geographical observation. If the rendering *circle* be
adopted (RV.), instead of *vault*, the reference will be to the horizon. — **28.** Synonymous, ternary. *Clouds* (AV.) as in 3[20], not
skies (RV.), the *heavens* (= skies) being mentioned in the preceding verse ; the Heb. word is used for the *sky* apparently conceived of as an expanse of clouds (Dt. 33[26] ψ 18[11(12)]). In the
second line *the fountains of the deep* might, from the parallelism,
be interpreted as the celestial sources of water, stored above the
firmament, whence descends the *rain* when *the windows of heaven
are opened* (Gen. 7[11]) ; the *sea* is mentioned in the next verse.
But the *deep* is elsewhere always the *sea*, and must probably be
so understood here — in this verse its formation, in v.[29] its limitation. In accordance with the phraseology of the rest of the paragraph we must read *fixed fast* (instead of *became fast* or *strong*,
or *burst violently forth*), a reading supported by the Greek, and
obtained by a slight change in the Hebrew. — **29.** A triplet (as
the text stands) ; the first and second lines form a couplet, synonymous, ternary, and the third line also is ternary. The *bounds* of
the *sea* are fixed, as in Gen. 1[9. 10] Job 38[8-11] ψ 104[6-9]. Lit. *when he
set to the sea its bound;* the rendering *when he ordained his decree
for the sea* does not accord so well with the following clause.
Nor, in second cl., is the translation *should not pass beyond its shore*
allowable, since the Heb. word (פי) is never used in the sense of

---

* Jastrow, *op. cit.; Il.* 18, 607 ; Herod. 4, 36.

shore. — The earth is described as founded, like a building, in many passages in OT. (Jer. 31^{37} Isa. 51^{13} Job 38^4 ψ 24^2 82^5 104^5), and the word is to be interpreted literally. — The Vatican Grk. omits the first and second clauses of this verse (probably by scribal oversight) ; Bickell, to avoid the triplet form, omits the third. The symmetrical arrangement of the other verses suggests that a line may have here fallen out of the Hebrew text, or been added to it. There is no trace of a missing line. The third line corresponds to v.$^{25.\ 26}$, and seems to be necessary ; but second line, an explanation of first line, is not necessary, and may be a gloss suggested by Job 38^{11}.

30, 31 describe Wisdom's manner of life at the side of Yahweh during the work of creation. Text and translation are difficult. Cf. WS. 7^{22}–8^1. — **30.** Apparently ternary ; v.^{30c} appears to belong with v.^{31a}, the two lines forming a couplet (ternary). The verb *was* refers the paragraph to the period mentioned above, the time of creation. The expression *at his side* implies intimate association, but not necessarily architectonic activity ; in itself it conveys only the idea that God's work was characterized by wisdom. — The word rendered *ward* in the translation above occurs only here in OT., and its meaning is doubtful. By a change of form it may be understood as having the same sense as the similar term in Cant. $7^{1(2)}$, *artist*, here *architect, master-workman ;* * the objection to this rendering is that in the preceding description Yahweh himself is architect, and in the following context Wisdom is represented as sporting, not as working.† A different change of the Heb. word gives the form found in Lam. 4^5, = *one brought up, cherished,* whence *alumnus (alumna), nursling, foster-child,* ‡ or *guarded, under protection, ward* (Frank.). Frankenberg understands the procedure of the paragraph thus : Wisdom is conceived (v.$^{22.\ 23}$), is born (v.$^{24-26}$), is present at the creation (v.$^{27-29}$), is, as young child, at Yahweh's side, under his care, living a joyous life. The sense *nursling* accords with the succeeding context, and with

---

* So Grk., Lat., Ew., RV., and most modern expositors. The expression in Jer. 52^{15} is too obscure to be cited in this connection.

† It is, perhaps, to the sense *artist* of the word here that WS. 7^{21} alludes in its τεχνῖτις.

‡ Aq., Rashi, AV., Schult., *al.*

the representation of the whole paragraph, and corresponds, as
passive, to the active *nurse* or *tutor*, male (Nu. 11[12] 2 K. 10[1]
Isa. 49[23] Esth. 2[7]) or female (2 S. 4[4] Ru. 4[16]).   The renderings
faithful (Targ.) and *continually* (Hoffman, *Schriftbeweis*, I., 97)
are not allowable ; the Heb. might be changed so as to give the
sense *continually*, parallel to *day by day*, and to the adverb in the
third line, but the change would be arbitrary and graphically hard.
— WS. 9[9], *Wisdom, who knows thy works, was with thee, was present when thou madest the world*, appears to be a philosophically
colored reproduction of this line. — In second line the Heb. reads
lit. : *I was delight*, which may mean " I experienced an emotion of
delight " or " I was a source of delight " (to God), = *his delight;* *
the latter is the sense of *delight* in most of the passages in which
the word occurs (Isa. 5[7] Jer. 31[20] ψ 119[24 al.]), but the former is
favored by the connection, in which is portrayed Wisdom's joy in
the contemplation of the divine creation (Wild., *al.*) ; cf. Job 38[7].
For the construction (*I was delight = I was full of delight*) cf.
ψ 120[7] : *I am peace*, = " I am for peace (or peaceable)," and
Gen. 12[2] : *be thou blessing*, = " be thou full of (or, a type of)
blessing." — The picture of enjoyment is continued in the next
line by the term *sporting* or *laughing* (RV., *rejoicing*), which in
like manner portrays Wisdom's delight in God's work.   The word
can hardly have the sense *joyously active*, which would be appropriate if Wisdom were represented as *master-workman*.† — **31**.   Ternary.   The first line seems to be identical in meaning with v.[30c].
His world is lit. *the world of his earth*, in which expression the
first term may represent as an organized whole that which the
second term represents merely as a mass.   The expression is,
however, more probably a rhetorical aggregation ; the two terms
are really synonymous (as in v.[26], ψ 90[2] *al.*), the first being poetic,
the second the ordinary prose word ; the first does not mean
specifically *the inhabited world*, $\dot{\eta}$ οἰκουμένη (as RV. interprets it)
— both terms are occasionally used in that sense (ψ 96[13]).   It

---

* So Grk., RV., Oort, Frank., *al.*

† The verb is used to describe the play of the people in a festival (Ex. 32[6]),
dancing etc. in a religious procession (2 S. 6[21]), and a military combat of cham-
pions (2 S. 2[14-16]) ; in the last case the "sport" was of the grimmest, but it was
apparently regarded as a spectacle in which the two armies found relaxation and
pleasure.

does not seem to be the intention of the poet to represent Wisdom as passing from the divine presence into the world of men; the point in the whole of the preceding description is her intimate association with Yahweh in the creation of the world — not as architect or adviser, but as companion — it is the poetical expression of the fact that wisdom is visible in the construction of the world. This being the theme, it seems improbable that at the end so important a point as Wisdom's dealing with men (which is treated at length in the first half of the chapter) would be introduced with a brief sentence, and with the term *sporting*. For this reason the second line, *and my delight was with mankind* (lit. *with the sons of men*), appears to be an addition by an editor or scribe who desired to see a reference to Wisdom's work among men. But, in the preceding description of creation man is not mentioned, the author choosing to confine his view to the physical world (cf. Job 38. 39, where only things non-human are mentioned). — Grk. regards Yahweh as the subject of the couplet: *when he rejoiced at having finished the inhabited world, and rejoiced among the sons of men* (following Gen. 1[31]), but the change of subject is improbable.

32-36. Wisdom's concluding exhortation to men. The Hebrew reads:

32. And now, my sons, hearken to me —
    Happy are they who walk in my ways.
33. Hear instruction that ye may be wise,
    Reject it not.
34. Happy is the man who hearkens to me,
    Watching continually at my gates,
    Waiting at the posts of my doors.
35. For he who finds me finds life,
    And obtains favor from Yahweh,
36. And he who misses me wrongs himself —
    All who hate me love death.

In the Hebrew text the order is unsatisfactory; v.[33] is closely connected with v.[32a], and v.[34a] with v.[32b] — this is nearly the order of Vat. Grk., which, however, omits v.[33]. Following this suggestion, with some modifications, we might read:

And now, my sons, hearken to me,
Hear my instruction, reject it not.

Happy is he who walks in my ways,
Happy the man who hearkens to me,
Watching, etc.

If v.[33] be retained, as in the Hebrew, its symmetry would be improved by reading the second line: *Reject not my admonition*. The lines in the Heb. text are ternary, except v.[33b], which has only one beat; in the emendation suggested above this exception disappears. The emendation also gets rid of the triplet (v.[34]), and gives a series of synonymous couplets. Bickell, by insertions, makes three quatrains. — The happiness of the devotee of Wisdom (the central thought of chs. 1–9) is here stated in general terms. Such an one waits at her doors (v.[34b]) like a suppliant for royal favor. The content of the happiness is expressed (v.[35]) by the equivalent terms *life* and *the favor of Yahweh*, the opposite of which is *wronging one's self* and *death* (v.[36]). The *life and death* are, as elsewhere (1^{32} $2^{21.\ 22}$ 3^{16}, etc.), physical, but with the connotation of general earthly well-being or failure, bodily and moral. The opposite of *finds* is *misses* (v.[36], RV., marg.), that is, fails to find — metaphorical expression taken from missing a mark; sin also in Heb. is conceived of as a failure to hit the mark, but the sense *sins against* (RV.), which the Heb. word might conceivably have, does not accord with that of the parallel clause. There is, however, in *misses* an element of conscious action (= *purposely fails to find*), which is definitely expressed in the parallel *hate* (v.[36]) = *deliberately disapprove and reject* (cf. v.[33]). It is the free human will that is appealed to (as in 1^{25} and throughout the Book) — of their own motion men accept or reject the highest things. Those who reject instruction *do violence to, wrong* themselves (*his soul = himself*), and, hating the source of life, *love death* (see 2^{22} 4^{19} 5^{23} 7^{27}); the rendering *his life*, instead of *himself* (v.[36a]), is less accurate. By change of text *despises* may be read (as in 15^{32}), instead of *wrongs*, but the change is not necessary. With the independent action of man accords the attitude of God — to those who choose aright he shows *goodwill, friendliness, favor* (v.[35]) — his opposite attitude toward the unwise is stated in 3^{32-35} (cf. ψ $18^{25.\ 26(26.\ 27)}$). The relation of God to human conduct is here described as that of a judge — he is not said to inspire or guide, but to bestow favor or disfavor according to desert (so generally in OT.).

This description of wisdom has played a prominent part in theological history, especially in the history of Christian dogmatics. It is imitated in BS. 1^{1-10} 24 ; in the latter chapter Wisdom is identified with the Law, and so generally in the later Jewish expository works.* In Wisd. Sol. 7 it is Wisdom's relation to the human soul that is expounded. The NT., chiefly occupied with other points of view, barely alludes (Mt. 11^{19} 1 Cor. 1^{24} Col. $1^{15, 16}$) to an identification of Wisdom with the Messiah. Philo's treatment of the conception hardly goes beyond the OT. point of view.† The Jewish schools appear to have laid no stress on the demiurgic function of wisdom as such. ‡ It is in the Christian Church that the idea first assumed importance. The whole passage, Pr. 8^{22-31} (especially v.^{22}) was early employed in the controversies respecting the nature of the Second Person of the Trinity, particularly in connection with the idea of eternal generation ; the argument turned in part on the question whether the verb in v.^{22} was to be translated by *created* or by *possessed.* The passage was used by the Sabellians,§ and is referred to as proof of the uncreated person of the Son by Irenaeus, ‖ Tertullian,¶ and especially by Athanasius (against the Arian position),** and later by Augustine,†† and Basil of Caesarea ‡‡ ; it has often since been cited as prooftext. §§ It seems obvious that it gives a personification, intended to affirm the wisdom manifest in the creation of the world — an approach (under Greek influence) to hypostasis, but not more than an approach.

---

22. 𝕳 יהוה; 𝕿 אלהא —𝕳 קנני; 𝕲$^{BNA\ al.\ plur.}$ (and so 𝔖𝕿) ἔκτισεν; H-P 23 (Venet.), 252, ΆΣΘ ἐκτήσατο, and 𝕷 *possedit.* — 𝕲 renders קרם by εἰς, and omits מֵאָז; the rendering appears to be an error of the translator, and not

---

* *Midrash Mishle* on Pr. 8^{22}, *Ber. Rab.*, c. 1, *al.*

† See Drummond, *Philo-Judaeus*, Bk. 3, ch. 6, p. 212; Siegfried, *Philo von Alexand.;* Briggs, *Messiah of Apostles,* p. 495–514; Toy, *Judaism and Christianity,* p. 99–102.

‡ See Weber, *Theologie* (on *Memra, Metatron,* etc.).

§ Dorner, *Person of Christ,* Eng. transl. I., 2, p. 183 f.

‖ *Cont. Haer.*, Bk. 4, ch. 20.

¶ *Cont. Prax.*, ch. 7.   †† *De Trin.*, Bk. I., ch. 12.

** *De Decret.*, 13, 14, and *Orat.* II., chs. 16–22.   ‡‡ *Letters*, 8, 8.

§§ In *Crit. Sac.* (on 8^{22}) by Calv. *Inst.*, 2, 14, 8, Turretine, *Inst.*, 3, 29, and (apparently) by Dick, *Theol.*, ch. 30, but not by Hodge and other recent writers.

designed to avoid the expression of primeval origin, which it brings out fully
in the context. אַ‎ל‎ טֶרֶ‎ם‎ מִ‎ן‎; 𝕃 *antequam.* — The construction of this verse,
and particularly of קֶדֶם‎, is difficult. קֶדֶם‎ is not a preposition in Heb. (RV.
before), nor does it elsewhere occur as noun = *foremost, first* (what was the
Heb. original of BS. 1⁴ προτέρα πάντων we do not know). Either (if the text
be retained) it must be read as an Aram. form, קְדָם‎ (which is not a probable
writing for the original text), or it must be conjecturally assumed to mean
first. If the context (v.²⁸) be held to call for the temporal interpretation
of the two predicates, we must read בְּרֵאשִׁית‎ (so Jerome, Ep. 140, *ad Cyp.*).
The difficulty with קֶדֶם‎ might be avoided by reading : מִקֶּדֶם פְּעָלַי מֵאָז‎, *of old he
created me, of yore;* there would then be no word in ᵇ answering to the דַּרְכּוֹ‎
of ᵃ, but this would not be an insuperable objection. — 23. 𝔥 נִסַּכְתִּי‎; 𝕲 ἐθεμελίω-
σεν, as if from יָסַר‎, and so 𝔖 אִתְקְנַנִי‎, and 𝕿 (pass.) אִיתַּתְקְנִית‎; 'A κατεστάθην;
𝕃 *ordinata sum.* The signification *put, set, establish* for the stem נסך‎ is
assured by ψ 2⁶, and by Ass. *nasak* (= *put, set,* De., *Hwbuch*); possibly this
signification and the *pour out* of Heb. are connected; Ass. has *nisakku*
(= *priest*), and both Ass. and Heb. have נָסִיךְ‎ *prince,* perhaps = *one set* (in
official position), possibly, like *nisakku,* = *a pourer* (of libations). But the
derivation of our word from סכך‎ is more satisfactory (Ew., Hitz., Frank.);
נסכתי‎ was read by Σ (and, according to one account, by Θ), προκεχειρισμαι,
probably for προκεχρισμαι, and (De.) by Graec. Ven., κέχυμαι. — 24. 𝔥 חֹלָלְתִּי‎;
𝕲, less well, ποιῆσαι. — 𝔥 נִכְבַּדֵּי‎, lacking in 𝕲, and perhaps to be omitted as
yielding no satisfactory sense; we may, however, read נִמְלָאֵי‎ or מְלֵאֵי‎ (cf.
Eccl. 11⁸). Böttcher's *noblest of waters* is not appropriate. Oort נִבְקְעֵים‎ *cleft,*
with omission of מַיִם‎, does not commend itself. The dag. forte in the ר‎ seems
to be due to the rapid pronunciation of stat. const. — 26. 𝔥 עַד לֹא‎; 𝕲 κύριος,
free rendering, or possibly = אֲדֹנָי‎. — 𝔥 חֻצוֹת‎; 𝕲 ἀοικήτους; the word is incompatible with אֶרֶץ‎ (perhaps inserted from Job 5¹⁰), and is better omitted.
𝔖𝕿𝕃 *rivers,* on which see Nöldeke's remark in Pink. — 𝔥 רֹאשׁ עַפְרוֹת‎; Graetz
noblest of dust, = *gold* (Job 28⁶). For עֲפָר‎ Dys. writes עֳפָלֵי‎ *heights,* an unnecessary change; 𝕲 οἰκούμενα, the origin of which is doubtful; Baumg., probably
rightly, rejects Aram. עֲמָרוֹת‎ *inhabited;* Heid. suggests עֲרָבוֹת‎, the name of one
of the seven heavens, according to *Pirke Eliezer,* c. 18 (see ψ 68⁵); cf. Levy,
Chald. Wört. — 27. 𝔥 חוּג‎ (see Isa. 40²² Job 22¹⁴); 𝕲 θρόνον, perhaps after
Job 22¹⁴. — 𝕲 ἀνέμων, = רוּחוֹת‎, or freely takes תְּהוֹם‎ to be the upper ocean, the
source of rain and wind-clouds, and so perhaps, in next verse, τῆς ὑπ' οὐρανόν.
— 28. 𝔥 עִזּוֹ‎; write עֻזּוֹ‎ (Oort, Bi.), from the connection, and 𝕲 ἀσφαλεῖς
ἐτίθει. — 𝕲 τῆς ὑπ' οὐρανόν (see preceding note), perhaps = הֵכִל‎ (cf. v.²⁶);
Just. and Iren. are cited in H-P as having ἀβύσσου, and Lag. holds this to be
the genuine reading of 𝕲. — 29. 𝕲ᴮ omits ᵃˑ ᵇˑ, apparently by scribal error;
Bi. omits ᶜ as induced by the erroneous Grk. text of v.²⁷ᵇ; probably 𝔥 has lost
a line. For 𝔥 חֻקּוֹ‎ 𝕲ᴮ had חֹזֶק‎, a good reading, but no change of 𝔥 is necessary. — 30. 𝔥 אָמוֹן‎; taken from stem אמן‎ *firm* by 𝕲 ἁρμόζουσα; 𝔖 מַתְקְנָא‎
arranger (or perhaps pass., = *firm, trusty*); ΣΘ ἐστηριγμένη; 𝕃 *cuncta com-
ponens;* understood as connected with אֹמֵן‎ *nurse* by 'A τιθηνουμένη (= אָמוּן‎,

cf. Lam. 4^5 Graetz); rendered as adj. by 𝕿 מהימנתא *faithful, trusty.* Nouns of the form קָטִיל are either abstract nouns of action (Inf. abs.), or of the nature of Pres. Parts., usually of stative vbs. (קטן), sometimes of active or voluntative vbs. (לשן, perhaps ארן *lord*); on the norm see Ew., § 152*b*; on the masc. form, Ges.[26], § 122, 2, c. Anm. 1. For the name of agent we expect the form קַטָּל, as in Cant. 7^2, and Ass. ***ummānu.*** Read אָמָּן. Cf. BDB., s.v. אמון and אמן. — 𝕳 ואהיה שעשעים; 𝕲 *ἐγὼ ἤμην ᾗ προσέχαιρεν*, reading שעשעיו, which, from the connection, is improbable. The expression, which looks tautologous, is omitted by Bi. as dittography from the context; if it be taken as scribal repetition, the יום יום also should probably be omitted. The line may, however, be retained; see note on this v. above. — **31.** 𝕲 understands יהוה as subject, and at end of [a] adds *συντελέσας*, perhaps reading תְּכַלִּיה for תבל (Lag.), perhaps free translation, since (Baumg.) *οἰκουμένην* suggests תבל. — **32.** The order in 𝕲[B] is v.[32a. 34a. 32b. 34b. etc.] (v.[33] is omitted), a natural arrangement, favored by the ו in ואשרי, which seems to point to a preceding parallel clause. Bi., after the Saidic Vrs., fills out v.[32a. 33] as follows: *And now, my sons, hearken to me; Hear the instruction* [*of my words! Live to length of days*] *and be wise, And reject not* [*my admonition*]! a possible but suspicious expansion; it introduces the reward (life) in anticipation of v.[35], and employs the doubtful expression חְיוּ לְאֹרֶךְ ימים (in ψ 23^6 the verb is different). If not the addition of the Coptic scribe, it is based on a doubtful Heb. text; cf. Bi.'s note. — **33.** The Heb. text is rhythmically unsatisfactory, and, if the verse be retained, we should perhaps, with Bi. (see preceding note), add תוכחתי at end. — **35.** K מצאי (Q מָצָא) seems to be scribal repetition of preceding word; 𝕲, *ἔξοδοί μου ἔξοδοι ζωῆς*, read מֹצָאַי and מֹצָאֵי, inappropriate and improbable. — **36.** 𝕲 has Part. and vb. plu. in [a] — probably a change of the Grk. scribe, in the interests of rhetorical symmetry; Heb. poetry is fond of variations of grammatical number in adjacent clauses.

IX. Wisdom and Folly as hosts. — This chapter, as it stands, consists of three parts. In v.[1-6] Wisdom is personified as a householder who prepares a feast (v.[1. 2]), to which she invites the uninstructed (v.[3. 4]), urging them to partake of her provision and live (v.[5. 6]); cf. 1^{20-23} 8^{1-21}. In contrast with this, stands, in the third part, v.[13-18], the invitation of Folly, who, noisy and seductive (v.[13]), sits in a prominent place and calls to the passers-by (v.[14. 15]), tempting the uninstructed youth by promise of secret delights (v.[16. 17]), he not knowing that her house is Sheol (v.[18]). Standing between these two descriptions, and interrupting their connection, is the paragraph v.[7-12], composed of separate aphorisms; it belongs by its contents in the succeeding division of the Book (10^1–22^{16}), and is here doubtless inserted by scribal error. The remainder of the chapter stands in specially close connection with ch. 7 as a warning against debauchery.

1–6. Wisdom's invitation to her feast — a semi-allegorical description of her gifts.

1. Wisdom has built her house,
   ‹ Set up › * her seven pillars,
2. Killed her beasts, mixed her wine,
   And prepared her table.

3. She has sent forth her maidens ‹ to cry › †
   On the thoroughfares of the city:
4. "Whoso is simple, let him turn in hither"!
   To him who is void of understanding she says:

5. "Come, eat my bread,
   Drink the wine I have mixed!
6. Forsake ‹ folly,› ‡ and live,
   And walk in the way of understanding"!

1. Synonymous, ternary. The building of the house is mentioned as a necessary preparation for holding a continual feast; it is an indication that Wisdom has set up a permanent establishment, in which she is ready at all times to entertain all who may come to her. Instead of Heb. *hewn* (the technical term of the stonemason) the parallelism favors the builder's term *set up, reared, erected* (so Grk. Syr. Targ.); the point is not that the pillars are hewn, but that they are put in place, so that the house is finished and ready for guests. The *pillars* are an ordinary architectural feature of the time, here introduced as a natural append-age to the house. The precise position of the pillars in the Jewish house of this period (c. 3d century B.C.) is not known; probably, as in Greek and Roman houses, they surrounded the hall or court which was entered from the street-door and was used for festive purposes; they served as support for an upper gallery. The number *seven* is not significant; either it is merely a round number, or it indicates the usual architectural arrange-ment of the time. — The verse easily lends itself to allegorizing

---

* Heb.: *hewn.*　　　　　† Heb.: *she cries.*
‡ Heb.: *ye foolish,* or, possibly, *the foolish* (or, *simple*).

and spiritualizing interpretation, and has been understood in this way from an early period. The Midrash takes Wisdom to be the Law, which created all the worlds; Procopius: the enhypostatic power of God the Father prepared the whole cosmos as its abode; Rashi: God by wisdom created the world. The *seven pillars* have been explained as the seven firmaments or heavens, or the seven regions or climates (Midrash); the seven days of creation, or the seven books of the Law * (Rashi); the seven charismata or gifts of the Holy Ghost (Procop., Bernard, De.); the seven eras of the Church (Vitringa); the seven sacraments, or the omnipotent word of the Son of God (Geier); the prophets, apostles, and martyrs (J. H. Mich.); the seven liberal arts (Heid.); the seven first chapters of Proverbs (Hitz.).† These interpretations carry their refutation on their face. The allegorical element in the paragraph is simply the representation of Wisdom as hostess, dispensing, in her own house, instruction, here symbolized by food and drink. — **2.** Parallels, quaternary- (or, binary-) ternary. In first cl. the Heb. is literally *slain her slaying* = killed her beasts. *Meat* and *wine* are mentioned as the chief materials of a feast (so 1 Sam. 16^{20} Dan. 10^3). Meat was eaten by the Jews probably not daily, but on special occasions (festivals), which had a religious character. ‡ Fermented wine (Heb. *yayin*) was a common article of food (1 Sam. 16^{20} Job 1^{13} ψ 104^{15}). It was *mixed* with spices to make it more pleasant to the taste (Isa. 5^{22} ψ $102^{9(10)}$). The Greeks commonly mixed their wine with water in a bowl (*krater*), and the Grk. here introduces this term: *she has mixed her wine in a krater;* to drink unmixed wine was considered by them unseemly (Plato, *Laws*, I. 9). Which sort of mixing is here intended is uncertain. — The *table*, originally a leather mat or other material laid on the ground (as among the Arabs to-day), came at an early time among the Hebrews to be a raised tray or board at

* Gen. 1^1 and Num. 10^{35} (*when the ark set forward*, etc.) were regarded, on account of their importance, as separate books.

† For other interpretations see notes of Geier, Vitringa, De.

‡ For the preëxilian custom see Dt. $12^{20.21}$ 14^{23-27}, and for the later usage Lev. $17^{3.4.13}$; cf. note on Pr. 7^{14}. The daily provision of meat on the king's table (1 K. 4^{23} [5^8]) was probably connected with a daily sacrifice. In our verse Grk. has *slain her offerings*. The use of meat is comparatively rare in Palestine at the present day.

which people sat on stools (so, perhaps, 1 Sam. 20[25]) or reclined on divans (Am. 6[4]); cf. the tables of the Temple (Ez. 40[39] Ex. 25[23]). — **3.** Continuous, ternary. The *maidens* are the necessary machinery of invitation, not to be explained allegorically as signifying preachers of righteousness; the householder (as in Mt. 22[3]) bids her guests through servants, who thus (as sometimes now) take the place of letters. The term is a general one for young women, sometimes free and unservile (Gen. 24[14] Ru. 2[5] Esth. 2[2]), sometimes, as here, attendants (so 27[27] 31[15]), apparently not slaves. — According to our Heb. text (*she cries*) she herself also, not content with sending messages, gives her invitation on the thoroughfares of the city (lit. *high places*), elevated places where one could easily be seen and heard (see note on 8[2]); these have, of course, no connection with the old shrines called *highplaces* in the prophetical and historical books. It is not clear whether it is thus intended to represent her (as in 1[20. 21] 8[1-3]) as going forth to places of public resort, or (as might be suggested by the parallel v.[14] below) as having her house and her seat in an elevated part of the city. But the syntax and sense of the Heb. are unsatisfactory, and the change of one letter gives the reading *she has sent forth her maidens to cry;* this is not out of accord with v.[4], in which the proclamation may be understood to be made by Wisdom through the messengers. In the Grk. she cries not *on the heights,* but *with a loud voice,* but this reading is improbable. — **4.** Synonymous, ternary. The invitation is addressed to the *simple* and *void of understanding,* those who have not moral insight and power of self-direction, the negative, unformed minds, not yet given up to sin, but in danger of becoming its dupes; the steadfastly good and the deliberately evil are not considered — the former do not need guidance, the latter will not accept it. Obviously, however, the author does not mean to exclude any class of persons from the counsels of Wisdom; he writes as a practical moralist, and represents the *simple* as her natural hearers. — The division of the verse is unusual; the second clause, instead of continuing the exhortation of the first, introduces a new formula of address; some expositors, following the Grk. of v.[16], would write: *whoso is devoid of understanding, I say to him,* etc.; but this would not be a natural form of address — see note on v.[16].

— **5.** Parallels, ternary. The invitation in figurative form. *Bread*, which here takes the place of the *meat* or flesh of beasts of v.[2], is also a necessary part of the feast. — **6.** Synonymous, ternary. The invitation in literal, explanatory form. The Heb. reads : *forsake, ye simple* (RV. incorrectly : *leave off, ye simple ones*), an incomplete sentence, since the verb requires an object, as in 2[13] 3[3] 4[2], etc. ; the object can hardly be the *simple* (AV. *forsake the foolish*), for this would be a singular admonition to the simple, and the parallelism calls for an abstract noun as object. Some (as Kamp.) suppose the object to have fallen out of the text, and leave a blank ; others (De., Now., Str.) supply *simplicity* as object : *forsake, ye simple, simplicity*. A better expedient is, by a slight change in the Heb. word, to read (as in the Grk.) *simplicity* or *folly ;* Luther : *verlasset das alberne wesen ;* cf. 1[22]. The word *folly* (which might easily have fallen out on account of its resemblance to the preceding) may be added ; but the resulting clause will be less rhythmical. — Grk. : *Forsake folly, that ye may reign forever ; and seek discretion, and direct understanding in* (or, *by*) *knowledge* — a misreading and expansion of the Hebrew. For the *reign* cf. Wisd. Sol. 6[21].

IX. 1. 狃 חכמוה; see note on 1[20]. — 狃 חָצְבָה; ᵴ ὑπήρεισεν, = הציבה (Vogel), from נצב; ᵴᴴ סבכרה; Ṫ עֲתִידַת; ᵴ אקימת; this reading is favored by the parallelism. — **2.** After כָּסְבָה ᵴ has εἰς κρατῆρα, = ב׃ ס, probably not in original 狃 (fallen out by resemblance to preceding word, Lag.), but addition of Grk. scribe for completeness. — On שלחן s. Moore, on Ju. 1[7]. — **3.** ᵴ δούλους, perh. rhetorical generalization of gender, or scribal error, possibly (Lag.) suggested to a Christian scribe by Mt. 22[3]. — 狃 תקרא עַל נַּפֵּי מרֹמֵי קרת; ᵴ συγκαλοῦσα μετὰ ὑψηλοῦ κηρύγματος, ק being taken as a form of קרא, and ק׃ as adverbial expression. ᵴ does not take מרומי as = *heights ;* the word appears to mean *raised streets* here and in 8[2] 9[14]. The addition ἐπὶ κρατῆρα of ᵴ appears to be erroneous insertion from preceding verse. 𝕃, freely ; *ad arcem et ad moenia civitatis.* 狃 הקרא makes a difficulty ; we expect a reference to the maidens, as in ᵴṪ𝕃, reading הקראנה or לקרא, and this form should probably be adopted, in spite of the 3 p. sing. אמרה of v.[5]. — 狃 וַף only here and in Ex. 21[3.4] where it = *body ;* Aram. and Assyr., *wing ;* the stem appears to mean *curved, arched ;* עַל וכי here = עַל, if the text be correct ; cf. בגפו Ex. 21[3], = *in himself.* — **4.** For 狃 אמרה Oort *al.* would read 1 p. אמר or אמרתי, but the change is unnecessary. — Gr. : מי פתי וחסר לב יסר הֵנָה ואמרה לו. — **5.** ᵴ plu. ἄρτων, as in 20[18] Gen. 14[18] etc., free use of Grk. idiom, not (Lag.) allusion to Eucharist (Jno. 6). — **6.** 狃 פראים; ᵴ ἀφροσύνην, and so all other Vrss.; read פתי, as the sense requires ; this word may have been read פרי׃ and so expanded into פריס and

פאיס. — Grk. expansion may have come from change of ζήσετε into ζητήσατε, and introduction of clause from Wisd. Sol. 6²³ (Lag.); Baumg. suggests that the Grk. translator wrote βιώσητε, which was corrupted (perh. under influence of WS. 6²³) into βασιλεύσητε, and that κ. ζητ. φρον. was then added to complete the parallelism. Cf. Lag., Pink.

13–18. The invitation of Folly.

— The section is parallel to v.¹⁻⁶, and should be transferred to this place. The central figure plays a part corresponding to and contrasted with that of Wisdom above. She is described as noisy (v.¹³), sitting in a public place (v.¹⁴), calling to passers-by (v.¹⁵), inviting the simple to come to her (v.¹⁶), promising them stolen pleasures (v.¹⁷), which, the sage adds, lead to death (v.¹⁸). The two sections give the contrast between rectitude and sexual debauchery. Cf. 5³⁻²⁰ 7¹⁰⁻²¹. From the "abrupt" way in which this paragraph is introduced (without such preparatory statement as is found in v.¹· ²), its only ground being the contrast with Wisdom's invitation, Frankenberg concludes that it is not the work of the author of chs. 1–9 ; the writer of v.¹³ᶠᶠ·, he observes, regarded the *harlot* of chs. 5 and 7 as merely a personification of Folly — a view which appears in the Grk. and has survived till now. Certainly the picture in v.¹³ᶠᶠ· is based in part on chs. 5 and 7, but this fact hardly points to difference of authorship ; nor is it introduced with undue abruptness (if it assumes v.¹⁻⁶) ; and it is not necessary to suppose because Folly is here the harlot of chs. 5 and 7 that the writer did not regard this latter personage as a real woman ; in chs. 2. 5. 6. 7 Folly is identified with sexual immorality.

13. [] Folly is loud and ‹seductive,›
     She knows no ‹shame› (?)

14. At the door of her house she sits,
     On [] * the thoroughfares of the city,

15. To call to the passers-by,
     To those who are going their ways :

16. "Whoso is simple, let him turn in hither "!
     And to him who is void of understanding she says :

17. " Stolen waters are sweet,
     And bread eaten in secret is pleasant "!

18. But he knows not that the Shades are there,
     That her guests are in the depths of Sheol.

---

* Heb.: *on a seat in* (or, *near*).

13. Rhythm uncertain. Folly's character. The text is doubtful. Heb.: *The foolish woman* (lit. *woman of folly*) *is boisterous*
(or, *loud*), *simplicity, and knows not what* (or, perhaps, *anything*) ;
Grk.: *A foolish and impudent woman comes to lack a morsel, she
who knows not shame ;* Syr.: *A woman lacking in discretion, seductive ;* Targ.: *A woman foolish and a gadabout, ignorant, and she
knows not good ;* Lat.: *A woman foolish and noisy, and full of
wiles, and knowing nothing at all.* — From a comparison with the
parallel v.[1] it appears probable that the *woman* of the Hebrew is
a gloss by a scribe who wished to call the reader's attention to the
fact that *folly* was a personification ; this being omitted, Folly
stands opposed to Wisdom. The rendering *Madam Folly* (taking
woman of folly as = *the woman folly* — so De., Kamp.) is hardly
allowable ; elsewhere (11^{16} 12^4 $21^{9.\ 19}$ 25^{24} 27^{15} 31^{10}) the defining
noun after *woman* has adjectival force. The word rendered *Folly*
(fem.) occurs only here in OT. ; the corresponding masc. form is
frequent in Prov.; see $1^{22.\ 32}$ 3^{35} 8^5. Instead of *boisterous* some
translators (Str., Kamp., Frank.) write *passionate* (sensuously
excitable), but this sense for the Heb. term is doubtful ; see notes
on 1^{21} 7^{11}. The expression *simplicity* of the Heb. text is suspicious both from its form (abstract noun) and from its meaning
— it is unnecessary to say that folly is foolish ; the connection
favors a reading (*seductive*, or *enticing*) like those given by Syr.
and Lat., and this is obtained by an inconsiderable change of text.
The sense of the last clause it is difficult to determine. The Heb.
hardly permits the translation *she knows nothing*, and this, moreover, does not comport with the address and power attributed to
Folly in the context ; *Folly* is primarily a moral, not an intellectual term — it does not exclude ordinary intelligence as the
sweeping expression *knows nothing* appears to do. Grk. *shame*
(which suits the connection) may be doubtfully adopted ; the
Heb. word which it implies is used elsewhere (18^{13} Jer. 51^{51} Isa.
50^6 ψ 35^{26} *al.*) only in the sense of *obloquy*, never as = the *sense of
shame*, though that may be an accident — the verb has this mean-
ing (Ez. 16^{61} *al.*). The Grk. rendering may be a free interpretation
of our Heb. text, as the Targ. *good* seems to be. — **14.** Synonymous, ternary. Folly sits in a prominent place, where she can be
seen ; Grk. *on a seat in public in the streets.* Wisdom (v.[3]) cries

aloud in such places — Folly sits and calls; the contrast in the methods of the two (the one sending out to seek men, the other sitting at home as seductress) does not indicate difference of zeal — the two descriptions seem to express the same earnestness — it is perhaps meant to say that Folly, like the unchaste woman whom she represents, the symbol of unlawful pleasures, prefers the privacy of her house (cf. ch. 7), while Wisdom, the preacher of righteousness, boldly gives her invitation in open day and in public places; but the text is not clear, and probably no difference is intended in the methods of the two, unless it be in the sending out of the maidens. — In second line we should probably read simply: *on the thoroughfares*, etc., as in v.^{3}, instead of the Heb. *on a seat in*, etc.; see notes on 8^2 9^3. Folly, like Wisdom, has a house, in which she sets a feast; the description of the preparations (cf. v.$^{1.2}$) is omitted, probably as an unnecessary repetition. — **15–17.** Her invitation, parallel to that of Wisdom (v.$^{4-6}$); v.^{16} = v.^{4}; v.^{17} corresponds to v.$^{5.6}$. — **15.** Synonymous, ternary-binary. She addresses herself to the passers-by (so Wisdom, $1^{20.21}$ 8^{1-3}), remaining, however, at the door of her house. The expression *those who are going their ways* (cl. 2.) = *the passers-by* (cl. 1.), not *who are going straightforward (right) on their ways* — the intention (as appears from the connection) is to represent these passers not as earnest persons bent on going forward without turning to right or left, but as ordinary wayfarers, to any and all of whom Folly addresses herself; a similar verb (*walk*) is used in v.^{6}; in 3^6 11^5 15^{21} the connection is different. — **16.** Synonymous, ternary. See note on v.^{4}. The expressions *simple* and *void of understanding*, here as there, mean *lacking in knowledge of the world, unable to recognize good and bad* (cf. v.^{17}). Instead of *she says* Grk. has *I say*, a reading which would give unity of form to the invitation in this verse, yet is not quite natural, since Folly would not address her intended victims as *void of sense;* cf. v.^{4}. — **17.** Synonymous, ternary. The inducement she offers is the delight of secret enjoyments, things prohibited by law or condemned by society, more tempting because they are forbidden. Folly here appears as identical with the *strange woman* of chs. 5 and 7. Her *water* and *bread* are parallel to the *bread* and *wine* of Wisdom (v.^{5}), only here the feasting is clandestine — the reference is to illicit sexual relations. *Stolen waters* (= any illicit thing) *are sweet* was probably a current proverbial saying ; and, in the term *water*, instead of the more festive *wine*, there may be an allusion to the figure of $5^{15. 16}$, on which see notes. —**18.** Synonymous, ternary. Comment of the sage : the fate of Folly's guests. In 2^{18} 5^5 7^{27} it is said that the licentious woman's ways lead to death; here, in sharper phrase, her house is identified with the Underworld — it is already in effect in the depths, and its inmates, though they have the semblance of life, are doomed and as good as dead. The death is physical, as in the parallel passages cited above ; the guests are no doubt regarded by the writer as morally dead, but that is not the statement here. On *Shades* (Refaim) see note on 2^{18}. The word rendered *depths* also = *valleys*, but, from the connection and from general OT. usage, this cannot be understood as a topographical description of Sheol, an assertion that it contains hills and valleys. It merely describes Sheol as lying deep beneath the earth, but there is possibly an allusion to the valley of Rephaim, near Jerusalem (2 Sam. 5^{18} Isa. 17^5). — The simple youth, who yields to Folly's invitation, is ignorant of his danger ; on the class of persons meant see note on v.^{4}. — Grk. here adds four couplets :

> But turn away, linger not in the place,
> Nor set thine eye on her;
> For thus wilt thou go through alien water,
> And pass over an alien stream.
> But abstain from alien water,
> Drink not of an alien fountain,
> That thou mayst live long,
> That years of life may be added to thee.

This is the addition of a scribe who felt that the curt ending of the text needed a hortatory complement ; it mars the poetic unity and vigor of the paragraph. The figure of the three first couplets is taken from $5^{15ff.}$; the last couplet (a familiar expression) is nearly the same as v.^{11} of this chapter.

13. 𝔐 כְּסִילוּת and פְּתַיּוּת are ἀπ. λεγ. (both probably Aram. forms); the latter may come from a st. פְּרִי (Ols.), the *a*-vowel being preserved by the doubling of the Yod; De., following Qamḥi (*Miklol*, 181 *a*), points פְּתַיּוּת; from פֶּתִי we should have פְּתָיוּת. Oort proposes Pi. כִּפְתָה, which may help to account for 𝔊 ἐνδεὴς ψωμοῦ (from יָן and כם); Jäger points out that 𝔊 in-

volves a form of פת. The connection favors the reading מפתה, = *enticing*. —
In אשת כסילות the כ׳ cannot be appositional definitive (De.). There is no
example in OT. of a determinative standing in apposition with a single noun
in stat. const. (בת ציון is not a case in point, for צ here is local definition of
כ׳); on the construction called suspended determination (where one noun
defines two in stat. const., these being in app. with each other) see Ew. § 289 *c*;
Ges.[26] § 130. 5; Moore, *Judges*, on Ju. 19[22]; Driver, *Deut.*, on Dt. 21[11]. Everywhere else in Prov. אשה is defined by the following noun. כ׳ here is parallel
to חכמות in v.[1], and אשת must be omitted as gloss, intended to indicate that the
כסילה was to be understood as a personification (a woman). Graetz would
write it אֵשֶׁב and attach it to preceding verse — a possible construction (though
אשב does not occur elsewhere with נשא), but the rhythm is against the addition of a word in v.[12]. — In מה Jäg., Hitz., Lag., Graetz, *al.* see the remains
of כלמה (𝕲 αἰσχύνην), an attractive reading (cf. Jer. 3[3]) if כ׳ may be understood as meaning the feeling of shame; this sense it has nowhere else in OT.
(though כלם, Ni. and Hof., is so employed) — elsewhere it = *opprobrium*.
מה is always to be taken as interrog., direct or indirect, even in Gen. 38[8]; we
might here read מאומה (as in Gen. 39[6]), but the connection does not favor
the resulting sense. We may doubtfully read כלמה — less well (Frank.) ר־יְלם
(Jer. 8[12]). — **14.** 𝔥 מרמי קרת, of which 𝕲 ἐμφανῶς ἐν πλατείαις may be free
rendering (see the wholly different wording of 𝕲 in v.[3]); it would seem that
𝕲 takes מרמי as = *streets* or *squares*; see note on this v. above. 𝕿 רמא ועשינא
and 𝕾 רמא (omitting the last word) also represent 𝔥, except that 𝕿 apparently read some form of יקר instead of קרת (Oort). 𝔥 is suspicious; for
כסא we should probably read גפי, as in v.[3]. If our text be retained, it would
be better to insert ב before מ׳ ק, which expression may, however (Fleisch.)
be taken as adverbial. — **15.** 𝔥 מישרים (𝕲 κατευθύνοντας) may be taken in
the sense of 𝕷 *pergentes*, or we may substitute the stem אשר, as in 4[14]. —
16. 𝔥 אמרה; 𝕲 and 𝕾 have 1 p. (the 3 p. occurs in Clem. Al.); the 3 p., as
the harder, is to be retained. — **17.** 𝕲 inverts the order of clauses of 𝔥, but
gives no suggestion for change of our text. — **18.** 𝕲 ὁ δὲ οὐκ οἶδεν ὅτι γηγενεῖς
(רכאיב) παρ᾽ αὐτῇ (שם) ὄλλυνται (שממו) καὶ ἐπὶ πέτευρον ᾅδου (ועמק שאול)
συναντᾷ (קרה). On γηγενεῖς cf. note on 2[18]; other renderings of ר in 𝕲 are
νεκροί, γίγαντες; see Schleusner. 𝕿, interpreting: דנגברי אפילת חמן תמן *that she
cast down the giants there.* — On the added couplets in 𝕲𝕾 see note above.

**7-12. A little group of aphorisms, belonging in the body
of the Book**; see parallel proverbs in 13[1] 15[12] 19[25] 10[8. 17] 16[21-23]
10[27] 11[19], and also 1[7] ψ 111[10]. They are probably the insertion of
a scribe who found this a convenient place for introducing into his
manuscript a collection which was in his possession, or, possibly,
they are here placed in order to separate the description of detest-
able Folly from that of divine Wisdom. Grk. (see below) expands v.[12] with remarks which are apparently designed to pave

the way to the following section. The Hebrew scribe makes six couplets, so that this may agree in length with the other sections. A certain logical order has been observed: v.[7] and v.[8] accord in thought, and so v.[8] and v.[9], and v.[10] and v.[11]; v.[12] stands by itself, and may be an afterthought.

7-9. Results of instruction given to different classes of persons.

7. He who corrects a scoffer gets insult,
And he who reproves a wicked man, reviling.

8. Reprove not a scoffer lest he hate thee;
Reprove a wise man, and he will love thee.

9. Give (instruction) to a wise man, and he will be yet wiser;
Teach a righteous man, and he will gain more instruction.

7. Synonymous, ternary. The scoffer. On *scoffer* see note on 1^{22}, and cf. $13^{1.\ 18}\ 15^{5}\ 23^{9}$. The term is here substantially equivalent to the *wicked* of second cl., but further describes the bad man, the enemy of wisdom, as one who actively rejects, despises, and mocks at true principles of life; the *wicked* is, in general, one who habitually does wrong, and is to be condemned in a tribunal of justice. Such persons are thought of as past reformation, so that he who tries to better them does them no good, but only brings on himself *insult* and *reviling*. The first of these terms signifies originally *littleness, despicableness* (so Partcp. in 12^{8}), then *disgrace* ($3^{35}\ 6^{33}$) and, actively, *belittling, reproach, reviling, insult* (18^{3}). The second, as it stands in the Heb., is literally *spot, blemish*, physical (Cant. 4^{7} Dan. 1^{4}), or ceremonial (Nu. 19^{2}, and so everywhere in the Pentateuch, except Dt. 32^{5}, where the text is corrupt); in Job 11^{15} (if the text be correct) it appears to mean *apprehension, fear*, or, perhaps, *consciousness of guilt* (but these interpretations are somewhat forced). Here the text is doubtful, but the parallelism calls for a word = *insult*.—The point of view of the verse is similar to that of those sociologists who recognize a class of "incapables."—**8.** Antithetic, ternary. The scoffer and the wise man. The first clause repeats the thought of the preceding verse, the second contrasts the conduct of the wise man under reproof; cf. $15^{5\ 10.\ 12.\ 32}$, with which verses our v.[7.\ 8] might properly be put.—**9.** Synonymous, ternary. The wise man. See $1^{5}\ 10^{8}\ 12^{15}\ 14^{6}$ 15^{32}, and especially 21^{11}. *Wise* and *righteous* are here put as identical, as throughout the Book, particularly in $10^{1}-22^{16}$. The teachableness of the *wise* is allied to humility — it is the opposite of the posture of mind implied in the term *scoffer*.

> 10. The beginning of wisdom is the fear of Yahweh,
> And the knowledge of the Holy One is understanding.

Synonymous, quaternary- (or, ternary-) ternary. The verse is related in a general way to the preceding context; the first cl. is found substantially in 1⁷ (with inversion of subject and predicate) and ψ 111¹⁰. In second cl., instead of *knowledge of* (= *fear of, obedience to*) *the Holy One* a number of versions and expositors * have *knowledge* (or, *counsel*) *of holy men* (the Heb. word is plu.), = either the knowledge which good men possess, or that which makes men good; but the parallelism obviously demands a reference to God. The plu. word is used of men (Israelites) in ψ 34¹⁰ Dan. 8²⁴, of angels in Zech. 14⁵ Job 5¹ 15¹⁵ ψ 89⁸ (and Aramaic, Dan. 4¹⁷⁽¹⁴⁾), but of God only here and 30³ (the sing. is common). The plu. (here probably used as expressing extent and majesty) may have been suggested by the plu. form *Elohim* for *God*, or it may have arisen in the same way (an original mass of divine beings in a community afterwards conceived of as one being); cf. plu. for *Creator*, Eccl. 12¹, † and Aram. *Heavens*, = *God*, Dan. 4²⁶⁽²³⁾. The term belongs to the later, more refined, vocabulary, which sought to designate the divine Being by his ethical qualities. — On the thought see note on 1⁷; knowledge of the divine will is theoretical wisdom, but cannot be separated from reverence (= obedience), which is practical wisdom. The divine law here had in mind is ethical, not ritual, and obedience to it is held to secure prosperity.

> 11. For by me will thy days be multiplied,
> And the years of thy life increased.

Synonymous, ternary. Instead of *by me*, Syr. Targ. (and apparently Grk., *in this way*) have *by it*, which effects some connection with the preceding verse, the *it* being the *fear* or the *knowledge* of God. But this connection is not quite natural (we should perhaps expect rather *them* than *it*, and the *for* is not appropriate), and it

---

* Grk., Vulg., Luther, AV., Procop., Rashi, J. H. Mich., *al.*

+ The clause Eccl. 12¹ᵃ probably does not belong to the original form of the verse, but it shows the linguistic usage of the later period. Bickell's emendation *thy wife*, instead of *thy Creator*, is, on exegetical grounds, out of the question.

may be just as well to retain our Heb. text, and regard the verse as the only surviving part of a paragraph, the *me* referring to *wisdom* mentioned in a lost couplet. The general sense is not affected by this difference of reading. There is no connection with v⁶. For the thought see 3². ¹⁶ 10²⁷ 19²³, in which long life is the reward of fearing God.

> 12. If thou art wise, thou art wise for thyself,
>   And, if thou art a scoffer, thou alone must bear (the consequences).

Antithetic, ternary. Of this verse (which is quite isolated, having no connection with the context, and no parallel in the whole Book) we have two forms, in the Hebrew and the Greek. The Hebrew, given above, affirms sharply the principle of individual responsibility, generalizing the idea of Ez. 18⁴ (*he who sins, he [alone] shall die*); the prophet declares that every Israelite shall bear the consequences of his sin — the sage extends the principle to all moral life, a principle certainly involved everywhere in Proverbs, but nowhere else expressed under the form of moral isolation. The writer has in mind, however, not a selfish isolation (it is not the command *thou shalt be wise*), but the impossibility of vicariousness in the moral life. — Grk. (followed by Syr.) reads: *If thou be wise, for thyself thou shalt be wise and for thy neighbors, but if thou prove evil, thou alone shalt bear the evil;* the first cl. may also be rendered: *if thou be wise for thyself, thou shalt be wise for thy neighbors also* — the general sense remains the same, the man is inseparably connected, on his good side, with his fellows. This pleasant, but untrue, affirmation, that a man's goodness benefits his fellows, while his evil affects only himself, looks like the effort of an editor to relieve the apparent selfishness of the verse. It is hardly correct to say (Jäger) that the *thou alone* of the Heb. in second cl. indicates, by contrast, the presence of *and for thy neighbor* in first cl.; the *alone* is merely the definite statement in one line of the aloneness which is involved in the parallel line. A change from the Grk. form to that of the Heb. is less probable than a change in the opposite direction, and the latter should therefore be retained as probably the original. After v.¹²
Grk. adds:

> Who stays himself on lies he feeds on wind,
> And he will follow after winged birds.

The ways of his own vineyard he forsakes,
And wanders from the paths of his own husbandry.
He passes through a waterless waste,
Through a land given over to drought,
And with his hands he gathers barrenness.

Before line 7 Bickell, to complete the couplet, inserts :

He sows on an untilled, waterless soil.

This paragraph appears to be an amplified form of a Hebrew
original, taken, perhaps, as Bickell suggests, from a current collection of aphorisms. The thought is vigorous, but the paragraph
certainly does not belong in this place, nor did it form a part of
the original Book of Proverbs, with whose literary style it does not
agree. The liar is compared to a neglectful husbandman who
comes to grief. With *feeds on wind* cf. Eccl. 1[14], and with the
second line, 27[8] 23[5].

7. 𝕳[b] is reproduced by 𝕲[AB∗ al.] 𝕷; instead of מכיח *reprover* H-P 23. 68.
109. 147. *al.* 𝕾[H] 𝕾𝕿 had (the Grk. and 𝕾[H] in a doublet line) הֹכָחֹת *reproofs*,
which does not agree with the parallelism (cf. Pink.). 𝕲[A al.] μωμήσεται ἑαυτόν
= מומו or מום לו, and so probably the μώλωπες αὐτῷ of H-P 23 *al.* (the Aram.
שוּם *wound, scar*, proposed by Lag., seems unnecessary). 𝕳 is better read
מום לו, though כ is suspicious; whether it can be taken as = *insult* or *indig-
nity*, as the parallelism requires, is doubtful, but no satisfactory emendation
of the text suggests itself; possibly we should read כלכה.— Gr. כֵּר רִק ומוכיח.
— 8. The 𝕲 MSS. add a positive doublet of ᵃ in varying
forms. — 9. The apparently incomplete expression רן is variously supplemented
by the Vrss.; 𝕲 (followed by 𝕾𝕷) adds ἀφορμήν *opportunity ;* 𝕿 writes אלף.
The rhythm does not suggest an omission in 𝕳, which is intelligible also as it
stands; but the insertion of a word (= *instruction*) in a translation is allowable.
— 10. 𝕳 קרשׁיב is rendered as plu. in all extant Vrss. (the readings of the Hex.
are not known) except 𝕾[Lee], and Saadia; it seems then to have been understood (except perh. in 𝕿) as = *righteous men.* — 𝕲 adds at end : τὸ γὰρ γνῶναι
νόμον διανοίας ἐστὶν ἀγαθῆς, the remark of a legalistic scribe, here out of place.
— For variant expressions in Clem. Al. (which, however, do not necessarily
mean different MS. readings) see H-P and Lag. — 11. 𝕳 בי is followed by 𝕷
only; 𝕾𝕿 בה; 𝕲 τούτῳ τῷ τρόπῳ, probably = בה; see note on this verse
above. — 𝕳 יוסיפו must be taken with indef. subject, but we should perh. read
Nifal. — 12. On the addition of 𝕲 in ᵃ καὶ τοῖς πλησίον see note on this verse
above, and on σεαυτῷ Deissmann, *Bibelstud.*, p. 120 f. On the added couplets
see notes of Lag. and Baumg., and for a translation of them into Heb. see
De. (the Germ. ed. — the translation is omitted in the Eng. translation).

II. DETACHED APHORISMS (X. 1–XXII. 16).

On the constitution and date of this division see the Introduction. The title *Proverbs of Solomon* belongs to the whole division. The proverbs will be arranged in groups as far as their subject-matter allows. Ben-Sira is to be compared throughout.

X. The main thought is that moral goodness and industry bring prosperity, and wickedness and indolence adversity — the portraiture is broad, not going into particulars. The parallelism is generally antithetic.

1. Wise and foolish youth.

> A wise son makes a glad father,
> But a foolish son is a grief to his mother.

Antithetic, ternary. Cf. 19^{26} 28^7. *Wise = discreet*, living a good life morally and industrially. We pass now from the philosophical conception of chs. 1–9, in which wisdom is a lore, the subject-matter and product of organized instruction, to the everyday common-sense view of wisdom as general soundness and propriety of conduct. The difference is not, however, to be pressed very far — it is largely one of shading; the aphoristic teaching of chs. 10^1–22^{16}, the outcome of observation under a general religious point of view, is expanded in chs. 1–9 into discourses in which life is regarded as an organized whole, with wisdom as central and governing principle. — The antithesis is symmetrical and exact: *wise* and *glad* are contrasted with *foolish* and *grief*. *Glad* and *grief* relate primarily to external conditions, such as the satisfaction or worry which come to parents from the good or bad conduct and reputation of their children; but the emotion founded simply on affection is not to be excluded. The interchange of *father* and *mother* is poetical variation; the meaning is not that the father is more interested in the wise son, and the mother in the foolish son (special maternal tenderness for a feeble or erring child), but *father* and *mother* stand each for *parents*. Similarly, the silence respecting the *daughter* is not to be interpreted as showing complete lack of interest in female children ; it comes in part from the relatively greater seclusion of young unmarried women, and their freedom from the grosser temptations of life — they might naturally be passed over in a book which deals not with the inward life, but with visible conduct in the outward world of society, and, in fact, the unmarried woman is not mentioned in Proverbs. The depraved woman is introduced as a warning not to women, but to men ; the good woman of ch. 31 is the married head of a household, and is praised mainly for the advantages of wealth and social position which she brings to her husband and family. The non-mention of daughters and of women in general may, however, be attributed in part to the relatively small estimation in which women were held in the ancient civilized world, among Chinese, Hindoos, Israelites, Greeks, and Romans.* — On care of daughters see BS. $7^{24. 25}$ 26^{10-12} 42^{9-11}. — Similar sayings concerning good sons are cited by Malan from the Ramayana, Confucius, Menander, etc.

2. Profits of wrongdoing and rightdoing.

> Treasures wrongly acquired profit nothing,
> But righteousness delivers from death.

Antithetic, ternary. The Heb. has *treasures of wickedness*, = wealth acquired unjustly (not stores or masses of evildoing) ; this is contrasted with *justice, righteousness* as a method of procedure in business-transactions and other affairs of life. Ill-gotten wealth, says the writer, though it may procure temporary triumph, profits nothing in the end, since violence and injustice are sure to bring divine or human (legal or private) vengeance on the man's head. Justice (= probity), on the other hand, by avoiding such vengeance (and having the blessing of God), secures to its pos-

---

* On the position of women in antiquity see *Revue Encyclopéd.*, vi. (1896), 825 f. ; A. Bebel, *Die Frau u. d. Sozialismus*, 1891 (Eng. tranl., 1894) ; Th. Matthias, *Zur Stellung d. griech. Frau in d. klassisch. Zeit*, 1893 ; Marquardt and Mommsen, *Hdbch. d. römisch. Alterthümer*, 1871–1888 ; Gardner and Jevons, *Manual of Grk. Antiq.*, 1895 ; Becker, *Char.* and *Gallus* As to Egypt cf. Wilkinson, *Anc. Egypt.*, chs. 2. 5. 8. etc.

sessor a long and peaceful life — exemption from premature death, which is regarded in OT. as a direct divine judgment. Wealth, says the sage, will not avert God's judgment, but righteousness secures his favor. For the nature of the *death* see notes on 1^{19} 2^{18-22}, etc.; cf. v.$^{16.\ 21.\ 27.\ 30}$ of this chapter. That there is no reference to rewards and punishments beyond the grave appears from the whole thought of the Book. On the terms *wickedness, righteousness* see notes on 4^{17} 8^{18} 1^{3}. — As early as the second century B.C. (and perhaps earlier) the term *righteousness* came to be used as equivalent to *almsgiving, alms*, as in Dan. $4^{27(24)}$, where the king is urged to rid himself of the guilt of sin by *righteousness* defined as showing kindness to the poor; and parallels to our proverb are found in Tob. 4^{10} 12^{9} BS. 3^{30} 29^{12}, with substitution of *almsgiving* for *righteousness;* in Tob. 12^{9} the two terms are employed as synonyms. This usage occurs also in NT. (Mt. 6^{1}), Talmud (*Succa*, 49 b), Midrash (on Pr. 21^{3}), Koran (9^{104}).* It is to be explained by the prominence which almsgiving always assumes in society (the care of the poor being the most obvious of social duties) — it naturally comes to be regarded as the special indication of a good heart, and as a means of wiping out guilt (cf. the analogous use in OT. of *afflict one's self* for *fast*). This idea, however, does not seem to be contained in our proverb; the contrast appears to be between probity and wickedness in general, though it is possible that the intention is to put treasure acquired wickedly and used selfishly over against wealth expended for the needy.

3. Desire fulfilled and unfulfilled.

> Yahweh suffers not the righteous to hunger,
> But he disappoints the desire of the wicked.

Antithetic, quaternary-ternary. *Righteous* and *wicked* are used in the most general sense. The Heb. has *the soul of the righteous*, where *soul* = the personality, with special reference to desire or appetite, as in Dt. 14^{26} ψ 107^{18} Pr. 13^{19}. *Disappoint* is lit. *thrust away, reject, put out of consideration*. The word here used for *desire* means *evil desire* (cf. note on 11^{6}); for good desire another

---

* It seems not to have existed among the Greeks and the Romans.

term is employed (10^{24} 11^{23} *al.*).   The point of view (found throughout OT., except in the speeches of Job and in Eccl.) is that the temporal wants of the righteous are provided for by God. This idea is expanded at greatest length in ψ 37 (see especially v.[19, 25]), a poem which seems to belong to the same period as the central part of Proverbs.   Elsewhere in OT. the application is to the nation, or rather to the righteous part of it (Isa. 7. 8 Ez. 36 Isa. 53, the Psalter *passim*).   Founded on the conviction of the divine justice, it survived all changes of fortune, and in Proverbs is applied without reservation to the individual man.   In Wisd. Sol. and NT. this view is abandoned, and the reward of the righteous is sought in the future life.

4, 5. Industry and sloth.

> 4. A slack hand makes poor,
>   A diligent hand makes rich.

> 5. He who gathers in summer acts wisely,
>   He who sleeps in harvest acts shamefully.

4. Antithetic, ternary.   Cf. 12^{24} 19^{15} 22^{7} 6^{6-11} 27^{23-27} 28^{19}.   Probably based on an old popular proverb; parallels are found among all peoples.   The second line is lit.: *the hand of the diligent makes rich.*   As *hand* in OT. often = *person*, we may also render : *The slothful becomes poor, the diligent becomes rich.*   By the change of a vowel *poverty* may be read instead of *poor*, with the sense : *The slothful gains poverty, the diligent gains wealth,* but the change is unnecessary.   The Vrss. give different readings : *poverty brings a man low* (Grk. Targ. Syr.) ; or, *a slack hand brings poverty* (Lat.).   In the first of these the verb is, from the parallelism, obviously wrong; the second is identical with a reading given above. — The Lat. and the Hexaplar Syriac here add the first couplet of the addition found in Grk. after 9^{12}, which see ; it seems here to be the random insertion of a scribe. — **5.** Antithetic, ternary.   Providence and improvidence.   Lit. *is a son who acts wisely,* and *is a son who acts shamefully.*   The last expression may be rendered, as in RV., *who causes shame* (cf. 28^{7}), but the parallelism favors the translation here given.   We may also reverse the order of subject and predicate, and render : *He* (or, *a son*) *who acts wisely gathers in summer, he* (or, *a son*) *who acts shamefully sleeps in harvest*. The meaning is the same in the two translations; but the first (characterizing the act as wise or unwise) is more natural than the second (characterizing the man as acting so or so). The statement is meant to be universal; the word *son* contemplates the man as a member of a family, but it is also assumed that he is an independent worker. The agricultural life, to which the proverb relates, existed among the Jews in Palestine from their first occupation of the land down to the destruction of Jerusalem by the Romans. On *summer* and *harvest* see note on 6[8]. — Grk. has:

> A son who is instructed will be wise,
> And shall use the fool as servant.
> A thoughtful son is saved from heat,
> But a lawless son is blighted (or, carried away) by the wind in harvest.

The first couplet appears in some MSS. at 9[12]; the second has a general resemblance to the Heb. of our verse, with great verbal variation.

X. 1. The title is lacking in 𝕲𝕾, and was perhaps not inserted in 𝕳 till after 𝕲 was made. — To אב 𝕾𝕮𝕿 attach suff., which may have fallen out through foll. וֹ; but the simple form accords with the curtness of aphoristic expression, and may be retained notwithstanding the אמו. — **2.** 𝕳 רֶשַׁע (and so 𝕷); 𝕲 ἀνόμους (and so 𝕾𝕿), less appropriate, since רֶשַׁע אצלת forms a contrast to צדקה. — For צדקה in the sense of *justice, aid, succor* to Israel (by Yahweh) see Ju. 5[11] Mic. 6[5], and cf. the similar sense in Sabean, in Hal. 188, 8 (צדק). Gr. adds ביום עברה, as in 11[4]. — **3.** 𝕳 צֶרֶק; 𝕲[AB al.] δικαίαν; between the two readings there is little to choose. — The primary sense of the stem הוה seems to be *go, move,* whence *blow* (of the wind), and Aram. *be* (perh. from *breathe,* perh. from *fall out, happen*), and specifically *go down, fall* (Arab.); the noun = *air* (Arab.), *desire,* connected with breathing (Arab., Heb.), *misfortune, destruction,* = that which *falls* on one (Heb.). In Job 37[6] הוה appears to mean *fall,* but Siegf. emends to רוֶה *water* (see König, p. 598). Cf. Fleischer, in De.[2], p. 94, Budde on Job 6[2] 37[6], BDB. Fleischer (in De., Job 37[6]) holds that the primitive sense of the stem is *gape, yawn.* 𝕾𝕿 הון *possession;* 𝕷 *insidias.* 𝕲 ζωήν, = חית, does not give so good an antithesis as 𝕳. — 𝕳 רשעים, for which a number of MSS. and printed edd. (see De' Rossi) have בגרם *treacherous,* apparently a gloss which expelled the text-word. The variation of number (sing. ע, plu. ר) is for rhythmical effect. — **4.** 𝕲 (foll. by 𝕾𝕿) πενία (ראש) ἄνδρα ταπεινοῖ, perh. taking 𝕳 as = *poverty makes the hand slack* (cf. Schleusn.), or reading some form of ענה or דך. Between רָאש and רָאש

there is not much choice; the parallelism (הָעֹשֵׁיר) rather favors the former.
The Hif. הֹ may be simple causative (*makes rich*) or causative-reflexive (*becomes rich*). On the couplet added in 𝔏𝔖ᴴ see Baumg.'s note. — **5.** The text
of 𝔊 seems to be based on that of 𝔥. Its first cl. υἱὸς πεπαιδευμένος σοφὸς
ἔσται = בן מוסר משכל, the בּ ומ being perh. paraphrase of אגר בקיץ; of this the
third cl. διεσώθη ἀπὸ καύματος ὑ. νοήμων is a doublet, κ. = קיץ (what Heb.
word δ. represents is doubtful); the second cl. τῷ δὲ ἄφρονι διακόνῳ χρήσεται
is scribal appendage as antithesis to the first; the fourth cl. ἀνεμόφθορος (read
ἀνεμοφόρητος) δὲ γίνεται ἐν ἀμήτῳ υἱὸς παράνομος = נרף בקצר בן מביש (cf. Isa.
19⁷). The whole is a paraphrase which may have taken the place of an
original Grk. text.

6, 7. The recompense of virtue and vice.

> 6. Blessings are on the head of the righteous
>
> .   .   .   .*
>
> 7. The memory of the righteous will be blessed,
>   But the name of the wicked will rot.

6. *Blessings* may be the good wishes or encomiums of men (as
in v.⁷), or the good things bestowed by God (so Grk.); the latter
interpretation is perhaps favored by the use of the expression *on
the head* (of Joseph) in Gen. 49²⁶ Dt. 33¹⁶; cf. De.'s notes here and
on Gen. 49²⁶. — The second cl. reads in the Heb.: *but the mouth
of the wicked covers violence* or *violence covers the mouth of the
wicked* (identical with second clause of v.¹¹). Neither of these
renderings gives any natural connection with the first clause. *Violence* is high-handed, oppressive conduct — it is said (ψ 73⁶ and
perhaps Mal. 2¹⁶) to cover the wicked man as a garment, he is
enwrapped in it (13² delights in it); so perhaps here, it covers his
mouth, that is, controls his speech, and therefore, his life. But
this affords no contrast to the first cl., from which we should rather
expect some such line as *evil pursues the wicked*. Grk. (representing a slightly different Heb. text from ours): *untimely grief
shall cover*, etc., which gives a contrast. Bickell emends: *but the
fruit of the wicked is sorrow and wrath* (cf. 13²). Graetz suggests *face* instead of *mouth*. We should perhaps read:

> The blessing of Yahweh is on the head of the righteous,
> But sorrow shall cover the face of the wicked.

---

* Heb.: *But violence covers the mouth of the wicked.*

The text appears to have been assimilated to that of v.[11b], on which see note ; or, possibly the original line has been lost, and v.[11b] substituted for it. — **7**. Antithetic, ternary. The antithesis is exact and complete. The common human desire to leave a good name behind shall be fulfilled, says the writer, for the good, but not for the bad : men will bless the one, or will regard him as an example of blessedness or prosperity ; the other they will forget.* The rule, in fact, holds in general, though it is not without numerous exceptions. The opposite point of view is expressed in *Jul. Caes.*, 3, 2 :

> The evil that men do lives after them;
> The good is oft interred with their bones.

Instead of *will rot* a slight change of text gives the reading : *will be cursed* (Frank.), which offers an exact contrast to *blessed*, and should perhaps be adopted ; this verb occurs in 11^{26} 24^{24}.

8. Obedience to law characteristic of the wise.

> A wise man heeds commands,
> But a foolish talker will fall.

Antithetic, ternary. Lit. *one who is wise of mind* (Heb. *heart*), and *one who is foolish of lips ;* the *prating fool* of RV. is inexact — it is not *a fool who talks,* but *a man who talks folly.* — The meaning of the first cl. is plain — the *wise man* (he who is sound in thought, practically judicious) abides by the prescriptions of competent authority. This characterization of the wise man is especially natural to the Jew of this period (4th or 3d century B.C.), for whom all right was embodied in his Tora, but is also of universal propriety, since all right conduct is conformity to law of some sort ; here the law is external, divine or human. — The second cl., also, is plain in itself (foolish talking brings misfortune), but stands in no obvious relation to the first cl., and seems not to be here in place. We may, indeed, suppose an elaborate implicit antithesis : language may be understood as the expression of thought and mind (so that *foolish talker = foolish man*), and *falling* as the result of *not heeding commands,* and the proverb, fully expressed, would then read : the wise man abides by law, talks sensibly, and pros-

---

* So in Gen. 12^3 : *in thee shall all nations bless themselves*, that is, take thee as the standard of success ; the explanation of the expression is given in Gen. 48^{20}.

pers; the fool rejects law, talks foolishly, and fails. But this roundabout mode of expression is contrary to the method of the Book, in which the antithesis of the clauses is obviously meant to be clearly set forth. The second cl. (which occurs again in v.[10]) was probably here inserted by error of scribe; it belongs properly in an aphorism in which the other clause declares the stability of the righteous. The reference is to earthly failure.

9. Safety in integrity.

> He who walks uprightly walks surely,
> But he whose ways are crooked shall ‹ suffer.›

Antithetic, ternary. In second cl. the Heb. has *shall be known*, that is, apparently, known as (= discovered to be) a wrong-doer, and punished. That a bad man's wickedness will be found out is probable; but the parallelism calls for the mention of punishment, and a natural expression is given in 11^{15}, where *suffer loss* or *evil* (RV. *smart for it*) stands in contrast with *sure;* this rendering requires only a slight change in one Heb. letter. We may also translate : *but it goes ill with him whose ways*, etc. The translations *will be taught* (that is, by his experience) (Ew.), and *will be seen through* (De.) are improbable. *Uprightly* is lit. *in uprightness, perfectness*, or *innocence ;* on *crooked* see note on 2^{15}. *Surely* = not *confidently*, but *safely*. The proverb seems not to contemplate divine intervention, but to refer to a common law of society : the man of upright life has nothing to fear from his neighbors or from the law — a dishonest man will be punished — nearly equivalent to *honesty is the best policy*.

10. Mischief-makers and friendly critics.

> He who winks the eye makes trouble,
> ‹ But he who reproves makes peace.›

Antithetic, probably ternary. On *winking the eye* (or, *with the eye*) as an expression for stirring up strife by malicious hints see note on 6^{12-14}. The second cl. reads in the Heb. : *and a foolish talker shall fall*, apparently repeated from v.[8] (where, however, it is not in place), here offering no antithesis — we expect the mention of something which causes the opposite of trouble. Grk. has

He who winks deceitfully with his eyes causes sorrow to men, but he who reproves openly makes peace. This furnishes the desired contrast, but in expanded form; the *deceitfully* and *to men* are explanatory additions, and perhaps also the *openly* (Bickell), though we might read (see 27⁵) *open reproof makes peace*, or *he who reproves evil*, etc. (cf. 24²⁵). In any case the suggestion is that frank reproof of wrongdoing will pave the way to repentance and amity. For the word *trouble* see 15¹³ Job 9²⁸, and cf. the similar term in 10²² 15¹ ψ 127² (sometimes = *labor*, 5¹⁰ 14²³).

11. Righteous and wicked speech.

> The mouth of the righteous is a fountain of life,
> But violence envelops the mouth of the wicked.

Antithetic, ternary. The second cl. (identical with second cl. of v.⁶, on which see note) is not to be rendered *the mouth of the wicked conceals violence*;* violence is represented as a garment which clothes the bad man's mouth, that is, it characterizes and is produced by his utterance — the idea of concealment is not in place, it is rather expression that is meant; in Prov. *mouth* is generally equivalent to *utterance*, and the idea that the wicked man uses language to conceal his thought (that is, is hypocritical), though here possible, does not accord with the first line. The contrast is between the speech of the righteous and that of the wicked — the former is a source of wisdom, peace, good earthly life, the latter brings hurt, misfortune; it is the effect on others that is referred to. The expression *fountain of life = life-giving water*, or, generally, *source of life*, is used of God in Jer. 2¹³ 17¹³ ψ 36⁹⁽¹⁰⁾ (De.), in accordance with the national theistic point of view of the prophets and psalmists; in Prov. it is used of wise, upright speech (so here), of the law of the wise (13¹⁴), of the fear of God (14²⁷), of wisdom or understanding (16²²), the reference in all cases being to prosperous and happy earthly life as the result of obedience to the highest wisdom, which is ultimately obedience to the law of God; see 3² 4¹³ 8³⁵, etc. The sage thus conceives of human life as a system ordered by law, this law residing in the mind of man, but being also the will of God, who thus

---

* De., Str., Kamp. *al.*

manifests himself in human thought. The *fountain of life* is a
natural figure, especially in Palestine, where springs played so
important a part in agriculture and life generally; there seems to
be no reason to suppose a reference to a primitive " spring of life "
corresponding to the " tree of life " of Gen. 2 (see note on 3[18]).
— The expression *living water* (Jer. 2[13] *al.*), = *running water*
(contrasted with standing water), is used in a different sense.

12. Hatred and love.

> Hatred stirs up strifes,
> But love hides all transgressions.

Antithetic, ternary. Cf. 17[9]. Hatred dwells on and exagger-
ates evil or unwise words and acts, and so causes misunderstandings and quarrels. Love hides trangressions, not by condoning
wrong, but by making allowance and forgiving; it leads a man to
cover up not his own faults (this is condemned in 28[13]) but those
of others (so 1 Cor. 13[7]). This clause is quoted in 1 Pet. 4[8] in
the form *love hides a multitude of sins* (that is, sins of others),
free citation, possibly from memory, but more probably (since it
occurs in Jas.) from some current Aramaic or Greek version
(which perhaps represented a Heb. text slightly different from
ours). A different application is given to the latter part of the
expression in Jas. 5[20], in which it is said that he who turns a sinner
from his evil ways *covers a multitude of sins*, conceals them, that
is, from the eyes of God, who no longer takes note of them —
a use of *cover* derived from OT., in which a verb * having this
meaning is employed in the sense *atone for* (Ex. 29[36], etc.), *for-
give* (ψ 78[38]), *appease* (Pr. 16[14]). The idea in these passages is
the same as in this verse — sin is hidden, ignored.

6. בְּרֻכַּת; $\mathfrak{G}$ (foll. by $\mathfrak{L}$) εὐλογία κυρίου, in which the κ. is perh. original
(Lag.), perh. interpretation. — It is doubtful whether there is any difference
of sense between לְרֹאשׁ and בְּרֹאשׁ; the former does occur in connection with
blessing (Gen. 49[26] Dt. 33[16]), and the latter, after verbs of *inflicting*, in connection with punishment (1 K. 2[37] Obad.[15] Joel 4[4, 7]); but elsewhere the two
are used in the same sense (cf. Ez. 16[12] with Pr. 4[9]). — For 歿 ח Graetz, with
probability, suggests פְּנֵי. 歿 ס:ח; $\mathfrak{G}$ πένθος ἄωρον (Lag. ἀθρόον, but cf. WS.

---

* *Kapar, kipper*, whence *koper, ransom, kapporet, covering* (of the ark), RV.
mercy-seat.

14^{15}), whence we may read כנס. — **7.** 獤 ירקב; 㿢 σβέννυται, = יוּעָך, as in 13^9 20^{20} 24^{20}; 㿢 have יעַך; Krochmal (cited by Gr.) יקב *shall be cursed* (cf. 11^{26}), a good reading if the ברכה be understood of men (Frank. ינקב). — **8.** 獤 אֱוִל; 㿢$^{B al.}$ ἄστεγος *babbling* (㿢^{70} 㿢^{II} ἄστατος *unsteady*); the σκολιάζων of 㿢 is gloss on this expression, or (Jäg.) on the διαστρέφων (獤 מֵעְקָשׁ) of v^9. 獤 ילבט; 㿢 ὑποσκελισθήσεται *stumble, fall* (as Arab. לבט); Frank. ילכד, which, how- ever, does not occur elsewhere without a defining term. — **9.** 獤 יֵרַע (foll. by all Vrss.) gives no satisfactory sense; read ירֵעַ (so Graetz) or ירע לו; cf. 11^{15} 13^{20} ψ 106^{32}. On 㿢 see Pink. — **10.** 獤^b (= 8^b) is here out of place. 㿢 ὁ δὲ ἐλέγχων μετὰ παρρησίας εἰρηνοποιεῖ, perh. = מכח בשפתים ישׁלם; Bi. מכח יעשה; ישׁלם; μετ. παρ. is rendered by Lag. למחיה (so in Lev. 26^{13}), by Gr. אל פנים. — **11.** For 獤^b פי 㿢 has ἐν χειρί, perh. scribal error for χείλει (Grabe, Lag.). — **12.** On 獤 מדון see note on 6^{14} — עַר after כסה occurs ψ 44^{20} 106^{17} Job 21^{26}, the primary sense of the vb. being perh. *lay, heap.* — 㿢 τοὺς μὴ φιλονεικοῦντας, = לא כשׁעב, the neg. being inserted to obtain a contrast with^a. 㿢 בהתרא *shame* (for 獤 ארבה) is scribal error, or emendation to avoid saying that love covers sinners (Pink.).

13, 14. The character and use of speech.

> 13. In the speech of the discerning wisdom is found,
>   But for the fool's back there is a rod.
> 14. Wise men conceal what they know,
>   But the talk of a fool is impending destruction.

13. Ternary. The two clauses, taken separately, give each a good sense, but there is no close connection between them. The first has congeners in 10$^{21.\ 31}$ 14^3 15^7, where there is well marked antithesis. The second is found almost word for word in 26^3, in which the meaning is clear — the fool, like a beast, must be driven or guided by force (cf. ψ 32^9). Such must be its sense here, and we should then expect in the first cl. the statement that the wise man is otherwise directed; possibly this is what is meant by saying that wisdom is in his *speech* (lit. *lips*) — he is guided by reason. But this sense is not obvious, and in v.^{31} the expression has another meaning, namely, that the lips of the good man utter wisdom, in contrast with which we should here expect to read that the fool utters folly (cf. v.^{11}). This sense may be got by a couple of changes in the Heb. text: *but folly is in the mouth of the fool* (lit. *of him who is devoid of understanding*, lacking in sense). It is doubtful, however, whether we should not rather retain the text, and regard the second cl. as here out of place.

As the verse stands, the meaning must be taken to be : An intelligent man's speech is wise, his thought is good, and he knows how to direct his life — a fool has no guiding principle in himself, and must be driven like a beast, or coerced like a child.   From Grk. we get no help : *he who brings out wisdom from his lips smites the fool with a rod.* — **14.** Antithetic, ternary.   The antithesis is obvious : wise men, knowing the power of words, are cautious in speech, and by sometimes keeping back what they know, avert misfortune, while fools, talking thoughtlessly, are constantly in danger of bringing destruction on people's heads, as by talebearing, revealing secrets, and the like.   Reticence is often praised in Prov. ; see v.^{19} 11^{13} 12^{23} *al.*   If the rendering *wise men lay up knowledge* (De., RV.) be adopted, the antithesis will be destroyed, and the two clauses cannot be regarded as belonging together. Cf. BS. 9^{18} 20$^{5-7}$.

15, 16. Wealth — its social value, and its proper use.

> 15. The rich man's wealth is his strong city,
> And the poverty of the poor is their destruction.
> 16. The wage of the righteous leads to life,
> The revenue of the wicked to ‹ destruction.›

15. Antithetic, ternary.   *Strong city* = protection against all dangers and ills.   The second cl. is lit. : *and the destruction of the poor is their poverty.*   Cf. v.^{29} BS. 40^{25}.   The Grk. omits the possessive pronouns.   There is probably no ethical thought in the proverb — the sense is that wealth smooths one's path in life, bringing supply of bodily needs, guarding against the attacks of the powerful, and giving social consideration (14^{20} 18^{23} 19^{4} 22^{7} 31^{23}), — while the poor man is exposed to bodily and social privations (19^{4} Eccl. 9^{16}). — It seems to be simply a recognition of the value of money, such as is found in all civilized lands.   Possibly, however, the sage has also in mind the moral dangers of poverty, as in 30^{9}. — A somewhat different sense is given to the first cl. in 18^{11}, on which see note.   The opposite side of the picture — the danger of wealth — is brought out in 11^{4} 13^{8} 23^{5} 28$^{6.\ 11}$ BS. 30^{14} 31$^{1-8}$, and it is declared in 19^{22} 28^{6} that poverty is preferable to vice. — **16.** Antithetic, ternary.   Lit. : *the wage,* etc. *is* (= *leads*) *to life, the revenue,* etc. *is to,* etc.   *Wage* (wages of labor) and *revenue* (what accrues to one) are synonyms — it is not meant to contrast the wealth of the righteous as gained by honest toil with that of the wicked as acquired without work (De., Str.) ; the former term is used also of the wicked (11^{18}) and the latter of wisdom (3^{14}). The contrast is between the tendencies and results of riches in different men. For the good man, who acquires and uses it properly, it leads to long life and earthly happiness (for this sense see notes on $3^{2. 22}$) — he does nothing to endanger his position. For the bad man it leads — we expect the antithesis *to death* (for which see 11^4) — instead of this the Heb. has *to sin*. If the text be correct, we must suppose that the sin involves punishment, ultimately death — the bad man comes into conflict with the laws of society, or incurs the anger and vengeance of God. But the word *sin* is here difficult. The point of the verse is not that wealth is an occasion of sin to the wicked man, but that, as the properly acquired and used wealth of the righteous secures life for him, so the improperly acquired and used wealth of the wicked secures death or calamity for him. The word *sin*, though supported by all the Vrss., appears to be a miswriting.* An easy change of text gives the appropriate term *destruction* (as in v.$^{14. 29}$). The meaning of the proverb is plain — even wealth, ordinarily regarded as a blessing, becomes a curse in the hands of a bad man. The point of view is that of chs. 1-9 : rightdoing is attended by earthly prosperity, wrongdoing by adversity.

17. Docility and indocility.

> He is in the way of life who heeds instruction,
> But he who neglects admonition goes (fatally) astray.

Antithetic, ternary. The first cl., lit. *the way to life is he who,* etc., might be rendered : *he is a wayfarer to life who,* etc., or *it is the way to life when one,* etc. ; the sense remains the same : he who follows right instruction will be led to a long and happy earthly life (see preceding verse), since he will be taught to avoid folly and so will escape danger. The second cl. states the reverse

---

* The sense *punishment*, which is given by some to the Heb. word in Isa. 5^{18} 1 K. 13^{34} Nu. 32^{23} Dan. 9^{24}, is doubtful, and in any case can hardly be assigned to it here.

side : rejection of instruction causes one to miss the way of life and happiness, and to wander into the paths of misfortune and death. The second verb is in form causative in the Heb., and we may translate : *he who heeds instruction is a way to life* (for others), *but he who neglects admonition leads* (others) *astray* (cf. Wildeboer) ; but this seems less natural than the sense given above (cf. the similar thought in 15^{10}). The proverb inculcates a teachable disposition — one mark of a fool is unwillingness to take advice. The *instruction* must be understood to be of the most general sort, including training in the higher divine ethical law, as well as guidance in smaller matters of everyday life.

18. Talebearing. The form is doubtful. The Hebrew most naturally reads :

> He who hides hatred is a liar (lit. lying lips),
> And he who utters (or, spreads) slander is a fool.

The verse is thus a synthetic parallelism, and AV. makes it (against the norm of the context) a single sentence : *he that hideth hatred with lying lips, and he that uttereth a slander, is a fool.* Luther : *false mouths cover hatred.* In the connection the expression *he who hides hatred* must mean the man who conceals hostile feeling under friendly words (26^{26}), and is thus false in speech. There might thence seem to result the antithesis of secrecy and publicity : a secret hater is a liar, an open slanderer is a fool. But this antithesis does not really exist in the verse — the suggestion rather is that concealed hatred expresses itself in slander (the two are related as cause and effect), which is itself an underhand, secret procedure. But, from the usage of Prov. (10^{12} 11^{13} $12^{16.\,23}$ 17^9 28^{13}) the verb *hide* (lit. *cover*), when undefined, would naturally mean to cover up, put out of the way, in a good sense, so that we might expect the clause to read : *he who covers up hatred is righteous,* and so Grk. *righteous lips conceal hatred.* — The text may be rendered : *Lying lips conceal hatred,* = *the liar conceals,* etc. ; but this general proposition is not true, and does not offer a distinct contrast to the second line. In 26^{26} the covering of hatred is defined as effected by *deceit,* and is thus stamped as evil ; without such a defining term it is doubtful whether the expression can be taken in a bad sense. We must adopt the construction of AV., or the reading of Grk., or else we must suppose that the original text has been lost, and that it referred to suppression of evil reports (as in v.[19] 17[9]), or gave some other antithesis to the second clause.

13. See note on this v. above. A possible reading for [b] is ואגלה בשפתי חסר לב. In [a] Bi. omits הנמצא for the sake of the rhythm. 𝕲[B] omits [a] by error. In [b] ῥάβδῳ τύπτει ἄνδρα ἀκάρδιον = חסר לב לגבר יבט. 𝕾 = 𝕲; 𝕿𝕷 = 𝕳. — **14.** 𝕲 ἐγγίζει συντριβῇ, = קרב למחתה. — **15.** 𝕳, דַּלִּים, 𝕲 ἀσεβῶν, prob. for ἀσθε-νῶν (𝕲[23] Grabe, Lag.). — **16.** For 𝕳 השאת we should read מחתה or מות. — **17.** The expression ארח לחיים, only here; cf. ψ 16[11] Pr. 2[19] 5[6] 15[24]; the prep. does not appear in the Vrss. We may read א׳ ח׳ לְשֹׁמֵר (cf. 15[24]), or Partcp. אֹרֵחַ, or באַרח ח׳ ש׳ — 𝕳 מַתְעֶה can be taken only in the causative sense, as everywhere else in OT. (the only other occurrence of the Hif. in Pr. is 12[26], on which see note). Read Qal תֹעֶה (the מ being omitted as erroneous repetition of preceding ה), or, with Hitz., point מתעה as Hith. — On the mistranslation of 𝕲 see notes of Vog., Lag., Baumg. — **18.** For 𝕲[B] δίκαια (for 𝕳 שקר) Grabe suggests ἄδικα, Lag. (with 𝕲[106]) δόλια, which may be conformation to 𝕳, or δ. may be free rendering to gain a good sense. The text of 𝕳[a] appears to be corrupt, and no aid is got from the Vrss. See note on this v. above.

19-21. The proper use of speech.

19. In a multitude of words transgression will not be lacking,
   And he who controls his tongue acts wisely.
20. The tongue of the righteous is choice silver,
   The mind of the wicked is little worth.
21. The lips of the righteous feed many,
   But the foolish die through lack of understanding.

19. Antithetic, ternary. *Tongue* is lit. *lips*. The second line may also be rendered : *the wise man controls*, etc. The caution is against much talking — in general, says the sage, it is impossible to talk much and be wise. The reference is to everyday life ; *transgression* is overstepping the bounds of sobriety and good sense. The preceding proverb is directed against gossip as injurious to others ; this is intended to guard the man's own character. It may be popular in origin, but its present form was given it by cultivated thinkers. Cf. BS. 20[8]. Malan cites a number of close parallels to this proverb, as *talkativeness is intemperance in speech* (Theophrast. *Char.* 8), and *silence is a hedge about wisdom* (*Pirke Aboth*, 3, 13), and cf. *Pirk. Ab.*, 1, 17, which is probably

based on this verse. — **20.** Antithetic, quaternary- (or, ternary-)
ternary. The antithesis rests on the identification of *thought* or
mind (lit. *heart*) and *speech* (*tongue*); it is assumed (and in
general it is true) that they correspond to each other. A good
man's speech, issuing from his good mind, makes for everything
good in life, and may be likened to *choice silver*, silver refined, of
highest value, and everywhere current. The *mind* of the *wicked*
(their inward being, attitude toward life, thought and opinion),
which naturally expresses itself in words, is of small account —
a contemptuous expression, doubtless = of no account, of no
value for speaker or hearer. The point of view is moral (as in
chs. 1–9); *righteous* and *wicked* are identified with *wise* and *unwise.* — **21.** Antithetic, quaternary- (or, ternary-) ternary. Speech
and thought are identified, as in the preceding verse, and *righteous*
(= *wise*) is set over against *foolish* (no doubt here = *wicked*);
understanding is lit. *mind* (*heart*), as above. The antithesis is
between the nutritive power of wise thought and speech, and the
incapacity of moral folly to gain life — earthly life, taken in the
widest sense, with physical and moral content. The good man
ministers to all the wants not only of himself, but also of others
(*many* here = all with whom he comes in contact), the bad man
cannot keep even himself alive; the death referred to is the
premature physical death which is the penalty of failure to grasp
and follow wisdom; see note on v.². The thought is substantially that of 3¹⁴⁻¹⁷, with substitution of *the righteous man* for *wisdom.* — A sharper antithesis would be gained by the reading *many
die through one who lacks understanding*, but the change of *fools*
to *many* is difficult; the rendering *fools die through one*, etc., gives
no appropriate thought. — In the first line the translation *the lips*,
etc., *gain many* (as friends) is hardly allowed by the Hebrew.
Cf. BS. 6⁴·⁵ 9¹⁸.

22. Happiness of work blessed by God.

> The blessing of Yahweh, it makes rich,
> And he adds no sorrow with it.

Continuous or extensive (the second cl. completing the first by
an additional detail), ternary. The first cl. affirms that physical
wealth is the gift of God, as in chs. 1–9 this gift is ascribed to

Wisdom.   The repetition of the subject by the insertion of *it*
indicates that it is the divine blessing and not anything else that
gives riches, that is, the divine blessing on the labor of men's
hands.   In the second cl. the term *sorrow* (sometimes = *painful
effort, toil*) is used, as in 15^{13} (*sorrow of heart* or *mind*), Gen. 3^{16},
for pain, suffering ; the wealth bestowed by Yahweh is distinguished, as being free from sorrow, from ill-gotten gain, which
brings evil with it (13^{11} 15^6 16^{19} 21^6 28^6).   There is an implied antithesis between the wealth of good men and that of bad men. —
Elsewhere in OT., when a preposition follows the verb *add*, it is *to*
(see Jer. 45^3), which would here be out of place. — This understanding of the term rendered *sorrow* is that of the Anc. Vrss.
Some expositors,* taking it in the sense of *labor*, render : *and toil
adds not to it* (namely, to the blessing), that is, human labor
counts for nothing in the acquisition of wealth — it is all God's
doing.   But such a sharp separation between man's work and
God's work is hardly an OT. conception (passages like Ex. 14^{14}
ψ 118^8 do not bear on this question) — man is everywhere represented as working under God's direction ; so ψ 127^2 (which is
cited by Ew., De., Str., as supporting their translation) affirms not
that labor in itself is useless, but only labor unattended by the
divine blessing.   In 14^{23} it is said that there is profit in all labor.

23. How wrongdoing appears to fools and to sages.

It is as sport to a fool to do wrong,
But it is ‹ abomination › to a man of sense.

Antithetic, quaternary-ternary.   The essential idea in the term
sport is not ease of performance (De. *al.: child's play*), but recre-
ation, enjoyment — so Gen. 17^{17} Ex. 32^6 Ju. 16^{25} Zech. 8^5 Job 40^{20}
Pr. $8^{30.\ 31}$ 26^{19} 31^{25} (the sense *derision* which the word sometimes
has, as in 2 C. 30^{10} Job 30^1 ψ 2^4 Pr. 1^{26}, does not come into consideration here).   It is the fool's moral superficiality that enables
him to enjoy sin — he has no deep sense of its sinfulness ; it is
involved that such conduct is easy for him — the assumption is
that wrongdoing may become part of a man's nature, his normal
and joyous activity. — The term here rendered *wrong* (RV. *wicked-*

---

* Saadia, Rashi, Luther. Ew., Hitz., De., Str., Kamp., Frank.

ness) is a strong one, sometimes expressing general enormity of conduct (21^{27} 24^9 Job 31^{11} ψ 26^{10}), frequently in the Prophetical and legal books = *lewdness* (Jer. 13^{27} Ez. 16^{27} 23^{21} Lev. 18^{17}), here badness in the most general sense. — The Heb. of the second line is lit.: *and wisdom to a man of sense* (or, *understanding*), which may conceivably mean that a man of sense is wise (an identical proposition), or that wisdom is as sport (natural enjoyment) to a man of sense (but *wisdom* is not parallel to *wrongdoing* — we should expect the name of the act, *rightdoing*). The natural subject of the second line is *wrongdoing*, and the predicate should be antithetic to *sport;* from the similar thought in 16^{12} we may here read *abomination*. Other proposed readings are: *a disgrace* (which does not furnish a distinct contrast to *sport*), and *as* (*object of*) *anger* (which gives the desired contrast, but the insertion of *object of* is unwarranted, and the *as* inappropriate). — The terms *fool* and *man of sense* have an intellectual and moral content.

24, 25. Fate of righteous and wicked.

24. What the wicked fears will befall him,
But the desire of the righteous will be granted.
25. When the tempest passes, the wicked is no more,
But the righteous is established for ever.

24. Antithetic, ternary. Lit. *the fear of the wicked*. The contrast is between *fear* and *desire*. Instead of saying that the desire of the wicked will not be granted, the author gives a more striking antithesis by declaring that the calamity apprehended by the wicked will overtake him. It is the ancient opinion of retribution in this world: every man desires happiness, and fears and apprehends misfortune — the good man shall have his desire (so ch. 3 and *passim*), the fear of the bad man shall be fulfilled. This opinion is combated in Job 3^{25}: Job, a good man, had feared evil, and it had come upon him. Our sage maintains the old view (which long continued to be the prevailing one), doubtless considering it to be necessary for the restraint of evil and the encouragement of good. The happiness had in view is general prosperity, without special reference to the satisfaction of a good conscience or the enjoyment of communion with God, and with no reference to the retribution of the future life. — In the second line the Heb.

has : *the desire*, etc., *he will grant*. The *he* is regarded by some
critics as indefinite (the resulting sense being *will be granted*), by
others as referring to Yahweh. Neither of these interpretations is
favored by the usage of OT., and the verb must be written as
Passive. — **25.** Antithetic, ternary. Lit. *at the passing over of the
tempest* (that is, of misfortune) *the wicked is not.* The Syr. has :
*as the tempest suddenly passes, so the wicked perishes and is not
found.* In 1^{27} the *fear* (= source of fear) of the wicked is
likened to a whirlwind or tempest, but (even if the Heb. allow it)
the comparison is not appropriate for the idea of impermanence,
and the Syr. is obliged to insert the word *suddenly* to get the
picture of swift destruction. The same construction (without the
suddenly) is given by Targ. Lat. and AV. — The second cl. reads :
the righteous is an everlasting foundation, not that he is a support
for others, but (as the contrast requires) that he himself is firmly
established. The verse sets forth the permanence and impermanence of the two classes of men : the wicked is swept away by
the tempest of divine punishment (1^{27}), the righteous is secured
against overthrow by divine protection (cf. 12^7 14^{11}). The thought
is adopted in Mt. 7^{24-27}.

19. For 𝔐 יֶחְדָּל 𝔖 has מתפצא (= יִנָּצֵל) and for פָּעַל, אולא (= פֹּשֵׁעַ), which
gives a less marked antithesis than that of 𝔐. — C. B. Mich. (quoted by De.)
compares the πολυλογία πολλὰ σφάλματα of Stobaeus. — **20.** 𝔊ᴮ πεπυρωμένος
(𝔐 נבהר), perh. for πεπειραμένος (Lag.) — **21.** 𝔐 ירעו; Frank., not well, *gain
as friends.* — The subst. חסר occurs in OT. only here and 28^{22}, the adj.
ten times in Pr.; לב is omitted by 𝔊, probably by scribal error. 𝔊 badly
ἐπίσταται ὑψηλά, = ירעו רמת (𝔐 ירעו רבם). — **22.** After Hif. of יסף the thing
to which something is added is introduced generally by עַל, sometimes by ל or
אל; here alone the vb. is followed by עִם — the prep. introduces the thing
along with which the עצב is not added. — 𝔊 follows 𝔐, but inserts explanatory
phrases : ἐπὶ κεφαλὴν δικαίου after εὐλογία κ., and ἐν καρδίᾳ after λύπη. —
23. חכמה in 𝔐 is to be taken as the antithesis to עָשׂוֹת זִמָּה. For ח Graetz suggests כלמה *disgrace*, as contrast to שחק, taken as = *sport*, a partial antithesis,
but hardly convincing. Read הֶבֶה. Frank.: כחמה. 𝔊ᵃ ἐν γέλωτι ἄφρων
πράσσει κακά, = ז בשחק כסל עשה, in accordance with which ᵇ might be rendered: *and (with enjoyment) a man of understanding (practices) wisdom*
(omitting ל), which has no advantage over 𝔐. In ᵇ 𝔊 takes הִבְנָה as pred.;
𝔖𝔗 follow 𝔊 in ᵃ (𝔗 עברתא for זמה), and 𝔐 in ᵇ. 𝕃 = 𝔐. — **24.** 𝔐 יִתֵּן,
hardly with subj. יהוה understood — there is no reason why י should not have
been written, if it had been meant (cf. ψ 21^8), and there is no trace of it in
the Vrss., except in Saad.; nor is there in OT. a clear example of the impers.

or indef. construction of יֵ֫רְ, not in 13[1] (on which see note below) or in Job 37[10] (on which see Budde's note). It is better, with 𝕾𝕿𝕷, to take it as Pass., and point as Hof. (cf. Job 28[15]), or (Vog.) as Nif. — 𝕮[a] ἐν ἀπωλείᾳ ἀσεβὴς περιφέρεται (and so 𝕾), where ἀπ. perh. = ארב, as in Jer. 49[28], and περ. = נבא (cf. Schleusn., Lag.). After [a] 𝕮[A] adds δουλεύσι δὲ ἄφρων φρονίμῳ (perh. from 11[23]), and after [b] καρδία δὲ ἀσεβοῦς ἐκλείψει (perh. corruption of [b], and cf. 15[7]). The additions do not belong to the Heb. original. — 25. In כַּנֵּד the ב is taken as compar. by 𝕾𝕿𝕷 Saad.; if this were the sense we should expect כ in [b], and so 𝕾𝕿 render; 𝕷 has *quasi* before *fundamentum*. 𝕮[b] δίκαιος δὲ ἐκκλίνας σώζεται εἰς τὸν αἰῶνα seems to be free rendering of 𝕳, and it is unnecessary (Semler, cited and approved by Lag.) to change ἐκκ. to ἀκλινής *unswerving*.

26. The sluggard.

> As vinegar to the teeth and as smoke to the eyes,
> So is the sluggard to those who send him.

A simple comparison, quaternary-ternary, based on some popular saying. The term rendered *vinegar* is used for any acid drink made from the juice of the grape (Nu. 6[3], forbidden, therefore, to Nazirites) — in some forms it was refreshing (Ru. 2[14]), in others unpleasant (ψ 69[21(22)]); see note on 25[20]. Hitz., Ew. render, in second cl., not so well: *to him who*, taking the Heb. word as plu. of majesty (like the word for *lord*). Grk., in first cl. *as unripe* (*sour*) *grapes*, perhaps scribal error for *vinegar*, and in second cl. *so is lawlessness to those who practise it*, which agrees well with the ethical tone of this chapter, not so well with first cl. It is probably a misreading of our Heb. text. Whether the proverb originally stood in this place is doubtful; it resembles in form the aphorisms of chs. 25. 26.

27-29. Contrasted fortunes of righteous and wicked.

> 27. The fear of Yahweh prolongs life,
> But the life of the wicked will be shortened.
> 28. The hope of the righteous will have a glad issue,
> But the expectation of the wicked will perish.
> 29. Yahweh is a stronghold to the ‹man of integrity,›
> But destruction to the workers of iniquity.

27. Antithetic, ternary. So 3[16] and many other passages — long life, a supreme blessing when there is no hope beyond the grave, is the reward of piety. The sage probably thinks both of natural causes (sobriety, etc.) as producing this result, and of im-

mediate divine action.   For *life* the Heb. has *days* in first cl.,
years in second cl. On *fear of Yahweh* see note on 1⁷.—**28.** Antithetic, ternary.   Lit. in first cl. *the hope of the righteous is gladness.*   The thought is substantially that of v.²⁶·²⁷—the aim of all
men, good and bad, is happiness—the cause is human law and
divine control—the good will, the bad will not, gain what they
wish.   Cf. Job 8¹³ ψ 112¹⁰, and so everywhere in OT., except in
the speeches of Job and in Ecclesiastes.   The aphorism looks to
the close of life.—**29.** Antithetic, ternary.   According to the
Masoretic punctuation the first line reads: *a stronghold to perfection is the way of Yahweh;* the parallelism requires that we read
(with Grk.) *perfect* (or, *righteous,* or, *pious*) instead of *perfection.*
But, as elsewhere in OT., it is always Yahweh himself, and not his
" way," that is called a stronghold, the line must be translated:
Yahweh is a stronghold to him who is perfect in his way, that is,
to a man of integrity.   The conception is the old-Hebrew one,
that the retributions of God in this life are determined by men's
moral character.—When (as in RV.) the " way of Yahweh " is
taken as subject of the sentence, the understanding is that the
divine government of the world produces the results named—an
idea appropriate in itself (see Ez. 18 ψ 18²⁵⁻³²⁽²⁶⁻³³⁾) ; but " stronghold " is a strange predicate of " way " (or " method of government "), and OT. usage is against such a construction.—In the
translation here adopted *Yahweh* is the subject of the whole
couplet, the antithesis being found in the two members of the
predicate, *stronghold,* etc., and *destruction,* etc.   We may also
take the second cl. as a separate sentence, and render: *but destruction will be to the workers of iniquity;* the antithesis will then
be simply between the protection given to the righteous and the
ruin visited on the wicked.   The objection to this rendering is that
it does not recognize the syntactical parallelism between *stronghold
to the perfect* and *destruction to the workers of iniquity* which is
suggested by the Heb.—both expressions appear to be predicates
of *Yahweh.*   The second cl. recurs in 21¹⁵, on which see note.

30. Permanence of the righteous.

> The righteous will never be moved,
> But the wicked will not abide in the land.

Antithetic, ternary. The general idea is the same as that of
v.²⁵, but there is special reference to the privileges of citizenship.
The sentiment of love of country was reinforced among the Israelites (and probably to some extent among other ancient Semitic
peoples) by a definite view of the relation between the deity, the
citizen, and the land. The favor of the deity was confined to his
own land and people, and the prosperity of the man was inseparably connected with his share in the soil. In ancient times this
view was held in a crude, unethical way (1 Sam. 26¹⁹) ; in Israel
it was gradually purified by intellectual and moral growth, but
never wholly given up — it was always in the land of Canaan that
the final blessing was to come to the people. The prophets interpreted exile as a temporary cessation of privilege, a preparation
for a higher destiny (Jer. 27²² Ez. 39²⁵⁻²⁹ Isa. 53). Thus possession of the soil, dwelling in the land, came to be the synonym of
the highest blessing (ψ 37⁹⁻¹¹, cf. Mt. 5⁵), and is so used here.
The expression retained its validity in the Greek period in spite
of the dispersion of the people (cf. Dan. 12 BS. 36¹¹ Enoch 85–
90). The reference in the first cl. (as the parallelism shows) is
to physical permanence, not to the maintenance of moral integrity.
See notes on 1³³ 2²¹·²².

31, 32. Speech of righteous and wicked : The expressions are
not perfectly clear; the text is perhaps in disorder. The Heb.
reads :

31. The mouth of the righteous utters wisdom,
    But the tongue of falsehood shall be cut off.
32. The lips of the righteous know what is acceptable,
    But the mouth of the wicked is falsehood.

31. Antithetic, ternary. The causative sense *utter* seems to be
required by the connection; but elsewhere (ψ 62¹⁰⁽¹¹⁾ 92¹⁴⁽¹⁵⁾) this
form of the verb means *sprout, grow, increase* (the causative form,
make grow, occurs in Zech. 9¹⁷). As the text stands, the antithesis is implicit. Instead of saying that the tongue of the wicked
utters folly or *falsehood* (as in v.³²), the verse, looking forward to
consequences, declares that it shall be *cut off;* the proverb in full
form would be : the righteous speaks wisdom, obeys God, and
lives — the wicked speaks folly, disobeys, and dies. It is a repetition of the familiar idea of precise compensation in this life; cf.

ψ 36³⁽⁴⁾ 37³⁰ 59¹²⁽¹³⁾ 144⁸ (the reference in the Psalms is generally to national enemies) Pr. 4²⁴ 10¹¹·¹³ 12¹⁶·¹⁹ 15²·⁷ Eccl. 10¹²·¹³, etc. — **32.** Antithetic, quaternary-ternary (or, ternary-binary). A simple statement of the difference between the utterances of the two classes of men. *Acceptable* is that which gives content, pleasure, to man (Esth. 1⁸) or to God (Pr. 8³⁵ 11¹ 12², etc., Isa. 49⁸, and, in the sacrificial ritual, Lev. 22²⁰, etc.). In the latter case the divine name is always expressed elsewhere in Prov., and the reference here must be to man. Good men, the proverb says, employ the sincere and kindly language that gives men pleasure. On the other hand, the *false* language of bad men, the parallelism suggests, stirs up strifes. The verb *know*, as predicate of *lips*, is somewhat strange. It might be taken, as in 12¹⁰, in the sense *regards, pays attention to*, but we should then expect *the righteous man* as subject; here we shall better, with Grk. and Hitzig, read *utter.** The proverb defines men's characters by the nature of their speech. — In the four clauses of the two verses there is possibly a chiastic arrangement, the fourth cl. answering to the first cl., and the second cl. to the third cl., so that the simple form would be :

> The mouth of the righteous utters wisdom,
> But the mouth of the wicked falsehood.
> The lips of the righteous utter what is acceptable,
> But the tongue of falsehood will be cut off.

26. In ᵇ 𝔊 παρανομία may = עַוְלָה (ℌ הֵיכָל); whether χρωμένοις represents שִׁלְחוֹ or some other word is uncertain. — **28.** ℌ תֹּחֶלֶת *hope;* 𝔊 ἐνχρονίζει, *lasts long* (because there is always hope), or, less probably, *is deferred* (because only a hope), or perh. represents some other Heb. word, as תְאַחֵר. — **29.** ℌ דֶּרֶךְ; 𝔊 φόβος, as in v.²⁷; 𝔖ᴴ (with note οἱ λοιποὶ ὡσαύτως) ὁδός, which may be conformation to ℌ, or may be original 𝔊. — ℌ הֹם must be pointed חָם; De. suggests that the Masoretes here pointed the word as subst. because the adj. is not found elsewhere with prefix. חָם occurs nine times in ethical sense (in poetical books only), twice of physical purity (Cant. 5² 6⁹), once of social habitude (Gen. 25²⁷); it is an ethical term of the later literature (Job, Pss. Pr.). — **31.** ℌ יָנוּב is doubtful, since it elsewhere means *sprout, grow*, and even Hif. is hardly satisfactory; Hitz.'s emendation יַבִּעַ is not improbable. 𝔊ᴮ ἀποστάζει may = יוּב or יָנַב (Jäg. in Lag.), or may be error for ἐπίσταται (so 𝔊²³·²⁵² 𝔖ᴴ) = ירעון (as in v.³²ᵃ). — **32.** ℌ יֵדְעוּן; we should probably read יַבִּעוּן (cf. 15²).

---

* Cf. Job 33³, where there is a similar difficulty, and the second cl. should perhaps read : *my lips speak what is sincere.*

XI. The contents are similar to those of ch. 10, but there are several new groups, as v.[10, 11], [19-21], [24-26].

1. Honesty.

> A false balance is an abomination to Yahweh,
> But a just weight is well-pleasing to him.

Antithetic, ternary. Honesty in commercial dealing. So 16[21] 20[10, 23], and cf. 20[14]; for the earlier legal precept see Dt. 25[15] Ez. 45[10] Lev. 19[36]. On *abomination* see note on 3[22]; originally ritualistic, it later acquired an ethical meaning. The moral rule is here connected with the divine will.

2. Pride and humility.

> When pride comes, then comes disgrace,
> But with the humble is wisdom.

Antithetic, ternary. *Pride* is here an overweening sense of one's deserts, and the *humble* man is one who does not overestimate himself; the latter term is in the Heb. a different one from that so rendered in ψ 9[12(13)] and elsewhere (which properly = *pious*); it occurs in Mic. 6[8] of humility before God, and might be so understood here *; but the context suggests the more general sense, referring to relations between man and man : as the haughty man makes enemies, is opposed and overthrown, so the humble man is complaisant, avoids antagonisms and disgrace, and is therefore wise. Such appears to be the antithesis : *wisdom* involves the *honor* or *peace* which we might expect to be put over against the *disgrace* of the first cl. *Wisdom* here = *good sense in worldly relations*, though it may also involve acquaintance with and obedience to the law of God, as in chs. 1–9. The term *pride* occurs 1 Sam. 17[28] Ez. 7[10] Jer. 49[16] (and the adj. in Pss.). With this proverb cf. 13[10] 15[33] 16[18, 19] 18[12] 22[4], and the Eng. "pride will have a fall," and for other parallels see Malan. — Instead of *the humble* the Lat. has *humility*, which gives a directer contrast to *pride*, though it is probably not the original Heb. reading.

---

* In the prophets and Psalms all things which come into rivalry with Yahweh are regarded as objects of his displeasure, to be cast down; this theocratic sense of *pride* is probably not the one meant bv the proverb.

3–6. The saving power of goodness contrasted with the destructive power of evil. The point of view is that of outward compensation in the present life according to moral character. The occurrence of these slightly varying forms of the same idea suggests the teaching of schools, in which sages would seek to inculcate a fundamental thought by repetition.

> 3. The integrity of the upright will guide them,
>   And the wickedness of the wicked will ruin them.
> 4. Riches profit not in the day of wrath,
>   But righteousness rescues from death.
> 5. The righteousness of the perfect smooths his path,
>   But the wicked will fall by his wickedness.
> 6. The righteousness of the upright will save them,
>   But the wicked are caught in their own desire.

3. Antithetic, ternary. *Integrity* is moral perfectness, freedom from misdoing — it is the quality of the *upright*, those who walk in the straight line of duty (rectitude) ; so (Job 1¹) Job is called *perfect and upright*. Opposed to this is the *wickedness* (deviation from the right way, wrongness) of the *wicked ;* this last term does not represent the Hebrew word usually so rendered; it sometimes means *faithless*, those who act secretly, treacherously, not keeping word with man or God, but, from the connection, commonly in Prov. = the morally bad in general. *Guide* = lead in the right way, procure wellbeing ; *ruin* = devastate, reduce to nothing. The proverb contemplates in the first instance the operation of natural, social law (the agencies mentioned are human qualities, *integrity* and *wickedness*), but doubtless with inclusion of the idea of divine reward and punishment (the upright, being perfect, are guided by God — the wicked, being bad, are destroyed by God). — **4.** Antithetic, ternary, or quaternary-ternary. The *day of wrath* may be the time of any crushing catastrophe, brought on by man or God ; here, from the parallelism, the reference seems to be to the crowning catastrophe, *death*, that is, death premature, sudden, violent, or otherwise unhappy (in second cl. Targ. has *evil death*) ; see note on 2¹⁸. In the prophets the *day of wrath* has a national signification — it is the day in which Yahweh visits the sin of Israel or of other nations with famine, pestilence, exile, or overthrow ; in the Wisdom books it is

the day (usually the final day) of retribution for the individual
sinner. The verse contrasts moral and non-moral defences
against misfortune; *riches* seems to stand for any social non-moral
power, with the implication, of course, that it is not allied with
rectitude; cf. ψ 49. Here, as in the preceding verse, the sage
may have in mind both natural and divine law, or ordinary social
law regarded as the law of God. It is not said that wealth is in
itself bad, but it is hinted that some men rely on wealth instead
of righteousness to save them from calamity — a condition of
things that holds good of Hebrew society from Amos down to the
second century B.C.; anywhere within this period such a proverb
may have originated. — *Righteousness* was sometimes interpreted
as = *almsgiving* (cf. note on 10²) ; see Tob. 12⁹, and cf. BS. 29¹².
— Saadia (10th cent. A.D.) renders in first cl. *day of resurrection*,
against the usage of Pr., which takes no account of the future life.
— **5.** Antithetic, quaternary-ternary. The figure is taken from
wayfaring : one man walks safely in a smooth, level road, another,
wandering from the main road, stumbles over rough places, and
falls irretrievably. See note on v.³; on the verb *smooth* (make
level or straight) see 3⁶. The agencies are here again qualities,
righteousness and *wickedness*, and the same union of human and
divine law as in the preceding verses is to be understood. —
6. Antithetic, ternary. An antithesis nearly identical with that
of v.³: goodness is socially helpful, badness is hurtful. The identity would be complete if we could render in second cl. *in* (or, *by*)
their own wickedness. The Heb. word (see note on 10³) has two
assured senses, *desire* (always evil) and *calamity* or *destruction*
(17⁴ 19¹³ Job 6³⁰ 30¹³); the latter is here inappropriate (RV. improperly, *mischief*), the former approaches nearly the idea of
wickedness. — The figure implied in *caught* (or, *taken*) is probably
that of a net (cf. 6² ψ 35⁸), possibly that of the capture of a city
(16³²). The term *wicked* of the second cl. is the same as that so
translated in v.³ᵇ.

7. The text is uncertain. The Heb. of first cl. reads :

When a wicked man dies, his expectation perishes.

The second cl., in its present form, can only be rendered : *and
the hope of strength* (or, *sorrow*) *perishes.* The abstract *strength*

is taken as = concrete *strong* by Rashi (who holds the reference
to be to the hope of the children of strong men), and by De.;
but the term (as De. points out) is never elsewhere used in an
ethical sense, and (though the inadequacy of strength, as of riches,
v.[4], might conceivably be referred to) we expect a definite ethical
term as equivalent or opposite to the *wicked* of first cl.; nor does
the concrete sense occur elsewhere.   The sense *iniquity, wickedness* or *wicked, unjust** is without support from OT. usage, the
plu. (found here) being never elsewhere so employed.   The rendering *sorrow* (Ew.) or *sorrowful* (Berth.) is not appropriate; it
is improbable that the expectation of the wicked would be described simply as *sorrowful hope*.   Failing a satisfactory rendering of the present text, emendations have been proposed: Graetz,
sons (= Rashi) ; Bi. *bad men;* or (by dropping the plu. termination) we get *iniquity*.   But, in the two last cases, we have the
proverb consisting of two identical propositions, which, in this
place, is a very improbable form.†   The Grk. supplies a desired
antithesis by rendering :

> When a righteous man dies his hope does not perish,
> But the boast of the wicked perishes.

This form, which is not supported by any other ancient authority,
looks like an interpretation of the Greek scribe, under the influence of the later belief in immortality.   The true text of the
second cl. must be left undetermined.   The form of the first cl.
suggests that the hope of the righteous man, in the sage's view,
would not perish at his death.   If such an interpretation were
certain (here and in 14[32]), it might help us to fix the time at
which the doctrine of immortality entered the Jewish world.   But
the doubt respecting the second cl. attaches itself to the first cl.
also, and we cannot regard its form as assured.   The more natural thought for Pr. is given in 10[28] 11[4]; cf. note on 14[32]. — One of
the clauses of the verse is perhaps a doublet, each clause having
originally read : *the hope of the wicked will perish*, and the doublet

---

* Saad., Luth., Hitz., Zöck., Noyes, Reuss, Str., Kamp.
† The change of form of the verb, from Impf. in first cl. to Perf. in second cl.,
is not to strengthen the thought (as if *perishes, will perish . . . has perished*), but
is rhetorical variation.

having ejected the proper antithetic clause which described the hope of the righteous.

8. Rescue of the righteous.

> The righteous is delivered out of trouble,
> And the wicked comes in his stead.

Implicit antithesis, ternary. *In his stead* means reversal of positions, not vicarious suffering (Isa. 53), an idea not found in Pr.; cf. 21[18]. The aphorism contains the sage's solution of the problem of evil. The righteous is sometimes afflicted — of this fact the sage (unlike the author of Job) attempts no discussion; but the affliction, he maintains, is temporary (so Job 20[5]) — ultimately the righteous is rescued (so 12[13]), and the wicked, cast down from his shortlived triumph, takes his proper place as sufferer. It is the doctrine of recompense in this world. The case of the good man's suffering and the bad man's prospering throughout life is not considered here or elsewhere in the Book. Cf. ψ 49. 73.

9. The righteous escapes the ruin which the wicked designs.

> With his mouth the impious man would destroy his neighbor,
> But by knowledge the righteous are rescued.

Antithetic, quaternary-ternary. The word here rendered *impious* seems to have been originally a ritual term, signifying the opposite of *pure, sacred* (so = *profane*), as in Isa. 10[6] (and the verb in Jer. 3[1] Isa. 24[5] Nu. 35[33] ψ 106[38]); then it passed to the sense of morally *impure*, out of relation with God (so RV. *godless*). Lat.: *simulator;* Aq. Sym. Theod.: *hypocrite.* The speech of such an one is false, malignant, likely to bring his fellowmen into trouble and death (as, for ex., by traducing them to men in power). There is probably no reference to the corrupting power of evil talk. As contrast to this we might expect in second cl. the statement (somewhat as in 10[21]) that the righteous saves his neighbor (and so perhaps we should read), instead of which it is said that he escapes (that is, apparently, the destruction of first cl.) by knowledge — either by general acquaintance with life (a result of devotion to wisdom, 14[15. 16] 22[3]), or by knowing the wiles of the impious and avoiding them. The converse statement is found in 10[21], where the righteous saves with his lips, and the

wicked die through ignorance. In general in Pr. the effect of
evil and good is confined to their possessors. — Grk.: *in the
mouth of the impious is a snare for citizens, but the knowledge* of
the righteous is prosperous, a free rendering of the Heb. (with
some changes of text), affected by next verse. — If we suppose
second cl. to be isolated, standing in no logical connection with
first cl., its meaning may be that *knowledge* (= wisdom) is the
saving thing in life — a conception which controls chs. 1-9.

XI. 1. 默 שׁלּמֹה; 𝕲 δίκαιον. On the use of δ. in the 2d century B.C. cf.
Deissmann, *Bibelstudien,* pp. 112 f. — **2.** On הרק see note on 3³ᵇ. — Stade
(*Wbch.*) suggests that זיד is Aram.; he refers to 13¹), which has the general
form of our v., only with מצב for הרן, and נסל *well-advised* for עני *humble,*
but such mutations of subjects and predicates are common in Pr., and there is
no good ground for changing the text here; cf. Lag. The occurrence of זיד
in Mic. 6⁸ is against regarding it as Aram. (Baumg.). — 𝕲ᵇ στόμα δὲ ταπεινῶν
μελετᾷ σοφίαν, in which στ. is perh. repetition from 10³², and μελ. insertion
for clearness. 𝕷, for the sake of formal symmetry: *ubi autem humilitas ibi
et sapientia.* — **3.** Kethîb ישׁד (adopted in 𝕿) is scribal error for Qerê ישׁבד. —
默 סלף; 𝕊 רבותא *pride* (a guess; cf. Pink.); 𝕷 *supplantatio;* 𝕿, verb נטרכלון,
shall be driven forth. The stem סלף = *move on;* Arab. *pass by* or *forward;*
Jew. Aram. *turn aside;* Heb. *turn aside, upside down.* — 𝕲ᵃ ἀποθανὼν δίκαιος
ἔλιπεν μετάμελον, perh. = ירם רנתה ... (Jäg., Bi.); cf. v.⁷ᵃ; see notes of Lag.,
Heid., Baumg.; 𝕲ᵇ = 默 v.¹⁰ᵇ. Θ = 默. — **4.** 默 ; 𝕿 כרבא *deceit,* = און. —
𝕲¹⁰⁹·¹⁴⁷ give 默; the v. is lacking in all other 𝕲 MSS., perh. by scribal oversight, possibly (Heid.) omitted from dogmatic considerations, because it seemed
to favor the rabbinical doctrine of justification by alms (cf. *Baba Bathra,* 10 a)
or by the study of the Tora (see the Midrash), against the Christian doctrine
of justification by faith. — **5.** 默 דרך; Bi. דִי. — 默 ישׁר; *Valkut* ילרד; *Ber.
Rab.* ידחה, both free renderings, or citations from memory; cf. v.⁶. — **6.** The
singular construction of ᵃ (וה without suff.) is not supported by Gen. 9⁵ (De.)
or ψ 32⁶ (Now.); these passages do not leave the reader to infer the subject
of the verb from a preceding predicate; read ברכב, with 𝕲𝕊𝕿𝕷. — **7.** See
note on this v. above. For the impossible אונים (elsewhere only Hos. 9⁴
Isa. 40²⁶·²⁹ ψ 78⁵¹, the last better דיע, cf. ψ 105²³) we may read (with 𝕲
ἀσεβῶν) אוילם (Bi.), or ייע (but this latter term cannot be taken as concrete);
but the form of the whole v. is doubtful. In ᵃ אדב, though sustained by 𝕲, is
better omitted, for the sake of the rhythm. — **8.** Impf. followed by ו + Impf.,
both expressing general facts, the second a sequel to the first; it is unnecessary
to point ו. — 默 יר; 𝕲 θήρας, = ירה (Jäg.) taken as = *persecution.* — 默 תחתו;
𝕲 ἀντ' αὐτοῦ, *for his sake,* or *in place of him.* — **9.** 默 רכה, *with the mouth,* as
ברעה, *by knowledge;* or we may write בפה. — הוף is *to turn away* (to good or
to bad), used in Arab. of persons in good sense, in Aram. and Heb. in bad
sense, of one who turns from religious faithfulness, *profane,* and so in Pr. of

the *wicked* in general. — 𝔊ᴮ ἀσεβῶν (אᶜ ἁμαρτωλῶν); ΑΣΘ ὑποκριτής; 𝔖 עָוֵל
wicked; 𝔗 נְבֵל *treacherous;* 𝔏 *simulator.* — 𝕳 וְיֵשְׁחָת רֵעֵהוּ; 𝔊 παγὶς πολίταις,
perh. = רי (or מֹשְׁחֵת) שַׁחַת.

10, 11. Relation of moral goodness to civil prosperity.

10. When it goes well with the righteous the city rejoices,
       And when the wicked perish there is shouting.
11. By the blessing of the upright the city is exalted,
       But by the mouth of the wicked it is overthrown.

Antithetic ; apparently quaternary-ternary. See 14^{34} 28^{12} 29^{8}.
The first couplet states the fact, the second the reason. The
counsels of the righteous, controlled by probity, bring blessing and
prosperity to the state ; those of the wicked, dictated by selfish
ambition and rapacity, bring destruction. This view of the relation of virtue to civil prosperity is found in substance in the
prophets (Am. 4^{1-3} Hos. 7^{3} Mic. 3^{9-12} Isa. $3^{14. 15}$ Jer. 22^{2-5} Ez. $22^{6. 15}$).
But, for them the nation is the unit, and the worship of other gods
than Yahweh the chief sin ; here the moral side alone is mentioned, and the civil unit is the city. It was in the Greek period
that the city-state became familiar to the Jews, and it seems to be
this later civilization that is here meant. — The expression *blessing
of the upright* might mean God's blessing on the upright, but the
parallel *mouth* (utterance, counsel) *of the wicked* (which is malefi-
cent) points to the beneficent words (involving deeds) of good men.

12, 13. Against contemptuous talk and talebearing.

12. He who mocks his neighbor is lacking in sense,
       But the man of discretion keeps silent.
13. A talebearer reveals secrets,
       But a trustworthy man conceals a matter.

12. Antithetic, ternary. Reversing subject and predicate in
first cl., we may read : *the fool mocks his neighbor* (so Grk. Str.
Kamp.) ; the sense is the same. The Heb. has *despises.* Contempt, lack of due regard for one's neighbor, may show itself in
various ways : in 14^{21} (where its opposite is care for the poor) it
manifests itself in indifference to men's bodily wellbeing; here, as
it stands in contrast with silence, it involves speech. A man who
speaks contemptuously of his fellow-citizens is said to be lacking
in *sense* (lit. *heart*) because he thus makes enemies and involves

himself and others in difficulties; it is obviously the part of *dis-cretion* (or, *understanding*) to keep silent. The reference is not immediately or mainly to the kindliness (to the neighbor) that should seal one's tongue, or to reflection on the fallibility of human judgments that should make one cautious (though these things would naturally be involved), but to a prudent regard for conse-quences in social relations. Nor is the line drawn between just and blameworthy criticism; the sage contents himself with de-nouncing contemptuous talk as a foolish thing. — Grk. *a man lacking in sense shows contempt for his fellow-citizens.* — **13.** Anti-thetic, ternary. A simple statement of two types of character. The Heb. expression describes the talebearer as one who goes about spreading malicious gossip — lit. *a walker of slander;* see Jer. 6^{28} $9^{4(3)}$ Ez. 22^9 Lev. 19^6. It is unnecessary to render by *he who goes about as a talebearer* (RV.); the *going* is included in the *bear*. In contrast with such an one the *trustworthy* man (*trusty of mind*) keeps silence respecting things which he has learned in confidential intercourse or otherwise — secrets of family or state; the reference is to things the mention of which is dan-gerous or undesirable. The first cl. occurs in 20^{19}; on *secret* cf. note on 3^{32}; the word is here to be taken in a general sense. The clause is understood by Grk. of political relations (cf. next verse): *a double-tongued man reveals the deliberations of the assembly* (or, *council*) — by the Lat. of private affairs: *he who is of faithful mind conceals his friend's act;* it is applicable to all the relations of life.

14. Value of political wisdom.

> Where there is no guidance a people falls,
> But in the multitude of counsellors there is safety.

Antithetic, ternary. A civil and political adage. *Guidance* is lit. *steering* — there must be some one at the helm; the guidance is assumed to be good (so RV., interpreting, *wise guidance*). The *multitude of counsellors* points not to any special political organi-zation, but simply to the need of manysided advice; that will be a well-governed city or state in which questions of policy are looked at from all points; Frank. refers to the "friends" of the Ptolemies and Seleucids. On the term *guidance* see note on 1^5; the word belongs to the poetical vocabulary. Instead of *counsellors* the

Anc. Vrss. have *counsel* or *counsels*. The proverb (which has no religious element) is not a folksaying, but the reflection of a man living in contact with public affairs. Hitzig cites, as representing the opposite point of view : "too many cooks spoil the broth."

15. Against giving security.

> He who is surety for another will suffer,
> But he who hates suretyship is secure.

Antithetic, ternary. A prudential maxim, the wisdom of which, as a general rule, is verified by universal experience, though there are obvious occasions when it should be disregarded. The word here rendered *another* (see note on 2^{16}) has three possible meanings : a person of a different nation ; one of a different clan, family, or household ; and a different individual. The strong Jewish national and family feeling might seem to favor the first sense, or the third, with exclusion of one's immediate family (father, son, brother). But the tone of the proverb appears to be universal, and in the later Jewish life the old relations of clan had partly vanished — the Jews became commercial, and needed commercial strictness ; exceptions might be left to the individual. *Suretyship* is lit. (as the Heb. text stands) *those who go security* (lit. *strike hands*) ; cf. 6^1 17^{18} 22^{26}. *Suffer* is *go ill*. RV. *he that hateth suretiship is sure* gives a good verbal play.

16. Honor to good women.

> A gracious woman obtains honor,
> Violent men obtain wealth.

Antithetic, ternary. This is the only verse in Pr. in which men are contrasted with women (such contrast is not made in 19^{13}). If the text be correct, the proverb relates to the struggle for riches and social position in communities in which women had some sort of influence, and the contrast is between upright gentleness and immoral force : an unscrupulous man may gain riches, but not esteem — a woman of gracious bearing, beautiful in manner (and presumably, in spirit) obtains honor. And as the industrious woman of 31^{23} helps to procure social consideration for her husband, so the honor here may be for husband and family, though women in Pr. (except those of licentious character) have no immediate relations with society at large ; but as there is no mention of family, it is probably better to understand the expression as referring to the esteem which comes to the woman herself from her family and her circle of friends. — The Grk. expresses a fuller antithesis by means of two couplets :

> A gracious woman obtains honor for her husband,
> But a woman who hates righteousness is a throne of dishonor.
> The slothful come to lack riches,
> But the manly lean (securely) on riches.

Lines 1, 4 represent the Heb. ; *for her husband* is interpretation. Lines 2, 3 are probably an addition by a Greek scribe ; *throne* is nowhere else used of a person (the expression perhaps comes from ψ 94[20]) ; *hates righteousness* indicates that *gracious* is taken as = *righteous;* line 3 may be rendered : *they who are slothful as to riches come to want.* — It is possible that the two lines of the Heb. verse are remnants of two independent couplets, the first relating to women, the second to men ; but the Grk. hardly gives the true text.

17. Kindliness is good policy.

> The kindly man does himself good,
> The cruel man does himself harm.

Antithetic, ternary. *Self* is lit. *soul* in first cl., *flesh* in second cl. ; the two terms are synonymous — the Heb. language expresses the idea *self* only by such words. It is on this term that the emphasis is laid ; it is *himself* that the kind man helps and the cruel man hurts — the one makes friends, the other makes enemies ; the commendation of kindness is based on its good results to him who practises it — a practical suggestion which would not prevent the sage's holding that it is in itself an obligatory thing. There is probably (to judge from the rest of the Book) no reference to the ennobling power of one quality and the depraving power of the other. The translation (Mich.): *he who does good to himself is kind (to others) and he who is hurtful to himself is cruel (to others),* is grammatically possible, but here improbable, because of the difficulty of supplying *to others,* and because in the context (v.[18-20. 24-26]) the subjects of the lines are such words as *righteous. wicked, kind, cruel.*

10, 11. קריה (v.[10]) occurs in preëxilian prophets (Hos. Isa. Hab.) and several times in Pr., קרת (v.[11]) only in poetical books (Job 29[7] Pr. 8[3] 9[3. 14] 11[11]); the use of the two words is not a ground for supposing difference of authorship in the two v. (so Hitz., who omits v.[10]), since both terms seem to have been common in the writer's time. — 𝔊[B] here omits v.[10b] (which it gives in v.[3b]) and v.[11a], making one couplet of v.[10a. 11b]; the omission, apparently scribal error, is supplied in 𝔊[AB b אּ c] (taken, according to 𝔖[H], from Θ). 𝔊 κατώρθωσε (העריץ) is changed to κατωρχήσατο by Lag., who refers the present 𝔊 text to Theodotion. — **12.** רֶעֶה; 𝔊 πολίτας, as in v.[10], a political interpretation natural in a city like Alexandria. — **13.** רכיל elsewhere = *slander;* so Ez. 22[9] אנשי ר׳, Jer. 6[28] 9[8], and probably Lev. 19[16] Pr. 20[19]. The vb. הרך has the sense of *going about,* Jos. 14[10]. For the construction here cf. Isa. 33[15] הלך צדק׳ *one who walks in righteousness;* cf. also the common construction in which ה׳ is defined by an Inf. abs. The st. is רכל *go,* whence the noun = *a going, gadding,* and, as the principal occupation of gadabouts is malicious gossip, *talking maliciously,* and so *slander.* הרך is sometimes followed by an adj. which describes the condition of the subject of the vb., as in Gen. 15[2] (*I go childless*), 2 S. 15[30] Job 24[10], and so ר׳ might perhaps be taken here (= *slanderer, talebearer*), but for the phrases in Jer. and Ez. above cited; but it is to be observed that the adj. after הלך describes the condition rather than the action of the subject. Cf. SS., in which both constructions of ר׳ are given, adj. under הלך, subst. under רכל. — On סֹ see note on 3[32]; 𝔊, freely, βουλὰς ἐν συνεδρίῳ. — **14.** יפל רֶעֶה; 𝔊 πίπτουσιν ὥσπερ φύλλα, = כַּעָלֶה, cf. v.[28] (Jäg.). — For 𝔐 יֵעַץ (sing., defining the category) the Anc. Vrss. read עֵצַה *counsel,* as in 12[15] 20[18], and this is perh. preferable as corresponding more precisely to התחבלת in first cl. — **15.** In 𝔐 רַע יֵרֹע the vb. must be taken as Nif. of רעע (not רוע, Ges.[26] § 67 t), and the רע as intensive nominal addition, performing the function of Inf. Abs. (cf. Ew. § 312 b); and we may point רֹע (Grätz). Siegfried, in *Wbch.,* proposes to omit ירע, or to read רֹ׳ ירע, Inf. Abs. + Impf. Qal, which is the usual construction; but, as Nif. occurs in 13[20] and the רע is intelligible, the change is unnecessary. — For 𝔐 כי ערב read יֵרֹב׳. — 𝔐 זר; Gr. לזר, as in 6[1]; see note on 20[16]. — The verb הקץ occurs in the sense of *making a bargain* only in Job and Pr.; this limitation is perhaps an accident. 𝔐 הֹקֵים, Act. Partcp., should perhaps be written הקץ Inf. — the ס may have arisen from following כ; SS. suggests Pass. Partcp. (cf. עָשֻׁק, Eccl. 4[1]); for Act. Partcp. as = abstract noun חבלם, Zech. 11[7], is not decisive. — 𝔊 πονηρὸς κακοποιεῖ (יֵרֵע) ὅταν συμμίξῃ δικαίῳ (זר) μισεῖ δὲ ἦχον ἀσφαλείας (הִקֵץ מבטה). In second cl. 𝔖 has *hates those who confidently hope;* 𝔗 *hates those who put their trust in God.* It was chiefly the word תקעם (𝔏 *laqueos*) that embarrassed the ancient translators. For further discussion of the readings of the Anc. Vrss. see notes of Jäg., Schleus. Lag. Heid. Baumg. Pink. — **16.** See note on this v. above. For 𝔐 חֵן we might read חָיִל, as in 12[4] (recalling also the אשת היל of ch. 31), but the הן also gives a definite and natural character. — Whether or not the expanded text of 𝔊 (adopted by Bi.) comes from a Hebrew MS. may be doubtful; but the strangeness of the expression θρόνος ἀτιμίας and the vigorous curtness of 𝕳 favor the originality of the latter. 𝕿𝕷 agree with 𝕳; 𝕾 follows 𝕲. — 17. 𝕳 שְׁאֵר; 𝕲 σῶμα; Σ οἴκους, probably for οἰκείους (Schl.); 𝕷 *propinquos*. — 𝕳 אכזרי; see note on 5⁹; 𝕿 writes a form of נכר, there properly, here improperly.

18–21. Contrasted rewards of virtue and vice. Antithetic.

> 18. The wicked earns delusive pay,
>   But he who sows righteousness real wages.
> 19. If one ‹ follows after › righteousness, (it leads) to life,
>   If one pursues wickedness, (it leads) to death.
> 20. They who are of wicked mind are an abomination to Yahweh,
>   But they who are perfect in their walk are well-pleasing to him.
> 21. The wicked will assuredly not go unpunished,
>   But the righteous will be rescued.

18. Ternary. The form of expression is taken from industrial life. *Real wages* is lit. *reward of truth*. The gain of a bad man is not real, for it is not enduring (10^{25}), and cannot save him from misfortune (11^4), but he who sows goodness shall reap prosperity (10^{24}) — his revenue is real and permanent, not illusive. The fact is here recognized that a bad man sometimes prospers, and the explanation offered is that his prosperity is only seeming; cf. note on v.⁸. The Latin has a slightly different form:

> The ungodly does unstable work,
> But to him who sows righteousness there is a faithful reward;

but the idea of *pay*, wages for work done, is clearly found in both clauses. Goodness, says the proverb, is commercially profitable — the pay is prosperity, insured by the laws of man and the favor of God. — **19.** Ternary. The second cl. is lit.: *he who pursues wickedness, to his death* (RV. *doeth it to his own death*). The general idea of the verse is plain : righteousness insures a long and happy life, wickedness a premature or otherwise unhappy death; see notes on 1³². ³³ 2²¹. ²² 3². The wording of the first cl. is doubtful. The more natural rendering of the Heb. is *so righteousness (tends) to life* (Saad.) ; this would connect the verse with the preceding as illustration or result (Luther has *for*, Noyes *as*) ; but such connection is contrary to the usage of this part of Pr., in which each verse is an independent affirmation, and besides, the relation of thought between this verse and the preceding does not suggest or justify a connective *so*. The word may be taken as adj., = *true, righteous* (Ew., see note on 15⁷, Jer. 23¹⁰), but *righteous in righteousness* is insufferable tautology; if it be taken as subst., = *that which is true, righteous, genuineness* (Rashi, Cocc. Schult. De. Str.), the resulting expression, *what is true in righteousness* (= not *true righteousness*, but *the true part of righteousness*) is unnatural; the renderings *firm, steadfast* (Zöck. RV.) are lexicographically unsupported, and this objection holds to Vogel's emendation *he who is firm in his walk*. The Lat. has *clemency*, Grk. and Syr. (by a change of text) *son* (Grk. *a righteous son is born unto life*). The expression *son of* is used frequently in OT. to denote doom or quality, but always evil quality: 31⁸ *sons of destruction*, ψ 79¹¹ *sons of death*, ψ 89²²⁽²³⁾ *son of wickedness*, and the common *son of depravity* (*belial*, 1 Sam. 25¹⁷, cf. note on Pr. 6¹²); the reading *son of righteousness* would give a not wholly unsatisfactory sense if *son* could be supposed to be properly used in a good sense. The Partcp. *he who pursues* suggests for the first cl. a Partcp. *he who follows after* (lit. *feeds on*, 15¹⁴); cf. 12²⁸, the form of which is similar to that of this verse. — **20.** Ternary. General statement of the moral demands of the divine favor; cf. 12²² 14² 15⁹. *Mind* (lit. *heart*) is the whole spiritual being. *They who are of wicked mind*, lit. *the wicked* (averted, perverted) *of mind*, are those who stray from the straight path of goodness. The *perfect* man is morally well-rounded, complete; the term in OT. involves general right feeling, but not absolute perfection of soul; see note on 2²¹. No heightening of effect or increase of intensity is involved in the sequence *mind . . . walk* (= *conduct*); the two terms are equivalent, each involving the other. The terms *abomination* and *well-pleasing* are opposites, originally ritualistic, here ethical; see Dt. 7²⁶ Lev. 22²¹, and notes on 3³² 8³⁵. — **21.** Ternary. The idea is a fundamental one in Pr., the reference being always to retribution in this life; see 1²⁶⁻³³ 2²¹·²², etc. *Assuredly* (so recent expositors and lexicographers generally) is lit. *hand to hand!*, the meaning of which is properly given in margin of RV.: *my hand upon it!* = *my word for it!* It appears to be a popular phrase of asseveration, derived from the procedure in a bargain, in which the parties clasped hands; so in v.¹⁵ above, 6¹, and Job 17³ *who will clasp my hand* (enter into a bargain with me, be my security)? The rendering *though hand (join) in hand* (RV.) = *though men unite their forces*, against which the form of the Heb. sentence is decisive; cf. 16⁵. The translation (Schult. Ges. after the Arab. usage) *from generation to generation*, = *through all time*, is not supported by Heb. usage. Saad.: *as the turn of hand to hand*, apparently = *suddenly*. Rashi explains the clause to mean: from the hand of God to the hand of the wicked the retribution will come. Targ. and Syr.: *he who lifts his hand against his neighbor shall not be held innocent of evil*, a mistranslation. In second cl. the Heb. has *the seed of the righteous*, the *seed* meaning simply *race*, as in Isa. 1⁴ (where the prophet calls his contemporaries a *seed of evildoers*), 65²³ (where *seed* is contrasted with *offspring*), and not *posterity* (a sense which the word often has); a reference to posterity (Berth. *al.*, in the sense: not merely the righteous, but also their descendants) would be inappropriate here, where the purpose is simply to contrast the fates of the wicked and the righteous.

22. Beauty without discretion.

> A golden ring in a swine's snout —
> Such is a fair woman without discretion.

A simple comparison, ternary, but with omission of the particle of comparison — the Heb. says: *a golden ring . . . is a fair woman . . .* The nose-ring was, and is, a common ornament of women in Western Asia, and in many barbarous and half-civilized tribes; see Gen. 24²² Ju. 8²⁴ Isa. 3²¹ Job 42¹¹, and Lane's *Manners and Customs of the Modern Egyptians*, Appendix A. The term rendered *discretion* signifies first *physical taste* (Ex. 16³¹ Job 6⁶), then capacity of *intellectual discrimination* (1 Sam. 25³³ Job 12²⁰), and apparently also ethical and religious judgment (ψ 119⁶⁶). It occurs in one other place in Pr. (24¹⁶), where it means *intellectual judgment, opinion, answer based on sound judgment*. Here the moral element is probably included. There is as great incongruity, it is said, in the union of beauty of person and deformity of mind and character in a woman as in the presence of a rich ornament on the coarsest and uncleanest of beasts (so the Grk.);*

---

* There is no allusion to a ring used to lead animals, for which process Heb. employs the word *hook* (2 K. 19²⁸ Ez. 19⁴).

this is no doubt the meaning of the condensed expression of the Heb. that such a woman *is a ring*, etc.

23. Character determines fortune.

> The desire of the righteous issues only in good,
> The expectation of the wicked in wrath.

Antithetic, ternary. *Desire = expectation.* Lit. . . . *is only good*, and . . . *is wrath* (or, *arrogance*). The proverb is susceptible of two interpretations, according as we take the predicates to express qualities or results of the subjects. In the first case (De.) the desire of righteous men is described as itself good, morally pure, embracing praiseworthy objects, that of wicked men as selfseeking, proud, arrogant (such is the sense of the word in Isa. 16^6, = Jer. 48^{30}). In the second case it is declared that the issue of hope will be in accordance with the character of the man — prosperity (divine favor) for the one class, wrath (divine punishment) for the other; the last word of the verse commonly means *anger*, of man (Gen. 49^7), or of God (Isa. 13^{13} Zeph. 1^{15}); such is its sense in 11^4, where *day of wrath* is parallel with (*doom of*) *death*. If the first interpretation be adopted, it will be understood that the hope of the righteous is fulfilled, that of the wicked denied (Grk. *is destroyed*). The second interpretation is favored by such proverbs as 10$^{24. 28}$ 11^7, and by the tone of the Book, which in general describes the consequences of actions. It is, besides, very nearly a tautology to say that the desire of a good man is good, that of a bad man bad.

24-26. Liberality or generosity, and niggardliness or avarice.

> 24. One man spends, yet still increases,
>   Another withholds what is proper, but (it tends) only to want.
> 25. The liberal man will be prospered,
>   And he who waters will himself be watered.
> 26. He who withholds corn, the people curse him,
>   But blessing is on the head of him who sells it.

24. Complete antithesis, ternary: one spends and grows, another hoards and declines. Lit. *there is one who spends*. The terms and the sense seem to be general — there is no special reference to almsgiving (as in ψ 112^9), but it is said that a just expenditure of one's wealth, in every way, is rational policy, tending to gain. That the reference is to physical wealth (and not to thought and act) may be inferred from similar expressions in Pr. ($11^{25.\ 26}$ 14^{23} 21^5), and that a general habit or policy is spoken of appears from the general character of the terms employed : experience teaches that the man of liberal methods prospers, and such an one, it is probably meant to say, has the blessing of God. The sage does not seem to have in mind a man's care of himself. *Proper* is that which is just, appropriate to the circumstances (the RV. rendering *more than is proper* is incorrect) ; *want* is lack, deficit. See a similar thought in BS. 11^{11}. In second cl. the Lat. (and so the Syr.) has, incorrectly : *Others seize what is not theirs, and are always in want.* — **25.** Synonymous (a form of rare occurrence in chs. 10–15), ternary. *Liberal man* is lit. *person* (lit. *soul*) *of blessing,* one who dispenses kindness, beneficence. *Prospered* is lit. *made fat,* metaphor derived from the condition of well-nourished animals or vegetables (Ju. 9^9 Isa. 30^{23} Jer. 31^{14} Job 36^{16}, cf. Pr. 13^4 28^{25}) ; the metaphor in *waters, watered* is agricultural. The reference appears to be specifically to kindly, generous conduct toward others ; the reward of such conduct is determined by social laws and by the divine approval. — **26.** Antithetic, ternary. Allusion to the practice of hoarding grain in seasons of scarcity in order to sell it at a high price. This is the only mention in OT. of this procedure so frequent in commercially developed communities ; Am. 8^{4-8} speaks only of eager desire to make money, and of fraudulent methods in trade. The practice here denounced probably became familiar to the Jews under Greek governments in great commercial and financial centres. Syr. and Targ. : *He who withholds corn in time of famine shall be abandoned to his enemies,* in which the last expression is based on a misreading of the Hebrew.

18. There is a paronomasia in שֶׁקֶר, שֶׂכֶר; the latter Stade would write שכר or שכרי (so 𝔖), since the usual noun-form is שָׂכָר; the assonance, however, may be intended; 𝔖 may be free rendering of 𝔐. The Participles express the general rule; עשׂה is to be understood in second cl. 𝔊 σπέρμα δὲ δικαίων, as in 𝔐, v.^{21b}, which see. — **19.** See note on this v. above. Omit the suff. in פֹּחוּ, as in all Anc. Vrss. — 𝔐 כֵּן; 𝔊 (followed by 𝔖) υἱός, and Bi. בן; 𝕿 הכנא מאן דעבד, apparently taking כן as = כאשר; 𝕷 *clementia,* perhaps taking צדקה

in the sense of *alms* (Baumg.), and נן from stem רעז, or possibly reading בן. The connection calls for a term parallel to the ברוך of ᵇ; Kamp. רֵעֶה, *he who associates with*, after 15¹⁴ Hos. 12² ψ 37³; Gr. בנן, graphically easy, but not appropriate in sense, even though, with Vogel, we supply דרכו; עשֹה is graphically possible in the old alphabet, but not easy; to חזן the same objection lies as to בנן; Kamp.'s emendation may be provisionally accepted. — **20.** In ᵃ 𝕲 has ὁδοί for רב, assimilation to ᵇ, and in ᵇ rhetorically inserts πάντες. — **21.** With יד דיו cf. the common expression תקע כף, *strike hands.* — צדקה ירֵע; 𝕲, not so well, ὁ σπείρων δικαιοσύνην, = צדקה ירע. — For ומלט 𝕲 has λήμψεται μισθὸν πιστόν, after v.¹⁸ᵇ (Lag.). — **22.** הב (favored by the rhythm) is lacking in 𝕲ᴮ, found in 𝕲ᴺ ᶜ·ᵃ; the epithet is often inserted in 𝕳, but sometimes omitted, as in Hos. 2¹⁵ Isa. 3²¹ Ez. 16¹². — **23.** חֵרָה; 𝕲 ἀπολεῖται, = אב־ה, and so De' Rossi 941, a natural reading, but not distinctly antithetic to the כב of ᵃ. — **24.** עֹשֶׁר; Perles, *Analekt.*, p. 88, עֹשֶׁר *wealth*, which is appropriate, but not better than 𝕳. — 𝕲, in ᵇ, εἰσὶν καὶ οἱ συνάγοντες, apparently free rendering of 𝕳. — **25.** In 𝕳 יִרֵא the א seems to be substitution, by an Aramaic-speaking scribe, for ר, which is found in many MSS. of Kenn. and De' Rossi (in which, however, it may be correction). The stem may be רוה, Hof. יִרְוֶה, whence רֵי, רָה, רֵה, or (Fleisch., De.), by metathesis, יֵרֶה; or, from st. ירה (Hos. 6³) we may get Hof. יֵרֶה, רה; it is, perhaps, better to emend to Hof. (Bi.) or Nif. (Gr.) of רוה; 𝕿 takes the form from Hif. הרה *teach*, 𝕾 from ארר *curse*, both improbable. 𝕲 is corrupt; its πᾶσα ἀπλῆ is perhaps for πιανθήσεται *will be fattened* (so 'ΑΣΘ), and its θυμώδης for μέθυσος (Σ), or perhaps = רעז one who excites anger; εὐσχήμων may = בב מראה, or may represent a form of יכה. — **26.** יקבהו; 𝕲 ὑπολίποιτο, = Aram. שבק (so 𝕾𝕿).

27. Kindness gains goodwill.

He who seeks good ‹wins› favor,
He who seeks evil, it will overtake him.

Antithetic, ternary. The word rendered *favor* may = *goodwill, acceptance* (12² 14³⁵), or *what pleases, what is acceptable* (10³², etc.); see note on 8³⁵. The *good* and *evil* are better taken in a wide sense, as embracing moral (as in Am. 5¹⁴) and general conditions (as in 3²⁷·²⁹ 13²¹ ψ 91¹⁰ Eccl. 2³), and as describing the man's conduct toward others. The second cl. declares that evil doing rebounds on its author — such is the implication in the expression *overtake*, lit. *come upon* (or *to*) *him*. The first cl. should give the antithesis to this: he who seeks good (for others), it will come to him as well. The Heb. has *seeks favor;* the *seeks* may be understood to mean *is thus really seeking (and finding) favor*, or, if this be thought to be putting too much into the word, we may change the text. The simple sense of *seeks* yields no satisfactory meaning for the clause. The *favor* can hardly be taken as = *God's favor*, for, if such reference had been intended, the divine name would have been expressed (De.), as in 12². If the favor be understood as referring to man, we have (in the Heb. text) the statement that he who wishes good fortune for himself must so act as to gain the goodwill of others, must do what is *pleasing* to them — an idea found nowhere else in Pr., and here offering no good contrast to first cl. Nor is the noun (*favor*, or, *what is acceptable*) elsewhere in OT. preceded by the verb *seek*, and it is better to understand some such term as *win, gain, obtain, procure* (so AV., Reuss). Yet this reading does not give a perfect antithesis, and it may be better to supply the divine name, and render : *he who seeks what is* (morally) *good secures God's favor, while he who seeks what is* (morally) *bad brings down on himself divine retribution.* Possibly the two lines belong to different couplets.

28. Folly of trusting in wealth.

> He who trusts in his riches will fall,
> But the righteous will flourish like the green leaf.

Antithetic, ternary. The antithesis assumes that the man who trusts in riches is ungodly, and that the righteous trust not in riches, but in God. *Riches* is here the representative of worldly power, and the admonition is directed not against legitimate confidence in wealth (as a means, for example, of doing good), but against the belief that it can save a bad man from the consequences of his deeds (that is, from human or divine wrath); see 10² 11⁴ ψ 62¹⁰⁽¹¹⁾. The metaphor is different in the two clauses — it is taken in the first from a building, in the second from a tree. Identity of metaphor may be gained by substituting *fade* for *fall* (see ψ 1⁸ 37²), by the change of one Heb. letter, or (as in the Grk.) by reading *rise* instead of *flourish*. The former of these changes gives a natural sense, but it is hardly necessary; difference of metaphor in two clauses of a proverb is not unnatural.

29. Economic folly of stinginess.

He who brings distress on his household will have the wind as his possession,
And the foolish will be slave to the wise.

Synonymous, ternary. For the verb *brings distress on*, or *harms* (RV. *troubleth*) see 11^7 15$^{6. 27}$ Gen. 34^{30} 1 Sam. 14^{29} 1 K. 18^{17}; *household* is lit. *house;* the rendering *inherit* for the second verb in first cl. (RV.) is possible (the man may be said to inherit poverty from his own folly), but the idea is rather that of coming to possess. The general sense of the verse is indicated in 12$^{7. 24}$ 14$^{1. 19}$ 17^2: the man who, by incapacity, negligence, or niggardliness, fails to nourish and build up his household will find his resources reduced to nothing; for *wind*, as = *nothingness*, see Jer. 5^{13} Eccl. 1^{14}. The second cl. restates the case: a man guilty of this economic and moral folly becomes literally or virtually a slave. The *wise* man (lit. *wise of mind*) is thrifty and successful, and neglect of one's own family is declared to be the sign of a *fool*. Slavery existed among the Jews throughout the OT. time (Neh. 5^5 Pr. 12^9 17^2 30^{10}, etc.), and later *; but whether the reference here is to the holding of Hebrew slaves by a Hebrew master is uncertain — foreign slaves might be possessed by a Jew, or Jewish slaves by a foreigner. — Possibly the two clauses do not belong together.

30. Life and death the outcome of conduct.

Our Heb. text reads:

> The fruit of a righteous man is a tree of life,
> But a wise man takes lives.

The *takes* is generally (as by RV.) interpreted to mean *wins:* a wise man wins souls (= persons) by his wisdom, which is understood to be morally good. But elsewhere in OT. the last expression of the couplet always means *takes away* (= destroys) *lives*, and must be so interpreted here; the resultant affirmation is, however, impossible. A better form is suggested by Grk., which has: *from the fruit of righteousness grows a tree of life, but the lives of the lawless are taken away untimely*, in which the word *untimely* probably represents an expression containing the Heb. term rendered *violence* by RV. (10^6 *al.*), and we may read:

> The revenue of righteousness is a tree of life,
> But rapine destroys men's lives.

---

* See A. Grünfeld, *Stellung der Sklaven bei den Juden*, etc.

Antithetic, ternary. *Fruit* = product, revenue (8^{19}) ; *rapine* involves the idea of revenue (or wealth) acquired by violence (injustice). The couplet may be paraphrased thus : the wealth which is gained by rectitude is a source of long life and happiness, while that which is gained by injustice brings death ; cf. 3^{14-18} 11^{18} 13^{11} 15^{16} 21^6. The result is stated in general terms — the agencies are divine and human. *Tree of life* is a familiar figure of speech, used in Pr. of wisdom (3^{18}), of fulfilled desire (13^{12}), of healing speech (15^4), and here of the product of integrity. — Another reading of the couplet is proposed by Grätz :

> The mouth of the righteous is a tree of life,
> But the wicked harms himself.

This gives an appropriate sense ; for the first line cf. 10^{11}, for second line 8^{36}. The changes required in the Heb. text by this emendation are, however, somewhat violent. Ewald and others arrange v.$^{29.\ 30}$ in the order : v.$^{29a.\ 30a.\ 29b.\ 30b}$, but nothing is thereby gained.

31. Certainty of retribution for sin.

> Behold, the righteous will be punished on earth —
> How much more the wicked and the sinner !

Progressive parallelism (advance from the less to the greater, or from the presence to the absence of a modifying condition), ternary. Instead of *behold* we may render *if* (so the Grk.) — the sense of the clause is not thereby changed. The verb *punish* is lit. *repay, give what is due* (for one's actions), the sense of punitive retribution obviously belonging to both clauses. The basis of the thought is the justice of the divine government : even the righteous will be punished for evildoing, then of course the wicked. The expression : " all the more will the wicked be punished " may appear to involve the idea that the divine justice, if relaxed at all, will be relaxed in favor of the righteous, and that, if it be maintained in spite of their claims, it will more certainly be maintained in the case of the wicked, who have no claims ; the meaning of the couplet may perhaps, however, be understood to be : " he who sins even a little will be punished, and he who sins much will receive greater punishment." It appears to be directed against those who fancied that sin might somehow escape God's notice ; cf. Eccl. 8¹¹, and, *contra*, Eccl. 3¹⁹ 9². By some expositors the verb is understood in first cl. as = *rewarded*, in second cl. as = *punished*, but this gives the unsatisfactory sense that God will more certainly punish the wicked than reward the righteous. Or, the verse is thus paraphrased (Str.) : the righteous are in general rewarded, though with real or apparent exceptions, but the wicked are most certainly punished — an interpretation which reads into the text what it does not contain. — The retribution is represented as coming from God (though it may come through man). *Wicked* and *sinner* are synonymous ; the terms appear to be separate grammatical subjects (not forming an hendiadys). The *righteous* are not perfect men, but men generally obedient to God, though capable of falling into sin. *On earth* does not express a contrast with a future life, but merely states that the world is the scene of life and retribution ; we might render *in the land*, as in 2²¹·²². The reading of Grk. (quoted in 1 Pet. 4¹⁸) *if the righteous is scarcely saved, where shall the ungodly and sinner appear ?* may be free translation of our Heb., the retribution inflicted on the righteous being taken as the means necessary to secure their final salvation, which is thus indicated as difficult ; but Grk. probably had a different Heb. text from ours.

27. For 𝕳 יבקש Grätz doubtfully proposes יפק *finds*, which occurs in 3¹⁸ 8⁸⁵ 12² 18²²; this is not graphically hard, and gives the desired sense. On שחר and בקש see notes on 1²⁸ 2⁴; ורש is frequently used of inquiry at an oracle (Gen. 25²² Ez. 14¹⁰), but means also simply *seek* (Dt. 22²). — 28. 𝕳 יבל; Ewald יבל. — 𝕳 יִפְרֶה; 𝕲 ἀντιλαμβανόμενος, = מעלה, as Partcp. (Jäg.) or בָּלִי (Ew.); Bi. reads מיברה as Subst., *höhe ;* Ew. יִיְרָל, as = *immer höher ;* Gr. כאהלם, *as aloe trees.* None of these readings offer decided advantages over 𝕳. — 29. 𝕳 עכר; 𝕲, periphrastically, ὁ μὴ συνπεριφερόμενος, *he who does not act humanely.* — In ª 𝕾 has a doublet, in one form following 𝕳, in the other 𝕲, in both cases with variations — an indication of the variety of sources from which our present 𝕾 text has been constructed; here it is probable that the 𝕳 form is the later. — 30. 𝕲 ἐκ καρποῦ δικαιοσύνης φύεται δένδρον ζωῆς, an inappropriate figure — the fruit should rather come from the tree; in 𝕳 the *fruit* (= *outcome*) is the *tree*, a mixed but not impossible metaphor. 𝕳 צדיק; point צֶרֶק, after 𝕲. For 𝕳 פרי Grätz reads ע, as in 10¹¹, which is, perhaps, better. — For 𝕳 לקח 𝕲 appears to have read לֻקָּה or נלקה, which it renders freely by ἀφαιροῦνται ἄωροι, *are untimely taken away*, and its ἄωροι probably represents סרם, for 𝕳 הכם (see 10⁶ 13²), ci. Frank. — 𝕾 follows 𝕲, with one variation.

— For 𝔐 נפשה הכב Gr. proposes ס.. היסי ה.., as in 8[36]; he should then read רשע
for דכה (cf. 10[11]). This offers a natural contrast, but the change of ־ to ר־ is
not easy. Read חטם for 𝔐 הכב (Frank.).— **31.** In place of 𝔐 בארץ, 𝔊 has
μόλις (a ἀπ. λεγ.), the origin of which is doubtful. 𝔊 may render 𝔐 וישֻׁרַט
paraphrastically by μόλις σώζεται, or μόλις may represent a separate Heb.
word, as כמעט (Gr.), or באלץ (Bi.), or באמץ (Jäg.); σώζεται may then = יישרם
taken in good sense, or it may = ־יְיר, or (Heid.) יבלט (it is nowhere else the
rendering of יערב). 𝔖 follows 𝔊, having רְיחֻפן for μόλις. 𝔗 appears to have
been influenced by 𝔖; it retains 𝔐 בארץ, but (here alone) renders יערם by
ימחסן, a term which elsewhere means *control one's self* (אפק), or *come into
possession of* (נהר), but here, from the connection, must = *strengthen one's
self, grow strong* (and in [b] it has : *but the wicked and the sinners vanish from
the earth*). 𝔐 and 𝔊 give two different texts, with different ideas; we cannot
combine them, writing בארץ יֻשֻׁלָב (Bi.) or כמעט י (Gr.), for ־י then gives no
appropriate sense (we get a good sense, however, by writing יערט). Either
text is possible; that of 𝔐 perhaps accords better with the general tone of
Proverbs. In [b] 𝔊 has ποῦ, = איכה, for 𝔐 אף כי; 𝔗 assimilates the form of the
clause to that of [a]. 𝔏 follows 𝔐. Saadia: *would to God the righteous might
be at peace in this world, then how the wicked and the sinner!* Cf. notes of
Hitzig, Heidenheim, Lagarde.

XII. 1. It is wise to desire instruction. — Antithetic, ternary.
The couplet admits of several translations. It may be rendered :

> He who loves knowledge loves instruction,
> But the stupid man hates admonition.

Here the man is defined by his attitude toward wisdom, — he
loves it or he is insensible to it, — and he will accordingly seek or
reject instruction. Or, reversing subject and predicate, we may
render :

> He who loves instruction loves knowledge,
> And he who hates admonition is stupid.

In this form the defining point is the man's attitude toward instruction, and the predicate states the result : in one case he gains
(and so shows that he loves) knowledge ; in the other case he virtually declines knowledge, and so proves himself stolid and irra-
tional. The general sense is the same in these two translations,
and either may be adopted ; but a more natural form is perhaps
gained by varying the order of subject and predicate in the two
clauses, and reading :

> He who loves knowledge loves instruction,
> But he who hates admonition is stupid.

The terms *instruction* and *admonition* are practically synonymous;
the reference is to moral and religious teaching; see notes on
$1^{2.23}$. *Stupid* (lit. *like a brute animal,* incapable of recognizing
what is reasonable) is here likewise an ethical term. The proverb
may allude to all sorts of teaching (by parents, friends, priests,
lawyers), but probably contemplates especially the schools or writings of sages, in which were given rules for the conduct of life.

2, 3. Contrast in fortunes of virtuous and vicious.

> 2. A good man will find favor with Yahweh,
>   A wicked man he will condemn.
> 3. No man stands by wickedness,
>   But the root of the righteous remains unmoved.

2. Antithetic, quaternary. *Good* is here used in the most general ethical sense. On *wicked* (מזמת, *wickedness, wicked devices*)
see note on 1^4. The word means *reflection, plan,* and is capable
of being understood in a good or in a bad sense; in Pr. 1–9 it
occurs in the good sense only, in chs. 10–24 (it is not found in
25–31) in the bad sense only, a difference of use which accords
with the view of difference of authorship for these two sections.
In the general sense of *thought, purpose* it occurs in Jer. 23^{20} 30^{24}
51^{11} ψ 10^4 Job 42^2. *Condemn* is a forensic term, = *pronounce
guilty:* in first cl. we might have the corresponding verb *pronounce right,* instead of which stands the equivalent expression
find favor; see notes on 1^3 2^{22}. The idea of the verse is divine
retribution in this life. — **3.** Antithetic, ternary. The thought,
familiar in Pr., that permanence comes only through goodness.
The result is no doubt conceived as effected by God, who, however, may employ human instrumentalities. *Stand* (or, *be established*) = stand firmly fixed in a position of earthly prosperity.
The figure is varied in the two clauses.

4. Wives, good and bad.

> A good wife is a crown to her husband,
> One who acts badly is as rottenness in his bones.

Antithetic, ternary. For other references to wives see 11^{16} 19^{14}
$21^{9.19}$ (= 25^{24}) 30^{23} 31^{10-31} BS. 7^{19} 25^{16-26} $26^{1.7.16.22-27}$ 36^{22-24} 40^{19} Eccl.

7^{28} 9^9; the treatment of family life belongs naturally to the gnomic literature both by the character and by the date of the latter. The wife of first cl. is described in the Heb. as a woman of *power*, *capacity* (חיל), a term which, when used of men, expresses the vigor or prowess of the warrior (Ju. 3^{29}, etc.), or intellectual strength (Ex. 14^{25}), or physical wealth (Ru. 2^1 Pr. 13^{22}, etc.). Of women it is used only four times in OT., once of Ruth (Ru. 3^{11}), and, in Prov., here and 31^{10-29}; in ch. 31 it describes a woman of good, vigorous character, especially of business capacity, and in Ruth it might be rendered *irreproachable* — the stress may be laid on general capacity or on moral worth ; here, probably, both shades of meaning are included. The words *virtuous* and *capable* are too narrow — the best English representative of the Heb. term is *good*, understood as including probity and housewifely capacity. Such a woman, it is said, is her husband's *crown*, his glory and joy, bringing him happiness at home and honor abroad by the excellence of her household arrangements, and the respect which her character commands. The *crown* signifies royal honor ; see 4^9 Lam. 5^{16} Job 19^9 Cant. 3^{11}. In contrast with her is the wife who *acts badly* (cf. 10^5) ; *bad* is here to be taken as the opposite of the *good* above ; such a woman destroys her husband's happiness and power as *rottenness* (*caries*) destroys the *bones*. The *bones* represent the substantial framework of the body (see 14^{30}). — Here and in ch. 31 the wife appears as manager of the economic affairs of the household, like the lady of medieval Europe. Though she is not spoken of as the intellectual companion of her husband or as the educator of her children, it need not be doubted that she acted in both these capacities. Her *teaching* is expressly mentioned in 6^{20} (cf. 31^{26}), and in the later history (Josephus, the Talmud) we meet with not a few Jewish women who, if not technically "educated," were capable of the best intellectual sympathy with their fathers and husbands.

5, 6. Contrast between virtuous and vicious in designs and words.

5. The plans of the righteous are just,
   The designs of the wicked are deceit.
6. The words of the wicked lie in wait for blood,
   But the speech of the upright saves [].

5. Antithetic, ternary. *Plans* and *designs* are synonyms — they are not contrasted as simple and not-simple (De.), and are not ethically distinctive; the first, here used of the righteous, is used of the wicked in 15^{26}, and the second is employed in a good sense in 1^5 11^{14}; they mean *designs* in general, and must be defined by distinctive predicates. *Just* is lit. *justice*. The statement of the verse — that good men deal fairly, bad men unfairly — is not an identical proposition, but is equivalent to *by their fruits ye shall know them.* — **6.** Antithetic, ternary. The first cl. is lit.: *the words . . . are a lying in wait*, etc., which may be interpreted, in accordance with 1^{11}: *relate to lying in wait* * ; but it is better to retain the lively figure of the text: the words (= plans) of bad men are assassins who treacherously lurk for their victims. *Speech* is lit. *mouth.* — In second cl. the Heb. has *saves them*, in which the *them* (which has no antecedent in first cl.) must refer to the *upright.* Such a reference, however, is not favored by the parallelism: the wicked, in first cl., attack others, and the upright, in second cl., should save others; good men, moreover, are, in Pr., saved not by their words, but by their righteousness (10^2 $11^{4.6}$) or by God ($16^{8.7}$ 18^{10} *al.*, cf. note on 14^3). To avoid the suspended *them* Bickell changes the *blood* of first cl. (Heb. *dam*) to *men* or *mankind* (Heb. *adam*); but so general a statement ("the wicked lie in wait for human beings, or for a man") is not probable; the wicked rather attack the innocent (1^{11}). It is simpler to omit the *them*, whereby we gain for the couplet the sense: "the words (= plans) of the wicked are hurtful, those of the upright helpful." — The reference in first cl. is to slanderous talk, accusations to great men, false testimony in courts of justice, and the like; the second cl. refers to the healing power of just and kindly speech.

7. Permanence and impermanence.

> The wicked are overthrown and vanish,
> But the house of the righteous stands.

---

* Wildeboer suggests that the author of 1^{11-19} had our verse in mind, and expanded its thought. This is possible, and would agree with the supposition that chs. 1–9 are later than chs. 10–22; but the idea may well have been a commonplace of the schools, and may have been expressed independently by different writers.

Antithetic, ternary. The same thought is given in 10²⁵. *Vanish* is lit. *are not,* = *cease to exist;* the sense of first cl. is : *the wicked shall be completely and finally destroyed, without hope of restoration,* that is, by judgment of God, with or without human instrumentality. The verse repeats the belief that virtue and vice are fully recompensed in this life.—The first cl. may be rendered : *overthrow the wicked and they vanish* (so the Latin, *verte*). It is taken by some (Saad. Ew. Reuss) to mean : "once overthrown, they vanish," that is, they have no power to recover themselves. Others (as Zöck.) interpret : "turn about and are not," that is, "vanish in the twinkling of an eye." These renderings are possible, and may be regarded as included in the Heb. words ; but a simpler and more natural antithesis is gained by the translation here adopted.

8. Intelligence commands respect.

> A man is commended according to his intelligence,
> A wrongheaded man is despised.

Antithetic, ternary (or, binary-ternary). *Intelligence* is capacity of sound thought and judgment ; so in 3⁴ (on which see note) 13¹⁵ 16²² 19¹¹ 23⁹ Job 17⁴ 1 Sam. 25³, and cf. the corresponding adj. (Partcp.) in 10⁵ ¹⁹ 14³⁵, etc. The opposite quality is *distortion, wrongness of intellect* (lit. *of heart*), incapacity to think soundly. The contrast intended is not of learning and ignorance, or of philosophical depth and shallowness, but of ability and inability to think justly in common matters of life. The proverb is a tribute to intellectual clearness, without special reference to, but doubtless with inclusion of, the moral and religious sides of life. The English term *perverse* (RV.) has an element of wilfulness which is not contained in the Hebrew ; the sense of the latter is better expressed by our *wrongheaded*, taken as = "incapable of just, discriminating thought, lacking in judgment," Lat. *excors*.

9. Comfort better than show.—The present Heb. text must be rendered :

> Better off is he who is socially low, yet has a servant,
> Than he who plays the great man, and yet lacks bread.

Antithetic comparison, ternary (or, ternary-binary). *Better off* is lit. *better.* That the term *low* (or, *lowly,* RV. *lightly esteemed*)

refers to social position appears from the connection, and from
1 Sam. 18²³ Isa. 3⁵ (RV. *base*).   The proverb does not commend
the social middle class as such (De.), but simply says that a man
of small social importance, if he be in comfortable circumstances
(this is implied in his having a *slave*), is really better off than one
who tries to keep up a certain state, while he lacks the necessaries
of life. *Plays the great man* is lit. *acts as if he were* (or, *pretends
to be*) *honorable* (or, *rich*) ; cf. 13⁷. We expect the man of the
second cl. to be described (in contrast with the *low* of first cl.) as
being really of high rank, not as merely assuming it.   But the
sage seems to have in mind a man of petty pride of rank, who
finds his pleasure in keeping up a vain show.   The proverb may
be a popular saying : comfort before show ; the case of a well-
born man struggling honestly and openly with poverty is not here
considered. — Some Anc. Vrss. and some modern expositors
(Schultens, Hitz. Ew.) render the second half of the first cl. :
and is a servant to himself (works for himself, is sufficient unto
himself), a sense which may be obtained by a slight change in
the Hebrew.   It gets rid of the statement (which to some seems
incongruous) that the socially unhonored man has a servant ; but
the possession of a servant, by no means improbable for a man in
moderate circumstances,* may well be put as an indication of
comfort, while, on the other hand, the expression *acts as servant
to himself* (*is his own servant, works for himself*) does not offer a
distinct antithesis to the *lacks bread* of the second clause.   Frankenberg, rendering : *it is better when one is despised for working
his field than when one plays*, etc., finds in the proverb proof that
manual labor, especially agriculture, was looked on as degrading.
But the opposite of this is true if we may judge from the respect

---

* At Athens the price of slaves varied considerably, but it was possible in Xen-
ophon's time (*Mem.* ii, 5, 2) to buy a slave for half a mina (in weight about ten
dollars, in purchasing power from five to ten times as much).   The possession of
only one slave was regarded as a sign of great poverty (Plut. *Apophth.* i, p. 696,
Phoc. 19).   In early Israel (Ex. 21³²) the value of a slave was 30 shekels of silver,
= about 18 dollars.   According to 2 Mac. 8¹¹ Nicanor (in the second century B.C.)
promised to sell 90 Jews for a talent, that is, at the rate of about 14 dollars a head.
A poor man might thus easily buy a slave.   It would happen, also, that a man
would inherit a slave, and, though reduced in circumstances, would then manage
to keep him.

with which work is spoken of in Pr. (6^{6-11} 10^5 *al.*) and in later books, as *Pirke Aboth* 1, 10; 4, 1. Ben-Sira, as sage (BS. $38^{25\text{ff.}}$), looks down on the ploughman and the handicraftsman who have no time for the contemplation of true wisdom, but he never speaks of work as socially despicable. — Some critics (as Kamp.) regard the expression as corrupt, and leave it untranslated. — A similar proverb, perhaps a modification of this, is found in BS. $10^{26.\,27}$.

XII. 2. 𝕳 is supported in general by the Vrss. 𝕲 παρασιωπηθήσεται, is prob. not from הרש (Jäg.), nor (Lag.) confluence of παρὰ θῶ (= מיהוה) and ἡττηθήσεται (= ירעץ Isa. 54^{17}), but free rendering of 𝕳 ירעץ. — **3.** 𝕲 ἀνόμου, perh. scribal error for ἀνομίας, perh. (Lag.) = רישע. — **4.** 𝕳 בצצשתיו; 𝕲 ἐν ξύλῳ, = בעץ (Jäg.), and following ἀπόλλυσιν, Jäg. thinks, represents the rest of the 𝕳 word, שתי. 𝕾 = 𝕲; 𝕿 = 𝕲, with transpositions. 𝕳 מבשה; 𝕷 *qui confusione res dignas gerit.* — For 𝕳 עברח Midr. Tanch. gives הפארת, citation from memory. — **6.** See note on this v. above. The suff. in 𝕳 יצרב is given in all the Vrss., but is better omitted, if 𝕳ᵃ be retained, so as to avoid the ambiguity of ᵇ, and gain the general form of statement which is found in ᵃ. — For 𝕳 רס Bi. reads ארם, which is too general a term in the connection; Gr. חמפם (see his emendation in 1^{11}), but this is not favored by the שרב. This objection lies against the reading רישעם יארבו לחמם, and 𝕳 דברי is besides supported by the פי of ᵃ. — **7.** 𝕳 הבד is better taken as Inf. Abs., = finite vb. (Ew., § 328 ᵇ), as in 𝕾𝕿; 𝕷 *verte;* 𝕲 οὗ ἐὰν στραφῇ. Gr., referring to 14^{11}, adds אהרי, but this is unnecessary, and mars the rhythm. — **8.** 𝕳 שכל is the specific Hokma term for intellectual sobriety. — 𝕳 ויעה occurs only here in Prov. (and elsewhere only 1 Sam. 20^{30}); the common terms are נפרל and עקש. — 𝕲 στόμα συνετοῦ ἐγκωμιάζεται ὑπὸ ἀνδρός, = לפי יכל יהרל אש יהלל; in 3 codd. of De' Rossi. — 𝕳 לבז; 𝕲 μυκτηρίζεται. 𝕾𝕿 = 𝕳. For 𝕳 יהרל 𝕷 has *noscetur,* and for לב נעוה לב *vanus et excors.* — **9.** Hithp. of כבד only here and Nah. 3^{15}; in Nah. = *show thyself* (really) *great,* or perh. *make a show of greatness,* here *act the part of greatness.* — 𝕿 = 𝕳. 𝕲 (followed by 𝕾) Σ δουλεύων ἑαυτῷ, 𝕷 *sufficiens sibi,* pointing עבד, and perhaps (though not necessarily) reading לנפשו instead of לו. Bi. עבד, and Gr. עבר (for ploughing), but 𝕳 עבד gives a satisfactory sense.

10. Kindness to animals.

The righteous regards the comfort (even) of his beast,
But the heart of the wicked is cruel.

Antithetic, quaternary-ternary. *Righteous* is sing. in the Heb., *wicked* plu. — rhetorical variation. The first cl. reads lit.: . . . *knows the soul of his beast.* *Knows* here = *gives attention to,* *comes into sympathetic relations with* (cf. Dt. 33^9 Job 9^{21} 35^{15}). *Soul* is the principle of life, common, according to OT. usage, to man and beast; it here signifies not the mere vitality (it is not that the good man refrains from killing his beast), but the sum-total of life as experience (cf. Ru. 4^{15} Job 10^1); the righteous man provides all things necessary for the animal's healthy and happy existence. The connection (cl. 2) indicates that the clause is of the nature of a meiosis: the good man is careful even of the lower animals, much more, then, of human beings. — The second cl. is universal in form: the bad man is cruel to all (beasts and men). The term rendered *heart* above usually means *compassion* (RV. *tender mercies*), and is here so under-stood by many Anc. Vrss. and commentators*; the oxymoron *cruel compassion* is possible, but occurs nowhere else in OT., and seems somewhat forced. In several passages (Am. 1^{11} 1 K. 3^{26}, and perhaps Isa. 63^{15}) the Heb. word in question appears to mean *bowels*, as seat of emotion, for which the Eng. equivalent is *heart*, and this sense may be adopted here (with De. Reuss, Str. Kamp. Frank.) as the more probable. — Kindness to domestic animals is enjoined in the Tora (Ex. 20^{10} 23^{12} Dt. 25^4), and the divine care of beasts is spoken of in Jonah (4^{11}) and in various Psalms ($36^{6(7)}$ $104^{14. 27}$, cf. 148^{10}); so also BS. 7^{22}.

11. Steady industry.

> He who tills his land will have plenty of bread,
> But he who follows useless pursuits is lacking in sense.

Implicit antithesis, ternary. Cf. 28^{19}, BS. 20^{28}. In second cl. the direct antithesis would be expressed by *will lack bread* (so nearly in 28^{19}), but the Masoretic form of the proverb, perhaps for the sake of variety, states not the result, but the quality of mind; such variations of apophthegms were doubtless common with the sages. Possibly, however, the second line should read:

> He who follows useless pursuits will lack bread.

The verse does not give special praise to agriculture, but takes it as a common pursuit, and as an example of legitimate and profita-

---

* Aq. Targ. Saad. Schult. Ew. Zöck. *al.*

ble industry; the sense is *he who seriously pursues a settled occupation will live comfortably.* The antithesis favors the sense *pursuits* in second cl. rather than *persons* (the Heb. gives simply the adj. *vain, unprofitable*); the reference seems to be not to idleness or slothfulness (Lat. *otium*), but to purposeless, unsteady occupations, perhaps also to immoral commercial and political practices. Agriculture was followed by the Palestinian Jews down to the destruction of Jerusalem by the Romans; see Joseph. *Ant.* 20, 9. 2; *War*, 7, 8. 3. — Grk. (followed by Lat.) here adds the couplet:

> He who indulges in banquets of wine
> Will leave dishonor (as a legacy) to his strongholds,

or, as Bickell emends,

> Will come to poverty and dishonor.

The idea is appropriate, but the couplet is more probably an editorial addition, or an extract from some current collection of proverbs, than part of the original Heb. text.

12. Text and translation are doubtful. The Heb. reads: *The wicked desires the net of evil men, but the root of the righteous produces* (lit. *gives*). If we understand the net of first cl. to be that which bad men spread for others, the result is an identical proposition: *the wicked desire the net of the wicked;* if the net be that in which bad men are caught, the resulting expression, *the wicked desire* (that is, in effect by their evil conduct seek and gain) *the net which entraps the wicked* is hard and unnatural. Others * render: *the prey of evil men*, taking the meaning to be that the wicked seeks (but in vain) to enrich himself by unrighteous gain; but, even if we accept the translation *prey, spoil* (which is without authority), the statement that the wicked desires the spoil of the wicked is in form unnatural. The second cl. also offers a difficulty: the verb there employed is used of a tree which produces fruit, but never of the root of a tree (RV.), and it cannot be rendered *shoots forth*, that is, sends forth slender stocks. Moreover, in all these interpretations a real antithesis is lacking. — Grk. has: *the desires of the wicked are evil, but the roots of the righteous are firm*, which gives a clear sense, accords in second cl. with v.³, and

---

* Fleisch. De. Noyes, Zöck. Str.

may be got from the present Heb. text without great changes, but it gives no good contrast in the two clauses. Targ., in second cl., *shall be established.* Syr.: *the wicked desires to do evil* (a change of one word in the Heb.). Lat.: *the desire of the wicked is a defence of the worst* (*things* or *persons*), *but the root of the righteous will grow.* — Various emendations have been proposed. Hitz.: *the refuge of the wicked is clay, but the root of the righteous endures* (or, *is enduring*); this form of second cl. is adopted by Ew. Zöck. Kamp. *al.* Grätz adopts the Lat. *defence.* Bi. transforms the couplet, reading: *the pillars of the wicked totter, but the root of the righteous is a fortress.* Kamp. omits the second half of first cl. (*the net of evil men*) as untranslatable. Reuss: *the wicked hunts for misfortune,* which he offers as a guess; Frank.: *wickedness is the net of bad men* (cf. v.[13a]), that is, they are caught by their own conduct. Hitzig's reading of second cl. (obtained by a slight change in the Heb.) seems probable (cf. v.[3]); in first cl. we should expect (as in v.[3a]) some figure of unsteadfastness (such as Bi. tries to supply); Frankenberg's emendation is the least open to objections, but it does not supply a satisfactory contrast to the second line. The two lines appear to belong to different couplets.

13, 14. The effects of speech.

> 13. By the sin of his lips the wicked is ensnared,
>   But the righteous escapes from trouble.
> 14. From the fruit of his lips comes [] requital to a man,
>   And what his hands do will return to him.

13. Antithetic, ternary. Cf. 10[11] 11[9] 18[7] 29[6]. *Sin* (or *transgression*) *of the lips* is any wicked, especially malicious, form of speech, which brings a man into danger by making enemies or exposing him to legal penalties; the reference is solely to the evil consequences of a man's own talk. The Heb. of first cl. reads: *in the sin of the lips is a snare to the wicked.* The form given by Grk. (requiring the change of one letter of the Heb.) is better: *the sinner falls into snares.* In second cl. the reference is to the guarded and kindly speech of the righteous. — Grk. adds:

> He whose looks are gentle will be pitied,
> But he who encounters (men) in the gates will afflict souls.

The reference in second cl. seems to be to litigiousness. De. suggests the emendation: *will afflict himself*. The origin of the couplet is doubtful. — **14.** Synonymous, ternary. Cf. 13^2 14^{14} 18^{20}. In first cl. the Heb. has: *from the fruit of a man's lips he is sated* (or *recompensed*) *with good;* but this does not give the general statement which we expect as parallel to second cl., and which is given in 18^{20}; the omission of the word *good* (which may easily have been inserted by a scribe) secures the symmetry of the couplet. We have then the declaration that every man must take the consequences of his words and deeds (cf. 14^{14}). The Heb. has in the two clauses two synonymous words for *man* (*ish* and *adam*). The marginal Heb. reading of second line is: *and what a man's hands do he will requite him for*, in which the *he* is regarded by some as indefinite subject (*one will requite*), by others as referring to God; but neither of these interpretations is supported by the usage of the Book. For the form of the text, *return*, see Obad. 15. — In second cl. Grk. (probably incorrectly) gets a completer parallelism by rendering: *and the recompense of his lips shall be given him;* the variant *hands* is better than *lips*. Syr., with slight difference of order from Heb.: *a good man shall be satisfied*, etc. — If the reading of the Heb. be retained, we have a progressive parallelism: in first cl. wise, kindly, righteous speech brings reward; in second cl. all actions bring requital. — In these two couplets the immediate reference appears to be to social law, not to the fact that God takes cognizance of words and deeds.

15, 16. Two marks of a fool.

15. The way of a fool seems to him right,
But a wise man listens to advice.
16. A fool's anger is displayed on the spot,
But a sensible man ignores an affront.

15. Implicit antithesis, ternary. It is assumed that the fool is stupidly self-confident and does not see the need of seeking advice. The reference appears to be solely to intellectual judgments, not to religious opinions, though these also will be included in the broader scope of the proverb. There is obviously here no condemnation of rational confidence in well-considered opinions.

— **16.** Antithetic, quaternary-ternary (or, perhaps, ternary). Lit. :
a fool, on the very day (on which he receives an insult, a disgrace),
his anger makes itself known (or, *displays his anger*), *but a sensible man covers up insult.* The proverb condemns thoughtless,
passionate resentment, and enjoins calmness and deliberateness in
the face of insult. It does not condemn self-defence, or resentment directed against wrongdoing, nor approve weakness, or cow-
ardice, or reticence under all circumstances; it does not relate
to forgiveness of injuries, or to the non-resistance described in
Mt. 5[38-42]; it simply enjoins calmness. The motive indicated is
not love or consideration for the author of the affront, but regard
for one's own interests, or for the general well-being. Quick
resentment is treated first of all as a foolish thing; doubtless it
was also considered morally wrong. On the term *affront* see note
on 3[35]. Cf. the sentiment of 11[2].

10. 𝕳 רחמי; 𝕲 σπλάγχνα; so 𝔖 (*the wicked, their bowels are closed*);
𝕷 *viscera.* On ר as = *bowels* see Ges. *Thes.,* and cf. רחם *womb* and (in Arab.)
relationship; whether the sense *mercy, love* is derived from a stem = *soft* (cf.
Arab. רחם), or is connected with the viscera considered as the seat of affection,
is uncertain. — **11.** 𝕳 הסר רב; Gr. הי לחם; Frank.: יחסר לחם. — For the additional couplet in 𝕲 see note on this v. above, and notes of Lag. De. Baumg.
Bi. — **12.** 𝕳 חֶמֶד; 𝕲 ἐπιθυμίαι, = חמדה; 𝔖𝕿 = 𝕳; 𝕷 *desiderium,* = חֶמֶד;
Hitz. הָֽמֵֽר; Bi. עָמֽוֹ. Frank. makes לחם (end of v.[11]) out of 𝕳 לב חבר (v.[11. 12]),
regards the ר of חבר as miswriting of ר (in following רעי), and attaching the
כ (of לב) to ר, reads: ברעע מצר רָעִים, an intelligible sentence. — 𝕳 מצר רָעִים;
𝕲 omits כ, for which 𝔖 has למעבד, = Heb. ירמעשה; 𝕷 *munimentum pessimo-
rum;* Gr. מצר רָשִׁים; Bi. (omitting מ) רעים. The simplest reading of ᵃ is that
of 𝕲, but it is not connected in its thought with ᵇ; the readings of Bi. and
Gr. are not natural; the true text can hardly be recovered. — In ᵇ we may
read איתן for 𝕳 ירן, 𝕿 ירירן, 𝕲 ἐν ὀχυρώμασιν (so Ew. Gr. Kamp.); Bi. מצר.
Lag. suggests that ירן may be corruption of the יין (𝕲 οἴνων) of ᶜ. For other
emendations see Nowack. — **13.** 𝕳 בקש; 𝕲 ἐμπίπτει εἰς παγίδας; read נקש
or יקש. — 𝕳 ויצא, ו + Impf., rhetorical sequence. — On the additional couplet
in 𝕲 see Lag. and Bickell; Bi.'s וקרא בשׁער (= 𝕲 ὁ δὲ συναντῶν ἐν πύλαις) is
suspicious (*cry in the gate* is not the natural antithesis to *have a gentle look*),
and the couplet, while it looks like a bad translation from Hebrew, is of
doubtful origin. — **14.** On the omission of מב see note on this v. above. —
𝕳 אישׁ; 𝕲 ψυχὴ ἀνδρός, in which ψ. is probably interpretation of the Grk.
translator (deleted by Lag.); a נכש in the Heb. would mar the rhythm. —
𝕳 ירו; 𝕲ᴮ, not so well, χειλέων (23. 157 χειρῶν, and so 𝔖ᴴ). — **16.** 𝕳 יודע;
the Vrss. understand the form as Hifil. — 𝕳 ביום; Gr. ביומו.

17–19. Good and bad speech.

> 17. He who speaks out the truth affirms justice,
> But a false witness (affirms) injustice.
> 18. Some men's chatter is like sword-thrusts,
> But the tongue of the wise is healing.
> 19. The lip of truth endures for ever,
> But the lying tongue is but for a moment.

17. Antithetic, ternary. The reference is to the depositions of witnesses before a legal tribunal. The verb rendered *speaks out* appears to have a technical legal sense; it is used of giving legal testimony in 6^{19} $14^{5.\ 25}$ $19^{5.\ 9}$; the first line, therefore, may be translated: *a true witness affirms*, etc. The rendering *injustice* (the word is usually translated *deceit*, as in 11^1) is supported by Job 15^{35} $\psi\ 43^1\ 55^{23(24)}$, and is here required by the antithesis if *justice* be written in the first line; but the antithesis may also be *truth . . . falsehood*. Testimony in a court of law, says the proverb, is public affirmation of justice and order, or of their contraries; a false witness sins against the fundamental principle of social life. The prominence given in the Book to the crime of perjury indicates that it was not uncommon. On the term *justice* see notes on $1^3\ 2^{20}$. — **18.** Antithetic, ternary. Lit.: *there is one who chatters like the thrusts of a sword, but*, etc. The person of first cl. is impliedly *foolish*. The verb of first cl. is used in Lev. 5^4 of the unwary utterance in which a man unconsciously binds himself by an oath (and so the corresponding noun in Nu. $30^{6.\ 8(7.\ 9)}$); in $\psi\ 106^{33}$ it describes a hasty, unadvised speech of which Moses was once guilty (Nu. 20^{10-13}); here it means the thoughtless talk which, taking no heed of what is due to men, wounds them by unkindness or imprudence. In contrast with this is the sympathetic and wise speech which heals suffering and saves from disaster. The proverb breathes a fine air of elevated benevolent feeling, the reference being not especially to testimony in court, but to general relations of life. — **19.** Antithetic, ternary. *For a moment* is lit. " for an eye-wink." The affirmation appears to be general: truth, supported by facts, and having the approval of men and God, is permanent; falsehood, unsupported and unapproved, speedily passes away. Similar aphorisms are found among other peoples; Delitzsch cites (from Dukes) later Heb. proverbs, which, however, are probably based on this. — Grk. (departing somewhat from our Heb. text) understands the reference to be to courts of law: *true lips establish testimony, but a hasty witness has an unjust tongue*, a reading which resembles v.¹⁷, but is here less probable than the form of the Hebrew.

20–23. Of falsehood and folly. — Antithetic, ternary.

> 20. Injustice is the purpose of those who devise evil,
>   But they whose plans promote well-being are ‹just.›
> 21. No mischief befalls the righteous,
>   But the wicked are full of misfortune.
> 22. Lying lips are an abomination to Yahweh,
>   But they who deal truly are his delight.
> 23. A man of sense keeps back his knowledge,
>   But fools proclaim their foolishness.

20. Lit.: *injustice is in the hearts of those who*, etc., is their purpose, belongs to their nature, and is the product of their acts. On *injustice* (RV. *deceit*) see note on v.¹⁷; lack of fairness and truthfulness is injustice. On *devise evil* see 3²⁹ 6¹⁴·¹⁸ 1 Sam. 23⁹. — The second cl. in the Heb. reads: *but to the counsellors of well-being there is joy.* The *counsellors of well-being* are those whose designs and plans are such as to promote the welfare of their fellow-beings; for this sense, *plan* or *design*, see Isa. 14²⁴. But the term *joy* of second cl. stands in no natural connection with the *injustice* or *deceit* of first cl. This latter term expresses the purpose of wicked men, and we should expect the corresponding term of second cl. to express the purpose of good men, their sincerity and equity. Such is the contrast given in v.⁵ of this chapter, and obtainable here by a slight change of the Heb., with the reading: *to the designers of well-being there is justice.* — If the *joy* of the Heb. be retained, the couplet must be interpreted to mean: wicked men design injustice, but the good men, purposing good to others, will be rewarded with joy or happiness. This is a possible but not natural and easy antithesis. In 21¹⁵ it is said that the practice of justice is joy to the just man, but the omission of the subject (the practice of justice), as is here assumed, would be hard. — On *well-being* (RV. *peace*), = "wholeness, completeness of being," see note on 3². *Counsellors of well-being = benevolent,* *righteous men.* The interpretation of *joy* as that which the good man procures for others is hardly allowed by the Heb.; see 10^{28} 15^{23} 21^{15}, where the joy is subjective, and similar constructions in 10^{16} 11^{26} etc. — **21.** The doctrine of full compensation in this life. *Mischief* and *misfortune* (RV. *evil*) are synonymous, and here refer not to moral depravation, but to outward suffering as the punishment inflicted by God. On *mischief* as = *misfortune* see 22^8 Job 5^6 21^{19}; on *misfortune* see notes on 3^{30} $6^{14.\ 18}$ 11^{27} 13^{17} 14^{16} 16^4 31^{12}. — Grk. Targ. Syr. give a different idea:

> No injustice is pleasing to the righteous,
> But the ungodly are (or, will be) full of evil.

This conception (representing a somewhat different Heb. text from ours) is appropriate, and may be the original form of the couplet. — **22.** The same general thought is found in $10^{31.\ 32}$ 12^{19} 13^5 16^{13} 20^{23}, and the same predicates in 11^{20}. On *abomination* see note on 3^{32}. — **23.** Wise reticence and foolish blabbing. *Keeps* (or *holds*) *back* (lit. *conceals*) = "holds in reserve, is not forward to display." The second cl. is lit.: *the heart* (= mind, nature) *of fools proclaims*, etc. The verse is an aphorism of prudence, sagacity, the quality to which Proverbs gives such prominence. The fool rushes in, displays his folly, is despised and gets into trouble; the man of common sense is cautious, reserved. The allusion is to circumstances which demand caution; outspokenness under certain conditions is approved in such passages as 15^2. But the Book reflects a society (large cities and arbitrary government) in which silence is golden. — For *keeps back* Grätz proposes to read *utters*, but this gives up the striking antithesis of the Masoretic Hebrew text, which is supported by $17^{27.\ 28}$ and other proverbs.

24. Industry brings success.

> The hand of the diligent will bear rule,
> But the slothful will be tributary.

Antithetic, ternary (or, binary-ternary). Praise of industry is found in 10^4 12^{27} 13^4 19^{15} 21^5, and satire on sloth in 6^{6-11} 24^{30-34}. While the idea is common to all times and peoples, this form of the apophthegm is suggested by political relations — it is learned rather than popular: a vigorous nation rules over its neighbors, a feeble nation pays tribute ; an industrious man attains wealth, high position, influence, power (22^{29}), a slothful man loses his wealth and becomes dependent (11^{29}). *Slothful* is lit. *slothfulness*. For *tributary* ($=$ *under tribute*) see Ju. 1^{28-30} I K. 4^6 Lam. 1^1 Isa. 31^8. — The couplet may be more tersely rendered :

> The diligent bear rule,
> The slothful are underlings.

25. Power of sympathy.

> Anxiety in a man's mind bows it down,
> But a kind word makes it glad.

Implicit or progressive antithesis, ternary : a kind word dispels anxiety and makes glad. Instead of *kind* (lit. *good*) *word* Grk. has *good news*, but the antithesis rather points to friendly, sympathetic words.

17. 頂 יֵרְדְּ, Hif. (without subject expressed), for which Lag. (p. vii) proposes יֵרֶד־, as in ψ 27^{12}; De. (here and on 6^{19}) defends 頂, but the construction is hard, and Lag.'s reading seems preferable; see notes on 6^{19} 14^5. De. remarks that elsewhere in Pr. 'י stands with כּוֹבֵם (he should except 29^8); but this may be accidental. — ᵹ: ἐπιδεικνυμένην πίστιν ἐπαγγέλλει δίκαιος; ἐπιδ. may perhaps (Jäg.) represent a form of הֵפִּ, taken as = *affirm* (in a court of justice), though elsewhere in Pr. (exc. $19^{5(2)}$ ἐγκαλῶν) 'ה is rendered by ἐκκαίειν; Lag.'s suggestion, יֵרְדְּ, is not probable, since this vb. is regularly represented by ἐλέγχειν (cf., however, ἐλ. *attest* and ἐπιδ. *demonstrate, prove*, in a court of law). — **18.** 頂 בְּמַה (בָּטָא), *to speak thoughtlessly* (understood by ᵹᏚᏛ as = simply *speak*) may be mimetic (hardly connected historically with βαττολογεῖν); ᎾᏞ render freely *promise* (according to Lag. they read בְּמַה). — ᵹᴮ μάχαιραι; read, with H-P 103 *al.*, μαχαίρᾳ, or insert ὡς, with 68. — **19.** 頂 רִבֶּן לְיֵר; ᵹ κατορθοῖ μαρτυρίαν, = הָכֵן לֵיֵר (Jäg.), the ל being taken (in Aram. fashion) as introducing the object, or perhaps the ל had fallen out; in ᵇ also the עֵד was read improperly as יֵר. — Ꮮ in ᵃ = 頂, in ᵇ = ᵹ; Ꮪ in ᵃ free, in ᵇ follows ᵹ; Ꮯ in ᵃ = 頂, in ᵇ follows ᵹ. ᵹ's rendering of ᵇ is thus strongly supported, but 頂 is favored by the antithesis. The form אַרְגִּיעָה is commonly explained as I pers. sing. Hif. Impf., but it is a noun, sometimes (Jer. 49^{19} 50^{44}) used adverbially; it appears to be an Inf. of Aram. form (less probably = אֶרְגִּע, from רֵיעַ, with א prosthetic). — **20.** 頂 חרש, in the sense of *mental construction*, is a Hokma term (3^{29} $6^{14.\,18}$ 14^{22}); but see also I Sam. 23^9 Hos. 10^{13} Job 4^8. — Note assonance in מֶרְפָּה, שִׂמְחָה; for the latter term Gr. proposes אֶמְנָה; it is better to read מִשְׁפַּט. — ᵹ βουλόμενοι; read βουλευόμενοι, with Ꮪᴴ ᵐᵃʳᵍ· 23 (Lag.). — **21.** 頂 יִאָנֶה; ᵹ (and so ᏚᏛ) ἀρέσει, = נָאוֶה, a not improbable reading. — **22.** 頂 יֵרֵ; Gr. suggests וּלְשׁוֹן, as parallel to שִׂפְתֵי, but the vari﹣

tion of 𝔐 is natural and effective. — **23.** For 𝔐 אֲוִלֶת, יְהְרָא, לֹסֵה, 𝔊 has θρόνος
(כסא), συναντήσεται (from יקרא), ἀπαῖς (אך), all misreadings. — 𝔗ᵇ, paraphrasing, סאני ייריא. — 𝔖 in ᵃ = 𝔊, in ᵇ apparently = 𝔐, rendering אזרז by בישתא;
cf. Pinkuss' note. — 𝕷 = 𝔐. — **24.** The adj. חרוץ, in sense of *diligent*, only in
Pr. (cf. the vb. in 2 Sam. 5²¹), elsewhere (Isa. 41¹⁵) *sharp ;* 𝔊 ἐκλεκτῶν, free
rendering, or (Baumg.) connected with ח־ *pure gold ;* cf. Job 37¹¹(¹⁰), where
ἐκλ. represents ברי, taken by 𝔊 as one word, and connected with בר *chosen,*
brilliant, and Pr. 12²⁷ where καθαρός = ח־. — **25.** 𝔊 renders freely: φοβερὸς
λόγος = רצוה; ταράσσει = ישחה; δικαίου is added to איש as interpretation;
ἀγγελία = דבר (it is unnecessary to suppose, with Gr., that 𝔊 read בשׂרה).
𝔐 is reproduced substantially by 𝔖𝔗𝕷, and ᵃ by Θ; but 𝔖𝔗 give the φοβ. and
ταρ. of 𝔊, which, here as elsewhere, appears to have influenced these Vrss.

26. A satisfactory translation of this couplet can hardly be
given. The second cl., *the way of the wicked misleads them* (or,
leads them to destruction) is intelligible, though in form somewhat
strange. A man's *way* (common metaphor for *conduct, manner
of life*) is described in OT. as easy or hard, or as leading to happiness or to misfortune, or it is said that men go astray or are led
astray (by God or man) in their way, but it is never elsewhere
said that the way itself causes men to wander; see 1¹⁹⁻³¹ 2¹²⁻²⁰ 3⁶. ¹⁷
4²⁶ 8²⁰ 13¹⁵ 14¹² 15¹⁹ *al.*; we should perhaps read: *the way of the
wicked is error*, or *the wicked goes astray in his way.* — In contrast with this we expect in first cl. some such statement as *the
path of the righteous is straight* (cf. 15¹⁹), or *the righteous departs
from evil* (cf. 16¹⁷), but the text offers no such thought. The
Heb., as it stands, must be rendered: *the righteous searches out*
(= explores, studies) *his friend*, which here yields no satisfactory
sense. A change in the Heb. preposition gives . . . *explores* (the
way) *for his friend* (or, *neighbor*), which is hardly apposite; and
the same remark holds of Ewald's translation (adopted, apparently, by RV.) . . . *is a guide to . . .*, in which, moreover, the
rendering *guide* is unwarranted. — The Anc. Vrss. give no material
help. Grk.: *a just arbiter will be his own friend*, perhaps corrupt for *the just is his own friend*, or *the just man knows his
friend;* Aq.: *he who makes his neighbor rich* (lit. *to abound*) *is
just* (or *righteous*); Targ. (followed by Saad. Rashi): *the righteous
is better than his neighbor;* Syr.: *the righteous gives his friend
good counsel* (= . . . *is a guide to . . .*) ; Lat.: *he who ignores
loss for his friend's sake is just.* — Most modern expositors (fol-

lowing Döderlein) prefer to change the vowels of one word and render : *the righteous searches out his pasture*, that is, superior to sinful desire, seeks (and finds) moral and religious nourishment *
—a figure taken from pastoral life in which good pasturage stands for well-being and happiness (Job 12²⁴). But the expression, used appropriately of the wild ox (Job 39⁸), is never elsewhere employed of man (not in Ez. 34¹⁴·¹⁸), and is somewhat strange and forced. The verb of the clause is suspicious ; it is used in the earlier literature of the selection of a camping-ground (Dt. 1³³ Nu. 10³³) or of a country, for example, by Yahweh (Ez. 20⁶), of the investigation of Canaan by the spies (Nu. 13², and frequently in Nu. 13. 14), perhaps of a specifically military reconnoissance (Ju. 1²³, but the text is doubtful), later of reflection (Nu. 15³⁹) and intellectual investigation (Eccl. 1¹³) ; it does not seem to be appropriate here. — The simplest emendation or interpretation is that of Targ., followed by AV. : *the righteous is more excellent* (marg. *abundant*) *than his neighbor*, but this is neither apposite in itself, nor related to second cl. We can only surmise, from comparison of 14²² 16¹⁷ 21¹⁶, that the general sense of the couplet is : *the righteous departs from evil, but the wicked strays from the (right) way*. The two lines may be, however, wholly unconnected with each other.

27. The two clauses are unrelated to each other ; there appears to be a displacement — each clause has lost its parallel. The first may read : *the slothful man* (lit. *slothfulness,* = *the man of slothfulness*) *does not hunt* (or, *rouse*, or, *roast*) *his game* — metaphor taken from hunting-life ; the meaning of the verb is doubtful, but the general sense appears to be that the slothful man is too lazy to provide food for himself, and must consequently suffer ; Kamp. regards it as too corrupt for translation. — The second cl. should express the idea that the diligent man does make provision for himself, but this meaning cannot be got from the present text. The following are some of the translations which have been proposed. Rashi (obtained, however, by an inversion) : *the substance of an industrious man is valuable* (and so AV) ; Qaṃḥi, Schult. (followed by De. Reuss, Now. RV. marg. Str. Kamp.) :

---

* So Hitz. Ew. De. Bi. Str. Kamp.

a valuable possession (wealth, substance) *of a man is diligence* (or, *to be diligent*), but the last word is the adj. *diligent*, and cannot be rendered *diligence;* Berth. Ew. : *a precious treasure of* (= *to*) *a man is one who is diligent,* that is, an industrious servant — an allowable rendering of the Heb., but an inappropriate idea ; the intention of the clause is to praise the diligent man for his value not to others but to himself. — Grk. (and so Syr.) changes the order of the words and reads : *a precious possession is a pure man,* which order is adopted by Umbreit, Bi. and others, substituting *diligent* for *pure;* Targ. : *the substance* (wealth) *of man is precious gold,* and Latin : . . . *is the price of gold.* — RV. (and so Noyes) inserts a preposition : *the precious substance of men is to the diligent.* If, in addition to this insertion, we transpose two words, we have the simple reading : *the diligent man possesses* (or, *gains*) *wealth* (lit. *there is valuable property to the,* etc.), a familiar idea in Prov., but not obviously connected with first cl. Cf. 10^4 12^{24} 15^{19} 19^{15} 20^4 *al.*

28. Antithetic, ternary. The first cl. reads : *in the path of righteousness is life* — the doctrine, abundantly dwelt on in Prov., that goodness insures a long and happy life ; see notes on 3^2 8^{35} 14^{27}. The second cl., in its present form, is untranslatable (*the way of its path — not death,* in which *not* is the imperative neg., and can qualify only a verb). Saad. Schult. De., mistranslating the negative : *the way of its path is immortality* (= *not death*) ; RV. (repeating AV.), adopting this mistranslation, inserting a preposition (without italicizing it), and writing *way of path* as one word, renders : *in the pathway thereof there is no death.* The definition of *way* by its synonym *path* is unexampled in Prov., and the resulting second cl. is a simple repetition of first cl. The form of the negative here employed is used only in voluntative sentences, and, if there were a verb, we might render : *and let not the way of its path be death,* an obviously impossible form of statement. The Anc. Vrss. and some Heb. MSS. and printed edd. have *to* instead of the negative (the difference involves merely the change of a vowel), and the clause should no doubt read : *but the way of wickedness leads to death,* or some equivalent expression (so most modern critics) — the idea that the bad man

will be cut off prematurely, or die some unhappy death. Cf. 2¹² ¹⁸
4¹⁸· ¹⁹ 5⁵ 7²⁷ 11¹⁹ 14¹² 15⁹, and, for the insertion of the verb *leads*,
see 14²³.

26. 𝖄ᵇ is reproduced by 𝕲𝕾𝕿𝕷, but can hardly be correct; דרך cannot
be subject of Hif. of הרה. — 𝖄 יהר gives no good sense whether pointed as
adj. or as Hif. of ר . The text is hardly recoverable; the Vrss. seem to have
had 𝖄. We might read: יָסֹר מֵרָיָה צֶדק (cf. 16¹⁷), but there will then be no
distinct contrast of expression between ᵃ and ᵇ. See Lag. Baumg. Pinkuss,
and note on this v. above. — **27.** The Vrss. in general support 𝖄, though, in
some cases, with inversions (see note on this v. above). 𝖄 חָרֻץ; 𝕲 (and so 𝕾)
καθαρός; 𝕿𝕷 *gold*. Gr. יקר הרוץ. Read in ᵇ ראדם ה'; הן יקר occurs in 1¹³ 24⁴.
The insertion of אדם between the two words is possible, but here hard. —
𝖄 חרך is taken by Rashi, Qamḥi *al.* to mean *roast*, = *burn*, as in Aram.
(Dan. 3²⁷), and cf. Arab. חרק; Schult. and others compare Arab. הרך *move*
(intrans.); Saad. *meet, encounter* (צדף III.); see Ges. *Thes.*, BDB, De.; the
word is perhaps corrupt. See De' Rossi. — **28.** In ᵇ for 𝖄 אֶל the Vrss. have
אֵל; and for this reading in MSS. and printed edd. see De' Rossi, B-D, Ginsburg. 𝖄 נִיבה; 𝕲 μνησικάκων *revengeful;* 𝕾 אכהון *wicked;* 𝕿 אבהנא, scribal
error for אנכ; 𝕷 *devium*, possibly for מנהבה (Baumg.). Some word, standing
in contrast with צדקה, must probably be substituted for נ־בה. Levy, *Chald.*
Wbch., suggests that 𝕲 read נרי־כ, but this is not probable; Jäg. מרבה; Buxt.,
Anticrit, 717, thinks μνησ. an insertion of the Grk. translator; Lag. prefers,
with 161 marg., ὃ δὲ μνησικακῶν; Bi. עֶברה (see 21²¹).

XIII. 1. Our Heb. text reads:

> A wise son his father's instruction,
> But a scoffer listens not to rebuke.

Antithetic, ternary. In first cl., if our Heb. text be retained, a
verb, = *hears* or *regards*, should, from the parallelism, probably
be inserted (so Targ. RV.) ; Kamp., instead of *his father's*, reads
loves (see 12¹, where, however, the verb in second cl. is *hates*) ;
Rashi inserts *seeks and loves;* Saad. *accepts;* Schult.: *one is* (or,
becomes) *a wise son* (*when*) *instructed by one's father;* Lat. (followed by De. Now. Str.) : *a wise son is* (= is the product of)
his father's instruction, which is a hard and improbable construction. The verb, by scribal corruption, has disappeared from the
Hebrew; probably we should read: *a wise son heeds* (or, *loves*)
instruction. — On first cl. see notes on 2¹ 3¹ 4¹; on *instruction* see
note on 1², and cf. 13¹⁸· ²⁴ ; on *scoffer* see note on 1²² ; *rebuke* occurs
13⁸ 17¹⁰ Eccl. 7⁵, etc. — In second cl. we might expect *foolish son,*

as in 15⁵, but *scoffer* (which occurs in 9⁸ as antithesis to *wise*) is a
more vigorous synonym of *fool*.   The Grk., assimilating the two
clauses, reads (its *destroyed* being corrected to *rebuked*) :

> A wise son is obedient to his father,
> But a disobedient son will be rebuked,

to which, however, the Hebrew form is to be preferred. — The
proverb lays stress on teachableness ; the *scoffer*, out of badness
of heart, refuses instruction.   Whether or not *father* be retained
in the text, the reference is especially to young men.

2. The outcome of conduct. — The Heb. is probably to be
translated :

> From the fruit of his mouth a man enjoys (lit. eats) good,
> But the desire of the wicked is violence.

So the couplet is rendered by many expositors * ; others † supply
in second cl. the verb of first cl.: *the appetite* (lit. *soul*) . . . *feeds
on violence*, but *appetite* in OT., though it desires or loathes, is
full or empty, is never said *to eat*.   The *violence* may be that
done to others (which is the natural interpretation), or (as first
cl. suggests) that which rebounds on the bad man ; but in this
last case the expression (= "the appetite of the wicked for
wrongdoing really brings violence on their own heads") is roundabout and hard. — The first cl. is substantially identical with 12¹⁴ᵃ,
in which, from the parallelism, we should probably omit the *good*
(and so Reuss here) ; but here the antithesis demands its reten-
tion. — The form of the Heb. couplet is unsatisfactory : the expressions "a man's words bring him good" and "the desire of
bad men is for violence" stand in no natural relation to each
other.   Grk.: *the good man eats of the fruits of righteousness, but
the souls of the wicked perish untimely;* Syr.: . . . *perish;* Targ.:
. . . *are snatched away;* Grätz (after 8³⁶) renders second cl.: *the
faithless do harm to themselves*.   We seem to have here a dislocation — the two clauses do not belong together.   The first cl.
should perhaps be assimilated to the corrected form of 12¹⁴, and
the second cl. might then be retained, with the sense that bad
men desire to act violently (that is, to gain wealth by unjust

---

* Lat. Saad. Rashi, De. Zöck. Str. Kamp.   † Schult. Berth. Ew. RV.

means). An antithesis is gained by adopting the Grk. reading, or by rendering : *a good man enjoys the (good) fruit of his mouth, but* (or, *and*) *the wicked harm themselves.* On *wicked* (or, *faithless*) see note on 2²², and on *violence* note on 3³¹; cf. also notes on 10⁶·¹¹ 12¹⁴ 26⁶.

3. Speech must be cautious.

> He who guards his mouth preserves his life,
> He who opens wide his lips — it is ruin to him.

Exact antithesis, ternary (or, quaternary-ternary). Warning against incautious speech, as in 10¹⁰ 17²⁸. The warning is always in place, even in everyday affairs, but is especially appropriate under a despotic government or in any ill-regulated society (such as abounded under the Persian and Grk. governments), where an imprudent word may cost a man his life. The reference is obviously to the physical *life*, not to the *soul* (as the Heb. term may sometimes be rendered) as the seat of moral and religious experience. Cf. BS. 9¹⁸, and the Syr. Menander, p. 70, l. 12.

4. Sloth and industry.

> The slothful desires and has not,
> The diligent is richly supplied.

Antithetic, ternary. Contrast of results of industry and idleness. Lit. *the soul of the slothful* and *the soul of the diligent*, in which *soul* is the physical principle of life, = desire, appetite. *Richly supplied* is lit. *made fat* (11²⁵ 15³⁰ 28²⁵ Dt. 31²⁰ ψ 23⁵) ; fatness, originally the sign of animal and vegetable health and vigor, is used as general symbol of prosperity. The shiftlessness of the lazy man is similarly denounced or ridiculed in 6⁶⁻¹¹ 12²⁷ 19²⁴ 20⁴ *al.* The Grk. (omitting the neg.) : *the idle desire, but the hands of the active* (or, *strenuous* or *manly*) *are diligent* (perhaps error for *prosperous*) ; Lat. (repeating the verb in first cl.) : *the slothful will and will not,* = is too lazy to decide or to act.

5. Men's relation to truth.

> The righteous hate deception,
> But the wicked act vilely and shamefully.

Antithetic, ternary. The subjects are sing. in the Hebrew. *Deception* (lit. *a false thing*) includes all words and deeds opposed to truthfulness (cf. Col. 3⁹ Eph. 4²⁴). As in first cl., so in second cl. the verbs more naturally express an attitude of mind (cf., for this rendering, 10⁵ 12⁴ 14³⁵ 17² 19²⁶) ; *deception =vile and shameful action.** Other translations (which, however, fail to bring out a distinct antithesis) are : *brings into evil odor* (or, *disgrace*) *and shame* (Schult. De. Str. RV. marg.) ; *is loathsome and comes to shame* (RV.) ; *is ashamed and without confidence* (Grk.) ; *is ashamed and put to the blush* (Targ.) ; *acts badly and brings shame* (Saad.) ; *confounds and shall be confounded* (Lat.).

6. Preservative power of probity.

> Righteousness preserves him whose conduct is perfect,
> But wickedness destroys the sinner.

Antithetic, ternary. Lit. *the perfect of walk;* the Heb. seems intended to read : *innocence of walk,* and, in second cl., *sin,* but the concrete terms are preferable in the Heb. text as well as in the Eng. translation. In second cl. the Anc. Vrss. have (not so well) *sin destroys* (or, *carries off*) *the wicked.* On the OT. conception *perfect* see note on 2⁷, and, on the general statement of the earthly consequences of good and evil conduct, notes on 1³². ³³ 3¹⁶ 10⁷, etc. — There seems no reason to hold, with Lag., that *righteousness* here = *almsgiving;* the natural opposite of wickedness is goodness in general. Lag. refers to v.⁷· ⁸ (on which see notes), and inclines to take *sin* (= offence against the theocratic order) as subject, but for this there seems to be no necessity. On the OT. relation between *righteousness* and *almsgiving* see note on 10². — Righteousness may save, and wickedness destroy, through the operation of natural causes, or through the directly manifested favor or disfavor of God, who remembers and reckons acts for or against men (Gen. 15⁶ Ez. 21²⁴⁽²⁹⁾). This verse is lacking in the Vatican MS. of the Grk., perhaps by scribal oversight.

7. Social pretence.

> Some, having nothing, pretend to be rich,
> Others, being wealthy, pretend to be poor.

---

* So Rashi, Ew. Kamp.

Antithetic, binary (or, ternary-binary). Apparently a condemnatory reference to two contrasted weaknesses, namely, foolish love of display, and equally foolish miserliness, conduct which is doubtless to be met with at all times. Or, there may be special allusion to a state of things which was common in the disordered period of the conflicts between the Greek princes of Syria and Egypt, when there were often pressing reasons for making a show of wealth or poverty. The moral is that men should be simply honest and unpretentious. In second cl. there might possibly be an allusion to desire to get rid of the obligation to give alms (see note on preceding verse), but such allusion is not obvious.

8. Wealth as a protection against enemies. — The text of second cl. appears to have suffered from scribal error. The Heb. of the couplet reads :

> A man's wealth is ransom for his life,
> But the poor man does not heed rebuke,

in which the predicate of second cl. is identical with that of v.[1b], and stands in no relation to first clause. It is not the characteristic of the poor to reject admonition, and the connection calls for the statement that the poor man, not having money with which to buy off his prosecutor or oppressor, must suffer the legal or illegal consequences of his crime or misfortune ; see similar references to the social disadvantages of poverty in 14[20] 19[4,7] 30[14]. Examples of a state of things in which money alone saves life abound in Jewish and other histories (and cf. the reference to murderous rapacity in Ez. 22[27]). The predicate of second cl. may be erroneous scribal repetition from v.[1], and should perhaps read something like *has no friends*, or *is a prey to his enemies*. Or, the second cl. may be repetition of v.[1b], with erroneous substitution of *poor man* for *scoffer ;* in that case it has nothing to do with first clause. — Various attempts have been made to establish a connection between the two clauses. Saad. : [wealth, rightly used in good works, saves life] *but he is poor who heeds not the admonition of God ;* Rashi : *the poor does not hear reproach* (from the good rich man, who, on the contrary, gives him alms), or *he who is poor* (in the knowledge of the law) *hears not the admonition* (of the law, and therefore does not escape evil) ; Midrash Haggada (cited by Rashi) refers the clause to the payment of the half-shekel obligatory on all Israelites equally (Ex. 30[13]), so that the poor man is not exposed to contempt for his poverty ; De. points out that the reference cannot be to the old legal commutation of the death-penalty to a fine, for this is restricted to one case (Ex. 21[30]), and even then the offender does not escape threatening or rebuke, and, if he cannot pay the fine, must suffer death (cf. Ex. 22[3(2)]) ; Schult. agrees in general with Saad., holding the meaning to be : true riches is that (namely, wisdom and virtue) which saves a man from death (ψ 49[8-10]), and he is poor who does not heed admonition ; Ewald takes the second half of the clause as subject (an improbable construction), and translates : *yet he became poor who never heard an accusation* (reference to legal proceedings) ; some * take *rebuke* as = *threat* (a sense which the word nowhere else has), and understand the meaning to be that the poor man, secure in the fact that he has nothing to be robbed of (*cantabit vacuus coram latrone viator*), hears or heeds not threats, is not concerned with the schemes of the powerful oppressor. — These renderings are all forced and improbable ; the first clause simply points out the value of wealth, apparently in evil or corrupt times, as a means of security (by bribery, and, in general, by procuring powerful protection), and the second cl. either belongs to another couplet, or must be emended so as to give a contrast to first clause. The emendation *wicked* for *poor* does not furnish a contrast. — On *ransom* see note on 6[35]. In the present case the rich man is exposed to the legal and other assaults of the powerful, and saves his life by a payment of money. See 10[15], and, *contra*, 11[28].

XIII. 1. In [a] שמע or קבל may have fallen out; cf. 1[8] 4[1] 8[33] 19[20] *al.* Dimock (cited by Dys.), אָרֵב, for 独 אב; Kamp. אָרֵב (if this be adopted, מסר and אהב should be transposed); Bi. inserts prep. מן before בסר, but the resulting construction is hard. 𝕲[a] ὑπήκοοs may represent שמע (so in 21[28], where, however, Jäg. proposes to read ἐπήκοοs), or may be free rendering of 独; in [b] ἀνήκοοs = לא שמע, and υἱόs apparently represents לי (assimilation to form of [a]); ἐν ἀπωλείᾳ (独 וערה) is perh. corruption of ἐν ἀπειλῇ (Jäg., see v.[8]). — 𝕿 inserts מקבל in [a], and 𝕾 משתכע. In [b] 𝕾 follows 𝕲 freely. On 𝕿 בעתא, to be read כאתא (so 𝕾), see Levy, s.v. בעתא, and Pinkuss. — For בסר 4 MSS. have ישמח,

after 10¹. — **2.** In ᵃ 𝕿 renders as in 12¹⁴ᵃ; for 𝕳 פי איש 𝕲 has δικαιοσύνης, perh. reading צדק, perh. imitating 11³⁾ (Baum.). 𝕲ᵇ ὀλοῦνται ἄωροι may represent 𝕳 חמס (the *evil fate* which overtakes the wicked), or חֵמֶם, from מסס (Capp. *Crit. Sac.*, iv. 4, 5, cf. Lag. Baum. Pink.). On ἄωροι cf. Frank. on 11³⁰. The word does not of itself render חמס, but only in conjunction with some other term, as *perish.* — A connection between ᵃ and ᵇ might be got by inserting כב after איש (so 𝕾), and supplying in ᵇ a verb parallel to יאכל. See note on this v. above. — Instead of יאכל 7 MSS. and Bibl. Sonc. have ישבע, and so 𝕾𝕿𝕷 Venet., as in 12¹⁴. — **3.** The stem פשׂק in Arab. = *go forth, separate one's self* (then *transgress, act unrestrainedly*) ; in Aram., *cause to go forth* or *away, cut off;* in Heb. *cause to go apart, open wide* (Qal only here, Pi. Ez. 16²⁵). — **4.** In 𝕳 עצל נפשו the ו may be petrified sign of Nom., as in חיתו, Gen. 1²⁴ *al.*, בנו Nu. 24³⁻ ¹⁵, מעינו, ψ 114⁸, perh. to be read מעיני (the form is not found elsewhere in Pr.), or Aram. anticipatory suff. (elsewhere in Pr. only 14¹³, on which see note), or we may (with Bi.) omit it as scribal error. 𝕿 adds the suff. to the second נפש also. — With רשן cf. Assyr. רישא, רשן. — 𝕲, not so well, omits אין; 𝕷 takes it as negation of מרׂאוה : *vult et non vult piger.* 𝕲𝕾𝕷 render עצל נ' as = עצל. — **5.** 𝕳 יבאש, from באש; better יבׂש, from בש. — 𝕲 οὐχ ἕξει παρρησίαν is free rendering of 𝕳 יהפר; on 𝕾 see Pinkuss. — **6.** One MS. has רשעם, and one חמאם. Read הַמֵאם instead of 𝕳 חמֵא. The subst. תם occurs a number of times in Pr. (2⁷ 10⁹ 19¹ 20⁷ 28⁶), the sing. adj. here, 10²⁹ 29¹⁰, the sing. תֻמֵם 1¹² 2²¹ 11⁵⋅ ²⁰ 28¹⁰⋅ ¹⁸. — For the stem סלף cf. the Arab. sense *go beyond*, and *turn over* (land for sowing); in Heb. Pi. *turn over, destroy*; subst. סלף *departure from* (*going beyond*) the right way, *falsity.* — The couplet, found in 𝕲ᴬ⋅ ⁶⁸⋅ ¹⁶¹⋅ ²⁴⁸⋅ ᵃˡ. 𝕾ᴴ Clem. Procop., is lacking in 𝕲ᴮ, probably by scribal inadvertence; its sentiment, though of the most general nature, is appropriate, and the style of the Hebrew is natural. — **8.** For 𝕳 רֵשׁ Frank. suggests רֻשׁע; see note on this v. above. If this emendation be adopted, the two lines of the v. must be held to belong to different couplets. 𝕳 וערה; 𝕲 ἀπειλήν. On this word, and on 𝕿 בעׂתא, 𝕾 כא־א, see critical note on v.¹ above.

9. Permanent prosperity of the righteous.

> The light of the righteous ‹ shines brightly,›
> But the lamp of the wicked goes out.

Antithetic, ternary. *Shines brightly* is in the Heb. *rejoices*, an expression not appropriate in the connection. Statement of the earthly fortunes of good and bad men under the figure of houses, one brightly illuminated (symbol of life, prosperity, joy), the other in darkness (symbol of adversity and death) ; see the full form of the figure in Job 18⁶. *Light* and *lamp* are synonymous (so in Job 18⁶), not symbols respectively of divine providence and human sagacity (De., who, inappropriately, refers to 6²³). For

some general parallels in Talmudic and other writings see Hitz.
De. (the references in Malan are scarcely appropriate). —
Another emendation (Frank.) is : *light rejoices the righteous*,
which gives a less marked antithesis than the reading here
adopted. Grk. : *there is light to the righteous always*, perhaps a
free rendering of our Heb., perhaps based on a different text.
The Grk. adds the couplet :

> Crafty souls go astray in sins,
> But the righteous pity and are merciful.

For the first cl. cf. 2^{15} 6^{12}, and, for second cl., ψ 37^{21} ; the two
clauses have no special connection with each other. The couplet
is not improbably a combination of glosses.

10. Pride as source of discord. The Heb. reads :

> Pride causes only strife,
> But with those who take counsel is wisdom.

Antithetic, ternary-binary. Cf. $11^{2.\ 14}$ 12^{2} 15^{22} 24^{6}. According to
this reading *pride* (haughty self-confidence) is set over against the
disposition to *take counsel*, which is the sign of rational self-dis-
trust ; and such pride, bringing one into conflict with others, is
thus foolish, while the opposite disposition is a mark of *wisdom*.
A distincter antithesis is gained if (with Hitz., after 11^{2}, on which
see note) we read : *with the humble is wisdom* (for which the
change required in the Heb. is not great) ; on the other hand,
the reading of the text is intelligible, and is perhaps a designed
variation of that of 11^{2}. The general sense remains the same —
those who take counsel (RV., not so accurately, *the well-advised*)
may be described as *humble* or *modest*. The proverb is directed
against litigiousness and general quarrelsomeness and offensive
assertion of one's supposed rights, perhaps, also, against the obstinate pride of rival princes, which frequently led to wars. — Grk.
(with different text) : *a bad man does evil by insolence, but they
who judge themselves are wise*, in which the antithesis is less clear
than in the Hebrew. The couplet should perhaps read :

> Pride engenders strife,
> But with the humble is wisdom,

humble being taken as = *unassuming*.

11. Results of legitimate and illegitimate accumulation of wealth.

> Wealth gathered ‹ in haste › grows small,
> But he who gradually amasses increases.

Antithetic, ternary. The Heb. reads : *wealth* (got) *from nothingness* (or, *vanity*), in which *vanity* is by some * taken as = *fraud, swindling;* but the word means only " a breath, something transitory, practically non-existent " (Dt. 32^{21} Job 7^{16} Eccl. 1^2), a sense which is here inappropriate (since wealth built up from nothing may be praiseworthy), and does not offer a good contrast with the following *gradually*. Comparison with 20^{21} 28^{22} makes it probable that the Grk. and the Lat. are right in reading *in haste* † ; the expression probably looks to abnormal methods, not according to the ordinary laws of industry or inheritance (as by son from father), but fraudulent business procedures, extortion, and the like. A man who becomes rich in this way, says the proverb, is likely to lose his wealth ; the reference is probably to reckless expenditure in luxuries, dissipation, speculations and illegal ventures, not to divine retribution ; and, on the other hand, legitimate industry will be accompanied by caution and thrift. This is obviously the observation of a man who lived in a commercial community. — The rendering *wealth dwindles away sooner than a breath* (Umbreit, Noyes) is in itself inappropriate (since a *breath*, here = *nothing*, cannot dwindle), and does not stand in contrast with second cl. — The translation *by labor* (RV.), instead of *gradually*, is improbable. — The Grk. inserts the explanatory phrases *iniquitously* (in first cl.), *righteously* (in second cl.), which latter Targ. renders *and gives to the poor* (see note on 10^2). — Grk. adds : *The righteous is merciful and lends*, on which see note on v.⁹.

12. Hope fulfilled and unfulfilled.

> Hope deferred makes the heart sick,
> But desire fulfilled is a tree of life.

Antithetic, ternary. *Hope* and *desire* are synonyms — each = " the thing desired or hoped for." *Fulfilled* is lit. *having come*. Instead

---

* Schult. De. Str.   † So Vog. Hitz. Ew. Reuss, Bi. Kamp. *al.*

of *hope deferred* we might render *extended waiting* — the sense would be the same. *Heart* is not the emotional nature, but the whole inward man; on *tree of life* see notes on 3^{18} 11^{30}. The proverb has no ethical bearing; it is true without reference to the moral character of desire. The Grk., misunderstanding the scope of the saying, writes *good desire*.

13. Safety lies in obedience.   The Heb. reads:

> He who despises the word is treated as debtor to it,
> But he who fears the commandment is rewarded.

Antithetic, ternary. *Is treated as debtor* is lit. *has been forced to give a pledge.* According to the Jewish law the debtor deposited with the creditor some article as pledge (Ex. $22^{26(25)}$ Am. 2^8 Job 22^6 Pr. 20^{16} *al.*) or mortgaged his house or land (Neh. 5^3), and the creditor, if the debt were not paid, might take possession of the debtor's property (Mic. 2^9), and even, if this did not suffice, of his person, and his wife and children (2 K. 4^1 Isa. 50^1 Neh. 5^8).* So, our text declares, he who offends against the word (that is, the law) is regarded as a debtor to it, and, if he do not meet his obligation, will be punished, while he who *fears* and obeys will be *rewarded* (cf. 11^{31}). The sinner, it is said, exists on sufferance for a time; at the end of that time he must discharge his obligation by obedience, or submit to his fate. This, however, is hardly a natural representation, and a slight change of the Heb. gives the simpler reading:

> He who despises the word will perish,
> But he who fears the command will be safe.

The term *word* may mean "law in general"; possibly it = *word of God*, with specific reference to the divine law given to Israel. The punishment and reward may come from man or from God. Cf. notes on 1^7 3^7 16^{20}. — Grätz unnecessarily emends to: *he who despises strife* . . . and *he who fears contention* . . . — Grk. adds the triplet:

> A crafty son will have no good thing,
> But the affairs of a wise servant will be prosperous,
> And his path will be directed aright.

---

* See Nowack, *Heb. Arch.*, pp. 353 ff.

This is apparently a scribal addition, taken, perhaps, from some current collection of proverbs (not from Ben-Sira) ; the second and third lines perhaps form a doublet. The thought is in keeping with that of our Book of Proverbs, in which, however, the only parallel couplet is 17^2. — The Lat. adds the couplet given in the Grk. after v.[9].

14. Wisdom is life-giving.

> The teaching of the sage is a fountain of life,
> Whereby one may avoid the snares of death.

Ternary, progressive (second cl. = predicate of first cl.), in form a single sentence, contrary to the norm of this part of the Book ; 14^{27} is nearly identical. The two lines give two different figures. The second cl. is lit. : *to avoid*, etc. On *fountain of life* see note on 10^{11}. *Teaching* (Heb. *tora*) = " content of the instruction." *Snares of death* are snares set by death (as fowler or hunter), or, more probably, snares of which the result is death, as in first cl. the result of the fountain is life. The *sage* (see 22^{17} 24^{23} 1^{2-6} 2^1) is the man of experience and wisdom, the teacher (public or private) whose instruction is designed to be a practical guide in everyday affairs. The sages appear to have formed a recognized class at this time, and to have performed the function of Heads of schools or Professors of the philosophy of life. Their teaching related to matters of common-sense prudence, and to the more nearly ideal conception of right and wrong ; it included the observations of practical sagacity, and the prescriptions of a strictly ethical-religious view of life ; see notes on 1^{2-6} 10^{11} 13^{11} 14^{27} *al*. In Proverbs the guide of life is not the immediate divine word of the Prophets or the divine rule of the Tora, but human reflection illuminated by divine wisdom — a difference which indicates a new phase of development of Israelitish moral and religious thought. — The Grk. gains a contrast by reading second cl. : *but the foolish dies by a snare*, an improbable form (cf. 12^{13}). An antithetic form might be expected, but cannot be got by any natural emendation of the Hebrew text. The idea of the proverb, as it stands, is that integrity (probably religious integrity) brings long and happy life, as in 3^{16} *al*.

9. 𝔐 יִשְׂמַח; 𝔖𝔗 נרון; 𝔏 *laetificat*, reading Pi. (so Frank.), but the order of words does not favor this reading; 𝔊 διὰ παντός, perh. paraphrase of 𝔐, contrast to the *extinguished* of ᵇ (Jäg.), hardly for ישבה *is extended* (Lag.), possibly for לנצה or חמר; see Schleusn. who thinks that a word (perh. χαρτόν) has fallen out. One MS. of De R. has יצמח. Grätz would emend to יורח (cf. 2 K. 3²² Isa. 58¹⁰ Job 9⁷), a more natural reading than that of 𝔐, and here, probably, to be adopted; שׂמר is nowhere else used of a light. — For Heb. translations of the couplet added in 𝔊 see Ew. and Bi.; cf. note on this v. above. — 10. 𝔐 נֶעֱצַב; Hi. (not improbably) יֵעָצֵב, after 11²; 𝔊, freely, ἑαυτῶν ἐπιγνώμονες (see 12²⁶). — 𝔊 רע for 𝔐 רק. It is better to omit רק and the ב of בִּיַד as corrupted repetition of preceding דִּינְך. — 11. 𝔐 מֵהֶבֶל; 𝔊 ἐπισπουδαζομένη, 𝔏 *festinata*. 𝔖𝔗 follow 𝔊, with modifications. Read (with Ew. Reuss, Lag. Kamp.) עַל מְבֹהָל. יד = "according to the task of the day, gradually" (cf. Levy, *NHW*., for the late Heb. use); בִּיד would mean "by the labor of one's hand." 𝔊 adds at end: δίκαιος οἰκτείρει καὶ κιχρᾷ. — 12. 𝔊 gives an elaborate paraphrase of ᵃ, making of it a full couplet: κρείσσων ἐναρχόμενος [Β—μένοις] βοηθῶν [ℵᶜ·ᵃ 106. 248. A *al*. βοηθεῖν] καρδίᾳ Τοῦ ἐπαγγελλομένου καὶ εἰς ἐλπίδα ἄγοντος, = *better speedy help than halting promise*. Some MSS. of 𝔊 (23. 106. 149 *al*.) and 𝔖ᴴ here add the line above given at end of v.¹¹, while others (106. 248) omit 𝔐ᵇ. As the form of 𝔐 is obviously original, these variations exhibit the liberties and uncertainties of Grk. scribes (see Baum.). — 13. On the Heb. represented by the addition in 𝔊 (found also in 𝔖) see Ew., Bi., and, on the texts of 𝔊 and 𝔖, Baum. Pinkuss. — Gr. reads רב for רבר, and מצה *strife* for מצוה. Better Frank., who omits י־, and reads ישלם (𝔊 ὑγιαίνει) for 𝔐 ישלם. — 14. In ᵇ 𝔊 has: ὁ δὲ ἄνους ὑπὸ παγίδος θανεῖται, = וּנְכַל יִמָּת מִמֹּקֵשׁ (so Baum.; Jäg. קָר); but the collocation *die + snare* is hard. We should perh. expect some such form as יָסָר צֶדֶק. — 𝔖 and one Heb. MS. have חכמה for 𝔐 חכם.

15. Value of intelligence. The first cl. reads:

Fine intelligence (or, good sense) wins favor.

The expression (שֵׂכֶל טוֹב) which stands as subject of the clause signifies intellectual *penetration* or *fineness* (1 Sam. 25³), or wisdom in the most general sense (ψ 111¹⁰) (in Pr. 3⁴ the text must be changed) ; the substantive is the distinctive term in Prov. for *sagacity, discretion, prudence* (12⁸ 16²² 19¹¹ 23⁹, and so Ezr. 8¹⁸). Here the reference is to that fine perception of propriety which makes a man discreet and courteous in his dealing with his fellows, whereby he wins their favor ; the term *culture* (suggested by De.), understood to include both intellectual and social fineness, may convey the idea of the Hebrew. — With this idea the second cl., as it now stands, cannot be brought into clear relation. Lit. it reads : *The way* (conduct, manner) *of the wicked* (faithless)

is permanent (enduring), in which *wickedness* is not a natural contrast to *intelligence,* and the conduct or manner of life of the
wicked is described not as bringing disfavor, but as *permanent,* a
term used everywhere else in a laudatory sense, as indicative of
strength, but never with ethical significance. It is employed to
describe a stream as perennial (Am. 5^{24} Dt. 21^4 ψ 74^{15}), or men
(Jer. 5^{15} 49^{19} 50^{44} Job 12^9), or their abode (Nu. 24^{21}), or the foundations of the earth (Mic. 6^2), as enduring, a bow (Gen. 49^{24}), as
standing fast, sure, the sea as having a permanent place or flow
(Ex. 14^{27}), and pain as perpetual (Job 33^{19}). The renderings
hard (AV. Str.), *rugged* (RV.), *unfruitful, desolate* (Reuss, Zöck.),
uncultivated (De.), are unwarranted by etymology or usage.
Schultens understands it as = *tenacious, inflexible,* that is, in a
bad sense, but such a sense does not belong to it; the clause cannot mean : the manner or conduct of bad men is characterized by
an immovableness which pays no respect to the claims of others.
Grk. Syr. Targ. : *are destroyed;* Lat. : *whirlpool.* — The true reading is uncertain. The translation of AV. : *the way of transgressors is hard* has been by many readers understood to mean that
transgressors have a hard time of it, or, that the modes of procedure of bad men are cruel — senses which are foreign to the
words. The next verse may perhaps suggest that the original text
contained some such expression as " the conduct of fools is hateful " (or, " breeds enmity "), or, less probably, " is their destruction " (Grk.), or (Frank.) " is emptiness " (cf. BS. 41^{10}). The
two lines appear to belong to different couplets. — After the first
cl. the Grk. adds the apparent variant :

> And to know the law is the part of sound understanding,

the first half of which reads like a gloss on the expression *wins
favor* — one, that is, gains the favor of God by a knowledge of
the law. But the line is found in the Grk. at the end of 9^{10} also,
where it is more appropriate ; and it was, perhaps, here inserted
merely because of the common expression *sound understanding*
(= *fine intelligence*).

16. Good sense and its lack shown in conduct.

The man of sense shows intelligence in all he does,
But the fool makes a display of folly.

Antithetic, ternary. The Heb. has, in first cl.: *Every man of
sense acts with knowledge* (or, *intelligence*); the transposition
(with Syr. Lat.) of the *every* (= *all*) gives a better form to the
sentence. The adj. *sensible* (= *of sense*, RV. *prudent*) is a common term in Prov. for the expression of intellectual sobriety and
acuteness; what is here said is that a man of this sort acts with
due regard to circumstances, while the fool *spreads out* or *displays*
his ignorance and folly like a pedlar who openly spreads his wares
before the gaze of all men. Cf. 12^{23} 15^2. The reference appears
to be solely to intellectual qualities.

17. Good and bad messengers.

> An ‹ incompetent › messenger ‹ plunges one › into misfortune,
> But a trustworthy envoy insures success.

Antithetic, ternary. In first cl. the Heb. has *wicked* and *falls into;*
but it is the business capacity of the messenger, and not his moral
character, that is in question (so in 25^{13}), and the predicate refers
(as in second cl.) not to the misfortunes of the messenger, but to
the unhappy consequences which his incapacity entails on his em-
ployers. The correction requires only the omission of one letter
and the change of two vowel-points. The term *envoy* occurs
again in 25^{13}; in Isa. 18^2 Jer. 49^{14} (= Obad.[1]), and perhaps in
Isa. 57^9,* it means a political or governmental messenger, an *am-
bassador*, but the more general name *envoy* is preferable as suiting
all the passages in which the word occurs. The reference is probably to private as well as public negotiations, and to affairs of
every description for the settlement of which an intermediator is
required. The terms *incompetent, trustworthy, misfortune, heals*
are of general (not primarily ethical) import. — *Insures success*,
lit. *is health*, that is, is a source of health, the agency by which a
sound, prosperous condition is attained. See 4^{22} 6^{15} 12^{18} 14^{30} 15^4
16^{24} 29^1 Mal. 4^2 (3^{20}).† The second cl. states not that the good
messenger heals or remedies the mistakes of the bad messenger of
first cl., but generally that such an one is helpful.

---

* In Jos. 9^4 the word should be changed so as to agree with v.¹².

† On the term in Eccl. 10^4 (= *quiet* or *conciliatory demeanor*) cf. Siegfried (in
Nowack) and Wildeboer (in Marti).

18. Financial success the reward of docility and caution.

> Poverty and shame will be the lot of him who rejects instruction,
> But he who regards admonition will be honored.

Antithetic, ternary (or, quaternary-ternary). Prudent regard to advice, says the sage, insures success in life; the maxim is a general one, and leaves room for cases in which, for moral or other reasons, one must go against the counsel of friends. The primary reference is to commercial success. The *shame* (*disgrace*) is that which usually attends *poverty*, and the *honor* is that which is given to wealth. The principle involved (caution in decisions) has, of course, a wider scope. Cf. 12^1 $15^{5.32}$. The *instruction* and *admonition* may be understood (but less probably) to refer to general moral and religious teaching. — The Grk., against the parallelism, inverts the order, rendering: *instruction removes* (or, *averts*) *poverty and dishonor*.

19. Two displaced lines, each of which has lost its proper parallel line:

> Desire accomplished is sweet to the soul,
> But it is an abomination to fools to depart from evil.

The first cl. is substantially identical with second cl. of 13^{12}, and the second cl. with second cl. of 29^{27}, in each of which couplets there is a distinct antithesis. A connection here between the two lines has been sought * by paraphrasing: " desire fulfilled is pleasant, and thus fools cherish their evil desire, and will not abandon it," or (Wild.): "the desires of good men are granted by God, but fools cannot expect such a blessing"; but these interpretations are forced, and contrary to the style of Proverbs, in which the connection of thought is simple and obvious; cf. 18^2, in which the fool's pleasure is defined, and see notes on 13^{12} 29^{27}. — Grk. (followed, with some variations, by Syr. Targ.) has:

> The desires of the righteous gladden the soul,
> But the deeds of the unrighteous are far from knowledge;

which in part represents a different Heb. text from ours, and seems to be in part a religious interpretation of our first clause. Similar religious interpretations of the first cl. are given by Rashi,

---

* Rashi, Schult. De. Reuss, Str. *al.*

Delitzsch, and others, but it obviously contemplates a general non-moral fact of human experience.

20. On choosing associates wisely.

Walk with the wise, and thou wilt become wise,
But he who associates with fools will smart for it.

Antithetic, ternary. In first cl. the Heb. margin (assimilating the construction to that of second cl.) reads : *he who walks . . . becomes.* *Will smart* (see 11¹⁵) is lit. *will be made* (or, *become*) *bad* (= *will come into evil case*) ; there is an implied contrast between this *evil*, the result of *folly*, and the *good* or *advantage* which is derived from *wisdom*. In the Heb. of second cl. there is an assonance : *rōʻé kᵉsîlîm yērôʻa.* The power of association to mould character is referred to in 1¹⁰ 2¹² 4¹⁴ 16²⁹ 22²⁴·²⁵ 23²⁰ 28⁷·¹⁹. The *wise* may be in general men of good sense, or the reference may be specifically to sages, men who sought and taught wisdom. The verse may be an admonition to attend the schools ; cf. BS. 39¹⁻³ Eccl. 12⁹⁻¹¹.

15. At end of ª Bi. adds וְהֹסֵר (presumably for the metre's sake). — 頂 אֵיתָן (on the stem see BDB), apparently an elative form, made (as in South Sem.) by pref. א, sporadic in No. Semitic ; ⅁ ἐν ἀπωλείᾳ (and so ℱ) ; ℭ (apparently following both 頂 and ⅁) ואראה חקפא רבזוי חבד ; 𝔏 *vorago.* Jäg. supposes that ⅁ read אֲדָם *their calamity* (1²⁷ 24²² Job 21¹⁷ *al.*), Gr. אברן ; neither of these would account for 𝔏 *vorago*. ⅁ may possibly be free rendering of 頂. Frank. חהו (see Job 6¹⁸ 12²⁴ BS. 41¹⁰), which is not satisfactory in itself, and secures no good contrast between the clauses. — 16. 頂 כל ערם יעשה ; better (as apparently ℱ𝔏) כל ר׳ ע׳ ; ℱ takes ר׳ ע׳ as defining relative clause (Pink.) ; cf. 16⁵. Grätz proposes שֵׂכֶל for 頂 כל. — 17. 頂 מלאך ; ⅁ βασιλεύς. — 頂 רשע ; read רע (so Grätz). — 頂 יפל ; read Hif. יפל (so Reuss, Now. Bi. Gr. Kamp. Frank.) ; cf. 7²⁶ 19¹⁵. — 頂 אמנה, plu. of extent and emphasis. — מרפא may be pointed as subst. or as Pi. Partcp. ; ⅁, freely, ῥύσεται αὐτόν. — 18. Before 頂 פרע insert ר׳. — 19. 頂 תַּאֲוָה נִהְיָה ; ⅁ ἐπιθυμίαι εὐσεβῶν (68. 106. *al.* Compl. ἀσεβῶν), in which εὐσ. is probably insertion to gain a religious tone, though it may represent a עברת צדקם (cf. note on 21³⁰) ; ⅁ ἔργα, = עברת (Jäg.) for 頂 תעבה ; ἀπὸ γνώσεως, = מדע, for 頂 מרע. — 𝔏 *qui fugiunt*, as if סרם or יסר. On a reading רשעם, for 頂 כסלם, see De' Rossi. — 20. Kethib ª (followed by ⅁), two Impvs. in conditional sentence ; Qeri (followed by ℱ𝔏) has Partcp. and Impf., as in ᵇ. — 頂 ירע ; ⅁ γνωσθήσεται, = Nif. or Hof. of ירע ; 𝔏, freely, *similis efficietur ;* in ᵇ ℱℭ = 頂.

21, 22. Recompense of righteousness and unrighteousness. — Antithetic, ternary. The doctrine of earthly reward according to conduct; see notes on 3^{13-18}.

> 21. Misfortune pursues sinners,
> But good fortune is the lot of the righteous.
> 22. The good man leaves wealth to his children's children,
> But the wealth of the sinner is laid up for the righteous.

21. *Misfortune* is lit. *evil; good fortune* is simply *good* in the Hebrew. On the terms *sinners* and *righteous* see notes on $1^{3.\ 10}$ 2^{20}. The second cl. is lit.: *he* (or, *one*) *recompenses the righteous with good.* The *he* is by some* taken to refer to God (Yahweh), but this is improbable, since such omission of the divine name as subject occurs nowhere else; others† understand the subject to be the indefinite *one*, and render the verb as passive (*the righteous are recompensed*), a construction possible, but hardly employed except where the connection points naturally to a definite subject; still others would construe *good* as subject (*good rewards the righteous*), taking it as = "the Good One," God (but God is never in OT. called simply "the Good One"), or as = "prosperity" (but this expression represents the reward, not the re-warder). It is perhaps better, following the Grk., to change the verb into *overtakes*, and make *good* (corresponding to *evil* in first cl.) the subject: *good overtakes* (= *is the lot of*) *the righteous;* for this use of the verb see Isa. 59^9 Job 27^{20}. The sense is un-affected by this change of text. The Pass. form of the verb in the Heb. is found in 11^{31} 13^{13}. — **22.** The term *good* describes that which is satisfactory of its kind, well adapted to its ends, as food (Gen. 3^6), or land (Ex. 3^8); used of persons it may mean *beautiful* (Gen. 24^{16} 1 Sam. 9^2), or *kind* (1 Sam. 25^{15} ψ 73^1), or *morally exemplary;* here, from the parallelism, it is equivalent to *righteous*, as in 12^2 $14^{14.\ 19}$. The reference is not to successful thrift, or to the kindhearted, liberal man who by dispensing bless-ing is himself blessed (as in 11^{25}), but to the morally good man whose obedience to law is rewarded with worldly prosperity. The ethical use of the term is frequent in Prov., less frequent in Pss., elsewhere rare. The bequeathal of wealth to descendants was in

---

* Saad. Now. Str. and apparently Schult.   † Lat. De. RV.

Israel (as among ancient peoples generally) a crowning test of
prosperity. This blessing is said to come to the *righteous*, but
not to *sinners*, whose wealth, on the contrary, passes (by natural
laws) into the hands of the good. On *sinner* see notes on 8^{36}
11^{31}.

23. The Hebrew yields no satisfactory sense. It reads:

> The fallow-ground of the poor yields (lit. is) abundance of food,
> But many a man perishes (or, is swept away) by injustice.

The statement of first cl. is opposed to common observation and
to the declaration of 10^{15}, and uses the strange term *fallow-
ground* instead of some general word for "land"; the second cl.
is vague (the *injustice* may belong to the perishing man or to his
destroyer), and between the two clauses there is no obvious relation — the productivity of a poor man's land has nothing to do
with a man's perishing by injustice. A sufficiently free paraphrase may, indeed, supply the needed connection: "even the
fresh land (which requires severe labor, and is presumably of moderate productive power) of a (pious or industrious) poor man
yields abundance of food, while many men (relatively rich) by
their unjust actions (fail to get nourishment from their land, and
in the end) are destroyed." * But these insertions overpass the
limits of allowable interpretation. There is nothing to indicate
that the *poor* man of first cl. is diligent or righteous — this cannot
be properly inferred (by contrast) from the *injustice* of second cl.;
nor is the poor man, as such, ever commended in Prov. (not in
19^{22}, and not in 3^{34}); moreover, a man supplied abundantly with
food is hardly to be called *poor* (cf. v.^{25}). — The Anc. Vrss. vary
considerably from the Heb., and from one another. Grk.: *the
righteous shall pass many years in wealth, but the unrighteous
shall be speedily destroyed;* and that there were variations in the
Greek versions is shown by the rendering of the Hexaplar Syriac,
which is based on the Greek text of Origen: *the great enjoy
wealth many years, but some men perish little by little;* Pesh. Syr.:
those who have no habitation (or, *means of subsistence*) [that is,
the poor] *waste wealth many years, and some waste* (*it*) [or, per-

---

* So substantially Ew. De. Reuss, Now. Str.

haps, by emendation, *perish*] *completely;* Targ. : *the great man devours the land of the poor, and some men are taken away* (= *die*) *unjustly* (or, *without judgment*) ; Lat. : *there is much food in the fresh land of the fathers* (= chiefs, heads of families), *and* (or, *but*) *for others it is collected without judgment.* The medieval Jewish commentators are equally at a loss in translating the verse. Saad. : *food* (that is, the manner of one's eating) *is often a sign of poverty, and many men are carried off without judgment* (that is, without knowing the judgment of God, or without dying a natural death) ; Rashi allegorizes. — Frankenberg emends :

> The fallow-ground of the wicked yields abundance of food,
> And wealth gathered by injustice.

But such a general affirmation is not found elsewhere in Pr., the translation *wealth collected* is not probable, and the difficulty of the *fallow-ground* remains. — The Hebrew text appears to be corrupt beyond emendation.

24. The rod for children.

> He who spares his rod hates his son,
> But he who loves him chastises him.

Antithetic, quaternary-ternary (or, ternary). *Spares* = withholds, fails to use (it does not mean "uses slightly") ; see 10^{19} 11^{24} 17^{27} 21^{26} 24^{11} Gen. 22^{12} ψ $19^{13(14)}$ Job 7^{11}. *Chastises* is lit. *seeks with chastisement,* = deals (with him) by chastisement ; the verb does not contain the idea of " early, betimes, diligently " (De. RV. *al.*) ; see notes on 1^{28} 7^{15} 8^{17} 11^{27}. The proverb simply commends bodily chastisement as a means of training ; details are left to the judgment of parents ; on *chastisement* see notes on $1^{2.8}$. Similar sayings are 22^{15} 23^{13} 29^{17} ; the regulation of Dt. 21^{18-22} (infliction of death on a disobedient son) seems, in the later postexilian period, to have fallen into desuetude.*

---

* On methods of corporal punishment of children among the Greeks and Romans see Becker, *Charicles,* Exc. to Sc. I, and *Gallus,* Exc. II to Sc. I, and A. Zimmern, *The Home Life of the Ancient Greeks* (transl. from the Germ. of H. Blümner), p. 98 ; for Chinese and other apophthegms relating to this point see Malan.

25. Relation of righteousness to supply of bodily wants.

The righteous has enough to satisfy his appetite,
But the wicked suffers lack of food.

Antithetic, ternary. Lit.: *the righteous eats* (= has food enough)
to the satisfying of his appetite, but the belly of the wicked lacks.
On *appetite* (= animal life or soul) see notes on 6^{30} 1^{18}. *Belly* is
the middle part of the body, rarely the outer surface (Job 40^{16}
Cant. $7^{2(3)}$), usually the interior, including the womb (Gen. 25^{23}
al.) and the cavity containing the bowels, regarded as the seat of
general feeling (Job 20^{20}) or as the receptacle of food (here and
18^{20}, on which see note); it thus comes to stand for the man's
being or personality (ψ 17^{14}), or the combination *soul and belly*
expresses the whole being (ψ $31^{9(10)}$). The reference in the proverb is to the satisfaction of all bodily needs, food standing for all
the physical necessaries of life — not to the satisfaction of spiritual
needs, of which there is no suggestion in the words; the inward
life of spiritual experience is alluded to in Prov. always under the
general terms *wisdom, fear of Yahweh,* and the like. On bodily
compensation in this life see notes on $1^{32.\ 33}$ $2^{21.\ 22}$, etc.— The distinctness of the phraseology of this verse brings out in sharp
relief the indistinctness of v.^{23}.

21. 𝔐 ישלם טוב; 𝕲 καταλήμψεται ἀγαθά; read טב ישג (Ew. Kamp.); Bi.
ישלם; Grätz ומנת צדקם ישלם; Lag. suggests that the word was written ישל׳,
out of which 𝕲 made ישגו; Jäg. regards ישבם as the word read by 𝕲, miswriting
of ישלב. — 22. To understand יהוה as subj. of יזהר is unnatural and unnecessary.
Before טוב Bi. inserts אש, but cf. 12^2. — 𝕷, fully, *filios et nepotes.* — 23. 𝕲 may
be based on 𝔐: δίκαιοι (Jäg. ישרם, for 𝔐 ראישם) ποιήσουσιν (perh. Aram. עבר
pass time, for 𝔐 אכל) ἐν πλούτῳ (𝔐 ניר *land,* taken as = *wealth*) ἔτη πολλά
(= 𝔐 רב), ἄδικοι δὲ (free rendering of 𝔐 ויש, to bring out contrast with
δίκαιοι) ἀπολοῦνται (= 𝔐 נספה) συντόμως (perh. free rendering of 𝔐 בלא
משבט, possibly = פתאם, omitting בלא). 𝕊 = 𝕲, except that in ᵃ it has periph-
rasis for *poor* instead of *righteous,* and renders 𝔐 אכל by אוכרו, and in ᵇ also
has אוכרו, which, however, may be scribal error for אכרו (Pink.). The Vrss.
appear thus to support the text of 𝔐, but furnish no suggestions for its
emendation. — Frank. reads רעיכב for 𝔐 ראישם, and takes יש as = *wealth;* this
latter is here hard, and the resulting couplet is unsatisfactory. On יש see
BDB. — 24. 𝔐 שהרו כסר, ע׳ with two objects, as קרם, 2 K. 19^{32}; the suff.
refers to the son, not (Ew. *al.*) to ע׳. — 𝕲 ἐπιμελῶς παιδεύει, probably not
reading מיסר (Pink.), but taking ע׳ as = *seek carefully,* and rendering the
phrase according to Grk. idiom (as RV. according to Eng. idiom). This

incorrect rendering of עהר is found in 𝔖 (which = 𝔊, except that it expresses the suff.) 𝔗 (בקר) 𝔏 (*instanter*) and an anonymous Grk. Vrs. (ὀρθρίζει, in Field), and is obviously due to a supposed derivation of this stem from שחר *dawn* (so Saad. Rashi). — Grätz suggests בצהרח מיסרי *corrects him in* (*his*) *youth*, but the change is unnecessary. — **25.** 𝔥 נכן; 𝔊 ψυχαί, perh. by assimilation to ᵃ, ב being usually rendered in 𝔊 by κοιλία (so ᾿ΑΣΘΕΣᴴ here); 𝔖𝔗𝔖ᴴ ס נ (Heb. ברט, Jer. 51³⁴); 𝔏 *venter*.

XIV. 1. Wisdom and folly in the home.

The Heb. text is in disorder, and the proper form is doubtful. The Received Text reads:

> The wise among women build (every one) her house,
> But folly with her hands tears it down.

The improbable collocation of concrete and abstract (*wise* and *folly*) may be got rid of by slight changes of text, as by reading, in first cl., *the wisdom of women* (so many recent expositors), or, in second cl., *the foolish* (Anc. Vrss. RV.). In all these readings the reference is to the wife as manager of household affairs, as in 31¹⁰⁻³¹, where, indeed, as to her acts she is called *capable*, and *wise* in her words only, but the difference is not significant. Elsewhere in OT. the epithet *wise*, used of women, indicates sagacity (Ju. 5²⁹ 2 S. 14² 20¹⁶· ²²), artistic skill (Ex. 35²⁵), or the profession of mourner (Jer. 9¹⁶⁽¹⁷⁾). The sense may thus here be: it is the wisdom of the wife especially that secures the prosperity of the household. This interpretation, however, assigns the wife a rôle which is more important than is indicated elsewhere in Pr., and is in itself not probable — the man is in OT. the more important person of the family. A simpler statement of the general efficiency of the housewife may be gained by further changes of the text, with the resultant reading:

> A wise woman builds her house,
> A foolish woman with her hands tears it down.

Builds her house = builds up her household. — It is possible, however, that (as 9¹ 24³ suggest) the word *women* of the present text is a gloss on the plu. adj. *wise*, and should be omitted. If, further, we change *wise* to *wisdom* and omit the unnecessary expression *with her hands*, we have the rendering:

> Wisdom builds the house,
> Folly tears it down.

The statement then is that wisdom is constructive, folly destructive, of the family and the best life. The objection to this emendation is that wisdom and folly are not personified elsewhere in chs. 10–29; an isolated case might, however, occur. — The word *women* being omitted, the first line of this couplet is identical with first line of 9[1], from which it may have been taken, and a different meaning given it. Or the expression may have been a common one in gnomic discourse, and may have been employed by different writers in different senses.

2. Identity of integrity and piety.

> He whose life is upright fears Yahweh,
> But he whose ways are wicked despises him.

Antithetic, quaternary-ternary (or, ternary). Lit. *he who walks in his uprightness* (but the *his* should be omitted), and *he who is wicked* (crooked) *in his ways*. That is, the good man shows by his conduct that he reverences God who demands uprightness, while the bad man practically sets him at defiance. — Subject and predicate may be reversed, so as to read: *He who fears Yahweh is upright . . . he who despises him is bad,* and the resulting sense is substantially the same as before. The first translation defines moral conduct by the man's relation to God, the second defines the man's attitude toward God by his moral conduct. The first is perhaps favored by the Hebrew order of words. — On *wicked* (= *crooked*, RV. *perverse*) see note on 2[15].

3. Discretion in speech. — The couplet reads in our Heb. text:

> In the mouth of the fool is a sprig of pride,
> But the lips of the wise preserve them.

Implicit antithesis, quaternary-ternary (or, ternary). The word rendered *sprig* occurs elsewhere in OT. only in Isa. 11[1], where it signifies a small branch shooting from the stock of a tree; here the branch of pride springs from its stem in the fool's mouth. The line simply characterizes the fool's language as proud; but, as second cl. declares the preservative effect of wise speech, we may probably infer that some effect of foolish proud speech is implied in first cl., and this effect, according to the parallelism in the present Heb. text, touches the fool himself — pride harms or destroys him (as in 11^2 16^{18} 29^{23}). It may be a question whether we should not omit the *them* in second cl., and interpret : "the fool's words are proud (insolent toward others), but the words of the wise are helpful (preservative of others)." This would accord better with the function ascribed in Pr. to utterance. — The Anc. Vrss., instead of *sprig*, have *goad* or *rod*. If this translation be adopted, we may regard the *rod of pride* as wounding others (Syr. Targ. Ew. Str. and perhaps Grk.), or as a scourge to the fool himself (De. Reuss, Zöck.), = *a rod for pride* (Kamp.) ; Hitzig (by a change of text) : *a rod for his back* (cf. 26^3, where, however, the word rendered *rod* is different). But the translation *rod* is doubtful, and the expression is not quite natural. The rendering *insolence* (Barth) instead of *sprig* (or, *rod*) is not probable. — Elsewhere the lips of the wise are said to give food (10^{21}), to dispense knowledge (15^7), or to keep knowledge (5^2), here to save (cf. 10^{11}). As the Heb. verb is sing., De. would assume *wisdom* as subject (*the lips of the wise, wisdom preserves them*), but this is violent and unnecessary ; it is easier to take the verb as plural. — The proverb, like many others, assumes the identity of speech and thought, and enjoins prudence in words.

4. Importance of the ox for the farmer. — Antithetic, binary. The Heb. text may perhaps be translated (as in RV.) :

> Where there are no oxen the crib is clean,
> But abundance of produce comes by the strength of the ox.

This form, however, does not offer a good contrast in the clauses — we expect : "no oxen, no produce" ; the rendering *clean* (in a physical sense) is doubtful (elsewhere, except Cant. 6^9, the word means "morally pure," Job 11^4 ψ 24^4, etc.),* and, in any case, the sense required is not *clean*, but *empty*, a meaning that the Heb. term never has ; nor would it be necessary to say that

---

* On the use of the word in Cant. 6^9 see the Comms. of Budde (in Marti) and Siegfried (in Nowack). In ψ $18^{20(21)}$ (= 2 S. 22^{21}) the corresponding noun is employed to describe the hands, but as a figure of moral purity.

where there are no oxen the crib is clean. A slight change of
text gives for the first line the rendering:

> Where there are no oxen there is no corn.

In the second line we should expect: "many oxen, much produce," a statement that may be got from the present text, since the
strength (= working power) of oxen is in proportion to their
number; the precise statement is that the crops depend on the
ox, the animal used in ploughing. — The couplet states a fact of
agricultural economy: a wise farmer will see to it that his oxen
are numerous and in good condition.   Care of animals is implied,
but not for their sake.   The duty of kindness to working animals
is enjoined in 12^{10} Dt. 25^4.

5. True and false testimony.

> A trustworthy witness does not lie,
> But a false witness utters lies.

Antithetic, ternary.   The thought is identical with that of 12^{17}, on
which see note; the man makes public affirmation of truth or
falsehood.   The proverb is aimed at the crime of false testifying
in a court of law.   Cf. 6^{19} 14^{25} 19^5.

6. Wisdom comes only to the serious.

> The scoffer seeks wisdom and finds it not,
> But to the man of understanding knowledge is easy.

Antithetic, quaternary-ternary.   *Wisdom = knowledge*, acquaintance with right principles and methods, here especially in things
moral and religious.   The term *scoffer*, as used in Prov., while it
is often a synonym of *wicked, ungodly*, always contains the element of lack of moral seriousness, and generally, also, that of positive opposition to truth; it here stands in contrast with the *man
of understanding*, that is, intellectual sobriety and insight, based
on moral earnestness.   The scoffer's desire for wisdom is not
explained; the sage means, we may surmise, that he valued it
because it gave social power and excited admiration — he did not
love it for its own sake, had no real sympathy with it, and therefore no receptivity for it (cf. 2 Tim. 3^7: "ever learning and never
able to come to a knowledge of the truth ").   These two classes,

here as elsewhere in Prov., are assumed as facts — no attempt is made to analyze the characters, to trace their origin, or to suggest methods of training, whereby the one may be strengthened and the other transformed.

7. Text and meaning are uncertain. The Hebrew text more naturally reads:

> If thou go from the presence of a foolish man,
> Thou hast not known lips of knowledge.

The first cl. has the Imperative *go*, = *if thou go*. If it be taken as a command proper, the second cl. must be understood as giving the ground of the exhortation: *go from . . . for thou hast not observed* (*in him*), etc., but this the Heb. does not warrant. The same is true of Saadia's rendering: *go from . . . else wilt thou not know*. Some (Schult. Ew. RV.) translate: *go into the presence of*, which is allowable, but less probable (it does not, however, change the general sense). As the couplet stands, the meaning is that a fool has no knowledge, and that from intercourse with him one gains nothing. This is an intelligible statement, but the form is strange, and the phraseology of second cl. is not natural — the expression *know lips* occurs nowhere else, and we expect the explanatory phrase *in him* (inserted by RV.). — The Anc. Vrss. give various turns to the couplet. Grk. (with several variations from the Heb. text): *All things are adverse to a foolish man, but wise lips are weapons of discretion*, an unsatisfactory form, followed by Syr. and (with a slight modification) by Bickell; Targ.: *Withdraw into another path from the presence of a fool, for there is no knowledge in his lips*, a simple and natural sentence, probably a free translation of our Hebrew; Lat.: *Go into the presence of a foolish man, and he knows not lips of prudence*, in which the verb *knows* (3 pers. instead of 2 pers.) may be the erroneous transcription of a Latin scribe. — These readings show that there was difficulty in the Hebrew text, but it is not easy to suggest a satisfactory emendation. The second cl. might be conformed to 20[15]: *wise lips are a precious adornment*, but this stands in no relation to the first clause, the form of which in the Grk. is not probable; after 26[1] we might read in first cl.: *there is no honor to a fool*, but this has no support from Versions.

The simplest emendation, perhaps, would be : *go from the presence of a fool, for his lips do not utter knowledge;* cf. 15[7].

8. Conduct must be carefully considered. — The couplet reads in our Heb. text :

The wisdom of a man of sense consists in understanding (or, considering) his way,
The folly of fools is deceit.

Free or loose antithesis, quaternary-ternary (or, ternary). The first cl. gives the gist of the practical philosophy of the sages : a man of good sense shows his wisdom not by fine words and theories or by boldness and display, but in the capacity to consider his actions, comprehend their real import, and choose that course of conduct which is best adapted to secure happiness. The *wisdom* referred to is practical sagacity; there is no mention of moral or religious elements, though the second cl. may perhaps suggest that these are involved. The second cl. does not offer an explicit contrast to the first. We expect the statement that the fool shows his folly by the absence of reflection and insight in the direction of his affairs, instead of which it is *deceit* that marks him — that is, craft, deception practised on others; such is the meaning of the term in Prov. (see 11[1] 12[15. 17. 20] 14[25] 20[23] 26[24]) and throughout OT. The contrast would be obvious if we could take the word in the sense of "self-deception" (so Berth. Ew. Zöck.), but the usage seems not to allow this. We may suppose that the sage chooses to pass over the obvious mental incapacity of the fool, to characterize him by his moral procedure, and to stigmatize or ridicule this as folly — folly, he may say, is best shown in craft and fraud; or, reversing subject and predicate, we may understand the line to say that deceit is essentially folly. Taking a suggestion from the Grk., the line may be read :

The folly of fools leads them astray,

which furnishes a direct and natural antithesis, and should perhaps be adopted. It is possible that the two lines did not originally stand together in one couplet.

XIV. 1. 湿 חַכְמוֹת, fem. plu. const. of חכם, is improbable because of the sing. vb. בנתה and the abstr. sing. אולת in [b]; read חָכְמָה, as in 9[1], on which see note.

נָשִׁם is best omitted as gloss to adj. חכמח. If a reference to wise and foolish women were intended, we should rather expect אשה הכמה (or אשת הכמה) and אוּלָה. — 𝕳 בִּיְרֶיה though logically unnecessary does not mar the rhythm (Bi.). On the Vrss. see note on this v. above. — **2.** The suff. in יָשׁרוּ may be retained, as in 𝕳 28[6] (on which see note), but is better omitted, as in 𝕳 10[9]. On לוז see note on 2[15]. 𝕲 renders the vb. in ᵇ by the passive, against the parallelism; 𝕷 further makes one sentence of the couplet: *ambulans recto itinere et timens Deum despicitur ab eo qui infami graditur via.* — **3.** הֹּטֶר occurs elsewhere only Isa. 11[1], where it = *shoot, stem,* or *branch;* the Heb. word may have had the meaning (which the word has in Aram.) *rod,* thoug⁚ that is probably not the sense here, and there is no need to regard our word as Aramaic. The sense *pride* (Barth., *Etymol. Stud.*), though it may have some support from Arab. (האטר = *walking with a proud gait*) is not favored by Aram. or by the connection here; cf. BDB. — 𝕳 השׁמורם is probably scribal error for תשׁמרום, so 𝕲 φυλάσσει αὐτούς; in the similar forms in Ex. 18[26] Ru. 2[8] the ו may be miswriting of י, or, more probably, erroneous scribal insertion. — **4.** אלף is half-poetical synonym of שׂר. — The large ס is scribal accident; see note in B-D. — On the first vowel in אֲבֻס see Ols. §§ 87, 175. The stem is apparently denom., == *furnish food;* so Partcp. אבס, 1 K. 5[3] (4[23]) Pr. 15[17], *provided with food, fatted,* and subst. מאבס, Jer. 50[26], *a place where food is kept.* But for אבס here we should probably read אֶרֶס, taking בר as = *corn.* — On the Mas. pointing of בר see Buxt. *Com. Crit.* — G. 𝕲 ζητήσεις σοφίαν παρὰ κακοῖς, = בַּקֵשׁ בלֵצֶם ח', which accords less well than 𝕳 with ᵇ. — וְהֵל is Nif. Partcp. or Perf. of קלל, masc. by poetic license, the subj. דעת being fem. — **7.** מִנֶּגֶד לֹ is here more naturally *from.* — ידעֶךָ may be taken as general Present, but, after Impv. לֵךְ, we expect Imperf. — 𝕲 πάντα, = כל (for 𝕳 לֵךְ), and ὅπλα, = כלי (for 𝕳 בל). In ᵇ we may perhaps read: שׂפְתֵיו דעת (or, יִפְהוּ) כִּי לֹא יֹזרו. — **8.** 𝕳 הבֵן; Bi. בֵּן; 𝕲 ἐπιγνώσεται, = רבן, or it may be free rendering of 𝕳. — 𝕳 מרמה; 𝕲 ἐν πλάνῃ, perhaps free rendering of 𝕳, perhaps = מַתְוּה, a reading better than that of 𝕳. — 𝕷 = 𝕳; 𝕊 seems to be affected by 𝕲.

9. Text and translation are doubtful. The natural rendering of the Hebrew is:

> The guilt-offering (or, guilt) mocks fools,
> But among the upright there is good-will.

The second cl. is clear. *Good-will* may be divine or human, but in the former case the divine name is expressed, as in 11[1] 12[2] 15[8] 18[22] *al.;* here the meaning must be that among upright men there is kind feeling toward one another, or (with a slight change of text), that the upright obtain the favor of other men, that is, are prosperous. — The subject of second cl. (*asham*) is susceptible of two renderings, both difficult in the connection. The representation of the sacrifice as mocking the sacrificer is unexampled—

elsewhere it is God who hates and rejects the formal offerings of
bad and unrepentant men (Am. 5²² Isa. 1¹⁴) ; and the verb here
used is never elsewhere employed in connection with sacrifice.
Further, the employment of the specific term *guilt-offering*
(which, in the later ritual, was confined to particular offences,
Lev. 5. 6. 19²², RV. *trespass-offering*) would be somewhat strange.
If the object had been to say that God does not accept the sacrifice of the unrighteous, it would seem that a different phrase
would have been chosen.   The rendering *guilt mocks fools* (Ew.)
is not natural.   Sin is said (Num. 32²³), by its consequences, to
reach men, find them out (Ew. compares the Grk. Nemesis), but
the sort of personification involved in *mocks* is violent and without example.   Nor is the rendering *fools mock at guilt* (RV.)
more satisfactory ; it is not at *guilt*, but at *sin* (AV.) that bad
men may be supposed to mock, but the Heb. word is not a natural expression for *sin*.   None of these translations exhibit a relation of thought between the two clauses, except by means of a
forced paraphrase, as : " the offering mockingly leaves fools unac-
cepted, but the upright do not mock one another (or, need no expiatory offering one from another)" ; or, " fools insolently laugh
at the guilt which their wrong-doing incurs, and thus bring hatred
on themselves, while among the upright there is that kindness
which is the natural product of well-doing."— Grk. (followed by
Syr.) : *the houses of transgressors will owe* (= will owe the law,
will need) *purification, but the houses of the righteous are acceptable* (that is, to God and man) ; Targ. : *fools speak in parables of
sin, but among the upright is favor;* Lat. as AV.   Natural forms of
the couplet would be :

> Fools incur guilt,
> Good men have the favor of God;

or :

> Fools suffer misfortune,
> Good men are prosperous.

The clauses may be displaced ; the original reading of first cl. is
lost.   For antitheses to the clauses see 11²⁷ 15⁸.

10. The Received text is to be translated :

> Every heart knows its own sorrow,
> And no other shares its joy.

Formal antithesis, with identity of thought, quaternary-ternary (or, ternary). Lit.: *the heart knows its own bitterness, and no stranger*, etc. *Heart* = not the emotional nature, but simply *man*. A simple statement of the familiar fact that every man in his deeper feeling stands alone. All experiences are included, but there is no special reference to moral or religious emotion; rather (since no religious or ethical term is used) it is the common, everyday experience that is mainly contemplated. This statement of psychological isolation is not at all in conflict with the natural obligation of sympathy with others, as expressed, for example, in Rom. 12[15]. For similar proverbs among other nations see Malan. In Eng.: "every man knows where the shoe pinches." — Bickell, on the ground that isolation is natural to sorrow, but not to joy, omits the negative in second cl., and reads: *others share its joy;* but the universality of the Heb. text seems preferable. The Anc. Vrss. have the negative. As second line the Grk. has: *and when he rejoices, he has no fellowship with* (or, *there is no mingling of*) *pride*, in accordance with which the couplet might be rendered:

> Every man knows his sorrow,
> And (therefore) with his joy no pride is mingled;

that is, the remembrance of sorrow makes one modest and moderate in times of prosperity and joy (see, on the other hand, BS. 11[25]). This is a proper sentiment, but (even after the change of *stranger* to *pride*) the construction (*when one knows*, etc., *then*, etc.) is not naturally suggested by the Hebrew. Cf., however, v.[13] of this chapter. — To the form of the Heb. it has been objected that the idea of emotional isolation is foreign to the thought of Prov.; but it is doubtful whether this is a less probable conception for the sages than that of the Greek.

11. The good endure, the bad pass away.

> The house of the wicked will be destroyed,
> But the tent of the upright will flourish.

Antithetic, ternary. *House = tent*, = dwelling-place, including the family-life, and the fortunes in general. The word *tent* is a survival from the old nomadic time; the old rallying-cry was: "to your tents, O Israel!" (2 Sam. 20[1] 1 K. 12[16]). On the doctrine of permanence and impermanence see notes on 1[32. 33] *al.*

12. Vice is a road that leads to death.

> There is a way that seems straight to a man,
> But the end of it is the road to death.

Ternary-binary. Identity in subject, antithesis in predicate, = "a way seemingly straight, but really fatal"; or, complete antithesis, = "the beginning of the way is straight, the end of it is death." The figure is that of a journey, in which the traveller imagines that he is pursuing a *straight* path that will lead him to his desired goal of success and happiness, but finds, too late, that it leads to earthly death, that is, to the destruction of happiness. The substitution of the ethical term *right* (RV.) for *straight* abandons the figure. The thought of the proverb is the illusive character of an immoral life: it seems to promise wealth, power, happiness, while its inevitable issue is destruction — wickedness fails, righteousness succeeds; see 2[22] 5[5. 23] 7[27] 9[18] 10[3] *al.;* the couplet occurs again at 16[25]. The process or method of delusion is not described. In second cl. the Heb. has plur. *ways* (or, *roads*). If the text be correct (we should perhaps read sing., with Targ.), the plur. is poetic conception of the road as consisting of numerous paths; it is not intended to indicate that immorality leads by many paths to death, while to life there is one way only; against this interpretation is the sing. *way* in first cl. (cf. Mt. 7[13. 14]). Grk.: *the end of it goes into the depths of Hades.* There is no reference to punishment in the other world. On *end* see note on 5[4].

13. Alternation of joy and sorrow in human life.

> Even in laughter the heart may be sad,
> And the end of joy may be sorrow.

Identical parallelism, binary-ternary (or, ternary). The text may be rendered: . . . *the heart is sad . . . the end . . . is sorrow.* The proverb will then say that joy always passes into sorrow, a pessimistic utterance, hardly in place in this Book. Nor does the sage mean to say that there is a deep-lying sadness in the human

soul which springs from a sense of the vanity of life (De.).   This
is a conception found nowhere else in OT., not even in Eccles.,
in which, while life is regarded as vanity, there is no distinct reference to a *universal sense* of failure; the OT. generally looks on
life as a good gift of God, and expects, by the divine blessing, to
find it full of joy (3^{18} 5^{18} ψ 16^{11}).   Nor, as Reuss remarks, can
there be reference here to a pervading sense of sin as the cause
of sadness; this conception also is foreign to OT. (and to NT. as
well, Mt. 6^{34} Rom. 12^{12} Phil. 4^4 Eph. 5^{20} Jno. 14^1).   The verse
probably speaks of the alternations of ordinary experiences, and
the mixed nature of emotions, and doubtless means to suggest
that men should not be surprised at the occurrence of these alternations, or yield themselves irrationally to either sort of emotion
(cf. v.^{10}).   The assertion of Eccl. 7^3, that sorrow is better than
laughter, represents a different conception of life.

14. Deeds determine fortune.

> The bad man reaps the fruit of his acts,
> The good man (enjoys the outcome) of his ‹ deeds.›

Antithesis of subject, ternary-binary.   Lit.: *From his ways the
bad man is sated, and from himself the good man.*   Instead of the
improbable *from himself* we may read, by the insertion of one
letter, *from his deeds* (Grk. *from his thoughts*) ; to take the Heb.
expression as meaning that the good man finds sufficient reward
in his inward experiences would be against the manner of thought
of Prov., which everywhere contemplates outward recompense ;
cf. Isa. 3^{10}.   In first cl. the subject is lit. *he who in mind turns
aside* (that is, from the path of right) = *the disobedient* or *wicked*
or *bad man* (Zeph. 1^6 ψ $44^{18(19)}$) ; RV. *backslider* conveys the
wrong impression of an apostate, one who declines from or abandons his own previous position of moral right; the Hebrew expression here implies simply non-adherence to the right.   On
good see note on 13^{22}; on the doctrine of the verse cf. $2^{21.\ 22}$ *al.*,
Gal. 6^7.

15, 16. Necessity of thoughtfulness and prudence.   Cf. 22^3 (= 27^{12}).

> 15. The simpleton believes every word,
>   But the man of sense takes heed to his step.

16. The wise man is cautious, and avoids misfortune,
   But the fool is arrogant and confident.

15. Explicit antithesis of subject, implicit antithesis of predicate, ternary. *Simpleton* is the person untrained, unformed intellectually (1^4 22^3 Ez. 45^{20} ψ $19^{7(8)}$) or morally (1^{32} 9^6); the term is here used in the former sense, in contrast with the thoughtful, prudent man. The point of view of 1 Cor. 13^7 is different: love has a largeminded, though not blind, trust in men; the simpleton is credulous, the man of love is sympathetic. — **16.** Antithetic, ternary. The reference, as in the preceding verse, is to intellectual qualities — such is the intimation of second clause. *Is cautious;* lit. *fears. Misfortune* (or, *harm*) is lit. *evil,* a term used in OT. in the widest sense. In second cl. the first adj. is lit. *passing beyond bounds;* the verb usually = *to be angry* (Dt. 3^{26} ψ $78^{21.\ 59.\ 62}$ $89^{38(39)}$), and the Partcp. in 26^{17} = *get excited, get into a passion;* for the meaning *arrogant* (which is suggested by the synonym *confident*) see the corresponding substantive in 11^{23} 21^{24} Isa. 16^6 Jer. 48^{30}. Other proposed renderings are *presumptuous, insolent, passionately excited.* — In first cl. if *fears* had been meant in a religious sense, the divine name would have been added; see 3^7 14^2 31^{30}, and cf. 1^7 8^{13} 16^6 22^4 *al.* The word here = "is apprehensive (of men and things) and on his guard." The predicates may be written: *cautiously avoids* and *is arrogantly confident.* Instead of *arrogant* the Grk. has *mingles with,* and Frank. renders:

> The wise man guards himself anxiously against evil,
> But the fool lightly takes part therein,

evil being taken as = wicked conduct. The context (v.$^{15.\ 17.\ 18}$) favors the translation given above.

9. וֶאֱ יָלִיץ; 𝕲 ὀφειλήσουσιν, perh. = some form of חב. In b 𝕲 has οἰκίαι (בית) for וֶאֱ בין, and it introduces this word in ª; the resulting couplet is intelligible, but not probable. A simpler reading, based on 𝕲, would be: אולם יחבו אשם ולישרם רצֹן; this assumes that the רצֹן exists, for the upright, without אשם. — 𝕿 read יָלִיץ, but renders it by מחלן, taking the stem in the sense *speak in parables.* — Lag. changes 𝕲 καθαρισμὸν to καθυβρισμόν, and gives as Heb. text of 𝕲: אויל מליצה נשה. See Baum. — 𝕾 has two forms of the couplet, one = 𝕲, the other nearer to וֶאֱ; the second reads: *fools commit* (עבר) *sin, but the sons* (בני for וֶאֱ בין) etc.; for ילץ it had, perhaps, some form of עלל (hardly a form of עלץ). Grätz, ילֹן; Frank. בֵּין אוֹ יָ ילֹן אשם: but the ילן is hardly appo-

site. — **10.** 獨 זֵר; 𝕲 ὕβρει, = זָדן, adopted by Frank.; see note on this v.
above. The suff. in שמחהו might then be omitted. — **11.** 獨 יִפרח; 𝕲 στή-
σονται; Gr. suggests ירוח *have free space.* — אהל, in Heb. *tent;* thence, in
Arab., *family, people;* cf. Ass. *alu,* = *city.* — **12.** 獨 דרכי; probably to be
read, with 𝕿, sing. — **13.** For 獨 יכאב לב Gr. proposes יכאב־לֵץ. — 獨 אחרתה
שמחה; the ה is probably not anticipatory suffix (though it may have been
added by an Aramaic-speaking scribe, see 13⁴), and is not to be prefixed, as
art., to following word (which would be against the usage of Pr.), but is better
deleted as scribal inadvertence. — Before verb of ⁿ 𝕲 inserts the neg., which
may be the slip of a scribe (Lag.), or may come from v.¹⁰, or from an altered
Heb. text. 𝕾 attaches suff. to שמחה. — **14.** 獨 מֵעָיו; read מִמְּעָלָיו (De. Str.
Kamp.). On 𝕲 διανοημάτων (hardly = מֵעֲלָלָיו, possibly דְּרָיו, taken as = *what
is in him*) see Capp. *Crit.* 4, 17. 6, Buxt. *Anticrit.* 579, Jäg. Lag. Baum.; on
𝕾 cf. Pinkuss. For the combination of דרך and מֵעָד see Ju. 2¹⁹ Hos. 4⁹ Jer. 4¹⁸
17¹⁰ 32¹⁹ Ez. 36²¹ Zech. 1⁴·⁶ *al.* — **15.** 獨 פתי; 𝕲 ἄκακος, *ignorant of evil,
simpleminded* in good sense; and, on other hand, 𝕲 πανοῦργος takes ערם in
bad sense. In 𝕲ᵇ, πανοῦργος δὲ ἔρχεται εἰς μετάνοιαν, it is not clear what
Heb. is represented by εἰς μετ.; Jäg. לאשמו; Schl., = 獨; Heid., להשבה.
𝕾𝕿 take 獨 אישרו as from אִשֵׁר *good fortune;* 𝕷 *gressus* is preferable. — 𝕷 adds
the couplet given in 𝕲 13⁹. — **16.** 獨 מהעבר is read by 𝕲 (followed by 𝕾𝕿
Frank.) as מהערב (Capp. *Crit.*, 4, 7. 3), ἀνόμῳ being addition of translator;
𝕷 = 獨.

17, 18. Good sense versus irascibility and stupidity.

> 17. A quick-tempered man acts foolishly,
>   But a wise man ‹ endures.›
> 18. Simpletons come into possession of folly,
>   But men of sense ‹ acquire › knowledge.

17. Antithetic, ternary. In second cl. the Heb. has: *and a
schemer* (or, *a man of wicked devices*) *is hated.* According to
this reading the proverb compares two bad dispositions by their
outcome and by the impression they make on men. The *quicktempered* man (he who is *easily angered*, RV. *soon angry*) often
acts foolishly, and thus loses the respect of his fellows; the *malicious plotter*, on the other hand, is *hated*. But a better contrast
is obtained if (by the omission of one Heb. letter) we read (with
the Grk.) *a man of thought endures*, bears much without getting
angry. The verb *bear, endure* is used absolutely in Isa. 1¹⁴ 46⁴
Jer. 44²² (and cf. Pr. 19¹⁹). In the subj. of second cl. the term
thought (or, *schemes, plans*) may be understood in a good sense
(hence *wise man*), or in a bad sense (hence *wicked plotter*); see

note on the word in 1^4; it is understood by all Anc. Vrss. except Lat. in the good sense.   The antithesis is chiastic : *angry* is contrasted with *endures*, and *foolish* with *wise.* — **18.** Antithetic, ternary.   *Simpleton*, as in v.^{15}.   In first cl. the verb should not be rendered by *inherit* (RV.), which may suggest the incorrect interpretation that the silly, unformed man falls heir to folly without effort, while the man of reflection or good sense acquires knowledge only by exertion ; the proverb affirms merely that a thoughtless person is ignorant and foolish, while a man who understands the needs of life gains knowledge. — The translation in second cl. *are crowned with knowledge,* or, *wear knowledge as a crown,** while it gives the same general sense as that of the emendation here adopted, is lexicographically doubtful.

19. Triumph of goodness.

> The bad bow before the good,
> And the wicked at the gates of the righteous.

Identical parallelism, ternary.   In second cl. we may supply some such verb as *stand suppliant.*   The adjectives are all to be understood in the ethical sense.   The form of expression is taken from Oriental custom : the inferior prostrates himself before the superior, or waits humbly at the great man's gate to implore his favor. The doctrine (based on belief in the immediate intervention of God) that moral goodness must in this life triumph externally over wickedness was held by Jewish philosophy till it accepted the broader doctrine of ethical immortality (Wisd. Sol. 2–5).

20, 21. Evils and claims of poverty. — Antithetic, ternary.

> 20. The poor man is hated even by his neighbor,
> But the rich has many friends.
> 21. He who despises his neighbor sins,
> But he who has pity on the poor, happy is he.

20. *Neighbor* is any one who stands in close social relations, from whom, therefore, sympathy may be expected (Lu. 10^{37}).   *Hated* is probably to be taken literally, = " detested " as a troublesome and obstructive person ; possibly, however, = " relatively disre-

---

* Theod. Targ. Saad. Rashi, Luth. RV. Schult. De Wette, Noyes, Reuss, De. Kamp. Frank. *al.*

garded " (cf. Lu. 14[26] with Mt. 10[37]).   The second cl. is lit.: *the lovers of the rich are many*.   The proverb states, without comment, a universal social fact. — **21**. *Neighbor*, as in the preceding verse, only he is here a person to whom sympathy is due, and it is assumed that he is poor; *despise* (= contemptuously neglect and repel) is substantially *hate*.   The first cl., thus, passes judgment on the coldhearted " neighbor " of v.[20], declaring that he *sins* against the law of God (see notes on 1[10] 8[36]).   The parallelism of the two proverbs points to the rendering *poor* (RV.) in second cl. (= physically poor), though the Heb. word may also mean *afflicted, suffering* in a general sense (De. Kamp. *al.*). — As he who despises the poor *sins* against God, so he who is kind to him is *happy* (not in the consciousness of well-doing, but) in the favor of God, who will reward such beneficence.   Here we see the starting-point for the later view (Dan. 4[24(27)]) that almsgiving has expiatory efficacy, and for the use of *righteousness* as = *almsgiving* (Mt. 6[1]).

17. 𝔐 מזמת אֵשׁ is taken in good sense by the Vrss., except 𝔒𝔏. — 𝔐 יֵשְׁנָא; 𝔊 ὑποφέρει; read יֵשְׁא; Hi. יֵשָׁאן *is quiet;* Ew., against the usage, יֵשׂוּא (= יִשְׁוֵה) *bears himself quietly, endures* (he refers to ψ 131[2]).   𝔏 = 𝔐.   On 𝔖 (= 𝔊) see Pink.   𝔗 paraphrases 𝔐, only taking מ׳ in good sense, and יֵשְׁנָא as Qal, making subj. in ᵃ the same as in ᵇ. — **18.** For 𝔐 יַכְתִּרוּ neither the Heb. meaning *surround* (as = *get possession of*, cf. Ez. 21[14]) nor the Aram. *wait for* (Job 36[2]) is here appropriate.   The denom. sense, from כתר *crown* (favored by a large number of authorities, ancient and modern) is more appropriate; but this use, which occurs nowhere else, is of doubtful correctness, nor does it furnish an exact or specially apt antithesis to the נחלו of ᵃ.   The term for *crown* in Pr. (4[9] 12[4] 14[24] 16[31] 17[6]) is עֲטָרָה; the noun כתר may be Heb. (cf. כֹּתֶרֶת *a capital*, 1 K. 7[16], and Ass. *kudur*, a sort of *cap* or *head-covering* [De. *Ass. Wbch.*]), but, as it occurs only in Esth., and as, according to Suidas, κίδαρις was said to be a Persian term for royal or priestly crown, it may be Persian.   The Pers. word may, however, come from the Babylonian. κίδαρις (= κίταρις), it seems, meant also a felt hat, a sense which Bab. *kudur* might well have.   Cf. Lag. *Gesamm. Abhandl.* 207.   De. compares post-Bibl. מכתר *giver of crowns*, and כֶּתֶר הדעת *crown of knowledge.*   Bi. יכרו *buy*, which is not decidedly apposite; Gr. יתפארו *glory* (as he and Cheyne read in ψ 142[8]), also unsatisfactory.   The connection calls for the sense *acquire*, but the reading is uncertain; we should, perhaps, emend to יורשו or יירשו, or to יאחזו, which 𝔊 κρατήσουσιν may represent. — **19.** The Anc. Vrss., except 𝔏, supply a verb in ᵇ: 𝔊 θεραπεύσουσιν; 𝔖𝔗 נֵחֹן *come.* — **20.** In 𝔐 לְרֵעֵהוּ the לְ expresses general relation, = *in respect to, for*.   The cl. may be rendered: *even to his* *neighbor the poor man is a hated person.* — **21.** עָנִי and עָנָו are identical in meaning throughout OT. In Prov. Keth. always gives the former (3³⁴ 14²¹ 15¹⁵ 16¹⁹ 22²² 30¹⁴ 31⁹· ²⁰), the latter is given by Qeri in 3³⁴ 14²¹ 16¹⁹. Possibly the Massoretes in the last-named passages, and in ψ 9¹³⁽¹²⁾ 10¹², take עָנִי in a physical and עָנָו in a religious sense (cf. the opposite change in ψ 9¹⁹⁽¹⁸⁾); the distinction is unwarranted, and it is difficult to see why they have altered the text in just these passages. 𝔖𝔗 (מסכן) understand the term in the physical sense. In ψ 9¹⁹ 𝔖 has מסכן, 𝔗 the vb. עני. — 𝔊ᵃ πένητας perhaps represents רשׁם (instead of רעהו), but may be interpretative assimilation to the πτωχούς of ᵇ. — 𝔏 adds at end the gloss: *qui credit in Domino misericordiam diligit.*

22. Recompense of beneficence and maleficence.

> Do not they go astray who devise evil ?
> But they who devise good meet with kindness and faithfulness.

Antithetic, ternary. The interrogative form is emphatic, = *verily, they go astray.* The derived sense *devise* is here better than the more primitive *cut, carve* (Reuss), or *plough* (Ew.) ; *devise evil, devise good* are general expressions for planning and doing wrong and right. The figure in *go astray* is that of travel : the bad man wanders hopelessly, and the expression may be rendered : *go to destruction.* The expression *kindness and faithfulness* (or, as hendiadys, *faithful kindness*) denotes honest, constant, friendly dealing, on the part of man or of God ; see Gen. 47²⁹ (Jacob asks of Joseph), Jos. 2¹⁴ (the spies promise Rahab), 2 Sam. 15²⁰ (David's farewell to Ittai), 2 Sam. 2⁶ (David's greeting to the men of Jabesh-Gilead) ; the phrase occurs in Pr. 3³ (on which see note) 16⁶ 20²⁸, in which passages the reference is to human relations, and such is probably the sense here. The proverb affirms that bad men are without the friendly help of their fellows, while good men meet with kindness. The translation *mercy and truth* (RV.) may be retained for its beauty, if it be understood in the sense given above. — The Grk. (followed by Syr.) has two forms of the couplet. One follows the consonants of the Hebrew, but changes the grammatical forms :

> They who err devise evil,
> But the good devise mercy and truth.

The other departs more widely from the Hebrew :

> The workers of evil know not mercy and faith,
> But acts of kindness and faith belong to good workers.

In second cl. the Lat. has : *mercy and truth devise good*. These readings offer no satisfactory suggestions for changes of the Hebrew.

23. Work versus talk.

> In all labor there is profit,
> But mere talk tends only to penury.

Antithetic, ternary. In second cl., lit. : *the talk of the lips is only*, etc. The Grk. interprets : *he who is merry and careless can only come to penury*. The verse (the simple reflection of which seemed bald) is paraphrased by the Syr. in a distinctly religious sense : *in all thine anxiety there is one thing which is profitable*, (namely,) *he in whose life there is lack shall have repose and comfort; the Lord heals every sorrow; but the talk of the lips of the wicked brings them to penury*. This is quite in the manner of the Jewish Midrash (but the Targ. here is literal). Lagarde thinks the paraphrase the work of a Christian scribe who had in mind Lu. 16$^{19-31}$ (parable of Lazarus) 10^{42} (Mary's "good part"). The proverb simply inculcates industry.

24. Coronets of sages and fools. The Hebrew reads :

> The crown of the wise is their riches,
> The folly of fools is folly,

which must be taken to mean that wealth is an ornament to those who wisely use it (better : *wealth is the* [or, *a*] *crown*, etc.), and that folly, when accompanied by wealth, remains always folly. But this interpretation requires too much to be supplied, and the statement of first cl. is strange ; elsewhere in Pr. the *crown* is the honor bestowed by wisdom (4^9), or a good wife (12^4), or the hoary head (16^{31}), or grandchildren (17^6) ; *wealth* is bestowed by wisdom (3^{16} 8^{18}), or is the reward of piety (22^4), but not elsewhere an ornament to wise men. The interpretation "wealth is that crown of honor which is bestowed by wisdom" (4^9 3^{16}) seems farfetched — the line here refers to the use made of wealth by the wise. A couple of changes in the Hebrew (based on the Grk.) give the reading :

> The crown of the wise is their wisdom,
> The diadem of fools is their folly.

This offers a natural antithesis (ternary). In second cl. Targ. has: *the glory of fools;* Syr.: *the subversion,* etc. Cf. BS. 13²⁴: *Wealth is good for him who is without sin, and poverty is bad in the mouth(?) of the pious* (or, according to another reading, *the ungodly*).

25. True testimony saves, false testimony slays. Our Hebrew reads:

> A true witness saves lives,
> But he who utters lies is (= causes) deception.

Antithetic, ternary. Instead of *is deception* we may read: *deceives.* The reference is to legal procedures. Truthful testimony saves men from death (when they are unjustly accused), and in general from loss and misfortune, while false testimony, according to the present Heb. text, deceives the judges and the public, and thus brings ruin or loss on innocent persons. Similar sayings are 6¹⁹ 12¹⁷ 14⁵. — But the form of second cl. is grammatically unsatisfactory, and does not give a clear antithesis to first clause. It is probably better, by a slight change of the Heb., to read:

> But he who utters lies destroys.

26, 27. The preservative power of godly fear.

> 26. He who fears Yahweh has strong ground of confidence,
> And his children will have a refuge.
> 27. The fear of Yahweh is a fountain of life,
> Whereby one avoids the snares of death.

26. Continuous parallelism, ternary, or quaternary-ternary. The Heb. has: *in the fear of Yahweh is,* etc., but this gives no antecedent for the *his* of second cl., which cannot refer to *Yahweh;* the usage of Prov., and the parallel aphorism, 20⁷, show that the children of the God-fearing man are meant: such passages as Dt. 14¹ (Ew.), ψ 73¹⁵, in which Israelites are called "sons of God," have no bearing on this verse. Nor is it satisfactory to consider the *his* as referring to a *he who fears* contained implicitly in *the fear* (De. Str. *al.*); this is rhetorically hard and unnatural. If the unity of the couplet is to be preserved, it is better (with Luther) to change the text and read as above. To *fear Yahweh* is to have reverent regard for his law, with its rewards and punishments, and this ensures his protection. The second cl. involves the idea of solidarity and inheritance, according to which children reap the fruits of the father's deeds (Ex. 20[5. 6], and *contra*, Dt. 24[16] Jer. 31[29] Ez. 18[2]). It is less likely that the reference is to the good training of pious fathers, whereby their children learn to fear God and thus have him as a refuge ; this, if it were the sage's thought, would be distinctly expressed. — **27.** Continuous, ternary or quaternary-ternary. Lit. : *to avoid.* The couplet is identical with 13[14], with substitution of *the fear of Yahweh* for *the law of the wise,* the two things being regarded in Prov. as mutually equivalent, and as of equal authority (cf. BS. 19[20]). The teaching of the sage rests on his own observation and conviction, but it involves the recognition of God as the supreme source of truth. — The change of figure (*fountain* and *snares*) is not rhetorically bad.

28. Population the measure of strength.

> A numerous people secures the king's glory,
> But lack of people entails his destruction.

Antithetic, ternary (or, binary). Lit. : *in the multitude of people is . . . but in the lack . . . is the destruction of the prince* (De., unnecessarily and improbably, *the destruction of his glory*). This political observation, which suits any time, refers to industrial activity and international wars, and declares that wealth and military strength are the decisive factors in national political life — a purely human point of view, standing in contrast with that of the prophets and psalmists ; see Isa. 7[11] 10[15] 37[20] 14[22] 49[7] Ez. 39[28] Joel 3(4)[12-16] ψ 33[16]. Cf. v.[34].

29-33. Various exhibitions of wisdom and folly.

> **29.** He who is slow to anger shows great wisdom,
> He who is of hasty temper shows great folly.
> **30.** A tranquil mind is the life of the body,
> But passion is rottenness of bones.
> **31.** He who oppresses the poor reviles his Maker,
> He honors him who has mercy on the needy.
> **32.** The wicked is overthrown by his wickedness,
> But the righteous may trust ‹ to his integrity.›
> **33.** Wisdom takes up its abode in the mind of men of sense,
> And ‹ folly › in the mind of fools.

29. Antithetic, ternary. *Wisdom* is, more exactly, *good sense;* the irascible man is characterized as a fool on general principles of personal and social well-being. In second line the verb of our Heb. text is lit. *lifts up, exalts,* which (if the text be retained) is best understood * as = *increases* (= *is full of, brings to a high pitch*), or † as = *proclaims aloud;* in any case the sense is that hasty temper is a sign of lack of sense ; the renderings : *takes folly up* (as it lies before his feet) ‡ and *carries* folly *away* (receives it as his portion in life), § while they give the same general meaning, are not favored by the parallelism. The text should probably be changed so as to read *increases.* — **30.** Antithetic, quaternary-ternary. *Tranquil mind* is lit. *heart of healing,* = a mind or nature which soothes its possessor ; its opposite is an excitable, passionate disposition which keeps the man in turmoil, which is to the soul as caries to the bones. *Body* (lit. *flesh*) and *bones* stand for the man's whole being (as often elsewhere), and are not to be understood (De.) as referring to the close relation between body and mind ; this physiologico-psychological observation is not found in OT. The rendering *passion* (for the word which often means *envy, jealousy, indignation*) is suggested by the connection (the term expresses the opposite of tranquillity) ; for a similar sense cf. Ez. 5[13] Isa. 42[13] Cant. 8[6]. *Jealousy* (if this translation be adopted) will express the pain one feels at the success of others ; but we should then expect in the first cl. the opposite feeling (sympathy, well-wishing). — **31.** Chiastic antithesis, ternary. The *his* may refer to the subject *he,* or to the *poor;* in the former case, the insult to God consists in the violation of his command to be good to the poor, in the latter case the consideration is that neglect of the creature is offence to the Creator. In either case the familiar duty is based on religious grounds, but in the latter case (as De. remarks) there is the implied recognition of a common humanity — the needy man is not merely an object of passing sympathy, he is respected as a creation of the divine wisdom. A similar idea is found in Mal. 2[10], and an exact parallel in Job 31[15]; in the well-known hymn of Cleanthes all men are said to be sons of God. Here a practical turn is given to the conception. Cf. 17[5] 19[17]

---

* So Grk. Targ. Syr. Fleisch. Kamp.   ‡ Ew.
† With Schult. Reuss.   § Rashi, De. Str.

BS 4⁵·⁶ (in which a special prudential motive is introduced). *Maker* is a divine name of the late reflective literature (Isa. 51¹³ 54⁵ Job 4¹⁷ 35¹⁰ ψ 95⁶) ; Hos. 8¹⁴ Isa. 17⁷, in which also the word occurs, are probably late editorial insertions. — **32**. Antithetic, ternary. In the reading given above (which follows the Grk.) the contrast is the common one between the results of righteousness and wickedness, the second cl. affirming that a good man, on account of his integrity, has ground to expect the protection of God. This does not involve self-righteousness (De.), but is simply the general teaching of Prov. as to the reward of the righteous. — As the text stands, it must be rendered :

> The wicked is overthrown by his calamity,
> But the righteous has hope (even) in his death,

in which the contrast is between the absoluteness of the fall of a wicked man, and the confidence or trust which the good man has even in the greatest of calamities. One objection to this rendering is that the term *hope* (or, *trust, confidence*) is nowhere else used absolutely, but always with the addition of the object or ground of hope (30⁵ Isa. 30² ψ 118⁸ *al.*). But the chief difficulty lies in the necessity of defining *hope* in accordance with the usage of Proverbs. The book does not recognize a joyful immortality, but everywhere retains the old idea of Sheol, and regards death as a misfortune. What hope could the righteous have for the hereafter? Delitzsch suggests that, though there was then no revelation of true immortality, yet the pious trusted God, and fell asleep, believing that they were going home to him ; this, however, is but another way of saying that they had the hope of immortal life. We must either suppose that Prov. here announces a doctrine which is ignored in the rest of the book, or we must recognize an erroneous reading in the Hebrew text. A slight change gives the reading of the Grk. — **33**. Antithetic, ternary. Lit. : *In the heart* (= *mind*) *of the intelligent man wisdom reposes* (or, *is at rest*), *but in the mind* (or, *inward part*) *of fools it makes itself known* (or, *is made known*). Since the meaning cannot be that true wisdom is possessed by fools, the *it* (= *wisdom*) of second cl. must be understood (according to the present text) in a sarcastic or ironical or humorous sense, and *known* must express a contrast

to *reposes*, so that we may paraphrase : " a man of sense, not
being ambitious to gain applause, keeps his wisdom to himself
(reserving it for fit occasion), while a fool, anxious to shine, or
ignorant of propriety, airs what he thinks his wisdom at every
opportunity." But this paraphrase contains too much explanation,
and the employment of *wisdom* in a sarcastic sense is unexampled
and improbable ; moreover the expression *it makes itself known in
the mind of fools* is strange and hard. Cf. 12²³, where a sentiment
of this sort is clearly expressed. The Grk. (followed by Syr.)
inserts the negative, and says that it is *not known* in fools, while
the Targ. reads : *folly is known* (or, *makes itself known*) ; these
emendations offer an intelligible statement, but they leave the
strange term *known*, which yields no satisfactory sense. The Lat.
gives the bold interpretation : *it will teach fools also* (cf. 8⁵), which,
however, the Heb. cannot mean. The rendering : (*that which is*)
in the inward part of fools is made known (Schult. RV.) is syntactically highly improbable, if not impossible. The present text
seems impracticable ; the change of *is known* to *folly* (not a violent one in the Hebrew) gives a syntactically natural sentence,
with a sense substantially that of 13¹⁶ 14⁸ 15². ¹⁴ (and cf. Eccl. 7⁹) :
practical wisdom is the permanent possession of men who have a
true perception of the relations of life, while folly in conduct
(אולת) characterizes those who are intellectually dull (כסל). The
distinction between perception and conduct is made elsewhere in
Prov. (10²³ 14⁸ *al.*).

34, 35. Relation of nations and kings to integrity and intelligence.

34. Righteousness exalts a nation,
    But sin is the disgrace of peoples.
35. The king's favor is bestowed on a servant who acts intelligently,
    His anger rests on one who conducts affairs badly.

34. Antithetic, ternary. *Righteousness* here = general moral
integrity, its opposite is *sin; exalts* = gives prosperity and power ;
disgrace = that which produces contempt, namely, on account of
lack of national vigor and power. The sentiment is substantially
that of the prophets, that national prosperity accompanies obedience to divine law — only, there is here no reference to the specific
Israelitish Law, and the relation between integrity and success is

conceived under the general laws of social life. It is not clear
whether there is reference to the nation as a political unit, whether,
that is, we have here a principle of international ethics; but, as
such a principle is nowhere else stated in OT., the reference is
probably intranational. The recognition of the necessity of integrity in the life of the people is distinct and noteworthy; the
motive, as elsewhere in Prov., is utilitarian: morality is commercially and socially profitable. — **35.** Antithetic, ternary. In first
cl. the predicate is *who acts cleverly, skilfully,* that is, in administrative affairs; the contrasted predicate is *who acts badly,* that
is, is incompetent. *Servant* = any subordinate, here an official
person. The verse may be rendered:

> A clever servant has the king's favor,
> An incompetent one his displeasure.

22. 𝔐 הַלּוֹא is not expressed in any Anc. Vrs. (𝔖 עוּלָא *the godless,* and so 𝔗),
but is good in sense and rhythm. For 𝔐 יתעו Hi. proposes יָרְעוּ, and for ה' י' Gr.
suggests יחעבו עלם; neither of these emendations is a distinct improvement of
𝔐. Before הרשׁי in ᵇ insert ר (cf. 13¹⁸ 16⁶); so 𝔊. — On the double rendering
in 𝔊𝔖 see Lag. Baum. Pink. Lag. regards the second form in 𝔊 as original,
but this is not clear. — **23.** 𝔊 appears not to give a double translation of 𝔐ᵃ
(Lag.), but to render 𝔐 דבר שׂפתים freely by ἡδὺς καὶ ἀνάλγητος. On 𝔖 (which
follows 𝔊, but also gives 𝔐ᵇ paraphrastically) cf. Pink. — **24.** 𝔐ᵃ עֵשָׂרם;
𝔊 πανοῦργος; read יָרְמֶם or עָרְמחם. — 𝔐ᵇ אוּלֶת (first occurrence), rendered
freely by 𝔊 διατριβή; read לִוֵֹת (1⁹ 4⁹). The second א is better written
אוּלֶחַם. — 𝔐 מַרְמֶה; read, with Hi., מַרְפֵּה *destroys.* — **26.** 𝔐 בִּירֹבא יהוה; read
לִירָא יְ, to gain an antecedent for the suffix in following בְּנָיו. — **27.** 𝔐 יִרְאַת;
𝔊 πρόσταγμα, = הֹרֶת, as in 13¹⁴ (Jäg. Baum.). — **28.** 𝔐 רֹזֶן, only here; elsewhere (8¹⁵ 31⁴ Ju. 5³ Hab. 1¹⁰ Isa. 40²³ ψ 2²) רוֹזְן; the stem (see the Arab.)
= *heavy, weighty, powerful;* 𝔊 δυνάστου; 𝔗 פָּרְנַס (πρόνοος) *provider, leader*
(so Heb. רעה); 𝔖 מֶלֶךְ; 𝔏 *principis;* cf. name of Syr. king רזן, I K. 11²³. —
29. 𝔐 חֶרַם; 𝔊 ἰσχυρός (ἰσχυρῶς Bᵃᵇ ᴬᶜ· ᵃ A); 𝔗 סני, apparently = מְרַבה (Gr.),
which we should probably here read. — **30.** 𝔊ᵃ (followed by 𝔖) πραΰθυμος
ἀνὴρ καρδίας ἰατρός is free rendering of 𝔐, the two first words (𝔐 חיי בשָׂרם)
having been conformed, by scribal caprice, to the beginning of v.²⁹, μακρόθυμος
ἀνήρ, and taken as subject; for 𝔐 רב מרפא 𝔊 appears to have read מרפא לב.
— **31.** 𝔐 עֹשֵׁק; 𝔊 ὁ συκοφαντῶν. — רל and אבין do not occur in chs. 1–9. —
32. 𝔐 הֹסה במֹחו; 𝔊 ὁ πεποιθὼς τῇ ἑαυτοῦ ὁσιότητι; read בתמּו (Bi. Kamp.
Frank.). — **33.** 𝔐 הֵרָיְעַ; read אוּלֶת. For ἀνδρὸς, in 𝔊 ἐν καρδίᾳ ἀγαθῇ ἀνδρὸς
σοφία, Jäg. proposes ἔνεδρος, which would satisfactorily represent 𝔐 תָּנַח (see
Lag.). — **34.** 𝔐 הסר (apparently an Aramaism); 𝔊 ἐλασσονοῦσι, = חסר (Jäg.).
— **35.** 𝔐 יְיַבְרְבוּ; 𝔊 τῇ δὲ ἑαυτοῦ εὐστροφίᾳ, = וערמָחו (Jäg.). — 𝔊 has another
rendering of ᵇ in 15¹ᵃ: ὀργὴ ἀπόλλυσιν καὶ φρονίμους (מֵבֶן).

XV. 1. Power of gentleness.

> A soft answer turns away wrath,
> But harsh words stir up anger.

Antithetic, ternary. *Soft* = mild, gentle ; see 25[15]. *Turns away;*
cf. 29[11] 24[18] Jer. 18[20] ; one Greek text has *causes to cease* (= destroys). *Harsh* (RV. *grievous*) is that which produces vexation
or pain. Hindu, Chinese, Greek and other parallels to this proverb are given by Malan ; see also Ptah-hotep (in Art. *Egyptian
Lit.*, in *Lib. of World's Best Lit.*). — To this couplet the Grk.
prefixes a modified form of second cl. of 14[35] : *anger destroys even
the wise.*

2. Speech of sage and fool.

> The tongue of the wise ‹ dispenses › knowledge,
> The mouth of fools utters folly.

Antithetic, quaternary (or, ternary). *Dispenses* is lit. *drops* (5[3]
Job 29[22] Am. 7[16] Ez. 20[46] [21[2]] *al.*), for which the Heb. has *makes
good*, that is, does or treats in a good, excellent way, RV. *uttereth
aright;* this does not give so exact a contrast to *utters* as the reading here adopted, which is obtained by a slight change in one
Heb. letter. The reference is to all wisdom and folly, religious
and other. Cf. 10[20. 31. 32] 12[18] 14[3].

3. God's criticism of life.

> The eyes of Yahweh are in every place,
> Keeping watch on wicked and good.

Continuous, ternary. The Participle in second cl. is used of the
watchman of a city (2 K. 9[17] Isa. 52[8]), of the prophet as moral
and religious critic (Ez. 3[17]), of the wife as guardian of the household (31[27]), and the verb of God as observer of men (ψ 66[7]).
This universal divine criticism is adduced as a warning against
wrong-doing (De.) : Yahweh will punish the bad and reward the
good — nothing escapes his eye. Possibly also (Frank.) the
couplet is aimed at the philosophical theory that God looks with
indifference on human actions (Epicureanism).

4. Gentle speech.

> A soothing tongue is a tree of life,
> But violent words wound the soul.

Antithetic, ternary. *Soothing tongue* is lit. *the healing of the tongue*, that is, its utterance which has power to heal or soothe the feelings of others, becoming thus to them a source of enjoyable life ; the two terms of the Heb. expression should perhaps be inverted, so as to read *a tongue of healing* (such is the order in 14³⁰, *a heart of healing*). RV. *wholesome tongue ;* De. *gentleness of tongue.* On *tree of life* see note on 3¹⁸.—The Heb. of second cl. reads lit.: *but violence* (RV. *perverseness*) *therein* (that is, in the tongue) *is a breaking of the spirit,* a crushing or wounding of the man to whom or of whom such words are spoken ; *spirit* = inner being or personality ; for the expression see Isa. 65¹⁴ (RV. *vexation of spirit*).— *Violent* is that which passes beyond the line of right, the immoderate, extravagant, or false ; see note on 11³, and, for the corresponding verb, notes on 13⁶ 19⁸ 21¹² 22¹². The parallelism here favors the sense *immoderate* (so the Lat.) or *violent,* which gives a contrast like that in v.¹.—The second cl. is misunderstood by all the Anc. Vrss. except the Latin.

5. Docility a mark of wisdom.

> A fool despises his father's instruction,
> But he who regards reproof acts wisely.

Antithetic, quaternary-ternary (or, ternary). Cf. 13¹ 15²⁰. *Acts wisely* = is wise, that is, shows his good sense in accepting reproof. The first cl. assumes that parental instruction is the basis of moral life, but the characterization of the fool as a despiser holds good, in Prov., in respect to all instruction (10⁸ 12¹ *al.*).

6. Financial reward of righteousness.

> In the house of the righteous are great stores,
> But the revenues of the wicked are ‹ cut off.›

Antithetic, ternary. Cf. 10² 11⁴ 15²⁷. Physical prosperity is represented as the reward of virtue. The Heb. reads lit.: *the house of the righteous is a great store* (or, *treasure*), *but in the revenue* (or, *produce*) *of the wicked is a thing troubled* (that is, brought into misfortune, calamity, or embarrassment, see Ju. 11³⁵ 1 Sam. 14²⁹ 1 K. 18¹⁷) ; cf. 11¹⁷·²⁹. This last expression is not here appropriate ; *calamity* (RV. *trouble*) would be logically correct, though the Heb. does not admit of this translation ; the antithesis favors the reading (found in one Greek text) *destroyed, cut off;* the prep. *in* should be removed from second cl., and inserted (as in RV.) in first clause. The form of expression of the couplet is drawn from agricultural life; the term *revenue* occurs in 3⁹·¹⁴ 8¹⁹ 10¹⁶ 14⁴ 16⁸ 18²⁰ Ex. 23¹⁰ Jos. 5¹² *al.* — The Grk. has two renderings of the couplet, one differing slightly from the Heb., the other conformed to it; the former is probably the older, the latter a revision.

7. Sages, not fools, seek knowledge.

> The lips of the wise ‹preserve› knowledge,
> But the mind of fools is without ‹intelligence.›

Antithetic, quaternary-ternary. The proverb contrasts the wise man's devotion to knowledge with the intellectual dulness of the opposite class. *Wise* and *foolish* denote tempers or constitutions of mind; *knowledge* is the product or the accumulated treasure of wisdom. *Lips* and *mind* (*heart*) are substantially synonyms; the lips speak what the mind thinks; so in v.²⁸, and cf. v.¹⁴. Here, as elsewhere in Pr., stress is laid on utterance and teaching. — In the first line the verb in the Heb. is *scatter*, a word elsewhere used of destructive dispersion (20⁸·²⁶ Ez. 5¹⁰ ψ 106²⁷ *al.*); the appropriate term *preserve* is obtained by the change of one letter. The last expression of second cl. reads in the Heb. *is not so*, or, *is not upright* (or, *honest*, or, *steadfast*, or, *trustworthy*). The first of these renderings is rhetorically lame and improbable, and is hardly bettered by RV. *doeth not so;* the verb *scatter*, retained by RV., suits *lips*, but not *mind*, though this difficulty disappears if we read *preserve*. The second rendering supplies no good contrast to first cl.; the point is not the fool's lack of uprightness, but his inability to appreciate knowledge. The contrast is gained by a slight change in the Heb. text, whereby we have the sense *does not understand;* for similar expressions see 18⁵ 23¹⁵ 28⁵ 29⁷. The *fool*, whose point of view puts him out of sympathy with the right, has no real comprehension of life.

8, 9. Two abominations of the Lord. — Antithetic, quaternary-ternary.

> 8. The sacrifice of the wicked is an abomination to Yahweh,
> But the prayer of the upright is acceptable to him.

9. Abomination to Yahweh is the life of the wicked,
But him who practises righteousness he loves.

8. This is one of the few places in Prov. in which the sacrificial ritual is mentioned (see 7^{14} 17^1 $21^{3.\ 27}$), and here, as in $21^{3.\ 27}$, it is introduced in a connection which calls for disapprobation. Sacrifice without righteousness, say the sages and the prophets, is abhorrent to God; sacrifice with righteousness is not mentioned in Prov., perhaps because it was obviously proper, and called for no remark. The sages recognize the ritual as a legitimate and binding form of worship, but they lay no stress on it — they never enjoin obedience to its requirements. — The contrast of *sacrifice* and *prayer* appears to be doubly significant: it intimates that the former is an outward service easily performed by a bad man, while the latter is an inward service appropriate to the sincerely pious; and it suggests that, in a certain circle, a movement had begun which, by laying stress on communion of heart with God, tended to bring about the abolition of the sacrificial ritual; a similar movement appears to be indicated in ψ 50^{14}, and is most fully visible in the Sermon on the Mount. — The two terms can hardly here be synonyms, standing each for a ritual complex which includes the commonly associated acts of sacrifice and prayer (see 1 Sam. 1^{12} 2 Sam. 7^{18}, and cf. Lu. 1^{10}); the antithesis is here marked. — For a similar attitude toward sacrifice cf. Am. 5^{22} Isa. 1^{11} Jer. 7^{22} 1 Sam. 15^{22} ψ 50^{9-14} $51^{16.\ 17\ (18.\ 19)}$. On *sacrifice* see note on 7^{14}, on *acceptable*, notes on 8^{35} 10^{32} 11^1, and, for the ritual use of the term, Lev. 1^3. The prayer of the morally good man is *acceptable*, is pleasing and is heard, simply because he is good — but it is not said whether or not he also offers sacrifice. — **9.** Parallel to the preceding couplet, with substitution of ethical for religious conditions. *Life* is lit. *way*, = line of conduct, manner of life; *practises* is lit. *follows after.* — Possibly the editor, in putting the two couplets together, meant to explain the first by the second.

10. He who will not learn must die.

There is stern correction for him who forsakes the way,
He who hates reproof shall die.

Identical, ternary. The *way* is that of truth and righteousness. The *stern* (hard, grievous, sharp) *correction* is death (second cl.

shall die). On *correction* and *reproof* see notes on 1². ²³. The person described is the morally wicked, disobedient man ; the punishment is physical and earthly. Life is represented as a discipline — woe to him who fails to profit thereby ! — Grk., interpreting : *shall die basely* (or, *a shameful death*).

11. The depths of the soul are known to God.

> Sheol and Abaddon lie open before Yahweh,
> How much more the hearts of men !

Extended parallelism, ternary. The couplet expresses a conclusion from the less to the greater ; it is assumed that the Underworld is a more remote and mysterious region than the human soul. On *Sheol* see notes on 1¹² 5⁵ *al.* The term *Abaddon* (= place of destruction, region of death) occurs elsewhere in OT. in 27²⁰ (in connection, as here, with *Sheol*), Job 26⁶ (parallel to *Sheol*), 28²² (in connection with *Death*, = the Realm of death), 31¹² (= Underworld), ψ 88¹¹⁽¹²⁾ (parallel to *Grave*, and = Underworld) ; it is thus a synonym of *Sheol*, to which it is here added for rhetorical emphasis. There is no authority for the opinion (De.) that *Abaddon* is the lowest region of Sheol. The OT. does not recognize strata in Sheol ; the expression in Dt. 32²² ψ 86¹³, *Sheol below* (AV. *lowest hell*, RV. *lowest pit*), simply describes Sheol as a place beneath the earth, like the *Netherland* (= Sheol) of Ez. 31¹⁴. In the NT. Apocalypse (9¹¹) Abaddon is the name of the Angel of the Abyss (= Angel who inflicts death, and sends men to Sheol) ; in the Talmud (*Shab.* 89ᵃ) it is used in a similar manner ; as the conception of the other life became more definite, the tendency was to personalize OT. expressions. Here, as in Job 26⁶, Yahweh is apparently represented as controlling Sheol ; a different view is expressed in Isa. 39¹⁸, where (as generally in the earlier literature) Yahweh has nothing to do with the Underworld (cf. note on 1¹²) ; the change of view was due to the completer development of the monotheistic idea. Even Job (Job 14¹³) is not sure that God's power controls Sheol ; the view of Prov. is more advanced, but still does not express a moral control exercised by God over the denizens of the Underworld. — *Men* is lit. *children of men; son of man* is a comparatively late Heb.

expression for "human being"; so Ez. 2^1 *al.*, Job 25^6 ψ $8^{4(5)}$ 33^{13} Dan. 8^{17} (and Aramaic, 7^{13}).

12. Indocility of the scoffer.

> A scoffer loves not to be reproved,
> And will not walk ‹ with › the wise.

Explanatory parallelism, ternary-binary. On *scoffer* see note on 1^{22}. In second cl. the Heb. has *go to;* the better reading is given in 13^{20} (so the Grk. here); cf. 22^{24} ("do not walk [associate] with an irascible man"). Cf. also 1^{15} 4^{14}. The scoffer is regarded as a man whose character is fixed. It is not suggested that he might be helped by association with the wise.

13. Joy enlivens, sorrow depresses.

> Joyous heart makes cheerful face,
> But by sorrow of soul the spirit is broken.

Antithesis partly implicit, ternary. RV. (= AV.) : *a merry heart maketh a cheerful countenance*, in which the word *merry* now implies more of movement and utterance than is contained in the Heb. term, which means *joyful, glad*. *Soul* is lit. *heart; heart* and *spirit* are synonyms, both signifying the inner nature or being, but, in the connection, *spirit* may have the connotation (in Heb. as in English) of courage and hope.—Exact antithesis in expression would require "sad face" in second cl.; the variant phrase implies that a broken spirit is manifested by sadness of countenance, while a cheerful face shows a high, courageous spirit. The proverb notes a fact of experience : joy is inspiring, sorrow is depressing — the advantage of the former is clear. The man's mood is shown by his countenance. Cf. BS. 13^{25}.

14. The aliment of sages is knowledge, of fools folly.

> The mind of the wise seeks knowledge,
> The mouth of fools feeds on folly.

Antithetic, ternary. The relation between *wise* and *knowledge* is the same here as in v.^{7}, on which see note. In second cl. the Heb. text has *face*, which Ewald retains; but the reading of the margin, *mouth* (which is found in all the Anc. Vrss.) accords with the verb *feeds*, and is obviously better; *mouth feeds* is a rhetorical variation of *mind seeks*. — Instead of *feeds on*, the verb of the second cl. may be rendered *is occupied with, strives after* (lit. *associates with*), or, *delights in*, but *feeds* better suits the noun *mouth*. — The word rendered *fools* denotes the highest degree of stolidity, insusceptibility and unreceptiveness; the mental furniture and nourishment of such an one is *foolishness* or *folly* in thought and deed, and this is the product of ignorance. Here, as in 14[33] *al.* and throughout chs. 1–9, virtue is allied with knowledge, vice with ignorance. The verbs express eager interest and devotion.

XV. 1. 﨟 יֵשֵׁב; *Berakoth*, 17 *a* מֵשֵׁב (Strack, *Proleg.*, 105) — 﨟 רַךְ; ⅏ freely ὑποπίπτουσα *submissive*. — 﨟 יַעֲלֶה; ⅏ ἐγείρει, free rendering of 﨟, or of מֵעִיר, as 𝔖 has it. — **2.** 﨟 תֵּיטֵב; read חַפֵּץ (Mic. 2[6] Ez. 21[2]); the stem occurs in Pr. only in 5[3], and then in the literal sense; ⅏ καλὰ ἐπίσταται = 﨟 דַעַת תֵּיטֵב. — 﨟 אַרְלִת; 𝔖 רוֹטִתוּ, = אָלַת (Jäg.). — **4.** In [b] ⅏𝔖𝔗 diverge widely from 﨟: ⅏ ὁ δὲ συντηρῶν αὐτὴν πλησθήσεται πνεύματος; πλ. = יִשְׂבַע; συντ. perh. from פרס or מִפְרָס *weighs* (Jäg. Gr.); Schl. suggests μὴ συντηρῶν and συντριβήσεται. 𝔗 (and substantially 𝔖) וראיכל מן פירוחי נשבע (𝔖 adds מנה), apparently free rendering of ⅏. Bi. writes סֶלֶף and שֶׁבַע. There seems to be nothing better than to retain 﨟, perh. omitting ב in בְּרָח (Isa. 65[14]); De., in support of the ב, adduces Arab. כשר בקלבי *he has broken my heart;* the ב would thus mark the place of the act of breaking. — כֶּרֶף (the stem in 𝔖 usually הפך, 𝔗 קלקל) occurs only here and 11[3], on which see note. — **5.** 﨟 יִנְאַץ; ⅏ μυκτηρίζει. — **6.** In 﨟 בתבאה omit the ב, and insert the same prep. before בַּת (so 𝔖𝔗). Bi. בהרבת. 﨟 וְנֶעְרֶת; read נֶכְרָת. — On ⅏ see Lag. Baum. — **7.** 﨟 יְזָרוּ; ⅏ δέδεται, from אזר; Σ φυλάσσουσι; read יצרו (Frank.). — 﨟 כֵּן; ⅏ ἀσφαλεῖς; 𝔏 (לֹא כֵן) *dissimile;* read יָכֵן (so also Gr. suggests). — **10.** 﨟 לְעוֹזֵב אֹרַח; ⅏ γνωρίζεται ὑπὸ τῶν παριόντων, = לְעַבְרִי אֹ' (Jäg.), γν. being supplied to make the sentence complete. — ⅏ ἀκάκου (﨟 רָע), probably error for κακοῦ (Jäg.). 𝔖 follows ⅏; 𝔗 מטעיא ארחה, perh. free rendering of 﨟. — 﨟 יְמַת; Gr. יִמְט (Hos. 13[1]). — **11.** 﨟 אֲבַדֹּן; ⅏ ἀπώλεια. — **12.** 﨟 אֶל; read אֶת (⅏ μετά). — **13.** In [b] ⅏ σκυθρωπάζει *is sad* maintains פָּנִם as subject, while 𝔖 follows 﨟 except that it makes the verb transitive; in both cases we have the natural freedom of translators. — **14.** Kethib פני; read Qere פִי (so ⅏𝔖𝔗). — 﨟 יִרְעֶה אַרְלֶת; ⅏ γνώσεται (ירד) κακά (perh. = 﨟); Gr. ירצה *delights in*, and Frank. ירעה as corresponding Aram. form; all the senses of the stem רעה seem to be closely related to one another.

15. Happiness is better than sorrow.

> Every day is hard for him who is in trouble,
> But the happy man has a continual feast.

Antithetic, ternary. A statement of ordinary experience (cf. v.[13]), without ethical import, but with implied commendation of cheerfulness and happiness. *Happy* is lit. *good of heart,* that is, in a good, joyous, or cheerful frame of mind. The *feast* is the enjoyment of the conditions of life. *Hard* here represents the same Heb. word that is rendered by *stern* in v.[10]. On the adjective translated *in trouble* (which elsewhere has also the senses *poor, afflicted, pious*) see notes on 3[34] 14[21] 16[19].

16, 17. Superiority of spiritual over physical wealth.

> 16. Better is little with the fear of Yahweh
> Than great treasure and trouble therewith.
> 17. Better a dish of herbs with love
> Than a fatted ox with hate.

16. Single sentence expressing an antithesis, ternary. Lit. *in the fear,* etc., that is, so held. *Trouble* (a different word from that rendered *in trouble* in preceding verse) is disturbance, anxiety, perplexity. It is assumed that the *fear of Yahweh,* morality based on or connected with religion, saves one from harassing care, since it brings divine protection. It is not said that wealth necessarily entails trouble and distress, but only that this may be the case — a statement which the experience of all men, especially in highly organized communities, abundantly confirms; and the couplet is a warning against rage for riches. — **17.** Antithetic sentence, ternary. Cf. 17[1]. The word rendered *dish* appears to mean primarily, "that which one offers to a traveller," and then, in general, "a portion of food"; Grk. *entertainment of a guest;* the allusion in the proverb may be to such entertainment, though the application is general, to all meals. The allusion, as in the preceding couplet, is to the perils of wealth (*fatted ox* stands for luxury in general). There is no polemic against wealth, but a reminder that it is not always an unmixed blessing. On *fatted* see note on 14[4], and cf. 1 K. 4[23] (5[3]).

18, 19. Commendation of patience and industry.

> 18. An irascible man stirs up contention,
> One slow to anger appeases strife.
> 19. The way of the slothful is ‹ hedged up with › thorns,
> But the path of the ‹ diligent › is well-built.

18. Antithetic, ternary. The man of first cl. is not one who is angry (RV. *wrathful*), but one prone to anger, quicktempered, in

contrast with the calm, patient man of second cl.   See the similar
statements in 14^{29} 15^1 BS. 8^{16} 28$^{8-12}$. — **19**. Antithetic, quaternary-
ternary.   Grk., happily : *the way of the slothful is strown with
thorns, that of the sturdy is smooth.*   Heb. : *is like a hedge of
thorns*, in which the *like* is to be omitted (in accordance with the
form of second cl.) and the *hedge* changed to *hedged* — a path
cannot be compared to a hedge, but may be said to be hedged
up, encumbered ; so Hos. 2$^{6(8)}$: *I will hedge up thy way with
thorns.*   The slothful man meets with obstacles at every point, and
makes no progress.   On the other hand, the path of the industrious man is *carefully constructed* and free from obstacles, like a
highway (so RV.) ; the adj. means *cast up*, roads having been constructed by throwing up earth (Jer. 18^{15} Isa. 57^{14}).   The antithesis
requires that the man of second cl. be described as *diligent;* the
Heb. term (*yashar*) may mean *honest, straightforward* (usually,
upright), but an inconsiderable alteration gives the ordinary word
for *industrious* (10^4 12$^{24.\ 27}$ 13^4 21^5).

20, 21. Wisdom and folly — their results for life.   Antithetic,
ternary.   Delitzsch makes v.^{20} (on account of its resemblance to
10^1) the beginning of the third section (see 13^1) of the collection
contained in 10^1–22^{16}.   It may mark the beginning of a separate
minor collection ; see the Introduction.

> 20. A wise son makes a glad father,
>   A fool scorns his mother.
> 21. Folly is delight to one who lacks sense,
>   But a man of understanding is straightforward in his ways.

20. The first cl. is identical with first cl. of 10^1.   In the second
cl., instead of the *is a source of anxiety to* of 10^1 (which furnishes
an obvious contrast), we have the variation *scorns*, which may
be taken to mean " despises advice and so brings sorrow to his
mother," or " shows by his conduct that he despises his mother's
teaching," or simply " scorns his mother and her advice " (so
the Grk.) — that is, the wise son honors and gladdens his father,
the foolish laughs at and saddens his mother.   The variation of
expression in a familiar apophthegm would be not unnatural ; it is
possible, however, that the second cl. stood originally with some
such line as *a wise son honors his father.* — In second cl. the

Heb. reads (as in 21[20]) : *a fool of a man* (RV. *foolish man*) — a
construction like that of Gen. 16[12], *a wild ass of a man* (a man
of the fool sort, of the wild ass species). The Anc. Vrss. and
some Heb. MSS. read *foolish son*, which may be assimilation of the
expression here to the more familiar form of 10[1]. — **21.** The term
folly here has a moral as well as an intellectual content. The
delight is made possible by intellectual and moral obtuseness —
the fool does not understand the consequences of his actions, and
therefore has no basis for his moral life; he takes pleasure in
things bad not because they are bad, but because he does not
know that they are bad, and does not see or believe that they will
bring punishment on him. — He who has insight into the laws of
life, human and divine, acts in a *straightforward* way, is wisely
upright, knowing that this is the only safe rule of life. Knowledge
is thus represented as the foundation of character.

15. Before 𝔥 כֹב insert י. — 𝔊[a] πάντα τὸν χρόνον οἱ ὀφθαλμοὶ τῶν κακῶν
(= עֵינֵי רָעָם) προσδέχονται κακά. Lag. supposes that the Grk. translator had
רַע רַע רַע, which he read רָעָם רֹאֵ֣ת רָעָה; perh., however, the Grk. stands for
לְעֵינֵי רָעָם רָעָה, Bi. עֵינֵי רַע רָעַת. — 𝔥 מִשְׁתֶּה; 𝔊 ἡσυχάσουσιν, = מַשְׁבַּת (Lag.). —
16. 𝔥 מֶהֱמָה; Gr. מֶרְכַה. The following בי is omitted by Bi. on rhythmical
grounds. — For 𝔥 מ׳ 𝔊 has ἀφοβίας, a singular expression (= *without the fear
of Yahweh*), but apparently chosen as contrast to the φόβον of ᵃ; the reading
ἀσεβείας (𝔖[H] 23. 252. Lag.) is scribal emendation; cf. Baum. On 𝔖 see
Pinkuss. — **17.** 𝔥 אֲרֻחַת; 𝔊 ξενισμός; 𝔖𝔗 שֵׁרַת *a meal;* 𝔏 freely, *vocari ad.*
Bi. omits שָׁם, instead of which 𝔊 has καὶ χάριν, perh. = וְחֵן (Bi.), perh.
rhetorical expansion. — 𝔖 רִשְׁמָא; not Rabbin. (love of) *the name,* i.e. *God*
(Baum.), but (love of) *reputation;* see Pinkuss. — **18.** On the two renderings
of 𝔊 see Lag. Baum.; ἀσεβής (חָסֹם), as being farther from 𝔥, is regarded by
Lag. as genuine; 𝔊 τὴν μέλλουσαν (= *the impending* or *threatening quarrel*)
is free rendering of 𝔥 רִב, or, possibly, = הבא; μᾶλλον, in like manner, may
freely express the contrast of the clauses, the מדן of 𝔥 being left untranslated.
𝔖 combines the two renderings of 𝔊, perhaps by alterations of successive
scribes. — **19.** 𝔥 מִשֻׂכָּה; read מְסֻכֶּת (so 𝔊, cf. Lag.). — 𝔥 יְשָׁרִים; 𝔊 ἀνδρείων;
read חָרֻצִם (cf. 𝔊 in 10⁴). — **20.** 𝔥 כֹסֵל אדם; 𝔊𝔖𝔗 and 7 Heb. MSS. have
בֵן כֹסֵל, probably assimilation to 10[1]. — 𝔥 בֹזֶה; 𝔊 μυκτηρίζει; 𝔖 בהתתא *disgrace* (the same stem is employed in 10[1]). — **21.** 𝔊 appears to leave שִׂמְחָה
untranslated, and to insert τρίβοι from the connection; Lag. emends ἐνδεεῖς tο
ἐνδεεῖ.

22, 23. Value of wise words.

> 22. Where there is no counsel plans are thwarted,
>   They succeed when many give advice.

23. Joy comes to a man from the utterance of his mouth,
And a word in season, how good is it!

22. Antithetic, ternary. The idea of the couplet is substantially that of 11^{14}, on which see note; variations of such aphorisms were doubtless common; see note on v.^{20}. The *plans* (RV. *purposes*) may be those of a government or those of a private family or person; *thwarted* (RV. *disappointed*) is lit. *broken; succeed* (RV. *are established*) is lit. *stand;* the last expression of second line is lit.: *by* (or, *through*) *the multitude of counsellors* (or, *advisers*). The king had his cabinet, and the private man his circle of friends. On *counsel* see 3^{32} 11^{13} 20^{19} 25^9, and cf. Am. 3^7 Jer. 23^{18} Job 19^{19} ψ $55^{14(15)}$. — **23.** Synonymous, ternary. *Utterance* is lit. *answer*, a term which is often used in OT. and NT. for expression or speech in general, where there is no obvious response. The meaning appears to be that a well-considered and apposite word may bring profit and joy to him who utters it. The general expression *utterance of the mouth* is defined in second cl. as a *word in season* (lit. *in its time*), appropriate to the situation. The reference will then be to all sorts of occasions of private intercourse (business relations, and other social and family relations) and public affairs in city and state. *Good* = useful, effective. — If the *word in season* be understood as a word of advice, consolation, or general friendliness, which is helpful not to the utterer, but to others, it will be necessary to omit the possessive pronoun in first cl., and read *from an utterance of the mouth.* — The omission of the pronoun still permits, however, the first interpretation of the couplet, which may be rendered: *a judicious utterance brings satisfaction, a seasonable word is useful.*

24. Wisdom is life.

The wise man's path goes upward, to life,
He avoids (the way to) Sheol beneath.

In form antithetic, in meaning identical, ternary. The second cl. is lit.: *so as to turn away from Sheol beneath* (= *so that he turns*, etc.) — appositional proposition put (as is not uncommon in OT.) in the form of result (or, what is the same thing in Heb., purpose). The first cl. is lit.: *the way of life upward is to* (= *is the way of*) *the wise man;* as *beneath* (or, *downward*) qualifies

Sheol, so *upward* qualifies *way of life;* the statement is that the way of life (which is described as an upward one) pertains to the wise and not to the unwise. *Sheol* stands here (as everywhere else in Prov.) for physical death, and the *life* of first cl. must, accordingly, be physical life; see, for example, 13¹⁴ 14²⁷. The significance of the term *upward* is given in the paragraph 2¹⁸⁻²² where the way that leads down to the dead is contrasted with the path of the righteous who continue to dwell on upper earth; the couplet repeats the familiar belief that good men (for *wise* includes *good*) will enjoy long and happy life in this world; see notes on 2¹⁹ 3¹⁸ 5⁶ 10¹⁷ 13¹⁴ *al.* The rendering of RV., *to the wise the way of life* (*goeth*) *upward* appears to imply that there may be a way of life which goes in some other direction; that of Reuss is better : *the wise man climbs the way of life.* There is, however, no reference to an eminence above the earth (heaven, for example) to which the wise man ascends; men in OT. (except Enoch and Elijah) go, after this life, not to heaven but to Sheol; the *upward* is simply the negation of the *beneath* (or, *downward*). — There is in this verse, therefore, when its terms are interpreted in accordance with the usage of the Book of Proverbs, no intimation of a doctrine of happy immortality.

25, 26. Divine antagonism to moral evil. Antithetic, ternary.

> 25. Yahweh uproots the house of the proud,
> But establishes the border of the widow.
> 26. Evil devices are an abomination to Yahweh
> [But pleasant words are pure.]

25. *Widow* here stands for any poor, helpless person, the natural prey of the powerful and unscrupulous, here called *the proud* (16¹⁹ Job 40¹¹ ψ 94²); Yahweh is described as the protector of the weak (so always the chiefs, kings, and national deities of antiquity); he is the father of the orphan, the judge who secures the rights of the widow (ψ 68⁵⁽⁶⁾). The word *border* alludes to the Israelitish law which endeavored to maintain intact the landed property of every family by forbidding its alienation (Dt. 19¹⁴); greed of land is denounced by the prophets (Isa. 5⁸ Mic. 2⁹) and the later moralists (Job 24² Pr. 22²⁸). The law, based at first on the inseparable connection between land and citizenship, became later more directly the expression of a sentiment of justice. — **26**. *Evil devices* are thoughts or plans which look to the injury of others. On *abomination* see note on 3[32]. The second clause, as it stands, cannot be original. The connection calls for the statement of something which is not an offence to Yahweh — the clause simply describes certain words. Many recent commentators and translators, in order to secure a connection between the two clauses, insert the words *to him* in the second ; but, if this is done, the difficulty remains that *pure* (*ṭahōr*) is not a proper contrast to *abomination* (*tōʿēbā*) ; even if it be taken in a ritualistic sense as = *clean*, its opposite is *unclean* (*ṭāmē*) ; in any case it is a singular epithet to apply to friendly speech. Grk. (with a different Heb. text from ours) : *the sayings of the pure are held in honor*, which gives a good thought, but not a satisfactory contrast ; Lat. (following Grk.) : *pure speech will be confirmed by him as very beautiful*. We should, perhaps, change the text so as to read : *pleasant* (or, *gracious*) *words are well-pleasing to him ; gracious words* will then stand as the sign of friendly intention. But even this reading does not give a satisfactory contrast to the first cl., and the line seems to be out of place as well as formally corrupt.

27. Against taking bribes.

> He who is greedy of gain destroys his own house,
> But he who hates gifts will live.

Antithetic, ternary (or, quaternary-ternary). The expression *greedy of gain* involves injustice in the acquisition of wealth (see note on 1[19]). A rebuke of avarice and highhanded dealing, with special reference, in second cl. (and apparently in first cl. also) to judicial and other bribery. Government in Oriental lands has always included the giving and taking of gifts. See 11[29], Ex. 23[8], Ez. 22[12], Eccl. 7[7]. A greedy unscrupulous man (that is, a corrupt judge or magnate) comes to grief, says the sage ; he is ruined by natural causes, or by direct intervention of God.

From this point onward the order of verses in the Grk. varies in an irregular manner from that of the Hebrew ; the nature of the material (isolated sayings) made such variation easy. The arrangement in the Greek (as in the Hebrew) seems to be sometimes determined by verbal resemblances, and there was here great play for the fancy of scribes. Whether the advantage in arrangement is with the Heb. or with the Greek must be determined separately in every case.

28. Speech of good and bad men.

> The righteous considers his words,
> The utterances of the wicked are vicious.

Antithetic, ternary. Lit. *the mind (heart) of the righteous considers* (RV. *studies*) *to answer, and the mouth of the wicked utters bad things;* the Heb. idiom likes to describe fully processes of thought and action. — The antithesis is ethical, not merely intellectual; the meaning is not that the righteous speaks cautiously, the wicked inconsiderately, but that the good man takes care to speak what is true and kind, while the bad man, feeling no concern on this point, follows the bent of his mind, and speaks evil. The propositions are put as universal, in accordance with the ethical system of Proverbs, which recognizes no nice distinctions, but regards men as wholly good or wholly bad. The verb rendered *utters* is lit. *pours out* (see 1^{23} 15^2), and is possibly, but not probably, meant to contrast the wicked man's unscrupulous deluge of words with the deliberate speech of the righteous. — Grk. in first line : *the hearts of the righteous meditate faithfulness,* which gives a better contrast with second line than the Hebrew, and should perhaps be adopted.

29. What prayers are heard.

> Yahweh is far from the wicked,
> But he hears the prayer of the righteous.

Antithetic, ternary. Cf. v.[8]. *Far from* = inaccessible to, deaf to the appeal of. It is involved that the wicked may pray (that is, ask for some favor), but their prayer will not be favorably received. The case of a bad man's repenting is not considered; such a man, in the view of the OT., would, by his repentance, be transferred from the category of the wicked to that of the righteous.

30. Good news.

> Pleasant news makes the heart glad,
> Good tidings make the bones fat.

Synonymous, with variation of terms, ternary. *Pleasant news* is lit. *light* (or, *shining*) *of the eyes*, that is, the light which shines in the eyes of the bringer of good news (as the second cl. suggests) ; cf. 16^{15} Job 29^{24} ψ 4^6 44$^{3(4)}$ 89^{15}. The expression is by some understood to mean *good fortune*, which gives the same general sense ; but this meaning is doubtful, and does not furnish so direct an antithesis as the rendering here adopted. Grk. (with a variation of text) : *the eye which sees beautiful things. Fat bones* are those which are full of marrow ; cf. ψ 63$^{5(6)}$, and notes on 11^{25} 13^4.

31–33. Docility and humility.

> 31. He who hearkens to life-giving admonition
>   Will dwell among the wise.
> 32. He who rejects instruction slights himself,
>   But he who regards admonition gains understanding.
> 33. The fear of Yahweh is instruction in wisdom,
>   And before honor goes humility.

31. Single sentence, quaternary-ternary. Lit. *the ear that hearkens to the admonition of life; the ear* = the man ; on *admonition* (or, *reproof*) see note on 1^{23}. *Dwell* is properly *lodge, pass the night* (Gen. 19^2 2 Sam. 17^8 Job 31^{32}), but the term is used in poetry to express permanent dwelling (19^{23} Job 19^4 ψ 91^1). Teachableness is the key that unlocks the door of the sages. The observation is a general one, but has an academic coloring. The *life* is of this world, and primarily physical (see 3^2 *al.*), but involves the higher moral and religious elements. To *dwell with the wise* is synonym of success and happiness, knowledge is the fundamental fact in life. — The abrupt and vigorous synecdoche which, in second cl., puts *ear* for *man*, is especially natural in gnomic poetry. — **32.** Antithetic, quaternary-ternary. On *instruction* see note on 1^2 ; *admonition*, as in preceding couplet. *Slight* is *despise, lightly esteem*, then *treat slightingly*, and *reject as being of small value* (1 Sam. 8^7 Job 5^{17} Pr. 3^{11}). One who refuses to be taught fails to become wise, and thus puts a slight on himself, treats himself as being of small account. The contrast to this is stated clearly in second clause. The Heb. has a formal antithesis which cannot be reproduced in English : *slights his soul*

(= personality, self) . . . *gains heart* (= understanding) ; the parallelism forbids us to take *soul* as = *life*. The Greek translator abandons the text in order to get the sharp contrast : *hates himself* . . . *loves his own soul*. Here, as in the preceding couplet, understanding, knowledge, wisdom, is the essential thing in life, the synonym of well-being. — **33**. Quaternary-ternary. The connection between the two clauses is not explicit — one of them is perhaps out of place ; but see below. The *fear of Yahweh* is elsewhere described as *the beginning of knowledge* (1^7) or of *wisdom* (9^{10}), and here, in substantially the same sense, as *the instruction of wisdom*, that is, the *instruction* which *wisdom* gives, or, more probably, *instruction in wisdom*. The latter expression is, therefore, the proper subject of the sentence : the material or the essence of wisdom is reverent regard for the divine law, for (as Pr. elsewhere declares) this law is the perfect expression of the truth of life, and obedience to it ensures safe guidance and perfect happiness. This fundamental conception, the identity of divine wisdom and human wisdom, is thus common to the two Divisions, chs. 1–9 and chs. 10^1–22^{16}. See notes on 1^7 9^{10}. — The proper antithesis to second cl. is found in 18^{12} : *pride* leads to *destruction* as *humility* to *honor;* but a connection between *humility* and *the fear of Yahweh* is given in 22^4, which is an expansion of this clause. According to 22^4 the two things are substantially the same : *humility* is a reverent attitude toward God as supreme and holy ruler. If the term be so understood here, the *honor* is the reward (as in 22^4) which God bestows on those who obey him, and our couplet contains an expanded parallelism : *the fear of God is wisdom, and it entails honor*—first the intellectual product of reverence, and then its reward. On the other hand, 18^{12}, compared with 16^{18}, suggests that it is the natural social law that is here contemplated : humble demeanor procures friends and honor, as pride makes enemies and leads to downfall. Probably both conceptions of the aphorism were held, and the gnomic writers used one or the other as suited their purposes. The identity of the two conceptions results from the doctrine that God is the author of natural law.

22. 𝕲 μὴ τιμῶντες = בֹּ זֵב (𝕳 בְּאֵין); ἐν καρδίαις = בְּלֵב (𝕳 בְּרֹב).— The insertion of עֵצָה *counsel* at end of ᵇ (𝕲𝕾𝕿) is adopted by Bi., who refers to

the sing. הָקֵב; this insertion is possible, but hardly necessary; Gr. חֶפְרָה מַחְשָׁבָה.
— On ﬡ, which follows 𝕲, but with arbitrary changes, see Baum. Pinkuss. —
23. 𝕲 οὐ μὴ ὑπακούσῃ ὁ κακὸς αὐτῇ οὐδὲ μὴ εἴπῃ καίριόν τι καὶ καλὸν τῷ κοινῷ
= וּדְבַר בְּעִתּוֹ מַה טּוֹב‎ = לֹא יִשְׁמַע אִישׁ בְּמַעֲנֶה פִיה‎, the man being interpreted as κακός,
and the couplet freely rendered throughout. — As to the original sense of the
stem עָנָה answer cf. Ges. *Thes.*, and Arab. עֲנִי, מַעֲנִי. — 24. 𝕳 לְמַעְלָה; 𝕲 διανοή-
ματα, perh. after Ez. 11⁶, perh. = מַחְשֶׁבֶת; cf. Jäg. Lag. — 𝕳 מַטָּה; 𝕲 σωθῇ,
perh. = מִצֵּל (Baum.), or יְרֵכָה (Jäg.). — 26. On ᵇ see note on this verse above.
𝕲 ἁγνῶν δὲ ῥήσεις σεμναί, in which it is doubtful what Heb. word σ. represents. For 𝕳 טָהוֹר we should perhaps read רַבּוֹנָי. — 27. Instead of σώζεται
(𝕳 יִהְיֶה) 23. 103. 252. 253 have ζήσεται, a correction after the Heb. — See
notes of Lag. and Baum. on the dislocation of couplets at this point. — 28. In
8⁷ 24², ψ 2¹ הגה is followed by the object directly, in ψ 77¹³ 143⁵ by ב and
object, here by ב in 𝔖𝕿; as, however, the object is here an act, the ל is
appropriate. — 𝕳 רְיָנָי; 𝕲ᴮ πίστεις; 𝕲ˣᴬ πίστιν; 𝔖𝕿 (following 𝕲) חיומנתא;
these Vrss. seem to have had אֱמוּנָה or אֱמֻנָה, which should perhaps be adopted
in 𝕳. — 30. 𝕳 מֵאַר עֵינָיו; 𝕲 16² θεωρῶν ὀφθαλμὸς καλά, free rendering of 𝕳
taken to mean "what the eye sees." The Heb. expression does not occur
elsewhere in OT., but appears to mean *the light that resides in the eyes* (cf.
ψ 90⁸); for the rendering *good fortune* there is no authority in OT.; מאר
occurs only in late writings (from Ez. on). — 31. Lacking in 𝕲, probably
by scribal accident. The rendering in 𝔖ᴴ appears to be based on that of
ΑΣΘΕ; these Vrss. and 𝔖𝕿 = 𝕳; 𝔖ᴴ differs from 𝔖 in a couple of words. —
32. 𝕳 כֹּאֵס and לְכֶד; 𝕲 16³, freely, to gain a distinct contrast, μισεῖ and
ἀγαπᾷ. — 33. 𝕳 יהוה; 𝕲 (16⁴) ᶜ ᵃˡ. θεοῦ; 𝕲ᴮᴬᴺ κυρίου; which of these is
original in the Grk. it is hard to say. — 𝕳 סֵר; Perles, *Analekt.* p. 60: מְסַר
basis, which is suitable, but the change is not necessary. — See H-P, Lag.
Swete.

XVI. 1–9. Divine control of life.

1. To man belong the plans of the mind,
   But from Yahweh comes the answer of the tongue.

2. All a man's conduct seems to him pure,
   But it is Yahweh who weighs the spirit.

3. Commit thy work to Yahweh,
   Then will thy plans succeed.

4. Yahweh has made everything for its own end,
   Yea, even the wicked for the evil day.

5. The proud man is an abomination to Yahweh,
   He will assuredly not go unpunished.

6. By kindness and truth sin is expiated,
   And by the fear of Yahweh one escapes misfortune.

7. When a man's ways please Yahweh,
   He makes even his enemies to be at peace with him

8. Better is a little with righteousness
   Than great revenues with injustice.
9. Man devises his way,
   But Yahweh directs his steps.

1. Antithetic, ternary (or, binary). This proverb is identical in meaning with v.⁹, and with our "man proposes, God disposes"; see Malan for Chinese and other parallels. *Plans* is *arrangements* (RV. *preparations*); *mind* is lit. *heart; the answer of the tongue* = the final outcome of one's reflections and purposes. To regard the couplet as contrasting merely thought and expression (De.) is to empty it of meaning; Mt. 10¹⁹ (referred to by De.) is different. The idea of God's absolute control of human affairs is found throughout OT., as, for ex., in Am. 3⁶ ψ 118⁸ Ex. 10¹, cf. Rom. 9¹⁶. In the term *answer* there is possibly allusion to the task of speaking (defending one's self, etc.) before great men (Frank.). See 22²¹, and note on 15²³. — 2. Antithetic, ternary. See 3⁷ 14¹² 21² 24¹². Contrast between human and divine moral judgments. The first cl. does not mean to affirm that men never condemn their own conduct, but states a general rule of human self-satisfaction, or is in the nature of a supposition, so that the couplet may be paraphrased: "though a man's actions may seem right to him, ignorant and prejudiced as he is, yet the final verdict on them comes from the infallible investigation of God." The suggestion is that men should not take their own judgment of themselves, but should test themselves by the judgment of God, that is, by the absolutely pure moral standard. *Conduct* and *spirit* are lit. *ways* and *spirits;* the latter term expresses the whole inward nature, its purposes and motives; *weighs* = measures, determines, tries, appreciates. — In 1 Sam. 16⁷ we have a somewhat different contrast, namely, between human judgment based on the merely outward and visible, and divine judgment which regards the mind. — 3. Continuous, ternary-binary. Lit. *roll on Yahweh thy works* (or, *deeds*), trust everything to him; so ψ 37⁵, cf. ψ 22⁸⁽⁹⁾. Syr. Targ. Lat. read *disclose.* — V.¹⁻³ are lacking in the Greek. — 4. Continuous, ternary. The Heb. permits the translation *for his own end,* but the rendering *its* is indicated by second cl., which states the end or destiny for which wicked men are created. The proverb declares, in a simple and direct

way, the principle (recognized everywhere in OT.) of the absoluteness of Yahweh's government of the world, and it is added that every one of his acts has a definite purpose; since the wicked are punished, it is Yahweh who has created them to that end. This predestination to evil (to use the modern expression) is held in OT., without metaphysical speculation and without embarrassment, in connection with the belief in human freedom — men are considered to be either good or bad, but the good man may at any moment become bad, or the bad man good; see Ex. 9^{16} Ez. 14^9 18, BS. 39$^{16-34}$, cf. Eccl. 3$^{1-11}$. — Grk. reads: *all the works of the Lord (are done) with righteousness, and the wicked man is kept for the evil day.* — The *evil day* is the day of judgment, retribution, punishment. — The prophets regard the nations of the earth as controlled by Yahweh in the interests of Israel; the sage considers individual men as created with a purpose. This larger view belongs to the philosophic period of Jewish history. What God's purpose is in creating the wicked for punishment the proverb does not say. According to Ezekiel (Ez. 38^{16} 39^{21}) Gog is punished that Yahweh may manifest his power and glory to all nations, and so in the Pentateuch Pharaoh is dealt with (Ex. 9^{16}, cf. Rom. 9^{17}). The sage's point of view is not clear — it is, perhaps, that the moral government of the world makes the punishment of the bad man necessary; but no explanation is given of why the bad man should have been created at all. There is no intimation of a belief that the wicked are a necessary element of God's education of the world (cf. BS. 15^{12}). — **5.** Continuous, ternary-binary. The first cl. is the same as first cl. of 11^{20}, with substitution of *proud* for *false;* the *proud* man is he who sets himself presumptuously against Yahweh, and refuses to obey the divine law. The second cl. is the same as first cl. of 11^{21}, with omission of *the wicked;* on the expression *assuredly* (lit. *hand to hand,* = *my hand on it!*) see note on 11^{21}.

Grk. here inserts the two couplets:

The beginning of a good way is to do justly,
And it is more acceptable with God than to offer sacrifices.
He who seeks the Lord will find knowledge with righteousness,
And they who rightly seek him will find peace.

These couplets (which may have been written originally in Hebrew) resemble proverbs in our Hebrew text; the first may have
been suggested by 16⁶, the second by 28⁵ (cf. 14⁶). It is probable that many aphorisms were in circulation which are not included in our Book of Proverbs; some of these are found in the
Greek text of Proverbs, others in Ben-Sira. — **6.** Synonymous,
ternary. The expression *kindness and truth* stands for morality
or virtue in general; so it is used in 3³, on which see note. By
such ethical integrity *sin* (or, *iniquity*) is *expiated* (lit. *covered*),
that is, the divine anger against sin is turned away, and the
man's relation to God is as though he had not sinned. The
priestly mode of expiating sin was by offerings, but prophets
and sages lay the greater stress on disposition of mind and
on conduct; see Hos. 6⁶ (where love to God and knowledge
of him are said to be more desired by Yahweh than sacrifice),
Jer. 7²². ²³ (where Yahweh is said to have commanded not sacrifice
but obedience); cf. Ez. 18 ψ 50¹⁴ 51¹⁶. ¹⁷⁽¹⁸. ¹⁹⁾; in Isa. 40² the sin
of Jerusalem is said to have been expiated by her suffering. — The
fear of Yahweh is parallel and equivalent to *kindness* (or, *love*)
and truth; and *misfortune* (or, *suffering*), lit. *evil*, is identical
with the punishment which is averted when sin is expiated. —
7. Continuous, ternary. Grk. (the couplet occurs after 15²⁸):
*the ways of righteous men are acceptable with the Lord, and by
them even enemies become friends,* which is identical in meaning
with the Hebrew; the form of the latter seems preferable. Instead of the *by them* of the Greek we should perhaps read *to them*.
In the Heb. couplet the happy condition of the righteous is
brought about directly by divine action; but human causes, such
as the kindliness and helpfulness of the good man, are probably
not meant to be excluded. — **8.** Comparison, ternary. Substantially identical with 15¹⁶. The proverb differs from the others of
the group in not containing an explicit reference to the divine
government; but *righteousness = the fear of Yahweh* (15¹⁶). —
9. Antithetic, ternary. Identical in meaning with v.¹. Lit. *the
mind* (heart) *of man devises* (or, *thinks out, plans*). Grk.: *let the
heart of a man think* (or, *reckon*) *justly, that his steps may be set
right by God,* which misses the striking antithesis of the Heb., but
gives a good thought; the *justly* is added from the connection. —

In v.[1] [9] we have two substantially identical aphorisms in close proximity. One is a variant of the other, perhaps in a different collection; the editors naturally took all good material that they found.

10–15. Functions of kings.

The couplets are extended parallelisms. The reference is to all sovereigns, not merely to those of Israel; if, as is probable, the paragraph is postexilian in date, it is the numerous non-Jewish monarchs of the Greek period (possibly, also, the Maccabean princes) that formed the writer's milieu. It is, however, the ideal king whose character is here sketched (except in v.[14. 15]), whether the proverbs be preëxilian or postexilian — the king who governs in wisdom and justice. In such ideal portraitures in the Prophets and the Psalms (Isa. 11^{1-5} ψ 72) the king is guided by God, and controlled by the divine law; here, and elsewhere in this part of Prov., the reference is to the human law of right (in 8^{15} to the personified divine-human wisdom). The term "theocratic" can be used of the Israelitish kings only in the vague way in which it is applicable to all ancient sovereigns — they all performed religious rites, and consulted the deity in important affairs. The kings of Israel were as arbitrary and absolute as the independent spirit of the clans, tribes, elders, and princes permitted them to be — hardly one of them paid much respect to the moral law of Yahweh in his political policy or his private concerns. Delitzsch observes that the OT. never speaks of the actual king as infallible; the idea "the king can do no wrong" did not exist in Israel. — Reference to kings is found both in chs. 1–9 and in chs. 10–31.

10. The lips of the king are an oracle,
    In judgment his mouth transgresses not.
11. [] Balance and scales are ‹the king's,›
    All the weights of the bag are his work.
12. It is abomination to kings to commit wickedness,
    For the throne is established by righteousness.
13. Righteous lips are the delight of kings,
    And they love him who speaks right.
14. The anger of the king is a messenger of death, —
    A wise man will pacify it.
15. In the light of the king's countenance is life,
    And his favor is like a cloud of the Spring rain.

10. Binary. Lit. *on the lips* . . . *is an oracular decision* (RV. *divine sentence*) : the decision of the ideal king is as just as if God himself had given it — that is, as second cl. puts it, he does not violate justice ; *judgment* = legal decision. The meaning (as may be inferred from the parallel proverbs in chs. 10–31) is not that God speaks through the king. Delitzsch's rendering : *let not his mouth err* is out of the question. — The term *oracular decision* is literally *divination*, the consultation of the deity (Ez. 21$^{21(26)}$ Nu. 23^{23}) ; the practice was condemned by the prophets as generally connected with the worship of other gods than Yahweh (1 Sam. 15^{23} Dt. 18^{10} 2 K. 17^{17}), or with false pretensions to speaking in his name (Jer. 14^{14} Ez. 13^{6}). Here the term is used figuratively. — Bickell emends to *oracle of Yahweh*, but the addition is unnecessary — the divine name is understood. — **11.** Ternary-binary. *Weights* is lit. *stones*, which were kept in a *bag*. From Am. 8^{5} we may, perhaps, infer that, as early as the eighth century B.C., the Israelites had a legal standard of weights and measures (and, for the sixth century, cf. Ez. 45$^{10-12}$; it is possible, indeed, that the Babylonians had introduced their system into Canaan in or before the fifteenth century.* It may be assumed that, after the Exile, under the Persians and the Greeks, the Jews had a regular system of stamped weights of stone or metal. — The *balance* is the steelyard — cf. 11^{1} 20$^{10, 23}$ Am. 8^{5} Hos. 12$^{7(8)}$ Mic. 6^{11} Lev. 19^{36} Jer. 32^{10}. — In the first cl. the Heb. has *are Yahweh's*, for which it seems better (with Grätz) to read *are the king's*, with the sense that the system of weights and measures is ordained by the king as supreme authority and fountain of justice ; this emendation brings the oouplet into formal accord with the context. As the text stands, God is the ordainer of the machinery of commercial transactions, a statement which is not elsewhere found in OT. — he is said (as in Lev. 19^{36} *al.*) to demand just weights, he is not said to make or establish them. The word *king* may have been interpreted by some scribe as meaning the divine king, Yahweh. — In the first line the Heb. reads : *balance and just weights are*, etc.

---

* The Babylonian predominance in Canaan is shown by the fact that the Amarna correspondence employs Babylonian script and language. On early Babylonian weights and measures see C. F. Lehmann, *Altbabylon. Maass- und Gewichtssystem*, 1893, and G. A. Reisner on Bab. metrology.

It is singular that the adjective *just* should be attached to one of
these, and not to the other.   The Lat. avoids this difficulty by
rendering (with a slight change of text) : *balance and scales are
(matter of) judgment for Yahweh,* that is, he has to decide all
cases in which a false use of them occurs.   But this interpretation
of the term *judgment* is difficult, and the resulting sentence does
not offer a proper parallel to the second line.   It would be better
to omit the word *balance* (which would get rid of the difficulty),
but a more satisfactory sentence is gained by omitting the adjective, which is here not appropriate — as second cl. states that *all
stones* are the work, etc., so first cl. must state that *balance and
weights* in general belong, etc.   A scribe might naturally think it
desirable to note that the balances are just. — The rendering *a
just balance and scales are,* etc., given by many commentators
and translations,* is grammatically incorrect. — **12**. Ternary.   Cf.
Dt. 17$^{19.\ 20}$ Isa. 32^1.   The affirmation includes all kings considered
as ideal rulers ; such rulers understand that justice is essential to
their permanence.   Grk., less well : *he who does evil is an abomination,* etc. — Cf. 2 Sam. 7$^{13\ ff.}$ ψ 94^{20} Isa. 16^5 ; similar aphorisms
are 20^{28} 25^5 29^{14}. — **13**. Ternary.   Good kings desire honest counsellors and servants.   The verb *love* is sing. in the Hebrew, either
individualizing ("every king loves"), or agreeing with a sing.
king, instead of the *kings* of the text, or error for plural. —
14. Binary.   The Heb. has plural *messengers*.   The sense of
second cl. is probably not "it may be pacified by a wise man"
(that is, by wise precautions or other measures), but "he who is
wise will seek to pacify it" (instead of braving it).   The point of
the couplet is to magnify the king, not the wise man, and the
second line is more naturally understood as adding something to
the statement of the first line : the king's anger is so terrible a
thing that a man shows wisdom in trying to pacify it.   The king
is represented as absolute, as was true, in many respects, of all
ancient monarchs ; this trait is not necessarily out of keeping with
his ideal character; the couplet, however, rather regards him
simply as ruler. — **15**. Binary.   The antithesis to the preceding

---

* Geier, Ew. De. Str. RV. *al.*   These assume an exception to the grammatical
rule.   Zöckler : *scale and just balances*,

aphorism.   The *light of the countenance* is *a friendly look*, = *favor*, *gracious reception;* the word for *light* is different from that used in 15³⁰, but the general sense is the same. — *Life* is long and happy life, = prosperity.   The king, here as in v.¹⁴, is regarded simply as the arbiter of fate ; his moral qualities do not come into consideration. — The *Spring rain* ("latter rain," March-April) was essential to the ripening of the crops, and the *cloud* which heralded it was a symbol of blessing ; see Jer. 3³ Zech. 10¹ Job 29²³ ; the Autumn rain (" former rain," October) preceded the sowing (Hos. 6³ Dt. 11¹⁴ Jer. 5²⁴ Joel 2²³ ψ 84⁶⁽⁷⁾).   For details of agriculture see Nowack, *Arch.* I. § 41.

XVI. 1. Wanting in 𝕲ᴮ, found in 𝔖ᴴ𝕲²³ ᵃˡ· 𝔖𝕿𝕷; 𝕲²⁵². ²⁵³ ᵃˡ· 𝔖ᴴ add ὅσῳ μέγας εἶ τοσοῦτον ταπείνου σεαυτόν καὶ ἔναντι κυρίου τοῦ θεοῦ εὑρήσεις χάριν, = BS. 3¹⁸, and perhaps thence taken by 𝕲²⁵²ᵃˡ·. — **2.** The adj. זך occurs only in the late priestly ritual (Ex. 27²⁰ 30³⁴ Lev. 24². ⁷), Job, Prov., but the verb זכה is found in Isa. 1¹⁶ Mic. 6¹¹. — The stem תכן, = *establish*, appears to be a second-ary formation from כן; the origin of the sense *weigh*, *test* is not clear. Gr., unnecessarily, בחן. — The couplet is not found in this form in 𝕲ᴮ; something like it appears in 𝕲 16⁶, which is nearly related to the added couplet given above under v.¹; cf. BS. 35¹⁷· ¹⁸. — **3.** Wanting in 𝕲ᴮ, found in Θ𝔖ᴴ𝕲²³ ᵃˡ·, perhaps a late addition to �, after ψ37⁵. — On v.¹ ³ see notes of Lag. Baum. Bi. — **4.**, = 9 in 𝕲. — 𝔥 פָּעַל; 𝕲 ἔργα. — 𝔥 ינם; 𝕲 φυλάσσεται, = שׁמר. This is probably a mere scribal variation, and not an attempt to avoid the statement that God destines the wicked to punishment (Pink., who refers to Baethgen, *JPT.* 8, 413). — 𝕲's rendering of למענהו by μετὰ δικαιοσύνης is accounted for by Heid. from the Rabbin. reference of the Heb. expression to students of law; but, like 𝕿 *those who obey him*, 𝕲 simply takes the form in 𝔥 as = *obey*. — In 𝔥 לַמַּעֲנֵהוּ the vowel-point under ל may be scribal error, or it may be anoma-lously inserted to distinguish this expression from the prep. למען with suffix (so Ew. De. Philippi). — **5.**, = 6 in 𝕲. — 𝔥 חֵיַבת; 𝕲 ἀκάθαρτος (cf. βδέλυγμα, 15²⁶). — **10.** קסם, originally *part*, *fragment* (Arab. *portion*), from stem = *divide;* *divination* is perhaps from the fragments (of stone, etc.) which were used in divining processes (Halévy, *REJ.*, 1887), perhaps from the verb = *divide*, *determine* fates. — **11.** The stems פלס and אזן (Arab. *wazan*) appear to express the idea of *evenness, equality*. — משׁפט qualifies only מאזני, not פלס; see Philippi, *Stat. Const. im Heb.*, p. 12 ff. 𝕲 ῥοπὴ ζυγοῦ δικαιοσύνη παρὰ κ. = פלס מאזנים משׁפט ליהוה, taking משׁפט as pred., and so 𝔖𝕷. The משׁפט is better omitted as gloss. — 𝔥 ליהוה; read, with Gr., למלך; see note on this v. above. — **12.** 𝔖 read חֵיַבה and עֶשֶׂם, the latter word qualifying מלכם; 𝔖𝕿 appear to have been influenced by 𝕲; see Baum. Pink. — **13.** 𝔥 יאֹרב, Qal; 𝕷 Nif. (and so Jäg.); if a change is thought necessary, it will be better to write the vb. Qal. plur., or (with 𝕲) the noun sing., מלד. — **14.** 𝔥 מלאכי; 𝕲, sing., is better. — **15.** מלקש is, perhaps, originally *time of gathering*, and מורה ירה *sprinkler*. On the reading of 𝕿 see Fleisch., in Levy, *Chald. Wört.*, I. 420, and on 𝕾𝕿 cf. the notes of Baum. and Pink.

16–19. Wisdom, integrity, humility.

> 16. Wisdom is better than gold,
> And understanding more to be desired than silver.
> 17. The path of the upright avoids misfortune,
> He guards his life who takes heed to his way.
> 18. Pride goes before destruction,
> And a haughty spirit before a fall.
> 19. It is better to be of a lowly spirit with the poor
> Than to divide the spoil with the proud.

16. Two equivalent comparisons, ternary. Lit. *the getting of wisdom* and *the getting of understanding;* for the terms see note on 3^{14}. Fully expressed : " the acquisition of wisdom is better than that of gold," etc. The Heb. of first cl. reads : *the getting of wisdom — how much better is it than gold!* but the *how much* is probably scribal error. The identity of the thought of this couplet with that of 3^{14} is an indication that the final form was given to the two sections, chs. 1–9 and chs. 10–22^{16}, about the same time. — **17.** Identical, ternary-quaternary. In second cl. he who pays careful attention to his (moral) conduct is said thus to guard or preserve his life (or, himself, lit. *his soul*) — that is, integrity is a guard against misfortune — this is the familiar teaching of Proverbs ; in accordance with the parallelism the *evil* of first cl. (as the Heb. lit. reads) is naturally *misfortune*, which the path of the upright avoids. The interpretation " the conduct of the upright consists in avoiding moral evil " is possible, but does not furnish an antithesis. — The second cl. may be rendered : *he who guards his life* (or, *himself*) *takes heed to his way*, that is, he who desires to have a good, happy life looks carefully to his conduct. Combining this with the second rendering of first cl., the couplet would mean : " a good man avoids wrong, and he who has care for himself looks to his conduct," which (if we may be guided by the context) is less satisfactory than the interpretation : " the upright man escapes misfortune, and he who is careful in his conduct saves his life " — the surrounding couplets deal not with the method of securing happiness, but with the results of good living. — Grk., adding three lines after first cl. of v.[17], and one line after second cl., makes three couplets, as follows :

> The paths of life turn aside from evils,
> And the ways of righteousness are length of life.
> He who receives instruction will be prosperous,
> And he who regards reproofs will be made wise.
> He who guards his ways preserves his soul,
> And he who loves his life will spare his mouth.

This is probably a scribe's expansion of the Hebrew couplet; the matter is all to be found in the Heb. Proverbs. — **18.** Identical, binary. Cf. 11^2 (pride brings disgrace), 15^{33} (humility brings honor), 16^{19} 18^{12} (contrast of pride and humility), 21^{24} 22^4 30^{13}. The reference seems to be to the social laws and conditions which tend to abase pride. The English "pride will have a fall" may be derived from this proverb. — **19.** Chiastic comparison, ternary. With *lowly* is contrasted *proud*, and with *poor* the rich who *divide the spoil*. Instead of *poor* we might render by *humble* (RV. marg. *meek*), but this would destroy the antithesis, and introduce a tautology, since *lowly = humble*. The terms *lowly* and *proud* are here ethical, = the unassuming or inoffensive, and the overbearing or oppressive : they have, perhaps, also a religious import, = those who submit themselves to God, and those who disobey and disregard him. — The expression *divide the spoil* is taken from military life (Gen. 49^{27} Ex. 15^9 Jos. 22^8 Ju. 5^{30} 1 Sam. 30^{22-24} Isa. 53^{12} ψ $68^{12(13)}$), or from the judicial and other civil injustices of the rich ; cf. 1^{13} 31^{11}.

20–25. Wisdom and graciousness.

20. He who gives heed to the word will prosper,
    And the man that trusts in Yahweh, happy is he!
21. The wise man is called a man of discernment:
    Sweetness of speech increases power of persuasion.
22. Wisdom is a wellspring of life to its possessor,
    And folly is the chastisement of fools.
23. The wise man's mind makes his speech judicious,
    And gives persuasiveness to his discourse.
24. Pleasant words are a honeycomb,
    Sweet to the soul and healing to the body.
25. There is a way that seems right to a man,
    But the end of it is the way to death.

20. Synonymous, ternary. *Gives heed* is *acts wisely* (in reference to) ; cf. 21¹². The *word* is the law of right as given by the sages and by God, and it is unnecessary to add *of Yahweh* (Grätz) ; see note on 13¹³ ; it is not improbable that the reference is in part to (postexilian) legal and prophetical documents. *Prosper* is lit. *find good.* — *Trust* substantially = *gives heed,* since trust and obedience involve each the other. The *good* and *happiness* include all desirable things of this life. The proverb gives the purely religious point of view : God blesses those who obey and trust him, and they need no other protection; see v.³ 3⁵·⁶. The expression *happy is he* occurs in 14²¹ 29¹⁸. — 21. Synonymous, ternary. The power of discreet gentleness of speech. Lit., in first line : *the wise of mind* [lit. *heart*] *is called discerning.* The *discernment,* as may be inferred from second line, shows itself in selecting proper language by which to influence men. *Is called* = "is recognized as, given credit for being." The last expression of second line (RV. *learning,* as in 1⁵) is to be rendered *persuasiveness,* as in 7²¹, on which see note ; such is the effect of *sweetness of speech* (lit. *of lips*). A man of true wisdom of thought shows himself intelligent, judicious, discerning (RV. *prudent*) by his attractive words, whereby he brings men to his way of thinking, or to a recognition of duty. The rendering *increases learning* does not convey a distinct sense ; in 1⁵ the sage adds, by study, to his own learning ; sweetness of discourse could increase the learning of others only, but the Heb. expression does not naturally convey that idea. — Instead of *discerning* (or, *intelligent*) Grätz, by change of text, would read *agreeable,* and Bickell *harp* (that is, as melodious as a harp) ; the latter reading is unnatural, the former furnishes a good antithesis, but the Heb. text is favored by v.²⁶. — *Sweetness* = graciousness, friendliness ; on *discerning* see note on 1⁵. — 22. Antithetic, ternary. On *wellspring* (or, *fountain*) *of life* see 10¹¹ 13¹⁴ 14²⁷ 18⁴ ; on *chastisement* (the word is also rendered *instruction* and *correction*) see 1² 3¹¹ 7²² 13²⁴ 22¹⁵. As *wisdom* secures for its possessor (by natural and divine law) all the blessings of life, so *folly* brings on its possessor loss of blessing, and positively punishment. The *chastisement* is not here a means of reformation, but merely a requital of wrongdoing ; the *fool* is once for all ignorant, inapprehensive, disobedient to human and

divine law. — **23.** Synonymous, ternary. Identical in thought
with v.[21] On *makes judicious* (a different term from the *discerning* of v.[21]) see notes on 1^3 $10^{5. 19}$ 14^{35} 15^{24}. Here it is the wise
man's *mind* (= good sense or sagacity) that makes his speech
persuasive; in v.[21] the agent is sweetness of expression; but the
epithet *judicious* or *sagacious* favors the reading *discerning* (instead of *agreeable*) in v.[21]. The two couplets are variations of one
theme. *Speech* and *discourse* are lit. *mouth* and *lips*. — **24.** Single
sentence (second cl. interpreting first cl.), binary (or, binary-
quaternary). *Honeycomb*, cf. ψ $19^{10(11)}$, 1 Sam. 14^{27} Cant. 5^1;
pleasant = graceful, gracious, friendly; *body* is lit. *bone*. Grätz
finds in this couplet a suggestion for his emendation in v.[21]; it
does give some support to his reading, yet it is to be observed
that the reference here is simply to charm of expression and manner, while there the connection between wisdom and speech is
considered. — **25.** Identical with 14^{12}.

---

16. On קנה cf. Ols. § 173 *g*, Ges.[26] § 75 *n*; it seems probable that the form
is here, as Ols. suggests, scribal error for קנת, since the latter occurs in [b];
𝕷 Impv. in both clauses, inserting *quia;* Stade takes it as Inf. abs., Bi. as
Impv., but the 𝕸 Infin. is more satisfactory. 𝕲 νοσσιαί, = קנת or קְנֵי. — Omit
מה (probably repetition of preceding זה), which is syntactically difficult, if not
impossible. — **17.** In [b] a reviser has brought the text of 𝕲 into accord with 𝕸,
which latter is obviously correct. Bi. makes two couplets, adopting the [b] and
the [c] of 𝕲; but no great advantage is thereby gained, and the preference
should probably be given to 𝕸 as the shorter. — **18.** On the ἅπαξ λεγ. כָּשֵׁרוֹן
cf. Barth, *Nominalbild.* § 196 *b*. — **19.** שְׁפַל, Infin., taken as adj. by 𝕾, which
inserts it also before עָי, pointed עֵינָיִם. — On the relation between עֲנָוִים (here
Qeri) and ענים (here Kethib) see critical note on 14^{21}. — **20.** 𝕸 עַל דבר, where
עַל = *according to, in respect to* (cf. ψ 119^9 (לִשְׁמֹר כִּדְבָרֶךָ); Bi. בִּדְבַר, after 𝕲 ἐν.
— Gr. דבר יהוה. In [b] the Grk. Codd. vary between θεῷ and κυρίῳ, a varia-
tion that appears throughout OT., and is adduced by Klost. as proof that
difference of divine names in the Heb. text is not a sign of difference of
authorship (for a criticism of Klost. see E. König, *Theol. Stud. u. Krit.*, 1893).
— **21.** 𝕲 expands 𝕸 חכם לב into σοφοὺς καὶ συνετούς. — 𝕸 ונבֹן; 𝕲 φαύλους, =
נבל (Jäg.), whence Bi. וְבֵל *harp;* Gr. suggests נֵבֶל. 𝕾 gives 𝕸 freely. See
note on this v. above. — **22.** Before 𝕸 בִּ׳רֹיו insert ל, with 𝕲; it fell out by
reason of the ל of preceding שֵׁכֶל. — **23.** 𝕲𝕾 vary from, but support, 𝕸.
— **24.** 𝕲 in [b], less well, γλύκασμα δὲ αὐτοῦ ἴασις ψυχῆς, = ומחקו לנפש כרפא. —
25. 𝕲𝕾𝕿𝕷 here vary slightly from their renderings of 14^{12}.

26. Hunger makes a man industrious.

> The laborer's appetite labors for him,
> For his mouth impels him to work.

Single sentence (second cl. explaining first cl.), ternary. Cf. Eccl. 6⁷. *Appetite* is Heb. *nefesh* (= *soul*), that part of the nature which desires or craves food ; so 6³⁰ 23² 27⁷ Dt. 14²⁶ 23²⁴⁽²⁵⁾ Job 33²⁰. The second cl. is lit. *for his mouth presses on him.* The paronomasia in first cl. is effective : man works, and his appetite works for him. Hunger, says the proverb, is a useful thing, since it drives a man on to work ; or, a man will work, whether he likes it or not, for hunger forces him to gain food. Industry, from this point of view, is not a virtue of high rank. Grk. : *A man who labors labors for himself, and drives away ruin; but the perverse brings ruin on his own mouth; ruin* is misreading of the Heb. word for *mouth*, and the last clause is the comment of a scribe. Syr. : *the soul that inflicts suffering suffers, and from its mouth comes ruin*, which in part follows the Greek.

27, 30. Mischief-making. Ternary. Cf. 6¹²⁻¹⁴, a paragraph which is out of place in chs. 1–9.

> 27. A wicked man digs (a pit of) mischief,
>   And on his lips there is as it were a scorching fire.
> 28. A false man scatters discord abroad,
>   And a backbiter separates friends.
> 29. A villain entices his neighbor,
>   And leads him in a way not good.
> 30. A slanderer devises falsehoods,
>   A backbiter consummates mischief.

27. A metaphor and a simile. *Wicked man*, lit. *man of belial;* see note on 6¹². *Mischief* (or, *misfortune*) is lit. *evil.* The second cl. indicates that the reference of the couplet is to slanderous talk : the man's lips *scorch*, burn those of whom he talks — he digs a pit into which they fall. — **28.** Synonymous. Cf. 17⁹. Lit. *a man of falsehoods, a liar;* on this term see note on 2¹²; *backbiter* is lit. *murmurer, whisperer;* in the second line, lit. : *separates a friend*, probably = not *alienates his friend*, but, as the parallelism (*discord*) and 18¹⁸ suggest, *separates* (= *alienates*) *one friend from another;* on *friend* see 2¹⁷ (the RV. rendering, *chief friends*, =

intimate friends, is possible but unnecessary) ; Rashi : *alienates the prince* (such is the meaning of the Heb. word in Gen. 36[15] Zech. 9[7]), that is, God ; Luther : *makes princes disagree.* — **29.** Extensive. *Villain* is lit. *man of violence,* here in general a man of immoral or criminal methods of procedure ; he *entices* his *neighbor* or *comrade* (as in 1[10-19]) into habits of vice and crime, not to some secret place where he may rob or murder him — this last does not suit the expression *in a way not good.* *Neighbor* = any associate or acquaintance, and, in general, any man. — **30.** Parallelism of expressions. The couplet is almost identical with 6[13. 14]. Lit. : *he who shuts* (or, *winks*) *his eyes to devise,* etc., *he who shuts* (or, *bites*) *his lips consummates,* etc. ; in first cl. the Infinitive expresses purpose, and the sentence is incomplete, or the meaning may be : *he who shuts,* etc. *(does it) to devise,* etc. (RV.) ; in second cl. the verb expresses the completed act. We may gain symmetry and completeness by changing the Infinitive into a finite verb, and reading : *he who shuts . . . devises,* etc., and *he who closes . . . consummates,* etc. ; this reading supposes that the acts of shutting or winking eyes and closing or gnawing lips are regarded as signs of evil purpose, which, from 6[13. 14], appears to be the case. On the other hand, if we change the finite verb of second cl. into an Infinitive, we have a natural expression, but, at the same time, two incomplete sentences, and it must be supposed that a final clause has been lost, the complete proverb reading : " he who closes (or, winks) his eyes in order to concoct mischief, and he who shuts (or, snaps) his lips in order to perfect (or, as a sign that he has perfected) mischief, let him be avoided (or, he will surely come to grief)." Such a couplet, however, would be contrary to the norm of this Division, in which every couplet is complete in itself. The construction with two finite verbs is the simpler and the more natural. The expressions *he who winks the eyes* and *he who closes* (or, *gnaws*) *the lips* are equivalent to *slanderer* and *backbiter.* The progression of thought, *devises . . . consummates,* is rhetorical — each of these classes of persons does both of these acts. — The Grk. reads :

> He who fixes his eyes devises falsities
> And marks out all evils with his lips;
> He is a furnace of wickedness.

Whence Bickell : *he who shuts his eyes is false, he who closes his ears is a furnace of wickedness.* — Lit. : *he who with astonished eyes meditates wickedness biting his lips perfects evil.* — The general sense of the couplet is plain, but form and translation are uncertain. Cf. BS. 5[14].

31. Righteousness gives long life.

> A hoary head is a crown of glory
> Which is gained by a righteous life.

Continuous, ternary. The second cl. is lit. *in the way* (= *life*) *of righteousness it is found* (= *come upon, acquired*). The Heb. hardly allows the rendering *if it be found in,* etc. (this idea is expressed eloquently in BS. 25[4-6]). The assertion is that old age is the reward of rightdoing : righteousness, = wisdom, bestows long life (3[2. 16] *al.*). The possibility that a bad man may live to be old is not here considered ; it is assumed that the wicked perish early (2[22] 12[7] 24[16] 29[1] ψ 9[17(18)] 55[23(24)]). This conception, which is the prevailing one in OT. (it is opposed by Job) and in BS. (1[12] 16[4]), was modified by the acceptance of the doctrine of happy immortality (WS. 4[8. 9] "honorable age is not . . . measured by number of years "), and is not found in NT.

32. Excellence of self-control.

> He who is slow to anger is better than a warrior,
> And he who rules himself than he who takes a city.

Synonymous, ternary-quaternary (or, ternary-binary). *Himself* is lit. *his spirit* (= his inner nature, soul). The sage extols the virtue of moderation, self-control, a familiar one to Greek thought (σωφροσύνη) ; in OT. it is referred to only in the Wisdom books. Numerous parallel sayings (Chinese, Hindu, Greek, etc.) are cited by Malan ; see Hor., *Ol.* 2, 2. Delitzsch refers to *Pirke Aboth*, 4, 1, *Par. Regained*, 2, 466 ff. — The Grk. adds, after first cl., its rendering of second cl. of 24[5] : *and a man of prudence than a great estate.*

33. God controls men's decisions.

> The lot is cast into the lap,
> But the whole decision of it is from Yahweh.

Implied antithesis, ternary-binary. The thought is substantially that of v.[1.9]: all human affairs are controlled by God — only, in this case, the arbitrament is consciously referred to him. The determination of the divine will by casting lots was probably universal in the ancient world; the deity was supposed to direct the throw; see *Iliad*, 3, 316 ff., Cic., *De Divin.*, 2, 41 (Cicero says that educated people of his time regarded the custom as a superstition). In OT. important public and private affairs are so determined (Ju. 1[3] Isa. 34[17] Lev. 16[8ff.] Jon. 1[7] *al.*, cf. Acts 1[26]); the priestly decision by Urim and Thummin was probably by lot (1 Sam. 14[41ff.] 28[6] Nu. 27[21] *al.*). The term *lot* was used also as = one's part or portion (Ju. 1[3] ψ 16[5]). On *lap* see notes on 5[20] 6[27]; the reference here is to the garment.

26. 𝔥 נפש עמל; 𝔊 ἀνὴρ ἐν πόνοις; but נ is better understood as = *appetite*. — 𝔥 פיהו; 𝔊 ἀπώλειαν, = פיד (Hitz.); in 𝔊 the line ᶜ is gloss on ᵇ. — The stem אכף appears to signify *lay on* (so in Arab.), *press*, *urge*, *impel;* in Syr. *to be solicitous;* for the Assyr. see De. *Assyr. Hdwbuch.;* in 𝔥 Job 33[7] the noun אכף is probably to be emended, after 𝔊, to כף (Ols. Siegf. Budde, *al.*). אכף על is regarded by Wild. as Aramaism. Cf. BDB. — 27. On בליעל see critical note on 6[12]. 𝔥 כרה; Gr. suggests (but unnecessarily) חרש. — Between Kethib שפחיו and Qeri שפתו there is little choice. — 28. נרגן was not understood by the Vrss.: 𝔊 λαμπτῆρα δόλου πυρσεύσει κακοῖς, in which λ. suggests נר (Lag.), and κ. is interpretation; ℭ *quarreller*, or *fiery*, *irascible;* ⅏ *empty*, *inane;* 𝔏 *verbose;* cf. Lag. Baum. — The small final Nun is doubtless due to some scribal accident in the archetypal MS. (cf. Lag.). — 30. The stem עצה = *compress* (so Syr.) or *strike* (so Arab.); see note above on this verse. Stade compares עצם, which stem, in its late-Heb. and Aram. sense, *shut*, should perhaps be read here (so Grätz, Frank.). In any case the *shut* may suggest *wink*. On קרץ see notes on 6[18] 10[10], and cf. ψ 35[19]. The sense *gnaw*, *bite*, found in Ass. (De. *Wbch.*) suits the connection (*lips*); cf. ἐπιδάκνων below, and the connection of קרץ in Arab. Aram. with *slander*. — In 𝔊 πάντα τὰ κακά is doublet of οὗτος κάμινός ἐστιν κακίας, but which is the earlier is uncertain; Bi. adopts κάμινος κακίας, = כר רעה. Instead of the ὁρίζει of 𝔊[B], = כלה (𝔊[A] ὀργίζει, perh. scribal error, perh. = קצף), a number of Codd. (23. 106. 109. 147. 149. 157. 252. 260. 295. 297) have ἐπιδάκνων *gnawing*, adding, however, ὁρίζει before πάντα, and ε. is probably the original 𝔊 reading (Lag.). — On ⅏ see Pink. — For קרץ Gr. reads הפך, a possible but unnecessary emendation. — 33. את הגרל after passive verb (so Gen. 4[18] *al.*); what is commonly grammatical subject is here presented as the object of the action, or rather, as the object of contemplation, as in Arab. after *'inna*, *'anna;* it is an attempt, on the part of the language, to give prominence and emphasis to the thing by holding it up as object of thought; see Ew. § 295 *b*, Ges. [26] § 121 *b*. —

𝔊, having rendered כל משפטו by πάντα τὰ δίκαια, assimilates ᵃ to ᵇ by writing πάντα τοῖς ἀδίκοις, גרל being left untranslated.

XVII. 1. Desirableness of a quiet life.

> Better a dry morsel and quietness therewith
> Than a house full of feasting and strife.

Antithetic comparison, ternary — the value of a quiet life. **Cf.** 15¹⁶. ¹⁷ 25²⁴. The word here rendered *feasting* is lit. *sacrifices;* in ancient Israel all eating of flesh was a religious act — the animal was first presented to the deity by the priest, and then eaten by the worshippers with the accompaniments of a feast; see 1 Sam. 9¹². ¹³ 20⁶. ²⁹. The ordinary term for this animal sacrifice is the one employed in our verse. Such sacrifice was offered at a shrine; but the Deuteronomic code, which abolished all shrines but the Jerusalem temple, expressly authorizes the killing and eating of animals at home (Dt. 12¹⁵. ²¹). The old term for the ritual slaying of beasts is, however, sometimes used to express private slaying (Dt. 12¹⁵ Ez. 39¹⁷ Isa. 34⁶), and thus comes to denote *feasting* (so RV.; AV. marg. *good cheer*); this word sufficiently expresses the contrast of the meagre *dry morsel,* bread without savory accompaniments, and the richness of a meal in which meat is the principal feature. It is uncertain whether the proverb contemplates a sacrifice proper, or a private preparation of animal food, but the general sense is the same in the two cases. Cf. note on 7¹⁴.

2. Cleverness succeeds.

> A wise slave will rule over a profligate son,
> And will share the inheritance among brethren.

Continuous sentence, quaternary (or, ternary). *Wise* = one who acts with sagacity, a clever, capable person; moral excellence is not expressed, but is possibly to be understood. *Profligate* = one who acts shamefully, in such a way as to bring disgrace on himself and his family (see 10⁵ 12⁴ 14³⁵). *Share* is lit. *divide.* The slave, in the case here supposed, is said, not to act, after the father's death, as executor of the estate, distributer of the property among the heirs (De.), but himself to be one of the heirs, promoted above the unworthy son; for this sense of the verb see 29²⁴ (RV.

is partner); *share the inheritance* need mean no more than *come into possession of part of the property*. Slaves in Israel, even when non-Israelite of origin, were considered as members of the family, adopted the religion of the master, and took part in the national festivals (Gen. 24[12] Dt. 5[14] 12[12-18] 16[11-14]) ; in the later law (Gen. 17[12]) the slave is required to be circumcised, though this rule is relaxed in the Talmud (*Yebam.* 48 b). Abraham (Gen. 15[3]) speaks of his homeborn slave Eliezer as his heir; a man sometimes gave his daughter in marriage to his slave (1 Chr. 2[35]), who thus came to be head of the household. So an unworthy son, it is here said, might be partly or wholly set aside in favor of a capable slave. Such a case was, no doubt, exceptional — the Old Testament law regards sons as the heirs, but it appears that, in later times, the father had considerable liberty in disposing of his property (see 30[23]).* In regard to the value set on sons compare what is said in Ben-Sira (16[3]) and Wisdom (4[1]) of the undesirableness of bad children. — For the idea cf. BS. 10[25].

3. God the judge of character.

> The fining-pot is for silver, and the furnace for gold,
> And Yahweh is the trier of hearts.

The couplet may be regarded (as in RV.) as expressing a contrast between material and spiritual testing, but is better understood as an implied comparison : *as . . . so ;* quaternary- (or, binary-) ternary. Other references to the process of testing and refining metals are Isa. 1[25] Jer. 6[29] Ez. 22[17-22] Mal. 3[3]; the figurative use is found in Isa. 48[10] ψ 17[3] 66[10] Dan. 12[10] *al.* The character of metals, says the proverb, is disclosed by the human process of refining, and the true nature of the human soul by God — it is involved, of course, that he alone can fully estimate the soul — man may know something of it, but not all. The first cl. of this verse occurs in 27[21].†

4. Moral badness of listening to evil talk.

> A bad man gives heed to wicked words,
> A ‹ false › man listens to mischievous talk.

---

* Cf. Ewald, *Alterthümer*, p. 240; Nowack, *Arch.*, § 29.

† See art. *Refining* in Smith, *Dict. of Bib.;* Now., *Arch.*, § 43. 4; Rawlinson, *Phoenicia*, p. 317.

Identical thought with variation of terms, ternary. *Words* and *talk* are lit. *lip* and *tongue; wicked words* is lit. *lip of wickedness* (Heb. *awen*) — the defining noun is employed in $6^{12.\,18}$ 10^{29} 11^{7} 12^{21} *al.*, and in OT. the majority of its occurrences are in Job, Ps. Prov.; *mischievous talk* is lit. *tongue of injury* (or, *destruction*) ; for *a false man* the Heb. text has *falsity*, hardly abstract for concrete, rather the text must be corrected; *false* is to be taken in the sense of *false* (or, *faithless*) *to friends and companions* (= unmindful of what is due to men), substantially equivalent to *bad*. The purpose of the proverb seems to be not to define *bad* and *false* as those who *give heed*, etc., but to assert that those who so give heed are bad and false. Another rendering of the couplet (Frank.) is : *deceit* (?) *results when one gives heed*, etc., *falsehood results when one listens*, etc., but this is scarcely natural. — Many MSS. of Grk. here add a couplet which in the Vatican MS. occurs after v.[6].

5. To laugh at misfortune is impious and dangerous.

> He who mocks the poor reproaches his Maker,
> He who is glad at calamity will not go unpunished.

The rhythmical form is that of v.[4]. The first cl. is a variation of 14^{31a}, on which verse see note. The *calamity* is apparently, from the parallelism, that which befalls the *poor*, and he who is glad at misfortune thus mocks the unfortunate ; such an one, inasmuch as he *reproaches* (contemptuously criticises) *his* divine *Maker* (by mistaking and blaming his providential control of the world), will incur punishment from God. The second cl., taken by itself, might refer to the punishment of heartlessness through the operation of natural laws. The sympathy with the poor here expressed is found throughout the Old Testament. The *mocking* is perhaps simply or mainly the failure to give sympathy and aid ; cf. BS. 4^{6}. — Grk. adds : *and he who is compassionate will find mercy*, a natural contrast, probably a gloss.

6. Parent and child — each the ornament of the other.

> Children's children are the crown of old men,
> And the adornment of children is their fathers.

Parallelism of form, two similar or complementary thoughts, ternary. Cf. ψ 127³⁻⁵ BS. 3¹¹ 25⁷. The intimate relation between parent and child, in general the value of the family, is expressed by the statement that each member is the crown or adornment of the others; mother and daughter are to be included. Parent and child form a social unit — each gives support, dignity, and happiness to the other. — The RV. rendering in second cl., *glory*, is possible, if the term be taken as meaning "honor received," but the parallelism shows that it is here equivalent to the *crown* of the first clause. — The value placed on children as procuring respect for parents is apparent throughout OT.; a sort of protest against this feeling occurs in Wisd. Sol. 3¹³· ¹⁴ 4¹. Originally this desire for children was connected with the belief that the childless man, having no one, after his death, to provide food for his Shade, would fare ill in the Otherworld. Of this primitive belief (and of the related cult of ancestors) there are no definite traces in OT. — The Grk. (Vat. MS.) adds:

> To the faithful belongs the whole world of wealth,
> But to the faithless not an obolus.

It is difficult to explain this couplet as a corruption of any Hebrew proverb, or to attach it to any distich in the context. The sentiment resembles that of 3¹⁶, but the form is Greek, and we must suppose that a Greek-speaking scribe has inserted the lines in this place (or after v.⁴) as a familiar saying, or from a current written collection of aphorisms.

7. Let fools be false, and good men true.

> Honest words do not become a fool,
> Much less do lies a man of rectitude.

Parallel between a less and a greater, ternary (or, ternary-binary). Lit. *lip of excellence* and *lip of falsehood*. The first cl. appears to be sarcastic and sardonic, = "a fool has no business to talk truth," or "true talk does not comport with a fool's character." *Fool* (Heb. *nabal*, in Pr. only here and 17²¹ 30²²) is a contemptuous and opprobrious term involving lack of intellectual and moral insight and weight (1 Sam. 25²⁵ 2 Sam. 3³³ Job 2¹⁰ ψ 14¹); the contrasted word in second cl. (*nadib*) elsewhere in Pr., except 17²⁶,

means *nobleman* or *prince* (8^{16} 25^7), but here, from the parallelism, better *man of noble character, of rectitude* (cf. Isa. 32^5,
where it is contrasted, as here, with *fool*). The general sense of
the aphorism is apparent from the similar sayings in 19^{10} 26^1; in
both of these something is mentioned which is obviously out of
keeping with the status of the fool, and in 19^{10} an advance is
made to something which is regarded as still less appropriate in
some other person. The precise sense of first cl. turns on the
meaning of the subject of the sentence. The term which there
in the Heb. defines *speech* signifies *remainder* or (in adverbial use)
exceedingly throughout OT. except in our verse and Gen. 49^3 (in
Job 4^{21} the form is probably corrupt), but neither of these senses
(*abundance, diffuseness*) is here appropriate; in Gen. 49^3 the
meaning suggested by the connection is *excellency* or (as Dillmann
explains it) *superiority, preëminence*, and the same sense is found
in Syriac and in a related Heb. word which occurs a number of
times in Eccl. (2^{13} 7^{12} *al.*). There appears to be no authority for
the meanings *elevated, noble* (Ew.) and *pretentious, arrogant* (De.
Reuss, RV. marg.). The proverb seems to offer a sharp and sarcastic antithesis — the sage would say: " let every man act in
character — excellent (here = honest, true) words do not become
a fool, nor lies a man of rectitude." According to De. the meaning is: " it is repulsive to us when an ignorant, vulgar man puts
himself impudently forward, and much more repulsive," etc.; but
this meaning (if it could be got from the Heb.) is not appropriate, since, from the tone of the second cl., we expect in first cl.
the mention of something which is alien to the fool. Nor, according to OT. usage, can the contrast between the characters be a
social one: *churl . . . nobleman.* Grk.: *faithful* (or, *true*) *words
do not become a fool*, in which the adjective may be chosen as
offering a distinct contrast to *false*, but the sense is appropriate,
and may rest on a Heb. term; Lat.: *verba composita* (feigned,
false words, which are in excess of the truth). — If the meaning
honest, true be regarded as foreign to the word of the Heb., it
may be got by a slight change of text.

XVII. 1. As זבח is rarely used of private slaughter of animals, Dys., not
without probability, proposes to read כבחי here, as in 9^2; the Vrss. had the
word of 𝕳. — 𝕲ᵃ μεθ᾽ ἡδονῆς probably = עֲרֵבָה (see 𝕳 20^{17}) for 𝕳 חרבה (Jäg.),

but may be interpretation of 𝔐; in ᵇ instead of the πολλῶν of B we should perhaps read πλήρης with אAC, and ἀγαθῶν καὶ ἀδίκων are expansion, ᵈᵈ· being
possibly scribal variation of μετὰ μάχης. — **2.** 𝔐 בֶּן מַבְשׁ; 𝔊 δεσποτῶν ἀφρό-
νων, apparently = בַּעַל מ׳; Bi., comparing BS. 10²⁵ (ἐλεύθεροι), reads בְּחֹרִם, but
this is hardly probable. — In ᵃ 𝔊 has free rendering of 𝔐; in ᵇ for בחן stands
ἐκλεκταί (א* ἐκλέγεται), from בחר. Instead of κυρίῳ 𝔊ᴬ has Θῶ (Θεῷ). —
4. 𝔐 מֵרִע is Hif. Partcp. of רעע; we therefore expect a corresponding concrete form in ᵇ, and may, with Gr., read מִשְׁקָר (cf. 1 S. 15²⁹) instead of שקר;
מֵזִין is for מַאֲזִין; both this verb and מַקְשִׁב are commonly and properly followed
by אל, and so we should probably here read instead of עֲל. — For an extraordi-
nary translation of this couplet see Schultens. — 𝔊ᴬᴮ ᵃˡ· δίκαιος δὲ οὐ προσ-
έχει, probably scribal alteration to gain an antithesis; 𝔐 is followed in
𝔊⁶⁸· ¹⁶¹· ²⁴⁸· Compl·. — On a couplet here added in 𝔊ᴬ ᵃˡ· see note on v.⁶. —
5. 𝔐 אֵיד; 𝔊 ἀπολλυμένῳ, perh. = אבד (Lag.). — After *misfortune* 𝔗𝔏 add,
as interpretation, *of another*. — **6.** On the couplet added in 𝔊 see note on this
proverb above, and cf. notes of Lag. and Baumgartner. — **7.** In ᵃ 𝔊 πιστά
may be free rendering of 𝔐 יתר to gain a contrast with the ψευδῆ of ᵇ; but
it is possibly error of Grk. scribe for περισσά (Grabe, Lag.); in ᵇ δικαίῳ
(representing 𝔐 נדב) may be miswriting of δικαστῇ or δυνάστῃ (Jäg.), or, the
Heb. may have been read צדק, but 𝔊 may be free translation of 𝔐. — יֶ־תֶ־ר must
mean either *remainder* or *abundance* or *excellence ;* see note on this couplet
above. The stem has the sense *over and above* in North Sem. (Ass. Aram.
Heb.) and South Sem. (Arab. Eth.); in all these dialects, except Ass. (so
far as reported in De. *Wbch.*) the noun also means *string* — whether this sense
is related to the other is uncertain. The word should here probably be
emended to יֹשֶׁר.

8. Power of a bribe. The Heb. reads :

A stone of favor (or, beauty) is a gift in the eyes of its possessor —
Whithersoever he (or, it) turns, he (or, it) prospers (or, acts cleverly).

Extensive (second cl. explaining first cl.), quaternary-ternary.
Gift here, from the connection, = *bribe*, as in Ex. 23⁸ (= Dt.
16¹⁹) Isa. 1²³ ψ 15⁵. The *possessor* (or, *owner*) is more naturally
the briber, who succeeds by bribing; if it be taken as = the
bribed, the meaning is that the latter, stimulated by the gift, does
his best (*acts cleverly, skilfully, wisely*), or *is successful*. The
stone, if characterized by *beauty,* = *precious stone* (cf. 1⁹ 3²²), and
the meaning will be that the bribe, as a costly, precious thing controls the action of venal magnates. But this sense is too nearly
tautologous to be probable — to say that a bribe is a precious
stone is to say nothing to the point ; a bribe was in fact often lit-

erally a precious stone, generally its equivalent in money. We
expect an expression describing the power of the bribe, and such
an expression is furnished by Frankenberg's interpretation of
stone of favor as = a stone that brings favor, a lucky stone or
magic stone. The Heb. expression does not occur in this sense
elsewhere in OT., but the Israelites had amulets (Ez. 13[18]), and
charms, sometimes made of precious stones, were widely employed in antiquity. The rendering: *a bribe is a source of good
luck* gives an intelligible thought. — The expression *in the eyes of*,
= *in the estimation of*, suits the bribed better than the briber,
though it may be understood of the latter; the reading *in the
hands of* would be more appropriate for the briber. — The couplet
must be taken to mean either:

> A bribe is a beautiful thing in the estimation of him who accepts it,
> And he (accordingly) in all respects acts skilfully (or, successfully);

or:

> A bribe is a thing of power in the hands of him who gives it,
> In all that he undertakes he prospers.

The latter interpretation is the more probable. If in second cl.
it be substituted for *he*, the general sense remains the same: the
bribe succeeds. — The two meanings of the verb (*acts wisely* and
succeeds) are substantially identical; one states the manner, the
other the result of action; see 1 Sam. 18[5] Isa. 52[13], and cf. Pr.
10[5. 19] 14[35] 15[24] 16[20] 17[2] 19[14] 21[12]. The sage states, without comment, a fact of experience: bribery is a potent means of success.
It is forbidden in Ex. 23[8] *al.*

9. Forbearance promotes friendship.

> He who covers up transgression seeks love,
> He who harps on a matter alienates his friend.

Antithetic, ternary. Similar reflections are found in 10[12] 16[28].
He who *covers up* (is silent about) the hasty speeches and ill-
advised acts of his friend thus puts aside occasions of quarrel,
and *promotes kindliness* of feeling; he who *repeats* (or, *spreads
abroad*, or, *harps on*) imprudent talk alienates his friend. The
proverb is concerned not with crime but with gossip. The inversion of subject and predicate, so as to read *he covers transgression
who seeks love* (De., who refers to 10[12]), is possible, but accords

less well with second cl., in which the man's mode of dealing with
his friend's slips of word and deed is the subject; in 10¹² the
point of view is different — *hatred* and *love* are the subjects. —
On *friend* see notes on 2¹⁷ 16²⁸; on *alienates* (= *separates*) notes
on 16²⁸ 18¹⁸, and cf. 18¹ 19⁴.

10. A wise man heeds criticism.

> A reproof enters deeper into a man of sense
> Than a hundred stripes into a fool.

Simple comparison, ternary. The Grk., following a different pointing of the Heb., has: "a threat humbles (lit. crushes) the heart
of a man of sense, but a fool, though scourged, does not understand." The general meaning is the same in the two forms;
there is no good ground for changing the present Hebrew. The
proverb is an observation of common experience, and has parallels in other literatures. *Hundred* is a large round number; cf.
the legal "forty stripes save one." We may render: "a reproof
affects (or, benefits)," etc. — *Enters* is lit. *descends;* Hitzig compares Sallust, *Jug.* 11 : *altius in pectus descendit.*

11. Rebellion is dangerous.

> A ‹rebel› seek to do mischief,
> But a terrible messenger is sent to him.

Continuous sentence, ternary (as the text stands). The first cl.
reads literally : *rebellion seeks only mischief*, or possibly, *rebellion
certainly seeks*, etc. — the translation above given involves a slight
change of text; there is no good authority in OT. usage for the
statement (De. Siegfried *al.*) that the abstract *rebellion* is used for
the concrete *rebellious* (in Ez. 2⁷ 44⁶ we should read, with Grk.,
house of rebellion). Grk. (followed by Lat. and RV.) inverts this
order of subject and predicate : *every bad man stirs up strifes*,
but so general an allegation does not account for the sharp threat
of the second clause. The statement *a bad man seeks only rebellion* (as the Heb. may be rendered) is not true unless the last
term is taken (as it is used elsewhere in OT.) as = "disobedience
to God"; so it seems to be understood in part by the Grk.,
which renders the second cl. : *but the Lord will send to him a pit-*

iless angel (or, *messenger*), that is, some frightful misfortune (storm, pestilence, or the like). This sense is, however, here improbable — if *Yahweh* were meant to be the subject, it would be expressed — and the second cl. suggests that some flagrant crime like rebellion is had in mind, and then the subject of the sentence is naturally *a rebellious man* or *a rebel*. *Rebellious*, in the sense of "disobedience to God," is distinctively a term of the Prophetic thought. If the text be correct (as to which there is ground for doubt) the proverb is purely political (like 23$^{1-3}$, etc.), affirming that rebellion against constituted authority is an evil and dangerous thing. Such an opinion might suit many different periods of history : it might possibly belong to the time of Ezekiel, who (Ez. 17) denounces Zedekiah for his rebellion against the King of Babylon, or to the fifth or fourth century B.C., when the Jews were accused (Neh. 6$^{6-8}$) of wishing to make themselves independent of Persia, or when (according to Euseb. *Chron.*, in the Armenian translation) a considerable body of Jews was deported, by Artaxerxes Ochus, to Hyrcania in punishment for an uprising ; but it more naturally falls in the Greek period when rebellions were rife in the various provinces into which Alexander's empire was divided. — The emendation : *the king will send a terrible one against him* (Dyserinck) gives a good sense (substantially identical with that of our Heb.), and should, perhaps, be adopted. On *terrible* (or, *cruel*) see 5^9 11^{17} 12^{10} Jer. 6^{23} Isa. 13^9.

12. A fool is dangerous.

> Meet a bear robbed of her whelps
> Rather than a fool in his folly.

Continuous sentence with implied comparison, binary. Lit.: *let a bear*, etc., *meet a man rather*, etc. For the picture of the bear see 2 Sam. 17^8 Hos. 13^8. The point of comparison is the danger involved in the two meetings ; in the animal the danger arises from her ferocious anger, in the fool from his intellectual and moral idiocy — he is capable of everything, his *folly* is an integral part of him. The couplet may be based on an old folk-saying. — Grk. (with a peculiar reading of the Heb.) : *care may come on a wise man, but fools meditate evil.*

13. Punishment of returning evil for good.

> Whoso returns evil for good,
> From his house evil shall not depart.

Simple affirmation, ternary.   Such base ingratitude, it is said, will
be punished — whether through the social laws that spring from
men's moral sense, or by direct divine action, is not said.   For
the phrase of first cl. see 1 Sam. 25²¹, and on returning good for
evil see Pr. 25²¹·²².

8. 𝔐 אבן הן השחר, for which 𝔊 has μισθὸς χαριτων παιδεία; Lag., with
probability, emends to σταθμὸς for μ., and ἐπιδοσις for π.; 𝔗, inverting, כפא
דשׁחדא הקרא; 𝔖 misunderstands; 𝔏 *gemma gratissima expectatio praesto-*
lantis. — **9.** 𝔐 שׁנה *repeat* (with ב introducing the thing in which the repetition occurs) gives a good sense; Gr. emends to שׁגה *errs*, and Winckler to
משׁנה *reports*, a meaning which occurs in Ass. (De. *Wbch.*) but not in Heb. —
𝔊 μισεῖ κρύπτειν, in which μ. = שׂנא (and so 𝔗), and κ. may be rendering of
דבר understood as = the idea contained in the מכסה of ᵃ (Lag.). On 𝔖, which
is based on 𝔊, see Pinkuss. — **10.** In 𝔐 יחת (from נחת) the first rad. is assimilated, and the tone, for rhythmical reasons, is retracted; the assimilation occurs
also in Jer. 21¹³ Job 21¹⁸, but not in ψ 38³; cf. Ols. § 237 a, Ges.²⁶ § 66 f. The
stem is perhaps Aramaic. — 𝔊 in ᵃ has free rendering of 𝔐; in ᵇ it seems to
have read בחפה כסל מאס (Jäg. Lag.) or to have taken תחת from חתת (συντρί-
βει), a reading which Frank. adopts; the derivation from נחת seems more
appropriate.   𝔗 expands 𝔐; 𝔖 follows 𝔊; 𝔏 = 𝔐. — **11.** 𝔐 אך (wanting in
𝔊𝔖𝔗, in 𝔏 rendered by *semper*) taken either as = *only* or as = *certainly*, is
inapposite, and the abstract מרי (read מרבה in 𝔊𝔏) is here very improbable, if
not impossible; read אישׁ מרי (as 𝔖𝔗 have it). — After שלח the Prep. ב seems
properly to introduce the object which one stretches out the hand to grasp;
we should here perh. read לו or אליו. — Before רע Bi., following 𝔊, inserts כל;
for 𝔐 מלאך Gr. reads מהלך (so 6¹¹), but the difference is not important; Dys.,
more probably, מלך and ישׁלח. — **12.** For the Heb. of 𝔊ᵃ Jäg. suggests פנשׁ
דאבה באשׁ שׂכל; in ᵇ 𝔊 read אל instead of אל: *to a fool is folly.* 𝔖 in ᵃ follows
𝔊, only doubling the subject (*care and fear*), in ᵇ = 𝔐, with אל for אל. 𝔗 in ᵃ
mingles 𝔐 and 𝔖, in ᵇ, reading אל, interprets 𝔐. 𝔏 = 𝔐.

14. Of quarrelling.

Text and translation are doubtful. Our Heb. may be rendered :
a letter out of water is the beginning of strife, and before getting
wrought up (= excited, angry) *leave off contention*, or . . . *before*
contention (or, *quarrelling*) *breaks out, leave off.* The word rendered *getting wrought up* (or, *quarrelling*) occurs elsewhere in OT.

only in 18^1 20^3, on which see notes.* The reference in the first line of our Heb. text seems to be to making a small aperture in a dam or in anything which prevents the flow of water : it is easy to let the water out, hard to stop it — the aperture grows larger, and the flow of water stronger. This construction is intelligible, though the language is somewhat indefinite ; we should expect mention of the point whence the water is let out ; in any case, we must, for grammatical accuracy, read : *a letting out*, etc. The Grk. gives what is perhaps a better text by reading *words* instead of *water*, whence we have : *outpouring of words is the beginning of strife*, a warning against thoughtless talk, as in 10^{19} 17^{27}. — In the second line the norm of the Book leads us to expect an assertion (parallel to that of first line) that something comes before something (as in 15^{33} 16^{18}) — perhaps (omitting the *leave off*) : *before conflict goes quarrelling*, a progression in the thought. Either the rendering of RV. (*leave off contention before there be quarrelling*) or that of Siegfried (*before contention break out leave off*) is, however, possible. Whatever the precise form of the aphorism may be, its general sense is clear — it is a warning against strife.

15. God abhors judicial corruption.

He who gives judgment for the wicked and he who condemns the righteous
Are both of them an abomination to Yahweh.

Simple affirmation, quaternary-ternary (or, binary-ternary). The offence described is that of the unjust judge, controlled by prejudice, passion, servility to governors, or a bribe. The Heb. of first cl. contains an assonance that cannot well be imitated in modern English, somewhat as *he who rights the wrong and he who wrongs the right* (the verb *right* as in Shakspere, *Rich. III.* 1, 3). The rendering of RV., *justifies* (that is, *pronounces just*), now conveys a wrong impression, one too distinctly ethical, and *acquits* is too narrow a term, since the bad man is not necessarily the defendant in the trial. From this Heb. word the forensic expression *justify* has passed into NT. (Rom. 3^{20}, etc.). *Wicked* is

---

* Schult. De. *al.* take it (from Arab. and Syr.) to mean *show the teeth* (in sign of anger), whence *quarrel;* according to others (Siegfried *al.*) it means *break forth* (in a hostile way).

he whose cause is bad, *righteous* he whose cause is good.   On *abomination* see note on 3[32].   For the idea of the couplet cf. Ex. 23[7] Dt. 25[1] Isa. 5[23] 1 K. 8[32] Job 34[17] ψ 94[21] Pr. 24[24].

16. Wisdom is beyond the fool's reach.

> If the fool has money to buy wisdom,
> What boots it, since he has no mind?

Question, really prose, but arranged in ternary form.   Lit. *why* (or, *of what avail*) *is there a price in the fool's hand to buy wisdom, and intellect* (lit. *heart*) *there is none ?*   Grk. : *why has a fool wealth ? for a dolt cannot buy wisdom.*   The term *fool* appears to refer to both intellectual and moral weakness, since *wisdom* in Pr. is commonly employed in the wider sense.   There may be an allusion to attendance, by mentally and morally weak persons, on the instruction of sages; but, as it is doubtful whether fees were taken by the Jewish teachers, the proverb may merely affirm that wisdom cannot be got without certain qualities of mind.   Here, as elsewhere in the Book, the *fool* is absolutely excluded from the domain of wisdom, and nothing is said of a change of mind whereby he may enter it.   De. cites the "golden proverb" of Democritus: "there are many who have learning without mind (νοῦν)"; but the antithesis of Pr. goes deeper — the fool is not merely lacking in breadth and fineness of intellectual apprehension, he is also unsympathetic toward all knowledge and wisdom.   *Mind* is properly "capacity to learn," which here probably involves "disposition to learn." — The Grk. adds a couplet made up from v.[19a] and v.[20].

17. Value of friendship.

> A friend is always friendly,
> A brother is born for adversity.

Identical, ternary.   As symbols of steadfast, helpful affection *friend* and *brother* are here (as in ψ 35[14], cf. 2 Sam. 1[26]) equivalents : one is loving at *all* times, even in times of trial ; the other is *born for* (= intended for, adapted to, exercises his specific function in) adversity, the occasion which most severely tests friendship. — Many recent translators (De. Reuss, Kamp. RV. marg. *al.*) adopt the rendering *and is born as a brother for* (or, *in) adversity*, that is, the true friend, in time of trial, is, as it were, born anew into blood-kinship and assumes the rôle of brother. This translation gives substantially the same sense as the other, identifying *friend* and *brother* in respect of faithfulness, but is less natural, and less exact. — Some interpret the second line as expressing a contrast to (and an advance on) the first line, with the sense : " a friend, it is true, is always friendly, but in time of trial it is the brother (at other times indifferent) that comes forward " ; but the term *always* appears to include times of trial ; the friend is not friendly in fair weather only, and the brother does not confine his kindness to seasons of adversity. A brother is a natural representative of unselfish love ; but Pr. in two places (18^{19} 19^7) represents the fraternal relationship as far from perfect, and in two places (18^{24} 27^{10}) puts it below the relationship of friend or neighbor — that is, it estimates the bond of social affection as higher than that of blood. — On the value of friendship see BS. 6^{14-16} 22^{23}. The love of sister for brother or of brother for sister is nowhere directly spoken of in OT. (in 2 Sam. 13^{20} Absalom is next of kin and natural protector), but the word *sister* is used as = *dear friend* (7^4 Cant. 4^9 *al.*).

18. Folly of going security.

> Void of sense is he who pledges himself,
> Who becomes security to another.

Identity of predicates, quaternary or ternary. *Pledges himself* is lit. *strikes hands ;* on the expression see notes on 6^1 11^{15}. The *another* refers to the creditor. *To another* is lit. *in the presence of his neighbor.* Grk. : *for his own friends*, with the same general sense. Similar warnings are given in 6^{1-5} 11^{15} 20^{16} 22^{26} 27^{13} BS. $29^{18(24)}$. The OT. law says nothing of such security ; the custom arose, doubtless, in the later commercial life.

19, 20. Strife and falseness are destructive.

> 19. He loves ‹wounds› who loves strife,
> He who ‹talks› proudly seeks destruction.
> 20. A false heart finds no good,
> A lying tongue falls into calamity.

19. Chiastic parallelism, quaternary (or, binary). **Instead of** *wounds* the Heb. has *sin*, not here appropriate, the corresponding term in second cl. being *destruction;* the emendation requires only a slight change in the Hebrew. In second cl. the text reads : *he who makes high his door,* which is understood to refer to the pride and ostentation shown by building the house-door high* ; but no such custom is known to have existed in antiquity, and the parallelism calls for an expression referring to strife ; the change of a letter gives the reading *makes high his mouth,* = speaks loftily, haughtily ; cf. the similar expression *speak loftily* in 1 Sam. 2³.† — The parallelism involves the idea that proud words occasion strife, and strife is always injurious, often destructive. Cf. 11² 18¹² 20³ 29²³. — **20.** Synonymous, binary-ternary. Lit. *he who is false in heart* (= mind, inward being) and *he who is false in tongue;* on the first of these terms for *false* see note on 2¹⁵ — it means "that which deviates from the straight line," "morally crooked" ; the second means "that which is turned away from the proper form." *Finds = meets with.* The *good* and *calamity* (lit. *evil*) relate not to moral advantage or disadvantage, but, as appears from the whole course of thought in the Book, to external prosperity or adversity ; it would, besides, be tautological to say that the liar is not morally good.

21. Children not always a joy.

> He who begets a dolt does it to his sorrow,
> And the father of a fool has no joy.

Identical, ternary. The two terms *dolt* (Heb. *kesīl*) and *fool* (Heb. *nabal*) are here practically identical in meaning. The former (which occurs nearly fifty times in Pr., see note on 1²²) is "dull, slow-witted," intellectually, morally, or religiously ; the latter (found elsewhere in Pr. only in 17⁷ 30²², and less than twenty times in the whole OT.) commonly, outside of Pr., relates to religious folly. Here the reference may be to intellectual and moral stupidity, or to the intellectual sort alone. Cf. v.²⁵ of this chapter, and BS. 22³. — Grk. (imitating 10¹) adds : *but a wise*

---

* The Grk. has : *who makes his house high.*

† Aben Ezra, Schult. *al.* interpret *door* as = *mouth*, but this is an improbable metaphor.

son makes a glad mother, an antithesis which might naturally have
been appended by a scribe.

22. Cheerfulness is health.

> A cheerful heart is a good medicine,
> But a broken spirit dries up the bones.

Antithetic, quaternary (or, binary). Cf. 15[13], to first cl. of which
our first cl. is conformed by some critics; but the variation of the
Heb. seems more probable. On *heart* and *spirit* see notes on 2[2]
and 11[13]; both terms here relate to temper of mind — in first cl.
we have a cheery, courageous nature, in second cl. a broken-spir-
ited, dejected, downcast nature. In first cl. the predicate is lit.
causes good healing (or, *recovery*). The *bones*, as skeleton, represent the whole body; they may be vigorous, fat, full of marrow
(3[8] 15[30] 16[24] Isa. 58[11]), or feeble, rotten, eaten by caries (12[4] 14[30]
ψ 31[10(11)] Job 30[30]); in this verse the *dryness* is contrasted with
the *fatness* (fulness of marrow) of healthy bones. The reference
is primarily to the physiological effect of temper of mind, and
then, perhaps, to the general effect on life; as to the old-Hebrew
conception of the relation of the bones to the rest of the body,
the process of nourishment in bones, and the relation of mind to
body we have no precise information. For similar sayings among
other peoples see Malan; on ancient medicine see art. *Medicine*
in Smith, *Dict. of Bible*.

14. פֶּטֶר or פֶּטַר is better than פֹּטֵר (so Gr.). — On the stem גלע see Schult.
Ges. *Thes.* BDB. From Arab. it appears to signify *uncover, disclose* (= Heb.
גלה), then *show the teeth, quarrel, rage;* the last-named meaning suits the use
of the Hith. in Pr.; Gr. (after *Nidda*, viii. 2) takes it as = *burst forth* (so also
Siegf.); Heb. גלח, Syr. גלע, Arab. גלע, seem to be different stems. Frank.,
in opposition to the rendering *before there be conflict*, says that לפני is never
used in dehortation, but always introduces something that actually precedes;
yet cf. Gen. 27[7] לפני מתי. — 𝕲 is partly corrupt, partly based on a different
Heb. text from ours: ἐξουσίαν δίδωσιν perh. = פטר *gives free course* (but Jäg.
refers to ψ 22[8]); λόγοις = מלם (instead of מים); δικαιοσύνης is perh. for διαδι-
κασίας and ἐνδείας for ἀναιδείας (התגלע) (Jäg.). — 𝕾 read דמם for מים, and
perh. הנרב for התגלע (Baum.); 𝕿 appears to expand 𝕾 (cf. Pinkuss); 𝕴[b] *et
antequam patiatur contumeliam* (perh. = *before he is stripped*) *judicium dese-
rit*. — 16. On the arrangement of lines in 𝕲 see note on v.[19] below. — 17. To
take לצרה as = *in adversity* is perh. possible, but is here hardly natural. — In [b]
𝕲 has a doublet, the second member of which is abridged; or this second line

may be an interpretative gloss. רֵעֶ֫ךָ הָרַע was, according to Jäg., understood by
𝕲 as Hif. Impv. of רעה *make thee a friend.* — **18.** 𝕲𝕃 take תקע כף as a gesture
of joy. — 𝕳 לפני רעהו; Gr., retaining sense of 𝕳, ו ' לימען; Bi., after 𝕲 (τῶν
ἑαυτοῦ φίλων) לְרֵעֶ֫הַ, making the reference general — the nature of the warning
is not thereby affected. — **19.** 𝕳 פשׁע; Gr. פב, which is preferable. — In 𝕲
the order of lines differs from that of 𝕳: after v.[16] come v.[19b] and a modified
form of v.[20], then v.[17] (with doublet). 18. 19a. 20; the change is due to an error of a
Grk. scribe. — 𝕳 פרחו; 𝕲 τὸν ἑαυτοῦ οἶκον, = בֵּתו or בּרהּוּ, a good sense, but
not preferable to that of 𝕳. It is better, however, with Frank., to read פי; cf.
the combination of גבה with בר , 1 Sam. 2[3]. — **21.** 𝕳 לֵר; 𝕲 καρδία, = לב.
here inapposite and against the parallelism; it is perh. induced by the κ. of
v.[22]. — **22.** 𝕳 וֵהָה is most naturally connected with the verb of Hos. 5[13], and
so, = *healing.* The similarity to 15[13] has suggested the sense *face,* for which,
however, there is no authority (see Arab. נחת and וגה). The primitive signification of the stem is uncertain; cf. Syr. גהא, *flee, withdraw* (whence perhaps
our noun, = *cessation, betterment*), and see notes of De. Now., and the lexicons. 𝕲 εὐεκτεῖν; 𝕾𝕿 read גויה *body,* and Dys. Gr. emend to גוה.

23. Wickedness of taking bribes.

> A wicked man accepts a bribe
> To pervert the course of justice.

Single sentence, ternary. Lit. . . . *accepts a bribe from the bosom*
(that is, of a briber) . . . *the ways of justice.* On *bosom* as = a
part of a garment, and on its use as pocket see notes on 6[27] 16[33];
on *bribe* (lit. *gift*) see v.[8] above, and on the power of gifts cf.
21[14]. The rendering . . . *takes a bribe from* (*his own*) *bosom*
(that is, in order to corrupt a judge and pervert justice), while
possible, accords with the Heb. and with parallel sayings less well
than the translation above adopted. The *wicked man* is here the
corrupt judge or other influential person.

24, 25. Inanity and oppressiveness of the fool.

> 24. The goal of the man of understanding is wisdom,
>   The fool's eyes roam over all the world.
> 25. A foolish son is a grief to his father
>   And bitterness to her that bare him.

24. Antithetic, ternary. Lit. *in front of the man of understanding is wisdom, but the eyes of the fool are on the ends of the earth.*
The *man of understanding* (see 8[9] 17[10] 2[5]) is he who compre-

hends the issues of life, and makes it his aim to attain the true principle and law of conduct (the divine law implanted in the mind of man); the *fool*, on the other hand (Heb. *kesīl*, see v.[21]), lacking in insight and stability, is incapable of fixing his attention on any one thing, and therefore does not seek wisdom. The interpretation " the man of sense sees wisdom everywhere, the fool seeks it unsuccessfully everywhere " (Ew. *al.*) is improbable — the fool is not represented in Pr. as seeking wisdom except in the moment of final deadly peril (1^{28}), while the reference here is to the man's ordinary thought, and the point is his lack of seriousness; cf., on the other hand, the attitude of the scoffer in 14^6. For the expression *ends of the earth* see Jer. 25^{33} Dt. 28^{64} ψ 135^7 Mt. 12^{42} *al.;* it denotes the extremities of the then known world, that is, the region south of Ethiopia, the south of Arabia, the region just east of the Tigris (perhaps to the centre of Asia), Asia Minor, and the coasts of the Mediterranean Sea. — **25.** Identical, ternary-binary. The proverb is a variation of 10^1 15^{20} 17^{21}. *Fool* (*kesīl*) as in v.[21, 24]. — Delitzsch makes 17^{25}–18^2 a separate section on the ground that it begins and ends with the same thoughts which open and close the preceding passage, 17^{21-24}; but the repetition of a proverb hardly warrants such a division; see the Introduction.

26. Against injustice under forms of law.

The first line of the Heb. is clear :

> Also to fine the righteous is not good.

The word *also* (= intensive *and*), which implies a conjunction or contrast with something that precedes, is here without significance, unless we suppose a lost line or couplet with which this line or this couplet stands in contrast (possibly 18^5) ; and even if the order of lines in the couplet be inverted, the word will still be inapposite, since the relation of thought between the two lines does not call for such an emphatic connective; the rendering *even* (Kamphausen : *already*) is, for the same reason, improper. — *Fine* (usually employed of a pecuniary mulct, Dt. 22^{19} *al.*) may = more generally *punish* (as in 22^3). *Not good = not proper.* — The second line may be rendered : *To smite the noble for upright-*

ness (RV.), or: . . . *against equity*, = *unjustly* (Frank. *al.*), or:
. . . *is against equity*, = *is unseemly* (Wild.). The first sense is
improbable : in first line the bad act is simply punishing a just or
righteous man (without the addition " for his justice or righteousness "), nor in fact is the " noble " man commonly assailed " for
(= on account of) his nobleness," but in a rapacious spirit which
cares not whether its victim be noble or ignoble, or his cause just
or unjust. The second rendering (in which the expression *is not
good* must be supplied from first line) involves a tautology — any
punishment of a righteous man must be unjust. The third rendering gives a distinct parallelism of predicates in the clauses.
Kamphausen changes the text and renders : *to smite the noble is
so in high degree* (that is, *is emphatically not good*), but the translation is doubtful, and a climax here is improbable. — If the word
noble be retained, it must, from the parallelism, be understood in
a moral sense, as = *righteous*. It may mean *nobleman, prince*
(8^{16} 25^7 Job 12^{21} ψ 118^9 *al.*), or *willing, freehearted* (Ex. 35^5), but
also, apparently, *morally noble :* thus in v.^{7} of this chapter it is
put over against *fool*, and in Isa. 32^{5-8} is contrasted with *fool* and
knave. — Another emendation of text (Frank.) gives the reading :
to oppress (*him*) *in court unjustly* (or, *inequitably*), to which the
tautology (*oppress . . . unjustly*) seems a decisive objection.
Probably the second line should be read either : *it is not seemly*
(or, *fair*) *to oppress the upright*, or : *it is not seemly to pervert
justice*. Cf. 18^5, which appears to be a variation of this couplet,
and after it our line might be read : *to oppress the upright in
court.*

27, 28. Value of silence. — Identical, quaternary-ternary (or, ternary).

> 27. He who is sparing of words is wise,
>   A man of cool spirit is judicious.
> 28. Even a fool, if he hold his peace, is accounted wise,
>   Sensible, if he keep his lips shut.

27. Cf. 10^{19}. First cl. lit. . . . *knows knowledge ;* cf. 4^1, *know
understanding*. The man of *cool spirit* (lit. *he who is cool of
spirit*) is one who maintains composure and self-control, is not
under the dominion of excited feeling, and is therefore cautious in

speaking; the proverb is primarily directed not against literary loquacity (though this may well be included), but against language which may stir up ill feeling. — Subjects and predicates may be inverted, so as to read : *The wise man is sparing of words, the judicious man is cool.* — The ancient Heb. editors (in the Masora) read, in second cl., *he who is precious* (= costly, dear, rare) *of spirit,* which is interpreted by Rashi (perhaps guided by first cl.) to mean *he who is sparing of words,* by others *of worthy bearing* (Saadia) or *character* (Schult. AV.). The two last renderings are tautological (cf. De.) ; the translation *cool* (which is generally adopted by recent expositors) seems satisfactory ; Grk. *longanimous ;* Targ. *humble.* — *Wise,* lit. *a man of wisdom* (or, *comprehension*). — **28.** The meaning is not that the fool shows wisdom in keeping silence, but that silence conceals folly, and is, moreover, commonly regarded as a sign of profundity. See many proverbs, similar to these two, in Malan's *Notes.*

23. 𝕲 gives a very free rendering of the whole couplet as a single sentence, and adds a doublet of the second half; see Lag.'s attempt to explain the wording, and Baum.'s criticism of Lag. — 𝕾 *he who receives bribes is wicked, and perverts the way of justice,* less probable than 𝕳. — **24.** 𝕳 את פני *alongside of, in front of ;* Gr. emends improperly to אל פני *toward.* Before מֵכִן Bi. inserts אִשׁ, unnecessarily; sense and rhythm in 𝕳 are good. In 𝕲𝕾𝕿 את is not rendered. — With 𝕲[103. 147. 253] the Grk. text is better read πρόσωπον συνετοῦ ἀνδρὸς σοφόν, 𝕲[B] giving no sense (Lag.). The הדן *rejoice* of 𝕿[Lag.] must be emended, after 𝕾, to חירן *look,* as in the Breslau Codex (Pink.). — **26.** Omit גם as meaningless (f. note on v.[28] below). The ל before צרק is improbable, since ענשׁ is elsewhere followed by noun without Prep. (see 21[11]); we should perh. read לַעֲנשׁ (see the ל in [b]); the insertion of the Prep. before the noun may be error of eye, or may be due to an Aramaic-speaking scribe. — 𝕳 לחכת; better לחשׁת (Frank.). For נָרב cf. Arab. נרב *active, excellent* (= physically or morally good), and Eth. מֻרַכ *exposed to peril* (= *pressed on*); the stem perhaps = *move on, press forward.* — 𝕳 עֲלֵי ישׁר affords no satisfactory sense; read כָּל ישָׁר (Gr.), as 𝕲 οὐδὲ ὅσιον (Dys. בְּלִי ישָׁר); the emendation עֲלֵי יֶהֶר *superabundantly* (Kamp.) does not accord with the context. 𝕾𝕿 *who say what is right;* 𝕷 *qui recta judicat.* — **27.** K וְקַר; Q יְקַר. The latter is followed freely by 𝕲𝕿𝕷 and the medieval Jewish interpreters, the former by 𝕾. — **28.** 𝕳 גם introduces a contrast between the אול and the naturally suggested חכם (in v.[26] there is no such natural suggestion of contrast between צדק and רשׁע). — 𝕲 ἀνοήτῳ ἐπερωτήσαντι (מדריש) σοφίαν σοφία (חכמה) λογισθήσεται, an improbable reading. On the unimportant couplet added in 𝕲[68. 161] to v.[27], and apparently a free variation of v.[28a], see Lag. — 𝕾 repeats מתחיב in [b].

XVIII. 1. Our Heb. reads: *One who separates himself* (or, *holds himself aloof*, or, *is alienated*) *seeks desire, quarrels with* (or, *rages against*) *all wisdom* (or, *quarrels by every means*). This is now generally held to mean that one who holds himself aloof from his friends or from society follows his own selfish desires and ambitions, and opposes everything reasonable.* This observation, however, does not accord with the tone of Proverbs. The character thus described is that of a man who, wrapped up in himself, ignores the interests and claims of the community, and thus becomes an enemy of society. The same thought, in ecclesiastical form, is expressed in Hillel's saying (*Pirke Aboth*, 2, 4): "separate not thyself from the congregation," that is, " be not a separatist, a free-lance or schismatic, do not withdraw thyself from the mass of belief and custom represented by the community " — an idea natural to an Israelite of the later time, but, in its broader form improbable for the sages of Proverbs. — Grk. (followed by Lat.) has: *a man who wishes to separate from friends seeks pretexts, but at all times he will be liable to reproach* (or, perhaps, *and . . . will be full of reproach*), which reads *pretext* for *desire* and *will be reproached* for *will quarrel*, and adds *from friends*. This reading is adopted substantially by Hitzig and Frankenberg. The latter renders: *the alienated friend seeks an occasion* [of quarrel], *seeks by all means to stir up strife*, which in its homely tone resembles other aphorisms of the Book, but appears to be over-cynical. The renderings *at all times* (Grk.) and *by all means* (Frank.) are doubtful. Hitzig's translation is not more satisfactory: *he who is excluded* [by men from their society] *seeks an occasion, gnashes his teeth against all that is beneficial* [to others]. It seems impossible to get a satisfactory sense from the Hebrew, and no good emendation presents itself.

2. The fool's fatuousness.

> A fool takes no pleasure in sound sense,
> But rather in revealing his nature.

---

* So Luth. RV. Ew. De. *al.* For the views of the early commentators see *Critici Sacri* and Geier. Aben Ezra explained it as referring to the traveller who leaves home in order to search out all knowledge. So nearly B. Hodgson (Oxford, 1788): *A retired man pursueth the researches he delighteth in, and hath pleasure in each branch of science*, a pleasing picture, but forbidden by the verb of the second clause.

Antithetic, ternary. On *fool* (*kesīl*) see notes on $1^{22} 17^{21}$. *Sound sense* is *comprehension* and the conduct which follows therefrom; see note on 2^2. The second cl. is lit. *but in his mind's* [*heart's*] *disclosing itself.* The fool, that is, having no inkling of what is wise and noble, has fatuous satisfaction in following out and manifesting his intellectual and moral feebleness, which he regards as wisdom.

3. Vice entails disgrace.

> When ‹ wickedness › comes then comes also contempt,
> And on ‹ insolence › follows scorn.

Synonymous, binary (or, quaternary-binary). The Heb. reads: *when the wicked man comes, comes also contempt, and with disgrace is scorn.* The reading *wickedness* (obtained by a change of vowels) is favored by the form of expression of first cl., by the second cl., and by the parallel line in 11^2 (*comes pride, then comes disgrace*). — Of the three other nouns of our Heb. the first and third are active (expressing one's feeling toward a person), the second is passive (expressing the state of the despised person). The relation of the nouns of first cl. to each other is ambiguous: the *contempt* may be felt by the wicked for others, or by others for him; the second sense is favored by the parallelism (the *scorn* of second cl. is directed toward the bad man), and by such proverbs as 11^2. — The second cl. in our Heb. affords no satisfactory sense. *Disgrace* cannot be taken (Zöckler) as = *shameful conduct* (synonymous with *wickedness*). The couplet is by some * understood to mean: " the wicked man despises others, but with the disgrace which he inflicts on others comes scorn from others for him," a forced interpretation of second cl. Others,† following the Grk., read: " When the wicked comes, comes also contempt, disgrace, and scorn," which is grammatically and rhythmically improbable. A slight change of text gives the reading for second cl. ‡ : *and with him are disgrace and scorn*, that is, he (the wicked man) inflicts these on others; this (identical in sense with Fleischer's rendering, but grammatically better) is intelligible, but is not quite natural. — A parallel to first cl. is got if

---

* Strack, *al.*   † With Fleischer.   ‡ Grätz, Bickell.

(by an easy change of consonants) we substitute *insolence* (or, *pride*) for *disgrace:* " with wickedness is contempt, with pride is scorn." The ambiguity of direction in *scorn* remains; for the reasons given above it is better to take it as felt toward the bad man. Grk. and Lat. regard the *contempt* of first cl. as inflicted by the wicked ; in second cl. Lat. makes him the sufferer, Grk. is doubtful. — On *contempt, disgrace, scorn* see notes on 12⁸ 3³⁵ 6³³. The distinction made by Delitzsch, that the first and third of these terms relate to words, and the second to conduct, is not warranted by OT. usage.

4. The Heb. text reads : *The words of a man's mouth are deep waters, a flowing brook, a wellspring of wisdom.* This unrestricted statement does not accord with the thought of Prov., in which no such excellence is ascribed to men in general (in 12¹⁴ the text is to be changed) ; nor can we take *man* as = " the ideal man," or paraphrase (Ew. De.) " it often happens that the words," etc. — this is not in the manner of the Book. As the couplet stands, the *man* must be qualified by some term like " good," or, " wise," and the second cl. must be regarded as continuing the predicate of first cl. To take second cl. as an independent sentence, and describe the *wellspring of wisdom* as *a flowing brook* (RV.) is to introduce an impropriety of language — a fountain is not a brook ; and the rendering *the words*, etc., *are deepened waters* [that is, of a cistern, which is exhaustible], *the wellspring*, etc., *is a flowing* [or, *bubbling*, = inexhaustible] *brook* (Hitz.) supposes a meaning (" deepened ") which the Heb. does not permit, and thus introduces an unwarranted antithesis between " man's words " and " wisdom."—The two lines of the couplet do not agree well together. A comparison like that of our first cl. is found in 20⁵, but in a sense which is hardly applicable here : there a man's secret thought is compared to " deep water," as hard to fathom and get possession of ; here the *deep water* is rather the symbol of inexhaustible supply, a sense which is given by the parallel terms *flowing brook* and *wellspring*. This inexhaustibleness cannot be meant to be affirmed of men in general ; the *man* must be defined. We may supply *righteous* (as in 10¹¹), or *wise* (cf. 13¹⁴ 16²²), but then the *wisdom* of second cl. will not be appropriate — it is not naturally related to "righteous," and, with "wise" in first cl., it would produce an identical proposition. Further, the term *fountain* (Heb. *māqōr*), when it is used metaphorically, always occurs elsewhere in connection with the idea of "life" (5^{18} 10^{11} 13^{14} 14^{27} 16^{22} Jer. 2^{13} 17^{13} ψ $36^{9(10)}$ $68^{26(27)}$), and the definition *life* here suits the context better than *wisdom*. The expression *fountain of life* may mean either "fountain of life-giving water," or "perennial fountain"; the latter sense accords with the parallel *brook*. The reading *life*, instead of *wisdom*, is found in the Grk. and in a few Heb. MSS.; the testimony of the latter is not of great value, and the Greek reading may be a correction after 10^{11}. But the usage of Prov. must be allowed to have weight, and we should perhaps read the couplet: *The words of the wise are deep waters, a flowing brook, a perennial fountain*, that is, an inexhaustible source of counsel and blessing. — On *word* as equivalent to *thought* see note on 10^{11}.

5. Against legal injustice.

> To favor the guilty is not good,
> Nor to oppress the innocent in court.

Identical thought with antithesis of terms, ternary. A forensic saying, $= 17^{26}$ (cf. 17^{15}); *guilty* and *innocent* are the terms usually rendered *wicked* and *righteous* respectively. *Favor* is lit. *lift up the face*, that is, "raise a suppliant from the ground in token of favor" (Lev. 19^{15} Mal. 1^8 2^9 Job 13^8 ψ 82^2, and the verb alone in Gen. 19^{21}, $= accept$); the implication here is that the favoring is unjust. — The Heb. of second cl. reads: *to oppress* (lit. *turn aside*, that is, from one's rights), etc., which may be taken to mean *so as to oppress*, etc. (RV. marg.), but it is more natural to understand second cl. as simply parallel to first cl. *Court* is lit. *judgment*, $= legal decision$. Lat.: *that thou mayest decline from the truth of justice* (reading *truth* or *righteousness* instead of *righteous*). Grk. (expressing the implied adjective): *nor is it holy to pervert justice in judgment*. Cf. 1 K. 21^{9-13} Am. 5^{12} Isa. 1^{23} Jer. 22^3 Ez. 22^{12} *al.*

XVIII. 1. מַאֲוָה; ⑤ προφάσεις, = לְאָנָה, as in Ju. 14^4 (Capp. *Crit. Sac.* 4, 5, 13), which should, perhaps, be adopted; cf. 2 K. 5^7. Possibly נִרְגָּן *slanderer* should be read instead of נִפְרָד; cf. 16^{28}; the לְ of מַאֲוָה appears to be taken by ⑤ as sign of Acc. — 𝔐 בכל חושיה; 𝕲 ἐν παντὶ καιρῷ, perh. free rendering of 𝔐; on ה' see Lag on this passage. — 𝔐 יהגלע; 𝕲 ἐπονείδιστος, = יתהגל or יתלען (Capp. 4, 7, 3). — On 𝔖 and 𝕿 see notes of Pink. and Baum. — **2.** 𝕲 ἄγεται (supplied by the translator) is apparently scribal error for ἀγαται (Jäg.), and ἀφροσύνη is interpretation of 𝔐 התגלת לבו, or perh. (Gr. Baum.) represents הללת (which, however, it does not represent in Eccl. 10¹³). — **3.** 𝔐 רָשָׁע and קָלוֹן; read רֶשַׁע and יָרוּן. — כֹּז, חֶלוֹן, חרפה, are general terms for contempt, which is naturally often expressed by words, sometimes also by deeds; see 12⁸ 6³⁰, 3³⁵ ψ 83¹⁷, 6³³ Ju. 5¹⁸. Bi. (and so Gr. doubtfully) reads וּמֵי. — 𝕲 εἰς βάθος is ingeniously explained by Jäg. as = בְּאֻגַּם *into the pool* (for 𝔐 גם נא), but it is doubtful whether βάθος would be used for אגם, a word which 𝕲 elsewhere in OT. perfectly understands; one might rather think of עמק; cf. βαθὺ in v.⁴, 𝔐 עֲמָקּב. — **4.** For פִי אִישׁ read חֶרֶם חָרַם (Gr. הבנה אִישׁ), and for חכמה read חַיִּם (so 𝕲 and several Heb. MSS.). — 𝕲 λόγος ἐν καρδίᾳ ἀνδρός, = רבר בלב אש, in which בלב appears to have arisen out of 𝔐 ברפ (in רבר פי), the ר and פ becoming ל and ב (Lag.). — 𝕲 ἀναπήδυει Lag. regards as error for ἀναπιδύει.

6–8. Foolish and slanderous talk.

> 6. The lips of a fool lead him into strife,
>   And his mouth brings on him stripes.
> 7. A fool's mouth is his ruin,
>   And his lips a snare to him.
> 8. The words of a slanderer are like dainty morsels,
>   They penetrate into the innermost recesses of a man.

6. Identical, ternary. Cf. 17¹⁴·¹⁹ 19²⁹ 20³. Lit. *come into strife,* = *lead,* etc.; or a slight change of the Heb. will give *lead* (so the Grk.). *Brings on him* is lit. *calls for.* The fool's thoughtless or malicious words involve him in disputes (legal or other), which, since he is in the wrong, entail punishment. — **7.** Identical, binary-ternary. Cf. 12¹³ 13⁸ 17²⁸. The thought is the same as in the preceding couplet. *Ruin* is to be taken as = "grievous calamity, crushing misfortune." The Heb. is lit. *a snare to his person* (lit. *soul*), = *to himself.* — **8.** Comparison explained, ternary. The couplet occurs again at 26²²; cf. 16²⁸ 26²⁰. The *slanderer* is one who whispers malicious gossip, which, says the proverb, is received by the hearers as eagerly as choice morsels of food, and, like them, pass into men's being, and so affect their thought and action. On other translations of the word here rendered *dainty morsels* (such as *sport* or *mockery, blows* [AV. *wounds*] *burning, tormenting, simple, reserved, soft*) see critical note below. The text does not express an antithesis in the two lines: *the words are soft* (or, *reserved*), *nevertheless they penetrate* (lit. *go down*); it is the quality of sweetness in the words that makes them acceptable. The Heb. has lit. in second cl. *go down into the inner chambers of the belly,* in accordance with the mention of food in first cl.; the expression *the recesses of a man* is more appropriate to the acceptance of gossip. On *inner chambers* (here = *interior*) see note on 7^{27}. The proverb simply states a fact — men's readiness to listen to malicious talk — without comment. For the concluding phrase cf. 20^{30}.

9. Sloth is destructive.

He who is slack in his work
Is brother to him who destroys.

Single sentence, binary-ternary. Against indolence and carelessness. The primary reference in *work* is probably to the ordinary bread-winning occupations of life, but the term may include all affairs, of friendship, statesmanship, etc. The slothful or indolent man, the proverb declares, ruins things as effectually as the spendthrift or traitor or any one who sets himself to destroy. Indolence, as an offence against physical well-being, is specially denounced in Proverbs; so in 6^{6-11} 10^{4} 12^{24} 15^{19} $20^{4.13}$ 21^{25} 24^{30-34} 26^{13-16} (cf. BS. $22^{1.2}$ 40^{28-30}). *Brother* = "one of similar nature" (so *companion* in 28^{24}). *Him who destroys* is lit. *a possessor* (= *a dealer*) *of destruction;* the reference is not to robbers and murderers, but simply to those who bring ruin on their own affairs and those of others. Rashi explains the expression as referring to Satan.

6. 𝔐 Qal יָבֹאוּ; 𝔊𝔗 Hif. יָבִאוּ, unnecessary. — 𝔐 לְמַהֲלֻמוֹת; 𝔊 *τὸ θρασὺ θάνατον*; the last word seems to represent the three last letters of 𝔐 (Jäg.), the rest is doubtful: Jäg. suggests that 𝔊 out of למה made הֵמָּה (comparing 9^{13} 20^{1}), Baum. suggests הַהֹמִיָּה (9^{13} *γυνὴ . . . θρασεῖα*), and Levy (*Chald. Wört.*, s.v. הַרְהָא) למהר (out of למהל); the reading החמה is the most probable. — **8.** On נִרְגָּן see note on 16^{28}. — 𝔐 מִתְלַהֲמִים (found only here and in the duplicate couplet 26^{22}) has been variously explained: 1. 𝔊 (in 26^{22}) *μαλακοί* (which elsewhere in 𝔊 = רך); cf. חלק 28^{23} *flattering* (so Kimḫi, Geier), and Arab. לחמה *soft* (Ew. compares נעם), or (Frank.) Aram. חלה *sweet;* possibly Σ (26^{22}) *ἐν παρέργῳ subordinate, incidental* is here to be included, in the sense of *feigned*, but see below under *sport.* 2. *Whisper, murmur* (= לחש); 'A (26^{22}) *γοητικοί jugglers;* Ew. suggests comparison with Aram. רעם as possible, = *murmur*, as expressing either the transient or the insinuating character of words.   3. 𝕿 ראבן *disturb*, *vex* (and so substantially 𝔖), as = הלם *strike;* so Immanuel (in Reuchlin), Rashi *wounds* (cf. לחם, Heb. and Arab.) or (26²²) *combatants*, Luther, AV. (see text and margin), Levi, Vatablus *those who feign themselves wounded*.   Similar is 𝕿 רכן (26²²) *strike down*, perh. scribal variation of ראבן (cf. Levy).   4. Σ in 𝔖ᴴ תמימן, = ἀκέραιοι (Middeldorpf ἄκα-κοι), 𝕷 *simplicia*, Θ (26²²) ἐξαπλούμενοι, perh. free rendering of 𝔊, perh. error of text.   5. *Sport*, *play*, taking להם as = לההׂ; so Saad. Mich. Zöck.   6. *Hidden* (Aben Ezra), perh. with reference to Arab. לחם, IV, or connected with *whisper*.   7. *Burning* (Ew.) = *destructive* (like poison), taking להם as = להב.— The comparison with Arab. לחם *swallow with avidity* seems to be the most satisfactory, though the rendering *sweet morsels* is possible. — 𝔊 omits the couplet, substituting 19¹⁵, but with changes (Jäg. Lag.). — 9. 𝕳 נס, with reference to other classes of persons who are destructive.   Originally it may have pointed to an immediately preceding statement; in the present connection it is without significance.

10, 11. God and wealth as fortresses.

> 10. The name of Yahweh is a strong fortress,
> To which the righteous runs and is safe.
> 11. A rich man's wealth is his strong city,
> It is like a high wall in his estimation.

10. Single sentence, ternary (or, binary-ternary).   The expression *name of Yahweh*, common elsewhere in OT. (except in Ju. Ru. Ezr. Esth. Job [discourses] Eccl. Cant.), is found in Pr. only here (a similar expression in 30⁹).   The *name* = the person, because it expressed his nature and qualities (as early names commonly did), and because in very ancient times the name was regarded (perhaps in consequence of its significance) as having an objective existence and as identical with its possessor,* and the locution which thence arose survived in later times when the old crude conception had vanished.   Every people came to associate with the name of its god all that it attributed to the god.   The name Yahweh was significant to the Jews at this time not because it was a "tetragrammaton" or had in it any mysterious meaning, but because, as the proper name of the national deity, it represented for them all ideas of divine guidance and protection.   On the period of the history during which the name was commonly employed see note on 1⁷.   The superstitious notions which were

---

* See Spencer, *Sociol.*, I. 263; Jevons, *Introd. to Hist. of Rel.*, pp. 245, 361; Brinton, *Rel. of Prim. Peoples*, pp. 92 f.

later attached to the "tetragrammaton" are unknown to the OT.*
Cf. Ex. 3¹⁴. — *Is safe*, lit. *is set on high* or *in a high place*, where
he is safe from the attacks of enemies.　The proverb affirms generally that God protects the righteous; it says nothing of the
means employed.　Cf. ψ 27⁵. — **11.** Parallel comparisons, quaternary-ternary.　*Estimation*, lit. *picture*, then, apparently, *imagination, thought;* cf. ψ 73⁷, and note on Pr. 25¹¹.　A better
parallelism is given by reading: *and like a high wall is his riches*.
The Heb. appears to say that wealth is a protection not really,
but only in the opinion of its possessor; this is possibly the correction of an editor who took offence at the rôle ascribed to
wealth.　Whichever reading be adopted, the couplet simply states
a fact; it is doubtful whether praise or blame is implied; cf. 10¹⁵,
in which our first cl. occurs.　Wealth is regarded in Pr. sometimes
as a desirable source of power, sometimes as associated with immoral and irreligious pride. — From the collocation of v.¹⁰·¹¹ it
might be surmised that the former is a correction of the latter, or
a protest against it.　Such protest may have been added or inserted
by an editor; v.¹¹ stood originally, no doubt, as a simple record of
observation.

12, 13. Danger of pride and hasty speech.

> 12. Pride goes before destruction,
>   And before honor humility.
> 13. He who answers before he hears,
>   It is folly and shame to him.

12. Antithetic, ternary-binary.　Lit., in first cl., *before destruction
a man* (lit. *a man's heart*) *is haughty;* see 16¹⁸.　The second cl.
occurs in 15³³. — **13.** Single sentence, ternary.　*Hears* = "gives
attention to"; *shame* = "disgrace."　Cf. BS. 11⁸, *Pirk. Ab.* 5, 7.

14, 15. Value of courage and wisdom.

> 14. The spirit of a man sustains misfortune,
>   But a broken spirit who can bear?
> 15. The mind of the intelligent acquires knowledge,
>   The ear of the wise seeks after knowledge.

---

* See Buxt. *Lex*. s. v. פרש and שם מפורש. In Lev. 24¹¹·¹⁶ "the Name" should
be read "the name of Yahweh"; the "Yahweh" was omitted *causa reverentiae* by
late scribes.

14. Implicit antithesis, ternary, = " an unimpaired spirit is strong, a broken spirit is weak." Frankenberg, in first cl., not so well: *He who soothes a man sustains* (= controls) *his anger. Spirit* is the inner being thought of as the seat of vigor and courage (as in Eng. *spirited*) ; *broken = stricken, crushed. Sustain* and *bear* are here synonyms ; the rendering *raise up* (RV. marg.), instead of *bear* (= *endure*), is here improbable. *Misfortune* is lit. *sickness* (RV. *infirmity*), here used of any suffering. The proverb records a fact of human experience, the sense being : when the spirit, which is the source of strength, is itself crushed, what help is there? (for the rhetorical form cf. Mk. 9^{50}), and the implied exhortation is : be brave, do not succumb to trouble. There is no reference or allusion to divine aid. There is here a near approach to the Greek conception of " courage " as a virtue, a conception hardly elsewhere formulated in OT. — **15.** Identical parallelism, ternary. The first cl., with variation of verb, occurs in 15^{14}, in which the second cl. introduces the *fool* as contrast. — *Intelligent* (see note on 1^5) and *wise* are synonyms, and so *acquires* and *seeks after*. The word *ear* points to oral instruction. A progression of thought, such as : " the intelligent (the higher grade of mind) already possesses knowledge, the wise (the inferior grade) is only seeking it," is improbable. No such distinction exists in Pr. between *intelligent* and *wise*.

16–18. Legal and other contests.

> 16. A man's gift makes room for him,
>   And brings him before great men.
> 17. The first comer is right in his plea,
>   Then comes the other and tests him.
> 18. The lot puts an end to disputes,
>   And decides between the mighty.

16. Synonymous parallelism, ternary. The *gift* is not intellectual endowment,* a sense foreign to the Heb. term, nor the bounty which a liberal man benevolently dispenses (19^6), thereby gaining friends,† nor precisely a bribe, but probably, as second cl. appears to indicate, a present made to *great* and powerful men, whereby they become well disposed to the giver, afford him protection and

---

* Hitzig.   † De. Str. *al.*

aid, and he thus has *room*, a free field, access (as in second line) to the presence of the patron. Cf. 17[8]. The custom of making such presents to the great, common in Israel and elsewhere, was notably prevalent in the Greek period of Jewish history ; see, for ex., the stories of Joseph, Hyrcanus, and Herod in Jos. *Ant.* 12, 4, 2. 9 ; 14, 12, 2. — **17**. Single sentence, with implied antithesis, ternary-binary. *First comer*, he who first presents his cause before the judge, and is naturally able to make out a good case ; *is right*, that is, in appearance ; *plea*, lit. *lawsuit* (RV. *cause*) ; *the other*, lit. *his neighbor*, the other party to the suit ; *tests him*, lit. *searches him*, examines his argument, and presents the other side. The first cl. may be translated *he who is first in his plea* (RV. *pleadeth his cause first*) *is right*** ; the sense remains the same. — In *Pirk. Ab.* 1, 8 it is said that the judge, so long as the parties are in his presence, must regard both as guilty, that is, must distrust both. — The proverb = *audi alteram partem*. — **18**. Synonymous, ternary-binary. On the employment of the *lot* among the Israelites see note on 16[33]. In this case the contending parties, instead of going into court, agree to refer their dispute not to an arbitrator, who would weigh the arguments and decide like a judge, but to God, who was supposed to order the drawing or casting of the lots in accordance with justice ; this divine decision, if accepted in good faith, would at once stop contention, even when the contestants were *powerful*. The questions in which the lot was resorted to in the later time were, it is probable, chiefly or wholly such as concerned property rights of private persons — political disputes would commonly be otherwise settled. *Decides* is lit. *separates*, that is, parts the contestants, so that the dispute ceases.

19. It is difficult, if not impossible, to construe the Heb. text. Lit. : *a brother sinned against* (?) *than a strong city, and disputes are like the bar of a fortress.* The translations *sinned against* (*treated perfidiously, injured, offended*)† and *who resists, sets himself in opposition* ‡ are grammatically doubtful. The insertions *harder, stronger, harder to be won*, etc., before the comparative sign *than*, are unwarranted ; it would be necessary, if the preced-

---

* So De. Reuss, *al.*   † Rashi, RV. *al.*   ‡ Ew. Zöck. *al.*

ing word should be retained, to change *than* to *like* (see second line). But even then the comparison of an injured friend and of disputes to a fortified city or a fortress is strange and improbable. It is not impossible that the couplet is a variant of v.[11] of this chapter (cf. 10[15]), and should read : *the rich man's wealth is a strong city, and his riches is like the bars of a fortress.* — Grk. : *a brother helped by a brother is like a strong and lofty city, and is as strong as a well-founded palace.* This is better than the Heb., but is still unsatisfactory — there is no reason why a brother helped by a brother should be thus singled out. — For the *bars* of cities and fortresses see Ju. 16[3] 1 K. 4[13] Isa. 45[2] Neh. 3[3], and cf. Nowack, *Arch.* i. 142, 368 ff.

10. 𝕲 ἐκ μεγαλωσύνης, = מִגְדָל (Jäg.). — **11.** 𝕳 מַשְׂכִּית (cf. 25[11]) apparently = "something graved or fashioned"; the meaning of the stem is uncertain. Frank. suggests נכשיו or נכסיו, which is, perhaps, to be adopted. — **12.** 𝕳 אש need not be omitted in the interests of the rhythm, since לֵב אִשׁ may be pronounced as one word. — **14.** 𝕳 יַחֲרֶה; 𝕲 θεράπων φρόνιμος, according to Jäg., = מַחֲרֶה (cf. 19[6]) *one who carefully attends to him* (see Lag.'s note), which Frank. adopts, rendering : *wer ihn schmeichelnd besänftigt*, and taking רח as = *anger*, but the resulting line does not offer a good antithesis to second line. — 𝕳 רִח נְכֵאָה; 𝕷 *spiritum ad irascendum facilem.* — **17.** K יִבֹא; Q וּבָא. Either reading gives a good sense, but a connective is natural, and we should perh. write ויבא; a ו may have fallen out by reason of preceding ו. — 𝕲 ἑαυτοῦ κατήγορος, = מרבי (1 Sam. 2[1]) or רָבִי (Isa. 45[9]). — **18.** 𝕳 הִגְרִיל; 𝕲[ABN] σιγηρός (= σιγηλός) *a silent man;* better κλῆρος, as in 𝕲[xc. a. marg.] 𝕾[H] *al.* — 𝕳 עֲצֻמִם; Gr. suggests יֵצֵא or מַצֵּב *contestants.* — **19.** 𝕳 אָח וְפִשַׁע; 𝕲 (followed by 𝕾𝕿𝕷) ἀδελφὸς ὑπὸ ἀδελφοῦ βοηθούμενος, = אָח נֹשָׁע, improbable in the connection. The isolated נפשע is suspicious; the Nif. occurs only here, and the Qal is always followed by ב or עַל; De. compares קְמֵם עֲלֵי = חֲמֵי, but to this it may be replied that the two forms are different (Frank.) — in the case of an Act. Partcp. the construction is possible, but not in the case of Pass. Partcp. See note on this v. above. — 𝕳 וּ מִקְרִית, though syntactically possible, is hard; the substitution of ב for מ is favored by ᵇ and by 𝕲𝕾𝕿𝕷. — On K מדנם, Q מְדִינָם see critical note on 6[14]. — 𝕳 וְכִבְרִחַ אַרְמֹן; 𝕲, inverting order, ὥσπερ τεθεμελιωμένον βασίλειον *as a firmly founded palace;* for τ. (AB𝔸 *al.*) Lag. would read μεμοχλευμένον (𝕾[H] *al.*) *barred.*

20, 21. Power of the tongue.

20. From the fruit of the mouth comes requital to men,
The outcome of the lips they must bear.

21. Death and life are in the power of the tongue,
They who use it must eat its fruit.

20. Synonymous, ternary (or, quaternary-ternary). The thought is that of 12^{14} 13$^{2.3}$, on which see notes — a man must take the consequences of his words, which are here regarded as expressing his thought and nature. Lit. *from the fruit of a man's mouth his belly is filled, the outcome* (or, *product*) *of his lips fills him.* *Fill* and *belly* belong to the figure employed (eating) — words are spoken of as something that a man feeds on, they, by their consequences, determine his position and fate, they bring *requital*, for good or for evil according to their character. On *outcome* (= *produce, product*) see notes on 3$^{9.14}$. — **21.** Synonymous, ternary. See 13^3. Good and bad speech are contrasted by their results. The *death* and *life* are physical; see notes on 3^2 5^5. *Are in the power of* = "are at the disposition of, are dealt out by." Caution in speech is suggested, since words may bring the greatest misfortune (the termination of earthly life) or the greatest good fortune (a long and prosperous life). — In second cl. the Heb. reads lit. *they who love it* (the tongue), which, in the connection, can mean only *they who are fond of using it,* but the verb is not natural, and the text is perhaps wrong. Grk. *they who control it* does not agree with the general form of the predicate of second cl., or with the thought of first cl.; the predicate to such a subject should be *will enjoy good.* The suggestions of De., that the *it* may refer to *wisdom,* or should be read *Yahweh,* are out of the question. Cf. BS. 37^{18}.

22–24. Wife, wealth, friend.

> 22. If one finds a wife, it is a piece of good fortune,
>   A favor bestowed on him by Yahweh.
> 23. The poor man uses entreaties,
>   The rich man answers roughly.
> 24. There are friends who only seek society,
>   And there is a friend who sticks closer than a brother.

22. Synonymous, ternary (or, quaternary-ternary). Lit. *he who finds a wife* (that is, a good wife) *finds good, and obtains favor from Yahweh,* that is, he finds not a good thing (RV.), but good fortune, which, says second cl., he must regard as a special favor from God, who bestows all good fortune (not "he may, in consequence, expect favor from God"). Reuss: *may congratulate* *himself, it is a favor from God.* On the sentiment and on the meaning of *good* (= capable) as used of a wife see 12⁴ 19¹⁴ 31¹⁰⁻³¹ BS. 7¹⁹ 25⁸ 26¹⁻³, ¹³, ¹⁴, ¹⁶, ²³ 40²³ (read *prudent wife*) ; cf. 5¹⁸ Gen. 2²⁴ Eccl. 9⁹ (for another view see Eccl. 7²⁸). Rashi: "he who finds the law " ; Saadia sees in the wife an allusion to Eve. — Cf. 8³⁵, in which our second cl. occurs, the reference there being to the finding of wisdom. Numerous similar sayings are cited by Malan. — The Grk. adds : "he who puts away a good wife puts away good, and he who retains an adulteress is foolish and ungodly," a scribal addition intended to bring the thought of the couplet out more fully. — **23.** Antithetic, ternary (or, binary-ternary). The social eminence and the rudeness of manner which sometimes accompany wealth, and the social dependence and humble bearing of the poor man — put by the proverb as a general rule ; this may be taken as a testimony to the manners of the time (probably the Greek period) ; cf. 22⁷ BS. 13³. — **24.** Antithetic, ternary. Heb., first line : *A man of friends is to be broken* [= *crushed, ruined*], that is, his nominal friends, so far from helping him, will only use him for their own purposes. This interpretation * is exaggerated in its statement, does not offer a satisfactory antithesis to the second line, does not follow the best Heb. text, and is in part a doubtful translation. The expression *man of friends*, with the sense "he who possesses (or, makes) many friends " is not quite in accordance with OT. usage, in which the defining noun after *man* states a personal quality or a characteristic occupation (see 3³ 10²³ 12² 19²² 29⁴ Isa. 53³ ψ 41⁹⁽¹⁰⁾) ; thus in Gen. 46³⁴ the *men of the flock* means precisely not "men owning flocks," but "men whose business is the tending of flocks." Apart from this the parallelism (supported by a Jewish tradition) favors the reading *there are* instead of *man* (the difference between the two is that of a vowel), and first line might be rendered : *there are friends for being crushed*, that is, who only bring ruin. But, since the second line speaks of a steady, reliable friend, we expect in first line a reference to superficial, untrustworthy (rather than to hurt-ful) friends ; this reference is gained by giving to the verb the sense of "friendly association," a sense which is found in several

---

* Adopted by Schultens, De. RV., and the majority of modern expositors.

Anc. Vrss.,* and is adopted by Luther, Mercer, Geier, AV. The
verbal form (the Prep. *to* + Infin. in the Heb.) must be understood to express the purpose and function of the *friends :* they
seek only society, and are found wanting in time of stress, while,
on the other hand, there are friends who stand by a man in his
darkest days, and are more to be relied on than the nearest blood-
kinsman. Friends, says the sage, are of two sorts : some are fair-
weather comrades, but some are stout and faithful helpers. — The
terms *friends* (first line) and *friend* (lit. *lover*, second line) are in
themselves synonyms — the difference between them here intended is suggested by the context. The second line has sometimes been understood to refer to the Messiah. Cf. BS. 6[8-17]
(especially v.[10]) 37[4. 5].

20. Bi. omits the Prep. in חברי, making the noun the subject of the verb —
possible, but unnecessary. — The reading אשׁ טב, suggested by Gr. (who refers
to 12[14]) is here inappropriate. — **21.** 頻 st. אהב; ⅁ κρατοῦντες, from אחז,
which affords no good sense; all other ancient authorities and most moderns
follow 頻, which can hardly be original. No good emendation has been suggested; neither דבר *(those who are subject to it)* nor שׁמר *(those who give heed
to it)* (Gr.) is satisfactory. Rashi: " he who loves his tongue and exercises
himself in the law." Saadia: "according as he loves one or the other"
(death or life). — **22.** The insertion of טבה after אשׁה (⅁⅁⅁⅁) is natural, but
unnecessary (cf. Eccl. 7[28]). — On the couplet added in ⅁ (and in ⅁⅁) see
note on this proverb above; ᵃ follows closely the norm of 頻ᵃ, and ᵇ is the
natural antithesis. — **23.** Lacking in ⅁ᴬᴮℵ, given in ⅁ᴴ and H-P 23. 103. *al.*;
see notes of H-P, Field, Lag. — **24.** 頻 התרעֵעַ, not from רע (Gr. Ven.), or רע
bad (Zöck. *al.*), but from רע *break.* Read התרעת, from רעה (so ⅁⅁⅁⅁[23]). —
頻 אישׁ is read ישׁ by ⅏ Hitz. Löwenstein, Frank. *al.*, and is, from the parallelism, to be adopted. Baer (in *App. Crit.* to the B-D ed. of Prov.) observes
(from the Masora) that this is one of the three occurrences of אישׁ, in which
ישׁ is to be expected, the others being 2 Sam. 14[19] Mic. 6[10]; see Kimḥi, *Libr.
Rad.*, s.v. אישׁ. — The couplet, like the preceding, is wanting in ⅁ᴬ ᵃˡ·, found
in H-P 23 *al.*; להתרעע is rendered by τοῦ ἑταιρεύσασθαι, cf. ⅃ *ad societatem.*
⅁ᴴ *a man loves himself in order that he may be loved,* either a free rendering
of ⅁, or a corrupt Syr. text. The construction of 頻 is periphrastic future,
= היה להת, *is going to be* (or, *is to be*) *ruined.* In the emended text ל + Inf.
expresses purpose. Cf. critical note on 19[8].

─────────────

* Targ. Lat. and some Grk.

XIX. 1-4. Poverty, wealth, folly.

1. Better is a poor man, upright in life,
   Than he who is false in speech, even though he be ‹rich.›
2. To act without reflection is not good,
   He who is hasty in action fails of his aim.
3. A man's folly ruins his affairs,
   And then he is angry with God.
4. Wealth adds many friends,
   But the poor man — his (one) friend withdraws.

1. Comparison, antithetic, ternary. In first cl., lit. *who walks in
his uprightness* (or, *perfectness*). *Speech* is lit. *lips;* on *false* (RV.
perverse) see note on 2^{15}. Instead of *rich* the Heb. has *a fool.*
The couplet occurs again at 28^6, with *rich* instead of *fool*, a reading here required both by the parallelism of the clauses (*poor
. . . rich*) and by the obviously intended antithesis in second cl. :
the *though he be* (lit. *and he is*) naturally introduces something
which might appear to oppose the *better*, but *fool* could only
strengthen the comparison. Ewald thinks that *rich* was the original reading, but retains *fool* on the ground that this expression
(= *haughty*) is a synonym of *rich* * ; but this is obviously not
true in Pr. — the *poor* may be *upright*, but he is never identical
with the *religiously humble;* and the *rich*, though he may be *arrogant*, is always the man of physical *wealth*. — **2.** Synonymous,
ternary. Against heedlessness. The Heb. begins with the word
also, which is significant here only in case it is intended to add
heedlessness to falsity (v.¹) as a thing *not good*, and this is hardly
probable. — The first half of first cl. is defective, lit. *without
knowledge of soul*, that is, "in the soul," = *without reflection*, as
appears from the parallel *haste* of second cl. ; the verb, *act* or *be*,
must be supplied, and *soul* should perhaps be omitted. The Heb.
word for *soul* may also mean *self* or *desire*, but the renderings *to
be without self-knowledge* (Ew.) and *desire without reflection*
(Hitz.) are not in accordance with the usage of the Book. The
translation *that the soul be without knowledge* (RV.) is grammatically untenable. So, also, the interpretation : *when one pays no
regard to his desires* (that is, denies himself all pleasures, in order

---

* So Zöck. De. Nowack *al.* The reading *rich* is adopted by Grätz and Kamphausen.

to save money), *that is not good*, is hardly to be obtained from the Heb., and is not a probable reflection for Pr. The last expression of first cl. means "not a good (or, sensible, useful, helpful) thing," nearly = *unsuccessful;* Reuss's *blind eagerness can only be hurtful,* and Wildeboer's *where there is no knowledge* (or, reflection), *there also* (even) *eagerness is not good* are grammatically doubtful. — In second cl. *is hasty in action* is lit. *hastes with his feet.* — If the proverb be taken in connection with the preceding, it must be interpreted as directed particularly against heedless pursuit of wealth; but it seems better to understand it as a condemnation of thoughtless eagerness and hastiness in general. *Fails of his aim = misses the mark* (see 8^{36} Job 5^{24}). — **3.** Continued thought, quaternary-ternary. *Ruins = overturns* (RV. *subverteth*); *affairs* is lit. *way; God,* lit. *Yahweh.* For the thought cf. BS. 15^{11-20} Soph. *Oed. Col.* 1693 ff., and other parallels in Malan. — The couplet is a criticism of the allegation that failure is the work of God; the reply is that the fault is with men themselves — a practical way of dealing with a much-debated question characteristic of Pr., and standing in marked contrast with the lines of thought of Job and Ecclesiastes. — **4.** Antithetic, quaternary-ternary. Cf. v.^7 and 14^{20}. The second cl. may also be rendered: *the poor is separated from his friend* (so RV). On the terms *wealth* and *poor* see notes on 1^{13} 10^{15}.

5–7. Perjury, liberality, poverty.

> 5. A false witness will not go unpunished,
>   He who utters lies will not escape.
> 6. Many seek the favor of the liberal man,
>   All are friends to him who gives.
> 7. All the poor man's brethren hate him —
>   How much more do his friends stand aloof!

5. Identical in thought, ternary (or, binary-ternary). For the expressions see 6^{19} 14^{5. 25} and v.^9 below, of which this couplet is a doublet, and here not in place; the reference is to legal proceedings, and the certainty of punishment is affirmed as a general rule — a testimony to the justice of the courts of law of the time. — **6.** Identical in sense, with increment of expression, ternary. The indefinite *many* is heightened into the definite *all*, and thus receives the suggestion of universality. *Seek the favor* is lit. *stroke* (or, *smooth*) *the face* (caressingly) or *make the face soft* (gentle, favorable) ; see Job 11¹⁹ ψ 45¹²⁽¹³⁾ 1 K. 13⁶ ψ 119⁵⁸, etc. The translation *liberal* (lit. *willing*) is suggested by the parallelism, but the Heb. word (*nadīb*) may also be rendered *potentate* (Grk. *kings*) or *noble ;* see notes on 8¹⁶ 17⁷·²⁶. The reference is probably to the munificence of the rich private man or prince who seeks, by gifts, to attach men to his person and his cause — such was the method in ancient political and social life. A more general reference to unselfish liberality is possible, but the proverb appears to contemplate the somewhat corrupt city life of the later period of Judaism. — **7.** Advance from the less to the greater, ternary (or, ternary-quaternary, or, binary-ternary). *Hate* is to be understood literally — a poor man, as likely to be burdensome, easily becomes an object of detestation ; *brethren* = kinsfolk in blood, and *friends* are associates, not bound by the tie of blood, whose friendship is superficial and untrue. It is assumed that blood-kinsmen are under greater obligation than friends to help.

At the end of this couplet the Heb. has a line which is now unintelligible, reading lit. *he who pursues words, they are not* (Heb. marg. *his they are*), which RV. interprets as meaning *he* [the poor man] *pursueth them with words, but they are gone,* a sense which is not contained in the Heb., and is forced and unnatural in form (RV. marg. is correct except the expressions *which are nought* and *he pursueth*). Lat. : *he who pursues only words shall have nothing,* which is intelligible (though not a rendering of our Heb.), but the expression *pursue words* is strange. The line appears to be the corrupt remnant of a lost couplet, but it is hardly possible, with our present means of information, to recover the original form.

8, 9. Wisdom is profitable, falseness is fatal.

> 8. He who acquires understanding is a friend to himself,
>   He who follows wisdom ‹ will › get good.
> 9. A false witness will not escape,
>   He who utters lies will perish.

8. Synonymous, binary- (or, quaternary-) ternary. *Understanding*, lit. *heart*, = mind, intellectual perception, with reference to all the affairs of life; the same idea is expressed by *wisdom*, lit. "apprehension, comprehension, insight" (see note on 2²); *follows = preserves, pays due regard to; is a friend to* (or, *loves*) *himself* (lit. *loves his soul*) = "has regard for his own interests"; as predicate of second cl. the Heb. has *to find* (or, *get*) *good*, which may be understood as = "is going to get," etc., but a simple change of letters gives the better reading *will get; good* = "what is advantageous." The sense is: intellectual insight (= clearness of thought, good sense) is profitable in this life, the moral as well as the physical life being probably included; cf. 3¹³⁻¹⁸, etc. — **9.** Synonymous, ternary (or, binary-ternary). The couplet is a variation of v.⁵, with the stronger expression *perish* in second clause.

10. Wealth and power befit only the wise and the free.

> Luxury is not a fitting thing for a fool,
> Much less for a slave is rule over princes.

Climax, ternary. *Fitting = appropriate* (not exactly *seemly* or *becoming*); see 17⁷ 26¹. The proverb compares two things in which there is no propriety: the value and use of luxury are not understood by an obtuse, uncultivated man, rather it develops his bad qualities, and he becomes ridiculous and disgusting; and a slave, with all the vices of a servile class, elevated to political power, is likely to become arrogant and tyrannical. Wealth was often acquired by men morally and intellectually dull, and the promotion of slaves to places of authority was not uncommon in Asiatic and African governments (Strack refers to the rôle played by eunuchs); cf. 30²² Eccl. 10⁷ BS. 11⁵. The *fool* of first cl. may be identical with the *slave* of second cl., but this is not necessary. On the other hand, slaves sometimes proved excellent governors; cf. 17² 14³⁵. — On the position of Heb. slaves see notes on 11²⁹ 12⁹ 22⁷.*

---

* Cf. Job 41⁴ [40²⁸], from which, however, it cannot be inferred that the relation of a slave to his master was based on an agreement between the two.

11. Forbearance is wise.

> It is wisdom in a man to be slow to anger,
> It is his glory to pass over transgression.

Synonymous, ternary (or, quaternary-ternary). On *wisdom*, = "sound sense," see note on 12[8] (in 3[4] the text is incorrect); the couplet in the Heb. is lit.: *a man's wisdom defers his anger, and his glory* (= that on which he may pride himself) *is to pass*, etc.; the translation given above is obtained by changing the vowels of one word, whereby we gain the exact parallelism *to be slow* (= *to defer*) . . . *to pass*, corresponding to the other parallel expressions *a man's wisdom . . . his glory*. The same thought is found in 14[17. 29], and cf. 25[21. 22] and Eccl. 8[1]. Forgiveness of errors and injuries is here represented as a sensible thing, probably because it promotes social peace and wellbeing; there appears to be no reference to divine reward, though there may be an implication of moral law. For the expression *pass over transgression* cf. Mic. 7[18].

12. A king's anger is dreadful, his favor refreshing.

> The wrath of a king is like the roaring of a lion,
> His favor like dew on vegetation.

Antithetic, ternary (or, quaternary-ternary). The first cl., with change of one word, occurs in 20[2], on which see note; similar references to royal power see in 16[14] 28[15] Eccl. 8[2-4]. The picture of the king suits many periods of history, but particularly the time when the Jews had special reason to fear the caprices of foreign rulers. The word rendered by *vegetation* includes grass, herbs and cereals.

XIX. 1. Wanting in 𝕾ᴺᴬᴮᶜ; 𝕾ᴴ *sub ast.* Compl. H-P 23. 103. 253 = 𝕳. — 𝕳 ‹כסל›; 𝕾 ‹עתירא›, 𝕷 *dives* (but adds *et insipiens* at end); read ‹עשר›, which the parallelism imperatively demands. The *insipiens* of 𝕷 and the ‹סקלא› of some MSS. of 𝕾 are corrections after 𝕳. — For 𝕳 ‹שפתיו› 𝕾𝕿 have *ways*, which may be free rendering of 𝕳, or may represent Heb. ‹רכיו› (cf. Pink.). — **2.** Lacking in 𝕾ᴺᴬᴮᶜ; H-P 23 *al. without knowledge of the soul there is no good;* 𝕾ᴴ *to be without knowledge* etc. *is not good;* Saad. Compl. *without knowledge the soul is not good;* 𝕾𝕿 *he who does not know himself, it is not good for him;* 𝕷 *where there is no knowledge of the soul it is not good;* Rashi as H-P 23 𝕷. — ‹לא טב› must be predicate; ‹בלא› + noun always qualifies a preceding word (noun or verb), and cannot here qualify נפש ("a soul without knowledge"). The Heb. text appears to be defective. Gr. proposes to attach ﬡ to the כסל of v.¹, change גם to נס (cf. Isa. 21¹²), and insert ﬥ before ﬧﬡ, but the resulting sense, "a fool flees without knowledge of soul to what is not good," is awkward, and כסﬥ is probably not original. The נפש is unnecessary and strange, and looks like a gloss on רעﬨ; if this be omitted, and גם be changed to עשה or עשﬨ (cf. 21⁸) or היﬨ, the clause becomes clear in construction and meaning. — נפש may be a gloss on היﬨ בﬥﬡ דעﬨ. — **4.** In 𝕳 מרעﬣﬡ﬩ the מ may be Prep., or nominal preformative. — **6.** The art. in הרע is to be omitted; Bi. כﬥﬣ רע. — **7.** 𝕳 מרעﬣﬡ﬩ is defectively written plu. — 𝕲 follows 𝕳ᵃˑᵇ with change of pointing. — Bi. adopts the additional couplet of 𝕲 and renders it into Hebrew. — **8.** 𝕳 ﬥﬨצﬡ; read מצﬡ׳, as apparently 𝕲𝕾𝕿𝕷 (and so Dys.), though these Vrss. may merely give idiomatic translations of ﬥﬨצﬡ; to take it as abridged periphrastic Future, = היﬣ ﬥמ׳ (De. Wild. *al.*) is allowable, but seems here less natural; cf. note on ﬩ﬣﬨרעשּׂ, 18²⁴. — **9.** See notes on v.⁵. — **11.** Point הﬡרﬥ as Inf. (so apparently A𝚯𝕾). 𝕲 is corrupt (see Jäg. Baumg.).

13, 14. Bad sons, bad and good wives.

13. A foolish son is ruin to his father,
   The quarrelling of a wife is like the continual dripping of a roof.
14. House and riches are an inheritance from fathers,
   But a wise wife is the gift of God.

13. Collocation of two similar things, ternary. The thought of first cl. is found in 10¹ 17²¹·²⁵ (and cf. v.¹⁸ below), that of second cl. in 27¹⁵. We expect, as contrast to first cl., a reference to the wise son, or, as contrast to second cl., a reference (as in v.¹⁴) to the good wife; the couplet is perhaps made up from two others. The noun *dripping* (or, *dropping*) is found elsewhere in OT. only in 27¹⁵, the verb *drip*, *drop* only in Job 16²⁰ ψ 119²⁸ Eccl. 10¹⁸, all late passages; the term *continual* (lit. *pushing, driving*) occurs in Heb. only here and 27¹⁵ (Aramaic in Dan. 4²⁵·³²·³³⁽²²·²⁹·³⁰⁾ 5²¹). Cf. Wisd. Sol. 3¹². — *Wife* is lit. *woman*, here possibly any "woman," but the special reference is more probable. An Arab proverb, which De. heard from Wetzstein, says that three things make a house intolerable : *tak* (the leaking through of rain), *nak* (a wife's nagging) and *bak* (bugs) ; other parallels are cited by Malan. — **14.** Antithetic, ternary (or, quaternary-ternary). Wealth, says the sage, is an accident of birth, while a wise wife is a special favor from God (lit. *Yahweh*). This seems to be a curious limitation of divine providence, which, we expect an Israelite to say, certainly controls a man's birth and inheritance of property as well as his choice of a wife ; the distinction made between social conditions established by social law and acts controlled by the will of the individual is popular, not philosophical or theocratic (the form in 18^{22} is better) ; it shows, however, the value set on a good wife. In early times the wife was usually chosen by the young man's parents (Gen. $24^{3. 4}$ 38^{6}), though not always (Ju. 14^{2}); at a later period considerable freedom was doubtless accorded the man, and a happy choice on his part is here represented as due to special divine guidance. V.^{13} suggests an unhappy choice. — *Wise = intelligent*, probably in the special sense of *thrifty;* cf. 31^{10-31}. This second cl. gives a contrast to the second cl. of v.^{13}. Cf. 18^{22} (and Eccl. 9^{9}) ; in BS. 26^{3} a good wife is the portion of those who fear God, and such is the implication in our passage.

15. Inconveniences of idleness.

> Slothfulness casts into a deep sleep,
> The idle man must suffer hunger.

Synonymous, ternary. The noun *deep sleep* is found in Gen. 2^{21} 15^{12} 1 Sam. 26^{12} Isa. 29^{10} Job 4^{13} 33^{15}, the corresponding verb in Ju. 4^{21} Jon. 1^{5} Dan. 8^{18}, the Participle in 10^{5} (on which see note) ψ $76^{6(7)}$ Jon. 1^{6} Dan. 10^{9}. The expression here signifies complete inactivity. *Man*, lit. *soul* ($= person$). Cf. $6^{9. 10}$ 10^{4} 12^{24} 20^{13} $24^{33. 34}$.

16. Obedience to law gives life.

> He who obeys the law preserves his life,
> He who despises the ‹ word › will die.

Antithetic, quaternary-ternary. Lit. *he who keeps the commandment keeps his life* (lit. *soul*), *he who despises his ways will die.* The *law* may be human (especially the teaching of the sages) or divine ; the principle of the couplet is the same in both cases, but in the latter case it is God who (directly or indirectly) deals out reward or punishment (as in 3^{33}), while in the latter the agent of retribution is the court of justice, or the natural law of human society. — We may also translate : *he who obeys* (or, *conforms to*) *law*, that is, regulates his conduct by an established (and, presum-

ably, wise) norm, instead of by his own caprice ; the general
sense remains the same. — For the Heb. *despises his ways* an easy
change of text gives the reading : *despises the word* (as in 13¹³),
which supplies the appropriate parallelism of nouns ; the verb
despises cannot well be used of a man's ways (Frank.). *Will die*
is the reading of the Heb. margin (Masoretic), the text has *will
be put to death*, that is, by decision of the judge — the common
legal expression (as in Ex. 21¹².¹⁵, etc.) ; the former is more in
accordance with the manner of Pr., which regards death as the
natural consequence of wrong-doing.   Cf. 13¹³ 15¹⁰ 16¹⁷.

17. God rewards kindness to the poor.

> He who has pity on the poor lends to Yahweh,
> And he will repay him his deed.

Continued thought, binary, or ternary-binary.   On *poor* see note
on 10¹⁵ ; cf. 22⁹ 29⁷ ψ 41¹⁽²⁾.   In second cl. we may render *good
deed* (as RV.), the adj. being supplied from the connection ; the
Heb. word signifies " something done," sometimes good (ψ 103²),
sometimes bad (ψ 137⁸), often with the suggestion that there is to
be retribution or recompense for the thing done, as here and 12¹⁴.
Kindness to the poor is regarded as done to God (cf. Mt. 25⁴⁰),
who will repay it, as the whole Book suggests, by bestowing long
life and worldly prosperity. — The ethical basis of the proverb is
the recognition of the natural duty of caring for the poor.   The
motive urged is not the obligation to do right, but the reward of
rightdoing.

18. Chastisement saves a child.

> Chastise thy son while there is still hope —
> Set not thy heart on his destruction.

Implicit parallelism, quaternary-ternary.   *Chastise* is teach (ψ 2¹⁰),
reprove (Pr. 9⁷), correct (Jer. 30¹¹), here punish bodily, as in
29¹⁷·¹⁹ Dt. 21¹⁸.   Instead of *while* the Heb. may be rendered *for*
(RV. *seeing*).   *Set not thy heart* is lit. *lift not up thy soul* (= *thy
desire*), as in ψ 24⁴ 25¹ 86⁴.   *On his destruction* is lit. *to kill him*.
Cf. 13²⁴ 23¹³ 29¹⁷.   The sense is : train thy son by bodily chastisement in the docile period of childhood — do not, through weak

or mistaken kindness, so neglect to control him that he shall go astray and finally suffer death as the natural (legal or other) consequence of his ill-doing. The second cl. can hardly be understood as a warning against excessive bodily punishment (*do not carry your chastisement so far as to kill him*). According to Dt. 21[18-21] a son, on the representation of his father that he was intractable, might be sentenced to death by the elders of the city; but the more refined feeling of later times revolted against this procedure.* In the family life contemplated by Pr. it is highly improbable that a father would ever think of carrying chastisement to the point of killing his son. The meaning of the couplet is given in 23[13]. — Bickell: *do not fancy that thou could'st kill him*, a violent and inappropriate emendation. The rendering *let not thy soul spare for his crying* (AV.)† is hardly permitted by the Hebrew.

13. Before רֶלֶךְ *dripping* כ should, perhaps, be inserted. — 14. 狠 משכלת *prudent;* 𝕲 ἁρμόζεται (with which Lag. compares the 𝕲 rendering of שכל in Gen. 48[14]) takes the Heb. word as = *is wisely adapted*, that is, *given in marriage* (and so 𝔖𝔗). — 15. The couplet occurs in 𝕲 in 18[8], with variations. — 16. Bi. changes the second שמר of 狠 to אהב to avoid repetition (referring to v.[8]); but the repetition is here effective. — 狠 דרכיו; read דבר, to agree with בוה. Keth. יְמַח; read Qerī יִמַח. — 18. 狠 אֶל המיתו; 𝕲 (followed by 𝔖) εἰς ὕβριν, = אל המיתו, from המה (Jäg.), or Aram. המא *neglect, despise* (Lag.); A𝔗𝔏 = 狠. — The text appears to be corrupt, but no satisfactory emendation offers itself. Bi.: ואל חרם תשא נפשו.

19. Text and translation doubtful.

The Heb. margin reads: *A man of great anger pays a fine* (or, *must bear a penalty*) (or, *he who pays a fine is very angry*), *for*, (or, *but*, or, *in truth*) *if thou rescue, thou must do so again* (or, *thou wilt increase*). In first cl. *great* is the reading of the Heb. margin; the text has an obscure word, variously rendered (*stony*,

---

* In the oldest known Semitic material there is no mention of the father's power of life and death over the son; see the Sumerian "Laws relating to the family" (found in Assurbanipal's library, and probably adopted by the Assyrians), in which the severest punishment that could be inflicted on a refractory son is expulsion from the father's house. But the law in Dt. 21[18-21] is probably a modification of an earlier Hebrew regulation, according to which the father had the power of inflicting death (cf. Ex. 21[15, 17]). Cf. W. R. Smith, *Relig. Sem.*[2], pp. 59 f. The power of life and death was originally included in the Roman *patria potestas*.

† Following medieval Jewish authorities.

hard, rough, frequent). Of the many interpretations offered of
second cl. the following are the principal: If thou save [thine
enemy] thou wilt add [good to thyself] * ; If thou save [thy son,
by moderate chastisement], thou mayst continue [chastisement,
and so educate him to virtue] † ; If thou save [the angry man
from the legal penalty, thine interposition is useless], thou must
do it again [since he will repeat his offence] ‡ ; If thou save [the
person who is the object of the angry man's wrath], thou increas-
est [the angry man's wrath]. § These interpretations supply a
great deal, and the two last assume (what is improbable) that
anger is a finable offence. With changes of text we may read:
The more he sins, the more he adds to his punishment ‖ ; or, [a
man who is fined is very angry] but if he show contempt [of
court], he has to pay more ¶ ; but such details of legal penalties
(even if they could be got naturally) are out of place in this
series of aphorisms. The text appears to be incurably corrupt,
and there is perhaps, in addition, a dislocation.

20, 21. Human counsel, human and divine plans.

> 20. Hearken to counsel, and receive instruction,
>   That thou mayst be wise in future.
> 21. Many are the thoughts in a man's mind,
>   But the plan of Yahweh, it will stand.

20. Continuous, ternary, or quaternary-ternary (possibly binary-
ternary). On *counsel* and *instruction* see notes on $1^{25.2}$; they are
the teaching of the sages, or of sagacious persons in general, and
they make one *wise* in all affairs. The thought may be simply
the commonsense one: "take advice if you would act sensibly —
only a fool refuses to take advice," or there may be a reference to
the philosophical, ideal conception of wisdom of chs. 1–9. *In
future* is lit. *in thine after-life* (RV. *thy latter end*), an expression
which generally means "the end of life" (see 5^4), but here, from
the connection, seems to signify "hereafter [after receiving
instruction] in thy life." The Syriac reading *in thy ways* is per-

---

* Rashi.   † Saad. Michaelis.   ‡ Bertheau, RV. *al.*
§ Str. Wild. Strack quotes Rabbi Simeon ben Eleazar (*Pirke Aboth* 4, 18): "do
not try to soothe thy neighbor when he is angry," for you thereby only exasperate
him.   ‖ Syr. Targ.   ¶ Frankenberg.

haps better.   It is not probable that the couplet, taken as an
address to the pupil, refers to technical teaching and promotion
in the schools : "thou art now only a beginner, but listen to
instruction, and thou wilt become a sage " (Wild.). — **21.** Antithetic, ternary.   *Thoughts* = *reflections, designs; plan* is in Heb.
the same word as that rendered *counsel* in v.[20], but here *decision,
design* (regarded as the result of deliberation).   The absolutely
wise and sure divine purpose in the government of the affairs of
men is contrasted with the diversity and uncertainty of human
plans ; cf. $16^{1.\ 9.\ 33}\ 20^{24}\ 3^{6}$.

22.   Form and sense are uncertain.

Lit. :   *the desire of a man is his kindness, and a poor man is
better than a liar.*   The meaning of first cl. is doubtful.   It may
be taken (with objective genitival construction) to be : "the
desire felt toward a man (our regard for him) is called forth by
his kindness" (to us or to others), but this* is an improbable
translation ; or "that which is desired by man is to receive kindness " (Saad.), or "man's desire and joy is to show kindness," †
both of which are doubtful as translations, and give a thought
which is not in accordance with the tone of the Book.   Many
recent expositors ‡ render : "a man's goodwill is his kindness,"
that is, beneficence lies in the intention ; but the Heb. word
hardly means "goodwill" — it is "desire" or "the thing desired," §
as in $10^{24}\ 11^{23}\ 13^{12.\ 19}\ \psi\ 10^{17}\ 78^{29}$ Gen. 3^{6}, and never elsewhere in
OT. has the sense of "intention."   And further, if it could be
held to have that sense here, the form of the Heb. sentence
would still be hard and improbable.   None of these translations
establish a relation between the two clauses of the couplet ; the
interpretation : "the essence of beneficence is the intention — a
poor man who would give, but cannot, is better than a rich man
who could give, but lies and says he cannot give " ‖ manifestly
imports into the text what does not exist there. — Grk. (with
change of text) "mercy is fruit to a man," whence Ew. "a man's
gain is his pious love," and so a poor man who has this love (Grk.

---

* RV. marg., Rashi and other medieval Jewish expositors, Schult. Noyes ("that
which makes a man beloved ").

† Bertheau, Zöck.   § Stade, Kamp. Wild.
‡ Euchel, De. Reuss, Now. Str., and so RV.   ‖ De. Str. *al.*

a righteous poor man) is better than one who has become rich by
lying (Grk. *a rich liar*) ; this, though more intelligible than the
Heb., is still forced.　It would give a better sense to read : *a
man's kindness is a revenue to him*, that is, "kindness is good
policy," but the Heb. would not be a natural form of expression
for this thought.　The Lat. gets the doubtful proposition in first
cl.: "a needy man is merciful."　Hitzig, taking the suggestion of
the Grk., renders : "from the revenue of a man is his kind gift,"
an insignificant truism.　Dyserinck, changing the text in second
cl. : "what is attractive in a man is his friendliness, but better
rough (or, crabbed) than false"; but the interpretation of "the
desire of a man" as = "what is desirable in a man" is not supported by OT. usage. — The second cl. should probably read : *an
honest poor man is better than a rich liar.*　The first cl. must be
left untranslated, as affording no satisfactory sense; and it cannot
be brought into natural connection with the second clause.

23. Piety gives safety.

> The fear of Yahweh leads to life,
> ‹ Who hopes in him › will be unvisited by harm.

Synonymous.　Lit.: *the fear of Yahweh (tends) to life, and he
dwells (or, abides) satisfied, he will not be visited by evil.*　The
enallage of subject in the Received Text is harsh, and not in
accordance with the style of Pr.—the *he* of second cl. has no
antecedent; the rendering *one dwells* (De. Zöck.) is not allowable, but, if our Heb. text be retained, this form, or the insertion
of "to man" in first cl. or the explanation "he who has it dwells"
(RV. and most recent translators) is necessary for syntactical
clearness; the Heb. text is in bad condition, and something like
the emendation above suggested seems necessary; cf. 29^{25} ψ 146^{5}.
Life = long life and prosperity, bestowed by God as reward of
obedience; see notes on 1$^{7. 33}$ 3^{2}.　On *dwell* see note on 15^{31}.
Satisfied = *content* (27^{7} ψ 17^{15}, cf. Pr. 30^{9} ψ 16^{11}).　With first cl.
cf. 14^{27}, with second cl. cf. 10^{3}.

24-29. Sluggards, mockers of parents and of truth, perjurers.

> 24. The lazy man dips his hand into the dish,
> And will not bring it to his mouth.

25. Smite a mocker, and the ignorant becomes wise,
   Reprove a man of sense, and he gains knowledge.

26. He who maltreats his father and drives away his mother
   Is a son who acts shamefully and disgracefully.

27. ? ‹ He who ceases › to listen to instruction
   ‹ Will › wander from words of knowledge?

28. A false witness scoffs at justice,
   And the mouth of the wicked ‹ utters › iniquity.

29. Penalties are prepared for scoffers,
   And stripes for the backs of fools.

24. Continuous, quaternary-ternary. A humorous and sarcastic rebuke of laziness, repeated, with variation of expression in second cl., in 26[15]. *Dips* is in the Heb. lit. *hides* (RV. *burieth*) ; *dish* occurs in 2 K. 21[13] (and nearly the same Heb. word in 2 K. 2[20] 2 C. 35[13]) ; the scene is a meal, and the method of eating is Oriental (cf. Mk. 14[20]). The verb of the Heb. (*ṭaman*) is hardly appropriate (Schult. Bi.), and should perhaps be changed (to *ṭabal, dip*). The last word of first cl. is rendered or read variously in the Anc. Vrss. : *bosom*** ; armpit*†; Rashi reports a rendering *slit in a garment* (= *bosom*), and Grätz suggests *garment.* There seems to be no good reason for changing the reading *dish*, though *bosom* gives a good sense. — **25.** Antithetic, quaternary or ternary. On *mocker* (= one who contemptuously rejects right teaching, is unteachable) see note on 1[22]. *Ignorant = simple*, moral simpleton (1[4.22]). The morally ignorant man, says the proverb, is warned when bad men are punished — it is an intelligible object-lesson ; a wise man learns in a more rational way, by giving heed to advice. — **26.** Continuous, binary-ternary. In second cl. we may render : *who is vile and despicable* (Reuss), or *who causes shame and reproach* (RV. De., cf. 29[15]). Cf. 10[5] 13[5] 17[6]. Nothing is said of the punishment of the unworthy son ; the old laws (Ex. 21[15.17]) had probably at this time fallen into desuetude. — *Maltreats* is probably equivalent to *drives away.* The son here seems to be in possession of the property in his father's lifetime ; the latter is presumably decrepit, the care of the property falls naturally to the son, whose unfilial conduct, though it may be condemned by public opinion, does not come under the cogni-

---

* Grk. Syr., and so some medieval Jewish commentators, AV. Bickell.
† Aq. Sym. Targ. Lat.

zance of the law. — **27**. Lit. *cease, my son, to listen to instruction, to wander from the words of knowledge.* The saying has been interpreted as a serious exhortation, = " cease to listen to that sort of teaching which will cause thee to wander," etc.,* but the Heb. term here rendered *instruction* can hardly be understood, when used without an adjective, to mean anything but right instruction, nor has it any other meaning elsewhere in Pr. ; or † " cease to listen to [good] instruction in order (that is, if thy purpose is, or, if the result for thee is to be) to wander," etc., but such an exhortation (= " better not hear than hear and not obey ") is foreign to the thought of Pr., which elsewhere divides men into the two classes, those who hear and those who do not hear, and does not deal with the case of those who dally with teaching or seek it in sport or know and act not (Wildeboer refers to Lu. 12^{47}). Ewald and Reuss regard the exhortation as ironical, = " only cease to hear, and you will soon wander," etc., but the latter thinks such a form unexampled in Pr. and doubtful. The grammatical construction of the Hebrew, also, is not clear, and the address *my son* does not elsewhere occur in this division of the Book (10^1–22^{16}). The text must be changed either as in the translation given above, or so as to read : *Cease, my son, to hate instruction, to wander,* etc., or, *do not cease, my son, to listen,* etc., *and do not wander,* etc. If the second or third reading be adopted, the couplet should be transferred to chs. 1–9 (cf. 5^{12}) or chs. 22^{17}–24^{22} (cf. 23^{12}). — **28**. Synonymous, quaternary or ternary. *False* is lit. *wicked;* for the meaning of the term (*belial*) see note on 6^{19}. The scene of first cl. is a court of justice (Ex. 20^{16} Lev. 5^1), and the second cl., from the parallelism, is to be so understood : the wicked witness inflicts injury by false statements ; the *iniquity* is the harm done by the perjurer not to his own soul (so the Grk.), but to the legal rights of others. Instead of Heb. *gulps down,* read *utters* (see 1^{23} 15^2 ψ 59$^{7(8)}$ 78^2). Cf. 6^{19} 14^{25} 25^{18}. — **29**. Synonymous, ternary. *Penalties,* lit. *judgments,* a term which occurs only in the plu., and is found elsewhere only in Ez. and later parts of Ex. Num. Chr. ; a change of one letter of the Heb. gives *rods* (so the Grk.), which offers an exacter parallelism to the *stripes* of second cl. On *scoffers* (to which *fools*

---

* Saad. Schult. Str. † Oetinger, De. Now.

is here equivalent) see note on 1²². The punishment spoken of is
that inflicted by men.

19. Kethib גרל, with which Arab. נרל *stony, hard* may be compared (Ew.
explains it by Arab. גויל *frequent*, but the interchange of ז and ר is improbable).
The stem גרל in this sense may be found in גרי *lot* (originally, perhaps, *pebble*,
Schult. *al.*), but as the adj. does not elsewhere occur in North-Semitic, the
Qeri גדל (so Θ) seems preferable. For 𝕳 הצר and הסף Frank. proposes ילך
and יסף. — 𝕳ᵇ appears to be corrupt, but a satisfactory emendation is difficult.
— **20.** 𝕳 באחרהך; 𝔖 באחריתך, perhaps to be adopted. — **22.** 𝕳 תַּאֲוַת; 𝔊 καρπὸς,
whence Ew. and Bi. emend to הבאת *revenue;* kindness may be said to be a
source of revenue, but cannot be called revenue. הסר is not "pious love"
(Ew.), but general benevolence and friendliness. — In ᵇ 𝔊 supplies the suggested adjectives. — **23.** 𝕳ᵇ שֶׁבַע יָלִין appears to be a corrupt expression. An
intelligible reading of ᵇ would be: שׂבר עליו בל יפקד רע; the same thought is
expressed in 29²⁵, with בטח instead of שבר. — **24.** 𝕳 צַלָּחַת; 𝔊 κόλπον accords
with the verb of 𝕳, טמן, and is perhaps a guess induced by this verb. The
noun in 𝕳 is more pertinent (for why should a man take his hand from his
bosom in order to carry it to his mouth?), and the verb should perhaps be
changed to שבל. — **26.** 𝕳 מְשַׁדֵּד; Gr. מוֹרֵד *ejects*, to secure exacter parallelism
with יברח, or, as he writes it, מַבְרִח. — **27.** 𝔊: הגה for 𝕳 ישנה, and רע for
𝕳 דעת; 𝔏: *do not cease . . . and be not ignorant* etc.; 𝔖𝔗: *cease, my son,
and hear . . . and thou wilt not wander* etc. The Heb. form is doubtful; we
may insert the neg. with 𝔏, or write שנא for 𝕳 שמע, or, omitting בני, read חדל
and ישנה for 𝕳 חדל and לשנות. — **28.** 𝕳 עֵד בליעל; 𝔊 ὁ ἐγγυώμενος παῖδα
ἄφρονα, = עֹרֵב בן ב׳ (Lag.). — יבלע; Frank., better, יבע. — **29.** 𝕳 שפטם;
𝔊 μάστιγες, = שבטם, perh. better.

XX. 1. Folly of drinking to excess.

> Wine is a mocker, mead is a brawler,
> Whoever is overtaken thereby is not wise.

Extensive, quaternary- (or, binary-) ternary. The sense is : it is
not prudent or sensible to indulge to excess in intoxicating drinks,
or : one thus overtaken (that is, drunk) does not in this condition behave or act wisely. *Wine* (*yayin*) is the fermented juice
of the grape ; of *mead* (RV. *strong drink*) all that appears from
OT. is that it was intoxicating (Isa. 28⁷), and, in the later legislation (Lev. 10⁹) forbidden to priests, that it was a common beverage of the people in the religious feasts of the preëxilic time
(Dt. 14²⁶), and that Nazirites (and probably also the Rechabites,
Jer. 35) abstained from it (not on account of its intoxicating

qualities, but because they represented the old pastoral life, and rejected agricultural novelties). It is not improbable that it was the fermented juice of fruits (other than grapes), such as the pomegranate (cf. Cant. 8²) and the date.* *Mocker*, scoffing at all things good and true ; *brawler*, violent, loud, uncontrolled. The drink is credited with the characteristics which it produces in men. *Is overtaken*, lit. *reels* (Isa. 28⁷), *is intoxicated* (cf. 5¹⁶) ; the rendering *errs* (RV.) or *is deceived* (AV.) is possible, but less appropriate.

2. Royal anger.

> The wrath of a king is like the roar of a lion,
> He who ‹ angers › him sins against himself.

Comparison and its explanation, quaternary-ternary. *Wrath of*, lit. *terror of*, = " terror inspired by " ; Grk. *threat* is formally a more appropriate expression — the lion's roar is properly an illustration of an utterance of the king ; the Heb. means to say : the terror produced by an angry king is as great as that produced by the roar of a lion. The translation *angers* follows the Grk. ; the Heb. is rather *is angry with* (RV. marg.). Instead of *himself* we may render *his own life* (*nefesh, soul*). For *sins against* we should perhaps read *harms*, as in 8³⁶. Cf. 16¹⁴ 19¹².

3. Folly of strife.

> It is an honor for a man to keep aloof from strife,
> Only fools are quarrelsome.

Antithetic, quaternary-binary. The second cl. reads lit. : *but every fool is quarrelsome* (or, *quarrels*, RV., *will be quarrelling*). On the word here rendered *quarrel* see notes on 17¹⁴ 18¹.

4. Sloth produces no bread.

> In the autumn the sluggard does not plough,
> And therefore in harvest he looks in vain (for a crop).

Continuous, ternary. *Autumn* is here particularly the season, following the last ingathering of crops, when the ground is to be

---

* Our words *sugar, saccharine* probably have the same stem as the Heb. term (*shēkār*). On its meaning cf. Lag., *Mittheilungen*, 2, 357 ; Nowack, *Arch.*, 1, 120.

prepared for sowing (the season of the "former" or "early" rain), beginning in October and lasting four or five months; the Heb. term is, however, generally used for the colder half of the year (Gen. 8^{22} Am. 3^{15} ψ 74^{17}) as opposed to the warmer half which includes harvest-time and summer. The *harvest* begins in April (barley) and lasts till September (grapes). The rendering *by reason of the winter* (RV.) or *of the cold* (Lat.) is improbable — the sluggard is deterred not by cold, but by laziness; *from the beginning of autumn on* (De. Str.) is possible, but less natural than *in autumn*. *Looks in vain*, lit. *asks and there is nothing;* he *seeks* food from his fields, but, owing to his neglect, there is none; the rendering *begs* (or, *shall beg*, Lat. RV.) is inappropriate — the man's slothfulness would not prevent his being helped by his neighbors, especially in the plentiful and joyous time of harvest.

5. Shrewdness discovers plans.

> The purpose in a man's mind is deep water,
> But a man of sagacity will draw it out.

Continuous, quaternary-ternary. A man's real thought, the proverb says, is hard to fathom, but may be discovered by one who knows how to sound the mind. *Purpose* is counsel, plan, the result of deliberation; *mind* is lit. *heart; deep water* (plu. in the Heb.) is the symbol of something hard to exhaust or apprehend. The figure is that of a mass of water which has to be drawn from a well or reservoir; the deeper the water the harder the task. The allusion is to men's disposition to conceal their plans. A clever man will discover a plan by shrewd inquiries and guesses. The proverb has no moral content. See 18^4, in which our first cl. occurs with *words* for *purpose*, and *mouth* for *mind*.

6. Rarity of real friendship.

> Many men profess friendship,
> But a trustworthy man who can find?

Antithetic, ternary. The first line is lit.: *many men proclaim every one his kindness* (or, *many a man proclaims his kindness*), = "professions of willingness to be helpful are frequent," with the implication that such professions are frequently hollow — it is not easy to find a man *trustworthy* or *faithful,* one who can be relied on for sympathy and aid in time of stress.* — The text has also been rendered : *many a man meets a man of kindness* (or, *a man who is kind to him*), taking *kind* in the sense of "kind in words only," or "kind in occasional matters" (with the implication that the friendliness does not go far).† The general sense in this translation is the same as that given above, but the meaning attached to *kindness* is hardly permitted by the Hebrew — the word means "real kindliness." The same general sense also is given by the rendering (which involves a slight departure from our Heb. text) : *many a man is called kind,* ‡ in which the antithesis is direct and natural. Either this translation or the one here adopted gives a satisfactory form to the couplet.

7–11. Rectitude of conduct. — Single sentences (partial parallelism in v.⁹).

> 7. A man of probity and righteousness —
> Happy are his children after him!
> 8. A king who sits on the judgment-seat
> Winnows all evil with his eyes.
> 9. Who can say : " I have made my heart clean,
> I am pure from sin "?
> 10. Divers weights, divers measures,
> Abomination to Yahweh are they both.
> 11. ‹ Even a child › is known by his deeds,
> According as his conduct is good or ‹ bad.›

7. Ternary. Lit. *one who walks in his probity as a righteous man.* The expressions *in probity* and *righteous* are to be taken together as hendiadys. The term *probity* (lit. *perfectness, integrity*) signifies hearty conformity to divine and human law, not absolute sinlessness (cf. v.⁹) ; see 2⁷ 10⁹ 19¹ Job 4⁶ ψ 26¹ 101², and cf. the adj. in Dt. 18¹³ Job 1¹ ψ 37⁷ Pr. 2²¹ 28¹⁸ 29¹⁰ *al.* Instead of *righteous* we may translate by *just*—each of these terms here = *perfect.* The first line may also (but not so well) be rendered : *the righteous man walks in his probity* (or, *in probity*). — The second cl. states the common OT. doctrine of the heritability of blessing for good conduct ; see, on the other side, Job 21⁸⁻¹¹

---

* So Saad. Ew. RV. *al.*   † De. Reuss, Wild. *al.*   ‡ Svr. Targ. Lat. Kamp.

ψ 17[14].—**8.** Ternary. The Oriental king (like the chief of the tribe or clan) acted personally as judge; cf. 2 Sam. 15[2-4] 1 K. 3[28] Isa. 11[3. 4] ψ 72[4] (so also, for ex., the Califs of Bagdad). The king (who is assumed to be just, see note on 16[10 ff.]) *winnows* all causes with his *eyes*, personally examines all claims and charges, sifts the evidence, especially sifts and exposes all crime and injustice. The verb of second cl. may also mean *scatters* (RV), = dissipates, destroys; but the other sense accords with the expression *with his eyes*, and is supported by the use of the verb in v.[26].—**9.** Ternary-binary. A declaration of human moral imperfectness. Such a belief was doubtless coeval with ethical reflection in Israel (Gen. 3 Isa. 6[5]), being a necessary result of observation. In the earlier literature (down to the sixth or fifth century B.C.) it is taken for granted without formal statement. The distinct recognition of sinfulness as an element of human nature begins to appear in Ezekiel (18. 33), and the formulation of the view is found in philosophical or reflective writings and utterances (1 K. 8[46] Job 4[17-19] 14[4] [apparently an interpolation] ψ 51[5(7)] 130[3] Eccl. 7[20]); in the Psalter we have only two or three occurrences of the general affirmation, the reference in ψ 14[3] and similar passages being (as the context indicates) to the enemies of pious Israel. The two conceptions, universal sinfulness (v.[9]) and the possibility of practical perfectness (v.[7]), were held together, without attempt to harmonize them logically — they furnish the raw material of later theological dogma; in our Book of Job the hero is pronounced perfect by God (Job 1[8]), yet is charged with sin not only by Elihu (Job 34[7. 8]) but also apparently by God himself (Job 40[8]). There is, in OT., no reference of human peccability to the event described in Gen. 3.— **10.** Binary. See 11[1] 20[23] Am. 8[5] Dt. 25[13-16] Ez. 45[10], and, for second line, 17[15]; cf. BS. 26[29], and v.[14] below. — **11.** Ternary. The Heb. reads: *also* (or, *even*) *by his deeds a child is* (or, *makes himself*) *known, whether his work be pure or right.* The initial particle here qualifies either the expression *by his deeds*, or the whole clause; in the former case it introduces a contrast between deeds and something else (conceivably, words) as mark of character, but of such other thing there is no trace; in the latter case it contrasts this clause with some other, but there is no

other with which it stands in contrast. The natural suggestion is
that the emphasis is on *child*, and the position of the particle must
be changed so that it shall qualify this word. Even a young child,
the sense is, shows character by conduct; the suggestion is that
conduct is always the test of character (Mt. 7^{20}), and that training
must begin early. In second cl. the form of the Heb. implies an
antithesis, and it is therefore better to read *bad* instead of *right:*
whether the child's conduct be good or bad, in either case it
indicates his character. The translation *good and right* (Lat.)
gives up the antithesis. The rendering *even in play* (Ew.) is not
supported by Heb. usage, and the sense *feign, dissemble* (Gen. 42^7)
for the verb of first cl. is here inappropriate. The rendering
whether his actions [hereafter] *will be pure* etc. is syntactically
improbable. In chs. 1–9 of Pr. *child* is used of mature young
manhood, in chs. 10–31 it signifies a person under the control of
parents, living (unmarried) in the father's house.

XX. 2. For 獨 אֵימַת Frank. suggests חמת; cf. the זַעַף of 19^{12}. — התעבר elsewhere = *to be* (or, *become*) *angry with;* the Vrss. take it here as = *provoke*,
and it may be so poetically used, in a sense for which we might expect Piel,
but this form is not found with such a meaning; a reading מִתְעָרֵב, as in v.^{19},
is here improbable. Hi. conjectures מִתְעַבְּרוּ, denom. Tiphel from the late
(Targumic) הִעֲבֹר *anger*, but such a verb does not occur. Possibly we should
read מְעַיֵּס (cf. Dt. 32^{21}). After הטא the object sinned against is elsewhere
introduced by ב or עַל; 8^{36} חֹטְאִי *he who misses me* appears, indeed, to show
that a direct object is possible, but we should perhaps here adopt the reading
of that passage חֹטֵא נַפְשׁוֹ (so Lag. Gr.); otherwise ב should be inserted before
נפשו; 獨 is supported by 𝔊𝔖𝔗𝔏. — **3.** 𝔊 ἀποστρέφεσθαι, = שׁוּב *turn away from*,
a good reading; 獨, from ישב or ע׳בח, is more vigorous; 𝔏 *separat se;* 𝔗 = 獨;
𝔖 trans. *to put away strife.* — **4.** The Prep. מִן may indicate the time at which
something is done. — **5.** The reading λόγος (= 獨 עֵצָה) of H-P 109. 147 *al.*,
instead of the βουλή of Codd. BאA, is regarded by Lag. and Baumg. as
original, on the ground that it could not have been a correction of the latter.
If this view be correct, the word presents a noteworthy instance of the preservation of an original reading by cursive MSS. But at most it can only be
looked on as probable; the possibility of a change of βουλή into λόγος, or of
an independent rendering of the Heb. by the latter term, must be admitted.
— **6.** In 獨 הסרו omit the suff., which may be scribal insertion from following ו.
— 獨 יקרא; 𝔊 τίμιον, = יקר. — **8.** 獨 מְזָרֶה; 𝔊 οὐκ ἐναντιοῦται, = Pass. מזרה,
which Gr. adopts with the sense *fastidio est.* — **10.** 𝔊, interpreting: στάθμον
μέγα καὶ μικρόν. — 𝔊^B here, varying from 獨, gives the order of couplets as
v.^{9}. 20–22. 10–13. 23–30; the order of 獨 is given in א 23. The reason for the differ-

ence is not apparent; but as there is no logical connection between couplets, accident or scribal caprice might easily vary the order. — **11.** Transpose נם to stand before נער, and for ישר read רשע. — 𝕃 Bi. omit the second אם. — 𝔖𝔗 refer זך to נער, and ישר to פעלו, which does not relieve the syntactical difficulty.

12–14. Man's faculties the gift of God. Industry, honesty.

> 12. The hearing ear, the seeing eye —
> Yahweh has made them both.
> 13. Love not sleep, lest thou come to poverty;
> Open thine eyes, and thou wilt have plenty of bread.
> 14. "Bad, bad!" says the buyer;
> But when he is gone, then he boasts.

12. Continuous, quaternary- (or, binary-) ternary. *Hearing* and *sight* here stand for all man's faculties — all, says the proverb, are the creation and gift of God. The suggestion is that he is greater than they, that he watches them, and that they must be used in obedience to him. Cf. ψ 94⁹. — **13.** Antithetic, ternary. Lit. *open . . . have plenty* (or, *be sated with*), two Imperatives, the first stating the condition, the second stating the result — a common construction in Hebrew. — Instead of *bread* we may say *food;* the same term means for the pastoral Arabs *meat,* and for the agricultural Hebrews *bread.* — **14.** Continuous, quaternary-ternary. A trick of trade. The purchaser disparages the ware, beats down the seller, and boasts of his cleverness.

15–18. Wisdom, fraud.

> 15. Store of gold and wealth of corals
> And precious vessels — (all this) are wise lips.
> 16. Take his garment — he is surety for another!
> For another hold him in pledge!
> 17. Sweet to a man is bread gained by fraud,
> But afterwards his mouth will be filled with gravel.
> 18. ‹Arrange› thy plans by counsel,
> Carry on war under advice.

15. Single sentence, ternary. *Wealth* is abundance ; *wise lips* is lit. *lips of knowledge;* the Heb. has sing. *a precious vessel.* The syntactical order is not certain, but the translation here given, in which the three first expressions all describe *wise lips,* is the most natural. The couplet is sometimes rendered in antithetic form :

store, etc., *but* (or, *yet*) *lips of knowledge are a precious vessel,* but this leaves first cl. syntactically suspended, and the resultant sense either suggests that a precious vessel is more valuable than gold and corals ("gold etc. is valuable, get wise lips" etc.), or puts wisdom and gold together as similar values ("gold etc. is valuable, and wise lips [also] are valuable") ; neither of these statements is probable. Most expositors render : *there is gold* etc., *but lips of knowledge are a precious vessel* (or, *jewel*). In this translation the antithetic form makes a difficulty, as above, and the expression "there is gold etc." is, in the connection, strange, feeble, and syntactically loose. Possibly the text should be changed so as to give a comparison like those of $3^{14.15}$ 8^{11}. — On *corals* (RV. *rubies*, or *corals*, or *pearls*) see note on 3^{15}. *Vessels* are articles of household furniture, sometimes made of precious metals, sometimes ornamented with precious stones (see Gen. 24^{53} Ex. 3^{22} $31^{7.8}$) ; the Heb. word is also used for articles of personal adornment, as of a bride (Isa. 61^{10}), comprising jewels and similar ornaments. — **16.** Synonymous, ternary. Lit. *for* (or, *when*) *he is surety* etc. ; in second cl. the Heb. text has plu. *others* (or, *strangers*), the margin fem. sing. *a strange woman* (= "another man's wife") ; the latter reading is less probable from the parallelism, which also favors masc. singular. — The couplet (which occurs again in 27^{13}) is an exclamation of contemptuous rebuke : "he has been foolish enough to become responsible for another man's debt — hold him to account, exact the legal penalty!" The garment, commonly given as security (Dt. 24^{10-13}), could be taken by the creditor if the debt was not paid. — In second cl. we should perhaps translate : *hold it* (the garment), for, though the person might be pledged for debt (Neh. 5^5), the reference, as first cl. suggests, is rather to the garment ; *hold him in pledge* may, however, be understood to mean not "hold his person as security," but "hold him to account as security." — On the term *another* see note on 2^{16}. — **17.** Antithetic, ternary. Lit. *bread of fraud* (or, *deceit*). *Gravel* is a mass of small *particles* (Lam. 3^{16}), here perhaps earth or sand. Pleasure fraudulently gained, says the couplet, is not lasting ; cf. 10^2 23^3 Job 20^{12-18}. — **18.** Synonymous, ternary. The necessity of consultation and deliberation in all proceedings ; the thought is substan-

tially identical with that of 24⁶.   *Counsel* is the advice of wise
persons.   The first cl. in the Heb. is declarative : *plans are
arranged by counsel,* to the form of which the second cl. may be
assimilated by reading : *and by* (or, *under*) *advice war is carried
on.*   But it is better to understand the couplet as an injunction,
and assimilate first cl. to second cl., with the sense : " when thou
formest plans or carriest on war, do it under skilful guidance "
(with the advice of able counsellors, statesmen, and generals).
In any case war is spoken of as a common incident of life ; nothing
is said of its moral accompaniments or its desirableness or undesirableness.   Cf. 21³¹ 24⁶ Ecc. 3⁸ Lu. 14³¹.   There seems to be no
ground for taking *war* to refer to the common affairs of life, such
as legal processes, and similar conflicts (Frank.) ; in the Psalms
(27³ 35¹ 120⁷ *al.*) terms relating to war are doubtless sometimes to
be understood figuratively, but such can hardly be the sense here.
On *plans* and *direction* see notes on 6¹⁸ 1⁵.

19–21. Gossip, filial impiety, unjust acquisition.

> 19.   A talebearer reveals secrets —
> Have nothing to do with a gossip.
> 20.   He who curses father or mother,
> His lamp will go out in midnight darkness.
> 21.   Property got prematurely at first
> Will in the end not be blessed.

19. Developed thought, quaternary- (or, binary-) ternary.   On
the terms in first cl. see the substantially identical first cl. of 11¹³.
— *Gossip* is lit. *one who opens wide his lips,* as in 13³ (where, however, the Heb. verb is different) ; the Heb. expression would ordinarily mean *foolish of lips,* which might possibly be understood as
= " gossip," but it is easier to take the Partcp. in the sense of
" opening," or else change the text.   Luther *false mouth* and AV.
him that flattereth (marg. *enticeth*) *with his lips* are incorrect ; RV.
openeth wide his lips. — **20.** Single sentence, ternary or ternary-
quaternary.   In the old law the punishment for cursing a parent is
death (Ex. 21¹⁷ Lev. 20⁹, and cf. Dt. 27¹⁶) ; the reference here is to
the natural consequences of barbarous impiety (so 30¹⁷) ; it is not
probable that the old law was in force in later times — the punishment for the offence in question was rather social, as now, and such

is the point of view of the Wisdom-books; cf. BS. 3^{16}, and see in BS. (7^{28}) the moral motive urged for honoring parents (another motive is given in Ex. 20^{12}). The old legal control of children was gradually replaced by the control of the family and of society. — *Midnight darkness* is lit. *the pupil of darkness,* = *deepest darkness;* on *pupil* (of the eye) see note on 7$^{2.9}$. On the meaning of the expression *his lamp will go out* see note on 13^9. — **21.** Single sentence, ternary, or ternary-binary. Instead of *property*, we may render *inheritance*, property which comes to one from one's father (cf. 17^2 19^{14}); the more general reference is the more probable. *Got prematurely* (one word in the Heb.) is the reading of the Heb. margin, which is adopted by most recent expositors; the verb means *to act hastily, precipitately,* and (if this reading be accepted) the suggestion here is that the man accumulates wealth unfairly (or that the heir does not wait to receive his inheritance in due course of nature, but obtains it prematurely, by foul means); no blessing, the proverb declares, will attend property so acquired. Saadia, referring the couplet to the impious son of the preceding couplet: *his inheritance will be full of trouble.* The meaning of the verb of the Heb. text is doubtful: Schult.: (an inheritance on which) *rests the curse of niggardliness;* Ew.: *is cursed;* Geiger: *full-grown;* modern lexicons: *is loathed, disgusting, abominable* (cf. Zech. 11^8), that is (if this reading be here adopted), because obtained by foul means. The marginal reading here adopted, which is that of the Anc. Vrss., appears to yield the more satisfactory sense. — *In the end* refers to the final outcome of the man's wealth (see note on 5^4), perhaps with connotation of divine retribution.

13. 頂 שֶׁנָה; 𝕲 καταλαλεῖν, for which Jäg. compares 17^9 BS. 19^7; Lag. refers to ψ 101^6, where κ. = a form of the stem לשן. — 頂 תּוּרַשׁ is by some derived from ירשׁ, and = *shall be expelled* (or, *deprived*), by others taken as metaplastic formation from רשׁ *to be poor;* better, perhaps, as Hof. of רשׁ. — **14.** לו is reference of the action to the personality of the grammatical subject, the so-called ethical Dative. — 頂 אזֵל; Gr. אזִל, = הוּזַל *bought cheap,* from זול. — V.$^{14-19}$ are wanting in 𝕲; they are supplied, from Θ, in 𝔖^H 23. 149. 253. 260. The omission is probably connected with the fact that our v.$^{20-22}$ are placed after our v.^{9}, but the origin of the change is uncertain; there is nothing in v.$^{14-19}$ to cast doubt on their genuineness. — **15.** 頂 זהב שׁיֵ; Gr. מו יַחַר. On שׁי see note on 8^{21}; it is better to take it here as noun, but it is possible to

understand it as verb. — **16.** The Impv. לקח is found elsewhere only Ex. 29[1]
Ez. 37[16]. — ‭‭זּר‬; Gr. ‭זור‬, as in 6[1], which is allowable, but apparently not
necessary; for noun without Prep. after ערב see 11[15] 27[13]. — K ‭נכרים‬, Q ‭נכריה‬;
read sing. masc. ‭נכרי‬. — ‭חבלהו‬ might, so far as its form is concerned, be Impv.
or Perf.; the latter would be possible only in the sense *he has pledged* (parallel to ‭ערב‬), which does not elsewhere occur; as Impv. it is to be taken as
Qal, not as Piel (König), which would = *injure.* — **17.** ‭‭אָחַר‬; Gr. ‭אהרתו‬
(see 23[32]), unnecessary. — **18.** For ‭‭ Impv. ‭עשה‬ we might, to secure completer parallelism, read Infin. (so Bi.), or Nif. Impf. (so apparently 𝔖𝕮𝕷),
but it is better to change ‭‭ ‭הכן‬ to Hif. Impv. ‭תָּכֶן‬. — **19.** ‭‭ פתה; 𝕮 משרגג
entices, = Piel of ‭פתה‬, here hardly appropriate; Θ, similarly, ἀπατῶντι;
𝔖 ‭מסרדבן‬ *hasten,* perhaps free rendering, = *open wide ;* 𝕷 *dilatat.* — ‭‭ can
mean only *foolish* (of lips), and this sense is here possible. If the text be
changed, we should take not ‭פתה‬ (which is used, in connection with *lips,* only
in a general sense, of speech, never in a bad sense) but ‭פשק‬, as in 13[3] (so Gr.).
— **20.** K ‭אישׁון‬; Q ‭אֶשׁון‬, a word of doubtful meaning, rendered in 𝕮 by the
equally doubtful ‭א־ונא‬, on which see De. and Levy, *Chald. Wbch. ;* the other
Vrss. render Kethib. Instead of Prep. ‭ב‬ (of ‭‭) 𝔖𝕮 read ‭כ‬, which suits the
connection less well. — **21.** K ‭מבחלת‬, Q ‭מבהלת‬. Schult. explains ‭בחל‬ as
= Arab. ‭بخل‬ *avaricious,* Ew. as ‭בהל‬ *curse,* the Lexicons as = Syr. ‭בחל‬, which
is appropriate in Zech. 11[8], but not here. Read Qeri. Ew. adopts *curse*
as antithesis of the *bless* of [b], but the contrast thus gained is not satisfactory —
we rather expect in [a] an explanation of why the property is not blessed. —
For MSS. and edd. which give the Qeri see De' Rossi.

22–24. God's control of life.

> 22. Say not: " I will take revenge for wrong";
>   Trust to Yahweh, and he will save thee.
> 23. Divers weights are an abomination to Yahweh,
>   And a false balance is not good.
> 24. A man's steps are ordered by Yahweh;
>   How, then, can man understand his way?

22. Sentence with implied antithesis, ternary, or binary-ternary.
The same injunction is given in 24[29], and is implied in 25[21]; so, in
NT., 1 Th. 5[14] Rom. 12[17] 1 Pet. 3[9], cf. Heb. 10[30]. It is the protest which the advancing moral feeling made against the prevalent
principle of retaliation ; see note on 24[29]. — The ground or motive
adduced in second cl. appears to be simply that God will deliver
his servants from the machinations and injuries of enemies (so
De.), there being no reference to revenge, an interpretation which
is favored by 24[18]. God is thus represented not as avenging, but as
saving. The conception of Yahweh's vengeance on enemies in

Dt. 32^{35} (quoted in Rom. 12^{19} Heb. 10^{30}) does not refer to private relations between man and man. — *Take revenge for wrong* is lit. *repay evil*, that is, with evil; *trust to* is *hope in, wait on*, that is, confide a matter to God, wait for him to act. — For similar sayings among other peoples see Malan.—**23.** Synonymous, ternary. See v.^{10} and 11^1.—**24.** Continuous, with implied antithesis, ternary. See 3^6 16$^{1.9}$ 19^{21} Jer. 10^{23}. Since, says the proverb, human life is controlled by God [a principle which is a necessary inference from the doctrine of divine omnipotence], it is obvious [as Jeremiah had already affirmed] that no man can comprehend fully the meaning of his own experiences. The suggestion is that man must throw himself on God, acknowledge, obey and trust him (v.^{22} 3^6) — then his life will be rationally and successfully directed. Exactly how this reliance on God is to be reached our couplet does not say; there is no mention of written law, of Tora or Prophets (though these a pious Jew would naturally have in mind) — here, as elsewhere in Proverbs, the sage rests on the conscience enlightened by all available means. — If, in the second line, we emend *understand* to *order*, the meaning of the couplet remains the same. — This Division of the Book is thus at one with the first Division in the recognition of absolute divine sovereignty, and no attempt is made to reconcile this belief with the belief (held with equal distinctness) in human freedom. — The first cl. is nearly identical with first cl. of ψ 37^{23}, and is perhaps taken from it (though the sentence may have been a commonplace of religious thought) ; but, while the psalmist uses it to point out that a good man will be upheld by God, to the sage it suggests the limitations of human knowledge (and so, it may be inferred, the necessity of intellectual and moral humility and reverence) ; the former is national-religious, the latter is philosophical-religious.

25. Text and translation are uncertain. Our Heb. may be rendered : *It is a snare to a man when he rashly says " sacred ! " and after vows to make search*, that is, perhaps, to try to avoid payment. To declare a thing *sacred* (or, *holy*) was to renounce ownership in it (for ever, or for a time), and make it the property of the Temple (Lev. 27). The Heb. is not syntactically or logically clear : the *snare* (or, danger) to the man is expressed in the

first line only; the second line appears to give the ground of this
statement, that is, the nature of the danger; and the word rendered *rashly says* is doubtful.   The Grk. is clearer: *it is a snare
to a man hastily to consecrate property, for after (such) vowing
comes repentance;* this may be a free rendering of our Heb., or
may represent a different text. — The precise meaning of the
expression *make search* is not certain.   Elsewhere in OT. it signifies *look after, look for, seek out* (Ez. 34[11. 12], of lost sheep; Lev.
13[36], of signs of leprosy on the skin), or *make inquiry* (Lev. 27[33],
of inquiring and distinguishing between good and bad parts of the
tithe), and perhaps *inquire of an oracle* (2 K. 16[15] ψ 27[4], though
the reading in these passages is doubtful); for the rendering
reflect on there is no authority, and the sense *make a selection*,
= "endeavor to substitute a less valuable thing for the thing
vowed" (Frank., who refers to the expression in Lev. 27[33]:
inquire between good and bad) is hardly here appropriate, since
there is no question of choosing particular objects out of a mass
(as was true in the case of tithes).   The more natural sense
appears to be: "make inquiry into one's affairs or into the terms
of the vow, so as to escape payment."   The couplet may be conjecturally rendered:

> It is dangerous for a man hastily to consecrate property,
> For, after vowing, he begins to make inquiry.

Under some sudden impulse, good or bad, men would sometimes
make gifts which they afterwards regretted: they would see (as
sometimes happens now to those who make religious or charitable
donations) that they had given beyond their means, or had been
unjust to other obligations, or, when the motive was one of selfish
personal interest, that they had failed to gain their ends.   Such a
procedure the proverb declares to be a *snare* as leading into difficulties financial and moral; in like manner Koheleth (Ecc.
5[2. 4-6(1. 3-5)]) ridicules hasty vows, when a man, called on to pay
(for rates of redemption see Lev. 27), has to say lamely to the
Temple collector that he made a mistake.   Against this thoughtless, immoral habit of giving to religious objects the sages protest;
a similar evil is rebuked in Mk. 7[21], where, however, the gift
(*corban*) is made advisedly, and for a bad purpose.   **On vows**

see note on 7[14]. The renderings *to devour holy things* (which were lawful only for sacred persons), and *destroy holy things* are improbable. Saadia, who has the first of these, explains the *search* of second cl. as referring to attempts to get possession of property consecrated by others, or to avoid paying one's own vows. Cf. the Talmud tract *Nedarim* [Vows] 21 *a*.

26, 28. The ideal king is just and kind. — The two aphorisms, by their contents, belong together.

> 26. A wise king winnows the wicked,
> And passes the wheel over them.
> 28. Kindness and truth guard the king,
> And by ‹justice› his throne is sustained.

26. Synonymous, quaternary-ternary. On first cl. see note on v.[8]; here the *king* is described as *wise*, and it is the persons, the *wicked*, who are *winnowed*, sifted, disposed of. The *wheel* is that not of fortune, but of the threshing-cart (Isa. 28[27.28]), which separated the grain from the straw,* and there is also the implication of destructive or serious punishment; the winnowing proper was done with fork and shovel (Isa. 30[24] Jer. 15[7]). In Am. 1[3] the devastation of the Syrian invasion is compared to the crushing power of the threshing-sledge — it was the custom of war of the time.† A slight change in second cl. gives the reading : *and repays them their iniquity*. Cf. Isa. 11[4]. — **28.** Synonymous, ternary. On *kindness* and *truth* see notes on 3[3], and cf. 11[17] 14[22] 16[6]. *Truth* involves faithfulness to all obligations ; *kindness* is not merely *mercy* (= compassion or clemency), but general benevolence. The combination of the two terms (frequent in OT.) gives an expression of high and attractive moral character. The two are applied to a king in Isa. 16[5] ; in the Prophetic portraitures of the ideal king it is more commonly *justice* that is emphasized (Isa. 11[4] ψ 72[2] Zech. 9[9]). — In second cl. the Heb. reads lit. : *and he sustains* (or, *supports*, or *upholds*) *his throne by kindness*. The repetition of only one of the two qualities men-

---

* See Nowack, *Arch.* I. § 41.

† On the interpretation of 2 Sam. 12[31] see Hoffmann, *ZAW.* 1882 (in which it is maintained that David did not torture the Ammonites, but only set them to work), Stade, GVI. I. 278, Driver, *Samuel*, and cf. Geier's note.

tioned in first cl. is strange, and the substitution, in the Grk., of the other quality which should characterize royal administration is probably right.

27. Conscience is God's search-light.

The spirit of man is the lamp of Yahweh,
Searching all the chambers of the soul.

Single sentence, ternary-binary. The *spirit* is the *breath* (Heb. *neshāmā*) which is breathed into the body by God (as in Gen. 2⁷), whereby man becomes a "living soul," that is, a complete living person. The OT. conception appears to be that into every human body, as soon as it is formed, there is introduced a new " breath," which is the inward moral and intellectual being * ; but there is no theory of preëxistence of souls, such as is found in *Wisd. Sol.* 8²⁰. — The *spirit* is here man's moral and intellectual perception, the conscience, represented as the critic of the moral life, and therefore the search-light of God, who is the supreme and final critic; the presupposition is that the conscience is not only the creation of God, but also morally identical with him. — On *chambers* (fully *secret chambers*) see 18⁸; *soul* (lit. *interior*, or *belly*, as in 18⁸, cf. Job 32¹⁸) = the whole inward being, here especially the moral nature. Though, in the expression " the spirit searches the soul," there is a formal antithesis of " spirit " and " soul," the two terms are really equivalent each to the other, as in our expression " the conscience judges the soul "; but the former denotes the moral nature in its capacity of judge, with reference to the moral ideal, while the latter exhibits it on the side of its actual life. — Cf. 1 Cor. 2¹⁰. — The rendering *the light of Yahweh searches the spirit of man and all* etc. (Grätz) is rhythmically unsatisfactory.

29. Strength in youth, wisdom in old age.

The glory of young men is their strength,
The beauty of the old is the hoary head.

Antithetic, ternary. *Glory = beauty*, = adornment, that which constitutes the highest attraction, and is thus an indication of per-

---

* Cf. the later theory of creatianism, as opposed to traducianism.

fectness. The proverb must be understood as giving one aspect of things : what is most characteristic, attractive, and admirable is, in the young (persons in the prime of life), physical strength and exuberant animal life, in the old, gray hair regarded as the indication of gravity and wisdom ; the sage would doubtless hold that a young man should have something more than bodily vigor, and an old man more than wisdom. Cf. 16³¹, and the references there given.

30. Text and translation are uncertain. The Heb. may be rendered : "wounds from stripes [RV.: stripes that wound] cleanse away evil (or, cleanse the bad man), and blows (cleanse) the inward parts (or, and reach the inward parts, or, and blows which reach the inward parts)." — Grk. (with different text) : *blows and contusions befall bad men, and stripes* (penetrate) *into the inward parts;* Lat. (followed by AV.) : *the blueness* (or, *bruise*) *of a wound cleanses away evil things;* Rashi : *bruises and wounds are remedies* [lit. abstergents] *for evil, and blows* (*entering into*) *the inward parts.* Modern expositors * generally adopt Rashi's rendering. In second cl. De. translates : *and reach the inward parts* (Partcp. *striking, reaching* instead of Subst. *blows*) ; RV.: *and strokes* (*reach*) etc. — The thought of the proverb appears to be (cf. 17¹⁰) that moral evil must be put away by severe chastisement. The word in first cl. representing "cleansing" occurs as noun in Esth. 2³· ⁹· ¹² in the sense of "cosmetics" (applications to the skin) for women of a harem, and as verb in Jer. 46⁴ Lev. 6²⁸⁽²¹⁾ 2 Chr. 4¹⁶ in the sense of "furbish" (of weapons and vessels). The text appears to be in bad condition, and we should, perhaps, adopt the reading of the Grk., or emend so as to read : *Stripes cleanse the body, and blows the inward parts,* in which *body* and *inward parts* may both refer to the moral being, or the first term may be taken literally, and the second as = *soul;* or, since it is difficult to understand how stripes (or bruises) cleanse the body, we may read : *Cosmetics purify the body, and blows the soul.*

24. Instead of יָכֵן several MSS. (and so 𝔖) have יכן (cf. ψ 37²³), which also gives a good sense. — **25.** 𝔐 ילע may be Impf. of לעע or לוע or לעה, or Perf. or Impf. of ילע. Lag. identifies the stem with Arab. ולע IV., = *incite,*

---

* Geier, Schult. Mich. Reuss, Zöck. Noyes, Kamp. *al.*

and so, *hasten*, and he would then point the following word קדשׁ; the two words, he observes, would thus be correctly rendered by 𝔊 ταχύ . . . ἁγιάσαι. Another proposed derivation (De.) is from לעה, = Arab. לעה, *speak carelessly* (cf. ימין לע, *a vow made lightly*); ילע may thus be taken as Impf. of לעע or לוע, = "that he should lightly say": cf. Job 6³ (in Obad. 16 some form of בלע should perhaps be read).—𝔊 may = בהל לקדשׁ (Frank.).—𝕿 נדר *vow*, free rendering, or guess based on ᵇ; 𝕃 *devorare*, = ברע.—𝔎 בקר; 𝔊, well, μετανοεῖν.—Gr. reads ילן and אֲרֵח, *procrastinate* in paying one's vows.— **26.** 𝔎 אפן; Gr. אנם (and requites them for) *their iniquity* (ψ 94²⁸).— **27.** 𝔎 נר; 𝔊 φῶς, = נר or אר, or is perhaps free rendering of 𝔎.—Clem. Al. 221⁴⁸ πνεῦμα κυρίου λύχνος ἐρευνῶν τὰ ταμεῖα τῆς γαστρός, affected by 1 Cor. 2¹⁰.—**28.** 𝔎 סֵדָר, the subj. being the מלך; Nif., Perf. or Impf., would perhaps be better (though Nif. does not occur elsewhere).—**30.** K תמריק, Q תמרוק, 3 sing. fem. of Hif. and Qal, or two nouns; 𝔊 συναντᾷ, = מקרה (Lag.), or הקרינה (Frank.), or, less probably, הקרים (Gr.).—𝔎 ברע; Kamp. מֵרע.—𝔎 חבריה and חֲצֵע are synonyms (Ex. 21²⁵ Isa. 1⁶), and the latter should perhaps be omitted as gloss. For 𝔎 ברע we may read כָּשֵׁר; better perhaps: הֲבֵר תַּמְרֻק כָשֵׁר; for Hif. of ברר see Jer. 4¹¹ 51¹¹.

XXI. 1–3. God's control of men.

1. Like watercourses is a king's heart in the hands of Yahweh —
   Whither he will he turns it.
2. All that a man does he thinks right,
   But Yahweh tries the heart.
3. To do justice and equity
   Is more acceptable to Yahweh than sacrifice.

1. Comparison with explanation, ternary. A king is generally supposed to be autocratic, but God, the proverb declares, controls even his decisions and actions. *Heart* = mind. The picture is that of a land (as Egypt or Babylonia, but not Palestine), or a garden, watered by canals (cf. 5¹⁶ Isa. 58¹¹), whose flow is regulated by officers or gardeners; in the fertilizing *water* there may be an allusion to royal deeds of kindness (cf. 16¹⁵), but the main reference is to the divine control of kings. Cf. Tob. 1¹³ Esth. (Grk.) 14¹³.—**2.** Antithetic, ternary. See note on 16², with which this couplet is nearly identical; cf. 16¹· ²⁵ 17³. Lit. *every way of a man is right in his eyes*. *Tries* is lit. *weighs* or *measures*. —**3.** Single sentence, ternary. Cf. v.²⁷ 15⁸ ψ 40⁶⁽⁷⁾ 51¹⁶· ¹⁷⁽¹⁸· ¹⁹⁾ Am. 5²²⁻²⁴ Isa. 1¹¹ *al.* (and see also Hos. 6⁶). The ethical conception of piety, announced by the prophets, lost none of its force with the sages; see BS. 34^{18-26} $35^{6.7}$.

4. Text and sense doubtful.

The couplet appears to contain fragments of two couplets. Lit.: *haughty look and proud heart* (or, *haughty of look and proud of heart*) — *the tillage* (or, *ploughing*) *of the wicked is sin.* This may be understood to mean that pride, which is the industry or occupation of the wicked, is sin; but the figure is strange and forced. In Hos. 10^{12} Jer. 4^3 preparing one's heart for a new life is called "breaking up the fallow ground"; so here in second cl. the bad man's preparation for life may be supposed to be called sin, but this is not a probable sense — the meaning is rather that his life itself is sin. — The difficulty is not diminished if, by the change of a vowel, we read (with Grk. RV.) *lamp* instead of *tillage;* the sentence *the lamp of the wicked is sin* conveys no meaning; cf. 13^9, where the figure of light and lamp is simple and clear. — The first cl. recalls 16^5, the second cl. 10^{16} 13^9 24^9; new couplets might be conjecturally constructed, but the recovery of the precise form seems impossible; see Lagarde and Wildeboer.

5. Industry and sloth. — Antithetic, ternary. The Heb. reads:

> The methods of the industrious lead surely to gain,
> But every one who hastes (hastes) surely to want.

Hastes can here be understood to mean only "hastes to be rich," as in 13^{11} 28^{20}; but in that case we expect the term to be defined, as in 13^{11} 19^2 28^{20} 29^{20}. *Hasty* (even if it be taken to mean "using improper methods") is not a proper antithesis to *industrious;* we rather expect *slothful,* as in 13^4 (so the Lat.). The parallelism also suggests, instead of *every one,* some term equivalent to *methods,* and the word *surely* (or, *only*) adds nothing to the meaning. We may thus read:

> The methods of the industrious lead to gain,
> The ways of the slothful to want.

Methods = thoughts, reflections, plans (12^5 15^{22} 16^3 20^{18}). The couplet is an exhortation to industry; so 10^4 12^{11}, cf. 6^{6-11} 24^{30-34}.

6-10. The way of the wicked.

6. The acquisition of wealth by a lying tongue
   Is a fleeting breath, a deadly ‹snare.›
7. The violence of the wicked will sweep them away
   Because they refuse to act justly.
8. Crooked is the way of the vicious,
   But the conduct of the pure is straight.
9. It is better to dwell in the corner of the housetop
   Than with a quarrelsome woman in a ‹large› house.
10. The wicked desires to do harm;
    He has no kindly feeling toward his neighbor.

6. Single sentence, quaternary (or, binary-ternary). Cf. 10². In first cl. *acquisition of wealth* may be understood as = *wealth acquired*. *Fleeting breath* is lit. *breath driven* (by the wind) ; cf. Isa. 19⁷ ψ 68²⁽³⁾. The last expression of second cl. stands in the Heb.: *seekers of death*, or (by a slight change of text) the sing. may be read: (the acquisition etc.) *is a fleeting breath, seeking death*, an obscure and improbable form. The reading *snare*, instead of *seekers*, comes from the Greek, which has: *he who gains wealth by a lying tongue pursues vanities to* (or, *on*) *snares of death.* — **7.** Single sentence, ternary (or, binary-ternary). For the thought cf. 1¹⁹. *Violence* is highhanded, oppressive conduct ; see 24² (RV. *oppression*). *Sweep away*, = "take away, carry off" ; see Hab. 1¹⁵ (RV. *catcheth*), and a similar verb in Ju. 5²¹. The instrument of punishment for the wicked is law, divine and human. — **8.** Antithetic, ternary. The word here translated *vicious* is by some rendered *sin-laden* (De. RV.), by others *false, dishonorable* (Barth), or, with the omission of a letter, *proud* or *insolent* (Grätz) ; the general sense is the same in all these translations ; the rhythm appears to favor the last (and cf. v.²⁴), of which *vicious* is a synonym. By some critics the word is regarded as a corrupt form, of which no translation is possible. — The second cl. reads lit.: *but the pure, straight* (= *upright*) *is his conduct* (lit. *doing* or *work*). — The sense is : bad men are underhand in their procedures, good men are straightforward — that is, no man, whatever his pretensions, can be called pure, if he does not act uprightly. — **9.** Single sentence, ternary-quaternary. The couplet = 25²⁴; cf. 19¹³ 21¹⁹ 27¹⁵. Lit.: *better the dwelling . . . than a*

quarrelsome woman etc.　It was customary to sleep on the roof
(so Saul, 1 Sam. 9²⁵, according to the Grk. and RV. marg.), and
there a simply-furnished guest-room might be built, such as Elijah
(1 K. 17¹⁹) and Elisha (2 K. 4¹⁰) occupied; but to live always in
so narrow a space would be lonely and inconvenient. — The sense
large (or, *wide*) is obtained by transposition of letters; the Heb.
text has *house of a companion*, which is interpreted to mean *house
of society,** *common house,*† or *house in common,* ‡ that is, a house
in which one has society; but the phrase is not a natural one —
we should at least expect the plu. *companions;* or the *companion*
is taken to be the wife, the man being thus described as a householder (Frank.), an interpretation equally difficult.　In any case,
the antithesis in first cl. is "loneliness" (cf. ψ 102⁸) and discomfort. — The *woman* is probably the wife, but any woman, as a
mother or a sister, may be meant. — Others § translate: *it is
better to sit on the pinnacle* etc., a situation of danger as well as of
inconvenience; but, though the word may mean *corner-tower*
(Zeph. 1¹⁵), the idea of danger is not probable — the point is
rather the discomfort of the situation: rather any privation with
peace than luxury with strife. — The Grk., with a different text, or
else moralizing, has *unrighteousness* instead of *a quarrelsome
woman.* — **10.** Synonymous, ternary.　Lit. *the soul of the wicked*
etc., and *his neighbor does not find mercy* (or, *kindness*) *in his
eyes.*　Cf. 4¹⁶ 10²³ 12¹⁰ Isa. 1¹⁷.

XXI. 1. 韻 יהוה; ⨳ θεοῦ. — 韻 עַל; read, with Bi., אֶל. — ⨳𝕷 interpret ᵃ as
comparison: *as . . . so;* 𝕾𝕿 have only *as;* 韻, as curter, is probably original.
— **2.** 韻 וישר; *Tosef. Yebam.* I, 11, זך, doubtless scribal variation, after 16².
For 韻 תֹכֵן Gr. (as in 16²) reads בחן, but unnecessarily, since תׁ may = *tries.*
תכן (from כן), = *fix accurately, determine,* and so, perhaps, *weigh.* — **3.** 韻 ליהוה;
⨳ παρὰ θεῷ. — **4.** 韻 נר; ⨳𝕾𝕿𝕷 יֵר. — ⨳𝕷 make ᵃ a complete sentence; 𝕾𝕿,
inserting ו before נר, make the couplet a single sentence; Bi. makes ᵃ an
exclamation, and inserts ו before נר.　Possibly some such word as זֶפֶת (cf. 24⁹)
should be substituted for נר. — **5.** Wanting in ⨳; 𝕺𝕾ᴴ = 韻. — 韻 וכל אך;
𝕿 *and the foot* (as if it read רגל) *of the hasty;* 𝕾 *and (those) of the wicked,*
perh. reading לֵי (Pink.), perh. free rendering of 韻; 𝕷 *omnis autem piger,*
= וכל עצל. — Read דרכי עצל; עצל is read by Gr.　The אך may be retained, but
is unnecessary, and the thought is better without it. — **6.** ⨳ reads Partcp. פעל.
— 韻 נדף; ⨳ διώκει, = רדף (Jäg.). — 韻 מבקשי; ⨳ παγίδας, 𝕷 *laqueos,* = מקשי

(so Rashi, Ew. Hitz. Reuss, Kamp. *al.*), obviously to be preferred to 𝕳. — 𝕲's
form of the couplet, adopted by Bi. Frank., is not clear. — **7.** 𝕳 יוֹרֵם; 𝕲 ἐπιξενω-
θήσεται, = יִגְרֵם (Hitz.), improbable. — **8.** 𝕳 זֵר, ἅπ. λεγ., may be a noun of
agency from a stem זור (Capp.), which occurs in Arab. in the sense *bear a burden*, and (as denom. from *wizr, burden, sin*) *commit sin;* it would then mean
not *sin-laden*, but simply *sinner*. The derivation from a stem זור, in Arab. =
turn aside, be false, is less probable (but cf. 𝕲 σκολιὰς ὁδοὺς). 𝔖𝕿𝕷 *foreign*
(זר). Gr., taking the ו to be scribal insertion from following וּזְ, reads זֵד, which
also gives a good sense, and is perhaps preferable to 𝕳. — **9.** On K מדונים,
Q מדינים, see note on 6¹⁴. — 𝕳 בית חבר is followed by 𝕲𝖘𝕿𝕷; 𝕿 ב׳ שׁרקא *a
closed house*, free contrast to "open roof," perh. after 𝕲 κεκονιαμένοις; 𝖘 omits.
For חבר read רחב (so Gr.).

11. How simple and sage are taught.

> When the scoffer is punished, the simple is made wise,
> When the wise man is instructed, he receives knowledge.

Antithetic, binary-ternary. On *scoffer and simple* see notes on
1² ⁴. The punishment of the bad man is a warning to the
morally untrained, who is too unripe, intellectually and morally, to
be benefited by instruction; the wise man, on the other hand, is
receptive and teachable. Cf. 19²⁵. — The three similar terms of
second cl. are here employed with different shades of meaning:
wise denotes general comprehension of the issues and needs of
life; to *instruct* is to *cause to know*, to *give insight* into practical
truth; and the result is *knowledge*, acquaintance with definite
rules of conduct.

12. Text and translation are uncertain.

The Heb. may be rendered: *the righteous considers the house
of the wicked man, overturns the wicked to misfortune* (or, *ruin*).
As the Heb. text stands the subject of the couplet must be God,
the *righteous one* (so most recent expositors, and RV. marg.) ; a
righteous man might be said to note the wicked, but could not be
said to hurl them to ruin; the rendering "one hurls the wicked
etc.," = "the wicked are hurled" (RV. *how the wicked are overthrown to their ruin*), is difficult if not impossible, and the same
thing is true of the interpretation: "the righteous man notes etc.,
he (= God) hurls etc."; see textual note on 10²⁴. The reference to God is favored by 22¹², in which it is said that Yahweh
overthrows (= hurls down) the affairs (or, words) of the wicked.

—On the other hand, the designation of God as "a (or, the) righteous one"* occurs nowhere else in Proverbs, and elsewhere in OT. only in Job 34[17] "the just-mighty one," where the context makes the reference obvious and natural; here, on the contrary, the word is isolated.† — The Heb. text seems not to be in its original form. Hitzig emends so as to read: *the righteous man considers his house, but wickedness hurls the wicked to ruin* (cf. 13[6]), a possible sense for the lines separately, but giving no natural connection between them. The repetition of the term *wicked* is strange — we expect a contrast in the lines, such as Hitzig gains, or, with closer connection: *Yahweh considers the righteous, but overthrows the house of the wicked;* cf. 3[33], and ψ 41[1(2)]. — *Consider* (or, *note*) is lit. *to act wisely* in reference to a thing, direct one's intelligence to it; cf. ψ 41[1(2)]. The *house* of the wicked is his household or family, which stands for his social position. On *hurls* (or, *overthrows*) see 13[6] 19[3] 22[12]. *Ruin* is lit. *evil, harm.*

13, 14. Kindness to the poor.   Bribery.

13. Whoso closes his ears to the cry of the poor,
    He also shall call and not be answered.

14. A gift in secret turns away anger,
    And a present in the bosom violent wrath.

13. Single sentence, ternary.   The *poor* is the physically needy. *Also* emphasizes the fact that the unkind man will suffer the same fate as the man whom he neglects; it is the law of retaliation. He will *call* not to God (Targ. Syr.), but to his fellow-men; the statement is that a hardhearted man need expect no sympathy in his misfortunes.   For *answered* we may write *heard* (RV.), in the sense *listened to.*   Cf. BS. 4[1-6] Jas. 2[13]. — **14.** Synonymous, ternary.   The *gift* and the *present* are bribes, carried by the briber in his *bosom* and given *in secret;* the reference is to dealing with

---

* Delitzsch's assertion that the word, being without the Art., cannot mean "the righteous one" is disproved by Job 34[17].

† The Anc. Vrss. all understand the *righteous* to mean *righteous man*, and so the body of interpreters (except Rashi) up to De Wette, Fleisch. Ew.; Rashi refers it to God, but this exegesis of his has no great weight, for the reason that he habitually introduces references to divine things (God and the Tora), often without ground.   "God" is supplied as subj. of second cl. by AV. Geier, Mich. Wordsw. *al.*

judges and other great men. For the use of the bosom of the dress as a pocket see 17²³. — For *turns away* some Anc. Vrss.* have *extinguishes* (RV. *pacifieth*), a probable reading. The Grk. makes second cl. antithetic : *he who withholds a gift stirs up violent wrath,* a sense good in itself, but less probable than that of the Hebrew. — The power of a bribe is here noted simply as a fact. Against bribery see 17²³.

15, 16. Punishment of bad men.

> 15. The execution of justice is a joy to the righteous,
> But destruction to evil-doers.
> 16. The man who wanders from the path of wisdom
> Will rest in the assembly of the Shades.

15. Antithetic, quaternary-ternary. The sense is : to those who are in sympathy with what is good, and are conscious of right-doing, the execution of justice (by courts or otherwise) can only be a source of satisfaction (making manifest their integrity), while to offenders against law and right it means destruction. Instead of *destruction* we may render *dismay, terror,*† which furnishes a more direct antithesis to the *joy* of first clause ; but *destruction* is the meaning of the Heb. word elsewhere in Pr., and gives an effective heightening of the thought. — The subject of first cl. is lit. *to do justice,* which may be taken to mean "rectitude of conduct," ‡ but this interpretation affords no satisfactory sense for the second cl.; the statement that "rectitude, or obedience to the law of God, alarms evil-doers" § is unnatural in itself, and is foreign to the tone of Proverbs. The rendering *there is destruction to the* etc. (AV.) is not favored by the parallelism, which suggests that *destruction* must be predicate of the subject of first clause. — **16.** Single sentence, quaternary-ternary. *Wisdom* here = "understanding, insight, intelligence" in the law of life, which is the law of God. The *assembly of the Shades* is the population of Sheol; to rest therein is to be numbered with the dead. The verb *rest* (= "take position") is the poetic equivalent of *dwell,* and is probably not meant to convey the idea of repose. In Job

---

* Sym. Targ. Lat.　　　　　　‡ De. Reuss, RV. *al.*
† So De. Wild. *al.*　　　　　　§ De. Wild.

3^{17} the "weary" find rest in Sheol from the wicked who trouble
them on earth ; but here it is the wicked themselves who are said
to rest.   There is possibly a tinge of sarcasm in the expression ;
but this is hardly probable.   The idea of the couplet is the old
one that bad men die prematurely — physical death is the punish-
ment of sin; cf. ψ $8^{17(18)}$ $55^{23(24)}$ Pr. 1^{32} etc. — On *wisdom* and
Shades (Rephaim) see notes on 1^3 2^{18}.

17-21. Thrift, righteousness, comfort.

> 17. He who loves pleasure will come to want,
>   He who loves wine and oil will not be rich.
> 18. The wicked is a ransom for the righteous —
>   Instead of the upright stands the bad man.
> 19. It is better to dwell in a wilderness
>   Than with a quarrelsome and vexatious woman.
> 20. There is precious treasure [] in the abode of the wise,
>   But the fool swallows it up.
> 21. Whoso follows after justice and kindness
>   He finds life [] and honor.

17. Synonymous, ternary.   Immoderate love of pleasure and of
luxurious living is meant; cf. 3^{10}, where wine is regarded as a
blessing, and, for the representation of wine and oil as common
sources of enjoyment, cf. 27^9 Ju. $9^{9.\ 13}$ ψ 104^{15} BS. 31^{27}.   Among
the Hebrews, as among the Greeks and Romans, they were usual
accompaniments of feasts ; see Am. 6^6 Dt. 14^{26} Neh. 8^{12} ; the oil
was used for anointing the person.   In first cl. the Lat. has *who
loves feasts,* but the reference is rather to unbridled luxury in general, which is likely to lead to excessive expenditure of money
and to poverty ; cf. BS. 19^1. — **18.** Synonymous, ternary.   *Ransom* is that which is given to free a person from a penalty to
which he is exposed ; in 6^{35} it is a sum paid to an injured
husband, in 13^8 it is money considered as securing its possessor
against legal judgment or the oppression of great men, and so in
ψ $49^{7(8)}$ a consideration paid to God for averting physical death,
the common lot of men ; it is the old legal term for weregeld (Ex.
21^{30}) ; in 1 Sam. 12^3 it appears to be equivalent to "bribe."
Here, as second cl. suggests, the idea is a more general one :
when punishment is inflicted (by God) on a community, it is the

bad man, and not the good, on whom it falls.   The form of the
couplet suggests the sense that the righteous would, in the ordinary course of justice, be punished, but that God takes the wicked
as his substitute ; but this is too crude a conception—the thought
appears to be simply that the bad and not the good suffer, a fact
which is poetically represented as a substitution of the former for
the latter.   See note on 11⁸.—On *bad* (or, *faithless*), here
= *wicked*, see note on 2²².—**19**.   Single sentence, quaternary-ternary.   See v.⁹ 25²⁴, from which this differs in putting *wilderness*
instead of *housetop*, both lonely and incommodious dwelling-
places, but at least affording peace.   *Wilderness* is pasture-land,
not wholly without houses and people, but sparsely settled and
quiet.—In second cl. we may render (so RV. marg.) *a quarrelsome woman and vexation;* the sense is the same, since the vexation comes from the woman.—The Heb. is lit. *better abode in a
wilderness than a quarrelsome* etc.—**20**.   Antithetic, quaternary-
ternary.   The meaning appears to be : the wise man amasses
wealth, the fool squanders it ; cf. 10⁵.   The form of expression is
somewhat strange : elsewhere in this Division of Prov. the sage is
not represented as rich, and here the fool seems to squander the
wealth amassed by the sage (as if he were his heir).   The *it* must
mean the fool's own treasure, and *wise* must = " provident."   On
treasure (physical, not spiritual, riches) see 10² 15¹⁶ 21⁶ ; *precious*
is lit. *desirable* (Gen. 2⁹ ψ 19¹⁰⁽¹¹⁾).   The Heb. has *precious treasure and oil;* the *oil* (wanting in the Grk.) is, however, here
inappropriate, and must be regarded as an incorrect scribal insertion (perhaps from v.¹⁷).   *Fool* is lit. *a fool of a man*, as in
15²⁰.—Grk. : *precious treasure will rest on the mouth of the
sage* (cf. 10¹¹·¹³·¹⁴), but how the fool can swallow this treasure is
not clear.—**21**.   Single sentence, ternary.   Probity, the proverb
says, brings long life and honor—the same thought as in 3²·¹⁶ *al.*
Instead of *justice* the Heb. word might be rendered *righteousness*,
but this general term would make the following *kindness* unnecessary ; a good life is summed up in the two qualities *justice* (see
8¹⁸ 1³) and *kindness* (see 3³), as in 3³ it is summed up in *kindness*
and *faithfulness*.—In second cl., after *life*, the Heb. adds *justice*
(or, *righteousness*), which is manifestly a scribal insertion (probably an error of eye) from first clause ; to say that he who follows

righteousness finds righteousness is meaningless. — On *life* and *honor* see notes on 2[19] 3[16].

11. In 𝔐 לחכם the Prep. is possible, after חשׂכל, but may be scribal repetition of preceding ל. — **12.** It is doubtful whether חשׂכל can be understood as = "observe in order to control." It occurs in the sense of *give heed to* (the law) for the purpose of obeying (Neh. 8[13] Dan. 9[25]), *consider* (one's ways) for the purpose of rightly ordering (16[2]), and *be (kindly) considerate of* (the poor, ψ 41[2]); nowhere else in OT. is the term used to express observation on the part of God. The difficulty would thus not be set aside if יהוה were substituted for צדק. The deliberate hostility, moreover, thus ascribed to Yahweh, is unexampled in Pr., even in 1[24–32]. These considerations would incline us to interpret צדק of the good man, but 𝔐, as the text stands, cannot be so understood. Dys. מַכְשׁל, for מַשׂכל, hardly helps; Gr. לביתו אשׁר, for לבית רשׁע, and יפלח, for מפלח, gains a contrast between the reward (*good fortune*) of the righteous and the punishment (*destruction*) of the wicked, but gives a text which is syntactically difficult. — 𝔏 apparently read לסלף רשׁעם מרע (*ut detrahat*), but such procedure is not elsewhere in Pr. ascribed to the צדק, and סלף is nowhere else in OT. used in a good sense. — It is probable that the original form of the couplet stated a contrast between the actions or fortunes of righteous and wicked men. We should, possibly, read: משׂכל יהוה צדק ובית; ;רשׁע הוא מסלף — **14.** 𝔐 יִכְבֶּה; ℭ מרעיא, 𝔏 *extinguit*, = .יכבה — **15.** 𝔐 מחתה; 𝔊 ἀκάθαρτος, perh. reading הטמאה; ὅσιος is then supplied as subject. — **16.** 𝔐 ירפאם; 𝔊 γιγάντων; 𝔖ℭ בני ארעא .— **18.** 𝔊 omits [b] (probably by accident), and v.[18b] was then wrongly attached to v.[17]. — **21.** Omit the second צדקה, with 𝔊[AB al.], Ziegler, Elster, Gr. Bi.

22, 23. Power of wisdom and prudence.

> **22.** A wise man scales the city of the mighty,
> And casts down the stronghold in which it trusted.
>
> **23.** He who is careful of mouth and tongue
> Saves himself from trouble.

22. Synonymous, ternary. Intellect or practical sagacity versus physical strength. Cf. Eccl. 9[14. 15] 7[19] Pr. 20[18] 24[3–6]. *Scales* is lit. *ascends* (Joel 2[7]). In second cl. lit. *stronghold of its confidence;* the Heb. has *strength*, which may be understood as = *stronghold*, or the text may be changed (by the addition of one letter).* — **23.** Single sentence, ternary. Lit. *he who guards* etc. *guards himself* (lit. *his soul*) *from troubles.* Cautiousness in speech is

---

* On the ancient Semitic methods of defending and attacking cities see Nowack, *Arch.*, §§ 71. 72; Billerbeck, *Der Untergang Nineveh's* (in *Beitr. z. Assyriol.*, iii.).

inculcated, as in 13^3 18^{21}. The troubles referred to are probably
social and legal difficulties into which imprudent talk brings one,
especially in a community in which there are gossips and professional informers (Eccl. 10^{20}) ; the reference is hardly to distress
of conscience (De.).

24. Definition of scoffer.

> Scoffer is the name of the proud, arrogant man,
> Him who acts with insolent pride.

Single sentence, ternary. The syntactical construction is not perfectly clear. The Heb. is lit. : *proud, arrogant, scoffer is his
name, acting in insolence of pride.* We cannot well translate " he
who acts with insolent pride is proud and arrogant and is called a
scoffer " (Reuss), or " the proud and haughty man, scorner is his
name, he worketh etc." (RV.), since this would be defining *proud*
by *pride*. The couplet must rather be taken as a definition of the
term *scoffer;* in that case it and 24^8 are the only examples of
formal definition in the Book. If this interpretation be correct. it
appears to point to the existence of a precise, philosophical form
of instruction in the schools, and to the distinct recognition of a
class of arrogant disregarders of moral law, both of which facts
suit the time when the Jews came under Greek influence. The
term rendered *proud* occurs only here in Pr., and is not found in
any preëxilian writing ; from such passages as Mal. 3^{15} ψ 119^{51} we
should infer that it was sometimes a designation of those Jews
who were faithless to the national law. The corresponding substantive occurs in 11^2 13^{10}, where it = *haughtiness* in the ordinary
individual sense. *Arrogant* (found elsewhere only in Hab. 2^5)
must here be a synonym of *proud. Insolence* is lit. *outbreak*, used
of anger and pride. On *scoffer* see note on 1^{22}. The definition
given in the couplet appears to include all persons who acted with
bold disregard of moral and religious law. The word does not
mean " freethinker " in the modern speculative sense (De.) — it
is conduct with which Pr. deals — nor (to judge from the general
tone of Proverbs) can it designate merely national enemies or
apostate Jews (as in the Psalms) ; it is simply " insolently wicked,"
one who scoffs not at belief, but at law.

25. Sloth kills.

> The desire of the sluggard slays him,
> For his hands refuse to labor.

Single sentence, ternary. The sluggard's *desire* is for ease, and this kills him, since his indolence prevents his acquiring food and clothing and other necessaries of life. For *desire* see 10^{24} 13^{19} Nu. 11^4 Job 33^{20}; the word has a wider sense than *appetite*. Cf. 19^{24} 24^{34}.

26. Text and meaning uncertain. Lit.: *All the day he desires desire, but the righteous gives and withholds not.* The second cl. apparently refers to the good man's kindness to the poor (cf. Mt. 5^{42}), but with this the first cl. stands in no relation, and in itself yields no sense. The repetition of the word *desire* points to the preceding v., and the clause (read *all day long he desires*) may be merely a variant of, or a gloss on, v.^{25a}. The meaning of the couplet is by some * taken to be : people are all the time wishing and begging, but the righteous man, so far from asking for himself, is always ready to give to others ; but the Heb. does not permit this interpretation. — No satisfactory emendation has been proposed. Grk.: *the wicked man desires . . . bad desires,* which gives no antithesis to second cl.; Bickell : *all day long there is request on request,* which fails to say who they are that request. The substitution of *diligent* for *righteous* in second cl. gives an improbable statement. The clauses appear to be dislocated. The first, by a violent emendation, may be read : *the sluggard desires and has not,* with antithesis as in 13^4, and a new couplet might be formed on the second clause.

27-29. The wicked man's methods and perils.

> 27. The sacrifice of the wicked is (in itself) an abomination —
> How much more when it is brought as atonement for crime !
> 28. A false witness will perish,
>   .   .   .   .   .   .
> 29. A wicked man hardens his face,
>   An upright man considers his acts.

27. Climax, ternary. The first cl. occurs in 15^8, with the addition *to Yahweh*, which ought perhaps to be inserted here, though

---

* De. Bick. *al.*

it is naturally taken for granted. The proverb declares (as Am. 5^{21-24} Isa. 1^{11-17}) that sacrifice without righteousness is displeasing to God. A bad man's offering, even in the ordinary performance of ritual commands (vows, passover etc.), is abhorrent; how much more when, offered without repentance, it is meant merely to relieve one from the consequences of evil-doing! Sacrifices were prescribed, in the law, for sins of inadvertence (Lev. 4) and for certain cases of fraud (Lev. 5 6^{1-7} [Heb. ch. 5]), but not for more serious crimes, such as murder and adultery; but it is not improbable that in the popular view an offering atoned for any offence (see ψ 50^{16-21}). The suggestion is that this superstitious and immoral conception of the power of sacrifice existed among the Jews of the writer's time. The case of genuine repentance is not considered; the *wicked* man is regarded as one who is given over to sin. — *As atonement for crime* (RV. marg.) is lit. *in crime*, that is, "in the case of a crime." The word here rendered *crime* means originally *plan*, but appears to be used in OT. always in a bad sense (10^{23} 24^{9}), often of unchastity (Ez. 16^{43} 22^{9} $23^{21 \ al.}$ Lev. 18^{17}).* — This seems to be the most probable understanding of the expression, the meaning of which is, however, doubtful. Grk.: *wickedly* (or, *unlawfully*), = "with evil design" (RV.: with a wicked mind); the "wicked design" is naturally to secure safety for the offerer, hardly to do harm to others. We know regrettably little of the customs and ideas of sacrifice of the later Jewish period. — **28.** The first cl. is nearly identical with first cl. in $19^{5. 9}$; there the false witness is punished, here he *perishes*, either by course of law (cf. Dt. 19^{19}), or by divine intervention. — The second cl. is obscure, lit. *a man who hears* (lit. *a man hearing*) *shall* (or, *will*) *speak for ever*. The expression *a man who hears* yields, in this connection, no good sense. It cannot mean *one who hears God* (Saad.) or *is obedient to the law of God* (Rashi), for such predicates are elsewhere either expressed ($1^{8. 33}$ $15^{31 \ al.}$) or clearly suggested by the context ($1^{5} \ al.$ Ez. 2^{5}). In 1 K. 3^{9} the *hearing mind* which Solomon asks for, in order that he may judge the people, is a mind which attentively considers, and in this sense the term is here understood by some interpreters †;

---

* In Job 17^{11} the text is doubtful; see Budde, *Hiob.*   † Saad. Ew. De. *al.*

but there the context clearly indicates the nature of the hearing, here there is no such indication; *a hearing man* is a strange phrase by which to express the conception *a man who carefully listens* (and so is able to give trustworthy testimony).—The predicate is not less obscure. To *speak for ever* is something which would not be naturally said of (or desired for) any man, good or bad, in a court of law or elsewhere. Delitzsch interprets it to mean "will never need to be silent," or, preferably, "what he says will stand" (RV. *shall speak unchallenged*), but these meanings are not contained in the words. Instead of *for ever* we may perhaps render *to victory* (or, *glory*) *; but this rendering is obscure and unnatural. Wildeboer connects this term with the preceding, and suggests the translation: *a man who is known as trustworthy may speak*, but the interpretations *known* and *trustworthy* are both lexicographically improbable. Graetz changes the text and reads: *a man of truth will be remembered for ever*, in which *truth* stands in satisfactory contrast with *false*, but *remembered for ever* seems to be too large a reward for the *man of truth*, if, as the connection would suggest, he is simply a "true witness"; cf. 10⁷, where such a reward is assigned to the *just*, the man of general probity. We expect a statement equivalent to "a true witness will be established."—In default of a satisfactory interpretation or emendation the clause is better left untranslated.—

29. Antithetic, ternary. On "hardening the face" see note on 7¹³. Here the expression (lit. *shows boldness in his face*) refers to the impudence with which a bad man deports himself toward facts and persons; he unblushingly maintains what suits him, without regard to truth. On the other hand, the *upright* or virtuous man, anxious to do right, carefully *considers* his *ways* (= *conduct, acts*). *Considers* is the reading of the Heb. margin (and of the Grk.); the text has *establishes*, which Reuss prefers, finding thus the admirable antithesis: "a bad man fixes his face, a good man his deeds" (cf. 4²⁶); so RV.: *ordereth his ways*. On the other hand, the marginal reading offers a better antithesis to the picture of effrontery which appears to be given in the first clause. On *establish* see note on 4²⁶, on *consider* notes on 2⁵ 14¹⁵.

---

* Aq. Sym. Theod. *will advance to victory;* Lat. *will speak victory.*

30, 31. Divine sovereignty.

> 30. There is no wisdom nor understanding
> Nor counsel against Yahweh.
> 31. The horse is prepared for the day of battle,
> But to Yahweh belongs the victory.

30. Single sentence, binary. In the second line the preposition may mean *over against, in comparison with,* or *against.* The two meanings give the same general sense for the couplet; the second meaning appears to be favored by v.[31]: "no human wisdom can avail against Yahweh." A similar thought is found in Job $5^{12.\,13}$, cf. Jer. 9^{23}. The three nouns of the subject are practically synonyms,* *counsel* involving "capacity for giving advice"; see notes on $1^2\ 2^2\ 1^{25}\ 8^{14}$.—**31.** Antithetic, ternary-binary. Victory in battle, the couplet says, is decided by God, in spite of human arrangements. A similar thought, from a national point of view, is found in $\psi\ 33^{17}\ 76^{6(7)}\ 124$; here the point of view is universal. *Victory* is *deliverance* from enemies; see 11^{14} (*safety*). *Prepared = set, harnessed.*— The *horse* is here spoken of as a usual (and apparently as a legitimate) feature in an army. The early Hebrews in Canaan, being mostly mountaineers, did not employ horses in war, and the use of them, as characteristic of foreigners, was not favored by the prophets; see Hos. 1^7 Dt. 17^{16} Zech. 9^{10} *al.* Horses were imported from Egypt by Solomon (1 K. 10^{28}).†

---

22. In 號 מִכְסֶה the suff. ה is written without Mappiq, and quiesces in the preceding vowel, the object being to secure a fuller vowel sound at the end of the couplet; for a list of occurrences of *He raphatum* in OT. see Böttcher, *Lehrb.* § 418. On the Segol under כ see Ges.[26] § 29 *m.*—𝕲 interprets the suff. as = οἱ ἀσεβεῖς; 𝕿 omits the suff., perh. by error of copyist.—**23.** Sing. צרה is given in Kenn. 30. 253, Bibl. Soncin., Brixiens., 𝕲𝕾𝕿.—**24.** On יהר see Ges. *Thes.* and De.'s note; the stem is probably יהר, with which היר is allied (cf. Arab.); the Aram. Vrss. render it by מרח, a stem (found also in Arab.) with a related sense.—**26.** 𝕾𝕿 = 號; 𝕷 in ª *concupiscit et desiderat;* Bi. האוה האוה. 號 האוה seems to be scribal repetition out of the preceding word.—On the unexpressed subj. see Ew. § 294, Ges.[26] § 144.—**27.** יהוה is

---

* Immanuel, cited by Delitzsch, interprets the first of theology, the second of worldly science, the third of politics; but no such distinction exists in the Hebrew terms.

† On Assyrian war-horses cf. Rawlinson, *Anc. Mon.* i. 414-427. The horse appears to be native in Central Asia.

read or supplied after חעבה (חעבה) in 𝔊 and 𝔖ᴴ, and is added by Dys. Reuss,
Kamp. — 𝔐 אף כי is inexactly represented in 𝔊 by καὶ γάρ; in the other
Vrss., including 𝔖ᴴ, אף is neglected. — **28.** 𝔐 שֶׁמֵע; 𝔊 ὑπήκοος, for ἐπήκοος.
— 𝔐 לָנֶצַח; 𝔊 φυλασσόμενος, = לִנְצֹר (Capp.), or possibly free rendering of 𝔐
(Baumg.); 𝔖ᴴ has נטר; 𝔖𝔗 rightly ; 𝔏 victoriam ; ΑΣΘ εἰς νῖκος. — Gr. ואיש
יזכר לנצח אמת.— The Heb. noun נצח appears to represent two stems: one
= shine (Syr. Arab.), whence glory, victory, clearness (of voice), purity
(of heart), and hence perh. מְנַצֵּה; the other = endure, whence continuance
(לנצח forever). Cf. Orelli, Syn., pp. 95 ff. — **29.** K יָכֵן is given in the great
mass of Heb. MSS., and in ΑΣ𝔖𝔗𝔏; Q יבן is found in 𝔊𝔄r, and about 50
Heb. MSS. — K דרכיו; Q דרכי.— **30.** 𝔐 יהוה; 𝔊ᴮ ᵃˡ. τὸν ἀσεβῆ (in some
cursives κυρίου); ἀσεβῆ is perh. error for εὐσεβῆ, perh. (Baumg.) represents
לבנֶר יהוה to him who is unfaithful to Yahweh (see ψ 73¹⁶); possibly the Heb.
expression was written בגר י (= כ׳ יהוה), and the י was overlooked by the
Grk. scribe.

XXII. 1, 2. Value of reputation. Mutual relations of rich and poor.

1. A good name is rather to be chosen than great riches,
   To be well thought of is better than silver and gold.
2. The rich and the poor stand side by side,
   Yahweh is the maker of them all.

1. Synonymous, ternary, or quaternary-ternary. The Heb. has
simply *name*, = " repute, standing," here involving the predicate
good, as in Gen. 6⁴, *men of* (military) *reputation*, Job 30⁸ *a name-
less race* (God-forsaken, without social standing), Eccl. 7¹ (good)
repute is better than oil, BS. 41¹² *be careful of thy* (good) *name*.
To be well thought of (lit. *favor*) is to have kindly appreciation,
good reception from others, to be *persona grata*; and, from the
parallelism, *name* is the estimation in which one is held by others,
during life, and after death. On *favor* see notes on 1⁹ 13¹⁵, cf.
Eccl. 9¹¹. A good reputation, the proverb appears to say, is valuable for the advantage it brings, respect, influence, material prosperity. Or, the sense may be the larger one that good repute,
involving high intellectual and moral character, is a more precious
possession than material wealth. The first interpretation is perhaps supported by the term *favor*. — RV. *loving* (lit. *good*) *favor*
is improbable ; *good* is not a proper epithet of *favor* (in which it
is implied), and does not so occur elsewhere in OT. See note
on 1⁹. — **2.** Single sentence with suggested antithesis, ternary.

Stand side by side is lit. *meet one another.* The meaning is: There are social differences among men — but all men, as creatures of God, have their rights, and their mutual obligations of respect and kindness. This conception of human equality, having its roots in the old Hebrew life, and recognized by the Prophets, is more definitely expressed in the later gnomic literature, which looks at men apart from accidents of birth and station. Cf. Job 34[19] BS. 11[14]; Frank. refers to Syriac Menander 66.

3–5. Sagacity, piety.

> 3. A prudent man sees danger and hides himself,
> Simpletons go on and are mulcted.
> 4. The reward of humility (and) of the fear of Yahweh
> Is riches and honor and life.
> 5. ‹Traps and› snares are in the path of the lawless,
> He who has regard to himself avoids them.

3. Antithetic, quaternary-ternary. The couplet occurs again in 27[12]. On *prudent* = " observant, sagacious," see notes on 12[16] 1[4]. *Danger* is lit. *evil,* anything which is a source of injury, financial, physical, or moral. *Simpleton,* a favorite term in Pr., occurs elsewhere only in Pss. (three times) and Ez. (once) ; it expresses lack of good sense, and is not properly represented by Eng. " simple " ; see note on 1[4]. *Mulcted* or *subjected to fine* (Ex. 21[22] Dt. 22[19] Am. 2[8] 2 C. 36[3]) here = *suffer injury* or *are punished* in general, but the legal coloring may be retained in the translation ; see 17[26] 21[11]. — The *prudent* man here is not a sneak or a coldblooded and selfish person, but simply a man of forethought and acuteness. — Grk., first cl. : *an intelligent man, seeing a bad man severely punished, is himself instructed* — a sense good in itself (cf. 21[11]), but not that of the Hebrew. — **4.** Single sentence, ternary or quaternary-ternary. The *and* of first cl. is not in the Heb., but should probably be inserted. The cl. may be rendered : *the reward of humility is the fear of Yahweh,*[*] but humility, in such a connection, is substantially identical with the fear of God, or if a relation of sequence be supposed, it is rather the fear that precedes. — The combination of the two terms is, however, somewhat strange. They might be taken as in apposition (Now.) : *humility* (which is) *the fear of*

---

[*] De. Wild.

Yahweh, in which case *humility* would have the religious sense, and would = *piety;* the sage must then be supposed to be guarding against the non-religious interpretation of the term — "humility," he would say, "provided it be the fear of Yahweh, is rewarded"; this construction, however, seems hardly natural, for elsewhere (15^{33} 18^{12}) honor is declared to be the reward of non-religious humility. The term *humility* may, however, be a gloss explaining *fear of Yahweh*. Or, the couplet may be based on 15^{33}, combining in one clause the two subjects there standing in two clauses (see note on 15^{33}) ; in that case *humility* may here be understood as non-religious. Cf. the similar expression in ψ $45^{4(5)}$. For *humility* see 15^{33} 18^{12}, and cf. ψ $18^{35(36)}$ (= 2 Sam. 22^{36}). — The general meaning of the text is clear : reward follows humility and piety. On the nature of the reward see notes on $3^{2. 16}$. —

5. Single sentence, with implied antithesis, quaternary. On *lawless* (= *crooked*) see notes on 2^{15} 11^{20}. *He who has regard to* (lit. *keeps*) *himself* (lit. *his soul*) takes care to *avoid* (lit. *be far from*) the dangers of the lawless life. Instead of *traps* the Heb. reading is *thorns*, an expression which, in the connection, is hardly appropriate ; if the word be correct, the reference may be to hedges, which bar the way of the vagrant. It is better to emend to a term synonymous with *snares* (see Job 18^9). *Snares* are set for trespassers. — Dyserinck reads : *snares are hidden in the path* etc., which gives a good sense.

6. Education forms the man.

> Train up a child in the way he is to go,
> And even when he is old he will not depart from it.

Single sentence (condition and consequence), ternary, or quaternary-ternary. *Train up = give instruction, experience. In the way he is to go*, lit. *according to his way*, that is, not exactly " in the path of industry and piety " * (which would require *in the right way*), nor " according to the bodily and mental development of the child " † (which does not agree with second cl.), but " in accordance with the manner of life to which he is destined," ‡ the implication being that the manner of life will not be morally bad; but

---

* Ew. AV. RV.   † Saad. De.   ‡ Now. Zöck Wild.

the point on which stress is laid is the power of education. Frank. renders: *train a child in the beginning of his way, then* etc.; but the translation *in the beginning* is without authority. The couplet reflects the opinion of a community in which the precise training of children was recognized as possible and obligatory.

7–9. Thrift, improbity, liberality.

7. The rich rules over the poor,
And the borrower is slave to the lender.
8. He who sows iniquity will reap calamity,
And ‹ the produce of his work › will come to naught.
9. The kindly man will be blessed
Because he gives bread to the poor.

7. Synonymous, ternary. Cf. 11^{29} 12^{24} 17^{2}. The couplet states a natural social law; the reference appears to be not to legal control, but to the state of dependence consequent on poverty and borrowing; this is expressed by the strong term *slave*, which is probably not to be taken literally. According to the old Heb. law a man might sell himself or his children into slavery (Ex. 21^{2-7} Neh. 5^{5}), or the creditor might sell the debtor (Am. 2^{6} 2 K. 4^{1}); how long this law continued in force is uncertain, but the parallelism in our couplet suggests the more general sense for the term *slave*. —**8.** Synonymous, ternary. *Iniquity* = moral badness in general (Hos. 10^{13}); see the similar term in 29^{27}.—The term (*āwen*) here rendered *calamity* (= *trouble*) commonly means *iniquity* (so in 6^{12} 10^{29} 21^{15} *al.*), sometimes *idolatry* or *false god* (as in *Beth-aven*, Hosea's contemptuous name for Bethel, Hos. 4^{15}), here the result of wickedness (as in 12^{21}).—In second line the Heb. has: *and the sceptre of his insolence* (or, *the rod of his wrath*) *will* (or, *shall*) *fail* (= *pass away*), the reference being apparently to the tyranny of bad and powerful men *; the interpretation *the rod of his punishment* (= the wrath that falls on him) *shall come to pass* (be fulfilled) † is improbable. Grätz, with change of text: *will destroy him*. The expression of the Heb. is, however, unnatural (whether *rod* be taken as emblem of rule or as instrument of punishment), and offers no good antithesis to first clause. The emendation above adopted ‡ (*work* being tilling) preserves the figure

* De. RV. † Schult. Ew. ‡ Frank.

of first line, and furnishes a precise antithesis. On the doctrine
see notes on 1^{32} 2^{22} etc. — **9.** Single sentence, ternary. *Kindly* is
lit. *good of eye;* the opposite, *evil of eye*, occurs in 23^6 28^{22}. *Eye*
here = look, expression; there is no immediate connection with
the idea in the magical "evil eye." — *Blessed*, by God, immediately or through natural laws, and by men; see 10^6 11^{26}. *Bread*,
lit. *of his bread*. Cf. 14^{21} 19^{17} 31^{20} BS. 7^{32} WS. 7^{23}.

10. Insulting words stir up strife.

> Expel the scoffer, and discord vanishes,
> And strife and insult cease.

Synonymous (second cl. = predicate of first cl.), quaternary-ternary. On *scoffer* see note on 1^{22}. *Strife* is lit. *decision* or *judgment*, then a *lawsuit*, here, from the connection, any quarrelling
or contention, = *discord*. *Insult*, lit. *disgrace* (3^{35} 9^7), here substantially the talk that tends to inflict disgrace. — The Grk., reading second cl. differently : *for, when he sits in a council* (συνεδρίῳ),
he insults (or, *dishonors*) *everybody*. The reference in the Heb.
is probably not specially to proceedings in courts of law. Cf. 17^{14}
20^3.

11. Defective text. The Heb. reads : *He who loves purity of
heart* (or, *the pure of heart*) *the grace of his lips the king is his
friend*, which is syntactically defective. A slight change of text
may give the sense : *he who loves* etc., *on whose lips is grace, the
king* etc.* ; this is intelligible, and the combination of ethical and
intellectual qualities (purity and eloquence), though not usual
(see $12^{19. 20}$ 14^{35} 15^{22} 16^{10} 18^4 $20^{8. 28}$ 25^5 $29^{4. 14}$ ψ $45^{2(3)}$ Eccl. 10^{22})
occurs in 16^{13}. Ewald : *he who loves with pure heart*, which the
Heb. does not allow. Lat. (followed by RV.), emending by the
insertion of a Preposition : *he who loves* etc., *for the grace* etc.,
which introduces an inconsequence in saying that, if a man is
morally pure, then he is loved not for this purity, but for his graciousness of speech. Grk. : *the Lord loves holy hearts*. Delitzsch
mentions a Jewish interpretation which, in second cl., translates :
his friend is a king, that is, the friend of an honorable and culti-

---

* Rashi, Luther (who takes *king* to be = God), De. Reuss *al.*

vated man is as fortunate and happy as a king — which, as De.
remarks, is a beautiful, but improbable, exegesis. — If resort be
had to conjectural emendation, we may suppose either that there
is a contrast between God and king, or that *king* is the subj. of
the whole couplet.   In the first case we may read : *God loves the
pure in heart, grace of lips pleases the king* (so Wild.) ; such a
contrast occurs nowhere else, and is not probable.   In the second
case the reading will be : *the king loves the pure in heart, and
grace of lips is his delight* (so substantially Rashi and Luther), and
this seems to offer the most probable sense (see 16^{13}).

12. Text and translation doubtful.   Lit. : *The eyes of Yahweh
guard knowledge, but he overthrows the words of the wicked.*   The
text of first cl. cannot be correct for several reasons.   The verb
can here (as predicate of *the eyes of Yahweh*) mean only *guard*
(not *obey*), and cannot be followed by the abstract term *knowledge*, nor does OT. usage permit the interpretation of this term as
= *him who has knowledge* * ; and the verb is not an appropriate
predicate of *the eyes of Yahweh*, which are said elsewhere to " rest
upon, be directed toward," but never to " guard, protect."   For
this latter reason the emendation (Ew.) *knowers of knowledge* is
unsatisfactory.   Somewhat better Grätz : *the eyes of Yahweh are
on those who keep* (= *observe, obey,* or, *preserve*) *knowledge ;* the
verb, in the sense *obey*, is elsewhere followed by a concrete noun,
as *law* (28^7 ψ 119^{34}) or *precepts* (ψ 119^{56}) ; in the sense *preserve,
guard*, it is followed by *sagacity* (3^{21}), which is a quality of
the mind, and *instruction* (4^{13}), which is concrete, and it is, in
any case, doubtful whether such technical philosophical terms
would be employed in a theocratic couplet.   Frank. interprets :
Yahweh possesses (all) *knowledge, and* etc., but the verb does
not mean *possess*, and this rendering offers no good antithesis
or synthesis of the two lines.   As the ordinary antithesis to
wicked is a term = *upright*, we may perhaps read : *the eyes of
Yahweh are on the righteous ;* cf. ψ $34^{15(16)}$ 101^6.   The expression
" the eyes are on " carries, in OT., an implication of benevolence.
— On *overthrows* and *wicked* (*faithless*) see notes on 13^6 2^{22}, and
cf. 21^{12}.

---

* Saad. De. Zöck. RV. *al.*

13–15. Sloth, adultery, folly.

13. The sluggard says: There is a lion without,
On the street I shall be slain.
14. The mouth of the adulteress is a deep pit,
He with whom Yahweh is angry will fall thereinto.
15. Folly is bound to the mind of a child,
But the rod of correction will remove it.

13. Continuous, with synonymous predicates, quaternary-ternary. Humorous sarcasm: to suppose that there was a lion on the street (Heb. *streets* or *open places*) was absurd, but any excuse would do for one who was determined not to stir from his place. In the Heb. the danger in second cl. is from the lion, in the Grk. from human murderers (*there are murderers in the streets*); see the parallel 26^{13}. On the sluggard see $6^{6.9}$ 10^{26} 13^4 15^{19} 19^{24} 20^4 21^{25} 24^{30} $26^{13.14.15.16}$. — **14.** Continuous, ternary. *Adulteress* (plu. in the Heb.) is lit. *strange woman*, on which see note on 2^{16}. *Mouth* is a reference to her seductive speech. — Except in this couplet and its parallel 23^{27} the term here rendered *strange woman* in RV. occurs in Pr. only in chs. 1–9 (2^{16} $5^{3.20}$ 6^{24} 7^5), and Ewald would therefore here read *harlot*. But a reference to this vice in the present section is not improbable, if the final revision of the Book be put in the Greek period.* — In second cl. De. has *cursed of God*, and RV. *abhorred of the Lord*, both possible, but the ordinary sense of the Heb. term, *angry*, is more appropriate. — **15.** Continuous, ternary. Children, the proverb says, are morally immature, and the rod is the best discipline for them; see 13^{24} $23^{13.14}$ 29^{15}. The fool is to be similarly treated (10^{13} 26^3). Corporal chastisement of children was probably universal in antiquity (so in Egypt, Greece, and Rome — Plato commends moral training, *Laws* v., p. 729). — The affirmation of the couplet is general, and is not to be put as conditional: "if folly is bound . . . then the rod" etc. — Cf. Menander, *Monost* 422 : *he who is not flogged is not educated.†*

---

* Another word for *adulteress* (lit. *strange woman*) occurs five times in chs. 1–9 (2^{16} $5^{10.20}$ 6^{24} 7^5), once (23^{27}) in the rest of the Book; still another is found once (in a gloss, 30^{20}). The term for *harlot* is found twice in chs. 1–9 (6^{26} 7^{10}), and twice in the rest of the Book (23^{27} 29^8).

† See Becker, *Char.*, Exc. to Sc. I., *Gallus*, Exc. II. to Sc. I., and, for Egypt, the maxims of Ptahhetep and Dauf.

16. Lit.: *He who oppresses the poor, to bring increase to him, he who gives to the rich, only to loss.* Interpretations have varied according as the couplet has been taken as a single sentence or as antithetic, and according as the *him* of first cl. has been referred to *he* or to *the poor*, and the *loss* of second cl. to *he* or to *the rich*. Hence a great number of forced translations.* Possibly, following 28[8. 27] (cf. 11[24]), the *oppresses* should be changed to *gives to: he who gives to the poor it is gain to him, he who gives to the rich it is only loss;* we should then have a double contrast, between *poor* and *rich*, and between *gain* and *loss*, and the couplet would be a commendation of benevolence and a condemnation of bribery and servility. Gifts were made to the rich not out of love, but to secure their favor. — Cf. 14[31] 19[17] 28[3].

XXII. 1. After 𝕳 שֵׁם an adj. = *good* is inserted by 𝕲𝕿𝕃 Bi., not by 𝕾; the adj. is probably not original — the usage permits, and the rhythm rather favors, its omission. — 𝕳 טֹב is not a proper epithet of חֵן, and must be taken as predicate. — **2.** Gr., referring to 29[13], supposes that there is a lacuna before עֹשֵׂ. The statement "Y. enlightens (or protects) them all" would be appropriate; but 𝕳 gives a good sense. — **3.** K יסתר, Q נסתר; between the two there is little choice — the time is present, the Impf. with ו would follow the general rule of sequence, with ו would isolate the act as inchoate, the Perf. would be parallel to ראה. — **4.** Before יראת insert ו. — עֵנָוה occurs outside of Pr. only in Zeph. 2[3] (where it is parallel to צדק), 2 Sam. 22[36], = ψ 18[36] (where it is an attribute of God), and ψ 45[5]; in the last passage it apparently forms a compound with צדק, but the text is doubtful (see Wellh. in *SBOT.*, and cf. Cheyne, *Psalms* and *Psalter*). Here it is unnecessary, probably a gloss. — **5.** 𝕳 צִנִּים; 𝕲 τρίβολοι *thorns* or *thistles;* 𝕃 *arma* (taking צנה as = *shield*); 𝕾𝕿 נשבא *snares*, = צִמִּים (Job 18[9]), which is the better reading; Gr. Ven. ἄκανθαι. The sense *thorns* for 𝕳 may perh. be inferred from צֵנֹת, Am. 4[2], parallel to סִירֹת דוּגה *fishhooks;* masc. plu. צִנִּם occurs elsewhere only in Job 5[5], where the text appears to be corrupt (cf. Budde, *Hiob*). — Dys. צִפֻּנם (*snares are hidden*), which is appropriate and should perh. be adopted, though צנם gives a more satisfactory parallelism in first line. — **6.** The couplet is wanting in 𝕲[BAN], found in 23. 109. 147. *al.*, and in 𝕾[H], where it is ascribed to Θ. — The stem חנך in OT. = *dedicate* (a building, Dt. 20[5] 1 K. 8[63] ψ 30[1] Dan. 3[2]) and, only here, *train.* In Arab., in the sense *give training, experience, sound judgment* (cf. Eth. *understand*), the verb is a denom. from חֵנֶך (Heb. חֵך *palate*); this sense may be supposed to come from taking the palate as the seat of taste, first physical and then intellectual (so Ges. *Thes.*), or from the guidance of an animal by a bridle in the mouth,

---

* See the Anc. Vrss. Saad. Luth. Ew. Hi. De. Reuss, Str. Wild. RV. *al.*

or from the rubbing of children's palates (with dates, etc.) as an act of initiation into full membership in the clan; this last appears best to account for the two senses of the verb in Heb. — The ל before נער may result from the meaning of the verb *give initiation* or *training* (to the child); otherwise it must be regarded as an Aramaism. — 担 מִמֶּנָּה is omitted by Bi. as having no antecedent; but it refers naturally to דַּרְכִּי. — 8. 担 שבט עברתו; for עֵ 𝔊 has ἔργων, = עבדתו (so Wild.); Frank., better: שבר עבדתו. 担 יִכְלֶה; Gr. יָכַלֵּהוּ. — 10. 𝔊 read בַּת רָן — 11. Read either אֹהֵב יהוה טְהָר לֵב וּמֵחַנַּן שְׂפָתָיו רָעֵהוּ, or, with transposition, אהב מלך טהר לב והן שפתים רצני. 𝔖 in ᵇ: *and he* (God) *loves* (= חֹנֵן) *the lips of those who love* (= רֵעֵי) *the king*. — 12. Ew. יֵרֵעַ; Gr. עַל נֹצְרֵי דֵּ; Hi. רעה for דעה. Read either עֵינֵי יהוה עַל יֹדְעֵי דֵּ (which, however, does not offer a good contrast to דברֵי בגר), or עֵינֵי יֵ בַּצַּדִּקִם. — 14. 担 זרות; Gr. זרה. — 16. 担 עֹשֵׁק; read perh. נֹתֵן, though this is graphically not easy.

III. SECOND COLLECTION OF APHORISMS
(XXII. 17–XXIV. 34).

This collection consists of two parts, 22^{17}–24^{22}, and 24^{23-34}, the second being an appendix to the first.   The collection is marked off from the preceding (10^1–22^{16}) by the introduction of the author (22^{17-21}) and by the title prefixed by the continuator (24^{23}). It differs also in tone and structure from the preceding collection : it is in the form of an address to the pupil (who is called the *son*), it is intimate, argumentative, descriptive, and it is arranged in strophes instead of couplets.   In the two last points it approaches Ben-Sira.   The moral and religious content is the same as that of the rest of the Book.   On the date see the Introduction.

XXII. 17–21. The author's introduction.

The person of the author of 22^{17}–24^{22} is unknown; he is probably not the same with the author of 1^7–9^{18}, the structure and material being very different in the two sections.   This introduction differs also from that (1^{1-6}) which is prefixed to the whole Book — it is more personal in tone, and less lapidary in style. The author speaks as a sage who has composed or collected a body of maxims which he regards as of high importance.

The text is doubtful ; the Greek form differs considerably from the Hebrew.

The Hebrew reads :

17. Incline thine ear, and hear the words of the wise,
    And apply thy mind to my knowledge.
18. For it is pleasant that thou keep them in thy mind,
    That they be ready on thy lips.
19. That thy trust may be in Yahweh
    I instruct thee to-day, thee also;
20. Did I not formerly (?) write for thee
    In plans and knowledge,
21. To cause thee to know the truth of words of truth,
    To return answer, truth, to him who sends thee?

17, 18. The expression *the wise* seems to be a marginal title (as in 24²³) which has got into the text; read *my words*. The description of *keep them* by *pleasant* is improbable; this term properly describes *knowledge* (so the verb in 2¹⁰), but "keeping" is rather characterized as wise or beneficial (2¹⁻¹¹ 3²¹·²² *al.*). The Grk. has in 17ᵇ: *apply thy mind that thou mayest know that they are good*, but the proper object of "know" is "instruction" (1² 4¹). Ewald, better: *apply thy heart to knowledge, because it is pleasant.* — *Be ready* is lit. *be fixed, established,* = ready for use. — **19, 20.** By the *to-day thee also* of the Heb. the sage appears to intimate that he had taught other persons at a former time, but he does not further explain this. In the *formerly* (?) there would be a reference to former instruction given to the pupil here addressed; the Heb. word may be a fragment of the common expression for *formerly* (lit. *yesterday and the day before*). This rendering is, in any case, improbable, for the reason that it introduces a strange contrast between the instruction now given to teach trust in Yahweh, and that formerly given to impart the capacity of answering (v.²¹). — The Heb. margin, instead of this word, has a term meaning *officers* (2 Sam. 23⁸ 2 K. 7² 9²⁵ Ez. 23¹⁵), which by most interpreters, from Saadia on,* is taken as = *noble* (or, *excellent*) *sayings*, a rendering which is without authority in Heb. usage, and cannot be called probable. Delitzsch, in support of it, refers to the *noble things* of 8⁶ (which is probably an error of text), to the *royal law* of Jas. 2⁸, and to Plato's μέρη ἡγεμόνες (*Tim.* 91 *e*), = "governing powers of the soul"; but neither of these references is in point, since the terms "royal" and "governing" are epithets of the nouns "law" and "parts," while here the word *officers* stands alone and undefined, and the designation of a maxim simply as a "captain" (or, "officer") is unexampled and unnatural. — In some Anc. Vrss.† the word is rendered *triply* (which Rashi explains as referring to the Law, the Prophets, and the Hagiographa), by Luther, freely, *manifoldly*. This rendering (which may perhaps be taken as = *repeatedly*) is intelligible in the Grk. translation (*do thou transcribe them triply for thyself*), but not in the Hebrew. — **21.** In the

---

* AV. Mich. De. Reuss, RV. Kamp. *al.*   † Grk. Syr. Targ. Lat.

Hebrew the first *truth* is superfluous, probably a gloss. Similarly
truth has been repeated, by scribal error, in second cl. — The
expression *to him who sends thee* (or, in some texts, *to those who
send thee*) could only be understood to mean "to thy parent or
guardian, who has sent thee to school, and desires an account of
thy progress." A better sense is given by the Grk. reading *to
those who question thee.** The pupil, as sage, would be consulted
by many persons, and the proof of his maturity would be his
ability to answer questions concerning the conduct of life ; cf.
1 K. 10³ BS. 39⁹·¹⁰ WS. 8¹⁰⁻¹⁵.

The text of the passage has suffered greatly ; the following
translation is an attempt at a restoration of the original.

> 17. Lend thine ear and hear my words,
>   And give heed to learn right things,
> 18. So that thou mayest keep them in mind,
>   And they be ready on thy lips.
> 19. That thy trust may be in Yahweh
>   I teach thee my words.
> 20. I write(?) for thee . . .
>   That thy plans may be intelligent.
> 21. I teach thee words of truth,
>   That thou mayest answer him who questions thee.

On the omission of *the wise* see the note on this verse above. *To
learn*, lit. *to know* (v.¹⁷) is adopted from the Greek ; *right things*
is suggested by 23¹⁶. The form of v.¹⁹ᵇ is taken from 1²³. The
term *write* is suspicious, since elsewhere in the Book the instruction given by the sages is oral ; but cf. Eccl. 12¹⁰. The verb suggests a very late date for the final recension of our passage. For
the word omitted in v.²⁰ᵃ I can offer no emendation ; the connection suggests a word = " wise counsel or instruction " or " excellent things." In v.²⁰ᵇ *plans and knowledge* may be understood as
hendiadys, = *plans of knowledge ;* on *plans* see note on 1³¹ (RV.,
there, *devices*) ; we might perhaps render : *that thy counsels* (to
others) *may be intelligent.*

Notwithstanding the difficulties of the text, the general thought
of the paragraph is plain : the pupil is to devote himself to study,
in order that his religious life may be firmly established, and that

---

* So Saad. Rashi. Ew. De. Reuss. Now. Bick. Frank.

he may be able to give wise counsel to those who seek advice. The exhortation supposes a community in which study is valued and provided for: there are teachers and recognized bodies of truth — this is the Jewish reproduction of the Greek schools of philosophy.

XXII. 17, 18. 𝕳 חכמם, though given in the Vrss., appears to be a gloss, a marginal title, perhaps originally להכמם; cf. 24²³. 𝕲 has a doublet, one form (καὶ ἄκουε ἐμὸν λόγον) apparently omitting ה. Read דְּבָרַי.— 𝕳 לדעתי כי נעם; 𝕲 ἵνα γνῷς ὅτι καλοί εἰσιν; read לְרַעַת מֵישָׁרִם —𝕾𝕿 *because they are pleasant, keep them* etc.—Bi. inserts לְאִמְרִי at the beginning of v.¹⁷, and makes v.¹⁷· ¹⁸ triplets; but the triplet is rather to be avoided than sought in this Section.— **19, 20.** 𝕳 הים אף אתה yields no good sense; 𝕲 τὴν ὁδόν σου may be interpretation, the אף אתה being carried over (Jäger) to the next v. (καὶ σύ); yet the connection favors some such reading, perh. דְּבָרַי.— K שְׁלֹשִׁם, Q שָׁלִישִׁם; 𝕲 τρισσῶς; 𝕷 *tripliciter;* 𝕿(𝕾) עַל תלחא זמנן. The embarrassment of the Grk. translators and expounders is shown by the variety of readings in v.¹⁹· ²⁰, on which see H-P, Lag. In 𝕳 בקשֶצֶת we should perhaps write ל for ב.— In *Megil.* 7 a 𝕳 v.²⁰ᵃ is cited (against the proposal to canonize the Book of Esther) as showing that the three divisions of the Canon were already made up: *have I not written three* (and no more)? — **21.** 𝕳 להֹדִיעֲךָ; better, perhaps, הֹרִעֲתִּיךָ.— 𝕳 קְשְׁט is the gloss of an Aramaic-speaking scribe. 𝕲 omits ק, but expands the line by a second clause; 𝕾 appears to have read שׁקט *quiet* instead of ק' (Pink.), and to have followed 𝕲 freely in its insertion; 𝕮𝕷 insert ו between ק' and אמרי.— 𝕳 לְשֹׁלְחֶךָ, and so all Vrss. except 𝕲; 𝕲 τοῖς προβαλλο-μένοις σοι, for which Lag. reads τοῖς προβάλλουσί σοι, = לִשֹׁאלֶיךָ. Read sing. לְשֹׁאֲלֶה.

THE MAXIMS OF THE SECOND COLLECTION (22²²–24³⁴).

22, 23. Against oppression of the poor.

22. Rob not the poor because he is poor,
And oppress not the lowly in the gate.
23. For Yahweh will plead their cause,
And rob their robbers of life.

22. Synonymous, ternary. *Poor* (see 10¹⁵) and *lowly* (see 3³⁴) are here synonyms, both referring to physical poverty, which carries with it low social position and defencelessness (*because he is poor*). *Oppress,* = *crush,* = " rob of possessions." The *gate* is the place of dispensing justice; cf. 1²¹ 24⁷.— **23.** Synonymous, ternary. Cf. Ex. 22²¹⁻²⁴(²⁰⁻²³) 23⁶ Dt. 24¹⁴· ¹⁷. The word rendered *rob* (different from that of v.²²) occurs elsewhere only in Mal. 3⁸· ⁹

(where Wellhausen changes the text so as to read *cheat*) ; its exact meaning is not certain, but some such sense as "rob, cheat " is suggested by the connection.

24, 25. Against passionateness.

> 24. Consort not with a man given to anger,
>   And go not with a passionate man,
> 25. Lest thou learn his ways,
>   And bring destruction on thyself.

24. Synonymous, ternary. *Consort not with* (or, *be not friendly with*) = *go not with*. Cf. 15$^{1.8}$. — **25.** Single sentence, binary-ternary. *Learn* (= *accustom thyself to*), a late, poetic word ; the stem is found elsewhere only in the causative form, = *teach* (Job 15^5 33^{33} 35^{11}). — *Ways* is the reading of the Heb. margin ; the text has *way*. — *Destruction* is lit. *a snare*, which is explained by some * as = *danger*, but the suggestion in the word is rather *death;* see 12^{13} 13^{14} 14^{27} 29^6. Anger is denounced not as immoral, but as injurious ; the obvious implication, however, is that it is morally bad. The destruction (or, danger) comes through the violation of human law, which the sage doubtless regards as also divine law. Cf. BS. 8$^{15. 16}$. — Bickell (v.$^{24b. 25a}$) : *and be not friendly with a passionate man, lest thou get in his way*, that is, the destruction comes from his passionate violence (see BS. *ubi sup.*) — but the translation is lexicographically doubtful.

26, 27. Against going security.

> 26. Be not of those who pledge themselves,
>   Of those who are surety for debts.
> 27. If thou have not wherewith to pay,
>   Thy bed will be taken from under thee.

26. Synonymous, binary. Similar cautions in 6^1 11^{15} 17^{18} 20^{16}. *Pledge themselves* is lit. *strike hands*. *Are surety for debts*, lit. *bind* (or, *pledge*) *themselves for* (other persons') *loans.*— **27.** Single sentence, ternary (or, binary-ternary). Heb. : *why should one* (or, *he*) *take thy bed* etc.? the *why* is scribal repetition (ditto-gram) ; the question would be appropriate only if the first cl.

---

* Ew. Reuss.

were omitted. On the legal right of the creditor to seize the debtor's bed see notes on the couplets cited above (on v.[26]).

28. Rights of property.

> Remove not the ancient landmark
> Which thy fathers set up.

Partially synonymous (second cl. explains predicate of first cl.), ternary. The couplet is substantially identical with part of Dt. 19[14]. As citizenship and a share in the protection of the tribal or national deity were regarded, among ancient peoples, as dependent on possession of land, boundaries were treated as sacred, and were placed under the protection of deities (Zeus Horios, Terminus etc.). The land of the poor was often encroached on by the rich and the powerful (1 K. 21[19] Hos. 5[10] Is. 5[8] Dt. 27[17] Job 24[2]). The antiquity of a boundary-line (= *landmark*) gave it special sacredness. Cf. note on 15[25], and see 23[10], which is a variation of this couplet. — Bickell omits the couplet as a shortened form of 23[10], with a gloss (the second cl.) on *ancient* taken from Dt. 19[14] (in which the Grk. has *thy fathers* instead of Heb. *they of old*). It is true that we expect a strophe of two couplets here, as above, and there is, perhaps, some derangement in the Heb. text.

29. Praise of business capacity.

> Seest thou a man skilful in business?
> Before kings he shall stand,
> Not stand before obscure men.

The triplet form, unusual in Pr., perhaps indicates the loss of a line. *Skilful*, as in Ezr. 7[6] ψ 45[1(2)]; the Heb. word may also be rendered *quick*, *swift*, and so, perhaps, *diligent* (RV.), but the suggestion is rather of readiness and skill. *Stand before = enter the service of. Obscure;* RV. *mean.*

---

23. On the meaning of קבע cf. Ges. *Thes.* and Lag. In Arab. the stem = *hide*, in Aram. *fix firmly.* Possibly we should read עקב; in Mal. 3[8. 9] 𝕲 has ἐπτέρνισε, = עקב. 𝔖𝕿 פרע *take revenge;* 𝕃 *configet* (= *transfix*). — **27.** The interrog. in ᵇ is not given by 𝕲𝔖𝕿. In 𝔐 למה the לם seems to be dittogram of preceding לם (in לשלם). — **29.** 𝔐 אׁש חָזִיתָ; 𝕲 ὁρατικὸν ἄνδρα, = אׁש חזות (Jäg.). — Bi. makes a couplet of ᵃ by inserting הבנה after אׁש.

XXIII. 1, 2. Good manners at a king's table. — The quatrain is a single sentence, ternary.

> 1. When thou sittest to eat with a ruler,
>   Consider well who is before thee,
> 2. And put a knife to thy throat,
>   If thou be a man of great appetite.

If one be in danger of excess in eating, one must be severely cautious — anything like voracity will excite the contempt, and perhaps the hostility, of the ruler.* — " To put a knife to the throat " is said by Fleischer to be a proverbial expression for self-restraint; one, as it were, threatens to kill one's self if one misbehaves. — In v.^{2b} we may render : *if thou have a great appetite* (on this particular occasion); the moral is the same. In v.^{1b} lit. : *consider him who* etc. The rendering *what is before thee* (= the dishes) is possible — it would enjoin a wise choice of food — but is less probable than the other; it is the ruler that the guest must have in mind. To this interpretation it may be objected that to describe the ruler as being " in the presence " of his guest is unseemly — rather the expression should be : *consider in whose presence thou art* (so Frank.) ; yet see Gen. 18^{22}, where it is said (in the correct text) : *and Yahweh was still standing before Abraham.* The modern courtliness of expression appears not to have been the rule in the OT. times. — Ewald : *thou wilt put a knife to thy throat* (= wilt bring ruin on thyself) *if thou give free rein to desire* (that is, if the avaricious ruler perceive that thou too art avaricious) ; but this does not so well accord with the place (the dinner-table). — Cf. BS. 31$^{12-18}$.

In the Heb. follows, as v.^{3}, the couplet :

> Do not desire his dainties,
> Seeing it is bread of deceit.

This appears to be out of place, since the point in the preceding quatrain is control of appetite, and not treachery or insincerity on the part of the king. The first cl. is identical with second cl. of v.^{6}, where it is appropriate, and whence it may by mistake have

---

* Cf. Prisse Papyrus, Sect. 2 (translated by Griffith, in *Lib. of the World's Best Lit.*, Vol. 13), and Malan.

got to this place (so Bickell). The second cl. also is misplaced — the sing. *it* does not accord with the plu. *dainties*. Bickell places it after first cl. of v.[8]. — *Bread of deceit* is food offered with deceitful purpose. Cf. *Pirke Aboth*, 2, 3 : "be cautious in intercourse with the powerful ; they are friendly only so long as they can use men for their own interests."

4, 5. Against anxiety for wealth.

    4. Toil not to make thyself rich,
       From such a ‹ purpose › desist,
    5. For ‹ riches › makes itself wings
       As an eagle that heavenward flies.

4. Synonymous, binary. First clause : "make not wearisome effort (= take no pains) to become rich," that is, it is not worth the trouble. The second cl. is lit. *from thy wisdom* (or *understanding*, or *intelligence*) *desist* (RV. *cease from thine own wisdom*), which appears to say that the man holds it wise to get riches ; this is a singular form of expression, and is certainly not the point of the couplet. Some such term as *purpose* must be understood. —**5.** The Heb. text is in disorder : lit. *shall thine eye fly to* (or, *on*) *it, and it is gone* (lit. *is not*) ? (or, Heb. marg., *make thine eye fly to it* etc.), *for it assuredly makes itself wings* etc., in which the "flying of the eye" is an impossible expression, and the *it* has no antecedent. The first *fly* appears to be a scribal insertion from the nearly identical form (*flies*) at the end ; the expression *thine eye (is) on it, and it is gone* is a gloss on the couplet (describing the fleeting character of riches) — cf. Job 7[8] ; the *assuredly* is miswriting of the word for *riches*. The couplet, thus restored, expresses simply and effectively the reason why one should not be anxious to be rich. The rendering of RV. : *wilt thou set thine eyes upon that which is not?* is not permitted by the Heb. ; see RV. margin, where the correct translation is given.

6–8[a], 3[b]. The niggardly (or, churlish) host.

    6. Eat not the bread of a niggard,
       And desire not his dainties.
    7 *a*. (?) For as he deals with himself,
    7 *b*. So he deals with thee (?).

7 *c*. " Eat and drink," he says,
7 *d*. But his heart is not with thee.
8 *a*. The morsel thou eatest thou must spit out,
3 *b*. For it is bread of deceit.

6. Synonymous, ternary-binary. *Niggard* is lit. *a man of evil eye*, illnatured, ungenerous, inhospitable ; the expression occurs in OT. only here and in 28²² (cf. 22⁹) ; see in *Pirke Aboth* 5, 13 four classes of the " evil-eyed." The *eye* represents the look with which one regards men, and *evil* (or, *bad*) is simply the opposite of good and kind. In our couplet either *niggard* or *churl* suits the connection. — **7**. The Heb. of the first couplet (which has apparently lost some word or words) hardly admits of a satisfactory translation. The renderings : *as he reckons within himself* (lit. *in his soul*), *so is he* (RV.) ; *as one who reckons* etc. (De. Reuss) ; *as he had decided* etc. (Saad.) ; *after he has reckoned in his* (*niggardly*) *soul, then he says to thee* etc. (Frank.) give no natural sense, and do not connect themselves with the context ; to describe the churl simply as a calculating person, looking after his own interest, is not what we expect, nor would this be a natural way of expressing that idea. Moreover the translation *reckon* (derived from the later Jewish usage) is open to doubt. Bickell emends so as to read : *for selfish and calculating is he in soul, but with his lips not so is he*, in which the two adjectives are both doubtful. Possibly : *for not as he is with his lips, so is he in his soul ;* or, *for kindness is on his lips, but in his soul he is not so ;* or, as the verse is rendered above : " he deals stingily with thee, as with himself." — **8**. According to a possible rendering, the sage, continuing the injunction (after *eat not*), bids the guest *spit out*, as something offensive, any *morsel* (= any small bit) which he may have eaten ; but it is probably better to translate by *thou must* (or, *wilt*) *spit out* (or, *vomit up*) the disgusting morsel which offends the taste or turns the stomach — the verb will then describe simply the result of the eating. — As second cl. the Heb. has : *and thou wilt lose thy pleasant words*, a statement which has only a farfetched relation to the preceding context (it would mean that the guest had thrown away his agreeable conversation or his thanks on the host), but connects itself naturally with v.⁹, to which it should be transferred. What we here expect is a line describing the disgusting *morsel*, and this may perhaps be given by second cl. of v.[3] : *it is bread of deceit*, that is, not offered in true hospitality. — In any case the paragraph is a maxim of social intercourse, a caution against indiscriminate dining out. Cf. BS. 29[22-24].

9, 8[b]. Do not try to teach a fool.

> 9. Speak not to a fool,
>   For he will despise thy wise discourse,
> 8 *b*. And thou wilt throw away thy goodly words.

Single sentence, ternary. Lit. : *speak not in the ears of a fool*, that is, so that he can distinctly hear, not merely "speak in his hearing" (RV.) ; the expression "uncover the ear," = "reveal a secret" (1 Sam. 22[8]) is different. — Lit. *despise the wisdom of thy words*. On *fool* and *wisdom* see 1[22] 12[8]. — The suggestion * that 8[b] be attached to this couplet commends itself as good; the change makes a natural connection. Lit. : *thou wilt lose* (or, *ruin*) *thy goodly* (or, *pleasant*) *words;* the adj. *goodly* (Grk. *beautiful*, or *good*) occurs nowhere else as epithet of *words* — it appears to belong to the philosophical vocabulary (Grk. καλός), in which "beautiful" and "good" are synonyms.† — A line, necessary to form, with 8[b], a couplet, has perhaps been lost — something like "thou wilt weary thyself in vain." — Cf. 9[8] 26[4. 5] BS. 22[13].

10, 11. Respect the land of widows and orphans.

> 10. Remove not the landmark of ‹ the widow,›
>   Into the field of the orphan enter not;
> 11. For their redeemer is mighty,
>   He will plead their cause against thee.

10. Synonymous, ternary. Heb. : *the ancient landmark*, probably taken from 22[28] or Dt. 19[14]; the parallelism favors *widow* (the graphic difference is not great in Heb.) as natural correspondent to *orphan* ‡ ; for the collocation of the terms see Dt. 10[8] 14[29] *al.*

---

* Pinsker, *Babyl.-Hebr. Punktations-system*, p. 134.

† Such terms may have been introduced in imitation of Greek phraseology. The question whether there was such borrowing is discussed in recent works on Ecclesiastes (Tyler, Plumptre, Renan, Wright, Siegfried), and cf. Siegfried, in *Z. Wiss. Theol.*, 1875, Pfleiderer, *Heraclit*, Bois, *Phil. Judéo-Alex*.

‡ So Dys. Bi. Wild.

Jer. 7[6] Job 22[9] 24[3] *al.* ψ 146[9].— **11**. Single sentence, binary-ternary. *Redeemer* (or, *protector*) is the technical term *goel*, the
next of kin, whose duty it was, under the Hebrew law, to redeem
the lands of kinsfolk which had for any reason been alienated.
Here the supposition is that there is no human *goel*, in which case
God himself will act as protector. For the function of the *goel*
in regard to land see Lev. 25[25] (cf. Nu. 5[8]) Ruth 4[3. 4].— Cf. note
on 22[28].

XXIII. 1. 𝕳 אשר לפניך את; 𝕲 τὰ παρατιθέμενά σοι (and so 𝕾𝕿𝕷).—
2. 𝕳 בלעך. The ἁπ. λεγ. לע has been rendered by *throat* from Saad. on
(Rashi: *throat*, lit. *jaws*), which seems required by the ושמת שכן. The verb
has the sense *swallow* in Ob.[16], and in Aram. = *lap* (cf. Arab. ולע); the noun
in Aram. = *chin*, and is here rendered by 𝕿 *chin*, by 𝕾 *mouth*. It was
perhaps a general designation of the parts concerned in swallowing, with
different special applications in the various dialects. Lag.: *in thy longing*,
from stem לע = ולע (in Arab. *desire*), but this does not go well with the
preceding words.— **4.** 𝕳 להעשר; 𝕲 πλουσίῳ, = לעשר (Hitz.).— **5.** 𝕳 עשה;
read עשר.— K ועוף; read Q יעוף.— **7.** 𝕳 שער; 𝕲 τρίχα, = שער, and so 𝕾;
𝕿 הרע, = שער; 𝕷 *quoniam in similitudine arioli et coniectoris aestimat quod
ignorat*, apparently free rendering of 𝕳 taken as = "guess, predict." The
stem = in Aram. *estimate, reckon*, in Arab. *know*,[*] neither of which senses
suits here; the word is probably error of text. Frank. takes כמו as conjunction (after the Aram.), = *after*, and regards the words אכל ושתה as citation
placed between the subj. הוא and the verb יאמר; but this rendering of כמו is
without authority, the corresponding sense of כן, *then*, is equally doubtful, and
the interposition of a speech between subj. and verb is unexampled in Hebrew.
Bi. כם ושער; the sense he attributes to the former of these, *holding back*,
= *self-seeking*, is doubtful, and the occurrence together of two Aram. words,
otherwise unknown in OT., would be somewhat strange. Possibly we should
read: כמו יעשה בנפשו כן יעשה בך.— **9.** The noun שכל occurs, in preëxilic
writings, only in 1 S. 25[3]; it became a term of the gnomic literature.— V.[8b]
(properly added after v.[9]) is expanded by Bi. into a couplet by the insertion
of לריק עמלך after the first word; it would be rhythmically better to keep v.[8b]
as a line, and insert a second full line parallel to it.— **10.** 𝕳 עלם; read אלמנה.

12. Introductory exhortation.

Apply thy mind to instruction
And thine ear to words of knowledge.

---

[*] On the old-Arab. *poet* as = *seer, diviner*, cf. I. Goldziher, in *Trans. of Tenth
Internat. Congr. of Orientalists*.

Synonymous, ternary-binary. The appeal is similar to that in
22^{17} $23^{15.\ 16.\ 19.\ 26}$; it is intended to call special attention to what follows, and perhaps once introduced a longer collection of apho-
risms. See note on 1^2.

13, 14. Training of children.

13. Withhold not chastisement from the child;
    If thou beat him with the rod, he will not die.
14. Thou must beat him with the rod,
    And rescue him thus from Sheol.

Ternary. The two couplets are mutually identical in meaning,
perhaps independent variations on the same theme. *Chastisement* represents the same Heb. word as *instruction* in v.^{12}; the
connection indicates that it here means corporal correction or
instruction. The second cl. of v.^{14} reads lit.: *and deliver his life*
(lit. *soul*) *from Sheol*. The implication is that ill conduct brings
physical death, by human and divine law; from this fate the child
is saved by instruction, in which corporal chastisement is recognized as a universal and necessary means; see notes on 19^{18} 22^{15}.
On *death* and *Sheol* see notes on 2^{18} 1^{12}.

15, 16. Exhortation to the pupil.

15. My son, if thou be wise,
    I shall be glad;
16. I shall rejoice
    When thou speakest right things.

The quatrain is chiastic, the fourth line being parallel to the first,
the third to the second. The first couplet is ternary, the second,
as the text stands, binary-ternary, but a word may be lacking.—
The second cl. of v.^{15} has lit.: *I also*, here = "I, on my side"—
"wisdom for thee, gladness for me." The same contrast exists in
v.^{16}, though the word *also* is not there written.—In second cl. of
v.^{15} the subject is *my heart*, = *my mind*, = *myself;* in first cl. of
v.^{16} the subject is *my kidneys* (RV. *reins*), = *my mind*, = *myself*.
The Hebrews regarded both the heart and the kidneys (on
account of their physiological importance) as seats of intellectual,
moral, and religious life, and the two terms are in this respect
treated as synonyms (Jer. 11^{20} 17^{20} ψ 26^2); both are regarded also

as seats of physical life. Whether or not there was some specific
difference in the intellectual functions ascribed to them the statements of OT. do not indicate. — On *right things* see note on 1³.
— It does not appear why this hortatory address is inserted just
here. Possibly the section is a collection of fragments, and the
following quatrain, which this address introduces, is only a part of
a paragraph.

17, 18. Reward of fearing God.

> 17. Do not envy sinners,
>   But fear thou Yahweh always,
> 18. For there is a future,
>   And thy hope will not come to naught.

17. Antithetic, ternary. The second cl. reads in the Heb. : *but
in the fear of Yahweh all the day*, an incomplete sentence. The
line has been rendered : *but those who are in the fear of Y.* etc.
(Saad.), but the insertion of *those who are* is not allowable, and
the verb *envy*, in this construction, is always used in a bad sense.
This latter objection applies to the translation : *but on account of
the fear* etc., that is, = "seek after not sinners but the fear of
God"* ; this rendering is forced and contrary to usage. By
others† the Subst. Verb is supplied in second cl. : *but be thou in
the fear* etc. ; this also violates the usage of the language. A simple
change in the Heb. gives the reading : *but fear thou Yahweh* etc.
(cf. 24²¹), which follows naturally on first cl. — In first cl. lit. *let not
thy heart envy* etc. — **18.** The second cl. expands and explains first
cl. The introductory particle of the Heb. is a compound, lit. "for
if." The renderings *for surely* (RV.) and *rather* (Ew.) are syntactically impossible. It is better (with Saad.) to omit the *if*, which
may be scribal repetition from the preceding couplet. — The word
future (lit. *end*) may signify the last part of a man's life (5⁴·¹¹ 19²⁰
Job 8⁷ ψ 37³⁷) or of a certain period of time (Isa. 46¹⁰), or the result
or outcome of a thing or act (14¹²·¹³ 16²⁵) ; here the reference is
to the termination (RV. marg. *sequel*) and the outcome of the
righteous man's life, and the word nearly = *reward* (so RV.).
The outcome (= the *hope*) is long life and prosperity, as in 2²¹

---

* Schult. Hitz. De. Zöck. Wild. *al.*   † Grk. Lat. Ew. Reuss, Bi. RV.

$3^{7.8}$ $10^{27.28}$ 13^{29} 14^{32} (*contra*, of the wicked, 10^{28} 11^{7}), not the life
beyond the grave.   Grk. : *posterity.* — The form of first cl. is
somewhat strange ; everywhere else (except in the identical
phrase in 24^{14}) the term *end* is defined by some special word or
(Isa. 46^{10}) by the context, and here Grk. adds *for thee*.   Reuss,
not so well : *everything has an end at last;* this expresses resignation, but the connection suggests confidence.

19–21. Exhortation.   Warning against drunkenness and gluttony.

19.   Hearken, my son, and be wise,
       And walk in the path of ‹ prudence.›
20.   Be not thou among winebibbers,
       Among gluttonous eaters of flesh;
21.   For drunkard and glutton come to poverty,
       And drowsiness clothes one in rags.

19. Synonymous, ternary.   The second cl. is lit. : *make thy heart
walk* (= *guide thy heart*) *in the way;* on the verb of the Heb. see
notes on 4^{14} 9^6.   The *way*, according to this reading, is the path
of rectitude or wisdom ; cf. Jno. 14^6 and the Buddhist and Moslem
use of the term for the rule of life which leads to perfection and
happiness.   But the term does not occur elsewhere in Prov. in this
absolute (undefined) sense, and the text must be changed so as
to read a word (as *prudence* or *understanding*, cf. 9^6) parallel to
the *wise* of the first line. — **20.** Synonymous, ternary.   *Winebibbers* = "those who drink wine to excess " or "drunkards in wine."
Gluttonous eaters (one word in the Heb.), lit. "squanderers,
excessive consumers."   The *flesh* is not their own bodies, as if
drunkards were described as self-destroyers (Ges. Ew. *al.*), but
(as the parallelism shows) meat consumed at table. — **21.** Parallel, ternary.   *Drunkard*, the same word as in v.^{20} above (*bibber*,
without the *wine*). — The *drowsiness* (or, *sleepyheadedness*) is the
torpor which follows excessive eating and drinking.   Cf. *Pirk Ab.*
3, 3.

22–25. Value of parental instruction and approval. — V.^{23}

(which is wanting in the Grk.) belongs more naturally with v.^{19}.
Bickell omits v.^{23}, makes a quatrain of v.$^{22.24}$, and regards v.^{25} as an
appendix of the editor.   The paragraph interrupts the series of

injunctions relating to definite lines of conduct, and was probably
here inserted by a scribe or editor. It belongs more properly at
the beginning of the series, just after 22²¹.

> 22. Hearken to the father who begat thee,
>   And despise not ‹ the words of › thy mother.
> 23. Buy the truth, and sell it not,
>   Wisdom, instruction, and understanding.
> 24. The father of a righteous man will be glad,
>   The ‹ mother › of a wise son will rejoice.
> 25. Let thy father [] rejoice,
>   Let thy mother be glad!

22. Parallel, ternary. Lit. *thy father who* etc. The injunction
relates not to honoring parents, but to heeding their instruction.
Hence the Heb. of second cl., *despise not thy mother when* (or,
because) *she is old*, does not accord with first cl.; BS. 3¹³ exhorts
a son not to despise his father when the old man's intellect fails,
and we might suppose a similar reference to the aged and failing
mother here, but the question in the paragraph is one not of age,
but of instruction, and it seems better to change the text accordingly; cf. 1⁸.* — **23.** Synonymous, ternary. Cf. 4⁵·⁷ 15¹⁶. The
nouns are here substantially synonyms: *instruction* is training in
truth; understanding and *wisdom* are perception and practical
knowledge of *truth;* see notes on 3³ 1². — **24.** Parallel, ternary.
In second cl. the Heb. has *the begetter of a wise man*, but the parallelism and v.²⁵ suggest mention of the *mother*. — **25.** Parallel,
binary. In first cl. the Heb. has *thy father and thy mother*, but
as *mother* (lit. *she who bore thee*) stands properly in second cl. as
obvious parallel to the *father* of first cl., it should not be anticipated.

26. Exhortation (introductory to the two following paragraphs).

> Give heed, my son, to me,
> Let thine eyes take note of my ways.

Synonymous, ternary. The first cl. is lit. *my son, give me thy
heart*, that is, thy mind, thine attention (not thy affection, or, thy
spiritual devotion). As all other introductory exhortations in
this Section are by the sage, there is no ground for holding that

---

* With the expression *thy father who begat thee* cf. the phrase, frequent in the
Assyrian royal inscriptions, *my father, my begetter.*

the speaker here is Wisdom, and that she is contrasted with the harlot of v.[27], as the two characters are contrasted in ch. 9 * ; the exhortation in 7[24] also is by the sage (cf. 7[4]). — The reading *take note of* (= "watch, for the purpose of following") is that of the Heb. margin and of most Anc. Vrss. ; the Heb. text has *delight in* (so RV.), which gives a good sense, but the other reading is a common term in Pr. (3[1] 4[13] 6[20] *al.*), while *delight in* occurs elsewhere in the Book only once (3[12]), and then does not refer to instruction. For the sense *take note of* cf. Nah. 2[1(2)] : "keep an eye on the fortification, watch the way." See note on 22[12]. — The *ways* of the sage are those which he enjoins ; cf. 22[17-21].

27, 28. Warning against the harlot.

> 27. The harlot is a deep pit,
> The adulteress a narrow well.
> 28. Yea, she lies in wait like a robber,
> Many are they she ‹ plunders.›

27. Synonymous, ternary. *Adulteress*, lit. *strange woman;* see note on 2[16]. She is a married woman, in character a *harlot;* see 7[5. 10]. The two lines apparently introduce the two classes of unchaste women, the unmarried and the married ; but the same destructive character is ascribed to both. For *pit* (RV. *ditch*) see 22[14] Jer. 2[6] 18[20. 22]. *Well* (RV. *pit*) is here used in its literal sense, not figuratively as in 5[15] (cf. ψ 55[23(24)] 69[15(16)]). The narrowness of the well (or, pit) would make it harder to get out when one had fallen in. — The conjunction *for*, with which, in the Heb., the couplet begins, may introduce it as the ground of the exhortation of v.[26], or may be incorrect scribal insertion. — **28.** Parallel, ternary. *Yea* (= *also*) introduces an additional thought : she is not only a pit into which the unwary may fall, a passive danger, she is also an active danger, like a robber who attacks. This word for *robber* occurs only here in OT. ; the expression cannot be rendered *as for a prey* (RV. marg.). — The second cl. reads in the Heb. : *and the faithless among men she makes many* (RV. *increases*). *Faithless* may mean "unfaithful to the law of God" (2[22] 11[3. 6] 13[2. 15] 21[18] 22[12]), or, "untrustworthy" (25[19]) ; the second cl. might be rendered : *she increases, among*

---

* De. Now. Str. Wild.

men, the sinners, or, *she increases the sinners among men.* But
the parallelism suggests for second line a term similar to the
robber of first line, and a change of vowels gives *treacheries* (Jer.
12^1 Isa. 24^{16}), = *wickednesses* (cf. 22^{12}), instead of *faithless* (or,
sinners) ; the woman's treachery is that of a robber or plunderer.
Render : *plundering of men she practises largely,* or, as above,
many are they etc.

13. 𝔐 כי is omitted by Bi., but this seems unnecessary. — **17.** 𝔐 בירֹאת;
read אֵת יְרֹא. — **19.** The Piel אשר means not *guide,* or *set right* (in Isa. 1^{17} the
word is probably error of text), and דרך cannot be taken as = *right way,* or
absolutely *the way ;* we might perhaps read ישׁר *make right* (Frank., and,
apparently, 𝔊), but the resulting sentence is not quite natural, and the
parallelism suggests a term corresponding to חכם; read אשר בדרך בִּנָה. —
20, 21. 𝔊 συμβολαῖς (cf. 𝔏 *symbola* in v.^{21}), in its sense of *feasts* may
well = κρεῶν ἀγορασμοῖς, and may represent 𝔐 וללי *consumers.* The Grk.
term is adopted in the Talmud (סֻבְלָה), but it seems unnecessary to suppose,
with Lag., that it here renders בסֻבְלָיִן, scribal repetition of 𝔐 יין. — נבּסְכאי
נגשה is ἅπ. λεγ. — **22.** On זה as Rel. Pron. see the grammars. — 𝔐 כי זָקְנָה אֵמָּך
does not accord with the rest of the strophe, and the כי ד appears to be a gloss
which displaced the original word אמרי or דברי or מֵסָר. Bi.: זְקַן מִמָּך, but
v.$^{24.\ 25}$ make it probable that the reference to the *mother* should be retained
here. — **23.** The couplet should perhaps stand at the beginning of this strophe,
or it may be omitted. — **24.** Read Q יָגִיל גיל. — If masc. יֵלֶד be retained, then
Q יִשְׂמַח must be adopted (the connecting ו of K would here imply that יָגֵל is
repeated); but it seems better to preserve the antithesis of v.$^{22.\ 25}$, and read
יֹלֶדֶת and תִּשְׂמַח, in which the ת may perhaps account for the וי of K ישמח. —
25. Omit 𝔐 וְאִמֶּך. — **26.** K הרצנה; Q, better, תִּצֹּרְנָה. — **27.** 𝔐 שָׁחָה עֲמֻקָה (of
the harlot), which 𝔊 (cf. 22^{14}) renders by πίθος τετρημένος; the expression is
taken (Jäg.) from a Grk. proverb, which is cited by Erasmus (I. 10, 33) from
Aristotle (*Econ.* i. 6) — to get riches without being able to keep it is "to draw
water in a sieve and a perforated tub"; thus the ἀλλότριος οἶκος (𝔐 זֹנה) is
wasteful and destructive (see Lag.). — **28.** The ἅπ. λεγ. חֶתֶף is, from the
connection, a concrete noun, = *robber* (in form like מֶלֶך); the verb חתף
occurs once (Job 9^{12}). The stem is written with ת here and Job 9^{12}; elsewhere (Ju. 21^{21} ψ 10^9) written with ט, as in Aramaic. — 𝔐 בֹּגְדִים; read, from
the parallelism, בֶּגֶד, or בְּגָרָם (cf. Frank.).

29–35. Against drunkenness.

29. Who cries "woe"? who "alas"? who has strifes? who complaints?
Who has wounds without cause? who redness of eyes?

30. They who linger long over wine,
Who often taste mixed wine.

31. Look not on wine when it is red,
    When it sparkles in the cup.   [] *

32. At the end it bites like a snake,
    It pierces like an adder.

33. Thou wilt see strange things,
    Queer things thou wilt say.

34. Thou wilt be like one who is sleeping at sea,
    Like one asleep in a ‹ violent storm.›

35. "I have been struck, but I feel no pain,
    I have been beaten, I am not conscious of it.
    When shall I awake ‹ from my wine ›?
    I will seek it yet again."

29. General parallelism, quaternary (or, a quatrain). A lively description of the bodily effects of excess in wine. Instead of nouns the first line uses interjections — lit.: *who has oh ! who has alas !* The man quarrels over his cups, gets into difficulties, whence *complaints* (Job 10¹ 21⁴ 23² ψ 64¹⁽²⁾) ; in scuffles he is wounded (cf. Zech. 13⁶) *without cause,* that is, unnecessarily, for those slight and groundless differences that arise among drunken men ; his *eyes,* by their dulness or redness (cf. Gen. 49¹²), proclaim his dissipation, and indicate that he is not fit for work. — **30.** Synonymous, ternary, or binary-ternary. How *mixed wine* (lit. simply *mixture*) was prepared is not known, perhaps by adding spices ; cf. note on 20¹. — Lit. *go to try,* = *investigate, test, taste ;* the man is a devotee — he drinks continually. — **31.** Second line = predicate of first line, ternary. Description of wine when complete fermentation has taken place. The wine of Canaan seems to have been red ; cf. the expression "the blood of the grape " (Gen. 49¹¹), and Is. 63¹⁻³. — *Sparkles* is lit. *gives its gleam* (the term rendered *gleam* is the ordinary word for *eye*), that is, is full of life. — The Heb. adds : *it goes straight* (cf. Cant. 7⁹⁽¹⁰⁾) ; this does not accord well with the rest of the couplet, and appears, as the text stands, to be a gloss, explaining that wine in this state glides straight or smoothly down the throat ; the expression was perhaps here inserted from Canticles, and was possibly meant as contrast to v.³². Or, it may be original, in which case we should perhaps read : *At first it glides smoothly down, over the*

---

* The Heb. adds : *it goes straight* (or, *smoothly*).

lips and the palate, but at last it bites etc. We should thus have a quatrain instead of the couplet, v.[32], or the triplet, v.[31c. 32].— **32**. Synonymous, ternary-binary (the second line is perhaps defective). Lit.: *its end is: it bites* etc. The rendering *adder* is uncertain — the species of snake meant is not known (Jer. 8[17] Is. 11[8] 59[5]). — The precise signification of the verb in second line is not sure (it must be a synonym of *bites*) ; it has been rendered *stings*,* = *pierces*, and *poisons*.† The point of comparison is the deadly character of the result, but there may also be allusion to the silent, treacherous attack of the snake. — **33**. Synonymous, ternary. Lit.: *thine eyes will see . . . thy heart* (= *thou*) *will speak*. Description of the erratic fancies and fantastic talk of the drunken man — perhaps reference to delirium tremens. — The connection forbids the interpretation of *strange* (fem. plu. adj. in the Heb.) as = *strange women*. — On *queer* (= *distorted, topsy-turvy, false*) see note on 2[12]. — **34**. Synonymous, ternary. Description of the man's unsteady, whirling brain. In both lines we may render : *like one who sleeps*, or : *like one who lies down ;* both renderings represent the disturbed rest, the perturbation of thought, occasioned by the motion of the ship at sea ; the first seems to be favored by v.[35], in which the drunken man is awaking from sleep. — In the first line the Heb. is lit.: *in the midst of the sea*, which means not at the bottom of the sea (a place where men do not usually lie down), or on the surface of the water (on a plank, for example), but (as in Ez. 27[25. 26] 28[2. 8] Jon. 2[3(4)]) surrounded by water, on the high seas, at sea. — The text of the second line appears to be corrupt. Literally it reads : *and as one sleeping* (or, *lying*) *on the head . . ;* the word left untranslated (RV. *mast*) occurs only here in OT., and its meaning, if it be a real word, is unknown ; it is similar to the term for *line, rope*, but can hardly mean *mast* (which is a mere guess). Grk.: *and as a pilot in a heavy sea ;* Targ.: *as a sailor who is asleep in a ship ;* and so Frank.: *as a sleeping sailor in a storm*. A sailor, however, is precisely the person who sleeps well in rough weather, or, in general, at sea. It is simpler to adopt the expression *in a violent storm* (see Jon. 1[4]), which requires no great change in the

---

* De. RV. † Grk. Lat. Saad.

Hebrew. The couplet apparently describes the broken, unsound sleep of the reveller — his head is whirling, his mind is confused. There is no reference to the danger of drowning; the main reference is not to any danger, but to giddiness. — **35**. The first couplet is synonymous, binary; the second couplet is two sentences, and, as emended, ternary. The words of the drunken man as he is awaking from his debauch. He recollects that he was beaten in a quarrel, and congratulates himself that he feels no bad effects from the blows. The first couplet may also be rendered : *I was struck but I felt no pain, I was beaten but I did not know it*, with reference to his former happy state of insensibility ; but the soliloquy appears to describe his present feeling. — Hitzig (by a slight change of text) reads : *it* [the wine] *has smitten me . . . it has beaten me;* but, though wine is represented in 20¹ as a mocker and brawler, its sudden introduction here unannounced is not quite natural. His experience teaches him nothing — his only desire is to get back to his debauch. *When shall I awake ?* that is, I hope I shall soon recover full consciousness and strength ; not *if I awake*, which the Heb. does not permit. — The expression *from my wine* is not in the Heb., but seems to be required by the following *it*, which otherwise, in the translation here adopted, would have no antecedent (so Bickell) ; it also gives rhythmical symmetry to the couplet. If Hitzig's rendering be adopted, the insertion will not be grammatically necessary. — This paragraph, v.²⁹⁻³⁵, gives the fullest and liveliest description of drunkenness in OT. ; cf. Is. 28⁸⁻¹⁰, BS. 19². In its length and vividness it resembles certain paragraphs of chs. 1–9 (see chs. 5 and 7).

29. On the form of מִרְנָם see critical note on 6¹⁴. — 𝔐 חנם; 𝔊, here and Job 2⁸ 9¹⁷ 22⁶, διὰ κενῆς, but usually in Pr. δωρεάν; Lag. calls attention to the difference of usage in the two books. — The stem חכל = *dark;* cf. Ass. *akal* (in De. *Ass. Handwbch.*), Schult., Ges. *Thes.* BDB.; the reference appears to be to the dull red effect produced by excessive drinking of wine, perhaps, however, simply to the dulness of stupor. — **31.** K כֻּם; read Q כֹּם. — 𝔐 עין here hardly refers to the round bubbles, like pearls, on the surface of the wine (Ges. Fleisch.), for which, as De. remarks, the plur. would naturally be used (for a possible Ass. use in this sense see De. *Ass. Wbch.*). Since the eye is the determining feature of expression, the word is used in Heb. for the appearance of a thing, and so here, perhaps, from the connection, *sparkle, gleam* (or perhaps from the sparkle of the eye). — In 𝔐 יתהלך במישרים the Hith.

is somewhat strange (Cant. 7[10] has Qal). — **32.** אחרתו is defined by the pred. כנחש ישך. — For the stem פרש cf. Ass. *paruššu staff* (De.) Aram. פרש *ox-goad*, which appear to involve "piercing," cf. Schult. Ges. De. — **34.** וכשכב בראש חבל; 𝕲 καὶ ὥσπερ κυβερνήτης ἐν πολλῷ κλύδωνι, whence Frank.: וכחבל (or שכב ברעש (בשערה. A preferable reading is: וכשכב בסער גדל. — **35.** 𝕲: *when will it be morning, that I may go and seek those with whom I may associate*, the suff. having perhaps been understood (Schult.) to refer to the symposium; but such a reference would be too remote.

XXIV. 1, 2. Bad men are not proper objects of envy.

1. Do not envy bad men,
   Desire not to be with them,
2. For they meditate harm,
   And talk of mischief.

1. Synonymous, ternary. *Envy* = "be stirred up by, seek to emulate," attracted by their apparent success. *Bad men* is lit. *men of badness*, with special reference not to disposition, but to deeds. — **2.** Synonymous, ternary. Lit.: *their mind* (lit. *heart*) *meditates* and *their lips speak*. They plot evil, and will come to grief; cf. 1[15-19] 3[31. 32] 24[19] ψ 37[1. 2]. We have here again a resemblance to chs. 1–9. *Harm* is "spoliation, robbery" (21[7] Job 5[21. 22] Am. 3[10] Hab. 1[3]); the term *mischief* (properly "harmful deeds") occurs in Job 4[8] ψ 7[14(15)] Isa. 59[4] etc.

3, 4. Domestic utility of wisdom.

3. By wisdom a house is built,
   By intelligence it is established,
4. By knowledge its chambers are filled
   With all precious and goodly wealth.

The quatrain forms one sentence; the first couplet is synonymous, binary (or, ternary-binary), the second is a single clause, ternary. The three nouns *wisdom, intelligence* (see 1[2]), *knowledge* are synonyms, all expressing practical sagacity, without reference to moral and religious qualities. The *house* is here not the family, but the building; its erection and furnishing are, however, put as the sign of domestic permanence and prosperity. On *chambers* see 7[27] 18[8] 20[27], on *precious*, 1[13], on *goodly* (or, *pleasant*), 22[18] 23[8] ψ 16[6] Cant. 1[16]. Cf. 14[1]. — This quatrain probably does not give the antithesis to the preceding.

5, 6. Military value of wisdom.

> 5. A wise man is ‹better than a warrior,›
>   And he who has knowledge ‹than he who› has strength,
> 6. For war is conducted by wise guidance,
>   And victory lies in counsellors.

5. Synonymous, ternary. Heb.: *a wise man is in strength, and a man of knowledge strengthens might.* The second couplet, however, indicates that a contrast is intended between intellectual insight and bodily strength. — *Warrior,* lit. *mighty man.* — *Has strength,* lit. *strengthens might.* — **6.** Synonymous, ternary. Lit. *thou conductest* (or, *makest*) *war;* cf. 20[18]. — Lit. *safety is in the multitude of counsellors,* that is, in well-considered advice. On *wise guidance* or *planning* (= *wise counselling, steering*) see 1[5] 11[14] 12[5] 20[18] Job 37[12]; as the *guidance* is civil, political, and military, the terms " statesmanship " and " generalship " are too narrow. — An exacter parallelism is gained by writing *counsel* instead of *counsellors.* For *victory* see 21[31] Ju. 15[18] 1 Sam. 11[9] 2 K. 5[1] *al.* Cf. Eccl. 7[19] 9[13–16. 18a].

7. Text and meaning doubtful. Heb.: *Corals to the fool is wisdom, in the gate he opens not his mouth.* This reading of first cl.* gives no satisfactory sense. *Corals* (or, *pearls*) is taken as = " unattainable treasure," of which the fool can make no use ; but the term is elsewhere (Ez. 27[16] Job 28[18]) used in the sense of a thing esteemed as valuable, and the addition " unattainable " is farfetched. Moreover, elsewhere in Pr. (17[28] 18[6] *al.*) the fool is only too ready to open his mouth, and the one moment in his life when he may be called wise is when he closes his lips. On *gate* see note on 1[21]. — The first clause may also (by a slight change) be rendered : *wisdom is high to a fool,* which is held † to mean *too high,* = " unattainable " (identical in sense, therefore, with the preceding reading) ; this interpretation of the Heb. is doubtful, and, if it be accepted, the difficulty of second cl. remains. — Bickell : *If thou art silent in the presence of a fool, thou art wise, If thou hold thy peace, it is to thy credit; For a wise man refrains from strife, In the gate he opens not his mouth.* This reconstruc-

---

* Adopted by Rashi, De. Reuss, Now. Str.
† By Saad. Luth. Mich. Ew. RV. *al.*

tion is ingenious, but in 31^{23} it is an honor to the man that he is
known in the *gate*, the place of public deliberation. We expect a
quatrain, in which the loquacity of the fool is contrasted with the
reticence of the wise man; an exact restoration of the text is
hardly possible.

8, 9. Public opinion condemns the mischievous man.

> 8. He who is intent on mischief,
>   Men call him an intriguer.
> 9. Sin is folly's intrigue,
>   And a scoffer is offensive to men.

8. Single sentence, binary-ternary. Lit.: *he who devises to do
evil*, that is, harm to others. *Intriguer* (*schemer, plotter, trickster*)
is lit. *master of* (*evil*) *plans*. The term was perhaps a popular
epithet of scheming, mischief-making men. On *plans* see notes
on 1^4 12^2. The couplet gives a definition of a current term; cf.
21^{24}. — **9.** Synonymous, ternary. The translation given above
imitates the paronomasia of the Heb. *baal mezimmot* (*intriguer*)
and *zimmat* (*intrigue*). The latter word means "scheme, plan,"
good or bad; see notes on 10^{23} 21^{27}. The first cl. is lit.: *the plan
of folly is sin*, in which *plan* may be taken as subject, and folly
will then be defined as sin (so Lat. RV. *al.*); but, from the parallelism (second cl. is lit.: *an abomination to man is the scoffer*),
it is better to regard *sin* as subject,* it being thus defined as the
scheme of folly, and therefore despicable, just as a scoffer is despicable to men. On *scoffer* (here equivalent to "mischiefmaker")
see notes on 1^{22} 19^{25}. — *Offensive* = "that which produces loath-
ing"; see note on 3^{32}.

10. Text in bad condition. Heb.: *If thou art inert* (or, *slack*)
in the day of adversity, narrow is thy strength; or: *If thou art
inert, in the day of adversity thy strength will be narrow.* The
general idea is intelligible (an exhortation to work while there is
opportunity), but the wording and form are doubtful. *Strength*
may be understood in the sense of *substance, wealth* (as in 5^{10} Job
6^{22}): indolence brings poverty. But *narrow* (as Hitz. points out)
is not a proper epithet of *strength*, whether the term = *power* or

---

* So De. Reuss, Wild, *al.*

= *wealth;* cf., for the use of this adj., 23[27] Nu. 22[26] Is. 49[20] (in Isa. 59[19] Job 41[7] the text is probably to be changed). We might suppose a paronomasia: *in the day of straits* (Heb. *ṣārāh*) *strait* (Heb. *ṣar*) *is thy strength,* but it is doubtful whether the word would be thus used out of its proper sense. — Bickell: *Trust not in thy good fortune, And let not thy hands be slack; If thou be slack in the day of prosperity, In the day of straits thy strength will be strait.*

11, 12. Duty of rescuing those who are going to death. — It may be a question whether we should take these verses separately, or regard them as giving a couplet followed by a prose comment. The couplet reads:

> 11. Deliver those who are taken to death,
>   Save those who are tottering to slaughter.

Synonymous, ternary. The expressions *taken* and *tottering* appear to describe the gait of persons who are condemned, by the political or judicial authorities, to death. The reference may be to the ransom of prisoners of war, or to the rescue, by legal means, of innocent men who have been condemned by the tribunals. Perhaps some time of persecution of Jews is referred to (see WS. 2[10-20] 1 Mac. 1[30-37] Jos. *Ant.* 12. 4. 1; 12. 5. 4); or, the injunction may be a general one, suggested by the customs of corrupt and tyrannical governments. The vigorous character of the expressions (*death, slaughter*) makes it improbable that the reference is merely to the ordinary oppression of the poor by the rich, who deprive them of wealth, and thus of livelihood (= life). It is still more improbable that the couplet should refer to the holding back of those who, by vice or imprudence, are hastening to death. The verb rendered *save* is lit. *hold back;* elsewhere (as in 1 Sam. 25[39] ψ 19[13(14)]) it implies restraint of the man's voluntary effort, but the parallelism (*deliver*) here requires the sense *save,* as in Job 33[18] ψ 78[50].

V.[12] of the Heb., of which the English translation may be written stichometrically, reads (with one slight change):

> 12. if thou say: "‹ I › did not know this,"
>   He who weighs hearts, does he not perceive?

He who observes thy soul, does he not know?
And will he not requite every man according to his deed?

In first line the Heb. has : *we did not know this;* it is better, with the Grk., to write the sing., in accordance with the *thou* and *thy soul.* — The *this,* in this reading, may refer to the situation described in the preceding couplet; if a man plead ignorance of the situation, the answer is that he ought to have known. Or, the *this* may possibly (though not probably) refer to the obligation to help the suffering ; the man would then say : " I did not know my duty," but this would be an extreme case of ignorance. Cf. Tobit 1[16-20]. It is an objection to both these interpretations that the *this* has no expressed antecedent, since v.[11] does not state a fact, but only enjoins action in a supposed case. The Lat. rendering : *it is not in my power,* is, therefore, perhaps preferable. The man pleads inability — but this plea will be scrutinized by God. If this reading be adopted, the *it* may be regarded as referring to the duty enjoined in v.[11] ; or v.[12] may perhaps be taken as an independent exhortation. Bickell omits first and second lines, and thus makes a quatrain of v.[11. 12], in which there is no excuse and answer, but simply the statement (the interrogative particle being omitted) that God observes and rewards deeds of kindness. The first and second lines may have been inserted by a scribe who supposed that the third and fourth lines contained a rebuke of negligence. Or, the whole verse may be regarded as the annotation of a scribe or editor who wished to enforce the exhortation of v.[11]. — For the expression *weighs hearts* cf. 16[2] 21[2]. *Heart* and *soul* here = " inward being " (or, " thought "). On the fourth line cf. 12[14] 24[20] Jer. 25[14] 50[29] Job 34[11].

XXIV. 2. 𝔐 שׂר, or *plene* שׂור ; 𝔊 ψευδῆ, = שׁוא, with א for ר, a confusion which appears to suppose the old alphabet (Lag.); cf. 10[24] 19[28] 20[4] 24[15] 28[2]. — **5.** 𝔐 גְּבַר חכם בַּעֹז ; 𝔊 (followed by 𝔖𝔗) κρείσσων (= גִּבֹּר) σοφὸς ἰσχυροῦ. Read : גבר חכם טֹב מֵעֹז, or גְּבַר חכם מֵעֹז. Similarly, in ᵇ, for 𝔐 מְאַמֵּץ כֹּח, read מֵאַמֶּץ כֹּח (cf. Job 9[4]). — **7.** Bi.'s reconstruction is as follows : רָמֹת לֶאֱוִיל חכמַת הֶחֱרַשְׁתָּ לְהִתְאָרְחֶךָ כִי חכם ישֵׁב מֶרֶב בַּשַּׁעַר לֹא יִפְתַּח פֶּה. It is hardly probable that so much of the Heb. text would have fallen out. — **10.** Bickell : אֶל תִּבְטַח בְּרֹב. — **11.** For אִם as hortative particle cf. ψ 81[9] 139[19]. It was treated by 𝔊𝔖𝔏 as if = אל, is lacking in 𝔗, and may be omitted without detriment to the sense, and with advantage to the rhythm. — **12.** 𝔐 יְדָעֵנוּ ; 𝔊 οὐκ οἶδα, = לֹא ירעתי ; 𝔏 *vires non suppetunt,*

= ‫יכלנו‬ ‫לא‬, or better ‫ידי‬ ‫לאל‬ ‫אין‬, a reading which may be adopted. — 聃 ‫חכן‬;
𝔊 γίνωσκε, = ‫הבין‬ (Jäg.).

13, 14. Comparison of wisdom to honey. — The Heb. has
first an incomplete quatrain :

> 13. My son, eat honey, for it is good,
>   And honeycomb is sweet to thy taste.
> 14. So know wisdom (to be) to thy soul,
>   If thou find it.

To this is appended the remark : *and there is an end, and thy
hope will not be cut off.* This remark is hardly here appropriate ;
elsewhere in Pr. there is reference to the *end* only when there is
direct question of retribution ; see $5^{4.\ 11}$ $14^{12.\ 13}$ 16^{25} 19^{20} 20^{21} $23^{18.\ 32}$
24^{20} 25^8 29^{21}. The sentence seems to be here improperly inserted
from 23^{18}, where it is in place. — Note the difference of statement
in v.^{13} and 25^{16} ; for other references to *honey* and *honeycomb* see
5^3 16^{24}. The address *my son* should perhaps be omitted, and for
eat we might write *thou eatest*. *Taste* is lit. *palate.* — In v.^{14} we
expect the statement, in couplet form, that wisdom is sweet to the
soul. The expression *if thou find it* is suspicious ; a reference to
finding is natural in such passages as 3^{13} 8^{35} 25^{16}, but not here
where the sweetness of wisdom is the point. Comparing 2^{10} 16^{24}
we may surmise that the original form of the couplet was in substance :
> So knowledge will be pleasant to thee,
> And wisdom sweet to thy soul.

The general sense of the quatrain is clear, though the form is
doubtful.

15, 16. Caution against assailing good men.

> 15. Lie not in wait [] for the home of the just,
>   And assault not his dwelling-place.
> 16. For seven times the just man falls and rises,
>   But the wicked are overthrown by calamity.

15. Synonymous, binary, or ternary-binary. After *lie not in wait*
the Heb. inserts *O wicked man;* this is stylistically out of place
(since throughout this Section it is the pupil who is addressed
and warned against the wicked), mars the rhythm, and is proba-

bly a gloss. — *Home* is *abode* (3^{33} 21^{20}) ; *just* = *righteous ; assault* = *do violence to, violently assail, injure, devastate* (see 11^3 19^{26} 21^7 Am. 3^{10} Jer. 5^6 Job 5^{21}) ; *dwelling-place*, properly *couching-place*, the *lair* of animals (Is. 35^7 65^{10}), used of Israel when the nation is called a flock of sheep (Jer. 50^6), the verb also, ordinarily used of animals (Is. 11^6 ψ 104^{22}), sometimes referring poetically to men (Gen. 49^9 ψ 23^2). The injunction is against secret and open attempts on the homes of righteous men, and contemplates a period of violence, probably in a great city. — **16**. Antithetic, ternary, or quaternary-ternary. *Seven*, a round number (cf. Job 5^{19} Mt. $18^{21. 22}$) — the *righteous*, it is said, shall never be permanently cast down (cf. Mic. 7^8) ; the *wicked*, on the contrary, has no power to rise above misfortune — once down, he does not rise. The couplet probably refers not to the natural inspiriting power of integrity and the depressing effect of moral evil, but to divine retribution. — *Are overthrown*, lit. *are made to stumble*, or *do stumble*. Instead of *by calamity* we may render *in calamity*, that is, " in time of calamity."

17, 18. Against taking pleasure in the misfortunes of enemies.

> 17. At the fall of thine enemy rejoice not,
> At his overthrow do not exult,
> 18. Lest Yahweh see and be displeased,
> And turn his anger from him.

17. Synonymous, ternary. Lit. *at the falling of* and *at his being overthrown*. In second cl. lit. *let not thy heart exult*. The verbs *rejoice* and *exult* commonly signify the audible expression of joy ; the exultation may be generous (as in 5^{18} 23^{25}), or malicious (as here and in ψ 35^{19}). The injunction is negative (cf. Job 31^{29}), against exultation over enemies ; the positive side, sympathy with enemies (see ψ 35^{13-15} Mt. 5^{44}), is not expressed, but is perhaps involved. — **18**. Single sentence, ternary. The *turn his anger from him* (that is, from the enemy) is not to be understood as affirming that God will cease punishing a wicked man because another man is pleased at the punishment ; the full form of the expression is " turn from him to thee," and the stress is to be laid on the " to thee." " Thou," says the sage, " wilt then become the greater sinner, and Yahweh will be more concerned to punish thee than to punish him." — The motive here assigned — fear of Yahweh's displeasure — belongs to the ethical system of Proverbs. But this motive does not impair the dignity of the moral standard presented. Yahweh's displeasure is the expression of the moral ideal : it is one's duty, says the proverb, not to rejoice at the misfortunes of enemies. This duty is enforced by a reference to compensation, but it remains a duty.

19, 20. It is unreasonable to envy the wicked, seeing their end is unhappy.

> 19. Fret not thyself because of evil-doers,
>   Envy not the wicked;
> 20. For there will be no (happy) end for the bad man,
>   The lamp of the wicked will be put out.

Both couplets are synonymous ; the first is binary, the second ternary, or ternary-binary. Cf. $3^{31.\ 32}$ $23^{17.\ 18}$ 24^1 ψ $37^{1.\ 2.\ 7-9}$ 73. *Fret* = "be not angrily excited," that is, at the apparent prosperity of the wicked. On *end* see note on 23^{18}. Lit. : *there will be no end*, no outcome of life — that is, no good outcome. This pregnant use of the term is found only here and in 23^{18} (see note on 24^{14}) ; everywhere else it is defined. Thus it might be rendered *future* (Saad. *al.*), or *reward* (RV.) in this life. Grk. *posterity* (as in ψ 109^{13}) is, in this connection, less probable. — On the figure in v.^{20b} see notes on 13^9 20^{20}. — The problem of the quatrain is that of the Book of Job ; the practical moralists retained the old view, holding that it furnished the strongest incentive to well-doing that could be urged.

21, 22. Duty of obedience to constituted authorities. — Our Hebrew text reads :

> 21. Fear Yahweh, my son, and the king,
>   And with those who change have naught to do;
> 22. For suddenly arises their ruin,
>   And the destruction of them both who can know?

The address *my son*, because of its strange position and because it mars the rhythm of the Heb., is better omitted as scribal insertion. *Have naught to do* is lit. *mix* (or, *join*) *not thyself.* — *Who can know ?* = "comes suddenly, unexpectedly." — The expression

who change (intransitive) has been variously rendered : Schult.
RV. : *them that are given to change,* which can mean only *nova-
rum rerum avidi,* political agitators ; a slight modification of the
word gives the sense *changers* (transitive), wrongly interpreted
(by Hitzig *al.*) as = *revolutionists, insurrectionists;* Mich. *al.:*
those who are of a different mind, that is, those who do not fear
God and the king—a rendering lexicographically inexact ; Ewald :
the quarrelsome; Reuss : *the discontented;* Syr. Targ. : *fools;*
Lat. : *detractors.* — Grk. : *do not disobey either of them* (= *to
them both be not disobedient*). If in the expressions *their ruin* and
the destruction of them both the pronouns be understood as referring to *God* and *the king* (with the sense : "the ruin and destruction inflicted by them "), the Greek reading is satisfactory. If
the expressions in question mean "the ruin etc. which befall them,"
the reference must be to persons mentioned in the second line of
v.[21], and the reading *them both* is impossible (since the expression
cannot designate the two classes, those who fear Yahweh, and
those who fear the king). If the pronouns be taken as objective,
we may read :

> Fear thou God and the king,
> With the wicked (or, with fools) have naught to do;
> For on them falls sudden ruin,
> And destruction unforeseen.

If the pronouns be regarded as subjective, a natural reading will be :

> Fear thou God and the king,
> Anger not either of them;
> For the ruin they inflict is sudden,
> And the destruction they send unforeseen.

The general sense is the same in the two forms : obedience to
God as supreme religious authority, and to the king as supreme
civil authority, is enjoined (so 1 Pet. 1[17]) ; opposition to them by
wicked conduct will be punished with destruction. — *God,* as the
more familiar word, may be substituted for *Yahweh.* — The translation of v.[22b] : *the destruction of their years who can know ?* * is
unnatural — in OT. years (as = life) are said to be increased or
lengthened (9[11]), or diminished (10[27]), but never to be destroyed.

---

* Syr. Targ. De. RV. marg.

— The Grk. here inserts 30¹⁻¹⁴ of the Heb., giving an improbable order.

13, 14. The Vrss. substantially reproduce 𝔐. The pointing of the Energic Impv. רְעֵה (Cod. *Hillel*), instead of רְעֵה, is due (as in the Art. before חָ) to the following ה, to which the vowel is made to conform; see Strack, *Proleg.*, p. 19, and notes of De. B-D, Ginsburg. — **15.** Omit 𝔐 רשע, with Bi., as the gloss of a scribe who incorrectly assumed that the warning must be addressed to wicked men; the word is represented in all Vrss., but Σ has ἀσέβειαν, and 𝕷 *impietatem*. — **16.** 𝔐 שֶׁבַע, = *seven times*, as in ψ 119¹⁶⁴. — **17.** K plur. אויביך; Q, better, sing. — 𝔐 בִּכְשְׁלוֹ, as if abridged form of Nif.; better Qal בכשלו. — **18.** 𝔐 וְרַע is better understood as 3 s. m. Perf. with ו consecutive; the adj. would properly be followed by הוא; 𝔊 καὶ οὐκ ἀρέσει. — **19.** 𝔐 תִּתְחַר; 𝔊 χαῖρε, = הֲחַד (Lag.). — **21.** Omit 𝔐 בְּנִי. — 𝔐 שׁוֹנִים; 𝔖 (and 𝔗) שׁטיא *fools*, = "those whose intellect is changed, witless" (cf. Aram. שׁנא); 𝕷 *detractoribus*, = "disparagers," perh. = "those who change their attitude, opponents," perh. = "haters"; Venet. τοῖς μισοῦσι, = שׂנאים. — 𝔊, in ᵇ: καὶ μηθετέρῳ αὐτῶν ἀπειθήσῃς, = עַל שְׁנֵיהֶם אַל תִּתְעַבֵּר (Jäg.). — See De' Rossi on v.¹⁹. — **22.** 𝔐 שְׁנֵיהֶם gives no satisfactory sense. Ew.: שְׁנֵיהֶם; Bi.: שְׁנֹתָם *their idiocy*, taking שׁנה in the Aram. sense. שְׁנֵיהֶם is perhaps corrupted scribal repetition of the שְׁנִים of v.²¹; in that case we should add suff. to 𝔐 פֶּר, and make it parallel to אָדָם. — On the added couplets in 𝔊 see Ew., *Jahrb. d. Bibl. Wiss.*, xi. pp. 18 ff., Bi. Baumg.

APPENDIX TO THE PRECEDING COLLECTION. 24²³⁻²⁴.

This appendix was added by an editor, probably by him who collected 22¹⁷–24²², possibly by the general editor of the Book. It is introduced by the title:

23 *a*. These also are by the sages,

in which the *also* appears to allude to the similar title in 22¹⁷ (according to the emended text). The plur. *sages* points to the existence of a special class of wise men, who were oral teachers or writers. The utterances of these men formed a distinct body of thought, part of which is preserved in the Book of Proverbs, and other parts are given in Ben-Sira and Ecclesiastes. While it is not probable that all that they said has been edited, it is likely that we have in the various collections the gist of their thought. — The present group is part prose, part in defective rhythm; its contents nearly resemble in tone those of the preceding part of the Section.

23ᵇ–26. Judicial partiality. Honest words. — The mutual relations of the lines are doubtful. V.²³ᵇ may be retained as prose, or emended into rhythmical form; v.²⁵ may be connected with v.²⁴ or with v.²⁶. The verses read in the Heb. :

> 23 *b*. Partiality in judicial decisions is not good.
> 24. Who says to him who is in the wrong: "Thou art in the right";
>   Him men will execrate, and people curse.
> 25. But (or, and) they who reprove fare well,
>   On them rests the blessing of prosperity.
> 26. He does a friendly act
>   Who gives an honest answer.

Here v. ²³ᵇ is a prose sentence, a legal maxim; its thought is continued in v.²⁴ by the statement that the partisan judge is universally execrated. Bickell, changing the text of v.²³ᵇ and dividing second line of v.²⁴ into two parts, makes a quatrain : *he who is partial in judgment, who says* etc. The emendation is attractive, and should perhaps be adopted; if *he who is partial* had been corrupted into *to be partial*, a scribe would naturally add the words *not good;* it is, however, doubtful whether symmetry of poetical form can here be insisted on. — As the text stands, v.²⁵ appears to describe, as contrast to v.²⁴, the happiness of the upright judge, the *reprove* (or, *rebuke*) being taken as = "reprove the wrong, judge justly" (RV., interpreting, inserts *him*, as explicit reference to the *wicked man* of v.²⁴); the *blessing* (the *of prosperity* being omitted, as in the Grk.) will then stand over against the *curse* of v.²⁴. But the verb *reprove* is not elsewhere in Pr. used in the sense "judge justly"; v.²⁵ may be understood to refer to those who frankly rebuke wrong in general, and will then stand in close connection with v.²⁶. Bickell transposes v.²⁵·²⁶, reading : [*he who rebukes*] *is a true friend* etc., *and they who reprove* etc., making the quatrain relate to honest rebuke, and gaining a natural position for the *and* of v.²⁵ as a connective of the two couplets. The only important difference between the two interpretations of the paragraph lies in the sense given to *reprove.* — **23ᵇ.** Lit. *to have respect of persons,* to look (with partial eye) on a person; see Dt. 16¹⁹ (and 1¹⁷), from which this line is probably taken; it occurs again, in slightly modified form, in 28²¹. — **24.** On the technical forensic expressions of first line (usually

rendered *wicked* and *righteous*) see notes on 2²⁰·²². The line may
be translated: *he who says to the guilty: Thou art innocent.* —
Execrate (11²⁶ Job 3⁸) and *curse* (22¹⁴ 25²³) are synonyms (Nu.
23⁸, where RV., for the second, has *defy*). *Men* is lit. "nations,"
and *people* is "peoples"; for the meaning see 11²⁶ 14²⁸ 29²·¹⁸
ψ 94⁸; the plu. form, if it be genuine, must be understood to signify "all bodies of the people." — **25.** Lit. *and* (or, *but*) *to* (or,
with) *those who reprove it is well* (or, *pleasant*); for the last
expression see 2¹⁰ 9¹⁷ 2 Sam. 1²⁶. — Second line lit. *on them comes*
(or, *will come*) *blessing of good*, that is, not "good (or, rich) blessing," but a blessing which consists in good fortune (cf. ψ 21³⁽⁴⁾).
The tone of the verse in the Heb. form suits the good man rather
than the just judge; if *of prosperity* be omitted, it may be understood of the latter. — **26.** Lit. *he kisses the lips who returns honest*
(or, *pure, upright*) *words:* the first expression signifies not "he
wins love," but "he shows love," he is a true friend.* Straightforward, honest speech, says the verse, is a mark of true friendship.

27. Preparation for marriage.

> Set in order thy work without,
> Make it ready in the field;
> Then thou mayest (take a wife),
> And build thee up a house.

The first couplet is synonymous, ternary; the second appears to
be defective. *Without* and *in the field* refer to agricultural life;
see note on 3¹⁰, and cf. Mt. 9³⁷ 12¹. — The Heb. has lit. *afterwards then* (lit. *and*) *thou mayest build* — a construction in itself
intelligible and good, but the defective rhythm suggests that after
the adverb a verb has fallen out. Most expositors, from Rashi on,
see in the second couplet a reference to the setting up of a
domestic establishment (*house = household, family*, cf. Ru. 4¹¹),
and understand that some such expression as *take thee a wife* is

---

* This is the only place in OT. where there is explicit mention of kissing the
lips; there seems to be reference to it in Cant. 4¹¹ (interpreted by Cant. 5¹). In
the ancient world one kissed the hand, breast, knee, or foot of a superior, and the
cheek of a friend. Herodotus (1, 134) mentions kissing the lips as a custom of the
Persians. Possibly from them it came to the Jews.

to be supplied in the first line.   The verse enjoins providence:
"first acquire the means of supporting a family, then thou mayest
marry, and accomplish thy desire to build thee a house."   The
establishment of a family was a main ambition in Israelitish and
all ancient life.

28, 29. Against revenge.

> 28. Be not a witness against thy neighbor without ground,
>   And mislead not with thy lips.
> 29. Say not: "I will do to him as he did to me,
>   I will repay the man for his deed."

The quatrain has parallelism of form, but, like v.[12] above, is prosaic rather than poetical.   The supposed scene is a court of
law, as in 3[30]. — **28.** *Without ground* = "when he has given you
no ground for testifying against him" (see note on 3[30]) ; Grk. :
be not a false witness.   The expression is sometimes (by Reuss
al.) taken to mean : "when you are not legally required to testify,
but come forward, actuated by the spirit of revenge, as a voluntary witness " — a sense possible, but opposed by 3[30].   Elsewhere
falsity of testimony is expressed by words meaning *deceit* (so 6[19]
12[17] Ex. 20[16] *al.*), or, *wickedness* (19[28]), or, *malice* (ψ 35[11]), here
by the term *groundlessness.* — In the second line the literal reading is : *and dost thou mislead* (or, *befool*) etc.?   It is better, with
the Grk., to take the cl. as a prohibition.   For the sense *mislead*
see Jer. 20[7] Ez. 14[9]; in Pr. 1[10] 16[29] the verb means *entice.* —
29. Bickell omits one clause in first line, and writes: *say not: as
he did to me, so I will repay* etc.; but this is stylistically bad —
the omission of the expression *I will do to him* is hardly permitted by Heb. usage.   There is possibly a reference or allusion
to v.[12].   The Lat. makes the second line a general statement: *I
will repay every one* etc.; this is less probable than the reference
to the particular case. — The quatrain (especially v.[29]) is a modification of the old law of retaliation, as given in Ex. 21[23-25] Dt. 19[21]
Lev. 24[19. 20].   This regulation, it is true, was, in the later legislation, not a matter of private revenge, but a legal right, controlled
by judges; it was, however, based on the old principle of retaliation, and breathed its spirit.   It was gradually modified by the
advance of moral and refined feeling, and would be substantially

set aside by the principle announced in this quatrain; the sage here expresses the higher moral idea of his time.*

30–34. The sluggard.

30. I passed by the field of the sluggard,
    By the vineyard of the thriftless,

31. And lo, it was all overgrown with thistles,
    Its surface was covered with nettles,
    And its stone wall was broken down.

32. I beheld and reflected thereon,
    I saw and learned a lesson.

33. A little sleep, a little slumber,
    A little folding of the hands to rest;

34. And thy poverty will come as a ‹ highwayman,›
    And thy want as an armed man.

See notes on 6^{6-11}, to which this paragraph is parallel. The two passages accord literally in only one quatrain: $6^{10. 11} = 24^{33. 34}$; it is hardly necessary to attempt to bring them into closer similarity — the sages doubtless had many variations on the same text. — We expect quatrains here, but Bickell's method of gaining them (omitting part of v.^{31} and inserting 6^9 after v.^{32}) is somewhat violent. — **30.** Synonymous, ternary. A supposed or imaginary case; we may render: *a sluggard and an unthrifty* (or, *a negligent*) *man*. *Thriftless* is lit. *the man void of understanding*, lacking in the good sense which would make him provident.† — **31.** Ternary, triplet. The first and second lines are mutually equivalent, the third line stands alone. We may obtain a quatrain by adding a line (parallel to third line), or a couplet by omitting second line or third line, or by combining the two first lines into one. The triplet is suspicious, but it is not clear how the text is to be treated. — The precise meaning of the words rendered *thistles* (RV. *thorns*) and *nettles* is not certain; the first occurs only here in OT., the second elsewhere only in Zeph. 2^9 Job 30^7, perhaps a sort of lathyrus or vetch. The two represent the growth that springs up in deserted and neglected places. *Stones* are abundant

---

* Similarly, in Mt. $5^{38. 39}$ it is assumed that the spirit of the old legislation was morally defective.

† On viticulture in ancient Israel see Nowack, *Arch.*, § 42, and the Bib. Dicts.; on the modern culture of the grape see Robinson, *Bibl. Researches*, ii. 81 *al*.

in Palestine, and have always been used for building walls about fields and vineyards (cf. Is. 5⁵). — **32.** Synonymous, ternary. *Reflected thereon*, lit. *applied my mind, observed, took note* (RV. *considered well*). — *Learned a lesson*, lit. *received instruction.* — **33, 34.** See notes on 6¹⁰·¹¹. In that passage the description of the sluggard's laziness is introduced by an address to him; here the introduction to v.³³·³⁴ is given by v.³², so that the insertion of 6⁹ (Bick.) is hardly necessary. — In v.³⁴ the Heb. has: *and thy poverty will come walking* (or, *a walker*); a slight change of the last word gives the sense *as a highwayman* (as in 6¹¹), which is obviously the right reading (RV. *as a robber*).

23. 韻 הֲכֵר; Bi. reads מַכֵּר and omits כל טב. — **25.** 𝕲 omits טב. Hif. of יכח occurs in the sense *decide, judge* (always with connotation of just decision) in Isa. 11⁸ *al.*, sometimes absolutely; in Pr., absolutely, only here. — **26.** 𝕲: *they kiss lips which answer;* 𝔖𝕿: *... the lips of those who reprove* (𝕿 *return right words*); Σ: *he who answers* etc. *will be kissed with the lips;* 𝕃, correctly: *he kisses ... who answers.* — **27.** On the ו in 韻 אַחַר וּבָנִיתָ as introducing the apodosis see Ew. § 344 *b*, Ges.²⁶ § 112, 5. *c.* It seems better, on rhythmical grounds, to insert תִּקַּח לָךְ אִשָּׁה. — **28.** 韻 וַהֲפֵתִיתָ, interrog. part. and Piel introduced by ו, a construction (הֲ preceded by ו) which is found in 2 S. 15³⁵. The ה is better omitted, and the neg. may then be continued from ᵃ, or we may read וְאַל תִּי; 𝕲 μηδὲ. The sense *make wide*, for Hif. (𝕲 πλατύνου) seems to be assured by Gen. 9²⁷. — On the reading והפתות, from פתח, see De' Rossi. — **30.** For עַל in both cases 𝕲 has ὥσπερ, and it omits עֲבַרְתִּי. — **31.** קִמְשׂנִים is written with either שׂ or שׁ; see B-D, Ginsb. On the meaning of the terms קִמְשֹׁן or קִמֹּשׁ (Hos. 9⁶ Is. 34¹³) and חָרֻל see Löw, *Aram. Pflanzennam.* — **33, 34.** See notes on 6¹⁰·¹¹. — 韻 מִתְהַלֵּךְ; read מְהַלֵּךְ.

IV. CHAPTERS XXV.–XXIX.

This Section falls, by its style, into two parts. The first (25^2–27^{22}) bears greater resemblance to III. (22^{17}–24^{34}), the second (28. 29) to II. (10^1–22^{16}); between the two stands a discourse (27^{23-27}) after the manner of III. The Section thus appears to have been formed by the combination of two collections. It has certain couplets in common with the other collections. See the Introduction.

THE TITLE. 25^1.

The title reads: *These also are proverbs of Solomon which the men of Hezekiah, king of Judah, transcribed.*

The verb has this sense only here in OT.; elsewhere (Gen. 12^8 Job 9^5 21^7 *al.**) it means *remove* (in space or in time), and its signification here (*transcribe* = "remove from one book to another") belongs to the late literary vocabulary.† This superscription thus belongs in the same category with the titles found in the Prophetical Books and the Psalter, and has no value as a witness to the date of the original collection or to the origin of the particular proverbs; it only bears testimony to the disposition, in later times, to ascribe all wise sayings to Solomon, and a special suggestion of Solomonic authorship may have been found in the mention of kings with which the collection opens. Internal evidence leads us to refer this Section to the same general period as that of chs. 10–24; see the Introduction. — The supposition of the title is that, in addition to Solomon's own book (10^1–22^{16}), other collections of his proverbs were in existence in written form, and that these were copied out (or, in modern phrase, edited) by Hezekiah's men. ‡ This indicates the opinion that our Section was

---

* Job 32^{15} appears to be an interpolation; see Budde, *Hiob.*

† On the Talmudic use see Buxt., *Lexicon.*

‡ If the meaning were that the proverbs were handed down orally, and committed to writing from the mouths of men, the verb would naturally be *wrote.*

later than II., an opinion which is supported by considerations of
matter and style.   Hezekiah's time may have been selected by
the author of the title (or by the tradition which he represents)
as being the next great literary period, in Judah, after Solomon,
the time of Isaiah and Micah, or, the selection may have been
suggested by the military glory of the period (the repulse of the
Assyrian army), and the fame of Hezekiah as a pious monarch
and a vigorous reformer of the national religious life ; the *men of
Hezekiah* are the literary men of his court.   The period would, in
these regards, be an appropriate one, but the history of Israelitish
literature makes it improbable that such a work should have been
then undertaken ; to regard Hezekiah as a Jewish Pisistratus
(De.) is to ascribe to the time a literary spirit of which our documents give no hint.   It might be supposed that the fall of
Samaria would have led the men of Judah to collect the literature
of the northern kingdom, and our Section has, in fact, been
regarded as Ephraimitic ; but the vocabulary, style, and matter of
the Section do not warrant such a supposition.

2–7ᵇ. On kings.

2. It is the glory of God to conceal,
    It is the glory of kings to search out.

3. The heaven for height and the earth for depth,
    And the mind of kings is unsearchable.

4. Take away the dross from silver,
    And ‹ it › comes forth ‹ perfectly pure.›

5. Take away the wicked from the king,
    And his throne is established by righteousness.

6. Claim not honor in the presence of a king,
    And stand not in the place of great men.
    Better that it be said to thee : " Come up hither,"
    Than that thou be humbled before the prince.   []

The paragraph consists of three quatrains, a structure similar to
that of the third Section.   The space devoted to kings is noteworthy ; cf., in the first Section, 8¹⁵, in the second, 14²⁸. ³⁵ 16¹⁰. ¹²⁻¹⁵
19¹² 20². ⁸. ²⁶. ²⁸ 21¹ 22¹¹, in the third, 22²⁹ 24²¹, in the fourth, 29⁴. ¹⁴,
in the fifth, 30²⁷. ²⁸. ³¹ 31³. ⁴, and similar sayings in Eccl. and BS.
The political condition assumed is probably not that of old Israel.

2. Antithetic, quaternary, or ternary. It belongs, says the proverb, to the greatness of God that his work (in nature and in history) is mysterious, and his purposes inscrutable ; on the other hand, the function of rulers is to investigate (not the purposes of God, but) all the affairs of the State — they should be open and straightforward in government. The saying is perhaps directed against the tortuous diplomacy and other underhand methods of the time. — Lit. : *conceal a thing* and *search out a thing*, that is, anything and everything. — Cf. Robert Hall's sermon entitled : " The glory of God in concealing." — **3.** Comparison, quaternary or quaternary-ternary. As heaven and earth are too large to be comprehended, so the purposes of kings. The couplet is complementary to the preceding ; both are to be taken as statements of political facts, not at all as sarcastic or disparaging. The sage has a great respect for kings. — The *heaven* is the sky, the indefinite visible upper region, somewhere in which is the abode of God (Eccl. 5^2) ; the *earth* is indefinitely deep, reaching down to Sheol (2^{18} 5^5 Jon. $2^{2.6}$). — Delitzsch regards the form of the couplet as that of the priamel, the three subjects having the common predicate *unsearchable;* but it is more natural to confine this latter to the second line, the first line having the two predicates *high* (*height*) and *deep* (*depth*). — **4, 5.** The quatrain forms a comparison (the couplets are ternary). In the second line of v.[4] the Heb. reads : *and a vessel comes forth to the smith* (RV. *finer*). The *vessel*, according to this reading, has, as its parallel, the *throne* of v.[5] ; both may be said to be products of skill, and the vessel (according to some expositors) may be poetically conceived of as emerging to (or, for) the artist out of the refining process (cf. Aaron's brief history of the golden calf, Ex. 32^{24}). But this is not a natural form of expression — the vessel (as Wildeboer remarks) does not come to the silversmith simply by the process of refining, and the parallelism points to a comparison between the purity of the silver and that of the throne. It is, therefore, better to follow the suggestion of the Greek, which has : *it will be purified entirely pure.* — For *dross* see Isa. 1^{22} Ez. 22^{18} ψ 119^{119}. — *By righteousness*, that is, by means of righteous counsellors and counsels ; the Heb. expression may be rendered *in righteousness*, that is, in the sphere of righteousness or justice. —

For the Heb. *smith* (*silversmith* or *goldsmith*, lit. *refiner*) see Ju. 17⁴ Isa. 40¹⁹. In postexilic times the goldsmiths formed a guild (Neh. 3⁸) ; the reference in Neh. is to general artistic work, elsewhere in OT. to the making of images.*—6. Synonymous, binary, or binary-ternary. *Claim not honor;* the sense is well given in RV. : *put not thyself forward.* One's place in the royal presence was determined by rank or royal favor ; the reference here seems to be to a feast. For an example of prudence see Jos., *Ant.* 12, 4. 9.—7. Single sentence, containing antithetic comparison, ternary. The scene is a dinner ; cf. Lu. 14⁸⁻¹¹. *Hither,* that is, near the prince ; Grk. *to me.*—*Be humbled,* = *be put lower* (RV.) at table.—After *prince* the Heb. has : *whom* (or, *what*) *thine eyes see* (or, *have seen*), a lame and insignificant expression in the connection. Grk. Syr. Sym. Lat. attach the words to the following line. Sym. (with v.⁸ᵃ) : *what thine eyes have seen do not bring out to the multitude quickly.*

7c–10. Condemnation of gossip and tattling.

—V.⁹· ¹⁰ form a quatrain, and v.⁸ gives three lines, for which a fourth may be found by adopting the reading of Sym. given above, and we then have two variant quatrains. Otherwise it is difficult to make anything out of the concluding line of v.⁷. We may provisionally render as follows :

> 7 c. What thine eyes have seen
> 8. Report not hastily ‹ in public › ;
> ‹ For › what wilt thou do in the end
> When thy neighbor puts thee to the blush?
>
> 9. Discuss the matter with thy neighbor (in private),
> And reveal not his secret ‹ to › another,
> 10. Lest he who hears put thee to shame,
> And thine ill-repute pass not away.

7c, 8. Single sentence, ternary. *What thine eyes have seen* (or, *see*), that is, of thy neighbor's affairs.—The reading of the second line of the couplet is got by changing two vowels ; lit. : *do not bring forth to the multitude hastily* (Heb. : *go not forth to strive* [or, *to strife*] *hastily*). Instead of a warning against lawsuits or

---

* On casting in metal see Now., *Arch.* § 43. 4 ; Rawl., *Phoen.*, ch. 7 ; Pietschmann, *Phoen.*, pp. 175, 246 *al.;* Moore, *Judges,* on Ju. 17⁸.

quarrels we thus have a caution against gossip (see note on 16^{28}),
which is the topic of the next quatrain. The term *hastily* implies
thoughtlessness, impropriety. — In the third line the Heb. has:
lest what wilt thou do etc.? or, *lest what thou wilt do* etc., which
is syntactically impossible, and the majority of expositors have
supplied a word after *lest*, as: *lest thou know not what to do* *;
lest it be said: "what wilt thou do"?† *lest the question "what
doest thou?" be the end of it.*‡ These insertions are not easy,
and do not produce satisfactory senses, and Ewald's translation,
lest thou do something (that is, something thou oughtest not to do),
is equally unsatisfactory. It is better to change *lest* to *for*, or (with
Reuss) to omit it. — The second couplet describes the confusion of
the tattler when he is charged with his fault. *Neighbor* here = any
man with whom one has relations (cf. Lu. $10^{29\,ff.}$). The situation
described is a private difficulty. Cf. BS. 27^{16-21}. — **9, 10.** Single sentence; v.^{9} is ternary, v.^{10} is binary (or binary-ternary). The injunction is identical with that of the preceding quatrain. Lit. *quarrel
thy quarrel* etc., = *debate thy cause* (RV.) or *discuss the matter*
(Hodgson) *with thy neighbor*, that is, with him alone, in private —
do not talk of his affairs to others. *He who hears thee* = any one
who hears thy talk, and thus becomes aware of thy gossiping, untrustworthy, and dangerous character; but we should perhaps, with
the Grk., read *thy neighbor*, as in v.^{8}. — On *secret* see notes on 3^{32}
11^{13}. The second cl. of v.^{9} reads, in the Heb.: *and reveal not another's secret;* Lat.: *do not reveal a secret to another*, which is a
more appropriate injunction than that of the Heb., being exactly
parallel to the preceding line. — *Ill-repute*, properly, *defamatory
talk*, usually active, concerning others (Gen. 37^2 Jer. 20^{10} Pr. 10^{18}),
here concerning the man himself, and so equivalent to his reputation; a babbler, the proverb says, is universally disliked and
despised.

XXV. 1. 𝔐 משלי; 𝔊^B παιδεῖαι = מסרי; 𝔊$^{Ν\,c.\,a.\,A}$ παροιμίαι, probably correction after 𝔐. — 𝔊 adds αἱ ἀδιάκριτοι (var. εὐδιάκριτοι, διάκριτοι), perh.
= *miscellaneous*, and representing 𝔐 נם (Jäg.); 𝔖𝔗 render 𝔊 by עמקי *pro-
found*, that is, "not (easily) comprehensible." 𝔗 omits 𝔐 שלמה, probably
by scribal error. — **2.** 𝔐 חקר; 𝔊 τιμᾷ (Grabe reads τιμᾶν), = הקר (Jäg.),
from יקר. — **4.** 𝔐 ויצא לצרף כלי; 𝔊 καὶ καθαρισθήσεται καθαρὸν ἅπαν (מצרף

---

* Saad. Rashi, Schult. RV.   † Hitz. De. Str. *al.*   ‡ Wild.

was read by 𝔖 and *Bemidbar Rab.* c. 7); read with Dys. Wild. וּיֵּצֵא נִצְרַף כְּלִי;
Frank. צְרַף, instead of נִצְרַף. — 𝔗 מִן צרפא, = מְצֹרֵף. — 7ᶜ, 8ᵃ. Σ ἃ εἶδον οἱ ὀφθαλμοί σου μὴ ἐξενέγκῃς εἰς πλῆθος ταχύ. Read, with Bi., in v.⁸ᵃ: אַל תֹּצֵא לְרֹב מַהֵר. Elsewhere לְרֹב = *in abundance*, and רֹב, except in such adverbial expressions, is always defined by a noun (so 12 times in Pr.); yet it is possible that from such an expression as רֹב אדם (20⁶) it may have come to be = *multitude;* cf. Syr. רוּרבא. If this sense be thought improbable, then for רֹב we might read דְּבַר. — For פֶּן 𝔐 read כי.

11, 12. Value of wise advice. — The meaning of several words in the quatrain is so uncertain, and the text is in such bad condition, that only a tentative translation can be given. The Heb. reads :

11. Golden fruits in silver carvings
    Is a word fitly (?) spoken.
12. A golden earring and a necklace (?) of gold
    Is a wise reprover to an ear that hears.

11. The first noun (RV. *apples* here and Joel 1¹² Cant. 2³·⁵ 7⁸⁽⁹⁾ 8⁵) is variously understood as meaning apple, apricot, quince, citron, orange ; all that is certain is that it signifies some sort of fruit.* — The second noun signifies *carved work* on a stone or image (Lev. 26¹ Nu. 33⁵²) or carvings or drawings or pictures on a wall (Ez. 8¹²).† Here it has been rendered *ornamental objects* (Saad.), *admirable things* (Sym. Theod.), *beaten work* (Syr. Targ.), *filigree-work* (RV. marg.), *pictures* (AV. Wild.), *salvers* (Luth. De.), *baskets* (Ew. RV.), *necklace* (Grk., possibly error of text for *basket*), *couches*, or *sofas* (Lat.). — The *golden fruit* of the Heb. text must be understood to mean an object of solid gold, which does not accord with " pictures of silver " or " baskets of silver " ; solid gold apples or other fruits were never put in such pictures or baskets, nor would the representation thus given furnish a natural simile for the thought of the couplet. The interpretation *golden-colored fruits* is not permitted by the usage of the language. ‡ — The interpretation *fitly* (that is, under proper cir-

* H. B. Tristram (*Survey of West. Pal.*, 4, 294, and *Nat. Hist. of the Bible*) *apricot;* W. R. Smith (*Journ. of Philol.*, 13, 65) and I. Löw (*Aram. Pflanz.*, p. 155) *apple;* Celsus (*Hierobot.*, 1, 254 ff.) and Houghton (*PSBA.*, 12, 1, 42) *quince;* De. takes *golden apples* (*aurea mala*) to be *oranges.*

† For the sense *thought, imagining* see 18¹¹ ψ 73⁷.

‡ Tristram : *golden apricots in silvery foliage*, a charming picture, but not obtainable from the text.

cumstances and conditions, in due season) is inferred from 15²³
and from the connection; the meaning of the Heb. expression is
doubtful. — **12.** *Earring*, as in Gen. 35⁴ Ju. 8²⁴; the word may
also mean *nosering*, as in 11²² Gen. 24²² Isa. 3²¹ Ez. 16¹². — The
rendering *necklace* (RV. *ornament*) suits Cant. 7¹⁽²⁾ (the only
other place where the word occurs in OT.), and corresponds well
to *earring;* the Anc. Vrss., however, take the word to mean some
sort of precious stone (a sense which also would suit Cant. 7¹⁽²⁾),
and its signification must be regarded as doubtful.   The second
gold (Lam. 4¹ Isa. 13¹² Job 28¹⁶·¹⁹ 31²⁴ ψ 45⁹⁽¹⁰⁾ Cant. 5¹¹ Dan. 10⁵)
is a poetic word (RV. *fine gold*).   By changes of text the quatrain may be rendered conjecturally as follows :

> Like graved work of gold and carved work of silver
> Is a word fitly (?) spoken.
> Like an earring of gold and an ornament of silver
> Is a wise reproof to an ear that hears.

Like is supplied (twice) as an expression more natural in Eng.
than the Heb. form.   The sense *graved work* is obtained by a
transposition of two letters in the Hebrew; the resulting word
occurs in Ex. 28¹¹·²¹·³⁶ 39⁶·¹⁴·³⁰ 1 K. 6²⁹ 2 C. 2⁷⁽⁶⁾·¹⁴⁽¹³⁾ Zech. 3⁹
ψ 74⁶. — The *and* (instead of *in* or *on*) follows the norm of the
third line, and secures a better sense — the rendering *like golden
graving on silver carved work* (or, *on a carved figure of silver*)
gives a combination hardly congruous. — In the third line the
term *silver* is substituted (by an easy change of letters) for the
word of the Heb., and the line is thus more nearly assimilated to
the first line.   *Reproof* (instead of *reprover*) is parallel to *word*,
and requires only a slight change in the Hebrew. — The point of
comparison in both couplets seems to be the adornment of character which results from wise advice given to receptive minds;
see 1⁹ 3²² 4⁹ 14²⁴, and cf. BS. 50⁹ 22¹⁷.   This last passage compares
a mind composed and fixed by wisdom to ornamentation (sculp-
tures) on a wall, and it has been held that in like manner the
thought of v.¹¹ is the fixedness and enduring character of counsel
given to a man of sense (Frank.).   To this interpretation it seems
to be an objection that it does not accord with v.¹², with which v.¹¹
is probably identical in meaning, whether the two couplets form a
real quatrain, or v.¹² be a variant of v.¹¹.

13. The faithful messenger.

> Like the coolness of snow in harvest-time
> Is a faithful messenger to those who send him.

Comparison, with added explanation, — ternary. The rhythmic norm here changes from the quatrain (as in III.) to the couplet (as in II.). On the time of *harvest* see note on 6^8. Grk. here understands a fall of snow, but this, as is suggested in 26^1, would be untimely (so Rashi) ; the reference is more probably to drinks cooled by snow brought from the mountains.* — As third line the Heb. adds: *he restores* (= refreshes) *his master's soul* (= spirit), an unnecessary explanation (contrary to the manner of proverbs), a gloss. — Bickell makes the Heb. text a couplet : *As snow in heat is a faithful* etc., *he refreshes* etc.

14. Braggart pretence of liberality.

> Clouds and wind and no rain —
> So is the man who boasts of gifts ungiven.

Comparison, ternary. The first line describes a deceitful appearance or attitude : clouds and wind, as it were, boast of rain, and there is none. In second line lit. *a gift of falsity*, which must refer not to what is received (Hitz.), but (Saad. Ew. *al.*) to what is bestowed. *Clouds*, properly *vapors*, *mists* (Jer. 10^{13} 51^{16} ψ 135^7), which ascend. For Arabic parallels see Schult. De., and, for others, Malan.

15. Power of patience and gentleness.

> By forbearance ‹ anger is pacified,›
> And a mild word breaks the bone.

Synonymous, ternary. The Heb. has *a prince* (instead of *anger*) ; but one does not show forbearance to a prince — it is he who may be forbearing. The emendation requires only the change of a letter. *Forbearance*, lit. *slowness to* (lit. *deferring of*) *anger* (14^{29} 15^{18} 16^{32} Ex. 34^6). On *prince* (Ju. 11^6 Isa. 1^{10} Dan. 11^{18}) see note on 6^7; the rendering *judge* (De. RV. marg.) is improb-

---

* For the ancient custom see Xen., *Mem.*, 2, 1. 30; Aul. Gel., 19, 5; a similar usage in Austria is mentioned by Michaelis; cf. notes of Hitz. and Zöckler, and, for the modern custom in Syria, Hackett, *Illust. of Script.*, pp. 53 ff.

able. Instead of *is pacified* the Heb. has : *is befooled, deceived, enticed* (1^{10} 16^{29} 24^{28} 1 K. 22^{20}), a strange term in the connection ; the emendation is taken from 15^{18}. *Breaks the bone* = " destroys power," that is, in this case, takes away desire and disposition to speak angrily.

16. Moderation in enjoyments.

> If thou findest honey, eat what is enough,
> Lest thou be surfeited and vomit it up.

Single sentence, binary. On *honey* see note on 16^{24}. With the couplet cf. v^{27a} below, and see 24^{13}. Cf. BS. 31^{21} 37^{29-31}.

17. Caution against wearying one's friends with visits.

> Let thy foot be seldom in thy neighbor's house,
> Lest he be sated with thee and hate thee.

Single sentence, ternary-binary. Lit. *make precious* (= *rare*) *thy foot.* Cf. BS. 21^{22} 13^9. — This couplet bears a general resemblance to the preceding, but is not so like it that the two should be considered as forming a quatrain.

18. The false witness.

> A maul, a sword, a sharp arrow —
> Such is the man who bears false witness against his neighbor.

Single sentence, virtual comparison, ternary. In the Heb. the couplet is a metaphor : *a maul* etc. *is the man* etc. The term rendered *maul* means " that which shatters," as a hammer or a club ; related terms are found in Jer. 51^{20} Ez. 9^2. — The second line has the expression of the Decalogue (Ex. 20^{16} Dt. $5^{20(17)}$), probably a common legal phrase.

19. The hope of a bad man is ill-founded.

> A broken tooth and an unsteady foot,
> Such is a bad man's ground of hope in time of trouble.

Metaphor, quaternary. *Such* is supplied as in the preceding couplet. The rendering *broken* requires a slight change in the Hebrew. *Unsteady,* or *out of joint,* or *palsied,* is lit. *wavering, tottering* (Job 12^5). On *bad* (or, *faithless*) see notes on 2^{22} 23^{28}. For the sense *ground of hope* (one word in Heb.) see 14^{26} Job 8^{14} 31^{24} Jer.

17[7] Ez. 29[16]. That on which the bad man relies will fail him, says the proverb, in time of stress. — To break a man's teeth is to deprive him of power (ψ 37[7(8)] 58[6(7)]), an expression derived, perhaps, from observation of wild beasts (cf. ψ 35[16] 112[10]) or of savage men. — The translation : (such is) *confidence in a bad* (or, *unfaithful*) *man* etc. (De. RV. *al.*) is in itself improbable, and gives a statement that is not quite correct : it is not confidence but the ground or basis of confidence that is as unreliable as a broken tooth etc. — The ground of hope referred to is wealth or power, or deceit and violence.

9. For 𝔐 סר אחר read סרו לאחר. — 11. 𝔐 חפחי; read פתחי. Write ו instead of ב before משכיח. See Lag.'s note. — 𝔐 על אפניו; see Geier, Ges. *Thes.* Ges.-Buhl, DBD. and De.'s note. 𝔊𝔅𝔖 omit; Σ (and so 𝔏) ἐν καιρῷ αὐτοῦ; 𝔗 פסיאית, perh. (Pink.) from פיס (πεῖσις), and = "in the way of argument (or, persuasion)"; 'ΑΘ𝔊א c. a ἐπὶ ἁρμόζουσιν αὐτῷ, perh. = "under suitable conditions, on appropriate occasions," perh. (Ges. Lag.) represents לאמנם, cf. 8[30], a reading (adopted by Frank.) which is not precisely parallel to *an ear that hears*, and is not quite natural in the connection. Ges. Orelli *al.* take the stem in אפניו to be אפן *turn* (as in אופן *wheel*), and the noun as = *time* (Ges.) or *circumstance* (Orelli); Barth. assumes st. פנה, and the expression (after the Arab.) as = "according to its propriety." Others compare the late Jew. use of אופן in the sense of *manner* (Rashi *according to its modes*, = *on its basis*). None of these explanations are satisfactory — the word may be scribal error — but nothing better suggests itself than to adopt the interpretation of Σ. — 12. 𝔐 כחם; read כסה. The origin of כחם is unknown. Neither *cover, conceal* for the stem (Ass. Arab.) nor *mark, spot* (Aram.) suggests a suitable sense; the meaning *blood-red* in Jew. Aram. is prob. merely a special sense of *mark*. 𝔐 מכח; 𝔊 λόγος; Bi. דבר; better תכחח. — 13. 𝔐 צנת and כיום; 𝔊 ἔξοδος (= צאת) and κατὰ καῦμα (= כחם). 𝔖 follows 𝔊; 𝔗 follows 𝔐. — 15-18. 𝔐 יפתה קצן; read וישקט קצף; Frank. לקצף. — 𝔐 מפף is regarded by Lag. as incorrect pointing for מפף (Jer. 51[20], cf. Ez. 9[2]) the stem נפ׳ *shatter* is more suitable than פ׳ *scatter.* — 19. 𝔐 רעה may be Qal Part. (for רֹעֶה), = *crumbling* (Fleisch.), 𝔏 *putridus*, which would answer to following *unsteady;* an equivalent sense is given by the reading רעה (𝔊𝔖𝔗 and perhaps 𝔏); it is better to read נרעה, the first letter may have fallen out after preceding ז (Frank.). — 𝔐 מֻעֶדֶת, as if abbreviated Pu. Part.; better Qal Part. מֹעֶדֶת. — On the haggadic interpretation of the couplet as referring to faithless Israel's reliance on other nations (tooth and foot of beasts) Wild. cites Houtsma, in *ZATW.* 1895, pp. 151 f.

20. Gayety in the presence of sorrow. — Heb. : *One who lays off* (?) *a garment in time of cold, vinegar on soda,* (*so is*) *he who* *sings songs to a troubled heart.* The rendering *lays off* is doubtful ; the verb usually means *adorn* (Isa. 61[10] Job 40[10] *al.*), once (Job 28[8]) *pass* (or, *stalk*) *by*, whence the Causative (which occurs only here) might = *put off* (as in Jon. 3[6], with a different verb, *laid off his robe* is lit. *made his robe pass from him*). But, even if this translation be correct, the line is not in place, for it describes an act of impru-dence, while the connection calls for something not only inappro-priate but painful. Nor does the translation *he who adorns himself with a garment* give a suitable sense. Moreover the line is sub-stantially, in the Heb., the repetition (with difference of vowels) of second line of v.[19], and is not found in the Grk.; it is better, there-fore, to omit it as dittogram. — There remains a couplet, in which also the form of first line is not clear. The Heb. *neter* is not our nitre (potassium nitrate), but native sodium carbonate, nearly our common *soda*, more precisely *natron* (Grk. νίτρον, Lat. *nitrum*) ; it is mentioned elsewhere in OT. only in Jer. 2[22], from which passage it appears that it was used in washing the person. The effect of the acid *vinegar* on the alkali *natron* would be to destroy the efficiency of the latter ; but destruction of efficiency is not the point of the aphorism, which rather calls for some painful effect. The Grk. has : *as vinegar for a wound* (or, *a sore*), which is suit-able, since the immediate effect of the application of vinegar to a wound is painful.* — If the reading of the Grk. be adopted, and be supposed to stand for another word than Heb. *neter*, there still remains the latter to be accounted for. It might be regarded as erroneous insertion ; but, from the norm of v.[18. 19], we expect the mention of two combinations. Bickell : *water on natron*, and Grk. : *as a moth in a garment and a worm in wood* do not suit the couplet ; possibly the missing expression is : *smoke to the eyes* (10[26]). The couplet may have read :

> Vinegar to a wound and . . . ,
> So is a song to a troubled heart.

In second line the Heb. is lit. : *and one who sings in songs*, in which, in any case, the *and* and *in* must be omitted, and the cor-

---

* On the medicinal use of vinegar for wounds see Lag.'s note. The modern Egyptians mix it with natron as remedy for toothache.

respondent to *vinegar* is rather *song* than *singer*. A joyous song
gives a pang to a sad heart.

21, 22. Repaying evil with good.

> 21. If thine enemy be hungry, give him to eat,
> And if he be thirsty, give him to drink;
> 22. For thou wilt heap coals of fire on his head,
> And Yahweh will reward thee.

The quatrain is a single sentence, ternary (as emended). The
quatrain form suggests that this aphorism properly belongs in III.
(cf. 24^{17. 18}) or in the paragraph 25^{1-12}. — *Enemy* is lit. *he who
hates thee.* The Heb. has *bread to eat* and *water to drink; bread*
and *water* (omitted in the Grk. and Rom. 12^{20}) appear to be
glosses. *Heap coals of fire on his head* = " produce sharp pain,"
and the pain can here be only the pang of contrition — the
enemy will be converted into a friend ; the reference, in the connection, cannot be to punishment inflicted by God. Or, less
naturally, v.^{22a} may be understood to mean : " thou wilt take vengeance on him," that is, the noble vengeance of returning good
for evil. — The ethical rule is lofty, though the motives presented
are those of advantage to self. Instead of urging the simple obligation of universal love, the sage insists on what he thinks the
strongest motive with men. The declaration *Yahweh will reward
thee* assumes that kindness to enemies belonged to the divine
ethical code. Cf. 20^{22} 24^{17. 18. 29} BS. 28^{1-7} Mt. 5^{44} Rom. 12^{20}. —
Bickell omits *on his head*, taking the meaning to be : " thou wilt
put away the burning coals of hate," and so make a friend of an
enemy — a sense not different from the one given above, but it is
doubtful whether the verb can have this meaning.

23. Malicious talk.

> A north wind brings rain,
> And a backbiting tongue makes an angry face.

Two parallel sentences involving an illustration, ternary. In Palestine rain comes usually from the west (cf. Lu. 12^{54}) ; it may
have come also from the northern mountains, or the word *north*
may be used here in a general sense, as = " northerly," including

northwest.* The word is possibly an error of text. — The last
expression in second line may be rendered by the plu., *angry
faces;* the reference is to the person or persons maligned. —
Backbiting is lit. *secret.* — Grk. and Lat., in second line, make
face subject.

24 = XXI. 9. — The natural suggestion is that this particular
collection (25^2–27^{22}) was made independently of collection II.
(10^1–22^{16}).

25. Good news from afar.

> As cold water to a thirsty man,
> So is good news from a far country.

Virtual comparison, quaternary. The Heb. puts the two statements side by side, and lets the comparison suggest itself: *cold
water* etc. *and good news* etc., better, however, *cold water* etc. *is
good news* etc. as in v.$^{18-20}$. — *Thirsty* is properly *weary*, the special
sense coming from the connection, as in Job 22^7. — *Man* is lit.
soul (= person). — The difficulty of getting news from a distant
place heightens the refreshment it gives. Cf. 15^{30}. Wildeboer
refers to Gen. 45^{27}.

26. The overthrow of a good man.

> A troubled fountain and a ruined spring —
> Such is the righteous man who falls before the wicked.

Virtual comparison, quaternary-ternary. *Troubled* is lit. *trampled*
(Ez. 32^2 34^{18}); it was and is the custom in Western Asia for men
and beasts to enter a fountain or pond, for drinking or washing,
and so to foul the water as to make it useless. — The verb *falls*
(properly *is moved out of one's place*) is the standing expression
for loss of position, that is, of wealth and all that makes life prosperous and enjoyable; usually in OT. it is said that the righteous
will never be moved (10^{30} 12^3 ψ 10^6 15^5 16^8 *al.*), will never be
ejected from his position by the machinations of his enemies. In
one passage (ψ 17^5) the verb signifies moral faltering, and in this
sense it is sometimes here understood,† with the rendering: *the*

---

* On Palestinian winds see Robinson, *Bibl. Researches*, 1, 429; Now., *Arch.* § 11.

† So Mercer, Geier, Lag. De. *al.*

righteous man who yields to (the temptation of) *the wicked* —
such an one is a melancholy picture of lost purity and usefulness,
like a ruined spring.   In this sense, however, it is the path of rectitude from which the man is moved (so in ψ 17⁵), the verb is
not naturally followed by such an expression as *before the wicked*,
and it seems better to understand our couplet as referring to the
loss of social standing and prosperity by the plots of bad men
(see 12⁶ 16²⁷ 24² ψ 11² 17⁹ *al.*). — For the reason given above the
couplet probably does not contain a reference to yielding to evil
through false modesty and fear of men (Reuss) ; nor can the
stress be laid on the *wicked* as contrasted with the *righteous*, with
the interpretation : " if a good man's fall is known only to good
men, it does not injure others, but if it is known to bad men, it
encourages them in mockery and all evil " (Str. Wild.) — this limitation of the range of the couplet is not suggested by first line or
by the general tone of the Book, and such a secret society of the
righteous, concealing the sins of its members from the outside
world, would be immoral, if it were possible.

27. The Heb. gives two unrelated lines.   With the first : *to
eat much honey is not good* cf. v.¹⁶.   The second reads lit. : *the
investigation* (or, *searching out*) *of their glory is glory,* an obviously corrupt text.   Some expositors, by change of vowels, get
the intelligible sentence : *the investigation of difficult things is
glory* (or, *honor*),* that is : " there may be a surfeit of honey,
there cannot be excess of investigation " — a not very attractive
antithesis, and the rendering *difficult* is doubtful.   Noyes : *so the
search of high things is weariness* (cf. 27³), which offers a sceptical sentiment, proper to Eccles., but strange in Proverbs.   Grk. :
it is proper to honor notable sayings, and Frank. : *therefore refrain
from complimentary words* (lit. *words of honor*), a sort of speech
as cloying as honey — a rendering in itself appropriate, but elsewhere in OT. the Genitive defining *words* is always subjective
(characterizing them as true or false etc.), never objective
(stating their aim or result). — Probably each line has lost its

---

* So De. Reuss, Str. Bi., and the same translation, without change of text, is
given by Zöck. *al.*   Hodgson's *in deeds of virtue to exceed is glorious* furnishes an
antithesis to the first line, but cannot be got from the Hebrew.

companion line, and the text of second line remains doubtful; it
is perhaps a corruption of v.²ᵇ. — For other attempts at translation
see the notes of De. and Zöckler.

28. Absence of self-control is fatal.

A city broken through, without a wall —
Such is a man without self-control.

Virtual comparison, ternary. *Broken through*, a breach made in
the wall, so that it is defenceless — the wall is practically
destroyed; the reference may or may not be to a siege. — In
second line, lit.: *a man to whose spirit there is no restraint* — he
has no defence against anger and similar emotions. — *Such* is
supplied.

. **20.** 𝔐 עַל נָתֵר; 𝔊 ἕλκει, whence Oort נֶתֶק *scab* or *scurf* (Lev. 13³⁰), but
this is not suitable; Bi. writes מֶצַע after עַל, and adds עַל מִים before נתר. —
𝔐 וְשָׁר בַּשָׁרִים; read simply יָשָׁר. — 𝔊 in ᵇ, שָׂר בָּשָׂר; 𝔊ᵈ is variation of ᵇ;
𝔊ᶜ is perhaps based on 𝔐ᵃ. — **21.** 𝔐 לחם and מים are probably glosses;
their absence from 𝔊 may, however, be free translation. — 𝔐 שׂנַאֲךָ; 𝔊 ὁ
ἐχθρός σου, perh. = 𝔐, perh. = אֹיִבְךָ (so Bi.). — **22.** 𝔐 חֹתֶה; 𝔊 σωρεύσεις,
𝕃 *congregabis*. The stem seems to mean *snatch, seize* in Isa. 30¹⁴ ψ 52⁷ Pr. 6²⁷;
see Ges. *Thes.* BDB.; here, in pregnant sense, *seize and put*, = *heap*. Whether
it = *snatch away* (Bi.) is doubtful; the sense *away* might come from the
context (as perh. in ψ 52⁷), but here, after the omission of עַל ראשׁוֹ, such
pregnant sense would be difficult. On the Ass. stem see De. BDB. —
23. 𝔐 תחולל, *brings forth*, from חול; 𝔊 ἐξεγείρει; 𝕃 *dissipat*, from חלל. —
25. 𝔐 ארץ is omitted by Bi. unnecessarily. — **27.** 𝔐 הַרְבּוֹת has been construed
(De. Wild. *al.*) as subject of the sentence and defined by אֲכֹל דְבַשׁ: "to make
great the eating of honey"; but this construction is unnatural (Stade), and
it is better to read הַרְבֵּה, as adj. *much* (so the Vrss.). — 𝔐 כְּבֹדָם; De. Dys.:
כְּבֹדָם. 𝔊 in ᵇ: τιμᾶν δὲ χρὴ λόγους ἐνδόξους, perh. = וְהֹקֵר נִכְבָּדִים כָּבֹד; Frank.:
וְהֹקֵר דִבְרֵי כָבֵד. — 𝕾𝕿 (and RV.) carry over the neg. into ᵇ.

XXVI. 1–12 (except v.²) form a Book of Fools — a string of
sarcasms on the class most detested by the sages. The folly
described is intellectual.

1. The fool and honor.

As snow in summer, and as rain in harvest,
So honor does not befit a fool.

Comparison, quaternary-ternary. *Honor* is high position, respect, especially public. The saying is probably aimed at the elevation of incompetent men to high places in the governments of state and city. On the seasons see notes on 6^8 25^{13}.

2. The groundless curse.

> Like the sparrow in its flitting, like the swallow in its flying,
> The curse that is groundless does not strike.

Comparison, quaternary-ternary. *Flitting*, lit. *wandering*. *Strike*, lit. *come*, RV. *light.* — The point in first line is the aimlessness of the birds' motion, which never reaches a definite place. The aphorism is a partial denial of the old belief (generally held among early peoples), that blessings and curses had objective existence, and, by whomsoever and howsoever uttered, always reached that at which they were aimed — that is, that the deity invoked (in the blessing or curse) was coerced by the utterance of his name, and could not but respond to the adjuration. This belief, held by the earlier Hebrews (Gen. 27^{33} Ju. 17^2), necessarily receded, to some extent, before the advance of a purer theistic faith. It is so far modified in the proverb that the power of an unjust curse is denied. How far the belief in the efficiency of well-founded blessings and curses remained we have no means of ascertaining. — In second line the Heb. margin reads : *the curse . . . comes to him*, the *him* referring to the curser or to the cursed (the old belief, never completely eradicated) ; but the neg. particle is required by the illustration of first line, in which the point is failure to reach, not certainty of reaching. — The translations *sparrow* (6^5 7^{23} Gen. 7^{14} ψ 11^1 $84^{3(4)}$ Eccl. 9^{12} *al.*) and *swallow* (ψ $84^{3(4)}$), though not certain, are probably substantially correct.*

3. Government of the fool.

> A whip for the horse, a bridle for the ass,
> And a rod for the back of fools.

Virtual comparison, quaternary- (or, binary-) ternary. A fool, says the proverb, is like a beast, not to be controlled by appeal to

---

* See Bochart, *Hierozoicon ;* Tristram, *Survey of West. Pal.*, and *Nat. Hist. of the Bib.* ; Now., *Arch.* ; Hastings, *Dict. of the Bib.* ; Cheyne, *Cyclop. Bibl.*

reason. The designation of whip for horse and bridle for ass may be in part rhetorical variation — both animals may at times have required both instruments of guidance ; but there may be special propriety in the terms ; the ass, the favorite riding-animal (Gen. 22³ Ju. 1¹⁴ 1 S. 25²⁰ Zech. 9⁹), hardly needed the whip in moving over the rough mountain roads of Palestine ; but for horses, rarely employed except in war and on plains (21³¹ 2 S. 15¹ 2 K. 9¹⁸ Isa. 31¹ Job 39¹⁸·¹⁹ ψ 20⁷⁽⁸⁾), the whip might be useful ; cf. note on 21³¹. See 10¹³ ψ 32⁹.

4, 5. How to answer fools.

> 4. Answer not a fool according to his folly
> Lest thou become like him.
> 5. Answer a fool according to his folly,
> Lest he become wise in his own conceit.

Each couplet is a single sentence, ternary ; the two form an anti-thetic quatrain. The first is a warning against descending in man-ner of thought to the fool's level ; the second enjoins rebuke of folly. The Talmudic interpretation,* which refers v.⁴ to worldly things, v.⁵ to religious things, misses the point ; such juxtaposition of contradictories belongs to the nature of gnomic teaching. The rabbis, however, took exception to these discrepancies, and hesi-tated to receive Proverbs into the Canon ; the objection was removed by such interpretations as that quoted above. Cf. *Aboth Rabbi Nathan*, i., and see notes on 7⁷ 11⁹. The second line of v.⁴ is lit. *lest thou also become like him.* Cf. BS. 22¹³.

6. The fool as messenger. — Heb.: *He cuts off (his) feet, drinks in violence, who sends a message by a fool.* The second line expresses an imprudent act, of which the injurious conse-quence is described in first line, but the text and meaning of the latter are not clear. *Cuts off (his) feet* is commonly taken to signify : "deprives himself of the power of locomotion" — that is, to send a fool is equivalent to not sending at all ; the expression is perhaps designedly bizarre. In the phrase *drinks in violence* the verb must mean not "practices" (as in 4¹⁷ Job 15¹⁶)

---

* *Shabbath*, 30 *b*, cited by De.

but " suffers " violence (as in Job 21[20]). The noun makes a difficulty ; the connection calls for a sense like " damage, injury " (so
De. RV. *al.*), but the word means "violent wrong, highhanded
injustice " (cf. 4[17]), an expression which seems here out of place.
— The text of first line appears to be in disorder ; we might read
for the second phrase : *prepares disgrace* (for himself) ; or, for
the line : *he cuts off his messenger's legs.* We get from the couplet
only the general sense that it is imprudent or dangerous to employ
a fool as a messenger.

7. The fool as proverb-monger. — The second line : *and a
proverb in the mouth of fools* is clear, but no precise translation of
first line can be given. The first word of the Heb. is taken to
mean either " draw up, elevate, take away," or " hang loose."
Hence : *take away the power of locomotion from the lame* (Grk.),
that is, if a lame man can walk, a fool can utter wise sayings * ;
the legs [of others] *are higher than those of the lame*, and so a
proverb is too high for a fool (Rashi) ; *like dancing to a cripple*,
so is etc. (Luth.) ; *the legs of the lame are not equal* (AV.) ; *the
lame man's legs hang too loose* (Ew.), or . . . *hang loose* (RV.) †
With change of text : *what the lame man's legs are to him*, so is a
proverb etc. (Reuss) ; (*as*) *the leaping of the legs of a lame man*,
(*so is*) *a proverb* etc., that is, both are impossible (Hi. Frank.,
= Grk. Luth.). The sense of the couplet perhaps is : a fool
fares with an aphorism as a lame man with his legs — he limps
and does not go far.

8. Honoring a fool. — The least improbable translation of the
Heb. is that of AV. : *As he who binds a stone in a sling so is he
who gives honor to a fool.* The first line then expresses an absurd
procedure, namely, the fixing a stone in a sling so firmly that it cannot be thrown out (so Ew.). Delitzsch (following Rashi) takes the
meaning to be : " as a stone is placed in a sling only to be thrown
out, so honor, bestowed on a fool, does not remain " ; but if the
author had meant this, he would rather have said : " as a stone is
slung from a sling, so honor vanishes from a fool." — The meaning

---

* So substantially Syr. Targ. Lat. Saad. Zöck. *al.*
† So substantially Ges. De. Str. Kamp. Wild. *al.*

sling given (in the Grk.) to the last word of the line is by no means certain ; it may also perhaps be translated *stone-heap*, but to *bind* (or, *enclose*) *a stone in a stone-heap* (that is, it is said, to do a use-less thing) is not a natural expression. — Nor, if we take the first word as = *bag* (or, *bundle*) (as in 7²⁰), does the rendering *as a bag* (or, *bundle*) *of stones* (properly *a stone-bag*) *in a stone-heap* offer any clear sense, and if, on the authority of Zech. 3⁹ 1 C. 29⁸, we make the first *stone = precious stone, gem* (Saad. RV.), this does not suit the verb *bind*, or the noun *bundle*. — It is equally inadmissible to give to the first word the meaning *put = lay*, *throw*, as in Lat. : *as he who casts a stone on the heap of Mercury*,* that is, as he who takes part in idolatrous worship ; the allusion is to the custom of casting stones on a sacred cairn, particularly at the foot of a Hermes-pillar, the survival of a very old usage.† Luther : *as one who throws a jewel on the gallows-heap* (that is, the heap of stones at the foot of the gallows). — The proverb may have had some such form as : " like him who puts a jewel on a swine's snout is he who gives honor to a fool."

9. The fool with an aphorism. — The second line is identical with second line of v.⁷. The first line may read, if we follow the usage of Biblical Hebrew : *a thorn grows up in the hand of a drunken man*, which is meaningless, or *a thorn goes up into the hand* etc. (RV.), which is contrary to fact (the verb does not mean *pierce*). Or, instead of *thorn* we may render *thornbush* (as in 2 K. 14⁹ Cant. 2²), and, with De., assuming that the expression contains a late-Heb. idiom, translate : *a thorn-branch comes into the hand* (= *into the possession*) *of a drunken man ;* the resulting sense is not inapposite : there is a touch of humor in the compari-son of a fool with a wise saw in his mouth to a half-crazy drunken man brandishing a stick. We may, perhaps, read : *like a thorn-stick in the hands of a drunken man is an aphorism in the mouth of a fool*.

10. Corrupt text ; lit. : *much produces* (or, *wounds*) *all, and he who hires a fool and he who hires passers-by ;* the word ren-

---

* So the Midrash; cf. the Talm. tract *Cholin*, 133 a.

† The god was often, in early times, represented by a cairn, and it was a pious duty to throw a stone on the heap.

dered *much* may also mean *master, lord,* and is by some (probably incorrectly) rendered *an archer.* Many combinations and modifications of the words may be made, but the text is in too bad condition to permit a translation, and no satisfactory emendation has been suggested.*

11. The fool as learner.

> Like a dog that returns to his vomit
> So the fool repeats his folly.

Comparison, ternary. Or, first line freely : *as a dog returns* etc. *Returns* etc., that is, to eat it ; the fool, how often soever warned, does not learn ; cf. Terence, *Adelph.,* i. 1, Hor. *Ep.,* x. 24.† — The Grk. adds a couplet which is word for word the same with BS. 4²¹ (Jäger) ; the addition is probably by a Christian scribe.

12. Folly versus self-conceit.

> Seest thou a man wise in his own conceit —
> There is more hope for a fool than for him.

Single sentence, quaternary-ternary. Lit. *in his own eyes,* and *more hope to a fool.* Folly is obtuse, but self-conceit is blind and unapproachable. The folly is intellectual. Elsewhere (except

---

* Of the innumerable attempts at translation and emendation the following are the principal : Grk.: *all the flesh of fools suffers much, for their fury is crushed ;* Syr. Targ.: *the flesh of fools suffers much, and the drunken man crosses the sea ;* Sym. Theod. in second line: *and he who shuts up* [Th. *muzzles*] *a fool shuts up* [Th. *muzzles*] *anger ;* Lat.: *judgment decides causes, and he who imposes silence on a fool mitigates anger ;* Saadia (connecting with v.⁹) : *he* [the fool] *repels* [= wounds] *all with it* [with his wise saying], *refusing it to the ignorant and the bygoers ;* Aben Ezra: *a lord* [= a ruler] *afflicts all, hiring fools* etc. [that is, to make them work]; Rashi: *The Lord* [= God] *creates all, giving pay to fool and passer-by* (cf. Mt. 5⁴⁵) ; Luth. Fleisch.: *a (good) master makes all right* [= fashions everything], *but he who hires a bungler* [= a fool] *ruins it ;* Reuss (cf. RV. marg.): *the master does everything himself, the fool hires the first comer ;* Ew. RV.: *an archer who wounds every one — and he who hires fools and loungers* [= bypassers] ; De.: *much produces all* [that is, he who has much gains much], *but the fool's hire and his hirer pass away ;* Bickell: (*like*) *an archer who wounds all bypassers is he who hires fools and drunkards.*

† The first line appears in 2 Pet. 2²² as part of a couplet different from ours. which is cited not as "Scripture" but as a "true proverb"; it would seem either that the line, taken from Pr., had been recombined in popular use in the second century of our era, or that Pr. took it from a popular saying. The reading in Pet. agrees with the Heb. and the Aram. of Pr., not with the Grk.

29²⁰) the fool is treated as incurable ; here a possibility (though a very small one) is granted him. The point of the proverb is the denunciation of self-conceit. See v.¹⁶ and 29²⁰.

Here ends the Book of Fools, and is followed by a **Book of Sluggards** (v.¹³⁻¹⁶) ; cf. 6⁶⁻¹¹ 24³⁰⁻³⁴.

> 13. The sluggard says : " There is a roaring beast without,
> A lion is on the street."
> 14. The door turns on its hinges
> And the sluggard in his bed.
> 15. The sluggard dips his hand into the dish —
> To bring it to his mouth costs him an effort.
> 16. The sluggard is wiser in his own conceit
> Than seven men who can answer intelligently.

13. Single sentence containing a parallelism, quaternary-ternary. *Without*, lit. *in the way*, that is, in the street. *Roaring beast*, lit. *lion*, a poetic word (Hos. 5¹⁴ Job 4¹⁰ ψ 91¹³ *al.*) ; for this animal Heb. has many names ; see Job 4¹⁰·¹¹. A variation of the proverb is given in 22¹³. — **14.** Comparison, ternary-binary. The sluggard turns *in* his bed without getting out of it. Cf. 6⁹·¹⁰ 24³³. — **15.** Single sentence, quaternary-ternary. *Bring it*, lit. *bring it again*. *Costs him an effort*, lit. *wearies him*, = *he is too lazy to bring it* etc. See note on 19²⁴, with which this couplet is nearly identical. — **16.** Single sentence, ternary. *His own conceit*, as in v.¹². *Answer intelligently*, lit. *answer good sense*, = *answer discreetly* (RV. marg.), not exactly *render a reason* (RV.), though this is involved. — *Seven* is a round number. — The proverb apparently means to say that the sluggard thinks himself wise in avoiding trouble and thus enjoying life — men about him are toiling, but he has repose. Possibly the sage has in mind some form of Epicureanism ; the intimation then is that the sluggard is blind to the higher pleasures of life. He is put beneath the fool in intelligence (cf. v.¹²).

17. Meddling with other men's quarrels.

> He seizes a dog by the ears
> Who meddles with a quarrel not his own.

Single sentence, ternary. In second line lit. : *excites himself over*, = *takes part in, meddles with* (Lat. AV.), or this sense may be

got by a simple change of text. — At the beginning of second
line or the end of first line the Heb. inserts the adj. *passing by*,
whence the translations *who, passing by, takes part* (or, *vexes
himself*, RV.), or *seizes a passing dog* etc.   The first of these
renderings is the more appropriate : it is folly in a bypasser to
mix in a quarrel, but there is no special propriety in designating
the dog as one that happens to be passing by.   This is understood (De. Bi. *al.*) to refer to a strange dog ; one may, it is
suggested, with impunity seize one's own dog, but not a passing
dog.   But the dog was not a domestic animal in Palestine, and to
seize any dog was dangerous.   The adj. in question is in any case
unnecessary and cumbersome, and is probably a gloss or an erroneous repetition ; its omission also improves the rhythm.

18, 19. Folly of deceiving for amusement.

> 18. Like a madman who hurls about
>   Deadly brands and arrows
> 19. Is he who deceives his neighbor
>   And says " I did it in jest " !

18. Single sentence, binary-ternary.   In first line the noun of the
Heb. text may mean " one who is exhausted " (Gen. 47^{13}), or
(Aram.) " stupefied " ; neither of these senses is here appropriate.
A slight change of text gives the sense *madman* (Jer. 51^7), or,
one who plays the fool, feigns madness (1 Sam. 21^{14}), that is, the
jesting deceiver is like a man really insane, or, like one who pretends to be insane ; the second interpretation agrees with the *jest*
of v.^{19}, but the first seems better to convey the sense of the quatrain. — The second line is lit. : *brands, arrows, and death*, the
last term qualifying the two preceding. — **19.** Single sentence, ternary.   In second line lit. : *was* (or, *am*) *I not in jest?* The
quatrain forms a comparison.

20–22. Malicious gossip.

> 20. When there is no wood the fire goes out,
>   And when there is no talebearer strife will cease.
> 21. Charcoal for embers, and wood for fire,
>   And a quarrelsome man to make strife hot.
> 22. = 18^8.

20. Virtual comparison, ternary-quaternary. On *talebearer* see 18[8]. — **21.** Virtual comparison, quaternary. The rendering *charcoal* accords with the term *wood* (that is, in each member fuel is mentioned), but is not certain; in the other passages in which the term occurs (Isa. 44[12] 54[16]) it may mean *burning coal*, a sense not here appropriate. A change of text gives the reading *bellows* (Wild.), which should perhaps be adopted.

23–28. Hypocritical words.

23. Impure silver laid over a sherd —
    Such is ‹ smooth › discourse when the heart is bad.
24. With his lips one who hates dissembles,
    But in his heart he nourishes deceit.
25. When he speaks fair believe him not,
    For seven abominations are in his heart.
26. One may conceal hatred by guile,
    But his malice will be revealed in the congregation.
27. He who digs a pit will fall into it,
    And he who rolls a stone, it will come back on him.
28. A false tongue ‹ brings about destruction, ›
    And an insincere mouth works ruin.

23. Virtual comparison, quaternary-ternary. *Impure silver*, lit. *silver of dross*, = the impure mass left when, in the process of refining, the pure silver has been removed (RV. *silver dross*, = the dross which contains silver).* A sherd overlaid with this mixture had a gloss which resembled that of silver, a false exterior which concealed a mean material. — In the second line the Heb. has *burning* (= *glowing, fervent*) *lips*, which is taken to mean fervent protestations of friendship, but it is hardly a natural expression; the *smooth* (= *flattering, specious*) of the Grk. accords with the first line and with v.[25a. 28]; on the word see note on 5[3]. — **24.** Antithetic, ternary. *Dissembles*, cf. Gen. 42[7] 1 K. 14[5]. *In his heart* is lit. *in his inward part*. *Nourishes*, lit. *puts, sets;* cf., for the verb, Job 38[36] ψ 101[3]; the rendering *arranges* is less appropriate. — **25.** Single sentence, ternary. With the preceding this couplet may be considered to form a quatrain. *Speaks fair,*

---

* It is probable that this dross was largely composed of lead oxide. See Rawlinson, *Phoen.*, ch. x., and the Bible-Dicts. under *silver* and *lead*.

lit. *makes gracious his voice;* cf. v.^{23b}. *Seven abominations,*
= "countless wickednesses." On *abomination* see note on 3^{32}.
— **26**. Single sentence, with one antithesis, ternary. The Heb.
reads : *hatred may conceal itself;* the insertion of *his* before
hatred (so RV.) gives a satisfactory sense ; a different change of
text gives the equivalent reading : *one may conceal hatred.* One
or the other of these changes is required by the following expression *his malice.* — The term *congregation* (5^{14} 21^{16}) means any
assembly. From the time of Deuteronomy on it is generally used
(but not in Job and Prov.) to designate Israel assembled in a
theocratic or ecclesiastical capacity (1 K. 8^{14} Joel 2^{16} *al.*). In
the Persian and Greek periods the Jewish communities in various
parts of the world acquired civic organization, with the right to
administer justice, and the allusion is probably to this function of
the *congregation.** — **27**. Two parallel sentences, quaternary (or,
ternary). Mischief recoils on the perpetrator — a widely diffused
proverb. The pit is supposed to be dug with malicious motive ;
Grk. adds *for his neighbor,* an unnecessary explanation. The
stone is apparently rolled uphill, so that it may descend and crush.
Cf. ψ $7^{15.\ 16(16.\ 17)}$ Eccl. 10^8 BS. 27^{25-27} Esth. 9^1 Dan. 6^{24}. — This general observation seems to receive a special application in the next
couplet. — **28**. Two parallel lines, ternary. *Ruin* is "a blow that
causes a destructive (or, fatal) fall," and so the "ruinous fall"
itself. — The form of the Heb. in first line : *a false tongue hates
its afflicted ones* is improbable, and has called forth a number of
forced interpretations, some of which may be seen in the notes of
Delitzsch and Zöckler. The rendering of RV. : *hateth those
whom it hath wounded* (marg. *crushed*) is incorrect : the last
word is a simple adj., = *oppressed, unfortunate* (ψ $9^{9(10)}$ 10^{18} 74^{21}) ;
and further, the tongue is said in OT. to speak and to smite and
pierce, but never to hate or to crush a person (in 25^{15} it is the
soft tongue that *breaks the bone,* a figurative expression, = "dis-
arms opposition"), and the rendering *crush* is not found in any
Anc. Version. The expression *works ruin* appears to require in
first line some such sense as *deceives its possessor* (or, *owner*), or
brings (or, *produces*) *hate* or *destruction;* Fleischer (assuming an

---

* On the later Jew. civil organization cf. Schürer, *Hist. of the Jew. People,* § 27.

hypallage) : *crushes those whom it hates*, but this is hardly allowable — it is better to change the text. — The couplet may refer to
the ruin brought by the false tongue either on others or on its possessor ; the latter interpretation is suggested by the sense of the
preceding couplet ; the former is the more natural suggestion of
the words.

XXVI. 2. K לא; Q לוֹ; the authorities are given by Ginsburg. The Anc.
Vrss. follow Kethib. — **3.** 𝔊 נֵז; 𝔊 ἔθνει, = גיו, improbable. On the form of
גו see Ols. § 153, Ew. § 146 f., Stade, § 184. — **5.** 𝔖𝔗, stumbling at the formal
contradiction between v.⁴ and v.⁵, put here הכמותך in place of 𝔊 אַוַּלְתּוֹ. —
6. 𝔊 מִקְצֶה; 𝔊𝔖 read מִקְצֵה (𝔊ᴮ ᵃˡ· ὁδῶν should be ποδῶν, as in 𝔖ᴴ 106 *al.*);
𝔏 *claudus ;* 𝔗 רהטא *he who runs*, a free rendering or guess; Bi. מַקְצֶה, which
he takes as = *at the end, finally*, a sense not supported by usage, and not here
specially appropriate; Ew. מִקְצֶה, perh. better than the Act. — 𝔊 חמס; 𝔊 ὄνει-
δος, = חרפה, which is better. 𝔊 ποιεῖται; read πίεται. — שתה is perh. corruption of שלח; we might read : מקצה רגלי מלאכו. — **7.** 𝔊 דַּלְיוּ, possibly intended
for Aramaizing Pi. Impv. of דלה, which, however, is here inappropriate in
sense; Ew. Stade דְּלָיוּ Qal; De. דְּלוּי, but the sense of verbal noun, which he
gives to this form, *the hanging down*, is doubtful (see Ols. § 186 *b*, Barth. *Sem.
Nom.-Bildung*); Hitz. Frank. דָּלֲגוּ (cf. Isa. 35⁶), but the expression *the leaping
of the legs* is strange and improbable. The form of ᵇ permits either a noun or
a verb as first word of ᵃ, but what noun or verb is not clear — the whole clause
is suspicious. — **8.** 𝔊 צְרֹר; better צֹרֵר (𝔊 ὃς ἀποδεσμεύει), parallel to נֹתֵן. But
the whole line seems to be corrupt; possibly it should read : כאבן יקרה באף
חזר. — **10.** The meaning *archer* for רב is doubtful. In Jer. 50²⁹ Job 16¹³ we may
point רבו (instead of רַבִּים); in the latter passage Budde retains the pointing of
𝔊, but renders, by conjecture, *missiles*. In Gen. 21²⁰ Ball emends רבה to רֹמֶה. —
17. 𝔊 אזני; 𝔊 κέρκου *tail*, = זנב (Jäg.). — Omit עֹבֵר as insertion out of following word (מתעבר). 𝔖𝔏 מתערב, which should be adopted. — **18, 19.** 𝔊 מתלהלה;
Frank. מתהלל. On להה in Gen. 47¹³ cf. Ball (in *SBOT.*); the stem appears to
be Aram. (not found in Ass. Arab.), but might occur in Prov. — **21.** 𝔊 פֶּחָם;
𝔊 ἐσχάρα *hearth ;* 𝔏 *carbones ;* Bi. פחת, Inf. of נפח; Wild. מַפֵּחַ (Perles,
Analekt. p. 90). — On 𝔊 מדונים see note on 6¹⁴. — **23.** 𝔊 דֹלְקִים; 𝔊 λεῖα; read
חלקים (Jäg.). — **24.** 𝔊 שֹׂנֵא; 𝔊 ἐχθρός, whence Bi. אִיב. — **26.** 𝔊 תכסה, Hith.;
𝔊 ὁ κρύπτων, = כסה or מכסה (and so 𝔖𝔗𝔏). Read (or שנאתו) מ׳ שנאה, or
תכסה שנאתו. — On the form of מַשָּׁאוֹן (from נשא) see Ols. § 215 *d.* 11. —
27. 𝔊 אליו; 𝔊 ἐφ' ἑαυτόν; read עליו. — **28.** 𝔊 יִשְׂנָא דַּכּוּ; 𝔊 μισεῖ ἀλήθειαν
(and so 𝔖𝔗𝔏), a guess from the connection, or reading Aram. דכא *pure.*
Possibly in יש׳ we have יָשִׂיא (from נשא), and for דכו we might read בעליו
(*befools its possessor*); שנאה יביא, *brings hatred*, is graphically easy, but ש does
not give a full contrast with מדחה; better (or, שָׂאֶה) שֶׁכֶר יָבִיא. — On the omission of the י in דַּכּוּ (Hahn רכיו) see B-D, Ginsb.; it is perhaps a scribal
accident, perhaps veils a different reading of the text.

XXVII. 1, 2. Of boasting.

1. Boast not thyself of tomorrow,
   For thou knowest not what a day may bring forth.
2. Let another praise thee — not thine own mouth;
   Some other — not thine own lips.

1. Single sentence, ternary.* The *boast* implies overweening sense of one's capacity and power. We may omit *day*, reading *what it may* etc.; the sense is the same. Cf. Isa. 56¹² BS. 10²⁶ 11⁴⁻⁶ Jas. 4¹³⁻¹⁶. — **2.** Synonymous, ternary-binary. *Another* and *some other* are lit. *stranger;* on these terms see note on 2¹⁶.

3, 4. Folly and jealousy.

3. A stone is heavy, sand is weighty,
   But a fool [ ] is heavier than both.
4. Wrath is ruthless, anger destructive,
   But before jealousy who can stand?

3. Comparison, quaternary- (or, binary-) ternary. Lit.: *the heaviness of a stone, and the weightiness of sand!* that is, these things are well known, but etc. — In second line the Heb. has: *a fool's anger is heavier* etc.; but *heavy* is not a proper epithet of anger — it is the fool himself that is burdensome; cf. BS. 22¹⁴ ¹⁵, where it is said that a fool is harder to bear than lead, sand, salt, or iron; *anger* is a gloss, perh. suggested by the next couplet. — On *anger* see 12¹⁶ 17²⁵ 21¹⁹; in the Heb. it is the effect of the anger not on the fool himself (Zöck.), but on others, that is meant. Frank., less well, regards the *anger* as that excited in one by the folly of the fool. — **4.** Comparison, quaternary, or binary-ternary. Lit.: *ruthlessness of wrath, a flood of anger!* The *flood* is probably here thought of as destructive; cf. Nah. 1⁸ Job 38²⁵ ψ 32⁶ Dan. 9²⁶ 11²². — On *jealousy* see notes on 6³⁴ 14³⁰. The reference is to the jealousy of a husband; cf. Cant. 8⁶ (the jealousy of married love).

5, 6. Healthy rebuke.

5. Better is open rebuke
   Than a love that is hidden.

---

* Each member of this couplet is composed of four Iambi, but it is evident from the punctuation that the Heb. editors did not so read it; they divided it not by feet, but by ictus.

6. Sincere are the wounds of a friend,
‹Deceitful› the kisses of an enemy.

5. Comparison, ternary-binary. *Open* (lit. *manifested*), frank, direct, from friend or foe. The *love* is hidden, invisible, manifesting itself by no rebuking word, and therefore morally useless; or, by change of vowels: *love that conceals*, that is, does not tell the friend his faults. Frank.: *love given up*, that is, the man, instead of telling his friend his fault, withdraws his friendship without a word; but the rendering *given up* is not possible. De.: "love that does not show itself by helpful deed in time of need," but this gives no antithesis. Cf. BS. 19¹³⁻¹⁵. — The Heb. text is not quite satisfactory — the antithesis *rebuke . . . love* is not clear, and possibly *hate* should be substituted for *love* (cf. v⁶) — "hatred hidden under pretence of friendship." — **6.** Antithetic, ternary. The adj. of first cl. is *faithful, trustworthy*, here = *sincere*. In second line we expect a contrasted term, instead of which our Heb. text gives a word which is represented in the Anc. Vrss. by *suppliant, confused, fraudulent, bad*, but is generally interpreted by modern expositors as = *rich, plentiful, profuse* (so RV.), that is, the enemy is profuse in insincere professions of love. This latter rendering is to be rejected as lexicographically doubtful, and as not furnishing a proper antithesis. For the reading *deceitful* (AV., after Lat.) a change of text is necessary. — For *faithful* cf. 25¹³ Dt. 7⁹ Job 12²⁰; for *wounds* cf. Job 9¹⁷; *friend* and *enemy* are lit. *lover* and *hater*.

7. Hunger is the best sauce.

> One who has enough refuses honeycomb;
> To the hungry any bitter thing is sweet.

Antithetic, quaternary. Lit.: *the full soul tramples on* (= disdainfully rejects) *honeycomb, but to the hungry soul every bitter thing is sweet.* *Soul* here = the person, especially as possessing appetite. RV. *loatheth*, = *rejects*. There is perhaps an allusion to praise and congratulation, which may be nauseous to him who has much of it, grateful to him to whom it rarely comes. — Cf. the references to *honey* in 25¹⁶. ²⁷.

8. There's no place like home.

> Like a bird that wanders from her nest
> Is a man who wanders from his home.

Synonymous comparison, ternary. *Home* is lit. *place*, a general term which may signify either the abode of the individual man or family (Ju. 7⁷ 1 S. 2²⁰), Eng. *home*, or the land of abode, Germ. *heimath* (1 S. 14⁴⁶). For "native land" the Heb. usually says simply "land"; for Eng. "home" it has only the terms "place" and "house" (cf. Fr. *chez lui*, Germ. *zu hause*), but the idea of "home" was doubtless coeval with that of "family." — The reference in the proverb appears to be to any withdrawal from the security and comfort of one's permanent dwelling-place — the wandering of a merchant or a vagrant, the enforced journeying of an exile, or the departure of one who is ejected from his house by creditors or enemies.* There is probably, however, no allusion to Jewish national exile, or to the absence of the Dispersed Jews from Palestine — for that the language is too general, and the Jews of the Dispersion were quite at home in their adopted countries. — The renderings *a bird scared from* and *a man driven from* are not exact.

9. Lit.: *Oil and perfume* (or, *incense*) *make the heart glad, and the sweetness of his friend from counsel* (or, *sorrow*) *of soul.* The first line describes a physical pleasure which is presumably the illustration of a spiritual pleasure to be next described. The second line of the Heb. is unintelligible: the *his* has no antecedent, the expression "sweetness of a friend" is strange and doubtful (cf. 16²¹), and *counsel of soul*, if it be a possible expression, means simply "counsel given," not *hearty* † (or, *highminded* ‡) *counsel*, or *one's own counsel*. § — Grk. (with different text) : *and* (or, *but*) *the soul is rent by misfortunes*, which offers neither par-

---

* De. calls attention to the pathos of the Germ. adj. *elend* "wretched," = *eli lend* "foreign land"; see the citations in Grimm's *Wörterbuch*.

† See Mich. De. Str. *al.* AV. RV.

‡ Ew.: *but a friend's sweetness comes from counsel of soul* (from a "deep, full soul," in contrast with *perfume*).

§ Saad. Rashi, Zöck. *al.*: *the sweetness* (= agreeable discourse) *of a friend is better than one's own counsel.*

allel nor contrast to first line; Lat. (by inversion) : *and the soul
is sweetened by the good counsels of a friend,* an appropriate parallel; Kamphausen: *but sweeter is one's friend than fragrant
woods* (cf. *perfume-boxes,* Isa. 3²⁰), but the introduction of
another physical illustration is improbable; Reuss: *sweet friendship* (= "the sweetness of a friend") *strengthens the soul,* a satisfactory reading but for the phrase "sweetness of a friend." Possibly: *sweetness of speech* (or, *of counsel*) *strengthens* etc.;
"sweetness" is an epithet not of persons, but of things; cf. 16²¹
ψ 55¹⁴⁽¹⁵⁾. — *Oil* (21¹⁷ Am. 6⁶ Ez. 16⁹ Cant. 1³ 4¹⁰) and *perfume*
(see the adj. in Cant. 3⁶) are cosmetics and accompaniments of
feasts. Cf. ψ 104¹⁵ BS. 40²⁰·²¹.*

XXVII. 1. 刵 יום is omitted by 𝕾, Bi.; 𝕮 ἡ ἐπιοῦσα. — **2.** The לא in ᵃ
distinguishes פיך from זר; in ᵇ the אל makes שפתיך the subject of the prohibition. It is a question whether this difference is rhetorical variation, or whether
the לא should be written אל, or the אל be written לא. — **3.** Omit 刵 כעס as
scribal insertion. — **5.** 刵 אהבה may have been induced by the אהב of v.⁶. —
6. 刵 נעתרות. The stem עתר, = *abundance,* is Aram., but can hardly be Heb.,
since the proper corresponding Heb. form עשר exists; cf. Smend, Cornill, Toy
(in *SBOT.*) on Ez. 35¹³, and 𝕮 in Jer. 33⁶. But, even if 刵 be accepted as
Aramaizing form, it is here inappropriate in the only sense (*abundant*) possible for it. The Vrss. give no helpful suggestion. 𝕮 ἡ ἑκούσια, whence Bi.
מנדבת *than the willingness.* Dys.: נערצות *dreadful.* But these emendations
do not furnish the desired antithesis. The form of the couplet does not favor
the introduction of ᵇ by מן (as in 𝕮); as correspondent to נאמנים we expect
an adj., possibly Nif. Part. of עקש (cf. 28¹⁸) or of עוה, = *crooked, evil, deceitful.*
— **9.** קטרת is used elsewhere only of the fragrant vapor or incense of the
ritual service; but the verb (Pu. Part.) = *perfume* in Cant. 3⁶, and the noun
may have this sense here. — 𝕮 οἴνοις is scribal addition for fulness. — 刵 מחק
ורעהו; 𝕮 καταρήγνυται, = מתקרעה (Jäg.), which reading (accepted by Hi. Bi.
Frank.) is incongruous with ᵃ. — 刵 מעצת נפש; Reuss מאמץ נ, good graphically
and in sense. Kamp.: מעצי נ, taking נ as = *fragrance.* Bi. ומתקרעה מעצת נ;
Frank.: וסי מעצבת נ. Possibly the line should read: ומחק עצה מאמץ נ.

10. Of friendship. — The verse is composed of three lines
which, in their present form, appear to have no immediate connection one with another. — **10ᵃ.** *A friend of thyself and of thy
father forsake not* (lit.: *thy friend and thy father's friend* etc.),
= "do not abandon an old family friend for new friends," as

* For Grk. and Rom. use of cosmetics see Beck. Mommsen and Marquardt,
Blümner (Eng. tr. by Zimmern).

youth is often disposed to do. The reference is not specially to seeking aid from such an one, but in general to maintaining friendly relations with him. Only one friend is spoken of. — **10**[b]. Lit.: *And to the house of thy brother go not in the day of thy calamity.* But to whom should one go if not to a brother? "A brother," it is said (17^{17}), "is born for adversity." And even if there be a friendship which is stronger than fraternal affection (18^{24}), this would be no reason for ignoring the family tie — nor is anything here said of such a stronger friendship (see note on v.[10c] below). It is futile to suppose that the prohibition wishes to save the brother distress (Saadia), nor is the reference to excessive visiting (as in 25^{17}), and it is impossible that the sage should lay down the general rule that one should not go to a brother in time of need — such scepticism and cynicism would be out of keeping with the tone of the Book. The text must be regarded as defective, or the clause must be taken as a gloss inserted by some scribe whose experience had made him bitter against brothers, as Koheleth (Eccl. 7^{28}) is bitter against women. We might omit the negative particle and read : *but go to a brother's house* etc., which would be an isolated and unnecessary injunction, unless, with Bickell, the *brother* be taken as = the *friend* of the preceding line, and this is improbable — if *friend* had been meant, it would have been so written. Cf. the warning, in 25^{17}, against wearying one's neighbor with visits. — **10**[c]. *Better is a neighbor who is near than a brother who is far off.* The *near* and *far* refer to space, not to feeling ; the saying is a maxim of common experience. But there is nothing to show that it is this " far-off brother " who is meant in the preceding line — on the contrary the " brother " of the second line is regarded as near. As the text stands, the third line is an independent aphorism, perhaps part of a full couplet, of which the rest has been lost. — A connection between the three lines may once have existed ; but if so, the links have disappeared. If the second line be omitted, a couplet might possibly be formed of the other two.

11-15. Wisdom, prudence, hypocrisy, strife.

> 11. Be wise, my son, and make my heart glad,
> That I may answer him who shall taunt me.

12. = 22⁸.
13. = 20¹⁶.
14. When one blesses another with a loud voice, [ ]
   It is to be reckoned as equivalent to a curse.
15. A constant dripping in a rainy day
   And a quarrelsome woman are alike.

11. Single sentence, condition and consequence, quaternary-ternary. The speaker is the teacher (whether the father or some other), who is concerned for the young man's career, and desires that he may so conduct himself as to furnish a triumphant answer to all assailants. *Wise* is to be taken in the most general sense. For the verb *taunt* (or, *reproach*) see 14^{31} 17^{5} ψ 119^{42} (in the psalm the answer is furnished by religious trust, in the proverb by wisdom) ; for the noun see 6^{33} 18^{3}. The *taunt* (here mentioned as a possibility of the future) will have been induced by some real or supposed misconduct or display of ignorance on the part of the youth. The teacher is held responsible for the faults of the pupil. Cf. 22^{21} 23^{15} BS. 30^{1-6}. — **13.** The text in second line has fem. sing. *a strange woman*, which is to be emended, from the parallelism, to masc. sing. (or, plu.) ; the reference is simply to going security for other persons. — **14.** Condition and consequence, quaternary-ternary. Heb. : *he who blesses his neighbor* (or, *friend*) *with a loud voice early in the morning* (or, *in the morning, rising early*), *a curse it is* (or, *will be*) *reckoned to him*. The expression *early in the morning* refers not to the dawn of good luck (this is not warranted by Heb. usage of language) but to the zeal of the blesser (Jer. 7^{13}) ; the *him* may be either the blesser (he shall be considered to have uttered a curse) or the blessed (he shall be considered to have been cursed). It may be man or God who *reckons*. In the former case the proverb is a rebuke of hypocritical loud-mouthed adulation, which public opinion will regard as concealing willingness to ruin its object, if profit is to be thereby gained. In the latter case the meaning is that a loud-mouthed blessing will excite the anger of the deity, and call down a curse on the person blessed ; in this interpretation the *early* is commonly held to mean " before the issue of the man's good fortune is known " — the deity is offended by this premature assumption. On divine jealousy of human pretensions cf. note on 6^{17} ; elsewhere in OT.

except in early mythical narrative (Gen. 11⁶·⁷), it is directed
against Israel's enemies, or against wickedness, not against mere
good fortune.   It seems better, therefore, to adopt the first interpretation mentioned above. — The *early in the morning* is unnecessary, mars the rhythmical symmetry, and is probably to be
omitted as gloss.   On *curse* see note on 26², and cf. 20²⁰. —
15. Comparison, quaternary-ternary.   The couplet is substantially
identical with second line of 19¹³, on which see note. — Grk. : *drops
drive a man on a wintry day out of the house, so a railing woman
also* [drives him] *out of his own house*.   Our Heb. may in fact be
translated : *dripping drives on a rainy day*, out of which the Grk.
expands its line.   Syr. better : *a drop which drops* (= continues to
drop).   Lat. : *leaking roofs in a cold day*, in which *roofs* is free
translation, and *cold* follows Grk. *wintry*, a sense less probable
than *rainy*.   The roof, made of board, with a layer of earth and
straw, was kept from leaking only by constant repairs.*

16. Lit. : *He who hides her hides wind, and oil meets his right
hand* (or, *his right hand calls for* [or, *meets*] *oil*), which conveys
no sense.   Lat. *he who restrains her is as one who restrains
the wind* † connects the couplet with the preceding, the sense
being supposed to be that he who undertakes to restrain the
woman of v.¹⁵ (whom Rashi regards as unchaste) might as well
try to hold the wind or slippery oil (or, according to Rashi, he
uses oil to get rid of the taint of her presence).   But the verb
does not mean *restrain*, and the interpretation is obscure, unnatural, and improbable.   Grk. : *the north wind is a severe wind, but
by its name is termed auspicious*. ‡   Bickell : *the north wind* [it is
true] *is the cheerfulest of winds, but the* [hot and oppressive]
southwind is called " auspicious."   But, whatever the Grk. translator might attempt, one hardly expects such subtle etymologizing
from the Heb. sage. §   No satisfactory construction of the couplet
has been suggested.   Cf. 25¹⁴·²³ 26¹.

---

* On Pal. roofs see Thomson, *Land and Book*, ch. 25 ; Now., *Arch.*; cf. Mk. 2⁴.

† So Saad. Rashi, Luth. Ew. De. Kamp. RV. *al.*, but not AV.

‡ The Heb. word for *hide* may also = *north ;* the *right hand* represents good
fortune in Grk. Lat. Aram. Arab., though apparently not in Bibl. Heb.; *its name*
comes from a slight change in the word for *oil.*

§ For other impossible readings see De. Wild.

12. Before נִסְתָּר insert וֹ. — **13.** עֲרַב זָר; 𝕲 παρῆλθεν ... ὑβριστής, = עָבַר
זֵד (Jäg.). — נָכְרִיָּה; read נכרי; the ה is insertion induced by following ח, or
else the incorrect interpretation of a scribe. — **14.** בְּבֹקֶר הַשְׁכֵּים; 𝕲 τὸ πρωὶ
may include both words. — לוֹ is to be retained. — **15.** Lag. regards דֶּלֶף
and סַגְרִיר as unintelligible, and thinks the sense *continual* for טֹרֵד "very
funny." But the signification *drop* for דלף (which is perh. Aram.) seems
assured by Job 16²⁰ ψ 119²⁸ Eccl. 10¹⁸ (cf. note on 19¹³) and by Aram. and
Arab. usage. — The origin of the ἅπ. λεγ. סַגְרִיר is doubtful; 𝕲 χειμερινῇ
(= סתו?); 𝕷 *frigoris;* 𝔖𝕿 סגר. The stem סגר in Heb. and Aram. = *shut,*
enclose; in Arab. it = *fill,* whence the noun = *a filling rain* (see the authorities in Lane). Or, our noun may be from a secondary *S*-stem, formed on גר
= *go* (used in Ass. of the running of water); cf. Levy, *NHW.* The connection, with the support of the Ass. or Arab., may justify the rendering *rain.* —
The stem טרד = *drive* in Aram. and Ass. (𝕲 here ἐκβάλλουσιν); for the
intransitive sense cf. Arab. טַרִיר, = *that which follows on, a successor.* — On
מדונים see note on 6¹⁴. — נִשְׁתְּוָה is regarded by some (Qamḥi, *Miklol,*
131 *a*) as Nithpael (cf. Dt. 21⁸ Ez. 23⁴⁸), with omission of Dagesh and transposition of ת and שׁ, by others (Ols. § 275 Stade, § 410 *b, A* Ges.²⁶, § 75 *x*
Hi. De. Str. *al.*) as Nifal. As the form stands, it may be regarded as masc.
(from שָׁוָה), or as fem., with metathesis of ו and ת (Böttch. Kön. i. 591 f.); it
is better, with Ols. Stade, to read fem. נשׁותה (see Str.'s note). — **16.** De.,
for **·**: צֹפְנֵי הוֹן צָפַן רוּחַ, = *he who lays up riches* etc. Bi., for the couplet:
וְחַמָּן יְמָנֵת יִקְרָא (= רוּחַ) צְפֹנָיָה צַחַת רְחִ. Wild.: צְפֹנָיָה צָפַן רוּחַ, and perhaps
וְשֶׁמֶן יְמָנֵת יִקְרָא, = *and oil the southwind is called,* or *the oil of the south is
named* (= *is famous*). These are all desperate expedients.

17–20. Influence, fidelity, sympathy, greed.

17. As iron sharpens iron,
    So man sharpens man.

18. He who tends a figtree will eat its fruit,
    And he who has due regard to his master will be honored.

19. As [] face answers to face,
    So men's minds one to another.

20. Sheol and Abaddon are never satisfied,
    And the eyes of man are never satisfied.

17. Comparison, ternary. Lit.: *Iron sharpens iron* (or, *iron is
sharpened by iron*), *and a man sharpens the face of his friend,*
= "friendly social intercourse develops character." *Face* (if the
word be retained in the text) = *person,* as in 18⁵ — the whole
man. *Friend* = neighbor = any associate. Ew.: *iron together
with iron, and one together with the face of another,* that is, as
iron attracts iron (a fact known as early as Homer), so should

men stand and work together — a good sentiment, but an unnatural translation. Reuss, not so well : *is polished.* — **18**. Comparison, quaternary-ternary. The reward of faithful devotion to one's master as to one's work. The proverb is addressed to servants, and contemplates only the human *master;* cf. Eph. 6[5]. *Has due regard to* is lit. *observes,* = *gives heed to* (Hos. 4[10]). — Grk. *he who plants a figtree* offers no advantage over the Heb. — **19**. Comparison, ternary. Heb. : *as water face to face, so the heart* (= *mind*) *of man to man* (breviloquence for *so the heart of man to the heart of man*), or, *the heart man to man.* The first line in the Heb. yields no sense, and the text has been variously changed. Those who read *as in water* etc.,* or, *as water shows face* etc. *so the heart shows man* etc. (RV. marg.), take the reference to be to the reflection of the face in water, and understand the couplet to state the psychological identity and mutual sympathy of men, or the supposed fact that every man sees only his own nature (pride, for ex.) in other men, or sees himself reflected in other hearts. The *as water* is, however, probably error of text for *as,* and the expression *as face to face* may signify either similarity † or diversity ‡ : men's faces and minds are like or unlike. The latter sense is favored by the fact that what most strikes the attention in men's faces is their unlikeness, and the proverb may = "many men of many minds" ; but the wording of the text rather suggests the former sense, and this interpretation is perhaps supported by v.[17]. — **20**. Comparison, ternary. Cf. 30[16]. On *Sheol* and *Abaddon* see note on 15[11]. The former is the ordinary name of the Underworld, the latter is a poetical synonym ; the combination of the two is rhetorical fulness. As, says the proverb, generations of men forever troop down to the land of Shades, which yet is never filled, so men's desires are never satisfied. On the eye as the symbol of desire see Eccl. 2[10] 4[8], and cf. Eccl. 1[8]. In the connection the reference cannot be to the wish to see new sights. — The Grk. adds the couplet : *he who fixes his eyes is an abomination to the Lord; and the uninstructed do not restrain their tongues;* cf. 16[30] 21[23]. The couplet is possibly a part of the original Heb. text, more probably a scribal addition.

---

* De. Str. Wild. RV. *al.*   † So most expositors.   ‡ So Grk. Frank.

21. Public opinion as test of character.

The crucible for silver and the furnace for gold,
And a man (is to be estimated) according to his reputation.

Comparison, quaternary-ternary. The second line is lit. : *and a man according to his praise,* probably the praise he receives from others. The proverb will thus state the half-truth : "public opinion is generally right" (another side is given in Mt. 5^{11}) — it tests a man as fire tests metals. Less probable are the renderings : *according to that which he praises,* and *that on which he prides himself* (= what he regards as his praise, that is, as his title to praise) — these fail to bring out distinctly the notion of test contained in first line. Fleischer : *a man is* (a test) *to him who praises him;* but obviously the couplet means to apply the test to the man himself. — In 17^3 it is Yahweh who is the tester; here it is man. Section IV. has less of the religious tone than II. — On methods of refining see notes on 17^3 26^{23}. — The Grk. adds : *The heart of the transgressor seeks evil, but the upright heart seeks knowledge* — a sentiment which has many parallels in the Book, and may belong to the original text, or to some similar collection.

22. Folly ineradicable.

Though thou bray a fool in a mortar, []
Thou'lt not ‹ get › his folly out of him.

Single sentence, ternary. The Heb. reads : *his folly will not depart from him;* the causative form *thou wilt not remove* (so Grk.) suits the first line better. — The proverb is a picturesque and forcible way of saying that a fool's folly is his nature; the folly is intellectual, not moral. — At the end of first line the Heb. adds : *in the midst of grit* (or, *bruised corn,* or, *pounded grain*) *with a pestle,* which mars the symmetry of the couplet by unnecessary additions : the "pestle" goes as a matter of course with the mortar, and the "grit" is out of place — it is the fool alone that is pounded. The phrase appears to be a gloss. — Vat. Grk. : *though thou scourge a fool, disgracing him in the council* etc. One Grk. text represents the process as beating the fool up in a mass of preserved fruit (figs, olives, or grapes).*

---

* On the word rendered *mortar* see Moore, *Judges* (on Ju. 15^{19}), and G. A. Smith, *The Book of the Twelve Prophets* (on Zeph. 1^{10}).

17. Omit פְּנֵי. — On יחד cf. Kön. i. 373 f.; the stem is probably חדד (Job 1⁸), and the first י may be Hof. (Ez. 21¹⁴) or Hif., the second Hifil. If the first be read Hif., the Prep. בְ should be omitted. — **19.** כַּמַּיִם 𝔐; 𝕲 ὥσπερ; read כְּמוֹ with Vog. Bi.; Böttch. De.: כַּאֲשֶׁר בַּמַּיִם. — 𝕲 οὐχ ὅμοια, which Böttch. explains as = כְּאֵין דֹּמִים, misreading of כַּאֲשֶׁר בַּמַּיִם; or, the negative particle may be interpretation of the translator. 𝔗 follows 𝔖, except that it inserts the מַיִם of 𝔐. — **22.** וּרְהַכְתֹּשׁ 𝔐; 𝕲 μαστιγοῖς. — On the stem see Ges. *Thes.* BDB.; cf. Heb. Aram. and Arab. כתת. The stem כתש seems to be used of any pounding or pressing of hard or soft substances. It is perhaps Aram.; cf. D. H. Müller, *Sendsch.* 58. — 𝔐 בַּמַּכְתֵּשׁ בְּתוֹךְ הָרִיפוֹת בַּעֲלִי; 𝕲 ἐν μέσῳ συνεδρίου ἀτιμάζων, after which Bi. omits בַּמַ, makes בַּעֲ the beginning of ᵇ, and also with 𝕲, omits מֶּעֱלָיו; ἀτιμάζων he refers to some form of עֲרל. N. Herz (cited by Cheyne) makes συν. = חֶבְרָה *a company* or *society* (Job 34⁸); Cheyne prefers חֲבֵרִיו, and renders the Heb.: . . . *a fool amidst his associates* (or, *equals in rank*, cf. ψ 45⁸), *you would not remove* etc. See *Expos. Times* for May, June, July, 1897. It seems better to retain בַּמַ, and omit the three next words of 𝔐; 𝕲 may have omitted בַּמַ from its similarity to following בְּתוֹךְ. — On הָרִיפוֹת see Hi. (who makes the stem הרף), Ges. The word occurs elsewhere in OT. only in 2 S. 17¹⁹; ʼΑΣ πτισάνας; Θ παλάθας; 𝔏 *ptisanas* (*barley-groats*); in 2 S. 17¹⁹ 𝕲 ἀραφώθ. The form of the stem is uncertain; perhaps רוף, רפף or רפה; cf. Job 26¹¹, and Arab. Aram. רפף, *strike, break*.

23-27. Importance of small and large cattle for the farmer.

23. Look well to the appearance of thy flock,
    Give careful attention to ‹ thy › herds,
24. For riches last not forever,
    Nor ‹ wealth › to all generations.
25. When the hay is removed, and the aftergrowth appears,
    And the grass of the mountains is gathered,
26. Then the lambs will supply thee with clothing,
    And goats furnish the price of a field,
27. And there will be goat's milk enough for thy food, []
    And (enough) for the maintenance of thy maidens.

The poem is a short treatise on the culture of animals, and gives us a glimpse into the life of the rural population of Palestine. The soil of Israelitish Palestine was better adapted to the raising of sheep and oxen than to the production of grain, and the writer points out that it is to the former that the country landowner must look as his chief source of wealth. The introduction of this subject is in accordance with the practical aim of the Jewish gnomic writings. Cf. the works and remarks on agriculture by

Aristotle, Theophrastus, Cato, Varro, Virgil, and others, and the
extracts in the Geoponica.

23. Synonymous, ternary, or quaternary-ternary. *Look well*,
lit. *know* (emphatic). *Appearance*, lit. *face*, = state or condition
(RV.). *Flock*, of sheep and goats. *Give careful attention to*, lit.
set thy mind on. The Heb. has simply *herds* (that is, of cattle
or of sheep and goats) ; the insertion of *thy* (so Grk. and Lat.)
is favored by the parallelism. The context (v.²⁶·²⁷) shows that
the writer has in mind sheep and goats, not large cattle ; so
Nabal (1 S. 25²·⁷·⁸) has sheep and goats. Oxen, however, were
owned in the south of Canaan (Isa. 7²¹ Dt. 8¹³), though the
country seems to have been better adapted to small cattle. See
7²² 14⁴ 15¹⁷ for mention of oxen. — **24.** Synonymous, ternary.
Exhortation to continual effort, which is necessary because one's
stores are constantly being consumed — if one would transmit
wealth, one must be all the time amassing it ; the *wealth* is then
that of rural products, especially sheep and oxen. Or, the wealth
referred to may be non-agricultural, ready money and the like,
and the meaning will then be that flocks and herds are the only
solid and permanent riches ; in that case we must think of the
writer as unfriendly to urban and commercial life. — In second
line the Heb. has *crown* as the term corresponding to *riches ;* this
is explained as = "princely dignity," but the expression is inappropriate to the condition of such a person as is here described ;
a slight change of letters gives the parallel *wealth* (cf. Jer. 20⁶).
— **25.** Single sentence, quaternary-ternary. Lit. : *the grass is
removed and* etc. The connection indicates that this verse gives
the protasis or condition of a conditional sentence, of which the
apodosis or result is expressed in the following verses.* The
grass is removed to the barn in the form of *hay* as food for the
animals. After it is stored appears the second growth of *grass*
(RV. *tender grass*), the *aftergrowth*. This is the growth of the
lower lands, but the high lands (*mountains*) furnished admirable
pastures (1 Sam. 25²), from which also, it appears, the grass (the
term including all herbage) was *gathered*. The haying began in
Nisan (March–April). — **26.** Synonymous, binary-ternary (the

* So Saad. Rashi, Fleisch. De. Str. Wild. Frank. *al.*

first member is perhaps defective). Provision thus laid up, the flock will be well nourished and profitable; animals may be sold, and will thus furnish money to buy *clothing* or a *field*. Probably also in first line there is reference to the making of clothing at home from wool (cf. Job 31[20]); the clothing of the household for the year was doubtless prepared at this time. — **27.** Parallel statements, ternary-binary (according to the emended text). *Goat's milk* here appears as a common article of food. In the enumeration of foods in Dt. 32[13. 14], besides cereals, honey, oil, flesh, and wine, we find *curd* (= sour milk) of kine and *milk* of small cattle (sheep and goats). Meat was rarely eaten; the staples of food were bread, honey, fruits, and the products of the dairy.* — The second line is lit.: *and maintenance* (lit. *life*) *for thy maidens*, but the Prep. (*for*) is probably to be continued. — After *for thy food* the Heb. adds: *for the food of thy household*, thus giving three terms after *enough*, of which Syr. omits the third, and Grk. the second; these two are really synonymous, and it is better to omit the second, which seems to be a gloss (explanation of the third).†

23. 㦮 פְּנֵי; ⑥ ψυχὰς, perhaps = נפש, perhaps (Jäg.) = פני in sense of *person*. — 㦮 עֲדָרִים; read, with ⑥, עֶדְרְךָ. — **24.** 㦮 גֶּזֶר; read אֹצָר (cf. Jer. 20[6]). — 㦮 וְאִם may be retained, or we may read וְלֹא (⑥ οὐδέ). — Before second דר insert ו (Qerē). — **27.** Omit 㦮 לֶחֶם בֵּיתֶךָ (as gloss) with ⑥, whose θεραπόντων represents 㦮 נְעָרֹת (Jäg.) rather than בֵּית. — The first ζωήν of ⑥ appears to be assimilation of the Heb. expression (לחם) to the following phrase, in which ζωήν = חַיֵּי (㦮 חיים).

XXVIII. 1. The courage of a good conscience.

> The wicked flee when no one pursues,
> But the righteous are as bold as a lion.

Antithetic, ternary. *Bold* = confident, secure (11[15] 31[11] Ju. 18[7]). A bad conscience suspects accusers everywhere.

---

* Cf. the standing expression in OT.: *a land flowing with milk and honey* (Ex. 33[8] Ez. 20[6] *al.*); cf. also Eurip., *Bacch.*, 142; Ovid, *Met.* I, 111. For modern customs in Arabia and Palestine see Robinson, *Bib. Res.*, i. 571 *al.*; Palmer, *Desert of the Exodus*, p. 239 *al.*; Thomson, *Land and Book*, I. xxii *al.*

† With this paragraph cf. those passages of the Avesta (as Fargard 3) in which similar prominence is given to the culture of cattle.

2. The first cl. reads : *By the transgression of a land many are its princes,* that is, unstable government (a rapid succession of rulers) is a result of social corruption. Rapid change of rulers may, however, be an accident of the political situation. Possibly we should read : *by* etc. *many are its enemies* (or, *misfortunes*). — The second line is lit. : *but by intelligent (and) instructed men right lasts long,* or, *by men intelligent (and) cognizant of right it* (the existing status) *lasts long;* the second translation (in which the verb is taken as indefinite) is not probable. To understand *right* (in the first transl.) as = "jurisdiction, political authority" (De.) is a somewhat forced interpretation. Still less natural is RV.'s rendering, *state* (= existing status), from the sense "place, basis," which the Heb. word sometimes has. Instead of *men* we may write *man* (De.), the meaning then being that by a single intelligent man political order will be maintained. — Grk., with different text : *by the sin of ungodly men disputes arise, but a clever man will extinguish them,* which is intelligible, but disputes are said in Pr. to arise from the nature of the wicked, not from their sin — the disputes are themselves sin. — If the expression *knowing right* be omitted (as gloss on *intelligent*), we may read : *by a man* (or, *by men*) *of insight it* [the land] *is made stable* (= *is established*) (cf. 29⁴) ; or, if *days* be inserted : *by a man of intelligence its existence is prolonged.* — The text puts "intelligence" as antithesis of "transgression"; this may be understood in accordance with the point of view of Pr., which makes moral error the result of ignorance. — The general sense of the couplet appears to be that moral ignorance and transgression is responsible for political distress or disorder (so the Heb.), or, perh., that quarrels and lawsuits are the work of bad men (so the Grk.), and that order, or peace, is maintained by a broad intelligence which recognizes the claims of the moral law. It is possible, however, that the two lines of the couplet do not belong together.

Oppression of the poor.

> A ‹ wicked ruler › who oppresses the poor
> Is a beating rain which leaves no food.

Virtual comparison, ternary or quaternary-ternary. The Heb. reads : *a poor man and an oppressor of the poor, a beating rain* *and no bread,* that is, *a poor man who oppresses* etc. *is* etc. But in Pr. (or in OT.) a poor man is not conceived of as an oppressor of the poor, is not thought of as being in position to oppress; nor does it add to the distress of the poor that their oppressor is one of their own class. — Grk.: *a bold* (or, *courageous*) *man by wickedness oppresses* (or, *accuses*) *the poor,* whence we might read: *a wicked man who oppresses* etc. By the change of a vowel the sense is obtained: *a ruler* (lit. *a man, a chief*) *who* etc.,* but it is doubtful whether this is an allowable Heb. construction.† The reading here adopted, which is suggested by v.¹⁵, is obtained by a couple of simple changes of the text.

4. Attitude of faithful and faithless toward the wicked.

Those who forsake the law praise the wicked,
But those who observe the law are zealous against them.

Antithetic, ternary, or quaternary-ternary. The special interpretation of the couplet depends on the meaning given to the word *law.* If this means the "law of Yahweh," the national code, then the reference is probably not only to the general fact therein announced, but particularly to the condition of things in the Greek period when many Jews did give up the national religion and attach themselves to foreign rulers and magnates, who are often in the Psalms referred to as the "wicked," and Reuss is substantially right in translating: *the apostates praise the heathen.* If this be the correct interpretation, the couplet forms the only reference in Prov. to such apostasy (cf. ψ 119⁵³ WS. 2–5). — If *law* be taken to be the instruction of the wise (3¹ 4² 7² 28⁷·⁹) the couplet will mean that he who refuses this instruction does thus in effect endorse the wicked, while he who gives heed to it will in effect oppose them. This precise form of expression is not elsewhere employed by the sages in speaking of their own instruction, but the idea is found throughout the Book, particularly in chs. 1–9. — The sense "law in general" does not accord with the verb *forsake,* which implies a body of instruction with which the man stands in

---

* Hitz. De. Bi. Str. Wild. *al.*

† It occurs elsewhere only in the title *chief priest* (2 K. 25¹⁸ *al.*); in Ez. 38² the construction is different, *Rosh* being a proper name.

special relation; for the general idea of law the appropriate verb
would be "transgress." The second interpretation seems to be
the more probable. — The interpretation: *they who praise the
wicked forsake the law* (De.) is not a natural rendering of the
Hebrew.

5. Piety comprehends justice.

> Wicked men do not understand justice,
> But they who seek Yahweh understand it completely.

Antithetic, ternary-quaternary. To "seek Yahweh" is to inquire
of him in order to learn his will in any given case. It was the
technical expression for inquiry at an oracle (2 S. 21[1] *al.*), and so
came to signify dependence on and devotion to the will of God.
— *Understand it completely* is lit. *understand all*, the reference
being to *justice* (in dealings with men). It is only, says the proverb, from the divine will (here = the divine law) that *justice* (here
= *right* in general) can be known. — The couplet has a national
tone rare in Proverbs.

XXVIII. 1. 狃 נסו with sing. noun, and צדיקים with sing. verb; ❺, sing.,
φεύγει and δίκαιος. — **2.** For 狃 שריה we should perhaps read צריה or צרחיה
(cf. Dt. 31[17]). ❺ᵃ read רשעים and רבם; ❺ᵇ, for 狃 יאריך, יֵדַע כֵן יאריך, κατασβέσει
αὐτάς, = ידעכו (Lag.). The reading of ᵃ is not probable; that of ᵇ is better,
but not satisfactory. — Bi. omits יאריך (as repetition out of the two preceding
words), and for ידע כן reads יֵדְעֻן. Dys.: ·ידעך ארי ריב. We may perh. read:
ובאום מבן תָעַמֵד or ·ואדם מ׳ יעמדה. — **3.** 狃 גֶּבֶר רָש; ❺ ἀνδρεῖος ἐν ἀσεβείαις;
read גֶּבֶר רשע, and omit the ו before עשק; Dys. גֶּבֶר קָש; Frank. גֶּבֶר רשע. —
狃 וְאֵין לָחֶם; ❺ καὶ ἀνωφελής, on which see Lag.

6. Honest poverty better than dishonest wealth.

> Better is a poor man whose life is upright
> Than one whose conduct is base, though he be rich.

Antithetic comparison, ternary. A variation of 19[1], on which see
note. Lit. *who walks in his perfectness* and *one crooked of ways*.
— The Heb. has the dual, *two ways*, which is commonly interpreted as referring to the good way and the bad way, between
which the man has to choose; but this representation (appropriate in BS. 2[18]) is here inappropriate — the expression *crooked in
ways* is a common one for "dishonest, base"; a change of vowels
gives the plu. Cf. v.[18] below.

7. Profligacy is unwise.

> He who obeys instruction is a wise son,
> He who consorts with profligates brings disgrace on his father.

Implicit antithesis, ternary-quaternary. Cf. 10^1 13^1 17^{25} $19^{13.\ 26}$ 23^{15} 27^{11}. *Obeys*, lit. *keeps, observes.* The *instruction* meant is that of the father and teacher, not the national law (cf. v.$^{4.\ 5}$). *Wise* is lit. *intelligent.* On *profligates* (= *spendthrifts, rioters*) see $23^{20.\ 21}$. The text assumes that he who heeds instruction will not associate with profligates, and that a wise son brings joy to his father. The first line may also be translated: *a wise son obeys instruction;* the antithesis of *wise* will then be *profligate.* The two lines belong perhaps to different couplets.

8. Against demanding interest on loans.

> He who adds to his wealth by taking interest and increase
> Gathers it for him who is kind to the poor.

Single sentence, quaternary-ternary. In the OT. legislation the taking of interest is regarded as oppressive and is strictly prohibited between Israelites (Ex. $22^{25(24)}$ Dt. $23^{19(20)}$ Lev. 25^{35-37}, cf. Ez. 18^8 ψ 15^5), though allowed in transactions with foreigners (Dt. $23^{20(21)}$) *; the law was, however, frequently violated (Ez. 22^{12} Neh. $5^{7.\ 11}$). Later, when the dispersion of the Jews forced them into commercial life, its provisions were made more stringent (*Bab. Meṣ.* v.). — The objection to charging interest was based on the fact that loans were made to poor men to supply the necessaries of life, not to be employed productively; to demand interest was to take advantage of a fellowman's distress, the antithesis being *kindness to the poor.*† The OT. rule was thus ethically good, except in so far as it excluded foreigners from its benefit. The punishment of the interest-taker here announced is loss of

---

* This interpretation of Dt. 23^{20} is denied, but on insufficient grounds, by Rabbinowicz in the Introd. to his transl. of *Baba Meṣia* (*Législ. civ. du Thalmud,* Vol. 3).

† Charging interest was from early times common in Egypt, Greece, and Rome, and evidently in Israel also; it was a natural condition of lending money and other property. In Greece and Rome it was regulated by law. The opposition to it came from the moralists (as Plato, Arist., Demosthenes), not from the people, and no prohibition of it (in Israel, for example) was effective. See Wilkinson, *Anc. Egypt.;* Erman, *Egypt;* Smith, *Dict. of Grk. and Rom. Antiq.*[8]

wealth, which comes through social laws and divine retribution ; the wealth, by these same laws, falls to the benevolent man (14^{31} 19^{17} 22^{16}). Cf. BS. 3^{12-16}. Whether there was any difference of meaning between the terms *interest* and *increase* is not clear.* RV. retains the word *usury* in its old sense of *interest*.

9. The prayer of a bad man is futile.

> He who refuses to listen to instruction,
> His prayer is an abomination.

Single sentence, quaternary-binary (or, binary). Cf. $15^{8.\,29}$ Isa. 1^{15} BS. $35^{16.\,17}$. Lit. *he who turns aside his ear from hearing :* the reference is to the instruction of the teacher or parent. On *abomination* see note on 3^{32}. — In second line the Heb. has : *also* (or, *even*) *his prayer* etc. ; the " prayer " is, doubtless, merely a petition for some physical gift, and the *also* probably = " on the other hand," the couplet expressing an antithesis, or a relation of reciprocity : " if a man, on his part, is deaf to instruction, then God, on his part, is deaf to prayer." Cf. ψ $18^{25.\,26(26.\,27)}$.

10. Malice rebounds on itself.

> He who seduces the upright to evil
> Will fall into his own pit. []

Single sentence, ternary-binary (in the emended text). Lit. *into an evil way,* that is, probably (as in 8^{13}) into morally bad conduct. The OT. assumes that good men may go astray (Ez. 3^{20} *al.*). For second line cf. 26^{27}. — The first line is sometimes rendered : *he who misleads the upright into misfortune ;* but it is doubtful whether, if leading into unwise investments and the like were meant, the statement would be restricted to the upright (cf. BS. 37^9). Elsewhere (5^{23} 19^{27} 20^1 Job 6^{24} ψ 119^{10} *al.*) the verb *seduce, lead astray,* is used in a moral sense. — The Heb. adds : *And the perfect will inherit* (or, *possess*) *good,* which may be a gloss on this couplet (a reminiscence of such passages as 2^{21} ψ $37^{4.\,9.\,11.\,22.\,29}$),

---

* A distinction is perh. made in Lev. 25^{37}, *interest* referring to loans of money, *increase* to loans of food, but the variation of terms may be merely rhetorical. In Dt. $23^{19(20)}$ the former appears to be used as a general term for interest, and the latter is so employed in *Bab. Meṣ.* v. 1. Cf. Fleisch. in De., Wild. *Litt des AT,* § 7, Now. *Arch.,* § 66.

to bring out the other side of the picture, or perhaps the half of a new couplet, of which the other line has disappeared.

11. A self-conceited rich man.

> A rich man may think himself wise,
> But an intelligent poor man will probe him thoroughly.

Single sentence involving antithesis, ternary. Lit.: *a rich man may be* (or, *is*) *wise in his own eyes; probe thoroughly = search out.* Rich men, the proverb holds, being financially successful, are inclined to have great confidence in themselves (cf. 18[11]), but wisdom does not always go with wealth. Here, as elsewhere, the sage takes a defensive attitude for the poor against the rich — doubtless from the conviction that the former need help (cf. Eccl. 9[14-16]).

12. Contrasted administrations of righteous and wicked. —

The text is uncertain. Heb.: *when the righteous rejoice, great is the glory, but when the wicked arise, men are sought out* (or, *searched*). Antithetic. *Rejoice* is explained as = *triumph*, equivalent to *arise*, that is, "come into power," and *are sought out* as = *must be sought out*, = *hide themselves*, or, *are plundered* (with reference to Ob. 6, in which, however, the text appears to be defective). These interpretations are strained; in the sense *search* (= examine) the last verb of the couplet is not elsewhere in OT. followed by a noun meaning a person. The couplet should probably be emended so as to read somewhat as follows: *when the righteous are exalted there is great confidence, but when the wicked come into power men hide themselves,* that is, when good men control a city or state, there is prosperity — when bad men are in power, the people suffer. Cf. for *exalted* ψ 47[9(10)] 97[9], and for *confidence* Job 4[6].

6. 𝕳 du. דרכים; point as plu. — 12. 𝕳 בַּעֲלֹץ; read, perh. בִּהְעָלֹת. — 𝕳 תִּפְאֶרֶת is possibly for תִּקְוָה. — For 𝕳 יְחֻפַּשׂ we may read יִסָּתֵר (v.[28]) which is graphically not impossible. Dys.: יֵחָשֵׂף or יְפֻשַּׁט; Perles and Frank. suggest חֻפַּז *tremble.* — In ᵃ Bi. omits רַבָּה on rhythmic grounds.

13. True repentance.

> He who conceals his transgressions will not prosper,
> But he who confesses and forsakes them will obtain mercy.

Antithetic, ternary. *Conceals* is lit. *covers*, = refuses to confess. The *confession* is made to God and the *mercy* is accorded by him. Cf. Hos. 14[2-4] Isa. 1[16-18] Job 31[33f.] ψ 32[5]. Forgiveness is here made to depend not on sacrifice, but on purely ethical conduct. Confession is assumed to be a necessary accompaniment of repentance. Kindness to a repentant sinner is enjoined in BS. 8[5].

14. Fear of sin.

> Happy is the man who fears always,
> But he who hardens his heart will fall into misfortune.

Antithetic, quaternary (or, ternary). *Fears* = not *reverences* (3[7] 24[21]), but *is afraid of, in dread of* (3[24] Job 3[25]). The object of the verb is here probably not "God," but "sin" considered as involving "punishment" : one who fears that he may transgress a divine command is said to be *happy* because he is on his guard, and will thus escape punishment. — *Hardens his heart* (that is, his mind, himself), braces himself in his own doings, does not dread sin. The *misfortune* (contrasted with *happy*) is sent by God, but is probably thought of as produced by natural agencies. The point presented is not directly fear of moral impurity, but dread of its physical consequences.

15. The oppressive ruler.

> A roaring lion and a ranging bear —
> Such is a wicked ruler over a poor people.

Comparison, ternary, or quaternary-ternary. Cf. v.[3]. *Roaring lion*, cf. 19[12] Jud. 14[5] Zeph. 3[3] Ez. 22[25] Job 4[10] ψ 22[13(14)]. *Bear*, cf. 17[12] 2 K. 2[24] Am. 5[19] Isa. 59[11]. The *lion* and the *bear* occur together in 1 S. 17[34]. — *Ranging* is roaming in pursuit of prey (cf. Joel 2[9]), or the word may = *greedy* (cf. Isa. 29[8] ψ 107[9]) ; we should perhaps read *robbed of her whelps*, as in 17[12]. — The reference in *a poor people* may be to any financially poor community, or there may be special allusion to the later Jewish communities.

16. Folly of oppression. — Lit.: *A prince* (or, *O prince*) *devoid of understanding and a great oppressor — he who hates unrighteous gain will prolong his days.* The first line may also be read : *a prince* etc. *is a great oppressor*, but the natural form

would be : *a prince who is an oppressor is devoid of intelligence.*
The word *prince* should probably be omitted as the gloss of a
scribe who interpreted this couplet by the preceding. We should
probably read : *he who is oppressive is lacking in intelligence, he
who hates unjust gain will live long.* The *live long,* = "be happy,"
forms an implicit contrast to *lacking in intelligence,* = "knows not
what is good for him."

17. Lit. : *A man oppressed by the blood of a person flees* (or,
must flee) *to a* (or, *the*) *pit — let them not seize him* (or, *support*
or *maintain him*). The words yield no sense. The term
oppressed cannot mean conscience-stricken (De.) — elsewhere in
OT. it always refers to external acts ; nor is it a natural expression for "weighted with guilt." The *pit* is not the grave (De.
Frank.) — a man cannot be said to "flee to the grave." The
criminal referred to is hardly the grinding, destructive oppressor
of the poor (Frank., see note on 1[11]) — if such an one should be
"fleeing to the grave" it would be quite unnecessary to forbid
men to help him. Possibly there is some reference to the *lex
talionis :* "if a man charged with homicide flee to a city, let no
one seize (or, protect) him." The sentence (which is prose)
perh. belonged in a lawbook, and was here inserted by mistake.

18. Profit in integrity.

> He who lives blamelessly will be kept in safety,
> But a man of vicious life will fall [].

Antithetic, ternary (in the text as emended). Lit. *he who walks,*
and *one crooked of ways.* The second line reads in the Heb. :
but one crooked (= *false, evil`, in two ways will fall in one.* The
dual *two ways* is improbable (see note on v.[6] above), but if it be
retained, the statement that a man doubly false is sure to fall in
one way or another seems an unnatural and improbable mode of
expression. The sense *at once, suddenly,* for the word above rendered *in one* is doubtful, and here not appropriate. Lagarde
emends : *into a pit.* This is possible, but it is better to omit the
word, and thus gain the simple and sufficient contrast of *be kept
in safety* (lit. *be rescued*) and *fall;* the *in one* (of the ways)
appears to be a gloss on the *two ways* of the Heb. text. — The

reward and punishment are to be referred to God. On *blame-lessly*, lit. *blameless, perfect*, see notes on 1[12] 2[21], and on *vicious* (or, *evil*), = *crooked*, see 2[15].

15. דב 𝔐; 𝔊 λύκος, apparently = Aram. דיב or ראב. For שקק 𝔐 we should perh. read שקל. — **16.** Omit נגיד 𝔐 (as gloss) and the ו before רב, and insert ו before שנא (Q). נגיד in sense of *prince* only here in Pr.; cf. Job 31[37] Dan. 9[25. 26] 11[22]. For ורב 𝔐 Dys. reads יָרֵב. — חבונות 𝔐; 𝔊 προσόδων, = תבואת (Trom.); Lag. cites Suet., *Calig.* 38. — **17.** For the expression דם נפש cf. Jer. 2[34]. — עד בור 𝔐; 𝔊 ὁ ἐγγυώμενος, = עָרְבוּ (Lag.). — אל 𝔐; 𝔊𝔏 render as if it were לא. — עשק 𝔐 and בור; possibly to be read שֹׁפֵךְ and עיר. — **18.** דרכים du. 𝔐; read plu. — בְּאַחַת 𝔐; 𝔊 ἐμπλακήσεται, to which 254. 297 add εἰς κακά; 𝔖 בגומצא, = בְּשׁחוּת (Vogel), cf. v.[10]. Lag. (and so Dys. Bi.) reads בְּשַׁחַת. The word is better omitted as gloss suggested by v.[10].

19–22. Industry, integrity, greed.

19. He who tills his land will have plenty of bread,
  And he who follows vain pursuits will have plenty of poverty.

20. A trustworthy man will be richly blessed,
  But he who hastes to be rich will not go unpunished.

21. To have respect of persons is not good —
  For a piece of bread a man may sin.

22. An avaricious man hastens to be rich,
  Not knowing that want will befall him.

19. Antithetic, ternary. Variation of 12[11], on which see note; the antithesis (*bread . . . poverty*) is here more direct. — **20.** Antithetic, binary (or, ternary). *Trustworthy* = faithful to commercial and other obligations. Lit.: *will be great in blessings;* the *blessings* are the products (and so the rewards) of honest labor, as in Gen. 49[25] Mal. 3[10], or, gifts, as in Ju. 1[15], the giver, however, being God. — The *hastes*, it is assumed, involves dishonest procedures; the man, in that case, will not be *unpunished*, or will not be (or, be held) *free from guilt* (cf. 6[29] 11[21] 16[5] 17[5] 19[5. 9]). The former sense gives a direct contrast to the *blessed;* possibly, however, the meaning is: "a man who is in a hurry to become rich will fall into dishonest practices and thus incur guilt" (see 1 Tim. 6[9]). — Cf. BS. 31[5-8]. — **21.** Synonymous, binary. On first line see notes on first line of 18[5] and second line of 24[23]. The couplet refers to corruption in courts of law — a man may be tempted (or, many a man is tempted) even by a small bribe (*a* *piece of bread*, cf. 6²⁶).— **22**. Single sentence involving antithesis, ternary. *An avaricious man*, lit. *one evil of eye*, one whose look is unsympathetic, self-seeking; the expression occurs in OT. only here and 23⁶ (on which see note), the opposite, *good of eye* (= kindly benevolent), in 22⁹. The man stints himself and others; but his parsimony is an economic mistake, and leads to poverty. There may also be the suggestion (as in v.²⁰) that greed leads to or involves sin, and will be punished.— *Not knowing*, cf. 7²³; the expression may also here = *not considering*, hardly *without his knowing* (= unawares).

23. Reproof vs. flattery.

> He who reproves [] will find more favor
> Than he who flatters with the tongue.

Single sentence, ternary-binary. An assertion that men's good sense will prefer honest reproof to flattery; cf. 15⁵·¹² 25¹² 27⁵·⁶ 29⁵.— Lit.: *he who reproves a man*, after which the Heb. has *after me*. This latter, if it here mean anything, can mean only "in accordance with my instructions," a strange and improbable direction for the sage to give.* The translation: *a man going backward* (De.), is out of the question. Better, by change of text: *will afterward find*, that is, though flattery at first be sweet, one will in the end be grateful for honest rebuke.† But the sense "afterward" is involved in the declaration, and the word is probably a gloss. Bickell, improbably: *than he who flatters with the tongue after him*, that is, servilely follows him with flattery.

24. On robbing parents.

> He who despoils father or mother
> (Saying: "there is no wrong in it")
> Is companion to him who is a destroyer.

Triplet (if the second line be original), single sentence, ternary-binary-ternary. *Despoils* = *robs* (22²²); *destroyer*, that is, of property (cf. 6³² 11⁹ 18⁹), or, of the family life — probably, from the connection, not *murderer*. The proverb appears to be aimed at

---

* Aben Ezra, Mich.: *after my* [Solomon's] *example and precepts.*
† Lat. Rashi, RV. Reuss, Kamp. Wild. Frank.

attempts (legal or other) by children to get control of the property of parents, and thus diminish their resources (cf. Mk. 7[11.12]).
For ordinary theft, or for simple unkindness, no such form of
condemnation would have been used. The practice in question
was evidently not uncommon, and (as appears from second line)
was sometimes defended as morally proper, probably on the ground
that the family was a unit, that what belonged to the parents belonged legally to the children. The OT. legislation, in fact, contains no provision bearing on this point; the declaration of the
proverb is based on general ethical grounds. The second line
states in a natural way the defence offered by the son; yet the
very naturalness of it suggests that it is a gloss. To the people of
the time the couplet would be complete and intelligible without it,
but such an explanation would easily occur to an editor. — The
couplet is sometimes understood to refer to the case of a son who
is master in the house and is bound to support his parents, but
withholds their proper maintenance. This interpretation hardly
credits the verb *despoil* with its full force ; nor does it appear how
a son could be master in the lifetime of his father. — Cf. Pers.,
Sat. 6 ; Juv., *Sat.* 14.

25, 26. On trust in self and trust in God.

25. A greedy man stirs up strife,
     But he who trusts in Yahweh will prosper.
26. He who trusts in himself is a fool,
     But he who walks in wisdom will be saved (from harm).

Antithetic, ternary. *Greedy* is lit. *large* (lit. *wide*) *of appetite* (lit.
soul) ; cf. Isa. 5[14] Hab. 2[5].* — *Prosper*, lit. *be made fat;* see 11[25]
13[4] 15[30].—To "trust in one's self" (one's *heart*, intellect) is
(according to the parallelism) to follow the untrained suggestions
of the mind (passion, selfishness, dishonesty), or, to rely wholly
on one's own mental resources, opposed to which is living in
accordance with the instruction of ethical wisdom. — *Will be
saved*, that is, in any emergency where true insight into life is

---

* On the similar phrase *wide of heart,* =*proud*, see note on 21[4]. De.'s statement that *nefesh* (*soul*) = the "natural heart," and *leb* (*heart*) = the "spiritual
heart," is without support in OT.

required. — The lines appear to be dislocated : v.[26a. 25b] form a natural couplet ; v.[25a. 26b] have lost their correspondents.

27. Kindness to the poor.

> He who gives to the poor will not lack,
> But he who disregards them will have many a curse.

Antithetic, ternary.   Similar exhortations to liberality and kind-
ness are found in $11^{24. 25}$ 14^{21} 19^{17} 22^9 BS. 4^4 7^{32} 29^{20}; cf. $31^{6. 7. 20}$. —
Disregards, lit. *hides his eyes*, so as not to see distress. — The
curse is uttered by the *poor;* cf. BS. 4^6, in which it is said that
such curse will be heard by God.   Cf. note on 26^2.

28. Wicked government.

> When the wicked are in power men hide themselves,
> And when they perish the righteous increase.

Antithetic, ternary (or, quaternary-ternary).   *Are in power* is lit.
rise.   Increase, that is, in numbers, being free from oppression.
See note on v.[12] above.   The reference is to political administration in the City and the State, perhaps especially to the later fortunes of the Jews.   Cf. notes on 11^{10} $29^{2. 16}$. — The interpretation
of *increase* as = *become mighty* is hardly allowable (in 29^2 the text
must be changed), and its emendation to *rule* is not appropriate ;
cf. 29^2.

20. In explanation of 𝕲 Lag. refers to 11^{21} $19^{5. 9}$. — **21.** 𝕳; פָּנִים; 𝕲[B al.] πρόσ-
ωπα δικαίων, and 𝔖ⁱⁿ. 𝔖[H] had apparently π. ἀδίκων, whence Bi. reads פְּנֵי
רְשָׁעִם; but it seems more probable that the insertion is interpretation, after
18^5; cf. Dt. 1^{17}. — **22.** Bi. omits 𝕳 כִּי, but his rendering: *he knows not —
want comes*, is doubtful. — **23.** 𝕳 אַחֲרֵי; 𝕲 ὁδοὺς perh. = כְּאָרְחוֹ (Lag.), a somewhat unnatural locution; Kamp. Wild. אַחַר; Frank. suggests that 𝕳 may be
an Aramaic form, = אחר. The word is better omitted as gloss or dittogram. —
24. If we omit 𝕳 פֶּשַׁע, וְאֹמֶר אֵין, then following הוּא is, on rhythmical grounds,
better omitted.   Bi. makes a couplet of the v., omitting וְאֹמוּ as dittogram,
and writing [a] : גֹּזֵל אָבִיו וְאֹמֶר אֵין פָּשַׁע — a division rhythmically and syntactically
good, if [b] be retained.

XXIX. 1–3. Peril of persistence in sin.   Value of probity.

> 1. He who, being often reproved, persists in wrong-doing
>   Will suddenly be destroyed, and that without remedy.
> 2. When the righteous ‹ rule,› the people rejoice,
>   When the wicked govern, the people groan.

3. A man who loves wisdom rejoices his father,
He who keeps company with harlots wastes his substance.

1. Single sentence, ternary. Lit.: *a man of reproofs who hardens* (or, *stiffens*) *his neck will suddenly be broken to pieces* etc.; cf. 6^{15} 13^{18} 15^{10}. Stiffening the neck, in obstinate persistence, is the opposite of bending the neck, in token of submission. — The term *suddenly* may refer to the law of divine intervention; more probably it signifies that the man, secure in his obstinacy, does not foresee misfortune. The reproof comes from human teachers and judges. — **2**. Antithetic, ternary (or, quaternary-ternary). The Heb. has: *when the righteous increase*, the suggestion being that they then have control of affairs (so Saad. RV. marg.) ; the change of a letter gives the reading *rule*, which is required by the *govern* of second line. Cf. $11^{10.\ 11}$ $28^{12.\ 28}$. — **3**. Antithetic, quaternary-ternary. On first line cf. 10^1 $23^{15.\ 24}$ 27^{11}; on second line cf. $5^{9.\ 10}$. Licentiousness is put as the opposite of wisdom, as in $2^{10.\ 16}$ 5^{1-3} $6^{23.\ 24}$ $9^{1.\ 13}$. — In second line the predicate *wastes* etc. (instead of the precise antithesis *grieves his father*) states that which causes the father sorrow.

4, 5. Royal administration. Malicious cajolery.

4. A king by justice gives stability to a land,
But he whose exactions are excessive ruins it.

5. A man who cajoles his neighbor
Spreads a net for his steps.

4. Antithetic, ternary (or, quaternary-ternary). *Gives stability*, lit. *establishes* (*causes to stand*) ; stability involves prosperity. In second line lit. *a man of exactions;* cf. *a man of reproofs* in v.[1]. — Everywhere else in OT. the word here rendered *exactions* denotes ritual offerings (2 S. 1^{21} Isa. 40^{20}), which in the Israelitish law were of the nature of imposts or taxes (Dt. 12^6 Ex. 25^2 Ez. 44^{30} 45^{13-16} Lev. 7^{14} Nu. 5^9 Mal. 3^8) ; here the term is employed in the non-ritual sense. The royal *exactions* might be legal taxes or demands for " voluntary " gifts; probably all sorts of demands for money are meant. Cf. v.[14].* — **5**. Single sentence, ternary. Cf. 2^{16} 7^5

---

* On the method of collecting taxes in Egypt in the middle of the third century B.C. see the great Greek papyrus discovered by Petrie, and published by Grenfell and Mahaffy (cf. *Recent Research in Bible Lands*).

26^{28} 28^{23}. *His neighbor* = any person.   The word *flatter* in first
line (RV.) does not exactly represent the Heb. term, which suggests guile and seduction.

6. Security and happiness of probity. — Antithetic, ternary.
Heb. : *in the transgression of a bad man is a snare, but the good
man is joyful and glad.*   In first line the Syr. has the simpler
form : *the bad man is snared in* (or, *by*) *his sin.*   The implication is that the righteous has no fear of snares, and may therefore
be lighthearted ; the text does not warrant the interpretation that
he rejoices because the sinner has fallen into the snare and been
destroyed. — A more satisfactory form is perh. given by reading
path for *transgression,* and *may run* for *is joyful.*

7. The cause of the poor. — Heb. : *the good man regards the
rights of the poor, the bad man does not understand knowledge.*
Antithetic.   *Good* = *righteous.*   *Regards* is lit. *knows,* = " has
sympathetic knowledge of," " considers favorably " ; see note on
12^{10}, and cf. ψ 1^6 37^{18} ; this pregnant sense of the verb belongs particularly to the later language.*   *Rights* = *cause* (properly the
legal judgment, the justice due) ; see 20^8 $31^{5.\,8}$ Jer. 5^{28} ψ $140^{12(13)}$.
The word *poor* refers to physical poverty (10^5 19^{17} 22^{22} ψ $41^{1(2)}$
al.). — The expression *does not understand knowledge* is usually
explained as = " has no knowledge of (= no concern for) the
poor," but the words will hardly bear this interpretation ; *understand knowledge* means simply " have understanding or knowledge
or insight " (19^{25} Isa. 32^4), and such reference to intellectual
clearness and vigor is not what is required in our couplet.   The
text may be changed so as to read *the wicked* (or, *bad*) *man does
not understand justice,* or . . . *does not plead for the needy* (cf.
31^9 Jer. 5^{28}).

8. Wisdom is a peacemaker.

> Unscrupulous men kindle discord in a city,
> But wise men turn aside anger.

Antithetic, ternary.   *Unscrupulous men,* lit. *men of scoffing* (see
1^{22}), men who laugh at moral obligations, and stir up the baser

---

* Cf. the early use " to know intimately (that is, carnally)," as in Gen. 4^1.

passions of their fellow-citizens (Isa. 28[14]). *Kindle discord in,*
Elizabethan Eng. *inflame* (RV. *set in a flame*), lit. *blow up* (a
fire) ; so in Ez. 21[31(36)], cf. Cant. 2[17] 4[6. 16]. Elsewhere in Pr. the
verb = *utter* (that is, "puff out words," 6[19] 12[17] 14[5. 25] 19[5. 9]) ; cf.
ψ 10[5], *puffs at, poohpoohs;* in ψ 12[5(6)] the sense is rather *pants
after, desires.* — The *anger* is that of the men (the parties) of the
city.

9. Lawsuits between wise men and fools. — Lit. : *A wise
man has a lawsuit with a fool, and he is excited* (lit. *trembles*)
and laughs and there is no quiet (or, *rest*). The subject of second
line may be the *wise man* (Lat.), with the sense : *whether he be
angry or laugh, there is no quiet* (no end to the contention), or
the *fool* (Grk.), who is then said to show, by his excitement (that
is, probably, his anger) and his frivolous or derisive laughter, that
he has no sense of the seriousness of the situation. The predicates *is angry* and *laughs* appear to belong more naturally to the
fool than to the *wise man,* who is rather marked by quiet (Eccl.
9[17]) ; the expression *there is no quiet* can hardly mean *constantly*
(see Job 17[16] Eccl. 4[6] 6[5]). — The general sense seems to be that it
is not advisable for a wise man to have a controversy with a fool.
According to OT. usage the predicate in first line signifies an
action at law (1 S. 12[7] Jer. 2[35] Ez. 17[20] Isa. 43[26] ψ 9[19(20)]), not any
quarrel or controversy. *Quiet* (or, *peace*) is understood by some
as = *silence,* that is, the fool talks so much that there can be no
profitable discussion.

XXIX. 2. 觀; רבת ; ⅎ ἐγκωμιαζομένων, = ברכח (Jäg.) or perhaps הברך
(Lag.); read רדח.— 觀 plu. צדקם ; better sing. (Bi.).— **3.** The parallelism
suggests the omission of איש.— **4.** 觀 איש חרומח; ⅎ (followed by ℌ) παράνομος, = איש תרמית (Lag.) or איש תרמוח (Baumg.), cf. Kethib in Jer. 14[14]. ⅃ *ava-
rus.*— **6.** 觀 רשע; Pinsker (*Bab.-Heb. Punktationssystem,* p. 156) רעשׁ (1 S. 20[8]).
— 觀 ירן; Pinsk. ירץ; Dys. ירם ; ℌ νικος . . . בפשעו.— **7.** 觀 ידן דעח is suspicious; possibly ירן עני.— **9.** את איש may be omitted.

10. Lit. : *Men of blood hate a perfect man, and upright men
seek his life,* the second line of which is impossible. To put a
pause after *upright men,* reading : *men of blood hate a perfect man
and upright men — they seek his blood,* gives an unsymmetrical
division of lines and a loose grammatical form. The renderings :

and as for the upright, they (the men of blood) *seek his* (the upright's) *life* (RV.) and (Zöck. RV. marg.) : *but the upright care for his life* (or, *soul*) are unwarranted (the construction is different in ψ 142⁴⁽⁵⁾). We may change *upright* to *wicked*, or *seek* to *seek out* (that is, " care for "). The emended verb occurs in 20²⁵ in the sense *examine into, reflect on* (vows), and in Ez. 34¹¹·¹² in that of *seek out* (scattered sheep) ; in this sense of *inquire after* it may = "look after the interests of" (cf. ψ 142⁴⁽⁵⁾). Bickell : *the upright seek to refresh* (or, *sustain*) *him.* — The second emendation calls for the less change in the Hebrew ; the first gives the more probable sense.

11. Restraint of anger.

> A fool utters all his wrath,
> But a wise man ‹ restrains his anger.›

Antithetic, ternary. In second line the Heb. reads : *but a wise man stills it back;* the *it* naturally refers to the fool's wrath, but it is obviously the wise man's wrath that the couplet contemplates. The verb *still* (ψ 89⁹⁽¹⁰⁾) does not accord with the adverb *back*, and the *constr. pregnans* (RV. *keepeth it back and stilleth it*) is improbable ; nor can *back* = " in the background of his soul " (De.), or "afterwards" (Siegf.). The Grk. suggests the appropriate term *restrain* (Bi.), and for the doubtful *back* we may read *his anger* (Frank.). — *Wrath* is lit. *spirit* (= *mind* or *frame of mind* or *temper*), here, from the connection (as in Eccl. 10⁴), a state of wrath.

12–14. Great and poor.

> 12. If a ruler listens to falsehood,
>   All his servants are wicked.
> 13. The poor and the oppressor meet together,
>   Yahweh gives light to the eyes of both.
> 14. A king who deals equitably with the poor,
>   His throne will be established forever.

12. Condition and consequence, ternary-binary. *Falsehood* is here any sort of untruthful statement, as unjust accusation (especially of the poor), falsity in civil administration and political relations ; the courtiers adjust themselves to the prince. — *Servant* is any

functionary in the service of the king (1 S. 16⁵ 2 S. 2¹². ¹³ 2 K. 5⁶
Pr. 14³⁵ *al.*). — **13.** Single sentence, ternary. A variation of 22²,
on which see note. *Oppressor* seems to be a general term,
involving all sorts of hard procedures, financial and other (cf. the
similar term in ψ 10⁷ 55¹¹⁽¹²⁾ 72¹⁴), but there may be special reference to money (cf. the *rich* of 22²) ; Grk.: *creditor and debtor*.
— *Meet together*, as in 22². — The second line = "God enables
both to see," that is, " gives to both the light of life " (ψ 13⁴ Job
33³⁰ Eccl. 11⁷), creates both, permits them to exist, and controls
them — that is, there must be social classes, but God governs all.
— **14.** Single sentence, quaternary-ternary. Lit. : *who judges the
poor in truth.* Cf. 16¹² 20²⁸ 25⁵ 31⁵. The perpetual duration of
the dynasty is made to depend not on physical or intellectual but
on moral character ; the sage has in mind probably divine blessing, possibly economic and other social laws ; cf. ψ 18⁵⁰⁽⁵¹⁾ 45⁶⁽⁷⁾
72¹⁷.

15–17. Training of children. Triumph of the righteous.

15. The rod of correction gives wisdom,
    But a child left to himself brings disgrace on his mother.
16. When the wicked ‹ are in power,› wrong increases,
    But the righteous will feast their eyes on their fall.
17. Correct thy son, and he will yield thee comfort,
    And give delight to thy soul.

15. Antithetic, ternary (or, quaternary). Lit. : *rod and correction*, hendiadys. Cf. 13²⁴ 23¹³. For *left to himself* (lit. *let go,
= unrestrained*) see Isa. 16² (*scattered nestlings*) 27¹⁰ (*a scattered
home*), and cf. Job 39⁵. *Brings disgrace*, cf. 10¹ 17²¹. The *mother*
appears to be named not as being the tenderer parent, perhaps as
the one who has most to do with the training of the young child,
possibly for rhetorical variation (cf. 17²¹ 23²⁴. ²⁵). Grk. *parents*
may be free translation. — **16.** Implicit antithesis, ternary. Cf.
11¹⁰. ¹¹ 28¹². ²⁸ 29². In first line, for Heb. *increase*, read *govern* (as
in 29²), or *are in power*. — The second line assumes that right
will prevail in civil government as in all other things. *Feast the
eyes on* is lit. *see in* (so Ez. 28¹⁷) ; the fall of the wicked is the
salvation of the righteous (ψ 3⁷⁽⁸⁾ 5¹⁰⁽¹¹⁾ 34²¹⁽²²⁾ and *passim*) — a
sentiment engendered by the conflicts of the later times (cf. the

English Puritans of the seventeenth century). — The couplet separates two similar couplets, and is perhaps out of place. In the Grk.
it stands both here and after 28[17]. — **17.** Single sentence (with two
identical consequents), ternary. See 19[18] and passages referred
to under v.[15]. *Yield comfort* is lit. *give rest*, relieve from anxiety ;
see Dt. 12[10] 2 S. 7[1] Ez. 5[13] Lam. 5[5] *al.*

18. Heb.: *where there is no vision people perish* (or, *become
disorderly*), *but he who obeys instruction* (or, *law*), *happy is he.*
Antithetic, ternary. The word *vision* must refer to divine com-
munications to prophets, and the text gives the two forms of Israelitish divine revelation. But the *vision* can hardly be genuine.
The statement of first cl. is historically incorrect : the most calam-
itous period of Israelite history, politically and morally, was that
during which prophecy was at its height (and foreign nations do
not come into consideration), and the people were obedient at a
time when God hid his face and there was no prophet (ψ 44. 74).
Moreover, Pr. nowhere else mentions prophetic teaching, its
guide being wisdom, the instruction of the sages. We should
probably substitute for *vision* some such word as *guidance* (see
11[14]). — *People* = "folk," as in 24[24] Ez. 36[3] ψ 22[6(7)], not *the people*,
the nation. The precise meaning of the verb of first line is
doubtful ; it appears to be equivalent to the "fall" of 11[14] ; the
signification "become disorderly, throw off restraint" is assumed
from Ex. 32[25].

10. 𝕳 יִבָּקֵשׁוּ; Dys. יבקרו. It is perhaps better to change רְשָׁעִים to רֶשַׁע. —
Bi. יבקשו נָפֵשׁוּ, citing, for such Aram. form, the רִחַת of Hos. 13[1]; but the form
רחת is doubtful (see 𝕲), and for a Heb. verbal noun נֶפֶשׁ there is no authority;
for נֶפֶשׁ *respiration, quiet* see Buxt. *Lex.* — **11.** On the sense *quiet* for stem
שׁבח see Lane (*Lex.*), who holds the fundamental meaning to be *far removed,
free* (from care), whence *declare free* (from imperfections) = *praise ;* cf. the
Talmudic use *to make better, more effective.* 𝕲 ταμιεύται; 𝔖𝕿 חֹשֵׁב; 𝕷 *differt
et reservat.* Read חֹשֵׁךְ, with Bi. — 𝕳 בְּאֹהֵר; 𝔖𝕿 בְּרֵעִינָא, *in thought.* Read
הֹרֵנוּ. — **13.** 𝕳 רָשׁ וְאִישׁ תְּכָכִים; 𝕲 δανιστοῦ καὶ χρεωφιλέτου (as if = τόκος, Lag.).
The sense of stem תך appears to be *press, repress, oppress* (so Aram. Arab.);
cf. תֹךְ. — **16.** 𝕳 בְּרַבָת; read בִּרְרֹת. — **18.** 𝕳 חָזוֹן; 𝕲 ἐξηγητὴς *guide*, perhaps
free rendering of 𝕳, possibly = רַחְבָלֹת, which, however, is elsewhere (except
in Job 37[12]) represented by κυβέρνησις or κυβερνῶσις. — 𝔖𝕿 avoid the statement of 𝕳 (which probably seemed to them disparaging to an age that had
no visions), and substitute, from v.[16], *when the wicked increase* (Pink.). — We

should perhaps read תחבלת; חֶבֶל *line* (not *curb*) hardly suits. — 狃 may have been influenced by the חוּת of v.²⁰. For 狃 יפרע Frank. suggests, as possible, יפרע *will be scattered*, which, however, is hardly suitable. On stem פרע see Ges. *Thes.* and note on 1²⁵; the sense *perish* may perh. be allied with the sense *free;* cf. Arab. פָּרַע.

19. The training of servants.

> Not by words must a servant be taught,
> For he understands, but does not obey.

Single sentence, ternary. The servant, so the proverb intimates, like the son (v.¹⁵), must be trained by the rod — words will not guide him — he is not quite a rational being. On *servant* (properly *slave*) see note on 11²⁹. *Taught = corrected, set right, disciplined* (9⁷ 19¹⁸ 29¹⁷, cf. 31¹). *Does not obey* is lit. *there is no answer.* — Grk., interpreting: *a stubborn servant.* The rendering: *that servant will not amend upon admonition who, understanding, will yet give no answer* (Hodgson) misses the point of the couplet. Cf. Ben-Sira's detailed instructions for the management of servants (BS. 33²⁴⁻³¹).

21. The couplet seems to belong with v.¹⁹. Heb.: *he who delicately brings up his servant from a child, in the end he will be*
. . . The subject of second line may be the subject (*he*) or the object (*servant*) of first line. *In the end =* at the conclusion of this mode of procedure — it denotes the outcome of the experiment, not necessarily the end of life. The omitted word, which occurs only here, has been rendered *refractory* (Lat.), *unthankful* (Ew.), *son* (Saad. RV.), *young gentleman* (Luth.) etc.; it is probably an error of text. De.: *he* [the master] *will finally become a nursery,* that is, his house will be overrun by the children of his pampered servant. — Grk.: *he who from a child lives luxuriously will be a servant, and in the end will come to grief.* Some such reading as this for second cl. should probably be adopted, though it is not clear whether it is the master or the servant or the child that comes to grief.

20, 22, 23. Of passion and pride.

> 20. Seest thou a man hasty in his words?
> There is more hope for a fool than for him.

22. An irascible man stirs up strife,
   And a passionate man is the cause of much wrong.
23. A man's pride will bring him low,
   But he who is of a lowly spirit will obtain honor.

20. Condition and consequence, ternary. The rendering *affairs, business* (RV. marg.) instead of *words* is possible — the general sense is the same : haste is destructive of reflection; cf. 10⁸. — For second line see note on 26¹². Cf. BS. 9¹⁸ Jas. 1¹⁹. — **22.** Synonymous, ternary. *Irascible man*, lit. *man of anger* = one given to anger (not *an angry man*, which expresses a merely temporary feeling), = *passionate* (lit. *possessor of wrath*). The predicate of second cl. is lit. *great* (or, *abounding*) *in transgression*, that is, causing sin in himself and others by occasioning and fomenting quarrels. Cf. 15¹⁸ 14¹⁷·²⁹ 16³² 22²⁴ *al.* — **23.** Antithetic, ternary. See notes on 11² 13¹⁰ 15³³ 16¹⁸·¹⁹. — The paronomasia *low . . . lowly* is found in the Hebrew.

24. Partnership in theft.

He who is partner with a thief is enemy to himself —
He hears the curse and discloses nothing.

Single sentence, quaternary-ternary. *Is partner with*, lit. *walks with*, that is, probably, belongs to a gang of thieves (see 1¹⁰⁻¹⁵). The case contemplated (if the text be correct) may be that of a theft in which the guilty person is unknown — a curse is pronounced on the unknown thief — the man in question hears it, but is afraid to say anything, and the curse, which has objective or magic power (see note on 26²), strikes him; cf. Ju. 17².* As an oath involved a *curse* (the vengeance of the deity being invoked against the violator of the oath), the word here used may also mean *oath* (as in Gen. 24⁴¹ 1 K. 8³¹ Ez. 17¹³); in Dt. 29¹⁴⁽¹³⁾·¹⁹⁽¹⁸⁾ the term is equivalent to *covenant* (a curse being pronounced against a delinquent). The case described in Lev. 5¹ is apparently that of a witness in court who, having heard the curse uttered on an unknown offender, fails to tell what he knows, and thus hinders the execution of justice; he is acquitted on presenting an offering. — The couplet is otherwise explained as referring

---

* See Moore, *Judges*.

to the accomplice in a theft who is called into court as witness, has an oath administered to him (RV. *he heareth the adjuration*), and perjures himself. But in that case the connection between the two lines is not clear. Partnership with a thief does not necessarily or usually involve being summoned as witness, it does involve moral injury to the man whether he is forced into perjury or not, and the perjury does not bring physical injury unless it is discovered; moreover, the verb *hears* is not the natural expression for taking an oath — we should rather expect: *he swears to tell the truth, yet discloses nothing*. Hitzig, therefore, interprets: "he is really partner with a thief who, being called on to testify, says nothing." Possibly second line is corrupt, or out of place. — The proverb may be aimed at men in high places who employed inferiors in acts of robbery or peculation, and shielded them in legal inquiries.

25–27. Of piety and probity.

> 25. The fear of man brings a snare,
>   But he who trusts in Yahweh is safe.
> 26. Many seek the ruler's favor,
>   But every man's case is decided by Yahweh.
> 27. The righteous abhor the vicious,
>   The wicked abhor the upright.

25. Antithetic, ternary. *Fear of man* = regulation of one's conduct by the opinion or attitude of morally untrained men, fearing to speak truth and do right lest it should provoke enmity. *Brings a snare* = involves in misfortune. *He is safe* (lit. *set on high* in a safe place, cf. $18^{10. 11}$ ψ $20^{1(2)}$) who *trusts* for protection in God, and does his duty. Cf. 10^{27} 12^2 *al.* — **26.** Antithetic, ternary, or, ternary-binary. Cf. $16^{2. 9. 23}$. *Favor* is lit. *face;* cf. ψ 27^8 and Pr. 6^{35} ψ 10^{11} 16^{11}. The face showed the disposition or temper of mind, and the term is equivalent in Heb. to *presence.* The proverb deplores immoral (cringing or corrupt) reliance on human (especially political) power — God decides every man's destiny. — **27.** Antithetic, ternary. Lit.: *the abomination of the righteous is* etc., and *the abomination of the wicked is* etc. On *abomination* see note on 3^{32}; *vicious,* lit. *man of iniquity; upright,* lit. *upright of way.* Cf. 8^7 15^9 24^9.

21. 𝕳 מנין, ἁπ. λεγ., is usually taken as = נין *scion, offspring,* a sense possible but not probable; Berth.'s emendation מדין does not afford a satisfactorily definite antithesis; אָדֶן (cf. 25¹³ 27¹⁸ 30¹⁰) would be better — the sing. form of this word is found in 30¹⁰ Keth., in the other instances the plur. The choice of a ἁπ. λεγ., = *son,* instead of בן, would be strange; the word is probably a miswriting. 𝕲 ὀδυνηθήσεται, = (Jäg.) יהיה בינן; 𝕾 מתחנה (from אנח); 𝕿 מנסח. For מנן Ew. (*Jahrb.* xi. p. 10 ff.) cites Eth. mannānī, *one who despises.* 𝕲ᵇ should probably be adopted; for ᵃ either 𝕳 or 𝕲 gives a good sense. — **23.** Note the assonance in תִּשָּׁפֵל and שָׁפֵל. — **24.** After 𝕳 גָּנֵב Bi. inserts כְגֹנֵב שָׁם גְּנֵבָה, and omits 𝕳ᵇ, which may be a gloss after Lev. 5¹. Bi.'s emendation is ingenious, and the resultant sense is not inapposite, but שֹׁם גנבה is an improbable expression (see, for ex., Gen. 43²²). — **25.** 𝕲 has two versions of the couplet, 𝕳 חֶרְדַּת אדם being rendered in the second by ἀσέβεια, free translation, opposite of θεοσέβεια (Lag.).

V. CHAPTERS XXX., XXXI.

CHAPTER XXX.

The chapter forms a separate collection of sayings, differing markedly in tone from the rest of the Book. Its contents lead us to refer it to the latest period of gnomic collections; it was probably added by the latest editor, that is, after collections I.–IV. had been made up. It appears also to have undergone editorial revision; see notes on v.[10. 17. 20].

It consists of the title (v.[1a]), what appears to be the "words of Agur" (v.[1b-4]), an exhortation to trust God (v.[5. 6]), a prayer (v.[7-9]), an isolated maxim (v.[10]), a series of tetrads (v.[11-31]), and a sextet on pride and anger (v.[32. 33]).

How much of the chapter the collector intended to include in the "words of Agur" it is hardly possible to say. By some expositors the whole ch. is referred to Agur, by others v.[1-9] or v.[1-10], by others v.[1-4]. The plu. *sayings* might suggest a number of gnomes, but cf. 31[1-9]. Since the paragraphs are in thought independent, and must be treated separately, the question of unity of authorship is not important. — The Heb. of v.[1] reads: *The words of Agur, the son of Yakeh (Jakeh), the prophecy* (or, *oracle*), *the prophetic utterance* (or, *divine utterance*) *of the man to Ithiel, to Ithiel and Ucal.* Since the expression *prophetic utterance* always introduces the words uttered (Gen. 22[16] Nu. 24[3] Am. 2[11] *al.*), the title proper consists of the preceding part of the verse. In this title the word *prophecy* (*massa*) is inapposite; it is a term of the Prophetic vocabulary (rendered in AV. RV. by *burden* [*]), and expresses a divine message or oracle, a form of utterance quite out of keeping with the individual and reflective tone of what follows. How the word is to be treated is uncertain. One Grk.

---

[*] It means *burden* as well as *prophetic utterance ;* in Jer. 23[33-40] there is possibly a play on the two senses of the word.

Vrs. and many expositors take it as the name of a place, or name derived from name of place, and emend to *from* (or, *of*) *Massa*, or, *the Massaite*. Others, by a different emendation, read : *the gnomic saying* (Heb. *mashal*), or, *the gnomic writer* (Heb. *moshel*). Those who regard it as a proper name identify it with the region *Massa* of Gen. 25¹⁴ 1 C. 1³⁰, of which the exact location is not known, though it was presumably not far from the Israelitish border (cf. note on 31¹). In that case Agur (like the personages of the Book of Job) would be a resident of a non-Jewish region ; it would not follow that he was not a Jew, or that, if a Gentile, he was unacquainted with Jewish thought. But, as we know nothing of the civilization of this Massa, the name adds nothing to the understanding of the passage. The second reading (Saad. Geig. Bick.) has the advantage of relieving the question from the geographical discussion. But, if it be adopted, it must probably be regarded as not original, since *sayings* is a sufficient description of what follows ; or, if it be original, it must have been defined in some way (see note on 31¹), but the text gives no definition (the Lat., improperly attaching following cl., has : *the vision which the man spoke*). The word of the third reading (Grätz), *moshel*, is found elsewhere only in Nu. 21²⁷ Ez. 16⁴⁴ 18² (the verb several times in Ez.), and then in the sense of "speaker, reciter, writer, or employer of proverbs," and it appears not to belong to the vocabulary of the philosophical school ; we should rather expect *sage* as the epithet of Agur. Failing a satisfactory emendation, we may regard the word of the text as a gloss or as unintelligible, and omit it without detriment to the sense, rendering provisionally :

1ᵃ. The title proper. *The words of Agur Ben-Yakeh*. Of the Anc. Vrss. Syr. Targ. and Venet. Grk. take *Agur* and *Yakeh* as proper names ; Lat. regards the words as descriptive appellatives, and translates : *the words of the assembler, the son of the vomiter*, in which *assembler* = " teacher, one who gathers the people for instruction," and *vomiter* = " one who pours out words of instruction." Agur is identified with Solomon (Yakeh then being David) by many Jewish and Christian expositors (Rashi, Aben Ezra, L. de Dieu, Stier *al.*) ; by others (Saad. Mich. *al.*) he is taken to be an otherwise unknown ancient sage. The name "Yakeh" is by some (Mühlau, De.) held to mean *obedient, pious ;* the Midrash explains *son of Yakeh* as = "one who is free from all sin and iniquity" ; Hitzig changes the word and renders : *Agur, son of her whom Massa obeys* (Zöckler : *son of the princess of Massa*), Agur being thus made into a brother of Lemuel (31¹). Grk. sees no proper names in the sentence ; it renders : *reverence my words, son, and receive them and repent.* — There seems to be nothing better than to keep the *Agur Ben-Yakeh,* and to regard Agur as a sage, Jewish or non-Jewish, not of the time of Solomon, but of the late reflective period, or else as a man (like Job) famous in tradition, and taken by some late writer as his mouthpiece for the expression of philosophic thought.

1ᵇ. Secondary title (?). Lit. : *inspired utterance of the man to Ithiel, to Ithiel and Ukal,* in which most of the older interpreters see the names of two ancient sages, some suggesting that Ukal might be the Calcol of 1 K. 4³¹[5¹¹]. The names were sometimes interpreted as significant, *Ithiel* (Neh. 11⁷) as = "signs (= precepts) of God," or "with me is God," or "there is a God," *Ukal* as = "I can" (that is, "I can maintain my obedience to God"), the reference being to Solomon or to some other man or men. — Very early, however, there were attempts to get rid of the proper names and explain the sentence as an expression of thought introductory to what follows. Grk. : *these things says the man to those who trust in God, and I cease ;* Aq. : *to Ethiel, and do thou finish ;* Th. : *to Ethiel, and I shall be able ;* Lat. paraphrases : *the vision spoken by the man with whom God is, and who, because God abides with him, is strengthened.* In 1669 Cocceius (Koch) in his *Lexicon* proposed to translate the words following the word *man : I have labored on account of God, and I have obtained,* and this form of rendering, which found little favor at the time, has been almost universally adopted, though with variations, by modern expositors. The clause (after the word *man*) is translated : *I have wearied myself about God* (or, *O God*), *I have wearied myself about God* (or, *O God*), *and I have pined away* (or, *am consumed* or *faint,* or, *have finished*) ; or, with the insertion of the negative : *I have wearied myself* etc., *and have*

not succeeded (or, *prevailed*, lit. *am not able*). In all such interpretations, if the letters of the present Heb. text be retained
unchanged, the Vocative, *O God*, must be adopted; the rendering *about God* is unwarranted. The expressions *have pined
away*, or *am faint*, or *am at an end* (that is, of my powers)
are somewhat forced; the form with the negative (Bick.) is
better. Apart from these differences of construction the sentence, thus emended, expresses Agur's complete failure in his
effort to comprehend God's nature and mode of procedure. This
confession of ignorance (agnosticism) may be a reverent acknowledgment of the transcendence of God (cf. Job 11^{7-10}), or it may
be an expression of purely philosophic doubt; see notes on v.[2-4].
— None of these emendations, however, can be considered satisfactory. In the first place, *the man* cannot stand isolated, but
must be followed by a descriptive phrase, as in Nu. $24^{3.\,4.\,15.\,16}$ 2 S.
23^1*; and Bickell accordingly changes the text and renders:
*utterance of the man who has wearied himself about God: I have
wearied myself* etc.; but this repetition is unnatural and improbable. It is more likely that the second of these expressions is
erroneous scribal repetition of the first, or a corruption of some
other word. In the next place, the word *utterance*, which is the
technical term for the message of the prophet or the chant of the
seer, is here out of place as definition of a philosophical dictum.
It is understood by some as an ironical designation (by Agur or
an editor) of the doubt expressed in v.[2-4]: "behold the exalted
effusion of the champion"; but such irony is extremely improbable. Probably a descriptive expression originally followed the
name *Agur Ben-Yakeh* (cf. 31^1) or some statement the ground of
which is introduced by the *for* of v.[2], but the text appears to be
corrupt beyond possibility of restoration. Fortunately the sense
of the following verses is independent of this clause.

2-4. Agur's dictum.

> 2. I am stupid, beneath man's level,
> Have not human intelligence.

---

* The text of $\psi\ 36^{1(2)}$ is corrupt; see Ols. Cheyne, and Wellh. in Haupt's *Sacred
Books*.

3. I have not learned wisdom,
   I do not comprehend the Holy One.
4. Who has ascended to heaven and descended,
   Gathered the wind in his fist,
   Bound the waters in a garment,
   Fixed the boundaries of the earth?
   What is his name, and what his son's name?
   Surely thou knowest.

2, 3. Synonymous, ternary. The Heb. begins the v. with *for*, the reference being apparently to some preceding statement now lost. Apparently a sarcastic avowal of intellectual dulness, = "there are some who profess to understand God perfectly, and can give a full explanation of all that he does — I am not one of these wise men" — a sarcasm possibly aimed at men like the Three Friends and Elihu in Job, Agur sympathizing with Job himself; only, while Job's doubt is agony of soul, Agur's interest is dispassionate. — The first cl. of v.[2] is lit.: *I am stupid* (or, *a brute beast*) *from man*, not, that is, "the most stupid (or, the least learned) of men," but "of a stupidity that separates me from humanity, and equals me with the lower animals," and this is the sense of second cl. also. — *Stupid*, cf. $12^1 \psi 73^{22}$; here it refers to the intellect. On *Holy One* see note on 9^{10}. Possibly there is here allusion to such declarations as that of 9^{10}; cf. Job 6^{10}. *Wisdom* = the pretended wisdom of the schools. — **4.** Five questions, ternary. The subject cannot be "God" (De. *al.*) — this interpretation is excluded by the sequence *ascended . . . descended* (the starting-point being the earth), and by the reference to the *son.*[*] Since the questions (which appear to be modelled on Job 38, cf. Pr. 8^{24-29}) express divine acts, they must be regarded as a sarcastic description of a man who controls the phenomena of the universe (cf. Reuss); only such an one (as Yahweh says to Job) can speak authoritatively of God's nature and administration. — The *garment* is the

---

* In support of the reference to God, Cheyne (*Job and Solomon*, p. 151 f.) cites *Rig-Veda*, 10, 129: "Who knows, who here can declare, whence has sprung, whence, this creation? . . . From what this creation arose, and whether [any one] made it, or not, he who in the highest heaven is its ruler, he verily knows, or [even] he does not know." But, as Cheyne himself intimates, between the speculations of an Indian philosopher and the skepticism of a Jewish sage there is a wide gulf.

clouds (Job 26[8]). Cf. notes on 8[27-29]. To know a man's *name* and *his son's name* is to be well acquainted with him. The satirical tone is continued in the last words : *surely thou knowest,* or less well *that thou should'st know,* or *if thou knowest.* Cf. Job 38[5]. — The questions are by some expositors supposed to be asked not by Agur, but by a doubter (the *man* of v.[1]), to whom Agur replies in v.[5, 6]; see notes on v.[1]. — On the supposition that the subject of the v. is "God" the *son* has been understood as = Israel (*Midrash*), or the demiurge (Levi ben-Gerson), or Christ (Procop. *al.*), or as an adumbration of the Alexandrian doctrine of the Logos (Ew.) or of the NT. doctrine of the Son of God (De.). But in all these cases both the name and the son's name would be known. — The brevity of Agur's discourse makes it obscure. But there is no reason to regard it as irreverent toward God or as a denial of his existence, or as scoffing at "revealed religion"; the conception of "revealed religion," in the modern sense of the expression, did not then exist. He seems to take the position of the discourse of Yahweh (Job 38[2-5 ff.]) ; his attitude is one of reverent agnosticism, and he belongs to the school of the last reviser of the Book of Job and Koheleth. Cf. the submissive tone of ψ 131 in the face of questions like that here raised.

5, 6. Exhortation to trust and obey God.

> 5. Every word of God is pure;
>   He is a shield to those who trust in him.
> 6. Add not to his words,
>   Lest he rebuke thee, and thou be found a liar.

V.[5] is a couplet, ternary, taken from ψ 18[30(31)] (= 2 S. 22[31]) ; cf. ψ 12[6(7)] 119[140]. V.[6] is a prose sentence, the first half of which is taken from Dt. 4[2] (or 12[32] [13[1]]), and the second half appears to be based on Job 13[4. 10]. — The word *God* is in the Heb. the sing. form (*Elo*[a]*h*, plu. *Elohim*), found in Prov. only here, often in Job, elsewhere rare, always in postexilian writings, except Dt. 32[15. 17] Hab. 1[11] Isa. 44[8] (and in the two last passages, and perhaps in the first, it is not a proper name, but a common noun) ; in ψ 18[30] the name is *Yahweh*. — The adj. in v.[5] may be rendered *pure, purified,* like a metal, morally perfect, a perfect guide, or *tried,* trustworthy, so that his promise may be relied on. — *Rebuke = reprove, correct, set right;* see 3^{12} $9^{7.8}$ 15^{12} *al.* — The passage is by some regarded as the editor's reply to Agur's preceding sceptical utterance, by others as Agur's reply to the sceptical opinion quoted by him. But the expressions are too general for a formal reply; in a polemic we should expect a more specific reference to what precedes. V.$^{2-4}$ assert that God is incomprehensible; v.$^{5.6}$ declare that God's word is pure, final, and complete, and that he protects those who trust him. The paragraph may have been here inserted by the editor to relieve the negative tone of v.$^{2-4}$, but hardly to refute the assertion of the latter. — The stress is here laid on the completeness of God's *words*, and the paragraph is aimed at certain persons who wished to add to them. The *words* are the written revelation, that is, the Law, and probably the Prophets, and also the Psalms, since one of these is quoted. The threefold division of the Jewish Scriptures (Law, Prophets, Writings) is first expressly mentioned in the Preface to Ben-Sira (B.C. 132), and this paragraph may have been written not far from that time. It is difficult to say what additions are referred to. In the preceding paragraph (v.$^{2-4}$) there is no indication of intention to add to the written word; rather, if any modification of the word is suggested, it is a subtraction (see notes above), but our sage, in quoting from Deut., omits the injunction *take not from it,* as if he had only additions in mind. These are more probably doctrinal than ritual, and more probably religious than philosophical. Possibly the allusion is to the new doctrines of resurrection and immortality, which began to take shape among the Jews in the second century B.C. The writer, in that case, belonged to the conservative party. The authority of the written word was universally recognized; but the progressive party (afterward known as the Pharisees) adopted suggestions from Persian and Greek thought, and thus made additions to the teaching of Law, Prophets, and Psalms. Koheleth (Eccl. 9^5) combats the doctrine of immortality; Daniel (ch. 12) affirms resurrection of Israelites, but says nothing of immortality proper; Wisd. of Solomon (ch. 3) accepts this latter doctrine, but says nothing of resurrection. The two ideas were not established without a struggle.

Omitting v.$^{10.\ 17.\ 20.\ 32.\ 33}$, the remainder of the chapter consists of proverbs in which groups of two or four things are named (as in 6^{16-19}). This numerical arrangement is found as early as the eighth century B.C. (Am. 1^3–2^6), and appears several times in late poetry (ψ $62^{11(12)}$ Job 5^{19} 33^{14} 40^5), but is most fully employed in this chapter. It is probably a very ancient form of the Heb. *mashal* or stanza, in which it was useful as an aid to memory. The peculiarity of enumeration seems to be merely a mode of expressing indefiniteness (= *three or four*), in accordance with the mashalic principle of parallelism (heightening). — Cf. BS. 23^{16} 25^7 26^5, and the Kalevala.

7–9. A prayer for preservation from the temptations of poverty and riches.

7. Two things I ask of thee,
   Deny me them not before I die:
8. Deceit and lying put far from me,
   Poverty and riches give me not —
   Provide me with the food I need —
9. Lest I be full and deny thee,
   And say: "Who is Yahweh?"
   Or be needy and steal,
   And profane the name of my God.

The form of the stanza is not symmetrical. Of the two things mentioned in the petition, namely, deceit and financial extremes, only the latter is referred to in v.^{9}; the poet, perhaps, thought the reason for the prayer against lying too obvious to need mention. The third line of v.^{8} looks like a gloss; it is involved in the second line. In v.^{7} we might expect, in accordance with the norm of several following stanzas, the enumeration *one . . . two* (De.). Also the expression *before I die* is somewhat strange. The similar expression in ψ $39^{13(14)}$ involves the meaning: "I am soon to die; grant me relief from my present suffering that I may taste some happiness before I die and lose the possibility of enjoyment." Here, however, the situation is different: the petitioner asks not for cessation of suffering, but for a lifelong provision; in the Ps. the relief might be deferred till death, here the petition involves life, so that the *before I die* is unnecessary, and, as it involves the present, the setting a future limit is inappropriate. The couplet should perhaps read: *one thing I ask of thee, two things deny me* *not;* the norm *one* . . . *two* is perhaps, however, intentionally departed from; cf. v.[11-14] below. — The insertion of *O Yahweh* after *of thee* (Bick.) is appropriate but not necessary. *Deceit* (RV. *vanity*) is synonym of *lying* (lit. *word of falsehood*); see ψ 24[4] 144[8. 11]. *Provide me,* lit. *cause me to secure.* *The food I need,* lit. *the bread of my determined* (that is, *proper*) *portion;* Reuss: *my sufficient bread;* De. not so well: *the bread allotted me* (by God) — the bread is of course allotted by God, but what the petitioner desires is that necessary provision which avoids extremes.* *Deny (thee):* because a man of independent means is apt to forget that all comes from God. The use of the national name *Yahweh* would seem unfavorable to the supposition that v.[9. 5] are by the same author. — *Profane,* lit. *lay hold of,* that is, not *use disrespectfully* (by venting discontent on God, reproaching him with his apparent injustice), but *bring into disrepute* (by stealing); cf. Ez. 36[20]. To *profane* is to make common (the opposite of sacred, holy), to cause (a divine person or a sacred thing) to be considered unworthy of reverence. — We might expect the prayer: "teach me to use both poverty and riches aright"; but the writer's experience and observation have apparently impressed him with the dangers of both.

10. Against speaking ill of a servant.

> Defame not a servant to his master,
> Lest he curse thee, and thou be held guilty.

Single sentence, ternary-binary. *Defame,* lit. *wag the tongue against, gossip about.* If the defamation be false, the act is *slander* (so ψ 101[5]); here it seems better to adopt the more general sense, since slander is always a crime, and a special prohibition in the case of a servant was not necessary. The proverb forbids meddling in other men's household arrangements. — The ground of the warning is the punishment that will fall on the meddler. The aggrieved servant will *curse* his traducer, and the curse will certainly affect the latter; see note on 26[2]. The verb *be held guilty* (or, *be guilty*) is a common technical term of the later ritual (Lev. 4[13] Nu. 5[6] *al.,* and cf. ψ 5[10(11)] 34[21. 22(22. 23)]); it occurs

---

* Cf. the τὸν ἐπιούσιον of Mt. 6[11] Lu. 11[3].

only here in Pr., but the corresponding noun is found in 14⁹. On *servant* see note on 11²⁹. — The proverb would stand more naturally in chs. 23. 24, and has probably been misplaced by a scribe, who connected its *curse* with the *curse* of v.¹¹. Ewald seeks to bring it into relation with the preceding context by rendering: *incite not the servant* [= the pious man] *against his Lord* [= Yahweh], but the translation *incite* is doubtful, and the sense then given to second cl. ("the pious man, when he perceives the error into which he has been led, curses his seducer") is improbable.*

XXX. The section 30¹⁻¹⁴ stands in 𝕲 next after 24²². — Some MSS. and printed edd. have יָקֵא instead of יָקֶה. — **1.** 𝕲 read דברי חזר בני וקחם; μεταυθει may be explanatory insertion (in which case המשא is not rendered), or may represent some form of נשא. — 𝕳 המשא; 𝕵𝕿 *who received a prophecy*, combining משא with נאם; 𝕃 *visio*, = 𝕳. It should perh. be read מָשָׁל, and regarded as a gloss on דברי; cf. notes on 31¹. — 𝕳 נאם is hardly the inflated expression of a late editor who wished to imitate the old Prophetic style. — 𝕳 הגבר is rendered in 𝕊 by *and he was strong*, = ונבר. — Ginsb.: לו אתי אל. — 𝕳 אכל may be pointed אָכֵל (from כלה) or אָכַל (from כלל) or (Geig. *Urschrift*, p. 61) אֻכַל (from יכל); Geig. takes it as interrog.: *how could I?* Bick. inserts לא. On the pointings אכל with כ raphatum (which is the better supported) and אכל see De. and B-D. — **3.** The neg. לא is to be continued into ᵇ, or inserted in the text; cf. v.¹⁸. 𝕲 θεὸς, = ואל. — **4.** 𝕳 בחפניו; 𝕲 ἐν κόλπῳ, = בחצנ. — 𝕳 חצני; 𝕲 τέκνοις αὐτοῦ. — For 𝕳 בנו Bi. writes הקם, and after 𝕳 הקם inserts ארץ, and ואדרשה על אל as introduction to the following questions. — **8.** 𝕳 לחם חקי, for which, in Gen. 47²², stands simply חק (Frank.). — Bi. converts ᵃ into a couplet by inserting נרפם ו after ודבר. — **9.** 𝕳 מי יהוה; 𝕲 מי יהזה.

11–14. Four depraved classes of men.

11. Men who curse their fathers,
And do not bless their mothers!

12. Men who count themselves pure,
Yet are not cleansed of filthiness!

13. Men of haughty looks
And supercilious bearing!

14. Men whose teeth are swords,
And their mouths armed with knives!

In the last verse the Heb. adds the couplet:

To devour the poor from off the earth,
And the needy from among men.

---

* Cf. the similar representation in Koran 14²³⁻²⁷ 34³⁰⁻³².

The four classes are the unfilial, the self-righteous, the arrogant, and the rapacious. — As the text stands, each couplet is the exclamatory mention of a class, with descriptive relative clause, but without predicate, and this is the most satisfactory reading. Grk. inserts an adj. and takes the verb as predicate : *a wicked generation curses* etc. ; others supply the substantive verb : *there is a generation who* etc. (RV. *al.*), or take the first noun as Voc. : *O generation, that curses* etc. (Ew.) ; the reading *woe to the generation* etc. is not in accordance with the norm of the chapter. The couplets appear to approach the rhythmical norm of the Heb. elegy, as if the writer mingled sadness with his denunciation. — **11.** Lit. : *a generation which* etc., the word *generation* meaning not a genealogical group, or a mass of people living in the same age, but a *class* or *circle,* = (*certain*) *men,* as in ψ 24⁶. — On the sin referred to see note on 20²⁰. — **12.** Lit. : *a generation pure in its* (*own*) *eyes, yet from its filthiness not washed,* men who thought themselves morally good because they observed certain conventional or ritual proprieties, yet at heart were bad. Cf. 20⁹ Mt. 23²³⁻²⁶. The term *filthiness,* or, *filth,* here (and in Isa. 4⁴) signifying moral defilement, is used in a physical sense in 2 K. 18²⁷ (= Isa. 36¹²) Isa. 28⁸ (cf. Dt. 23¹³⁽¹⁴⁾ Ez. 4¹² Zech. 3³·⁴). — **13.** Lit. : *a generation, how lofty are their eyes, and their eyelids are lifted up !* Cf. 6¹⁷ ψ 131¹. — **14.** Lit. : *a generation, their teeth are swords, and their teeth knives.* The Heb. has two words (synonyms) for *teeth;* the second (a poetic word, Job 29¹⁷ Joel 1⁶ ψ 58⁶⁽⁷⁾) does not mean *jaw-teeth* or *molars* (Grk. RV. *al.*). — The sin denounced is unscrupulous use of power to gain one's ends ; the figure is that of a ravening beast. — It was natural that this description of rapacity should be interpreted (as in the appended couplet, v.¹⁴ᶜ·ᵈ), by a scribe, as a reference to oppression of the poor. But the addition of an interpretation is not the manner of the numerical groups of this chapter ; the aphorism is supposed to carry its own interpretation. The couplet may refer, in general, to oppression of the poor, or the terms *poor* and *needy* (which are synonyms) may = Israel (as in ψ 35¹⁰ 82⁴ *al.*) ; the former interpretation appears to be favored by 31⁹·²⁰. On *poor* and *needy* see notes on 3³⁴ 14³¹. — The whole stanza may refer to Israelitish offenders, or to rich and powerful foreigners (cf. ψ 13. 14. 101. 120. 123 *al.*).

Here begins the series of tetrads proper, the progressive form of numeration, *three . . . four*, being employed, except in the group in v.²⁴⁻²⁸. V.¹⁵ᵃ, however, stands out of connection with what follows.

15ᵃ. Lit.: *Aluka has two daughters, give, give.* The word *aluka* means *leech* in Syr. and Late-Heb. (and the Arab. has nearly the same form), is here so rendered in the Anc. Vrss., and is so understood by the great body of recent expositors. Allegorical interpretations, such as *the Underworld*, with its two daughters, *Paradise* and *Gehenna* (*Midrash* of Pss. Rashi), or simply *Gehenna* (*Aboda Zara* 17 a. Midr. of Pr.), or *Nonentity* (Saad.), or *Wicked Desire* (Calvin), or *Greediness* (De.), are without foundation. Nor is there any philological ground (Ew. *al.*) for regarding the word as the name of a bloodsucking or cannibal demon, similar to Heb. *lilith*, Rom. *lamia*, Arab. *ḡūl*, Hindoo *vetala*, Egypt. *ka.* — The *two daughters* are explained as the two mouths of the leech, or two young leeches, or paradise and gehenna, or avarice and ambition, or two sorts of nothingness etc. There is a difference between calling a hill a " son of oil," that is, " fruitful " (Isa. 5¹), and saying not " Sheol etc. are daughters of the leech," but " the leech has two daughters." The double *give, give* is regarded by some as giving the names of the daughters, by others as an exclamation or cry uttered by them : *daughters [who continually cry:]* *give, give !* — Various emendations of the text have been proposed. Ewald : *the bloodsucker has two daughters,* " *hither, hither* " ! *three that say:* " *hither, hither, hither the blood! the blood of the bad child* " !, to which he then attaches v.¹⁷. De. supposes a triplet, which ran : *the Aluka has two daughters: Give ! give !* — *Sheol and the barren womb ; there are three that are never satisfied,* the three being Aluka and her two daughters ; and on this, he suggests, followed a quatrain (of which only a part remains), beginning : *four say not enough* (v.¹⁵ᶜ). Bickell : *three things are not satisfied; four say not: enough! Aluka has two daughters: give, give, Sheol and the womb,* and the rest as in the Heb. text. These reconstructions, all arbitrary, are called forth by the desire to bring v.¹⁵ᵃ into logical connection with the following lines. The first word in the Heb. has also been taken as a title : *By Alukah*, which adds nothing to our knowledge, and, from the norm of the chapter, is highly improbable. The line is a fragment, or a gloss, whose text has suffered, so that the original sense is no longer visible. An illustration may have been drawn from the habits of the leech ; the persistency of the animal, in clinging to the object on which it fastens itself till it is glutted with blood, was well known to the ancients (Horace, *Ep. ad Pis.* 476).— The remainder of the paragraph accords with the norm of the following groups (characterized by *three . . . four*), and obviously forms in itself a complete proverb.

15ᵇ, 16. Four insatiable things.

> 15 *b*. Three things are never satisfied,
>   Four say not : " Enough " :
> 16. Sheol ; the barren womb ;
>   The earth is unsated with water ;
>   Fire says not : " Enough."

In v.[16] a quatrain (as in the following groups) may be obtained by expanding first line, possibly : *Sheol is never satisfied with dead, the barren womb never sated with children.* *Sheol* is described in 27^{20} as never satisfied ; cf. Isa. 5^{14} Hab. 2^5. *The barren womb* is lit. *the closing of the womb ;* cf. Gen. 16^2 30^1 20^{18} ; the reference is to the desire of a childless wife for children. The *earth*, desiring to be fruitful, is always thirsty ; *fire* ever needs fuel.— Cf. the Indian proverb : *Fire is not sated with wood, nor the ocean with the streams, nor death with all the living, nor women with men* (*Hitopadeça* 2, 113) ; and an Arab. proverb (Freytag *Prov-erb. Arab.* iii. 1. p. 61), in a long list of triads of insatiable things, has, as two of its three things, *wood by fire*, and *the earth by rain.* Whether the Heb. and Arab. proverbs can be traced to the East is uncertain.— Our proverb has no ethical meaning or application ; it is simply a record of observation, which may broaden the pupil's knowledge of the world.

17. Punishment of filial disobedience.

> The eye that mocks a father,
> And scorns ‹ the old age of ›(?) a mother,
> The ravens of the valley will pick it out,
> And vultures will eat it.

A quatrain, both couplets synonymous, the first ternary, the second binary, or ternary-binary. This serious quatrain, out of place in a string of satirical and descriptive tetrads, naturally attaches itself to v.[11], to which it was perhaps added as commentary or admonition. — The *eye* is named as the organ of the expression of feeling (cf. Job 16[9] Ez. 28[17]). The reading *old age* is from the Grk.; the word of the Heb. text, now commonly rendered *obedience*, is doubtful in form and meaning, and this sense is here hardly appropriate — the proper object of *scorns* is the person of the mother. The *raven* and the *vulture* (so, and not *eagle*, the Heb. is probably to be rendered) picked out the eyes and ate the flesh not of the living, but of the dead (1 S. 17[44] 1 K. 14[11] Jer. 16[4] Ez. 29[5] 39[17]).* Disobedient children are to die violent deaths, their bodies are to lie unburied and be food for birds, they will be honored with no funeral rites, and their position in Sheol will therefore be an inferior one. The verse is an expression of the high estimation in which regard for parental authority was held (cf. 23[22] Ex. 20[12]). — *Valley* is the bed of a water-course, or a depression through which a winter stream runs (Arab. *wady*). *Vultures* is lit. *sons of the vulture*, that is, not "young vultures" (RV. *young eagles*), but "members of the species vulture," like "sons of the prophets," = members of prophetic guilds, and "sons of the Elohim," = beings of the Elohim class. — The verse is by some regarded as a polemic against Agur's alleged repudiation (v.[2-4]) of parental instruction; but of this there is no hint in the text.

18, 19. Four mysterious things.

18. Three things are beyond my ken,
    And four I do not understand:
19. The way of the vulture in the air;
    The way of a serpent over a rock;
    The way of a ship on the high sea;
    And the way of a man with a woman.

The first couplet is quaternary-ternary, the others are ternary. — *Beyond my ken*, lit. *too wonderful for me*, or *wonderful beyond me*.

---

* Cf. *Iliad* i. 4. 5 and the imprecations ἐς κόρακας, βάλλ᾽ ἐς κόρακας. Geier refers to Arist. *Hist. Animal.* c. i, and Epictetus: *ravens destroy the eyes of the dead, flatterers the souls and eyes of the living*.

— It is held by many expositors (Mercer *al.*) that the characteristic intended in the four things is that they leave no trace behind;
on the tracelessness of a ship and a bird see the fine passage in
Wisd. of Sol. (5¹⁰·¹¹). This characteristic holds of the three first
cases, but hardly of the fourth; and as to the second, there would
be no reason for particularizing the serpent, since no trace is left
on a rock by the passage of any animal. The point is rather the
wonderfulness of the things named (Geier). The soaring flight of
a great bird (Job 39²⁶·²⁷), the mysterious movement of the serpent,
performed without feet (Gen. 3¹⁴),* the path of the ship through
the trackless deep (WS. 14¹⁻⁴),† and the procreation of a human
being (ψ 139¹³⁻¹⁶ Eccl. 11⁵) excite the admiration of the writer.
Apparently no religious sentiment is involved; the stanza is rather
a lesson in natural history and physics. — On *vulture* see note on
v.¹⁷. *On the high sea* is lit. *in the heart of the sea;* cf. 23³⁴.
Woman, properly *young woman* (Gen. 24⁴³ Ex. 2⁸ Isa. 7¹⁴ ψ 68²⁵⁽²⁶⁾
Cant. 1³ 6⁸), married (as in Isa.), or unmarried (as in Gen. Ex.
ψ and probably in Cant.). ‡

20. To the last line of v.¹⁹ an annotator has added a prose
explanation: *So is the way of an adulteress: she eats and wipes
her mouth, and says: "I have done nothing wrong."* The *eats
and wipes her mouth* is a humorous figurative expression of the
woman's non-moral indifference. The annotation misses the
point of the aphorism: the latter is concerned with the wonderfulness of the act, the former with the supposed moral carelessness
of one of the actors; the gloss assumes that the *young woman* is
unchaste. On *adulteress* (lit. *adulterous woman*) and *wrong* cf.
notes on 6³²·¹² 10²⁹. — The v. is regarded as a gloss by Hitz. De.
Reuss, Strack, Frank. *al.*

12. On the Mas. change of צָאָה to צָאָה (as if from יצא) see Geig. *Urschrift*,
p. 410. — **15.** The section 30¹⁵⁻³³ stands in 𝕲 next after 24⁴⁹; the order in
𝔚 is better. 𝔚 עֲלוּקָה, from stem = *stick to;* cf. Ass. *ilḳitu* (De.), name of an
animal. — 𝔚 הַב הַב; 𝕲 ἀγαπήσει ἀγαπωμέναι, from חב, and so 𝕊 חביבן, from

---

* The Jerusalem Targum inserts, as part of the curse: *thy feet shall be cut off.*

† In ψ 104²⁶ the word *ships* is doubtful; or the first cl. may be an interpolation;
the second cl. connects itself immediately with v.²⁵.

‡ That the term does not mean *virgin* (RV. in Isa. and Cant.) may be regarded
as certain.

which (or from ‎מ‎) 𝕿 incorrectly writes ‎מהבהבן‎, *burning* (= *destructive*).—
16. ‎עֲצַר רָחַם‎; 𝕲 ἔρως γυναικὸς, ‎ר‎ being taken as = *woman* (cf. Ju. 5⁸⁰,
Inscript. of Mesha, l. 17), and ‎ע‎ guessed at or rendered freely (cf. the force
of ‎עצר‎ in 2 C. 14¹⁰ Dan. 10⁸), or it was perhaps not in 𝕲's Heb. text. The
word should perh. be omitted (Bi.); it may be scribal explanation.—
17. ‎יִקְּהַת‎, elsewhere only in Gen. 49¹⁰, on which cf. Ball, in *SBOT*.
On the form see De. Ols. § 83 *a*, Ges.²⁶ § 20 *h*. The possibility of a Heb.
stem ‎יקה‎ *obey* seems to be proved by Ass. *aḳu* (De. *Wbch.*), but the noun ‎יקהה‎
is doubtful. It was not understood by the medieval Jew. commentators (who
generally render it *collection* or *weakness*), and was not read by any extant
Anc. Vrs. 𝕲 (and so 𝕾𝕿 Rashi) γῆρας, = ‎זקנת‎; 𝕷 *partum*. The rendering
obedience appears to have been first proposed by Abu'l Walid (c. A.C. 1000),
from Arab. ‎וקי‎, but is here inappropriate. Read ‎זקנת‎. Bi. further inserts
‎שיבת‎ before ‎אב‎.— 19. ‎בְּעַלְמָה‎; 𝕲 ἐν νεότητι, = ‎בַּעֲלֻמָיו‎ (Lag.).— 20. ‎וּמָחֲתָה‎
‎פִּיהָ‎; 𝕲 ἀπονιψαμένη = ‎מ‎.— Bi. omits ᵃ; but the whole v. is a gloss.

21-23. Four intolerable things.

> 21. Under three things the earth totters,
>   And under four it cannot bear up:
> 22. A servant when he becomes a king;
>   A fool when he is prosperous;
> 23. An unwooed woman when she (at last) finds a husband;
>   A maidservant when she is heir to her mistress.

The couplets are apparently ternary. The tone seems to be
humorous or whimsical: the earth is said to *totter* (or, *tremble*)
under the intolerable burden of the characters named. The
expression may be taken (but less probably) to mean that by the
changes of fortune here described the moral order of society is
subverted. The cases cited are all of persons of relatively inferior position who come into power, and the intimation appears to
be that they are then excessively pretentious, arrogant, and dis-
agreeable; it is hardly probable that the writer was so bitter a
conservative that he viewed with horror any departure from established rules. The examples are taken equally from the two sexes.
— The rendering *for, on account of,* instead of *under,* is weak and
not quite accurate. The word *servant* (or, *slave*) may denote an
officer of high rank (like Zimri, 1 K. 16⁹), who, however, is far
beneath a *king;* such sudden elevations have always been common in Oriental lands (for example, the Mamluk [that is, Slave]
dynasty of Egypt) ; see notes on 11²⁹ 19¹⁰.— The term *fool* (Heb.

nabal) means, in the early narrative literature, a person of low grade, socially (2 S. 3³³), or intellectually (17⁷·²¹), perhaps also (cf. 1 S. 25²⁵) a boorish person; in Prophetic writings its signification is religious and ethical (Dt. 32⁶ Ez. 13³ Isa. 32⁵·⁶), in the devotional literature it is used in the sense of "ungodly" (ψ 14¹ *al.*); here, as elsewhere in the Wisdom books (Job 2¹⁰ 30⁸), it appears to be employed in the intellectual sense. *Is prosperous*, lit. *is filled* (or, *satisfied*) *with bread,* = *is wealthy.* — *Unwooed,* lit. *hated,* that is, the object of dislike, or, not liked, not beloved (and so, nearly, not attractive); the term is used of an unloved wife in Gen. 29³¹·³³ Dt. 21¹⁵ᶠᶠ·; here it means not *odious* (RV.), but simply *unattractive, unsought,* and describes a woman who has long remained unmarried, and has felt the disgrace of her position (Hitzig). The couplet supposes a society in which a woman's personal attractiveness entered into her chances of marriage, in which, that is, there was freedom of choice to the man; this appears to have been the case in old, pre-monarchical, Israel (Gen. 29¹⁸ Ju. 14¹⁻⁴ 1 S. 25³⁹), and in the Greek period, doubtless, considerable freedom existed.* — The term *hated* is by some (Dathe *al.*) understood to mean *divorced* (Dt. 24¹⁻⁴). But the word never has this sense. *Hatred* (that is, dislike) on the part of the husband was, under the law, a ground of divorce, but the divorced woman is never called simply *one hated* (not in Isa. 60¹⁵). Moreover, a divorced woman was not necessarily *persona ingrata* to others than her former husband; the law allowed her to marry again, and such a second marriage would be looked on not as subversive of order or offensive to the common sense of propriety, but as natural and proper. Grk. *a hated woman, if she obtain a good husband* appears to understand the term as = *disliked.* — *Is heir to,* that is, inherits property, and herself becomes a mistress. The verb may mean *supplants,* that is, gains the favor of the husband, and thus becomes the real mistress of the household. Between these two senses of the verb it is not easy to choose, but both give the same general meaning for the clause. — In the OT. law the next of kin inherits, usually the son (Dt. 21¹⁷, cf. Gen. 21¹⁰), and (in the late legislation, Nu. 27⁸), if there were

---

* Cf. Moore, *Judges,* on Ju. 14¹ᶠᶠ·; Now. *Arch.* § 27.

no son, the daughter ; in late times a man or woman may have had the legal right to bequeath property at pleasure (cf. Job 42[15]). In the present case, if the rendering *is heir to* be correct, the property-holder is a woman, a case not contemplated in the OT. legislation (in Nu. 27[36] the heiress must marry a man of her own tribe, who then becomes the owner of the property), nor do we know what the property-rights of Israelitish women were in the fourth, third, and second centuries B.C.; in the Roman law a woman could make a will, and this freedom had not improbably crept into Jewish society. See note on 17[2].*

24-28. Four things little but wise.

24. Four things there are, small in the earth,
    But yet exceedingly clever :
25. Ants — a people not strong,
    Yet they prepare their food in summer;
26. *Shaphans* — a people not mighty,
    But they make their houses in the rocks;
27. Locusts — they have no king,
    But they march all in ranks;
28. Lizards — one may be grasped in the hands,
    Yet are they in kings' palaces.

Ternary. Small animals which show contrivance and skill. The proverb is simply descriptive of the habits of the animals, a bit of natural history, without expressed reference to human life, but perhaps with the implied suggestion that success is not confined to bigness ; cf. Aristotle, *Hist. Anim.*, cap. 1. — **24.** The number *four* alone is given, not the sequence *three . . . four;* the variation is possibly purely rhetorical, the predicates in the two lines being antithetic, not, as in v.[15. 18. 21. 29], synonymous. — *Exceedingly clever*, lit. *wise, endowed with wisdom;* Grk. : *wiser than the wise.* — **25.** See note on 6[6]. The word *people*, here and in next v., appears to refer to the industrial organization of the animals in question. The intimation is that *ants* lay up in the summer their food for the winter. — **26.** The *shaphan*, as is now agreed by naturalists, is the Syrian *hyrax*, a small pachyderm, which lives in crevices of rocks.† This habit (mentioned here and in ψ 104[18])

---

* For the Talmudic law of inheritance see *Baba Bathra* 120 a (cf. *Taanith* 30 b).
† See Tristram, in *Survey of West. Pal.;* Wood, *Bible Animals.*

is proof that it is not a "cony (or, coney)," that is, rabbit. It was erroneously supposed (Lev. 11⁵ Dt. 14⁷) to chew the cud, an inference from its habit of moving its jaws from side to side. — **27.** *March*, lit. *go forth.* *In ranks,* = *in orderly array.* In Joel 1⁴ four species of locusts are mentioned, of which one (Heb. *arbeh*) is the sort here named; a vivid description of their warlike array is given in Joel 2 (cf. Ju. 6⁵ Job 39²⁰). In the OT. legislation locusts are "clean" (Lev. 11²², cf. Mk. 1⁶).* — **28.** The fourth animal is probably not the *swallow* (Saad. *al.*), or the *ape* (Aben Ezra *al.*), or the *spider* (Levi, Luther, AV.), but the *lizard* (Grk. Lat. and modern expositors generally). The first line may be translated (RV. *al.*) : *the lizard seizes with its hands,* but, as in the other couplets the first line refers to the animal's weakness, it is better to render : *the lizard thou mayest grasp,* or, by a change of vowels, *may be grasped.* The form given above : *lizards* etc., is assimilated to that of the preceding couplets. — The lizard's habit of running over the walls of houses, in pursuit of food, is well known.

29–31. Four stately things. — Heb. :

29. Three things there are of stately step,
    Yea, four of stately gait :
30. The lion, mightiest of beasts —
    He turns before no foe;
31. .   .   .   .   ; the he-goat;
    A king   .   .   .   .

29. Quaternary-ternary. The form recurs to the sequence *three . . . four,* the two lines of this couplet being synonymous. The characteristic fact is noble carriage, which, in the case of the lion, is associated with power, and this last is probably to be understood in the others. The proverb is an admiring remark, without moral or religious suggestion. Lit. *are good* (or, *excellent*) *in step* (or, *march*), and *are good in gait* (or, *going*). *Step* occurs in 4¹² 5⁵ 16⁹, *gait* in 2¹³ 4¹² 15²¹. — **30.** Synonymous, ternary-binary. Lit. *a mighty one among beasts,* and *turns not back before anything.* This term for *lion* is found elsewhere only in Isa. 30⁶ Job 4¹¹ (in

---

* See Tristr. Wood. A description of a recent invasion of locusts is given by Thomson, *Land and Book,* ii. 102–108.

the last passage RV. has incorrectly *old lion*). — The word here
used for *beasts* commonly signifies domestic animals as distinguished from wild animals (Gen. 1²⁴ Lev. 1² ψ 148¹⁰, RV. *cattle*),
but in poetical or elevated and gnomic style is sometimes
employed for animals in general (Ez. 8¹⁰ Isa. 30⁶ *al.*). — **31.** The
couplet enumerates three objects (so v.¹⁶ᵃ has two objects), of
which only one is clear. The first expression (omitted above)
appears to be lit. *girded* (or, *girthed*, or, *compressed*) *about the
loins*, and has been understood to be a description of some animal,
as *cock* (so all the Anc. Vrss., except Venet. Grk.), from its warlike strut, or *eagle* (Saad.), or *greyhound* (Ven. Grk. Luth. RV.
al.), as being narrow in the flanks, or *zebra* (Ludolf), from its
girding stripes, or *warhorse* (Ges. Wild. RV. marg. *al.*), as accou-
tred for battle (cf. Job 39¹⁹⁻²⁵). Of these renderings *warhorse*
suits best in respect of stateliness, but *cock* has the best ancient
support. If this sense be adopted for the first word of the
expression, a change in the following word gives the reading:
the cock lifting himself up (or, *holding his head high*), or *the
proudly stepping cock*. The Grk. fills out the picture: *the cock
marching bravely among his hens.* — The *he-goat* is the leader
of the flock (Grk. adds: *who leads the flock*). Cf. Dan. 8⁵
(where, however, the Heb. term is different). — The last clause
reads: *and a king alk̲ūm with him* (or, by the change of a vowel,
his people), in which the word *alkum* is unintelligible. Grk.: *a
king who harangues a people* (that is, stands up to address a
nation); Lat.: *nor is there a king who can resist* (= *stand up
against*) *him* (that is, the goat); Saad. RV.: *the king against
whom there is no rising up.* These renderings are all grammatically impossible. Others (Gesen. De. *al.*) take *alk̲ūm* as pure
Arabic, and render: *the king who has authority to call out the
host;* but the employment of a foreign term, for which Heb. had
an equivalent (2 S. 20⁴), is improbable. Löwenstein: *King Rest-
less,* that is, one who does not stand still or pause in his career of
conquest. — Failing a natural sense in the Heb. expression, emendation of the text has been resorted to. As the Jews, in Talmudic times, sometimes, to avoid profanation of the divine name
Elohim, substituted a *k̲* for its *h,* Hitzig here reads: *a king with
whom God is;* but the religious expression is out of place in this

series of non-religious tetrads. Dys.: *a king with whom are thousands;* Bick.: *. . . who stands up for (the protection of) his people.* — Halévy (*Mélanges*, p. 123) regards *alkūm* as the name of an Arabian deity (*Ḳaum*), but the king who had the support of Ḳaum would hardly excite the admiration of an old Jewish gnomist. Geiger (*Urschrift*, pp. 61 ff.) takes it to be the anti-Maccabean highpriest Alcimus (1 Mac. 7[5-22] 9[1. 54-56] Jos. *Ant.* 12, 9, 7; 12, 10, 6), here ironically called "king," a title to which he possibly aspired; the introduction of a personal name, however, in this series is not what we should expect, and the reference to the *king* is obviously not ironical, but serious. We can only surmise that *king* and *alkum* are corrupted forms, and that the original text referred to the majestic mien and movement of some animal.

In v.[32. 33] the tetradic form is lacking, and the expressions, though quaint, are not humorous or ironical. In the present state of the text it is impossible to say whether there was originally (as the *for* of v.[33] appears to suggest) a connection between the two verses. — **32.** Heb.: *If thou . . . in exalting thyself, and if thou hast planned — hand to mouth.* The omitted word is usually rendered *hast acted foolishly* (or, *art foolish*), but this sense is found nowhere else in OT., and is doubtful; the translation *thought evil* (RV. *al.*) for *planned* is possible only when the connection shows that the plan is evil. Before *hand* the verb *lay* is commonly inserted. The sense thus obtained is: "if thou exaltest thyself in mere folly or by deliberate plan," or, "if thou art foolish in exalting thyself or in planning," or, "if thou art foolishly elated and plannest evil," or, "if thou art contemptible, it is by boasting; and if thou art wise (= plannest well) " — "then preserve silence." Taken in connection with what follows, the meaning of the v. would be that silence is pacific; but text and sense are doubtful. — **33.** *For, pressing milk brings out curd, and pressing the nose brings out blood, and pressing anger brings out strife.* The first line is perh. a scribal addition; *blood*, but not *curd*, is allied to *strife;* in *nose* (Heb. *ap*) and *anger* (Heb. *appayim*) there is a play upon words. — *Curd*, or, *sour milk* (not *butter*, or, *cream*), is produced by shaking milk in a vessel; it is a refreshing drink, and was a favorite beverage of the pastoral

Israelites (Ju. 5²⁵ Gen. 18⁸ Dt. 32¹⁴ 2 S. 17²⁰ Isa. 7¹⁸·²² Job 20¹⁷), as it is of the Bedawin to-day.*

23. 𝔐 תִּירֹשׁ; 𝔊 ἐκβάλῃ. — 𝔐 תִּבְעֵל; 𝔊 ἐὰν τύχῃ ἀνδρὸς ἀγαθοῦ. — **26.** 𝔐 שְׁפַנִּים; 𝔊 χοιρογρύλλιοι, *hedgehogs;* 𝔖𝔗 חגס, probably the *hyrax,* Arab. *wabr* (cf. Payne-Smith, *Thes. Syr.*); 𝔏 *lepusculus.* — **28.** Of 𝔐 בְּיָדַיִם תְּתַפֵּשׂ 𝔊 has two renderings: χερσὶν ἐρειδόμενος *supports itself by its hands,* reading Piel or Qal; and εὐάλωτος ὤν, *easily taken,* reading Nifal. — **31.** On the post-Bibl. Jew. interpretation of זַרְזִיר as a bird of the raven species see De. For 𝔐 מָתְנַיִם we might read מְוֻבֶּה, which would suit the *cock* or the *horse,* hardly the *raven.* — Arabic זִרְזִר (or זֻרְזֻר) is *starling;* if the name be mimetic, it might have been applied to more than one bird. The derivation from אזר, *bind,* is improbable. Cf. 3 Mac. 5²³. — 𝔏 אַלְקוּם עִמּוֹ; 𝔊 δημηγορῶν ἐν ἔθνει, perhaps = קוּם אֶל עַמּוֹ (Jäg.), less probably קֹם לְעַמּוֹ (Bi.), better קָם אֶל עַ; and so substantially 𝔖𝔗; 𝔏 *nec est rex qui resistat ei,* = וּמֹלֵךְ לֹא קָם עִמּוֹ; Hitz. אלהים; Dys. אלפים. The n. p. Alcimus is written אלקמס in the great bilingual Palmyrene inscr., col. 2, l. 28. אלקם might be corruption of אֵקֶן (A. S. Waldstein, in an oral communication), though *wild goat* (Dt. 14⁵) would be very near *he-goat.* מלך may be corruption of אלקם, or *vice versa.* For 𝔐 או היש read וְהִישׁ. — **32.** Everywhere else in OT. the Qal נבל = *fade, languish* (on Job 14¹⁸ and ψ 18⁴⁶ see notes of Budde and Wellh.); cf. Ass. *nabālu, dry (land),* and *nablu, flame;* in Arab. the stem has the sense of *skill, capacity.* Whether Qal is ever denom. may be doubtful; it is so taken by 𝔊𝔖𝔗𝔏, but their rendering may be a guess. What Heb. text is represented by 𝔊 ἐὰν πρόῃ σεαυτὸν ἐν εὐφροσύνῃ is not clear. — **33.** Bi. makes a quatrain by inserting after first מִץ : שֶׁלָּן יוֹצֵא מַיִם וּמִץ.

XXXI. 1–9.

A manual for kings or judges, a warning against such indulgence of appetite as might hinder the execution of justice. The Aramaizing diction suggests a late date (not earlier than second century B.C.). Cf. the aphorisms in 16¹⁰⁻¹⁵ *al.,* the national religious admonitions of Dt. 17¹⁵⁻²⁰, the theocratic portraiture in Isa. 9⁶·⁷⁽⁵·⁶⁾ 11¹⁻⁵ 32¹⁻⁸ *al.,* and the religious tone of WS. 1–9.

1. Superscription. — Heb.: *The words of Lemuel, a king, the oracle which his mother taught him;* or: *The words of L., king of Massa, which* etc. (or, *whose mother taught him*). The translation . . . *of king L.* (RV.) requires a change in the text. The

---

* See Rob. *Res.* ii. 405; Thomson, *Land and Book,* ii. 149; Doughty, *Arab. Desert.* i. 263; Now. *Arch.* i. 113; Moore, *Judges,* on Ju. 5²⁵; Driver, *Deut.,* on Dt. 32¹⁴.

rendering *oracle* is out of the question; see note (on *massa*) on 30¹. "Lemuel" might be regarded as "king of Massa" if there were any good ground for supposing that there was a country Massa, governed by a king, and somehow associated with wisdom and learning; but of such a land nothing is known.* Nor is there any reason for interpreting the name *Lemuel* (= "to God," that is, "devoted to God") symbolically (De. *al.*). The superscription is not necessarily by the author of the manual; it may be from the hand of a late scribe, representing his guess at the origin of the counsel; the word *king* may be scribal insertion (Frank.), or *Lemuel* may have been introduced from a corruption of text in v.⁴ (Bick.). The advice is not inappropriately put into the mouth of the mother, but of her nothing is known, and her introduction into the title may be the result of a wrong reading of v.². — On *taught* (= *set in the right way*) see 9⁷ 19¹⁸ 29¹⁷. ¹⁹.

2–9. The counsel.

2. What, my son? and what, son whom I bore?
   And what, son granted to my vows?
3. Give not thy strength to women,
   Nor thy heart to ‹those who› destroy kings.

4. It is not for kings [] to drink wine,
   Nor for rulers ‹to mix› strong drink,
5. Lest, drinking, they forget the law,
   And disregard the rights of the suffering.

6. Give strong drink to him who is perishing,
   Wine to him who is in bitter distress,
7. That, drinking, he may forget his poverty,
   And think of his misery no more.

8. Let thy decisions be ‹true,›
   Uphold the rights of all who ‹suffer›;
9. Pronounce thy judgments with equity,
   Maintain the cause of the poor and the needy.

2. If the text be correct, the repetition expresses earnestness, and the *what* refers to the content of the advice, = "what shall I say to thee?" But the form of expression is strange and doubtful; possibly, taking a suggestion from the Grk., we should read:

---

* See Dillm. on Gen. 25¹⁴, De. *Paradies*, p. 302, Ptol. 5, 19, 2.

give heed, my son, to my sayings, and observe my words (see 5^1 7^1 *al.*, and cf. Frank.) ; the speaker will then be the sage. — The word for *son* is Aram. On *vows* in general see 7^{14} 20^{25} Eccl. $5^{4(3)}$ ψ 50^{14}, and, in connection with prayer for a son, 1 S. 1^{11}. — **3.** Synonymous, ternary. Second line lit. : *nor thy ways so as* (or, *in order*) *to destroy kings;* the change of a vowel gives the reading *those who destroy*, as the parallelism suggests (*women = destroyers of kings*) ; *that which destroyeth* (RV.) is not allowed by the Heb. ; Targ. : *to daughters of kings;* Syr. : *to the food of kings* (against luxurious eating). *Ways* may be freely rendered by *heart*, or the text may be changed to gain this sense, or, by another emendation, to read *love*. *Strength* apparently = *virility*, not *wealth*. The couplet seems to be directed against such debauchery as is described in chs. 2. 5. 6. 7. 9. — **4.** First line lit. : *be it not to* (= *far be it from*) *kings, Lemuel, be it not to kings to drink wine;* the repetition *be it not to kings*, though rhetorically intelligible as emphatic, mars the rhythm, and is probably a scribal error, and the *Lemuel* also appears to be repetition of a part of the preceding word. The text is, however, doubtful ; one Grk. reading is : *do everything prudently, drink wine prudently.* — Second line lit. : *nor for rulers where* (or, *or*) *strong drink*, in which *where* is probably scribal error for a verb meaning *mix* (Isa. 5^{22}), or one meaning *drink, indulge in* (Isa. 56^{12}). On *wine* and *strong drink* see notes on 9^2 20^1. — **5.** Synonymous, ternary. The reason for the preceding warning. The verbs in the Heb. are sing. ; the connection (the plu. subjects in v.⁴) favors the plu. The *law* is the civil law of the land. On *suffering* (or, *poor*, or, *lowly*) see note on 3^{34}. *Disregard* (RV. *pervert*) is lit. *change*. — **6, 7.** Synonymous, ternary. Two proper occasions for the use of alcoholic drinks : bodily suffering (from hunger and want) and mental distress. In v.⁶ᵇ lit. : *to those who are bitter of soul.* The quatrain is symmetrical — v.⁶ᵃ is explained by v.⁷ᵃ, and v.⁶ᵇ by v.⁷ᵇ. V.⁷ is parallel to v.⁵. — **8.** Synonymous, ternary. Lit. : *open thy mouth for the dumb.* The term *dumb*, if it were the right reading, would obviously not refer to physical incapacity of speech (for the man, in that case, would depend not on the king, but on his nearest friend or his legal representative), but would mean (as is commonly understood) " one who, from poverty, or timidity, or some such cause, is unable to defend himself, by pleading, against his oppressor." This sense is, however, inappropriate : the Oriental man or woman, when wronged, is anything but "dumb" (see, for ex., 1 K. 3[16 ff.] 2 K. 6[26 ff.]) — the king is always accessible ; and the parallelism suggests a term synonymous with the *equity* of v.[9a] (v.[9a] is parallel to v.[8a], and v.[9b] to v.[8b]). Read : *open thy mouth in truth* (cf. 20[28] 29[14] ψ 45[4(5)]) ; *in truth* = "with faithful regard for justice." Another emendation (Bick.) reads *for the widow*, but this, though simple and attractive, does not so well accord with the parallelism. *All who suffer* is an emendation (Dys.) of the Heb. *all the sons of the passing-by*, interpreted (but without ground) to mean *those who disappear*, = *those who are perishing* (Ew. De. *al.*), or *those who are left behind*, = *left desolate* (RV.), and this is taken to mean orphans (Noyes, Bick. Frank.) and other persons destitute of protectors. — 9. Synonymous, ternary. Lit.: *open thy mouth, judge justly, and judge the poor and the needy*. On *equity* see note on 1[3], on *poor* and *needy*, notes on 3[34] 14[31].

XXXI. In 𝔊 the section 31[1-9] stands just before 𝔐 25; the date and cause of the dislocation are unknown. — **1.** 𝔊 had אל משא מלך למו רבי (Jäg.). — **2.** The plus of 𝔊 is mainly rhetorical expansion, though πρωτογενές may = בכר. — **3.** 𝔐 חֵילָך; 𝔊 σὸν πλοῦτον. — 𝔐 דרכיך; Dys. דריך (Cant. 7[13]); possibly we should read לָבְנַךָ. — 𝔐 לְמָחוֹת; read למחות (Ges. Bött. Dys. *al.*); 𝔊 εἰς ὑστεροβουλίαν, = מלכן לנחם (Lag.). — **4.** The second אל למלכם appears (from the rhythm) to be scribal repetition, and למאל to be miswriting of preceding למלכם (Bi.). — On the form of this name (Prep. + divine name) cf. Gray, *Heb. Proper Names*, p. 207, where similar forms are given (Heb. לָאֵל, Palmyrene לשמש *al.*). 𝔐 אי (Q אֵי) can hardly be read אל (as 𝔊 and Saad. seem to have understood it). The rendering *cupiditas* (Schult.) is without lexicographical support, and (*to say*) *where is* etc. (Mich. De. RV. *al.*) is forced and unnatural. Read מסך or סבא. — 𝔊 βουλῆς supposes מֶלֶךְ for 𝔐 מִלֶכָם; its πάντα ποιεῖ perhaps = לְכֹל, for 𝔐 למאל. — 𝔖𝔗 *of kings take care*, = 𝔐, and so 𝕷ᵃ *noli regibus dare vinum ;* 𝕷ᵇ *quia nullum secretum est ubi regnat ebrietas* is interpretation, with allusion (Baumg.) to Aram. רָז *secret.* — **5.** 𝔐 כל should perhaps be omitted, with 𝔊. — **8.** 𝔐 אֵלֶם; 𝔊 λόγῳ θεοῦ (perhaps = מלה, with the divine name added), which Lag. emends to μογιλάλῳ (see Isa. 35[6]) ; 𝔗 *those who do not pervert judgment*, free rendering from the connection, the sense *dumb* seeming improbable; 𝔖 *the word of truth*, based, Lag. suggests, on a Grk. reading λόγῳ ἀληθεῖ (a corruption of μογιλάλῳ) — possibly it represents Heb. אֱמֶת. — Something like this latter should be read as parallel to 𝔐 צדק in v.[9]. Bi. אַלְמָנָה. — 𝔐 דָן אֶל; better דין, as in v.[9]. — 𝔐 חֲלוֹף בְּנֵי ;

read, with Dys., בִּ׳ חֲלִי (see Jer. 6[7] Eccl. 6[2]). — 9. Before שָׁפַט we may insert ו or לֹ.

10–31. The ideal housewife.

— This description, the Alphabetic Ode or "Golden ABC" of the perfect wife, is notable both for what it includes and for what it omits. She is the industrious, sagacious business manager of the house, a kindhearted mistress, the trusted friend of husband and children, honored in her own person for what she does — a picture not romantic, but also not "Philistine." On the other hand, nothing is said of intellectual interests or pursuits. Nor is religion mentioned (see note on v.[30]); this is due (as in ch. 30, Esth. Cant.) to the fact that the author is concerned with something else. The husband takes no part in the domestic administration — he is occupied with public affairs (v.[23]).* — The alphabetic structure is complete, twenty-two letters (as in ψ 119). This arrangement (found in the Pss. and other late writings), mnemonically useful, is often rhetorically bad, inducing an unnatural diction and order of couplets (see, for ex., v.[27]). The rhythmical norm is ternary.

10.   A good wife who can find?
      Far above the worth of corals is her worth.

11.   To her her husband trusts,
      And has no lack of gain.

12.   She does him good and not harm
      All the days of his life.

13.   She gathers wool and flax,
      And works it up as she will.

14.   She is like the ships of the merchant,
      From afar she brings her food.

15.   She rises while it is still night,
      And gives food to her household.   []

16.   She examines a field and buys it,
      With her earnings she plants a vineyard.

17.   She girds herself with strength,
      Makes her arms strong (for work).

18.   She perceives that her profit is good:
      Her lamp goes not out at night.

---

* Cf., for Egypt. life, Wilkinson, *Anc. Eg.*, ch. 8, Art. *Egypt. Lit.*, in *Lib. of World's Best Lit.*, and for Grk. and Rom., Becker, *Char.* and *Gallus.*

19. She lays her hand on the distaff,
    Her hand grasps the spindle.

20. She stretches out her hand to the poor,
    Extends her hand to the needy.

21 *a*. She fears not snow for her household,

22 *a*. Coverlets she makes her.

22 *b*. Her clothing is linen and purple,

21 *b*. Her household are clad in scarlet.

23. Her husband is distinguished in the council,
    When he sits among the elders of the land.

24. She makes linen cloth and sells it,
    Girdles she delivers to the merchant.

25. Strength and honor are her clothing,
    She laughs at the time to come.

26. Her speech is full of wisdom,
    And kindly instruction is on her tongue.

27. She looks well to the ways of her household,
    She eats not the bread of idleness.

28. Her children congratulate her,
    And her husband praises her (saying):

29. "Many women do well,
    But thou excellest them all."

30. Beauty is deceitful, and comeliness is transitory,
    A woman ‹of intelligence,› she will have praise.

31. Give her credit for what her hands have wrought!
    Let her works praise her among the people!

10–12. First stanza: praise in general terms. — **10.** On the rendering *good wife* see note on 12⁴; on *corals*, note on 3¹⁵. The sense is: "a good wife is not easily found, but, when she is found, she is of inestimable value." — **11.** Lit.: *the mind* (lit. *heart*) *of her husband;* the reference is not to the husband's affection, but to his confidence in her capacity as manager of household affairs. — The second line is ambiguous — lit. *spoil* (or, *outcome*) *is not lacking*, in which we may supply *to her* (Grk.), or *to him* (Lat.), or *to the household* (Ew.) ; probably, from the connection, *to him*, as representative of the household. — *Spoil* everywhere else in OT. means "booty taken in war"; the more general sense *acquisition*, *gain* appears in the verb (RV. *pull out*) in Ru. 2¹⁶. The military term came to be employed in a peaceful sense. — **12.** The *good* and *harm* refer, according to the connection, to the general (more particularly, the financial) prosperity of the household. — **13–15.** Second stanza: the industrial pursuits of the household. —**13.** *Gathers*, lit. *seeks.* On *wool* and *flax* as industrial products see Hos. 2⁵· ⁹⁽⁷· ¹¹⁾ Jos. 2⁶ Dt. 22¹¹; the preparation of cloths and garments from this material was the work of women.* — Second line lit.: *and she works in* (or, *according to*) *the pleasure of her hands* — she works up the raw material into such forms (of garments, girdles etc.) as seems to her best. The interpretation *with her hands' pleasure,* = *willingly, cheerfully, diligently* (Ew. RV. *al.*), involving a personification of the hands, is unnatural (it is not supported by ψ 78⁷²). Hitzig's rendering: *she works in the business of her hands* (cf. Isa. 58³ Eccl. 3¹· ¹⁷ *al.*) is allowable, but the statement has no special connection with first line. — **14.** She does not rely solely on local supplies, but from all quarters provides maintenance for her household. — **15.** In the Heb. the v. is a triplet, but it seems probable that the third line *and portions to her maidens* is a gloss, a repetition or explanation of second line. *Portion,* from the parallelism, = *food* (30⁸ Gen. 47²² Ez. 16²⁷), not "appointed work" (RV. *task*). Bickell omits first line, but it would then be hard to account for its presence in the text. — *Food,* as in ψ 111⁵ (cf. Mal. 3¹⁰ Job 24⁵); the Heb. word usually means *prey.* — **16–18.** Third stanza: the housewife's financial enterprise. — **16.** *Examines* (RV. *considers*) (see 30³²) = *reflects on,* that is, examines from a business point of view. — *Buys,* lit. *takes, gets possession of* (see Neh. 5³). One might almost say: " she speculates in land " (Frank.). Bick., not so well: *Considers . . . in order to buy it.* — *Plants* is the reading of the Heb. margin; the text has: [considers] *the planting of* etc. *Her earnings* is lit.: *the fruit of her hands.* — The culture of the vine was, and is, an important industry in Palestine (see 24³⁰ Ju. 9²⁷ Neh. 5³ *al.*). — **17.** Lit.: *she girds her loins with strength,* that is, probably, not *strongly* (Grk.), but, by a figure, with strength as a girdle; the gathering up the robe with a girdle was a necessary preparation for serious work (2 K. 4²⁹). — The expression *for work,*

---

* See Schröder, *De vestitu Mul. Hebr.;* Hartmann, *Die Hebräerin* etc.; H. Weiss, *Kostümkunde;* Palmer, *Desert of the Exodus,* p. 74.

added above, is obviously implied. — **18**. The verb here rendered *perceives* means generally *taste*, physically (1 S. 14^{24} Job 12^{11} *al.*), and so, by natural transference from the physical to the intellectual (like Lat. *sentire*), *perceive;* the transition of meaning is visible in ψ $34^{8(9)}$: *taste* ($=$ find out by trial) *and see* ($=$ become convinced) *that Yahweh is good*. So here the housewife learns by trial that her work is bringing pecuniary profit, and this statement is repeated and expanded in second line, the meaning of which is not : "she is indefatigable in work," but (Wild.) : "her house is prosperous." In a well-ordered house the lamp burned all night as a sign of life (see note on 13^9) ; its extinction marked calamity (Jer. 25^{10} Job 18^6).* — **19, 20, 21ª, 22ª**. Fourth stanza : her provision for her household and for the poor. — **19**. *Lays on* is lit. *stretches out to*. The translation *on the distaff* is inferred from the connection. The Anc. Vrss. (except, perh., Targ.) understand the expression as adverbial : Grk. *to useful things;* Lat. *to strong things;* Aq. Sym. Th. Syr. *strenuously.* — **20**. This couplet belongs, by its contents, with v.$^{25.\ 26}$; it was placed here perh. because the phrase *stretches* occurs in v.^{19}. — **21**. On the occurrence of snow in Palestine see notes on 25^{13} 26^1. — As the text is arranged the reading of the Heb. (v.^{21b}) *are clothed in scarlet* is improbable. The connection calls for the mention of some warm sort of clothing ; a scarlet robe, though made of woollen material, was not necessarily warm enough for winter — and, if it were, it is unlikely that the writer would use this term instead of saying directly that the clothing was warm.† If the Heb. order of lines be retained, we might change the text so as to get the meaning *warmly*. But it is easier to change the order of lines as above. According to this arrangement the *coverlets* (v.^{22a}) are the protection against the cold, and the colored garments come together in one couplet. — Lat. (followed by AV. marg.) improbably : *clothed in double garments.* — **22ª**. On *coverlets* see note on 7^{16}.

---

* Cf. Now., *Arch.*, p. 144; Benzinger, *Arch.*, p. 124.

† Scarlet robes were articles of luxury and magnificence (Ex. 25^4 2 S. 1^{24} Jer. 4^{30}, cf. Lam. 4^5). On the cochineal insect, from which the coloring matter was obtained, cf. Rawl., *Phoen.*, ch. 8.

The section 31¹⁰⁻³¹ stands in 𝕲 next after 𝕳 29. — 16. K נטע; read Q נָטְעָה.
Bi. retains K, and omits the connective ו in 𝕳 וַהֲקִחָה. — 18. The K לַיִל, poetical form (Isa. 16³ Lam. 2¹⁹), may be retained; Q gives the usual form לַיְלָה.
— 19. 𝕳 בַּכִּישׁוֹר; 𝕲 (followed by 𝖘) ἐπὶ τὰ συμφέροντα, = בַּכֹּשֶׁר (Lag. בכשרת),
see ψ 68⁷, and cf. Esth. 8⁵ Eccl. 10¹⁰ 2²¹ al.; ΑΣΘ ἀνδρείᾳ, and 𝕷 ad fortia,
from קשׁר or קשׁה, or perh. = 𝕲; 𝕿 בכשׁרא (so ed. Ven. of 1568, Lag.), written
also בכנשׁרא (Buxt.) or בכנשׁרא (MS. of A.C. 1238); the second form (of which
the third is a variation) is a rendering of 𝕳 שׁר navel in 3⁸, and is not elsewhere
found in any other sense (Levy's rendering distaff is a mere conjecture); the
first form is repetition or transference of the word of 𝕳, and its meaning is
unknown (it can be only guessed to be = distaff); comparison of the stem
כשׁר as probably = straight, and of Targ. and Talm. כָּשׁר beam makes it probable that the word in 𝕿 and in 𝕳 = distaff, which sense is suggested by the
correspondent 𝕳 פֶּלֶךְ spindle. Frank. emends to Talmud. כוש spindle (Shab.
Mishna 17, see Buxt. Lex.), but it seems more likely here that the expression
would be varied; possibly, however, כוש and פלך are not exactly synonymous.
— 21. 𝕳 שָׁנִיב; 𝕲 δισσάς, which it makes the beginning of v.²²; 𝕷 duplicibus;
hence it has been proposed to emend 𝕳 to שָׁנִים, which, however, is lexicographically improbable, and the emendation להם for warmth (Hag. 1⁶) is
graphically hard. The change in the order of the lines, as given above,
appears to remove the difficulty in the interpretation of 𝕳.

— 22ᵇ, 21ᵇ, 23, 24. Fifth stanza : the distinction which she gains
by her industry. — 22ᵇ. The term here rendered linen (RV. fine
linen) signifies some fine material, made of flax or of a mixture of
flax and cotton, and was probably an Egyptian product (Gen.
41⁴² Ez. 16¹⁰· ¹³ 27⁷ Ex. 25–39). — The purple coloring matter was
obtained from a Mediterranean shellfish (murex, or purpura),
and its preparation was an important Phoenician industry (Rawl.,
Phoen., ch. 8). Garments dyed with it indicated wealth or high
rank (Ju. 8²⁶ Jer. 10⁹ Ex. 25–39 Cant. 3¹⁰). — The housewife's
wardrobe is costly and luxurious. — 21ᵇ. See above, under v.²¹. —
23. Distinguished, lit. known, a prominent well-known man. —
Council, lit. gates, the place of assembly of the elders of the city ;
see notes on 1²¹ 24⁷. The old-Israelitish government by " elders "
(somewhat similar to that of the old-Aryan village *) appears to
have continued to a late period (Ju. 8¹⁴ 11⁵ ψ 107³² Joel 1¹⁴). —
The husband thus derives civil benefit from his wife's reputation
— it is assumed by the people that the head of so well-ordered a
household must be a worthy man, though it is probably not his

---

* Cf. the Saxon witenagemot and the New England town-meeting.

dress (as v.^{22} might suggest) that gives him distinction. The order of couplets is not good. — **24.** The *linen cloth* (a different term from the *linen* of v.^{22}) was some fine fabric, the precise nature of which is not known, though it may be inferred from the ancient Jewish authorities that its material was linen. What the housewife made and sold was probably a square piece of cloth that could be used as an outer garment or as a night-dress. The term occurs elsewhere in OT. only in Ju. 14$^{12.\ 13}$ Isa. 3^{23}; cf. Mk. 14^{51} (*sindon*) Herod. 2, 86 *al.* The *girdle* was probably of similar material (Jer. 13^1 Ez. 16^{10}) ; for the various sorts of girdle see the Bib. Dicts. The weaving of fine material appears to have been a Palestinian industry from a comparatively early period. — *Delivers,* lit. *gives,* that is, in exchange for money or for other articles; cf. Tob. 2^{11}. — *Merchant,* lit. *Canaanite,* that is, here, Phoenician. From the commercial character of the Canaanites the name came to be used as = *merchant* (Zech. 14^{21} Job 41^6 [40^{30}], cf. Hos. 12$^{7(8)}$ Isa. 23^8 Zeph. 1^{11} Ez. 17^4). Later the commerce was largely in the hands of the Tyrians ; and it would appear that trade between Israelites and Phoenicians began as early as the tenth century B.C.* — **25-27.** Sixth stanza : her wisdom and prosperity. — **25.** The *strength* and *honor* which she enjoys come from her firm financial and social position. She is so well established that she *laughs at* the future, is without anxiety. — In v.^{17} the *strength* is physical, here it is social. — **26.** Her *wisdom* is common sense, good judgment, discretion. *Kindly instruction* is lit. *instruction of kindness* (RV. *law of kindness*), instruction, to her children, servants, and friends, which springs from a kindly, friendly nature : though firm in her administration, as becomes a business woman, she is not domineering or harsh. The interpretation : "instruction in the duty of kindness to others" does not so well suit the connection, which rather marks the *kindness* as a quality of the woman herself. — The first line is lit. : *she opens her mouth in* (or, *with*) *wisdom.* — On *kindness* see notes on 3^3 11^{17}. — **27.** *Looks well to* = acts as *watchman for* (15^3 2 S. 18^{24} Ez. 3^{17} ψ 37^{32}). — *Ways* = "conduct, doings" ; she supervises all that goes on. — This couplet would stand more

* On Phoen. commerce see Rawl., *Phoen.;* Now., *Arch.,* § 44.

properly next after v.[24]. — **28, 29.** Seventh stanza : her merits are
recognized by her family. — **28.** Lit. : *her children rise up and
call her happy — her husband* [rises up] *and praises her.* She
has the praise of her own immediate circle, those who know her
best. — Bick. inverts the order of lines of the couplet, but the language of v.[29] is more appropriate for the husband than for the
children. — Frank. : *Her sons prosper, therefore people congratulate her — her husband, therefore people praise her.* This sense is
in itself appropriate — the community congratulating a woman on
the success of her husband and sons — except that it seems to
give her all the credit for their good performance. But the Heb.
hardly permits this interpretation : the verb *rise up* cannot mean
prosper (the *rise to power* in 28[12] is different), and the supplying
people (that is, *they*) as the subject of the other verbs is very
doubtful, if not quite out of the question. For the verb *call
happy* see Mal. 3[12. 15] ψ 72[17] Gen. 30[13]; the *rise up* describes the
movement preparatory to a formal utterance (Gen. 37[35]). —
29. Lit. : *many daughters do* etc. The use of the word *daughter*
as = *woman* (only here and Cant. 2[2] 6[9]) is a survival (found only
in poetry) from the time when the woman, even after marriage,
remained always a member of her father's family, and was defined
as his "daughter." — *Well* represents the same Heb. word as *good*
in v.[10], = "vigorously, effectively, admirably." — These words of
praise are obviously uttered by the husband as the spokesman of
the family ; the writer speaks of his heroine in the third person.
— **30, 31.** Eighth stanza : laudatory summing-up by the poet. —
30. The author's point of view : what he values in a wife is
domestic efficiency. He need not be understood as despising
beauty — he says only that it is transitory, while intelligence is a
lasting source of domestic happiness. — On *beauty* and *comeliness*
(here synonyms) see notes on 1[9] 11[16] 6[25]. The two adjs., also,
deceitful (lit. *deceit*, see 6[17] *al.*) and *transitory* (lit. *a breath, a
nothing*, see 13[11]) are probably meant as synonyms : beauty is
said to be deceitful because it passes away, and with it passes the
hope of happiness based on it. The meaning may, however, be :
he who judges a woman merely by her beauty may be disappointed in her character. — The second line reads in the Heb. :
a woman who fears Yahweh, she etc. But this, while a sentiment

natural in itself, is improbable in the connection : the ode elsewhere makes no reference to religion, confining itself to a portraiture of the woman's domestic ability ; in the second line of
this couplet the verb *praise* obviously contemplates the same characteristic (namely, housewifely skill) that the same verb in v.[28]
has in view, and, from the tenor of the ode, the contrast to *beauty*
is not *piety*, but *intelligence, thrift, administrative capacity, industry ;* in accordance with this view v.[31] refers solely to her industrial
achievement. Following a Grk. text, we may read *of intelligence*
instead of *who fears Yahweh ;* the latter reading may be the correction of a scribe who thought that a poem describing the ideal
woman should not fail to mention piety as an element of her character. — **31.** Lit. : *give her of the fruit of her hands,* that is, as
second line indicates, let her have recognition and credit for her
industry and skill — such ability as hers deserves general praise.
The woman is regarded by the author as an independent individual, not merely as an appendage to her husband. The expression
perhaps contains an intimation that women, by reason of the privacy of their life, did not always get public credit for their administrative ability or for the important part they played in securing
the well-being of the family. — *Among the people* is lit. *in the gates,*
the place where the people gathered and talked over the affairs of
the community ; see note on v.[23]

24. פֶּ סָדִין; ⅏ σινδόνας (followed by 𝕃 *sindonem*) *muslin garments.* In
Targ. (Lam. 2[20-22] ψ 104[2]) סָדִין signifies an enveloping cloth or garment, and
it is used in Talmud for any covering for day or for night (Kimchi *nightdress*);
cf. Ass. *sudinnu, garment* (in De. *Ass. Wbch.*), and Arab. *sidn,* = *a curtain,*
whence *sādin, curtain-keeper* or *doorkeeper* (to the Kaaba or any shrine).
See notes of Geier, Mich. De. on this v., Moore on Ju. 14[12. 13], Cheyne and
Davidson on Isa. 3[23]. — Grk. σινδών seems to be derived from the Sem. word.
Herod. uses it of a cloth through which the Babylonians sifted pounded fish
(1, 200), of a similar material in which the Egyptians wrapped the bodies of
their dead (2, 86), and of bandages which the Persians used for the wounded
(7, 181). To the derivation from *Sindhu* (the Indus) the objection lies
(Schrader, *Forsch. zu Handelsgesch.,* I. 199 ff.) that the old Grk. name for the
Indus was not σινδός, but ἰνδός (from the Eranian form); and no appropriate
Egypt. etymology has been proposed. If the sense *garment* for Ass. *sudinnu*
be correct, the Heb. word is undoubtedly Semitic, and from such a form the
Grk. could come by the insertion of *n*; the ω of the Grk. perhaps points to a
form *sudān* or *sudōn.* Syr. סְדִינָא appears to be a loan-word from the Grk.,

influenced, perhaps, by the Heb. form. No verb סרן occurs in Semitic, and the meaning of the stem is unknown. See Bochart, *Phaleg*, col. 751, and H. Lewy, *Sem. Fremdwört. im Griech.*, p. 84. — **25.** 𝕳 אהרן; Bi., unnecessarily: מחר *the morrow.* — In 𝕲 v.25 follows v.26 (of 𝕳), the order of letters being thus Pe . . . Ayın, as in Lam. 2. 3. 4 (the order in ψ 10 Nah. 1[2-10], cited by Bi., is uncertain); this arrangement may indicate an early variation in the order of the letters of the alphabet.* — In the Sahidic Vrs. the order of lines is: v.[25a. 27b. a. 25b. 26a. b]. — **26.** 𝕳 הרת הסף; 𝕲 τάξιν ἐστείλατο, perh. = הר. ההשך. — **27.** K הירכות is scribal error for Q הליכות. — 𝕲 adds the greater part of v.26; see also 𝕲's addition at 3[16]. — **30.** 𝕳 אשה יראת יהוה, for which 𝕲 has the doublet γυνὴ συνετή and φόβον Κυρίου; the former appears to be the original reading, since it would be less easy to account for its introduction by a scribe; read אשת בינה (cf. 30²) or אשה נבנה (cf. 1⁵). — **31.** 𝕲 χειλέων, for 𝕳 ידיה, should probably be emended to χειρῶν (so 𝔖[H], Compl.). — 𝕳 מעשׂיה; 𝕲 ὁ ἀνὴρ αὐτῆς, = בעלה or אישה (the preceding word ends in ם).

---

* Accidental variations of order are perhaps found in ψ 25. 34.

INDEX

	PAGE
ABOTH RABBI NATHAN,	473
Adultery, punishment of,	141
Agnosticism,	520
Agricultural life,	63
Alcimus, the high priest,	537
Alexander (J. A.), hymn of,	29 n.
Angel, mediating,	8
Antiochus Epiphanes,	9, 37
Apostates,	496
Aristotle, proverb of,	438
Asidean,	37
Ass, use of,	473
BEATITUDES of Proverbs,	67
Bowels,	33, 98
Brain,	33, 98
CAIRN, sacred,	475
Children, education of,	
14, 86, 278, 376, 419	
Cloths, preparation of,	544
Cock, the,	536
Conscience,	163
DAUGHTERS,	198
Death, violent,	530
Demon, bloodthirsty,	528
Determinative, appositional,	192
Divine jealousy of human pretensions,	487
Divorce in later times,	141
Dog in Palestine,	478
EARLY marriage,	114
Early rising,	124

	PAGE
Eccl. 12^1,	112 n.
Education of Jewish children,	14, 86
Elo^{n}h,	522
Elohim,	35
Epicureanism,	43, 46, 104, 303, 376, 477
Esoterism,	8
FOURTH Gospel,	26, 169, 174
GENERATION, eternal,	181
God, connection of, with land,	52, 218
Greek element in Pr.,	22
thought,	35
Guest-room,	401
HARLOTS,	44
Haying, season of,	493
Hermes pillar,	475
Horses, use of,	412, 473
Hyrax, the,	534
IMMORTALITY,	300, 522, 523
Indefinite construction,	215
Indra,	128
Interest on money,	498 n.
JEWISH communities, jurisdiction of,	110
Jews, apostate,	23
in Palestine, agricultural life of,	201
of the dispersion,	484
Job 5, date of.	65
15^7,	xxxiii
book of,	80
Justice,	**39**

	PAGE		PAGE
ḲAUM, Arabian deity,	537	Retaliation, law of,	454
Kidneys,	98	Revelation, divine,	32
Kings, attitude of OT. toward,	168	Rigveda,	521 n.
functions of,	323		
Koran,	112, 199	SACRIFICE,	410
		Schools, 8, 9, 14, 51, 65, 84, 270, 424	
LEECH,	529	Seasons,	124
Liver,	98	Shaphan, the,	534
Lot,	363	Sheol, 15, 131, 307, 314, 338, 404	
Luck,	487	see also Underworld, Yahweh.	
		Silver dross,	479
MARRIAGE,	533	Sinner, attitude of sages toward,	27
ceremonies,	47	Sister,	347
Mashal,	3, 524	Slavery among the Jews,	238
Massa, land of,	539	Slaves as rulers,	371
Mazdean sacred books,	43	price of,	246 n.
Mead,	382	Socrates,	22
Midrash, 185, 475 n., 519		Soul,	40
Moshel,	518	Suretyship,	121
NAME, significance of,	360	TALMUD, the, 14, 47, 107, 152,	
Naukratis,	45	155, 199, 225, 307, 336,	
Nazirites,	382	395, 401, 473 n., 475 n., 498	
Night-patrol,	151	Taxes, Egyptian,	507
		Israelitish,	507 n.
PAITAN,	3 n.		
Parents, obligation to,	505	UNDERWORLD, Babylonian,	158
Peccability, human,	386	Urim and Thummim,	16
Perfection, human,	386		
Pharisees,	522, 523	VOWS,	394
Pirke Aboth, 354, 377, 429, 430			
Piyut,	3 n.	WEIGHTS and measures,	324
Prometheus,	128	Wife, how chosen,	374
Prostitution,	45	Wine, use of,	185
Ptahhetep,	142, 303	Wisdom identical with God's	
Punitive blindness,	28	moral law,	27
		Wisdom of Sol.,	531
RAIN in Palestine,	468	Women, divorced,	533
Rechabites,	382	position of, 103, 149, 198, 228, 243	
Repentance,	28	property rights of,	534
Resentment,	252		
Responsibility, individual,	195	YAHWEH, name of,	360
Resurrection,	522, 523	use of the name,	10
		and Sheol,	307

ABBREVIATIONS *

A.C.	After Christ.	𝕲	Alexandrian Version of OT.; 𝕲ᴮ, Vat. MS. of 𝕲, etc.
Ald.	Aldine Grk. text of OT.		
Aq.	Aquila.	Geig.	A. Geiger.
Ar.	Arab. Version of OT.	Ges.	W. Gesenius.
AV.	Eng. Authorized Version.	Ginsb.	Ginsburg's masoretic text of OT.
Baumg.	A. J. Baumgartner.		
B-D	Baer and Delitzsch, Liber Proverb. (textum masoreticum).	Graec. Ven.	Codex Venetus (= H-P 23).
BDB.	Heb. and Eng. Lex. of OT., ed. F. Brown, S. R. Driver, C. A. Briggs.	Gr.	H. Grätz.
		𝔅	Masoretic text.
		Heid.	M. Heidenheim.
		Hi. or Hitz.	F. Hitzig.
Beck.	W. A. Becker, Charicles or Gallus (Eng. trans.).	H-P	Holmes and Parsons, Vet. Test. graece.
Berth.	E. Bertheau, Die Sprüche Salomo's.	Houb.	C. F. Houbigant, Biblia Hebr.
		Jäg.	J. G. Jaeger.
Bi.	G. Bickell.	JAOS.	Journ. of Amer. Oriental Soc'y.
Bött.	F. Böttcher, Neue Aehrenlese.		
BS.	Ben-Sira (Ecclesiasticus).	Kamp.	A. Kamphausen (in Kautzsch's Heilige Schrift).
Buxt.	J. Buxtorf, Lex. Chald. Talmud. et Rabbin.		
		Kenn.	B. Kennicott, Vet. Test. Heb.
Cappel.	L. Cappellus, Critica Sacra.	Klost.	A. Klostermann.
Cl. Al.	Clement of Alexandria.	Kön.	F. E. König, Lehrgebäude d. hebr. Sprache.
Cocc.	J. Cocceius (Koch), Lex. Heb. et Chald.		
		𝕷	Jerome's Version of OT.
Compl.	Complutensian Polyglot.	Lag.	P. de Lagarde.
Copt.	Coptic Versions of Prov.	Luth.	Martin Luther.
De.	Franz Delitzsch, Das Salomon. Spruchbuch.	Mich.	C. B. Michaelis.
	Friedr. Delitzsch, Assyr. Handwörterbuch.	NHW.	Levy, Neuhebr. Wörterbuch.
		Now.	W. Nowack.
Deism.	Deissmann, Bibelstudien.	Ols.	J. Olshausen, Lehrbuch d. heb. Sprache.
De R.	J. B. De-Rossi, Var. lect. Vet. Test.		
		Pesh.	Peshiṭa Syr. Version of OT.
Dr.	S. R. Driver, Deuteronomy.	Pink.	H. Pinkuss.
Dys.	J. Dyserinck.	Pirk. Ab.	Pirke Aboth.
Ew.	H. Ewald.	Proc.	Procopius.
Fleisch.	H. L. Fleischer.	Rawl.	G. Rawlinson.
Frank.	W. Frankenberg.	RV.	Eng. Revised Version.

---

* Cf. Bibliography, p. xxxv.

𐎂   Peshiṭa; 𐎂^{Lee}, ed. of Lee, etc.

𐎂^H   Hexaplar Syriac.

Saad.   Saadia's Arab. tr. of Prov.

SBOT.   Haupt's Sacred Books of OT.

Schl.   J. F. Schleusner, Lex. in LXX.

Schult.   A. Schultens.

Siegf.   C. Siegfried (in SS.).

SS.   Siegfried and Stade, Heb. Wörterbuch.

Str.   H. L. Strack.

Sym.   Symmachus.

𝕿   Targum.

Th.   Theodotion.

Venet. (or, Ven.) Grk. Codex Venetus.

Vog.   G. J. L. Vogel.

Wellh.   J. Wellhausen.

Wild.   G. Wildeboer.

Zöck.   O. Zöckler.

A, or 'A Aquila.

Σ   Symmachus.

Θ   Theodotion.

DIACRITICAL MARKS

()   Insertion for clearness.

' '   Emendation of mas. text.

[]   Omission of Heb. word or words.